GORBACHEV

GORBACHEV

HIS LIFE AND TIMES

WILLIAM TAUBMAN

W. W. NORTON & COMPANY

Independent Publishers Since 1923

NEW YORK | LONDON

Photograph on page 622 courtesy of the Cold War Studies Archive,
Harvard University. All other photographs courtesy of the Gorbachev Foundation.

For information about permission to reproduce selections from this book,
write to Permissions, W. W. Norton & Company, Inc.,
500 Fifth Avenue, New York, NY 10110

For information about special discounts for bulk purchases, please contact
W. W. Norton Special Sales at specialsales@wwnorton.com or 800-233-4830

Manufacturing by LSC Communications, Harrisonburg
Book design by Barbara Bachman
Production manager: Julia Druskin

Library of Congress Cataloging-in-Publication Data

Names: Taubman, William, author.
Title: Gorbachev : his life and times / William Taubman.
Description: First edition. | New York, N.Y. : W.W. Norton & Company, Inc.,
2017. | Includes bibliographical references and index.
Identifiers: LCCN 2017015009 | ISBN 9780393647013 (hardcover)
Subjects: LCSH: Gorbachev, Mikhail Sergeevich, 1931– | Heads of state—Soviet
Union—Biography. | Soviet Union—Politics and government—1985–1991.
Classification: LCC DK290.3.G67 T39 2017 | DDC 947.085/4092 [B]—dc23
LC record available at https://lccn.loc.gov/2017015009

W. W. Norton & Company, Inc.
500 Fifth Avenue, New York, N.Y. 10110
www.wwnorton.com

W. W. Norton & Company Ltd.
15 Carlisle Street, London W1D 3BS

1 2 3 4 5 6 7 8 9 0

TO JANE—

and for our grandchildren:

Milo, Jacob, and Nora

CONTENTS

THREE ISSUES—RELATING TO POLITICAL LABELS, records of meetings of the ruling Communist party Politburo, and translit-eration of Russian language—deserve special attention.

It became common practice during Gorbachev's years in power for Soviet observers (and Westerners, too) to label his opponents as left-wing and right-wing. Hard-liners in the Communist party, the military, the security police, and elsewhere who resisted Gorbachev's reforms were dubbed right-wingers. Democrats, especially radical democrats who pushed Gorbachev to make haste in creating a market economy, were known as left-wingers. But given the way such markers are generally used outside the USSR—with Communists usually described as left-wing, and true believers in a market economy known as right-wing—to use these labels in this book would be misleading. As a result, I have gen-erally referred to those who resisted reforms as hard-liners or conserva-tives (even though the latter term can also be confusing), and to those who criticized Gorbachev for going too slowly as radicals or, when their stance was more moderate, liberals.

Beginning in 1966, official working transcripts (*rabochie zapisi*) were made of Politburo meetings, initially on the basis of notes taken by the head of the Communist party Central Committee's general department, and later by professional stenographers. When Gorbachev was party general secretary, his aides Anatoly Chernyaev, Georgy Shakhnazarov, and Vadim Medvedev, the first two of whom attended Politburo meetings without the right to speak, also took detailed notes. Many of these aides' accounts have been available in the archive at the Gorbachev Foundation (*Gorbachev Fond*) in Moscow. Quite a few "official" working transcripts have also become available, many of them in a collection called *Fond* 89, made public by then Russian president Boris Yeltsin in 1992. The *Fond* 89 documents at the Russian State Archive of Contemporary History (RGANI) in Moscow were subsequently microfilmed by the Hoover Institution at Stanford University. The Dmitry Volkogonov Collection at the Library of Congress contains Volkogonov's own selection of Politburo working transcripts. The National Security Archive (NSA) in Washington, where I did much of my work, possesses working transcripts from *Fond* 89 and the Volkogonov Collection, as well as other Politburo documents collected by the archive's staff. As far I can tell, official working transcripts and Gorbachev aides' notes on Politburo meetings are not substantially different when they cover the same conversations, but the official transcripts are longer since Gorbachev aides' notes naturally devoted particularly detailed attention to his words. The official transcripts pay more attention to comments by other Politburo members, some of them critical of Gorbachev, perhaps also influenced by the man supervising preparation of these transcripts, Gorbachev aide Valery Boldin, who was increasingly disenchanted with his boss.[1]

Both sets of Politburo records are cited in this book. Unless otherwise noted, it can be assumed that those cited from the READD-RADD collection at the National Security Archive are official transcripts, whereas those read at the Gorbachev Fond Archive (GFA) are notes taken by Chernyaev, Shakhnazarov, or Medvedev, who are named in this book's endnotes when their notes are attributed to them in the documents. The sources of other records I cite from other books, including the (so far) twenty-six volumes of Gorbachev's collected works, *Sobranie sochinenii*, and other collections of documents published in Russia and the West, are identified in those books.

There are several systems of transliteration of the Russian language. Throughout the text of this book, I have used transliteration that will be most familiar or most accessible to the non-Russian reader and most likely to capture the sound of Russian. However, when I cite specific Russian-language material in the notes and bibliography, I employ the Library of Congress transliteration system, which is often used in library catalogs. So, for example, although Anatoly Chernyaev, one of Gorbachev's longtime, close aides, appears as such in the text, when I refer to his Russian-language publications, I spell his name, Anatolii Cherniaev.

During the period covered in the bulk of this book, Ukraine was part of the Soviet Union. In that time, Russian versions of Ukrainian personal and place-names were used in official, and often in unofficial, discourse. For that reason, and to avoid confusing the reader, I use the Russian versions—except for material published after Ukraine became an independent state.

CAST OF CHARACTERS

ABALKIN, LEONID Economist, deputy chairman of USSR Council of Ministers, 1990–1991.

ABULADZE, TENGIZ Georgian film director of *Repentance*.

ADAMOVICH, ALES Byelorussian writer and critic who served as USSR Supreme Soviet deputy after 1989.

AFANASYEV, VIKTOR Editor in chief of *Pravda*, 1976–1989.

AFANASYEV, YURI People's deputy of the USSR, cochair of the Interregional Deputies Group, 1989–1991.

AITMATOV, CHINGIZ Soviet and Kyrgyz author.

AKHMATOVA, ANNA Famed Russian poet (1889–1966).

AKHROMEYEV, SERGEI Marshal of the Soviet Union; chief of General Staff of the Soviet Armed Forces, 1984–1988; military adviser to Gorbachev, 1988–1991.

ALEKSANDROV-AGENTOV, ANDREI Foreign policy adviser to Communist party general secretaries from Brezhnev to Gorbachev, 1966–1986.

ALIEV, GEIDAR First secretary of the Azerbaijan Communist party, 1969–1982; first deputy chairman of the USSR Council of Ministers, 1982–1987; Politburo member, 1982–1987.

ALLISON, GRAHAM Professor at Harvard University Kennedy School of Government.

ANDREOTTI, GIULIO Italian foreign minister, 1983–1989; prime minister, 1989–1992.

ANDREYEVA, NINA Chemistry teacher and rank-and-file Communist party member who wrote article in *Sovetskaya Rossiia* in 1988, accusing Gorbachev of going too far with his reforms.

ANDROPOV, YURI General secretary of the CC CPSU, November 1982–February 1984; chairman of the KGB, May 1967–May 1982.

ARBATOV, GEORGY Founder and head of Academy of Sciences Institute for U.S. and Canada Studies, 1967–1995; member of the Central Committee;

deputy of the USSR Supreme Soviet, 1985–1991; close adviser to Andropov and Gorbachev.

BAKATIN, VADIM Minister of the interior, 1988–1990; member of the Presidential Council, 1990–1991; chairman of the KGB, September–November 1991.

BAKER, JAMES, III George H. W. Bush's secretary of state, 1989–1992; Reagan's White House chief of staff, 1981–1985; secretary of the treasury, 1985–1988.

BAKLANOV, GRIGORY Russian writer.

BAKLANOV, OLEG Participant in the August 1991 coup; Central Committee secretary in charge of military-industrial matters, 1988–1991; minister of general machine building, 1983–1988.

BEKOVA, ZOYA Gorbachev classmate at Moscow State University.

BIKKENIN, NAIL Central Committee functionary.

BILAK, VASIL Slovak Communist leader.

BILLINGTON, JAMES U.S. librarian of Congress, 1987–2015.

BLACKWILL, ROBERT Special assistant to President George H. W. Bush for national security affairs, 1989–1991.

BOGOLYUBOV, KLAVDY Head of Central Committee's general department, 1982–1985.

BOGOMOLOV, OLEG Economist, adviser to Andropov and Gorbachev; director of the Institute of Economics of the World Socialist System.

BOLDIN, VALERY Participant in the August 1991 coup; Gorbachev adviser, 1982–1991; head of Central Committee general department, 1987–1991; member of Presidential Council, 1990–1991; presidential chief of staff, 1990–1991.

BONDAREV, YURI Russian writer.

BONNER, ELENA Wife of Andrei Sakharov.

BOVIN, ALEKSANDR Foreign policy consultant to Communist party general secretaries.

BRAITHWAITE, RODRIC British ambassador to Soviet Union, 1988–1991.

BRAZAUSKAS, ALGIRDAS First secretary of the Lithuanian Communist party, 1988–1989; chairman of the Presidium of the Lithuanian Supreme Soviet, 1990.

BREZHNEV, LEONID CPSU general secretary, October 1964–November 1982.

BROVIKOV, VLADIMIR Chairman of Byelorussian Council of Ministers, 1983–1986; ambassador to Poland, 1986–1990.

BRUTENTS, KAREN First deputy head of Central Committee international department, 1986–1991; deputy director of international department, 1976–1986.

BRZEZINSKI, ZBIGNIEW National security adviser to President Jimmy Carter, 1977–1981.

BUDYKA, ALEKSANDR AND LYDIA Gorbachevs' close friends in Stavropol and Moscow.

BURLATSKY, FYODOR Editor of *Literaturnaya gazeta*.

BUSH, GEORGE H. W. U.S. president, 1989–1993.

CARTER, JIMMY U.S. president, 1977–1981.

CEAUŞESCU, NICOLAE General secretary of the Romanian Communist party, 1965–1989; president of Romania, 1967–1989.

CHAZOV, YEVGENY USSR minister of health, 1987–1990; chief Kremlin physician.

CHEBRIKOV, VIKTOR Chairman of KGB, 1982–1988; Central Committee secretary, 1988–1989; Politburo member, 1985–1989.

CHENEY, DICK Secretary of defense under George H. W. Bush, 1989–1992.

CHERNENKO, KONSTANTIN CPSU general secretary, February 1984–March 1985.

CHERNYAEV, ANATOLY Close Gorbachev aide from 1986 onward; principal foreign policy adviser; head of Central Committee international department consultants group, 1961–1986; member of Central Committee, 1986–1991.

CHIKIN, VALENTIN Editor of *Sovetskaya Rossiia*.

CHIRAC, JACQUES French prime minister, 1986–1988.

CLINTON, BILL U.S. president, 1993–2001.

CZYREK, JÓZEF Top aide to Polish president and Communist party general secretary Wojciech Jaruzelski.

DANIUSHEVSKAYA, GALINA Gorbachev classmate at MGU.

DE MICHELIS, GIANNI Italian foreign minister, 1989–1992.

DEMICHEV, PYOTR Politburo candidate member, 1965–1988; Soviet minister of culture, 1974–1986.

DOBRYNIN, ANATOLY Soviet ambassador to Washington, 1962–1986; head of Central Committee international department, 1986–1988.

DOLGIKH, VLADIMIR Central Committee secretary, 1972–1988; Politburo member, 1982–1988.

DOLINSKAYA, LIUBOV Gorbachevs' neighbor in Stavropol.

DUBČEK, ALEXANDER First secretary of the Czechoslovak Communist party during and immediately after Prague Spring, January 1968–April 1969.

DUBININ, LIANA Wife of Soviet ambassador to Washington.

DUBININ, YURI Soviet ambassador to Washington, 1986–1990.

FALIN, VALENTIN Head of Central Committee international department, 1988–1991; Central Committee secretary, 1990–1991; Soviet ambassador to Federal Republic of Germany, 1970–1978.

FROLOV, IVAN Adviser to Gorbachev, 1987–1989; chief editor of *Pravda*, 1989–1991; Central Committee secretary, 1989–1990; Politburo member, 1990–1991.

GANDHI, RAJIV Indian prime minister, 1984–1989.

GATES, ROBERT CIA director, 1991–1993; deputy national security adviser, 1989–1991; CIA deputy director, 1986–1989.

GENERALOV, VYACHESLAV Deputy director of KGB directorate no. 9 in charge of Gorbachev's security.

GENSCHER, HANS-DIETRICH Foreign minister and vice chancellor of Germany, 1974–1992.

GERASIMOV, GENNADY Soviet Foreign Ministry press spokesman.

GOLOVANOV, DMITRY Gorbachev classmate at MGU.

GONOCHENKO, ALEKSEI Gorbachev speechwriter in Stavropol.

GONZÁLEZ, FELIPE Spanish prime minister, 1982–1996.

GOPKALO, PANTELEI Maternal grandfather of Gorbachev.

GOPKALO, VASILISA Maternal grandmother of Gorbachev.

GORBACHEV, ALEKSANDR Mikhail Gorbachev's brother.

GORBACHEV, ANDREI Paternal grandfather of Gorbachev.

GORBACHEV, MARIA Mother of Gorbachev.

GORBACHEV, SERGEI Father of Gorbachev.

GORBACHEV, STEPANIDA Paternal grandmother of Gorbachev.

GORBACHEV, RAISA Wife of Gorbachev.

GRACHEV, ANDREI Gorbachev press spokesman, 1991; deputy head of Central Committee international department, 1989–1991; section head in Central Committee international information department, 1986–1989; Gorbachev biographer.

GRANIN, DANIIL Soviet writer and USSR people's deputy after 1989.

GRISHIN, VIKTOR First secretary of the Moscow city committee of the Communist party, 1967–1985; Politburo member, 1971–1986.

GROMYKO, ANDREI Soviet foreign minister, 1957–1985; chairman of the Presidium of the Supreme Soviet, 1985–1988; Politburo member, 1973–1988.

GRÓSZ, KÁROLY General secretary of the Hungarian Communist party, 1988–1989; prime minister, 1987–1988.

GURENKO, STANISLAV Ukrainian Communist party first secretary, 1990–1991.

GUSENKOV, VITALY Raisa Gorbachev's chief aide; Soviet diplomat in Paris in 1970s.

HAVEL, VÁCLAV Czech writer, dissident; Czechoslovak president, 1989–1992.

HONECKER, ERICH General secretary of the Central Committee of the Socialist Unity Party of (East) Germany, 1971–1989.

HOWE, SIR GEOFFREY British foreign secretary, 1982–1989.

HURD, DOUGLAS British foreign secretary, 1989–1995.

HUSÁK, GUSTÁV President of Czechoslovakia, 1975–1989; general secretary of Czechoslovak Communist party, 1969–1987.

IGNATENKO, VITALY Editor of *Novoe vremia*, 1986–1990; assistant and then director of press for President Gorbachev, 1990–1991.

IVASHKO, VLADIMIR First secretary of the Ukrainian Communist party, 1990; deputy to General Secretary Gorbachev, 1991.

JAKEŠ, MILOŠ General secretary of the Czechoslovak Communist party, 1987–1989.

JARUZELSKI, WOJCIECH President of the Republic of Poland, 1989–1990; first secretary of the PUWP, 1981–1989; Polish prime minister, 1981–1985.

KÁDÁR, JÁNOS General secretary of the Hungarian Communist party, 1956–1988.

KAGANOVICH, LAZAR Close associate of Stalin; rival to Khrushchev.

KALYAGIN, VIKTOR Rural district party boss near Stavropol.

KARAGODINA, YULIA Childhood friend and sweetheart of Gorbachev in Privolnoe.

KARMAL, BABRAK Communist leader of Afghanistan, 1979–1986.

KAZNACHEYEV, VIKTOR Gorbachev associate and deputy in Stavropol.

KHASBULATOV, RUSLAN First deputy chairman of the RSFSR Supreme Soviet, 1990–1991; chairman of the RSFSR Supreme Soviet, 1991–1993.

KHRUSHCHEV, NIKITA CPSU first secretary, 1953–1964; chairman of Council of Ministers, 1954–1964.

KIRILENKO, ANDREI Politburo member, 1962–1982.

KISSINGER, HENRY U.S. secretary of state, 1973–1977; national security adviser, 1969–1975.

KOCHEMASOV, VYACHESLAV Soviet ambassador to the GDR, 1983–1990.

KOHL, HELMUT Chancellor of Germany, 1990–1998; chancellor of Federal Republic of Germany, 1982–1990.

KOLBIN, GENNADY First secretary of the Kazakhstan Communist party, 1986–1989.

KOLCHANOV, RUDOLF Gorbachev classmate at MGU.

KORNIENKO, GEORGY USSR first deputy foreign minister, 1977–1986; first deputy head of CC CPSU international department, 1986–1988.

KOROBEINIKOV, ANATOLY Gorbachev speechwriter in Stavropol.

KOSYGIN, ALEKSEI Chairman of the Soviet Council of Ministers, 1964–1980; Politburo member, 1948–1952, 1960–1980.

KOVALEV, ANATOLY USSR deputy foreign minister, 1986–1991.

KRAVCHENKO, LEONID Chairman of Soviet Radio and Television, 1990–1991; head of Soviet Telegraph Agency, 1989–1990; first deputy chairman of the USSR State Committee for Television and Radio, 1985–1988.

KRAVCHUK, LEONID President of Ukraine, 1991–1994; chairman of Supreme Soviet of Ukrainian SSR, 1990–1991.

KRENZ, EGON General secretary of the Socialist Unity Party of the GDR, October 1989–December 1989.

KRIUCHKOV, VLADIMIR Leader of August 1991 coup; KGB chairman, 1988–1991; Politburo member, 1989–1991.

KULAKOV, FYODOR First secretary of Stavropol party committee, 1960–1964; Central Committee secretary, 1965–1978; Politburo member, 1971–1978.

KUNAYEV, DINMUKHAMED First secretary of Communist party of Kazakhstan, 1964–1986.

KVITSINSKY, YULI Soviet ambassador to West Germany, 1986–1990.

LANINA, OLGA, AND TAMARA ALEKSANDROVA Secretaries of Anatoly Chernyaev.

LAPTEV, IVAN Editor of *Izvestiia*, 1984–1990; chairman of the USSR Supreme Soviet's Council of the Union, 1990–1991.

LATSIS, OTTO Researcher at Institute of the Economy of the World Socialist System, 1975–1986; journalist, 1986–1991.

LEBED, ALEKSANDR Soviet general; candidate for Russian president in 1996.

LENIN, VLADIMIR Main organizer of Bolshevik Revolution in 1917; leader of the Russian Soviet Federative Socialist Republic, 1917–1922, and of the Soviet Union from 1922 until his death in 1924.

LEVADA, YURI MGU classmate of Raisa Gorbachev; Russian sociologist.

LYAKISHEVA, NINA MGU classmate of Raisa Gorbachev.

LIBERMAN, VOLODYA Gorbachev classmate at MGU.

LIGACHEV, YEGOR Politburo member, 1985–1990; Central Committee secretary, 1983–1990; first secretary of the Tomsk regional committee, 1965–1983.

LIKHACHEV, DMITRY Russian scholar; USSR people's deputy.

LUKYANOV, ANATOLY Chairman of the Supreme Soviet of the USSR, 1990–1991; Central Committee secretary, 1987–1988; accused of participating in August 1991 coup.

MALENKOV, GEORGY Stalin associate; Khrushchev rival.

MAMARDASHVILI, MERAB MGU classmate of Raisa Gorbachev; Soviet philosopher.

MASLYUKOV, YURI Deputy chairman of the USSR Council of Ministers, 1985–1988; first deputy chairman of the USSR Council of Ministers and chairman of State Planning Commission, 1988–1991; member of Presidential Council, 1990–1991; Politburo member, 1989–1990.

MATLOCK, JACK F., JR. U.S. ambassador to Soviet Union, 1987–1991; special assistant to President Ronald Reagan for national security affairs, 1983–1986.

MATLOCK, REBECCA Wife of U.S. Ambassador Matlock.

MAZOWIECKI, TADEUSZ Polish prime minister, August 1989–December 1990.

MEDUNOV, SERGEI Krasnodar region party first secretary, 1973–1982.

MEDVEDEV, ROY Soviet dissident historian; USSR people's deputy.

MEDVEDEV, VADIM Senior adviser to Gorbachev, 1991; Central Committee secretary, 1986–1990; Politburo member, 1988–1990.

MEDVEDEV, VLADIMIR Head of Gorbachev security detail.

MIKHAILENKO, VITALY Gorbachev associate in Stavropol.

MIKHALEVA, NADEZHDA Gorbachev classmate at MGU.

MITTERRAND, FRANÇOIS President of France, 1981–1995.

MLYNÁŘ, ZDENĚK Close friend of Gorbachev's at MGU, 1950–1955; secretary of Czech Communist party, 1968–1970, and intellectual who played key role in Prague Spring.

MODROW, HANS Prime minister of GDR, 1989–1990.

MOLOTOV, VYACHESLAV Stalin associate; Khrushchev rival.

MURAKHOVSKY, VSEVOLOD First deputy chairman of USSR Council of Min-

isters and chairman of the State Agro-industrial Commission, 1985–1989;
first secretary of the Stavropol regional party committee, 1978–1985.

MURATOV, DMITRY Russian journalist, editor of *Novaya gazeta*; close Gorbachev friend.

MUSATOV, VALERY Central Committee official.

MUTALIBOV, AIAZ President of Azerbaijan, 1990–1992; first secretary of the
Azerbaijani Communist party 1990–1991; chairman of the Azerbaijani
Council of Ministers, 1989–1990.

NAJIBULLAH, MOHAMMAD President of Democratic Republic of Afghanistan, 1987–1992.

NAZARBAYEV, NURSULTAN First secretary of Communist party of Kazakhstan, 1989–1991; president of Kazakhstan, 1991–.

NÉMETH, MIKLÓS Prime minister of Hungary, 1988–1990.

NICHOLAS II Last Russian tsar, 1894–1917.

NIKONOV, VIKTOR Central Committee secretary specializing on agriculture,
1985–1989; Politburo member, 1987–1989.

NIXON, RICHARD U.S. president, 1969–1974.

OCCHETTO, ACHILLE Secretary-general of the Italian Communist party,
1988–1994.

PALAZHCHENKO, PAVEL English interpreter for Gorbachev and Shevardnadze, 1985–1991; director of international relations and press contacts
at the Gorbachev Foundation.

PATIASHVILI, DZHUMBER First secretary of Georgian Communist party,
1985–1989.

PAVLOV, VALENTIN Soviet prime minister, January–August 1991; participant in August 1991 coup.

PETRAKOV, NIKOLAI Economic adviser to Gorbachev, 1990.

PLEKHANOV, YURI Head of KGB directorate in charge of Gorbachev's security, 1983–1991; participant in August 1991 coup.

POLTORANIN, MIKHAIL Russian Republic minister of press and information, 1990–1992.

PONOMAREV, BORIS Head of international department of the Central Committee, 1957–1986; Central Committee secretary, 1961–1986.

POPOV, GAVRIIL Mayor of Moscow, 1990–1992; liberal politician.

POROTOV, NIKOLAI Deputy director of Komsomol cadres department in
Stavropol and Gorbachev's first boss.

PORTUGALOV, NIKOLAI Central Committee official.

POWELL, LORD CHARLES Private secretary and foreign policy adviser to
British Prime Ministers Margaret Thatcher and John Major, 1983–1991.

POWELL, COLIN President Reagan's national security adviser, 1987–1989;
chairman of the Joint Chiefs of Staff, 1989–1993.

POZGAY, IMRE Hungarian politician.

PROKOFIEV, YURI First secretary of Moscow city party committee, 1989–
1991; Politburo member, 1990–1991.

PUGO, BORIS Minister of internal affairs, 1990–1991; first secretary of the Latvian Communist party, 1984–1988; participant in August 1991 coup.

PUTIN, VLADIMIR Russian president, 2000–2008, 2012–; prime minister under President Boris Yeltsin, 1999–2000, and President Dmitry Medvedev, 2008–2012.

RAKHMANIN, OLEG First deputy head of Central Committee department on relations with Communist and workers' parties of socialist countries, 1968–1987.

RAKOWSKI, MIECZYSŁAW Polish prime minister, 1988–1990.

REAGAN, NANCY First lady, 1981–1989, wife of Ronald Reagan.

REAGAN, RONALD U.S. president, 1981–1989.

REGAN, DONALD White House chief of staff under President Reagan, 1985–1987.

REMNICK, DAVID *Washington Post* Moscow correspondent, 1988–1991.

REVENKO, GRIGORY Chief of staff of the Gorbachev presidential administration, end of 1991.

RICE, CONDOLEEZZA Director of Soviet and East European affairs, U.S. National Security Council, 1989–1991

RIMASHEVSKAYA, NATALIA Gorbachev classmate at MGU.

ROMANOV, GRIGORY Central Committee secretary, 1983–1985; first secretary of the Leningrad regional party committee, 1970–1983; Politburo member, 1976–1985.

RUSAKOV, KONSTANTIN Central Committee secretary and head of Central Committee department of relations with Communist and workers' parties of socialist countries, 1977–1986.

RUST, MATTHIAS West German amateur pilot whose plane landed in Red Square on May 28, 1987.

RUTSKOI, ALEKSANDR Vice president of Russia, 1991–1993.

RYABOV, YAKOV Sverdlovsk province party first secretary, 1971–1976.

RYBAKOV, ANATOLY Soviet writer.

RYZHKOV, NIKOLAI Chairman of the Council of Ministers, 1985–1991; head of the Central Committee economic department, 1982–1985; Politburo member, 1985–1990.

SAGDEYEV, ROALD Soviet space scientist.

SAKHAROV, ANDREI Russian nuclear physicist who helped design Soviet H-bomb; later turned Soviet dissident and human rights activist; freed from exile in 1986; deputy to Congress of People's Deputies in 1989.

SCOWCROFT, BRENT National security adviser under President George H. W. Bush, 1989–1993.

SHAKHNAZAROV, GEORGY Close aide to Gorbachev, specializing in Eastern Europe and political reform in USSR, 1988–1991.

SHAPKO, VALERY Gorbachev classmate at MGU.

SHAPOSHNIKOV, YEVGENY Last Soviet minister of defense, August–December 1991.

SHATALIN, STANISLAV Member of State Commission on Economic Reform, 1989; member of Presidential Council, 1990–1991.

SHATROV, MIKHAIL Soviet playwright.

SHCHERBITSKY, VLADIMIR First secretary of the Ukrainian Communist party, 1972–1989; Politburo member, 1971–1989.

SHENIN, OLEG Central Committee secretary and Politburo member, 1990–1991; participant in August 1991 coup.

SHEVARDNADZE, EDUARD Soviet foreign minister, 1985–1990; first secretary of Communist party of Georgia, 1972–1985.

SHMELYOV, NIKOLAI Soviet economist; USSR people's deputy.

SHULTZ, GEORGE U.S. secretary of state, 1982–1989.

SHUSHKEVICH, STANISLAV Chairman of Supreme Soviet of Belarus, 1991–1994.

SILAYEV, IVAN Chairman of the RSFSR Council of Ministers, June 1990–end of 1991.

SOBCHAK, ANATOLY Soviet legal scholar; USSR people's deputy; member of Presidential Council; mayor of St. Petersburg, 1991–1996.

SOKOLOV, SERGEY Soviet defense minister, 1984–1987.

SOLOMENTSEV, MIKHAIL Politburo member, 1983–1988.

SOLOVYOV, YURI First secretary of Leningrad province party committee, 1985–1989.

STALIN, JOSEPH (ALSO IOSIF DZHUGASHVILI) Succeeded Lenin as Communist leader of the Soviet Union in 1922; died in office in 1953.

STANKEVICH, SERGEI Soviet scholar; USSR people's deputy; leader of Inter-regional Deputies Group.

STARKOV, VLADISLAV Editor of *Argumenty i fakty*.

STARODUBTSEV, VASILY Participant in August 1991 coup attempt.

STRAUSS, ROBERT U.S. ambassador to the USSR, 1991.

ŠTROUGAL, LUBOMÍR Prime minister of Czechoslovakia, 1971–1988.

SUSLOV, MIKHAIL Central Committee secretary, 1947–1982.

TARASENKO, SERGEI Main adviser to Soviet Foreign Minister Eduard Shevardnadze, 1985–1990.

TELTSCHIK, HORST National security adviser to Chancellor Helmut Kohl, 1982–1990.

THATCHER, MARGARET UK prime minister, 1979–1990.

TIKHONOV, NIKOLAI Chairman of the Council of Ministers, 1980–1985; Politburo member, 1979–1985.

TITARENKO, ALEKSANDRA Mother of Raisa Gorbachev.

TITARENKO, LUDMILA Raisa Gorbachev's sister.

TITARENKO, MAKSIM Father of Raisa Gorbachev.

TITARENKO, YEVGENY Raisa Gorbachev's brother.

TIZYAKOV, ALEKSANDR Participant in August 1991 coup attempt.

TOPILIN, YURA Gorbachev classmate at MGU.

TRUDEAU, PIERRE ELLIOTT Canadian prime minister, 1968–1979; 1980–1984.

TVARDOVSKY, ALEKSANDR Soviet writer; editor of *Novyi mir.*

ULYANOV, MIKHAIL Soviet actor; USSR people's deputy.

USTINOV, DMITRY Soviet defense minister, 1976–1984; Politburo member, 1976–1984.

VARENNIKOV, VALENTIN Deputy defense minister and commander of ground forces, 1989–1991; participant in August 1991 coup.

VARSHAVSKY, MIKHAIL AND INNA Close friends of the Gorbachevs in Stavropol.

VELIKHOV, YEVGENY Director of Institute of Atomic Energy; USSR people's deputy, 1989–1991; member of President Gorbachev's Political Consultative Committee, 1991.

VIRGANSKAYA/GORBACHEV, IRINA Daughter of Mikhail and Raisa Gorbachev.

VIRGANSKAYA, ANASTASIA (NASTYA) AND KSENIA Granddaughters of Mikhail and Raisa Gorbachev, daughters of Irina.

VIRGANSKY, ANATOLY Son-in-law of Gorbachev, married to his daughter, Irina.

VLASOV, ALEKSANDR USSR minister of internal affairs, 1986–1988; chairman of the Russian Council of Ministers, 1988–1990.

VOLSKY, ARKADY Head of the Central Committee machine-building department; special emissary on Nagorno-Karabakh, 1988–1990.

VORONTSOV, YULI Soviet ambassador to the United Nations, 1990–1991; ambassador to Afghanistan, 1988–1990; first deputy foreign minister, 1986–1989; ambassador to France, 1983–1986.

VOROTNIKOV, VITALY Chairman of Russian Republic Council of Ministers, 1983–1988; chairman of the Presidium of the Supreme Soviet of the RSFSR, 1988–1990; Politburo member, 1983–1990.

VYSOTSKY, VLADIMIR Soviet actor and bard.

WAŁESA, LECH Polish president, 1990–1995; founder of Solidarity trade union.

WEIZSÄCKER, RICHARD VON President of West Germany/Germany, 1984–1994.

XIAOPING, DENG De facto leader of China, 1978–early 1990s.

YAKOVLEV, ALEKSANDR Politburo member, 1987–1990; Central Committee secretary, 1986–1990; Soviet ambassador to Canada, 1973–1983.

YAKOVLEV, YEGOR Chief editor of *Moskovskie novosti/Moscow News*, 1986–1991.

YANAYEV, GENNADY Vice president of Soviet Union, December 1990–August 1991; leader of Soviet trade unions, 1986–1990; participant in August 1991 coup.

YAVLINSKY, GRIGORY Soviet/Russian economist: deputy chairman of the Russian Council of Ministers and of the State Commission for Economic Reform, 1990.

YAZOV, DMITRY Soviet defense minister, 1987–1991; participant in August 1991 coup.

YEFREMOV, LEONID First secretary of Stavropol region, 1964–1970.

YELTSIN, BORIS Russian president 1991–1999; chairman of the Russian Supreme Soviet, 1990–1991; Politburo candidate member, 1986–1988; Central Committee secretary, 1985–1986; first secretary of Moscow city party committee, 1985–1987.

ZAGLADIN, VADIM Adviser to Gorbachev, 1988–1991.

ZAIKOV, LEV First secretary of the Moscow city committee, 1987–1989.

ZASLAVSKY, ILYA USSR people's deputy.

ZASLAVSKAYA, TATYANA Soviet economic sociologist.

ZDRAVOMYSLOVA, OLGA Executive director of the Gorbachev Foundation.

ZHIVKOV, TODOR Bulgarian Communist party leader, 1954–1989.

ZIMYANIN, MIKHAIL Central Committee secretary, 1976–1987.

ZOELLICK, ROBERT U.S. State Department counselor, 1989–1992.

ZUBENKO, IVAN Gorbachev speechwriter in Stavropol.

ZYUGANOV, GENNADY Leader of the Russian Communist party.

GORBACHEV

The Gorbachevs vacationing at Foros, August 1990.

"GORBACHEV IS HARD TO UNDERSTAND"

"GORBACHEV IS HARD TO UNDERSTAND," he said to me, referring to himself, as he often does, in the third person. I had begun working on his biography in 2005, and a year later he asked how it was going. "Slowly," I apologized. "That's alright," he said, "Gorbachev is hard to understand."

He has a sense of humor. And he was correct. The world is deeply divided when it comes to understanding Gorbachev. Many, especially in the West, regard him as the greatest statesman of the second half of the twentieth century. In Russia, however, he is widely despised by those who blame him for the collapse of the Soviet Union and the economic crash that accompanied it. Admirers marvel at his vision and his courage. Detractors, including some of his former Kremlin comrades, accuse him of everything from naïveté to treason. The one thing they all agree upon is that he almost single-handedly changed his country and the world.

Before Gorbachev took power in March 1985, the Soviet Union was one of the world's two superpowers. By 1989 he had transformed the Soviet system. By 1990 he, more than anyone else, had ended the cold war. At the end of 1991, the Soviet Union collapsed, leaving him a president without a country.

He did not act alone. The sad state of the Soviet system in 1985 prompted Gorbachev's Kremlin colleagues to choose him to embark on reforms, although he ended up going much farther than they intended.

He had liberal Russian allies who welcomed his far-reaching reforms and worked to support them, but then chose Boris Yeltsin to lead them to the promised land. He had hard-line Soviet adversaries who resisted him, covertly at first, then openly and all-out. He had personal rivals, especially Yeltsin, whom he tormented and who tormented him in turn, before ultimately administering the coup de grâce to both Gorbachev and the USSR. Western leaders doubted Gorbachev, then embraced him, and finally abandoned him, refusing him the economic assistance he desperately needed. And, perhaps most important, he had to deal with Russia herself, with her traditional authoritarian and anti-Western ways: after rejecting both Gorbachev and Yeltsin, she finally embraced Vladimir Putin.

As Communist party general secretary, Gorbachev had the power to change almost everything. Moreover, he was unique among his peers. Other Soviet citizens, some of them in fairly high places, shared his values, but almost none at the very top. The only three Politburo members who backed him almost to the end, Aleksandr Yakovlev, Eduard Shevardnadze, and Vadim Medvedev, were in a position to do so only because Gorbachev appointed them or kept them on. Longtime British Soviet expert Archie Brown has written, "There is absolutely no reason to suppose that any conceivable alternative to Gorbachev in the mid-1980s would have turned Marxism-Leninism on its head and fundamentally changed both his country and the international system in an attempt to reverse a decline which did not pose an immediate threat either to the [Soviet] system or to him."[1]

The late Russian scholar Dmitry Furman framed Gorbachev's uniqueness more broadly: he was "the only politician in Russian history who, having full power in his hands, voluntarily opted to limit it and even risk losing it, in the name of principled moral values." For Gorbachev to have resorted to force and violence to hold on to power would have been "a defeat." In the light of Gorbachev's principles, Furman continued, "his final defeat was a victory"—although, one must add, it certainly didn't feel that way to Gorbachev at the time.[2]

How did Gorbachev become Gorbachev? How did a peasant boy, whose high-flown tribute to Stalin won a high school prize, turn into the Soviet system's gravedigger? "God alone knows," lamented Gorbachev's longtime prime minister, Nikolai Ryzhkov, who eventually turned against him.[3] One of Gorbachev's close aides, Andrei Grachev, called him "a genetic error of the system."[4] Gorbachev described himself as "a product" of that system and its "anti-product."[5] But how did he turn out to be both?

How did he become Communist party boss despite the most rigorous imaginable arrangement of checks and guarantees designed to guard against someone like him?[6] How, asks Grachev, did "a not entirely normal country end up with a leader with normal moral reflexes and common sense?"[7] An American psychiatrist who profiled foreign leaders for the Central Intelligence Agency remained "mystified" as to how such a "rigid system" could produce such an "innovative and creative" leader.[8]

What changes did Gorbachev seek for his country when he took power in 1985? Did he favor merely moderate economic reforms, as he said at the time, only to be radicalized by their lack of results? Or did he seek from the start to liquidate totalitarianism, concealing his aim because it was anathema to the Politburo members who selected him? What inspired him in the end to try to transform Communism in the USSR? What made him think he could transform a dictatorship into a democracy, a command economy into a market economy, a super-centralized unitary state into a genuine Soviet federation, and a cold war into a new world order based on the renunciation of force—all at the same time, and by what he called "evolutionary" means? What possessed him to think he could overcome Russian political, economic, and social patterns dating back centuries in a few short years: tsarist authoritarianism morphing into Soviet totalitarianism, long stretches of near-slavish obedience to authority punctuated by occasional bursts of bloody rebellion, minimal experience with civic activity, including compromise and consensus, no tradition of democratic self-organization, no real rule of law? As Gorbachev himself would later say of the Russian mind-set that thwarted him: "Our Russian mentality required that the new life be served up on a silver platter immediately, then and there, without reforming society"?[9]

Did Gorbachev have a plan? What was his strategy for transforming his country and the world? He didn't have either, critics claim. But no one did, admirers reply; no one could have had a blueprint for transforming his country and the world simultaneously.

Whether or not Gorbachev was a master strategist, wasn't he a brilliant tactician? How else could he have gotten a Politburo majority opposed to his most radical reforms to approve them? Was he nonetheless "insufficiently decisive and consistent," as one of his closest aides, Georgy Shakhnazarov, said?[10] How could he have been, when the risk he ran for six years was sudden ouster and even imprisonment?

How did Gorbachev react when many of his own Kremlin comrades turned against him and so many of his own appointees mounted a coup against him in August 1991? Or was it he who betrayed them, leading them to believe he aimed to modernize the Soviet system, but then contributing to its destruction?

Was Gorbachev vengeful and unforgiving? Does that help to explain his fateful inability to get along with Boris Yeltsin? But he forgave or forgot some of his closest aides' sharp criticism of him and kept them by his side at the foundation he established after losing power in 1991. "I can't bring myself to take vengeance on anyone," he said late in life. "I can't not forgive."[11]

Given all the obstacles to success, wasn't Gorbachev a utopian idealist? Not at all, he insisted: "I assure you that starry-eyed dreaminess is not characteristic of Gorbachev." Yet he himself recalled, "The wise Moses was right to make the Jews roam the desert for forty years . . . to get rid of the legacy of Egyptian slavery."[12]

As leaders go, especially Soviet leaders, Gorbachev was a remarkably decent man—too decent, many Russians and some Westerners have said, too unwilling to use force when force was needed to save the new democratic Soviet Union he was creating. Why, when his enemies were willing to use force to crush the freedom he had introduced, was he unwilling to use force to save it?[13] Was he intellectually convinced, after all the blood that had flowed in Russia's history, especially in the wars and purges of the twentieth century, that more must not be shed? Was it an emotional aversion based on personal exposure to the terrible cost of war and violence?

Gorbachev's decency showed in his family life. His wife, Raisa, was a woman of intellect and good taste (even though Nancy Reagan didn't think so). Unlike too many politicians, Gorbachev loved and cherished his wife, and, rare for a Soviet boss, he was a committed and involved father to his daughter, and grandfather to his two granddaughters. What, then, made him feel, after his wife's agonizing death from leukemia at the age of sixty-seven, that, as he put it, "I am guilty. I am the one who did her in"?[14]

If Gorbachev was indeed unique, if his actions differed so drastically from what other leaders would have done in his place, then his character is central to explaining his behavior. But his character is hard to define. Was he a great listener, as some say, a basically nonideological man willing to learn from real life? Or was he a man who didn't know how to stop talking? Gorbachev was extraordinarily self-confident, and self-woundingly narcissistic, according to Aron Belkin, a leading Soviet psychiatrist who didn't know Gorbachev personally, but whose diagnosis one of Gorbachev's closest aides, Anatoly Chernyaev, found credible.[15] But if narcissism is a spectrum at the "healthiest end" of which are "egotism" and "extreme self-confidence," is that so unusual among political leaders?[16] Whatever term one uses, Gorbachev was extraordinarily sure of himself. But when asked what characteristic he found most off-putting in another person to whom he has just been introduced, Gorbachev answered, "Self-confidence." And what in general irritated him most in other people? "Haughtiness."[17] Did he feel threatened by other self-assured men? Or did he see himself in others and not like what he saw?

Aleksandr Yakovlev, Gorbachev's closest collaborator in the Soviet leadership, but somewhat estranged from him in later years, thought Gorbachev found himself hard to understand. Yakovlev felt at times that Gorbachev "was afraid to look into himself, afraid to communicate candidly with himself, afraid to learn something he did not know and did not want to know." According to Yakovlev, Gorbachev "always needed a response, praise, support, sympathy, and understanding, which served as fuel for his vanity and self-esteem, as well as for his creative acts."[18]

If so, how did Gorbachev react when, within sight of the mountaintop, he had to watch so much of his grand vision evaporate around him? Was he in fact a truly great leader? Or was he a tragic hero brought low in part by his own shortcomings, but even more by the unyielding forces he faced?

CHAPTER 1

CHILDHOOD,
BOYHOOD, AND YOUTH

1931–1949

MIKHAIL GORBACHEV WAS BORN on March 2, 1931, in the village of Privolnoe, some ninety miles north of the Russian city of Stavropol in the North Caucasus. His parents named him Viktor, possibly a prudent way of honoring the coming "victory" of the first five-year plan that Stalin predicted. But his mother and grandmother insisted on a secret baptism, during which his paternal grandfather christened him Mikhail, a name with more biblical connotations. The port-wine-colored birthmark on his head, which according to Russian folklore is a sign of the devil, apparently didn't faze his parents or grandparents.

Privolnoe could be translated roughly as "free and easy," but in his childhood it was neither.[1] In Privolnoe, as in the rest of the Soviet Union, land was being collectivized in 1931, a violent process that took the lives of millions of peasants. During the terrible famine of 1932–1933, two of Gorbachev's uncles and one aunt perished. Stalin's Great Terror of the 1930s swept up both of Gorbachev's grandfathers: his mother's father arrested in 1934, his other grandfather in 1937. Then on June 22, 1941, the Nazis invaded the USSR, occupying Gorbachev's village for four and half months in 1942. Famine struck again in 1944 and 1946. And following the war, when the Soviet people hoped for a better life at long last, Stalin cracked down again, forcing them to sacrifice once more for the glorious future that Communism promised but never delivered.

A more horrible time would be hard to imagine. Living through it clearly influenced Gorbachev's later views—on Stalinism and the need to condemn it, on force and violence and the obligation to avoid their use. But there is another side to the story. Throughout the horrors, the regime insisted that Soviet schoolchildren ritually "thank Comrade Stalin" for their "happy childhood." And, to a surprising degree, Gorbachev's childhood actually was happy. That had something to do with his naturally sunny, optimistic temperament. But it also reflected silver linings that miraculously appeared in the dark clouds over his head. How horrible could collectivization be if one of his grandfathers, who particularly doted on him, chaired a collective farm? Both grandfathers survived the Gulag and were soon released. Just when the Nazis seemed about to seize the Gorbachev family as relatives of a Communist collective farm chairman, the Germans were forced to retreat from Privolnoe. His father, whom Gorbachev dearly loved, was reported killed in the war, but the report was mistaken: Sergei Gorbachev somehow survived four years at the front and returned home in triumph. After the war, in addition to doing well in school and becoming a Komsomol (Young Communist League) activist, Gorbachev won one of the USSR's highest medals, the Red Labor Banner, for helping his combine-driver father break harvesting records.

Psychologists report that when personal misfortunes and tragedies-in-the-making manage to have happy endings, whether by chance or owing to the efforts of their potential victims, the latter are likely to end up more confident and optimistic, less susceptible to depression.[2] Moreover, it wasn't just that the worst didn't happen to Mikhail Gorbachev, but that much of what happened was nearly ideal. His father, Sergei Gorbachev, was apparently a wonderful man, adored by Mikhail and respected by his fellow villagers. In his youth, Gorbachev recalled, he not only had "filial feelings" for his father but was "closely attached" to him. True, they never put their feelings for each other into words: "they were just there."[3] Gorbachev's maternal grandfather, Pantelei Gopkalo, treated him with "tenderness." Tenderness is not a feeling that Russian men frequently admit having. But there were also tensions in the extended family. His paternal grandfather, Andrei Gorbachev, was "very authoritarian," Mikhail Gorbachev remembers. Andrei and Gorbachev's father, Sergei, grew estranged, even coming to blows on at least one occasion. But Grandfather Andrei, too, had a soft spot in his heart for his grandson, as did both of Gorbachev's grandmothers. Gorbachev's mother, Maria, could be cold and punitive: she had resisted being married to her husband, and she disciplined her son with a belt until he was thirteen. The family tensions took a toll on Mikhail; as he grew up, and even after he matured, he seemed to have a special need for the kind of attention and respect that he thought he deserved.[4]

His parents were poor, but worked hard and well and trained him to do likewise. To survive the war Gorbachev had to leave childhood behind when he was barely into his teens. After the war, he became a star pupil and exemplary citizen in school. And to top it all off, he won that medal for harvesting grain. By 1950, when Gorbachev left Privolnoe to attend Moscow State University, he was strong, independent-minded and self-

Young Mikhail Gorbachev with his maternal grandparents, Pantelei and Vasilisa Gopkalo.

confident to the point of arrogance. Gorbachev summarized his own outlook this way: "We were poor, practically beggars, but in general I felt
wonderful."[5]

THE PREHISTORY OF THE STAVROPOL area where Gorbachev was raised
can be traced from the first millennium B.C., when various tribes entered
the northwest Caucasus region. Stavropol itself was created in 1777 as
a military base and proclaimed a city in 1785. At its center was one of
several fortresses built along a line from Azov to Mozdok by Prince Grigory Potemkin (of Potemkin village fame), at the bidding of his lover,
Empress Catherine the Great, to defend the southern border of the Russian Empire. Cossacks settled the area, eventually joined by serfs fleeing oppressive landowners, then by other peasants sent into forced
exile. In the second part of the nineteenth century, Gorbachev's paternal ancestors migrated from Voronezh in southern Russia, his mother's from Chernigov in northern Ukraine. The southern periphery of the
empire, Gorbachev notes, had a "turbulent character" to it: leaders of
two peasant rebellions, Stepan Razin and Yemiliyan Pugachev, came
from nearby, as did Yermak, the sixteenth-century Cossack leader and
explorer of Siberia. "Apparently," he continues with pride, this spirit "got
into the blood of those who lived here, and got transmitted as a legacy
from generation to generation."[6] It was in this same fertile region that
the conservative anti-Soviet dissident Aleksandr Solzhenitsyn was born
in 1918.

The village of Privolnoe itself, in the far northwest corner of the Stavropol region, close to its borders with Rostov and Krasnodar provinces,
was founded in 1861. To get there nowadays, one drives northwest from
Stavropol past fields of wheat and sunflowers. The entrance to the village
boasts a large, multicolored sign proclaiming, "Welcome to Privolnoe!"
From the village square, a road, at first asphalt, then dirt, winds a mile
or so to a wide, open spot where the earth rises slowly up from the Yegorlyk River. In the 1930s the town's population was almost equally divided
between Russians and Ukrainians. Back toward the village center,
ethnic Russians lived on one side of the river, with people of Ukrainian
origin on the other. The land where the Gorbachevs settled, dropping

down to the river, is now uninhabited. Equally empty, except for scrub grasses and bushes, is the terrain stretching up toward the steppe. Only a couple of outbuildings are visible on the horizon. The rest of Privolnoe, with its wooden houses and large church, to whose construction the former president of the USSR, Mikhail Gorbachev, made a substantial contribution, isn't visible either.

It was here, at what was then the very edge of the village, that Gorbachev's great-grandfather, Moisei Gorbachev, built a hut for his wife and three sons, Aleksei, Grigory, and Andrei. Many years later, after Mikhail grew up, the Gorbachev family abandoned this frequently flooded plain and moved closer to the village. As a child, all he could see beyond their hut, located about two hundred yards up from the river, was the Russian version of an American prairie: "steppe, steppe, and more steppe."[7] In Moisei Gorbachev's time, the extended family, all eighteen of them, crowded together in one large hut with several chambers; other relatives lived nearby. Later, the three sons built huts for themselves, and Gorbachev's recently married grandparents, Andrei and Stepanida, set up life on their own. Gorbachev's father, Sergei, was born here in 1909.

By all accounts, Grandfather Andrei, who fought in World War I on the western front, was tough and stubborn. "He didn't spare himself or others," his grandson remembers. "Everything had to be in order."[8] "He was "stern and merciless."[9] "Stingy," says another source. "Sullen and irascible, although strong and strong-willed," add others.[10] Yet the old man who intimidated so many softened at the sight of his grandson. "He would invite me to follow him around, tell me stories, feed me, and insist I eat."[11] Stepanida was "good and caring" and a particularly good "friend" to her grandson, he recalls. In this, too, he was "lucky."[12]

Andrei and Stepanida had six children, but only two boys, so the peasant commune, which counted only males when allotting land, assigned them too little. As a result, says Gorbachev, all members of the family, including the smallest, had to work "day and night." They managed to lift the family from poverty, becoming what were called "middle peasants." But to provide dowries for the daughters, grain and livestock had to be sold. What rescued the family was a huge garden plot where Grandfather Andrei managed to grow almost everything his family needed. "It was such a stupendous garden," his grandson remembered.

"It stretched all the way down to the river. Grandfather grafted apple trees so that you could see various kinds, red and green. It was beautiful, tremendous. But it was dangerous to run off down there. Grandfather was a hard man, very hard."[13]

Grandfather Andrei was also hard on Communism. Asked whether Andrei ever joined the Communist party, an uncle of Gorbachev's on his mother's side laughed and answered, "No, not for anything."[14] Andrei refused to join a collective farm and got away with it, at least for a while. He remained an individual peasant proprietor, obliged to raise a prescribed amount of grain and sell a portion of it to the state, but not allowed to own property. When famine struck, leaving the family to eat anything that was edible and some things that weren't, Andrei fed them frogs; Gorbachev's first memory, he recalled, was watching them boil in a big cauldron until their white stomachs rose to the surface. He didn't remember whether he ate them or not, but he remembered all too well when he and his youngest uncle, who was only five years older than he, "ate the seeds that were supposed to be planted."[15]

In 1934 Andrei was arrested for "not fulfilling the plan [for sowing] when there was nothing to fulfill it with," says his grandson. Sent to a forced labor camp near Irkutsk in Siberia, where prisoners cut and hauled lumber, Andrei managed to earn four work commendations. He was released early and returned to Privolnoe (where he hung his four camp medals next to religious icons on the wall) more sullen than ever, but with no choice but to join the kolkhoz (collective farm). For the next seventeen years, he was in charge of a pig farm within the kolkhoz, which he turned into one of the best in the region. "So you see," Gorbachev said in an interview, "wherever they put him, he worked hard and forced others to, as well."[16] The lesson was not lost on his grandson.

Gorbachev's other grandfather, Pantelei Gopkalo, was the antipode, politically and psychologically, of Andrei Gorbachev. Grandfather Pantelei welcomed the Bolshevik Revolution. "It was Soviet power that saved us, that gave us land," said Gopkalo, who came from a dirt-poor peasant family and had slogged through the First World War on the Turkish front. Repeated over and over in the Gopkalo family, these words made a big impression on his grandson. So did the fact that after raising himself from a "poor" to a "middle" peasant, Gopkalo helped organize a new peasant commune in the 1920s, where he worked along with his wife, Vasilisa (also of Ukrainian origin), and their daughter, Maria, Mikhail Gorbachev's mother-to-be. In 1928, Pantelei Gopkalo joined the Communist party. Not long after that, he helped organize the first collective farm in Privolnoe in 1929. When young Mikhail asked his grandmother what that involved, "she laughed and said, 'All night your grandfather organized people, gathered them together, and the next morning, they all ran away.'"[17] Or as she put it more grimly to her grandson on a later occasion, which Gorbachev recalled at a Politburo meeting in October 1987: "What enmity collectivization created! Brother against brother, son against father, through whole families it rolled. The quotas came down from above—so many kulaks to evict, whether they actually were kulaks or not."[18]

So-called kulaks (the Russian word literally means "fist") were supposedly "rich" peasants; in fact, most were small proprietors who by dint of hard work and enterprise had managed to raise their status slightly above that of "middle" peasants. Gopkalo's son, also named Sergei, helped in the effort to "smash the bloodsuckers." "I was in a Komsomol cell," Gorbachev's maternal uncle continued. "We went homestead by homestead, driving out those who were pointed out to us. We cleaned them out. I was sorry for them. The head of my squad was always drunk. In one hut, he told me to crawl up in the loft and pull everything out. I took a quick look and shouted, 'Nothing there.' 'Crawl out,' he said, 'I'll take a look myself.' And though he was so soused he could barely see, he noticed several sheepskin coats. Boy, did I get it after that."[19]

"Dekulakization," like so much else in the Soviet Union, was supposed to proceed according to a plan, complete with monthly targets. Families were stripped of their property and herded into exile, some dumped in the barren steppe of the northeastern Stavropol region, others crammed into cattle cars in which many perished, heading much farther east. Just what role Pantelei Gopkalo played in all this is not known, but he obviously pleased his bosses, who assigned him to head a kolkhoz named "Red October."

Whatever his role in the brutal collectivization process, Pantelei Gopkalo seems to have been a decent chairman once the kolkhoz was established. A Stavropol journalist, who much later interviewed collective farmers about him, reported positive recollections from almost every-one.[20] By 1937, Pantelei had become head of the regional land depart-ment. "But he was still one of us," Gorbachev adds. "He was such an interesting person with so much authority, he talked quietly and slowly."[21] Gorbachev's grandfathers provided two models of authority: Andrei's rough, independent, and authoritarian, Pantelei's, as least as far as his grandson encountered it, milder, more considerate, and sym-pathetic to collectivized agriculture.

For several years beginning when he was three years old, Gorbachev lived with his maternal grandparents, rather than his parents, on their collective farm some twelve miles from Privolnoe. He would run along behind his grandfather's long, deep, open wagon, Gorbachev recalled. "I had almost complete freedom with them, and they loved me whole-heartedly. I felt as if I were the most important person in their family. No matter how much they tried to leave me with my parents, even if just for a short while, they didn't succeed. Not only was I satisfied with the arrangement, my father and mother were, too. . . ."[22] "That way they were free."[23]

In a time of famine, it made sense for Gorbachev's parents, who had barely turned twenty when he was born, to leave him with his doting and relatively well-off grandparents, themselves still young. (His grand-mother Vasilisa was only thirty-eight.) But was he really so satisfied with this arrangement, and if so, what did that mean? Once, when his grand-father tried to take him back to his parents in a horse-drawn wagon, Gor-bachev jumped out and dashed back a mile or so until Gopkalo caught up with him and took him back to the kolkhoz. Granted, he felt he was the most important thing in his grandparents' lives: Vasilisa often repeated that he was her favorite grandson. But what about in his parents'?[24]

GORBACHEV'S FATHER HAD ONLY four years of formal education, although he later received tutelage in the Bolsheviks' "literacy cam-paign" and training as a tractor driver/mechanic. According to his son, Sergei Gorbachev was "a simple village man, but endowed by nature with such a good mind, so much intelligence, inquisitiveness, human-ity, and many other good qualities. All this set him apart from his fellow villagers, but they regarded him with respect and trust: he was someone they could 'count on.'"[25]

Gorbachev's testimony is supported by others. Sergei Gorbachev "was a wise man," recalled a contemporary, "modest but extremely hard-working. . . . People loved him. He was always calm, a good man. People went to him for advice. He didn't say much, but he weighed every word. He didn't like speechifying."[26] According to a Komsomol colleague of Mikhail's, the elder Gorbachev "never raised his voice, was levelheaded, orderly, and decent."[27] Raisa Gorbachev remembered, "Mikhail Sergeyevich and his father were very much alike. They were friends. Sergei Andreyevich never got a systematic education, but he had a natural cultivation, a sort of nobility, a certain breadth of interests."[28]

Given these qualities, so at odds with those of Grandfather Andrei, it's not surprising that the two didn't get along. Nor did it help that Sergei chose to follow his father-in-law, rather than his father, by joining a collective farm. While Sergei and Maria were still living in Andrei Gorbachev's household, the grain was stored in the yard, where it was

Gorbachev's father, Sergei Gorbachev.

divided among members of the family. Once when Sergei was at work
in the fields, his father grabbed some of that grain for himself and hid it
in the attic. When Sergei climbed a ladder to search for grain under the
roof, his father tackled him. At twenty-three, Sergei was strong enough
to wrestle his father to the ground, but in the process broke his arm.
Sergei tried to keep the episode secret. In the end they divided the grain,
"but the episode certainly complicated relations between them," Gorbachev recalled.[29] Asked whether relations between his two grandfathers remained strained, Gorbachev at first said, "No, they were normal,"
but then added, "Of course, Andrei was jealous of Pantelei."[30]

Pantelei's daughter, Maria Gopkalo, born in 1911, was seventeen
when she married Sergei Gorbachev in 1928; her husband was nineteen.
"She was a beautiful woman," Mikhail Gorbachev recalled, but she was
also "tough and strong-minded."[31] Others agree that Maria, who was
and remained illiterate, was a "powerful woman, direct, with a sharp
tongue and a hard character."[32] Fellow villagers considered her coarse in
comparison with her husband. Gorbachev doesn't disagree: "It was as if
my father and Pantelei had somehow come out of the intelligentsia; they
resembled each other in that, and in their manner of treating others. My
mother was completely different."

Gorbachev revealed in an interview that his mother had not wanted
to marry his father at all. At age seventeen, she would have had a choice
of other suitors, especially if she was so beautiful. As for Sergei, he "loved
my mother deeply. Later in life, wherever he came to visit us in Stavropol,
he always went to a store to buy a present for Maria before he returned.
Wherever he went, he always brought her presents."[33] Asked whether
she ever came to love her husband, Gorbachev paused. "Later, I think,
when they had a family, when they had children." Yet in sharp contrast
to most Russian peasant women of that time, who bore many children,
Maria had her second and only other child, Gorbachev's brother, Aleksandr, in 1947, when Mikhail was sixteen years old. "After the war,"
Gorbachev added, "all the women fell in love with their husbands who
somehow managed to return alive."[34]

In accordance with peasant tradition, Maria and Sergei Gorbachev
began their married life in his father's house. It was a long adobe-walled
hut stretching from east to west with a straw-thatched roof. Describing

it in a 2007 interview, Gorbachev scribbled a picture on a piece of note-paper: "This first chamber, on the left, was the clean part, presentable," its earthen floor partly covered with carpet runners woven by women in the family. "For receiving guests?" he was asked. "No, no. What do you mean, guests? I remember it well. My grandparents' bed was here. And in the corner, a huge iconostasis consisting of ten to twelve gilded icons. The icon lamp was next to it." (In the home of Grandfather Pantelei, he being a collective farm chairman, the iconostasis was occupied by por-traits of Lenin and Stalin.) Through the door was another room with a huge stove, on which the women baked bread, and a smaller stove, on which they prepared everything else. Children slept on top of the big stove. In the corner by the wall stood a dining table and a bench. Another corner of this room was partitioned off for Gorbachev's parents so they could have a slice of privacy when they were first married. There was no bath, he added. They bathed in water heated in a tub.[35]

The next chamber, on the other side of a little vestibule, was the place where farming equipment—harnesses, whips, and the like—and grain were stored. Above was a loft where Gorbachev used to clamber up, "a cozy spot where I sometimes fell asleep." Here he once found a sack full of thick wads of paper, full of old tsarist currency. "They were useless, but Grandfather Andrei thought, 'maybe someday . . .'"[36] On at least one occasion, Mikhail slept next to a recently born calf, with a goose sitting on her eggs not far away.[37]

Another door led to a room where livestock were kept. The only heat in the whole complex was from the stove, plus that generated by the ani-mals and by the people who lived there. "I remember it all well," Gor-bachev recalled. "As a little boy, I climbed all over everything."

Prompted by crowded conditions and tensions between generations, Gorbachev's parents set up their own household. Pantelei built a hut for his daughter and son-in-law not far from Grandfather Andrei's, and arranged for Sergei Gorbachev to receive training as a tractor and com-bine driver.

Meanwhile, famine struck, taking the lives, according to Mikhail Gorbachev, of "between a third and a half of the villagers. Whole fami-lies perished, so that long before the war itself, half-destroyed huts, aban-doned by their owners, stood out like orphans in the village."[38] Next came

Grandfather Andrei's arrest in 1934. Grandmother Stepanida was left with two younger children, so Gorbachev's father had to care for everyone. Andrei's arrest marked his family as one that "nobody needed," and the family's location at the edge of the village intensified their isolation. But Andrei soon returned, and Grandfather Pantelei helped his son-in-law land a job at the local Machine Tractor Station (MTS). In contrast to collective farms, a state-owned MTS was a "higher form of property," with its employees classified as proletarians rather than peasants. Sergei would have higher status and more pay than his peasant relatives, on top of which he was soon breaking records for the harvest and being hailed in the district newspaper.[39]

IN 1937 PANTELEI WAS promoted to the district procurement office that oversaw deliveries of grain and other crops. That same year he was arrested during the Great Purge. "Quotas" sent down from Moscow determined the minimum number to be detained. Chided later for exceeding his quota, a police official in a neighboring district replied, "But others were arresting so many. What am I, worse than they are?"[40] Pantelei was an inviting target for those who envied his authority, or had suffered from his use of it. One of the terrible ironies of Stalin's purges was that they were genuinely popular among peasants who hated the local officials who had collectivized them.[41] In standard Stalinist fashion, Pantelei was seized in the middle of the night. His wife, Vasilisa, moved to Privolnoe to live with Gorbachev's parents. "I remember," he recalled, "how after his arrest, our neighbors began to avoid our home, as if it were plague-stricken, how only at night and in secret someone close to us would drop by for a moment. Even kids who lived in the vicinity would avoid contact with me. All this stunned me, and it has remained in my memory for my whole life."[42]

Pantelei was in prison for fourteen months. Sentenced to death, he survived when the regional procurator reduced the charge from the capital crime of heading an "underground right-Trotskyite counterrevolutionary organization" to the lesser "malfeasance in office," and he was released in December 1938 to return to Privolnoe. That same winter evening, Gorbachev remembered, his closest relatives sat around the rough-hewn table in his parents' hut while Pantelei, weeping, recounted what had been done to him. "The interrogator blinded him with a bright lamp, broke his arms pressing him against the door, and beat him brutally. When these 'standard' tortures didn't work, they thought up new ones: they wrapped grandfather tightly in a wet sheepskin coat and placed him on a hot stove. Pantelei Efimovich endured that and a lot more."[43]

Pantelei was an entirely "different" man on his return from prison.[44] He never talked about his ordeal again, nor did anyone else in the family. But the fact that he recounted it even once was rare, and it had a searing effect on his grandson. Most survivors of the terror never recounted the details of their ordeal at all, so their families preserved a more favorable view of the regime, a view that later turned sharply negative when the truth was finally revealed by Nikita Khrushchev in his 1956 "secret speech" denouncing Stalin.[45] In that sense, Gorbachev had a more balanced view all along, even though his grandfather, despite his ordeal, seemed to remain a believer: "Stalin doesn't know what the organs of the NKVD are up to," he said. The Gorbachev family's silence didn't mean they were trying to forget; they were afraid to remember. And Gorbachev, too, remained silent. Even after he became a high party official in Stavropol, even when he was a member of the party Central Committee, even after he became party general secretary and then president of the USSR, even after he fiercely condemned Stalin and Stalinism, Gorbachev never asked to see the records of Pantelei's arrest and interrogation until the August 1991 coup nearly drove him from power. During the 1960s and 1970s, when Brezhnev's regime was partly rehabilitating Stalin after Khrushchev's attacks on him, it would have been risky for Gorbachev to do so. But even after he himself was the nation's leading de-Stalinizer? "I couldn't cross some sort of psychological barrier," Gorbachev recalled.[46]

BY 1941 LIFE WAS improving in Privolnoe. Shoes, cotton cloth, salt, herring, matches, soap, and kerosene had reappeared in the stores. The collective farm had actually begun to pay its farmers in long-promised grain. Grandfather Pantelei replaced his hut's straw roof with tile. Gramophones appeared for sale. Very occasionally silent movies from portable

projectors were shown in the village. "The height of bliss for us children,"
Gorbachev recalled, "would be ice cream which appeared from somewhere now and then. And on summer Sundays, families picnicked in
the forests, where men sang languid Russian and Ukrainian folk songs,
drank vodka and sometimes squared off in fights. Little boys kicked balls
around, while women gossiped and kept track of their men-folk."[47]

Before dawn on Sunday, June 22, 1941, the Germans attacked the
USSR. At noon that day, villagers in Privolnoe gathered in front of a
radio loudspeaker (the only one in town) in the central square and listened, hardly breathing, to the official announcement. "It might seem an
exaggeration," Gorbachev continued, "but I remember everything about
the war. I've forgotten much that I had to live through after the war, but
the images and events of wartime are engraved in my memory forever.
When the war began I was ten years old."[48]

First of all, he remembered his father's departure for the front. When
the first call-ups came, delivered in the evening by men on horse-
back from the district draft board, Sergei Gorbachev got a brief defer-
ment until the harvest was gathered. Then one August morning, the
family crowded into a cart and headed for the district center, Molotovskoye (later Krasnogvardeisk), twelve miles away. There the square was
filled with other families, the sobbing of women, children, and old people
"blending into a heart-rending wail of sorrow." Gorbachev's father
bought him ice cream for the last time (which young Mikhail downed in
one gulp on a blisteringly hot day), and a balalaika as a keepsake, onto
which Gorbachev carved the date, August 3, 1941.[49]

With all able-bodied men gone, only women and children, the sick,
and old men remained in Privolnoe. The first winter came early and
hit hard. A fierce blizzard blanketed the village on October 8, covering
everything with snowdrifts. For the time being, there was enough to eat,
although not for the livestock, and little or nothing with which to heat
the huts. It took all the women, working together, to clear the road and
haul in hay. Once, Maria Gorbachev and several others failed to return
from road clearing for three days. They had been arrested and imprisoned for loading hay from state-owned haystacks onto their sledges, but,
as the wives of soldiers serving at the front and with children to feed at
home, they were released.[50]

Boys like Gorbachev had to do the work of their absent fathers, "moving from childhood," Gorbachev recalled, "to adulthood, right then and there."[51] When spring came, he took care of the garden that fed the family. Arising before dawn, his mother would start digging and weeding, then turn the work over to him when she left to work in the kolkhoz fields. His main job was to haul hay for the family cow and fuel for the stove. Since forests were scarce on the steppe, villagers used compressed cow dung for baking bread and cooking, and pricker bushes to heat the hut. Gorbachev worked alone, "but once in a while, forgetting about everything on earth, bewitched by a winter blizzard, or by the leaves whispering in the garden during the summertime, I'd find myself transported to some faraway place, unreal but greatly desired, the kingdom of dreams of a child's fantasies."[52] Was Gorbachev dreaming of anything like the brilliant future that awaited him? "I wasn't dreaming of anything in particular," he replied in an interview, "just of being someplace far away from where I was."[53] He may have been trying to sound modest. He later told another friend, "For some reason I believed that an entirely different future awaited me."[54]

When letters arrived from Gorbachev's father, his illiterate mother would dictate a reply to her son, or he would write back himself. Gorbachev's father subscribed to the Communist party newspaper, *Pravda*. Now, when it arrived, it was Mikhail who read it, first by himself, then, while sitting atop a huge stove, to the women who gathered at someone's hut in the evening to be together and hear the latest news. One day, a booklet arrived tucked into a copy of *Pravda*, recounting the heroic and widely reported story of a young partisan girl, Zoya Kozmodemianskaya, who was hanged by the Nazis. He read it aloud to everyone who had assembled. "They were stunned by the Germans' cruelty, and the courage of the young Communist girl."[55]

For a long time, the news Gorbachev read to his neighbors wasn't good. Before 1941, he and other boys had often played "war" in the gardens behind their huts, marching around, "storming" empty, run-down huts that had been abandoned in the famine of 1932, "shooting" each other, and singing rousing patriotic songs. They assumed the Germans would "get it in the mouth" if they invaded. All too soon, though, the enemy was at the gates of Moscow and near Rostov-on-Don, about 215 miles from Stavropol. By the summer of 1942, refugees were shuffling through Privolnoe, lugging rucksacks and kit bags, pushing baby carriages or handcarts, trading their goods for food, driving cows, horses, and sheep ahead of them.[56] Pantelei and Vasilisa, fearing what the Germans would do to a collective farm chairman, fled to parts unknown. Local authorities emptied fuel tanks into the Yegorlyk River, and burned fields that had not yet been harvested. On July 27, Soviet troops who had abandoned Rostov straggled through Privolnoe, heading east, looking grim and exhausted, their faces marked, Gorbachev recalled, by "sorrow and guilt." Bomb blasts, the rumble of heavy weaponry, the sound of shooting drew closer, and then, suddenly—two days of silence. On the third day, Germans roared into the village on motorcycles, followed by infantry troops. When the Nazis first appeared, Misha Gorbachev and two of his cousins stood watching. "Let's run," one cousin shouted, but Gorbachev says he stopped him: "Stop! We're not afraid of them!" he remembers saying.[57]

At least one German soldier seemed friendly, showing the boys photos of his children. Others seized everything they needed: cattle, pigs, chicken, grain. Finding Gorbachev and his friends hiding in a well, the Germans forced them to haul water.[58] "We had to serve them," Gorbachev insists. "We had no choice." Soon most of the Germans moved on to Molotovskoye, leaving Red Army deserters, theoretically assigned to police Privolnoe, to run amok—drinking, thieving, raping.[59] Gorbachev's mother and grandmother tried not to show their fear. Vasilisa had returned when the Germans got to Stavropol. (Pantelei managed to sneak away through cornfields and gullies.) Soon she was arrested by policemen, who ransacked the Gorbachev homestead. "Mother did not flinch," Gorbachev recalls. "Her courage reflected not only her character—she was a strong woman—but her despair at not knowing how all this would end." Some villagers had threatened her, saying, "Just you wait. . . . You're not living under the Reds anymore." The Gorbachevs heard rumors of mass executions in neighboring towns and of a massacre of Communists supposedly planned for January 26, 1943. So Maria and Grandfather Andrei decided to hide Mikhail on Andrei's farm several miles from Privolnoe. Late one night, Gorbachev and his mother set out but got lost in the dark, finding the farm only when, in the midst of a violent storm, flashes of lightning illuminated their way. But on January 21, Soviet troops liberated Privolnoe.[60]

During the occupation, the Germans drafted an old man, known to villagers as Grandpa Savka, to serve as the village elder. According to Gorbachev, Savka resisted the assignment until neighbors convinced him it would be better if one of their own represented them to the occupation forces. "Everyone knew that he had done everything he could to protect people from harm," and some even dared to say so when Savka was later arrested by the Soviets and sentenced to ten years for "betraying the Motherland." On top of what had been done to his grandfathers, this was another early sign to Misha Gorbachev of Soviet injustice. Not that a twelve-year-old could fully understand that, but he knew that Grandpa Savka was taken away, and later learned that he died in prison as an "enemy of the people."

The German retreat left Privolnoe in ruins without machinery, kolkhoz livestock, or seeds. When spring came, cows belonging to individual peasants pulled the plows. "I can still see the scene," Gorbachev continued, "the women in tears, the melancholy eyes of the cows." Except that since cows were all they had to feed their families, the women sometimes pulled the plows themselves. The harvest that fall was minuscule, yet it was requisitioned by the state, leaving the peasants almost nothing to eat. Famine struck again that winter and spring. Gorbachev survived only when his mother and a few other women hitched two surviving bulls to a cart and set off for the Kuban region. She had taken two pairs of her husband's calf leather boots, and a suit he had never worn, intending to trade them for corn. She left her son at home, although his aunt Sanya spent the night in the hut. "Mother took the last corn we had and measured out a cupful for me for each day," Gorbachev remembered. "I made groats and cooked kasha. A week went by, then two, and mother didn't return. Only on the fifteenth day did she arrive with a sack of corn, thirty-two kilos. That was our salvation."[61]

Fifteen days was a long time for a twelve-year-old to be left mostly alone in the midst of war, with no guarantee that either of his parents would ever return. It was a longer time still until goods were delivered to Privolnoe. Meanwhile, Gorbachev recalled, we had "no clothes, no shoes, no salt, no soap, no kerosene for the lamps, no matches." Villagers mended their footwear and clothing, and when these disintegrated, grew hemp to be made into shirts ("which felt as if they were made from wood"), made outer garments out of wool, boots out of hides soaked in petroleum, fire by striking flint and kindling ash-impregnated cotton, and "matches" with TNT from antitank bombs. "We had to learn everything from scratch," Gorbachev remembered with pride, and "I learned it to perfection. I found an old handle, adapted it, attached it to the axle of a piece of machinery, and turned it into a device for planting corn seed. . . . Just imagine, beginning when I was thirteen, it was my job to stack hay for our cow, scythe down the bushes that we used for fuel, and stack them. The work broadened my shoulders. It was tough physical work."[62]

Coping with the trials of wartime strengthened Gorbachev's self-confidence and self-esteem. A pivotal event in his relationship with his mother occurred in 1944. Gorbachev was thirteen when "she picked up a belt and raised it, threatening to whip me again. I grabbed it, tore it from her, and said, 'That's it! No more!' She burst into tears—because I was the last object she could control, and now that was gone."[63] Usually, fathers did the beating in peasant households. To be whipped by his mother when he was thirteen and doing the work of his absent father was devastating. Had his mother always been responsible for disciplining him? "She wasn't responsible for anything," he answered grimly. Rather, when he misbehaved, she would threaten to tell his father when he got home. "But father and I had a special relationship." And Gorbachev's mother resented that, too. "She never could forgive me for the way I defended my father. 'Your father is your favorite,' she would say to me. I'd say, 'You're my favorite, too, but you haven't noticed that I've grown up.'"[64]

He and his mother had to "settle things between us," he says, "and we began to do so pretty quickly." Nearly seventy years later, recalling how his mother had always been beside him during the war, he insisted, "I loved my mother. As did my father—until he died. She was a beautiful woman, very strong, and businesslike. Father was proud of her; he forgave her swagger, and helped her in everything. And that set a good example for me and my brother."[65] But it wasn't an easy example to follow.

When Gorbachev was promoted to Moscow in 1978, he asked Raisa Gudarenko, the young female party boss of a district near Privolnoe, to

Mikhail Gorbachev with his mother, Maria Gopkalo, on the day
his father departed for the front in World War II, August 1941.

look after his aging mother. According to Gudarenko, Maria Gorbachev
was physically strong (having once, when no longer young, actually
thatched her family hut's roof), "extremely direct" about what she liked
and didn't like, and "outwardly severe." Gorbachev's mother was a stick-
ler for order: everything in her house had to be just right. When guests
came she herself "covered the table" with food and drink, even when
others could have done so for her. She refused to have domestic help
and washed her own clothes. Although her home had a modern bathroom, she insisted on using the outhouse to save scarce water for other
villagers.[66]

Whatever Gorbachev thought of his mother, he chose a wife who
resembled her in her perfectionism.

———————

IN THE SUMMER OF 1944, Gorbachev and his mother received a letter from the front containing Sergei Gorbachev's documents and family photos, informing them that he had "died the death of the brave" in the Carpathian Mountains. "The family wept for three days," Gorbachev recalled, "and then—received a letter from Father himself, saying he was alive and well." Both letters were dated August 27. Had he written his before falling in battle? Four days later another letter from him arrived, proving he had survived. Gorbachev wrote back to his father, complaining about those who misinformed the family. "No, son, you're unjustly blaming the soldiers," Sergei Gorbachev replied. "Anything can happen at the front." Gorbachev was upset at having been reprimanded by his father, but learned another lesson from his fair-mindedness.[67]

The war ended for Sergei Gorbachev in late 1944 when he was seriously wounded by a bomb blast that lodged a large shrapnel fragment in his leg. "He could have been killed dozens of times," Gorbachev marvels. He had received a Medal of Valor for crossing the Dnieper River under relentless bombardment, and two Orders of the Red Star. One day in 1945, someone ran up to Misha and cried, "Your father is coming." "At first I didn't believe it, but then I saw him. We walked toward each other. He looked at me. What we were feeling is hard to describe. He grabbed me and embraced me. He saw that I was wearing a rough shirt made out of hemp, and rough, wool pants, homemade, too. I was barefoot, but I was healthy. I stood there. He looked at me again and said something that I've remembered my whole life: 'We fought until we ran out of fight,' he said. 'That's how you must live.'"[68]

Sergei Gorbachev never got over what he had seen and experienced in the war—and neither did his son. Both then and especially later, when father and son worked together for long hours in the fields, Sergei recounted the horrible first months of the war, when Red Army soldiers had to fight without rifles, or two men would share one rifle, or they would grab rifles from fallen comrades and fight on. He described fellow soldiers being mowed down by machine guns. He recalled hand-to-hand combat so brutal and bloody that it took him hours afterward to pull himself together: "It was either you or him; you hit, you struck, you shot, like a beast." Gorbachev's father fought at Kursk (the biggest tank battle in history), and helped liberate Kiev and Kharkov. One time, when Sergei Gorbachev's group of sappers failed to blow up a key bridge, they were threatened with execution by their own officers. Mikhail Gorbachev himself experienced war's horrors close up. Late in the winter of 1943, when he and some friends were searching for abandoned German weapons in a remote stretch of forest, they stumbled upon the remains of Red Army soldiers, which he observed closely and describes movingly: "decaying corpses, partly devoured by animals, skulls in rusted helmets, bleached bones, rifles protruding from the sleeves of the rotting jackets. . . . There they lay, in the thick mud of trenches and craters, unburied, staring at us out of black, gaping eye-sockets."[69]

Do such experiences help explain Gorbachev's extraordinary reluctance, once he became supreme Soviet leader, to use force and violence to preserve the Soviet empire? Perhaps because that reluctance, so admired in the West, is as strongly condemned in Russia, he declined in an interview to answer the question.

GORBACHEV WAS FOURTEEN YEARS OLD when the war ended. During the war, the Privolnoe village school closed for two years, reopening in the fall of 1944. By then, Gorbachev had no particular desire to study. "After all I had lived through, it didn't seem like a serious undertaking. Not to mention that I had nothing to wear to school." When his parents and maternal grandfather heard this, Gorbachev recalled, they were appalled and "surrounded me as if I were a wolf."[70] "Sell everything we have," Sergei Gorbachev wrote to his wife from the front, "clothes and shoes, and buy books. Mikhail must study."[71] "Take my boots," Grandfather Pantelei added. "But I have no coat," his grandson objected. "Wear my coat," Pantelei replied. "You've got to study, Mishka. That's what it takes to become a real person. Study well!"[72]

Gorbachev went off to the school, one and a half miles from his hut, in clothes too big for him. But he had "fallen behind." "I arrived, I sat there, I listened, I understood nothing. I didn't stay, I went home, I threw away the only book I had, and announced to my mother that I wasn't going back." His strong-minded mother burst into tears when he told her, but then left with possessions that she traded for pile of books with which she returned that evening. Gorbachev insisted he wouldn't go back. But "then I began to glance through them, to read, and got carried away. Mother lay down to sleep, but I kept reading [particularly a Russian language textbook]. Something must have happened in my head that night because in the morning I got up and went to school. By the end of the year, I had earned a certificate of merit, and from then on I got 'distinction.'"[73]

What happened that night was a revealing turning point. For a moment, a sharp shadow of fear—of failure and humiliation—fell across Gorbachev's growing self-confidence. But then his so often harsh mother again showed her love. After that, Gorbachev began to identify success in life with reading and thinking, and also with leading his peers. "From my earliest days," he later would say, "I liked to be a leader among my peers—that was my nature."[74] But first he, his fellow pupils, and their teachers had to make the schools usable. They had only a few textbooks, maps, and visual aids and some chalk. "The rest we had to prepare with our own hands."[75] Instead of a notebook, he wrote in the margins of his father's tractor instruction manual. Students made their own ink. They pitched in to feed weak and emaciated horses so they could haul fuel to heat the classrooms. Gorbachev helped mount an evening of amateur entertainment that raised 1,385 rubles, which purchased ten pairs of shoes and four sets of underwear for the pupils even poorer than he was.[76]

In 1946, while still attending Privolnoe's small primary school, he joined the Komsomol. In the much bigger high school (located in the district center, with around a thousand students), he became the Komsomol leader, organizing his fellow students in a variety of "political" activities: an evening discussion of "The Ulianov [Lenin's real name] Family"; a "political information session" on events overseas; a debate about a novel, much favored by Stalin, by Viktor Nekrasov, titled *In the Trenches of Stalingrad*; putting out a magazine called "The Little Dawn"; preparing an article, "Let's Talk about Our Study Schedule," for the "Young Stalinist" wall newspaper.[77] Gorbachev was a star in school, but not quite beloved by all. "From childhood on," he later confessed, "I wanted to amaze everyone." Or as he put it on another occasion, "I got used to lording it over people; I always wanted to develop myself." When it came time to elect a Komsomol leader, seven groups of students from seven nearby villages each nominated one candidate. As Gorbachev sat down after speaking, someone pulled away his chair and he collapsed on the floor. Did that mean some of his peers weren't as eager to be led by him as he was eager to lead them? "Actually," he joked to an American student audience sixty-five years later, "that helped me get elected."[78] Soon, he was appointed to the Komsomol committee for the whole district.

The graduating eighth-grade class of the Privolnoe school, 1947. Gorbachev is on the extreme left in the top row.

Gorbachev read everything he could get his hands on. He spent three days in a hayloft reading Thomas Mayne Reid's *The Headless Horseman*. Reid (1818–1883) was an Irish American author whose adventure tales about the American West were a staple among Soviet adolescents. Inspired by his stories, they played cowboys and Indians, except that in the USSR the Indians were the "good guys." Over the next few years, Gorbachev graduated to higher culture; he found in a meager school library a one-volume collection of the work of Vissarion Belinsky, the radical philosopher and literary critic of the first half of the nineteenth century. A bitter foe of the tsarist regime, a firebrand of the Westernizing intelligentsia, who proclaimed himself a socialist as early as 1841, the extraordinarily intense Belinsky was both a revelation and an inspiration to Gorbachev. The book "became my bible. I was carried away by it. I read and reread it, and carried it with me everywhere." When he wrote his memoirs in the early 1990s, Gorbachev still had the copy presented to him in 1950 as the first boy from his village to study at Moscow University: "I have the book in my hand right now. What interested me, what I paid special attention to, were the critic's *philosophical* pronouncements."[79]

From Belinsky, Gorbachev moved on to Pushkin, Gogol, and especially Lermontov. That early nineteenth-century poet of the Caucasus died young in a duel in Piatigorsk, approximately 120 miles from Privolnoe. Lermontov's romanticism captivated him; "I knew not only his short poems but his long ones by heart." Next, he was fascinated by Mayakovsky—more poetry full of romantic love, erotic longing, and rebelliousness. "What struck me then, and still strikes me now, was how these young writers managed to lift themselves to a level where they made philosophical generalizations. That was a gift of God!"[80] Initially attracted to writers' philosophical reflections, later, as Soviet leader, he aspired to approximate that intellectual level himself.

First, however, came ninth grade. He attended the high school in Molotovskoye, the district center twelve miles down the road from Privolnoe. Nowadays that distance is traveled quickly by car, on a good highway, which, in the summertime, runs between broad, green fields, where acres of tall yellow sunflowers stretch almost to the horizon. Back in 1948, Gorbachev and his classmates from Privolnoe covered the dirt road on foot in a little less than two hours, heading home after classes ended on Saturday afternoon, trudging back toward evening on Sunday. Once in a while they hitched a ride on an oxcart transporting milk to a cheese factory in Molotovskoye, but often they bushwhacked through fields and gullies, even in the dead of winter. At home they got provisions for the coming week (lard, pork, bread, and sweets), and their mothers did their laundry. During the week Gorbachev and two other boys from Privolnoe lived in a room in town.[81] He was now, as he later put it, "a fully independent person." No one "monitored my studies." How could they, since his parents and other relatives were minimally literate? "My parents considered that I was enough of an adult to take care of myself, without their goading and urging. Only once was I able to persuade my father to come to school for a parents' meeting. But when I was old enough to start attending parties and hanging around with kids, my father once said to my mother, 'It seems Mikhail has started coming home late. Say something to him.'"[82]

Gorbachev's mother with her two sons,
Mikhail and Aleksandr, not earlier than 1948.

The school, housed in a former tsarist era *gymnaziium* still in use decades later, and now bearing a plaque near the entrance saying, "The First President of the USSR Studied Here," is a large two-story building with classrooms on either side of a long corridor leading to an iron staircase decorated with intricate metal ornamentation. In 2005 teachers showed guests a classroom with rows of wooden desks facing a blackboard, pointing out the one at which Misha Gorbachev sat. (As far as could be determined, he did not carve his initials into it.) According to a classmate, "We were all getting educated, but Gorbachev was a particularly avid student with a huge appetite for knowledge. After school we would all study. Then we would meet and walk back to school, which was a sort of second home to us. Or we would go to a movie. If we encountered a teacher, it was considered improper to disturb them, but, and I'll never forget this, he would go up to a mathematics teacher and explain there was something he hadn't understood in class. Then he would sit next to her for ten or fifteen minutes before the film started, and she would explain."[83]

Others turned to Gorbachev to resolve disputes and referee fights. He himself didn't like to fight, they recall—not that he was afraid; it just went against his grain—but he could stand up for himself. A relative his age remembered punching Gorbachev and another kid, "just making mischief. I was a little older than Mikhail, who was the same age as my brother. I pounded them both, but when they got older they grabbed me, piled on, and wrestled me to the ground."[84]

Gorbachev seemed a natural leader. "He was a great organizer," his high school classmate remembered. "People liked and trusted him. He was honest and fair, he worked hard, and he knew how to make friends." Five decades later, Gorbachev commented, "I've been used to being a leader since I was a kid. That was an ambition I always wanted to realize."[85] He organized sports and social activities. He led the morning gym class, shouting into a big megaphone, "Ready, class! One, two, three, four! One, two, three, four!"[86] "Mikhail loved weight lifting," recalled his classmate. "We would lift thirty-two kilograms [70.5 pounds] 60 or 70 times, first jerk them up, then push, then press." But most of all, he loved acting.

The school's drama group was so popular that members couldn't just join but had to be selected. The group's adviser was a beloved literature teacher, Yulia Sumtsova; members often gathered at her home (where some who lived far away resided), both to rehearse and to study. They made their own costumes out of material provided by their mothers (mostly cheesecloth, his classmate recalls, since "there was nothing else") and cadged props, including a carpet someone's father had brought from Germany as war booty. Gorbachev became the group's leading man. What attracted him to acting, he says, was "the wish to socialize with my peers, but also the desire to express myself, to get to know what I didn't know." It didn't hurt that Yulia Karagodina, a girl in whom he had more than a passing interest, was his leading lady. Together they starred in Ostrovsky's *Snegurochka* (*The Snow Maiden*) and Lermontov's *Masquerade*.

The setting for high school performances, including Pushkin's *Rusalka* and several Chekhov plays, was not a stage but the end of the school corridor next to the iron staircase. Adults attended and the troupe even took the show on the road, performing in villages throughout the district, charging admission, with the proceeds going to buy shoes for classmates who had none to wear to school. Gorbachev reports that he and his fellow players never asked themselves whether the shows they wanted to mount were doable. "We performed the work of all sorts of playwrights. You can imagine how some of it turned out, but we weren't embarrassed. . . ." A traveling theater group from Stavropol came by to take a look. After Gorbachev and his colleagues staged *Masquerade*, the professional actors "praised us and made at least one comment that I still remember: They told us not to grab each other by the sleeve . . . during the clash between Arbenin and Zvezdich. They said that in high society sharp arguments were carried out somewhat differently."[87]

Gorbachev's impish sense of humor is visible in that recollection. So are the pride and relish with which he remembers performing. "The

Gorbachev (center) in a production of Lermontov's *Masquerade*,
in high school, 1948–1949.

truth is, he was a very good actor," recalled Karagodina. There was a time when he even talked with me . . . about trying for a theatrical institute."[88]

BEGINNING IN 1946, Gorbachev spent five summers in a row helping his father operate a mammoth combine harvester. From the end of June until the end of August, they worked away from home. Even when rains interrupted the harvesting, they remained in the field, taking care of the machinery. "Father and I had many discussions during these 'idle' days. We talked about a great variety of topics—work and life alike. Our simple father-son relationship developed into a bond between two people who shared a common cause and a common job. Father treated me with respect, and we became true friends."[89]

The two of them worked twenty hours a day until two or three in the morning. Rushing to gather the crop in dry weather, they labored without a break, each replacing the other at the wheel of the giant machine while it was still moving. "It was hotter than hell," Gorbachev remembered. "There was dust everywhere, the unceasing din of the machinery. If you looked at us, all you could see were eyes and teeth: the rest of our faces were caked with dirt and fuel oil. There were times, after fifteen to twenty hours at work, when I fell asleep at the wheel. The first year my nose often bled. . . ."[90]

The work paid relatively well, both in money and in kind, but even a combine driver's family depended on an individual garden plot to feed itself. And every household was overwhelmed with taxes and other obligations. Whether or not they kept cattle, peasants owed the state 120 liters of milk, plus butter and meat. They had to pay taxes on fruit trees whether or not they bore fruit, Gorbachev remembered, "so peasants cut down their orchards. There was no escape: Peasants weren't issued passports. . . . How did this differ from serfdom?"

Reflections like these probably came later. So did the revealing dilemma Gorbachev faced when giving fulsome speeches on agricultural policy: "It wasn't easy for me to refrain from extremely negative evaluations since I knew what peasant life was like."[91] At the time, however, he felt himself gaining strength and confidence. He lost at least ten pounds every summer, but "I was getting stronger." Yulia Karagodina remembered his face in those days. "It was scorched by the sun. His hands were covered with bubbly, bloody calluses."[92] "I was even proud of those calluses," Gorbachev adds. His father taught him so well that "in a year or two I could fix any part of the machine. I was particularly proud of my ability to detect a problem in the machinery immediately, just from the sound of it, and equally proud that I could clamber up on it from any direction, even where the reel was revolving and the cutters were gnashing their teeth."[93]

This passage to manhood was marked by another rite. When the first postwar harvest was over in 1946, the men in Sergei Gorbachev's brigade, most of them former frontline soldiers, decided to "wash it down" and insisted that young Mikhail, who was fifteen, do the same. "Go ahead, have a drink!" they shouted. "It's time for you to become a real man." Gorbachev looked at his father, who laughed. When Gorbachev was handed a mug, he thought it was full of vodka, but in fact it contained pure alcohol. For that there was a drill: First exhale, then gulp it down, then quickly down a mug of cold water. But Gorbachev just drank it straight. "What a state I was in! The men roared with laughter, my father most of all."[94]

The year 1946 was a lean one, with famine in many regions. The Soviet grain harvest was down to 39.6 million tons, from 95.7 in 1940. Stavropol was spared the worst, and refugees poured in from other provinces hoping to trade their possessions for grain. In 1947, another dry year, the yield was better (65.9 million tons) but far from enough. The spring of 1948 brought dust storms, but then rains that promised a good harvest. Sensing the chance to break harvest records, earning glory as well as bonuses for everyone involved, local authorities prepared their team for battle: two powerful "Stalinist 6" combines manned by the best drivers in the district, Sergei Gorbachev and his son, and Yakov Yakovenko and his; two potent S-80 tractors driven by another war veteran and a reliable party member; a truck to deliver fuel to the fields; two more party members to off-load grain from the combine, and another vehicle to haul it away. Combines and tractors were equipped with lamps for night harvesting

"Comrade Gorbachev Is Ready to Harvest" blared the June 20, 1948, edition of the district newspaper, *Road of Ilich*.[95] As of July 25, 1948, Sergei Gorbachev's combine was in the lead, with 870 hectares harvested. Several days later they were still ahead, with 1,239.[96] Meanwhile, the USSR Supreme Soviet's Presidium had decreed that a combine driver who harvested 8,000 centners of grain (a centner being one-tenth of a ton) would be awarded the Order of Lenin. Sergei Gorbachev and his son harvested 8,888. According to a Gorbachev classmate, the authorities planned to reward only the father, but he asked them to share the honor with his son. At first they refused, saying that an Order of Lenin could not be divided. At his father's suggestion, however, at age seventeen, Mikhail Gorbachev received one of the USSR's highest honors, the coveted Order of the Red Banner of Labor, signed by Joseph Stalin himself, while Sergei received the Order of Lenin.

When the award was announced that fall, the students in Gorbachev's school assembled to congratulate him. "It was the first time this sort of thing had happened to me. . . . I was embarrassed, but, of course, I was glad."[97] Yulia Karagodina kept a newspaper clipping quoting his speech: "All our happiness, all our future, depends on labor, the most important factor moving socialist society forward. From the bottom of my heart, I thank the Bolshevik party, the Leninist Komsomol, and my teachers, for teaching me love for socialist labor, steadfastness, and staying power." It is entirely possible, Karagodina added in 1991, "that he actually said those words. . . . We didn't know any other style of communication, and that way seemed natural to us."[98]

Yulia was in the tenth grade, Gorbachev in the ninth. "Strong, stocky, and determined," in her words, "Gorbachev had a remarkable talent for subjecting everyone to his will." She recalled his correcting teachers in history class, and once when he was angry at a teacher he said, "'Do you want to keep your teaching certificate?' He was the sort who felt he was right and could prove it to anyone."

One day at Sumtsova's house, where Karagodina was studying, he dropped by to ask her for help with a mathematical theorem. Math was her strong suit, while Gorbachev preferred literature and history. As she started to explain the theorem, he glanced around and noticed an empty space in the page she was editing for the school wall newspaper. "You mean you still haven't finished it?" he chided her. "It's supposed to be up tomorrow. Make sure you get it done before then!" Yulia remembered thinking to herself, "So now he's going to be my boss, too," and decided "to do absolutely nothing" in response. Two days later, at a meeting of the Komsomol committee, he reprimanded her in front of everyone. "I turned red as a crab," she recalled. "He was shouting a bit, disciplining me."[99] "I felt terribly hurt. I'm walking away from school, about to cry, when Mikhail comes running up, and asks me to go to a movie with him that same day." Members of the drama group often watched movies together, sometimes the same one over and over, while Sumtsova tutored them on acting. But Karagodina was now even more offended: How could Mikhail ask her to the movies when he'd just hurt her that way? "My dear," Gorbachev replied, "these things have nothing to do with one another."[100]

The school director admired Gorbachev. According to a classmate, she told Mikhail, "A great future awaits you. Once you leave here you can choose your place. With that medal, any university will accept you." Perhaps that's why, when she wanted to criticize Mikhail and Yulia for "spending so much time together so that classmates, looking at you, get the idea that they don't have to concentrate on their studies," she reprimanded her, not him. Karagodina obediently replied that she would see less of Gorbachev. When he learned that, he marched straight into the director's office. The director, reports Yulia, emerged "red-faced and agitated," followed by a smiling Mikhail. "What did you say to her?" Yulia asked. "Oh, nothing much. I just said, I'm a model student, and so is Yulia. I'm active in social service, and so is she. The fact that we are friends doesn't interfere with anyone. Let them model themselves on us." Naturally, according to Yulia's account, the director couldn't object.[101]

Gorbachev had extremely high standards for everyone. "I felt I was really not good enough for him," Yulia recalled, "or we really didn't fit. He was too energetic, too serious, so organized. And he was smarter than I was. He was the center of attention." For a while "it was love, yes it was, for both of us," but they never said things like "I love you" to each other, and at times he played at it. Once during a rehearsal of *The Snow Maiden*, when Yulia's character said, "Dear Czar, ask me a hundred times if I love him, and I will answer a hundred times that I do," Gorbachev leaned over, with the school director sitting nearby in the audience, and

The Gorbachev family, 1949.

whispered in her ear, "Is it true?" "My God," Yulia remembers, "I was shaken. I could hardly go on with my monologue. Everyone was asking what happened, and there was Gorbachev off to the side, smiling."[102]

When she graduated a year before Gorbachev, Karagodina left for Moscow to enroll in a teacher training program. But with the dormitory full and nowhere to live, she soon returned home. "How could you not stand up for yourself and your plans?" he demanded. "You should have lain down in the door to the rector's office and not left until you were given a room in the dorm." "That's the sort of thing he could have done," Karagodina remarked many years later. "But not I." Instead, she found a job teaching in a village school near Molotovskoye. Gorbachev visited her, she adds, but "things didn't work out, he could never make up his mind to pursue me. We never talked about love, and didn't make plans for the future. I guess we just didn't suit each other. He respected people who were strong-willed and determined. It's probably not accidental—I read it somewhere—that he jokingly referred to Raisa Maksimovna [Gorbachev's wife] as 'my general.' As for me, I didn't accept his maximalism."

If by "maximalism" she meant Gorbachev was determined to achieve what seemed impossible, she was right. When Karagodina was in her third year at a college in Krasnodar, she got a postcard from Mikhail. He closed with the Latin words *Dum spiro spero*. Her girlfriend from the Baltics translated: "While I breathe, I hope." This could have been his motto when his dream of transforming the USSR came crashing down around him. In a postcard back, Karagodina's answer to Gorbachev constituted a warning to the man who tried to change the world: "Breathe, but don't hope for too much!"[103]

CHAPTER 2

MOSCOW STATE UNIVERSITY

1950–1955

"WHAT YOU DO WHEN YOU finish school is up to you. If you like, we can work together. If you want to continue your studies, I'll help you as much as I can. But this is a serious question, and only you can decide for yourself." An unusual peasant patriarch, Sergei Gorbachev didn't try to dictate to his son. But Mikhail knew his father's and grandfather's real feelings. Neither of them had much education, and they could feel how much they had missed. Gorbachev had no doubt about what he wanted to do: "I wanted to keep studying."[1]

Many of his peers felt the same way.[2] The Soviet Union was rebuilding. It needed engineers, agronomists, doctors, teachers, and other professionals to replace those lost in both the war and the purges that preceded it. "Even the weakest students" sought out places where the entrance exams "weren't particularly demanding," Gorbachev admits. As for himself, he was "a particularly prideful, ambitious [*ambitsioznyi*] fellow. Why? Nature, I guess. Why do five to seven percent of people born in the world turn out to be capable of running their own business, whereas the rest become hired hands? It's a question of character."[3] In Russian, the word *ambitsioznyi* is not a positive term, usually translated as "arrogant" rather than "ambitious." In 1950 it was clear to Gorbachev what an *ambitsioznyi* country boy should do next—"apply to nothing less than the most important university of all, Moscow State University."[4]

MGU was to the USSR what Harvard is to the United States—except that in the Soviet Union there was almost nothing else, no Yale, Princeton, or Stanford, no Ivy League, no equally distinguished state universities, no elite liberal arts colleges. Moscow the city was itself unique: Washington, New York, Chicago, Los Angeles all rolled into one, the seat of government, industry, culture, even the film industry: the place to shine if you wanted to rise. To be sure, the Soviet Union had its own version of "affirmative action": students like Gorbachev of working-class origin enjoyed special favor in university admission. Although he was from a peasant family, his father's job as a combine driver lifted him to "most-favored" proletarian status. And his Order of the Red Labor Banner certainly wouldn't hurt; in fact, in the end he was admitted without having to take the required entrance examination.

Half a year before he finished school in Stavropol, Gorbachev wrote for information about MGU's programs. In return, he received a booklet listing all its faculties (departments), along with admissions requirements. In high school he had liked a variety of subjects: physics and mathematics as well as history and literature. So, in addition to MGU, he considered applying to several other institutions specializing in engineering, energy, and economics. Gorbachev's local draft board informed him he would be called up unless he enrolled in a military academy like the Baku Naval School, to which they urged him to apply. "I liked that idea," he recalled, "you know, young men like ships and uniforms. But something stopped me; I don't know what. I'd like to know. I was ready to serve, but then they told me I could be deferred if I enrolled in either a law school or a transport institute."[5]

At one point Gorbachev focused on the Institute of Railroad Transportation, in nearby Rostov, then briefly pondered a career as a diplomat. Finally, he sent off his application to MGU's law school, which in the Soviet (and now Russian) system is an undergraduate course of study.[6] The study of law in a country without the rule of law did not enjoy great intellectual prestige, but Gorbachev couldn't know that. Although he was "impressed by the role of judges and prosecutors," he had, he admits, but a "foggy notion" of law and jurisprudence.

Perhaps that's why MGU didn't initially respond to his application. At first he went off to his job on the combine. But after a while he left his father in the steppe (with his permission, of course), hitched a ride to the nearest town, and dispatched a telegram with a prepaid reply, reminding the university of his existence. "Admitted with dormitory accommodation included," read the notice he miraculously received three days later, brought to him in the fields by a postman. He attributed the miracle less to the medal he had been awarded at graduation (silver rather than gold because he had received a grade of 4 rather than 5 in German) and more to his Red Labor Banner and his worker-peasant background. But the main thing was he got in—"got in without taking an exam, without an interview, without anything. No one asked me a thing! Well, in my opinion, I deserved to be admitted. I was someone you could count on, and that's how it turned out at the university."[7] For the rest of the summer, he continued working on the combine with his father. But the work no longer felt hard. "I was overflowing with joy. My head kept ringing with the words, 'I am a student at Moscow University.'"[8]

Gorbachev understates his efforts to gain admission. During June 1950, at the very time MGU was deciding whether or not to admit him, he managed to become a candidate member of the party, a credential that certainly enhanced his case. Gorbachev's application for party membership, handwritten on June 5, 1950, declares, "I would consider it a high honor to be a member of the highly advanced, genuinely revolutionary Communist party of Bolsheviks. I promise to be faithful to the great cause of Lenin and Stalin, to devote my entire life to the party's struggle for Communism." In a supporting letter, his school principal described him as "one of our school's best students," "sensitive and responsive to his comrades," "morally steady and ideologically firm." Another recommendation reveals that even in the Russian provinces in 1950, when it came to university admission, it helped to be an athlete: the school's physical education teacher reported that Mikhail assisted him for the last two years. The district Komsomol committee, of which Gorbachev was a member, confirmed that he was "politically literate," i.e., that he "understands the policy of the party of Lenin-Stalin correctly." It also provided an assurance even more important during the last years of Stalinism—that although Gorbachev had lived in Privolnoe under Nazi occupation when he was twelve years old, "there is no *kompromat* [compromising material] concerning him."[9]

Gorbachev had never seen a train until he was thirteen. He first traveled to Stavropol at seventeen, and had never been outside the province. Now, at nineteen, accompanied by his father, with a battered old suitcase in which his mother had packed the few clothes he had, plus food to sustain him on the trip, he arrived at the Tikhoretsky Station, some thirty-two miles from Privolnoe. Grandfather Pantelei, who bid farewell as Gorbachev and his father clambered aboard the truck taking them to the station, "was very emotional; he was very happy for me, but sad to see me go. He had tears in his eyes. It was very sad."[10] Gorbachev's father was so emotional that he stayed on board until the train started moving, then jumped off, and forgot to give his son his train ticket. The conductor might have thrown Gorbachev off the train if the rest of the passengers in the lowest-class car hadn't come to his aid: "What are you doing?" they yelled at the conductor. "His father fought at the front. Did you see all the medals he's wearing?" The conductor retreated—on the condition that Gorbachev buy another ticket (which he could barely afford) at the next station.[11]

On this and later trips, the Moscow trains stopped in places Gorbachev had only heard about and imagined—Rostov, Stalingrad, Kharkov, Orel, Kursk, Voronezh, all of them still partly in ruins from the war—before pulling into the capital itself. It was not an easy beginning: Gorbachev didn't "feel very comfortable" at first. His new acquaintances said, "Moscow itself is a big village," but it didn't feel like a village to him. Privolnoe had no electricity, no radio (except the loudspeaker in the central square), no telephone, but the air was clean and fragrant and "at night the stars shone as if someone had hung lanterns in the sky." By contrast, in Moscow, rumbling with the roar of trams and the metro, "everything was new for me: Red Square, the Kremlin, the Bolshoi Theater, my first opera, my first ballet, the Tretyakov and Pushkin Museums, my first ride on a Moscow River boat, my first trip to the outskirts of the city, my first anniversary of the Revolution demonstration. Every time, I was overwhelmed by an incomparable sensation of novelty."[12]

During Stalin's last years, peasants were held in particularly low regard in Moscow. They had always seemed backward to Marx (who referred to the "idiocy of rural life"), Lenin (who claimed to have made a "proletarian revolution"), and Stalin (who exploited and brutalized them), and they still seemed like "dark people" to sophisticated Moscow urbanites.[13] And Gorbachev at first struck his Muscovite classmates as hopelessly underdeveloped. They lived at home in their parents' apartments, while he and other out-of-towners lived in a dormitory. "We represented the Moscow elite," fellow student Dmitry Golovanov, explained. "Gorbachev wasn't very interesting to us."[14] "He was deeply provincial," according to Zoya Bekova. "That was quite clear. He had the look of a peasant."[15] "You could tell from his pronunciation," Golovanov remembers.[16] He spoke with a southern Russian accent, softening hard *g*'s into *kh*'s. "He had one suit, and he wore it all five years," added Nadezhda Mikhaleva.[17] "And there were times when he went around without socks, because he had none."

But that impression disappeared after Gorbachev's first year, another student, Rudolf Kolchanov, remembered. "After that, there was no more condescension; everyone treated him as an equal."[18] Gorbachev's ego did not suffer from his exposure to the elite; instead, he emerged five years later ready to take on the world. The night before leaving MGU in 1955, he thought about what those years meant to him. The "peasant boy" who entered the university in 1950 and the man who graduated five years later were "quite different people." His family had shaped him "as an individual and as a citizen," as had his schools and teachers. He was grateful to his fellow harvest workers, who "taught me how to work and helped me understand the working man's system of values." And yet, it was Moscow University that gave him "the basic knowledge and inner strength that were decisive in the choices I made. It was there I began the long process of rethinking my country's history, its present, and its future. I know one thing for sure: Without those five years there would have been no Gorbachev the politician."[19]

Gorbachev was not the only university graduate in the world from a humble background who felt empowered by his higher education. But higher education under late Stalinism was permeated by propaganda and indoctrination. Still, even before Stalin's death in 1953, there were ways to get a real education at MGU. Some professors trained before or just after 1917 introduced students to a wider realm of philosophical and political ideas. Gorbachev's student years, with his exposure to the intellectual and cultural life of the capital, turned him into a man who thought of himself as an intellectual, with what he considered a philosophical cast of mind, a fact that helps to explain the vision he later brought to political leadership, as well as some of his limitations as a leader.

MGU also gave Gorbachev two life-changing friendships. One was with the Czech student Zdeněk Mlynář, who would go on to become the chief ideologist of the Prague Spring in 1968. The other was with his wife-to-be, Raisa Titarenko.

STALIN DIED ON MARCH 5, 1953. His last years were marked by new waves of repression. The "Leningrad Affair" of 1949 eliminated party leaders with roots in the former imperial capital. The "anti-cosmospolitanism" campaign of 1952 targeted Jews. In January 1953, Stalin's minions claimed to have uncovered a "doctors' plot," in which Kremlin physicians, most of them Jewish, had conspired to murder Soviet leaders. The publicity given to the "plot" sparked mass hysteria: rumors about infants killed in hospitals, a drop in visits to clinics and pharmacies. One arrested physician, the well-known pathologist Yakov Rappoport, later recalled the mother of a child with pneumonia, who refused to administer the penicillin prescribed by a doctor: "Let him die from illness, but not from poison that I gave him with my own hands."[20]

Moscow University could hardly escape the contagion. "The atmosphere was saturated with ideology," Gorbachev recalls. The teaching seemed aimed at "brainwashing young minds." Both professors and students were "under close surveillance."[21] And yet, the postwar years saw stirrings of change in Soviet society. Because of its prestige and the Soviet need for highly trained specialists, Moscow University was somewhat insulated from the general atmosphere of fear.

Members of Gorbachev's generation emerged from the dreadful war with optimism and a fierce determination to improve their lives. Still believing in the equality promised by Communist doctrine, students from the impoverished countryside thought themselves no less worthy than children of the elite. War veterans, with preferential access to universities, stood out from younger students. Having survived, won the war, and returned in triumph, they were particularly determined to build the future. "All of us in our generation had a strong faith in socialist values," remembered Leonid Gordon, a history student at MGU from 1948 to 1953. "We had contempt for wealth and everything we considered bourgeois. Our Soviet patriotism was strong." Nail Bikkenin, a future adviser to Gorbachev, recalled that he and his friends had "faith in their country and its proclaimed ideals . . . the USSR was a country of enormous possibilities and we had a lot of work ahead of us." MGU's philosophy department, where Raisa Titarenko enrolled in 1949, seemed to its students a hotbed of intellectual excitement. Yuri Levada, a pioneer in Soviet sociology (which was taught by the philosophy faculty) and opinion polling, recalled, "It seemed as if there had never been such interesting people there before or since." Boris Grushin, another distinguished sociologist, remembered that war veterans at MGU inspired their fellow students "with new perceptions and assumptions, with a new vision of life, of the world."[22]

Gorbachev recalled the pressure to conform: "The slightest deviation from the official line, any attempt to question anything, was fraught with consequences, culminating, at best, in scrutiny before a Komsomol or party meeting."[23] He himself became the Komsomol leader of his entering class, then deputy Komsomol secretary for agitation and propaganda for the entire law school. One of his first Komsomol assignments, for which he was given time off from his studies, was to monitor election polling places in Moscow's Krasnopresnensky district—to make sure that enough citizens actually voted to reach the Communist party's goal of a nearly 100 percent turnout. What he observed was that most voted "out of fear."[24]

In 1952, at the tender age of twenty-one, he was elevated to full membership in the party. This, along with his Komsomol role, could be taken (and has been by some) to mean that Gorbachev served as a political watchdog over his fellow students.[25] But the truth is more complicated. Of course, he had to pay obeisance to Stalin and his works. At a meeting of law school party members in early 1953, he rejoiced that "study of the works of J. V. Stalin and of the materials of the 19th Party Congress [held in 1952] obliges us to raise the level of our scientific-scholarly work," while regretting that "our professors and teachers have obviously not studied these materials deeply enough. As a result the quality of our seminars is weak."[26] But the haste with which he was elevated to full party membership suggests a lapse in political oversight. And testimony from his classmates confirms that, when it came to monitoring them, he did only the minimum.

Gorbachev's promotion from candidate to full party member had to be approved by the authorities of Moscow's Leninsky district, in which MGU is located. When he hesitantly informed them about the arrests of his two grandfathers, which qualified as *kompromat* in some circles, they brushed it off: "Don't worry! Just write it down. That will be enough."[27] Classmates trusted him to keep secrets. Nadezhda Mikhaleva explains that while Gorbachev's Komosomol mandate was to ensure "discipline" in the dorm, his main target was drunkenness, not political dissidence. Galina Daniushevskaya remembers a meeting called to condemn the "doctors' plot," at which she expected Gorbachev to lead the condemnation. Instead, she still marvels, "he didn't even show up."[28] For the most part, it seems, he actually concentrated on his studies.

No subject at MGU, not even natural sciences, was free from politicization. Biology and physics had been under ideological attack for years. Law was deformed by Stalinist doctrine: rejection of presumption of innocence, and acceptance of confessions as proof of guilt. But the curriculum included Roman law, the history of political thought, the constitutions of "bourgeois" nations, especially the United States, and instead of shunning the ideas of ideological adversaries, students were encouraged to study them carefully, if only to be better able to understand the class enemy. Even as they followed the party line, some professors tried to signal their reservations. One professor with a dry throat always sipped water while he lectured. "Even the best lectures," he smilingly confided to his students, "have to be watered down."[29] Another old-timer, Serafim Yushkov, had devoted his life to the study of Kievan Russia, the medieval predecessor to Moscovite Russia, yet he was suddenly accused of "rootless cosmopolitanism," the label usually attached to Jews. The "absurdity of the charge was so obvious," Gorbachev recalled, especially given Yushkov's old-fashioned Russian way of dressing. He went around wearing a wide-brimmed straw hat, and an embroidered shirt with a waistband outside of his trousers. Nonetheless, Yushkov was "worked over" by the law school's scholarly council, before which, holding his old straw hat in his hand, he uttered just three words in his own defense: "Look at me!" The Yushkov inquiry was dropped. "We loved his lectures," recalls Gorbachev, but their way of showing it was to play an ideological prank on the old man. They asked him how he could analyze Kievan history without more references to Marxism-Leninism. "He frantically opened his large, overflowing briefcase, extracted from it one such classic, donned his spectacles, and searched for a pertinent passage."[30] The point of the prank was to lampoon political monitoring by sardonically engaging in it themselves.

WHEN HE FIRST ARRIVED at MGU, looking and sounding like a country bumpkin, Gorbachev was teased by his classmates: "What was new to me they said they had learned way back in school, but mine was a village school." But he convinced himself that his innocence was a virtue: the Muscovites often were "afraid to display their own ignorance; they were afraid to ask for explanations in class," whereas he was "burning with curiosity and a desire to learn and understand." Granted "I had never suffered from an absence of pride, and whatever was new came easily to me," he still had to study extra hard. Before long, he could "hold my own in student discussions with even my most talented classmates."[31]

Gorbachev claims to have studied "greedily, feverishly." "We all worked a great deal," Rudolf Kolchanov remembered, "but he worked more than anyone."[32] "What others would study for an hour or two," Mikhaleva recalled, "he would devote three or four to." "He was assiduous," she continued. "When others went to sleep, he kept working." "I know for a fact," says Zoya Bekova, "that he never stopped until two or three in the morning, after getting up at 5 or 6 a.m. He studied, he read, he did everything he could to bring himself up to the level of the Muscovites."[33] "There was nothing country boy about his intelligence," recalled Volodya Liberman, a member of Gorbachev's study group, along with Mikhaleva and Zdeněk Mlynář.

Gorbachev conspicuously displayed his superiority in the realm of labor. That Order of the Red Labor Banner, recalled Liberman, "he wore it the whole first year and it drew attention to him." Nevertheless, Mikhaleva added, it seemed Gorbachev "had no complexes: he understood that he lacked culture and he set out to get help." Mikhaleva, green-eyed and raven-haired, was someone whose assistance he sought. She remembered saying, "Misha, you live in the dormitory, poor dear. You cannot live on bad sausages. Come home with me to study. . . . Mama is a splendid cook!" Nadezhda also introduced Gorbachev to Moscow's cultural life. "He would come to me and say, 'Nadezhda, if you go to a museum maybe you'll take me and tell me what this artist feels.' Or, 'If you're going to the conservatory, take me with you and tell me what that composer is thinking.' It was not embarrassing to him at all to ask." Another friend remembered Gorbachev asking what ballet was: "I've heard talk about it, but I've never seen it."

Gorbachev wearing the Order of the Red Labor Banner, not earlier than 1949.

"Gorbachev seemed to like me," Mikhaleva remembered, "but he never showed his attraction to girls." "He didn't care about alcohol or playing cards," Liberman explained. "And though he was very handsome with great hair, he never showed much interest in women." In a photo from those years, Gorbachev does indeed look like a French movie star with dark hair and eyes, wearing a fedora. But "Gorbachev always had this amazing ability to work. . . . No hobbies. No side interests. Just work."[34] Gorbachev himself puts it this way, "I had made a firm decision—I would devote all five years at MGU to study. No love affairs."[35]

That soon changed in the intense social environment of the MGU dormitory. The old academic buildings housing MGU's departments were still downtown, on the Mokhovaya, not far from the Kremlin. The dormitory, however, was four miles away in the Sokoloniki district, at 32 Stromynka, near the banks of the Yauza River.[36] Built in the early eighteenth century by Peter the Great as a military barracks, the vast yellow, four-story structure housed several thousand students. Undergraduates and graduate students were grouped according to the faculties in which they studied: historians, philosophers, physicists, biologists, students of literature and law, and others. As many as twenty-two first-year students lived in one room, furnished mainly with beds (under which students kept personal belongings in their suitcases), small bedside tables, one big table with a few chairs, a bookshelf or two, and one wardrobe. During their second year, "only" eleven had to share a room, by the third year as "few" as six. Each floor boasted one collective kitchen, shared by hundreds of students, and one large bathroom without hot water. Raisa Gorbachev, who also grew up in the provinces, remembered that the women's bathroom contained only toilets and sinks.[37] Kolchanov remembered no stalls or doors in the men's bathroom, only toilets. Zdeněk Mlynář, accustomed to better plumbing in his native Czechoslovakia, recalled a "collective latrine with a washing area," adding that "for everyone in the building there was a single Russian *banya* (bathhouse) in the courtyard."[38] The *banya* was open to men and women on alternate days.[39]

Dmitry Golovanov, who lived with his parents, remembered Stromynka as "horrible, like a prison."[40] But for a country boy like Gorbachev it seemed almost luxurious. His minimal wardrobe wasn't out of place: students often dressed in secondhand pants, beat-up jackets, and old high school or army uniforms.[41] There was a cafeteria and snack bar, Gorbachev recalled, "where we could buy a cup of tea for a few kopecks, with unlimited amounts of bread available on the table. There was a barbershop and a laundry, although we usually washed our own clothes for lack of money or want of a change. We had our own clinic, which also was new for me since our village had only a first-aid station. We had a library with spacious reading room [although Kolchanov recalled that because there were never enough seats, students worked there in shifts at all hours of the day and night], a student club with all sorts of cultural activities and sports. It was a world of its own, a fellowship of students with its unwritten laws and rules."[42]

A student city that never slept, with its lights burning all night, Stromynka boasted its own main avenues (long corridors where students gathered to gab), informal debating societies (often meeting in bathrooms), markets (where students like Gorbachev, who had little money, but occasionally received food parcels from his parents, traded and swapped), even strategies for commuting downtown: students swarmed onto trams in such numbers that harried conductors had no way of checking to see that they had paid—they usually hadn't. In late 1953, Stromynka's denizens moved to luxurious new dorms on Lenin Hills, a mammoth Stalinist wedding cake–shaped skyscraper in which students lived in "blocks," i.e., two individual bedrooms sharing a bathroom. But in his memoirs and in person, Gorbachev radiates much more nostalgia for Stromynka than for Lenin Hills.

Did he stand out at MGU as someone who might one day lead his country and the world? "He was *not* the most impressive student in our class by any means," said Rudolf Kolchanov. "It's not as if he were always a great reformer and world leader just waiting to happen."[43] Natalia Rimashevskaya, later a distinguished sociologist, remembered that Gorbachev "never tried to stand out, but rather stayed in the shadows. In class, he used to sit in the next to last row of seats. Those who wanted to be known as leaders made sure they occupied center seats in the first row. As a joke, we addressed Gorbachev as 'Distinguished Combine Driver' in recognition of the medal he wore."[44] But Gorbachev had noticeable virtues. He had a way of "locking on" when he talked to you, several fellow students remembered. "Misha was never greedy, materialistic," said Liberman.[45] According to Kolchanov, Gorbachev was "open, warm, and sociable" and had "a lot of friends."[46]

Gorbachev claims he despised the rigid teaching and rote learning. So he continued his high school pattern of challenging teachers. He was about to contest a particularly deadly professor, he recalled, when Valery

Shapko, the official "elder" (*starosta*) of Gorbachev's cohort, suggested waiting until after the final exam. Gorbachev didn't wait, the teacher took revenge by giving him a B instead of an A, and Gorbachev forfeited extra scholarship support on which he heavily relied. When Stalin's latest work of "genius," *Economic Problems of Socialism in the USSR*, appeared in the fall of 1952, one professor's lectures consisted simply of reading the great work aloud. Gorbachev passed him an unsigned note saying, "This is a university, and they admit people who graduated from ten years of schooling, that is, people who can read by themselves." The professor contemptuously read the note aloud, remarking it must have been written by someone with no respect for Marxism-Leninism, the Communist party, and the USSR. That's why "the hero" who wrote it hadn't dared to sign it. Slowly, Gorbachev stood up and identified himself. His act of "defiance" was referred all the way up to the Moscow city party committee, but they decided to quash the matter. Once again Gorbachev's proletarian-peasant origins helped.[47]

Classmates confirm his outspokenness. Andrei Vyshinsky, chief prosecutor at the 1930s purge trials, had established as a Soviet jurisprudential norm that a suspect's confession of a crime was sufficient proof of guilt. "Many of us took it as gospel," admitted Gorbachev's friend Golovanov, "but Gorbachev didn't. He couldn't refute it openly because he would have been thrown out. But he expressed another view among friends: 'It's wrong, just plain wrong. Confessions can be forced.'"[48] In the midst of the hysteria over the "doctors' plot" in 1952, Gorbachev's close friend Volodya Liberman arrived three hours late for class, looking "depressed, deathly, faceless." In tears, he explained he had been spotted as a Jew and thrown off a bus. Later, at a meeting in the law school, another student questioned Liberman's loyalty. A decorated veteran and the class orator, Liberman demanded to know, "Should I, as the only Jew among you, take on the entire responsibility for all Jews?" At this point, Liberman recalled, Gorbachev leaped to his feet, pointed at Liberman's accuser, and shouted, "You are a spineless beast!"[49]

"I wasn't making a political protest," Gorbachev recalled. "The time for that hadn't come yet. It was an intellectual protest against how a veteran and a human being had been treated."[50]

The hottest arguments and debates took place late at night. "We divided up into various ideological camps and factions," remembered Kolchanov. "Someone would cite Trotsky, someone else would criticize Lenin for signing the peace [accord with Germany in 1918] at Brest-Litovsk, or even criticize Stalin for, say, the primitive way he expounded philosophical ideas. I myself championed [Peter] Struve [a leading pre-1917 liberal reformer]. . . . Of course, we were out of our minds to talk like this, and we could have paid dearly for it. Several people who were about to graduate got ten years for such debates. But we were lucky, no one denounced us to the authorities."[51]

No one could be an open dissident, but Kolchanov testifies that Gorbachev was "a doubter." "He had a very clear understanding of Stalinist [agricultural] collectivization, and he thought it as an incredible injustice. He couldn't say it openly, but he was much more knowledgeable about this than we city boys." Gorbachev developed a reputation as someone who tried to mediate debates. "You think this," he would say, "you think that, but let's talk this through." Rimashevskaya remembered he would defuse hot arguments with a Marxist expression, "One must approach [this question] dialectically," that is, by juxtaposing thesis and antithesis, and then looking for a synthesis. "Maybe that eventually transformed [him] into a person who would work for compromise."[52] Or, to put it another way, into a politician. Well into retirement, Gorbachev told his aide/biographer Andrei Grachev that though his "passion and curiosity" grew at MGU into a "steady interest in philosophy and political theory that remains with me until this day, I don't consider myself a theoretician. What I am is a politician, a politician."[53]

ZDENĚK MLYNÁŘ WAS ONE of Gorbachev's closest friends at MGU. "Misha admired him no end," recalled Golovanov. "Zdeněk was amazingly smart."[54] "We lived in the same quarters for five years," Mlynář remembered, "belonged to the same study circle, prepared together for examinations, and both obtained our degrees cum laude. We were more than just fellow students: we were known to all as a pair of close friends."[55] Mlynář had joined the Czechoslovak Communist party in 1946, and was by his own account a true believer. "My communist faith was a closed system, which could not be penetrated in any fundamental way by an idea, argument, or even by any real experience from the outside." So politically reliable was Mlynář that he served as party leader of Czech students in Moscow. Nonetheless, he was denounced by Czech compatriots at MGU as a "wrecker." The snitching there echoed the purge of Rudolf Slansky, general secretary of the Czech party, who was condemned to death at a show trial in Prague in 1952. Fortunately for Mlynář, Czech Communist leaders came to Moscow that December and told the assembled Czech students that the party had not sent them there to "go around suspecting one another but rather to trust each other and study." This advice "confirmed my party faith: everything had been examined in the spirit of justice and found to be a misunderstanding."[56]

Zdeněk Mlynář, Gorbachev's friend at Moscow University— later, a key colleague of Alexander Dubček's in the Prague Spring.

Mlynář admitted, "It was my five-year stay in Moscow that gave rise to my first serious ideological doubts." He refused to trace them to "the wretched living standard of the Soviet people, the poverty and backwardness of their everyday lives. The problem was not chiefly the fact that Moscow was a huge village of wooden cottages, that people scarcely had enough to eat, that the most typical dress, even then, five years after the war, was old military war-issue uniforms, that most families lived in one room, that instead of flush toilets there was only an opening leading to a drain pipe, that both in the student residences and on the street people blew their noses into their hands, that what you didn't hang onto tightly would be stolen from you in a crowd, that drunks lay unconscious in the street and could be dead for all the passers-by knew or cared. . . ." This extraordinarily incriminating passage damns not with faint praise but by eschewing even that.

Mlynář didn't blame Commnism for all this, but saw it as "a direct consequence of the war and of the terrible backwardness of czarist Russia." The Soviet people's fortitude in bearing their burdens actually demonstrated "the human strength . . . of the 'new Soviet man.'" What really bothered Mlynář was not "the negative aspects of Soviet life," but "the absence of anything positive in its place," the absence of Communist values themselves. Most Soviets he met "tried to keep politics utterly separate from their personal lives. . . . While we took it for granted that what we said in public we also thought in private." Mlynář shared a dorm room with six former frontline Red Army soldiers. On their wall was a classic socialist realist poster, a reproduction of a famous painting of Stalin standing before a huge map of the USSR, outlining a plan for a green belt of trees along the steppe of the Volga basin. When vodka appeared in the room, however, the poster was turned to face the wall, revealing an amateur's obscene drawing of a pre-1917 Russian courtesan. What followed were several hours of hard drinking, during which the usual public "duplicity was unnecessary and people whose intoxicated tongues became increasingly tangled still managed to make more and more real sense."

Mlynář heard war stories utterly at odds with what he had seen in Soviet films and literature. Had he ventured to express his "highly correct" opinions, he would have been viewed "as a fool in the same class as Kadet Biegler in Hašek's *Good Soldier Švejk*." One student, a party member, told him how collective farmers had looked forward to the Germans' arrival, hoping they would dismantle the collective farms and give the land back to the peasants. Mlynář's roommates revealed their "contempt for their own moral weakness and self-pity for being powerless to change the things that aroused the contempt in the first place." It took him five years of living in Moscow to discover that "if you want to understand the inner world of the Soviet people, it is far more important to read Tolstoy, Dostoyevsky, Chekhov, and Gogol than all the literary productions of socialist realism put together."

Mlynář knew a young party functionary who voted to expel a friend who ran through Stromynka in his underwear to win a bet. In a drunken state, the functionary begged Mlynář, "I'm a swine—go on, tell me I'm a swine!" Why should he do so? Mlynář asked. "Because you're not a swine—you believe in it," was the reply. Mlynář explained that running around in dormitories in underwear wasn't exactly a crime (especially since in less puritan Czechoslovakia "it happens all the time"), but his weepy interlocutor would have none of it. "Nonsense, that's not the point. You actually read Lenin. You understand it because you believe it."

Mlynář worked as an intern in the procurator's office. (Procurators were charged with ensuring the strict observance of the law by officials and citizens, but in practice, they focused on implementing the party's dictates.) Exposure to the workings of the Soviet justice system deepened his doubts. On the one day a week reserved for hearing oral "complaints by the working people," crowds jammed the office, hoping to convey pressing personal legal problems to the duty officer. "Each case generally took five or ten minutes. The 'new Soviet people' . . . stood before him cap in hand, with timid deference, and stammered out their feeling of injustice and injury, while the prosecutor, who was usually doing some other paper work at the same time, sat behind his massive desk listening with only half an ear. Inevitably, he would dismiss 99 percent of the complaints as groundless."[57]

Despite his doubts, Mlynář found a way to keep believing: Whatever the faults of the Soviet Union, he later explained, there was no capitalist exploitation, no army of the unemployed, no foreign policy based on aggression and war. He and Gorbachev "were convinced communists," Mlynář insisted. "We believed that communism was the future of mankind and Stalin was the one great leader."[58] In high school Gorbachev had received high marks for an essay on the theme "Stalin Is Our Wartime Glory, Stalin Gives Flight to Our Youth"—so high that for several years the composition was held up to other students as a model. "Even in high school," Gorbachev remembered, "we talked about many things in a critical way . . . , but only on the local level. . . . We took it for granted that the system we lived under was socialism."[59]

Gorbachev's and Mlynář's doubts deepened as they confided them to each other. Together they watched the classic film *Cossacks of the Kuban* (1950), a Stalinist musical comedy. (Yes, these oxymorons not only existed but also were wildly popular just when real life was at its worst.) In the film, happy collective farmers joyfully bring in the harvest. "It's not true," Gorbachev whispered to his friend. "If the leader of a kolkhoz does not use brute force against the farmers, they would probably not work at all." In one scene, pretty blond milkmaids in sparkling summer dresses, who have just won a "socialist competition" by overfulfilling their plan, storm local stores for their own harvest of prizes (hats, shoes, candy, balloons), and even prepare to buy a piano for their kolkhoz. "Pure propaganda," Gorbachev informed Mlynář. "You actually can't buy anything."[60]

Together, the two friends studied the official history of the USSR, which insisted that anyone guilty of "antiparty deviation" had to be liquidated. "But Lenin did not have [his Menshevik opponent] Martov arrested," Gorbachev said. "He let him emigrate." According to Mlynář, Gorbachev had a favorite philosophical maxim, that "the truth is always concrete," which he used to cite when a lecturer in Marxist philosophy babbled on about general principles "regardless of how little they had in common with reality." Gorbachev was "well balanced and optimistic," Mlynář remembered, "highly emotional," but with "iron self-control." "Open-minded, curious," he had "an ability to listen, learn, and he's able to adapt. All this is the root of his self-confidence."[61]

Stalin's death shook them both. In a conversation with Gorbachev in the 1990s, Mlynář remembered standing next to him in a law school auditorium on Herzen Street during two minutes of silence in Stalin's honor. "I remember asking you, 'Misha, what's going to happen to us now?' And you, in a voice full of alarm and uneasiness, answered, 'I don't know.' Our world, the world of true-believing Stalinist Communists, was beginning to fall apart."

"Yes," Gorbachev replied, "That's the way it was."[62]

Mlynář and Gorbachev joined the crowd, tens of thousands, moving toward the House of Columns, where Stalin's body lay in state. Many were silent and sincerely mournful. But Mlynář also recalled "thieves and pickpockets, men [who] felt under women's skirts, and vodka drunk straight from bottles hidden in pockets. It was a crowd united by determination not to miss a spectacle, whether it be a funeral or a public execution." Funneled by mounted policemen into narrow streets leading to the bier, people were crushed together in dangerous bottlenecks. At first, they chanted rhythmically, "Heave ho!" Then, when "the density of the crowd reached unimaginable proportions," people began to be trampled. "I myself saw dozens of wounded and unconscious people," Mlynář wrote, "and some I saw were dead."[63] Mlynář didn't make it to the bier on first try. The next day, pretending not to know a word of Russian except for "boss," he got permission from a policeman to go to the head of the line. As for Gorbachev, he bypassed the bottlenecks and stood in line all night. "I could see Stalin close up for the first time—dead, stone-like, waxen-faced, devoid of any signs of ever having been alive. I searched his face for any signs of greatness, but something disturbed me, evoking mixed feelings."[64]

In the months after Stalin's death, especially after secret police chief Lavrenty Beria was arrested in June and executed in December, the press began to publish articles criticizing the "cult of personality," without mentioning Stalin's name. Newspapers ignored the first anniversary of Stalin's death in 1954. It wasn't until February 1956, after Gorbachev had graduated from MGU, that Khrushchev directly attacked Stalin in his famous secret speech to the Twentieth Party Congress. Meanwhile, the mood at MGU, as in society at large, began to change. Mlynář realized that his MGU friends "sensed and knew far more about the reality of Stalinist terror in their country than I had gathered from them while Stalin was still alive. In 1954 and 1955, such things were spoken of more and more openly." Upon his return to Prague in 1955, he found that his compatriots were more afraid than his fellow students in Moscow. "Of course," Gorbachev remembered, "we had a long, long way to go to truly open pluralism. For although the Party and other organs loosened the ideological reins, they were certainly not about to let them out of their hands."[65]

———————

BALLROOM DANCING WAS the rage at Stromynka in the early years after the war, but Gorbachev was known for avoiding it. "I preferred to read books," he recalled, even when friends dropped by to report on the girls they had met on the dance floor. One evening in 1951, Volodya Liberman and Yura Topilin ran into the reading room and summoned him urgently: "Misha, what a babe! A new one! Come on, take a look!"

"Do you think there's a shortage of them?" he sneered, but then reconsidered: "Ok, Ok. You go ahead. I'll catch up."

"The guys departed," Gorbachev recalled. "I tried to continue reading, but curiosity got the better of me. I walked over to the club and met my fate."[66]

Raisa Titarenko was a year younger than her future husband but a year ahead of him at MGU. She was studying in the philosophy faculty, one of the most prestigious at MGU, with students who were considered particularly ambitious. Raisa herself was especially "orderly" and "correct"; it was no accident that she ended up on the student council's sanitary commission. She was also particularly feminine. Although conditions in the dorm (including a total lack of privacy) were rough, and Raisa's friends couldn't afford cosmetics and jewelry, Raisa, her roommate remembered, managed to look beautiful without trying. She had a "fantastic figure"; she piled her braids on top of her head in a crown; she didn't have many clothes (women wore each other's for variety), but anything she put on looked wonderful, particularly a blouse with frills that looked on her "as if it had emerged from a full closet." The idea of "home" seemed very important to Raisa, perhaps because of her nomadic childhood on the Siberian railway. It extended to wanting to cook for herself and roommates, rather than rely on cafeteria food, so at one point they resolved to shop for themselves and prepare their meals in the communal kitchen. But the experiment didn't last long, because of the dorm tradition that required them to share what food they had with their fellow students.

Raisa always seemed calm and collected. Only once did her roommates see her angry—at a woman they regarded as a social climber who had a fling with a young man they saw as a "creature of biology." And

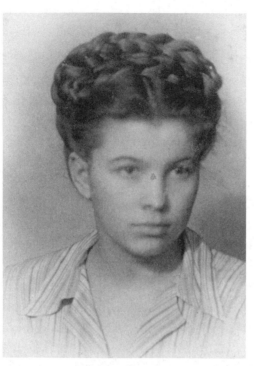

Raisa Titarenko,
later Gorbachev's
wife, during her
first year at Moscow
University, 1949.

only once did they see her cry—when a young man to whom she was
engaged broke off the engagement.[67]

The philosophy faculty was in the same downtown building as the
law school, and she, too, lived in the Stromynka dormitory. Gorbachev
couldn't understand how he had never caught sight of her until he did
at the dance. She was "elegant, very slender with light brown hair," but
extremely serious. Several boys were competing to dance with her when
Gorbachev walked in, but she chose Gorbachev's friend Yura. "We are
colleagues," she announced. She and Yura were both on the dorm committee. "So I'll dance with him. We have things to discuss."[68]

According to Gorbachev, he fell for her at first sight: "The days that
followed were tormented and joyous. It seemed to me that our first meeting had produced no impression at all on Raya. Judging by the look in her
eyes, she seemed calm and indifferent." He tried to meet her again; Yura
Topilin invited the girls from Raya's room over to his. They prepared
tea, and talked with the girls. "I very much wanted to impress her," Gorbachev recalled, "but think I made a fool of myself." Other young men
in the room were war veterans, and a girl asked Gorbachev where he

had fought. He sheepishly admitted he was only fourteen when the war ended. Raisa couldn't believe he was so young, so he pulled out his internal passport to prove it, and was immediately mortified by what he had done. "I must have been nervous," he recalled. "To put it mildly, she must have thought I was eccentric."[69] Raisa was reserved; during their short conversation, they used the formal, second-person plural, *Vy*, to refer to each other; and she soon suggested breaking up the gathering.[70]

After that, he tried many times to encounter her, to see her, or be seen by her. Occasionally they crossed paths in the dorm, but all she did was nod and walk on. "She bewitched me," he recalled, even in "a modest dress, all the more when she wore a "small hat with a veil." But male graduate students swarmed around her, and once he caught sight of her with a tall male student who wore glasses and was treating her to a chocolate. Gorbachev learned from friends that Raisa's admirer, Anatoly Zaretsky, a budding physicist, was engaged to her. "So, that's how it goes," Gorbachev thought to himself. "I guess I'm too late."[71]

Raisa Titarenko with her friend Nina Lyakisheva, near the Moscow University dormitory, May–June 1952.

Two months later, however, in December 1951, at a concert in the student club, he was searching for a seat in an overflow crowd, when he "suddenly sensed that someone was looking at me. I greeted Raisa, and said that I was looking for an empty seat." "You can have mine," she replied getting up. "It doesn't interest me much." Sensing that Raisa felt unwell, Mikhail offered to accompany her, and she didn't object. They walked for a long time along Stromynka Street, and the next day he took her to a movie. Soon they were taking daily walks. One day she invited him to her room, where her roommates were entertaining friends, and this time he had the wit to remain mostly silent—partly because he couldn't take his eyes off her—"not a classic beauty, but very, very sweet and attractive—with a lively face, shapely with an elegant figure . . . and a tantalizing voice" that sixty years later "still rings in my ears."

Soon Gorbachev and Raisa were spending all their free time together. His friends joked that they had lost Mikhail. "Everything else in my life somehow faded into the background. Frankly, I even abandoned my studies, although I managed to pass the tests and exams."

One winter day, however, as the couple walked back to Stromynka from their classroom building downtown, Raisa was silent, answering his questions in monosyllables. Suddenly she said, "We mustn't meet anymore. I've been happy all this time. I've come back to life. I had a breakup with a man I trusted. I'm grateful to you, but I won't survive if anything like that happens again. Better to stop seeing each other now, before it's too late." They walked on in silence. "I told Raisa that I couldn't agree, that for me it would be a catastrophe." At the dormitory, he walked her to her room and said he would wait for her two days later, near the same classroom building downtown.

"We mustn't meet any more," she insisted.

"I'll be waiting," he replied.

"Two days later," Gorbachev recalls, "we met again."[72]

The man Raisa had trusted was Zaretsky. His father was the director of railroads in the Baltic republics. His mother, according to Raisa, was a "striking, imposing woman with high ambitions," who demanded to inspect her son's bride-to-be and arrived in Moscow in a special railroad car. They were too "high ranking," Raisa's roommate Nina recalled. Zaretsky's mother didn't approve of Raisa, because of her humble origins, and her son, Raisa later told Gorbachev, "felt obliged to obey." After the breakup, Gorbachev recalled, Raisa had "tons of potential suitors," but she chose Gorbachev. She and her roommates had often talked about what sort of man they wanted to marry—a good man, intelligent, handsome, of course, nice if he were a Muscovite (so they could reside in the capital), preferably with a higher degree, ideally a professor, but, best of all, a foreigner. Raisa, who claimed she herself had no such plan, pledged herself to Gorbachev, and they swore to stay together forever. "I got married when I realized I loved him," she insisted.[73] Another thing about Gorbachev that qualified him to win Raisa, her roommate recalled, was he was not "a creature of biology."[74] For a year and half, he insists, although they went everywhere together, the most he allowed himself to do was hold her hand.

The young couple had a great deal in common. Both of Raisa's parents, like Mikhail's mother, were Ukrainian. Both Mikhail and Raisa were the firstborn in their families. According to Raisa's close friend Lydia Budyka, the two sets of parents resembled each other. Both fathers were "calm, quiet, and sweet." Her father, like Sergei Gorbachev, was "particularly attached" to his child. He chose her name, based on the Russian word *rai*, paradise. "He was very proud of me," Raisa said. "In the last months of his life, when he lay in a hospital in Moscow, he told me that for some reason he kept thinking of his mother and of me as a little girl. 'I always knew, always felt that it would be you who would save my life.'" Unfortunately, he couldn't be saved. He had a complicated operation and died in 1986.

All four of her grandparents were peasants. Raisa's father, Maksim Titarenko, was born in 1907 in Chernigov, where Mikhail's mother's family had come from, but in 1929 Maksim moved to Siberia, where he met his wife, Aleksandra. Raisa was born there in the village of Rubtsovsk, no larger than Privolnoe, in the Altai region. Neither set of parents had an easy childhood. "It was hard and hopeless labour," Raisa's mother told her. "Your poor grandmother! . . . She ploughed, sowed, washed the clothes and fed six children. And throughout her life not a word of complaint." Yet Raisa's mother, like Gorbachev's maternal grandfather, was grateful to the Bolsheviks. "Lenin gave my parents land—that is what my mother always says," remembered Raisa.

Even though he worked on the railroad, a prime breeding ground of Bolsheviks before and after 1917, Raisa's father never joined the party, though he warmed to it, his daughter said, after she married Gorbachev. Her maternal grandfather, like Gorbachev's grandfathers, was arrested during the 1930s. Labeled a "kulak," he lost his house and land during collectivization, then was accused of Trotskyism and taken away, never to return. "My mother still has no idea who Trotsky was," Raisa said in 1990, "and my grandfather certainly didn't know. . . . My grandmother died of grief and hunger as the wife of an 'enemy of the people.' And the four children she left to the mercy of fate."

Like her husband's mother, Raisa's was minimally educated. Gorbachev has praised her highly: "A talented woman. At a minimum, capable enough to have become a [government] minister. She was very capable, but from a kulak family."[75] According to Raisa, her mother was a naturally bright person who regarded her lack of an education as her "tragedy" and saw her main purpose in life as providing her own children with a proper upbringing. Aleksandra Titarenko remained a housewife, living in heated boxcars or barracks or movable huts, continually moving with her husband along the railroad, mother of three children by the age of twenty-five, spending her whole life "sewing, mending, darning, knitting, cooking, embroidering or cleaning." She "kept everything tidy, worked in the garden and, when it was possible, kept a cow or a goat so that the children could have milk."

Since life made it impossible for Raisa's parents to "realize themselves as they would have wished," she said, they "made it their aim in life at least to achieve through their children those precious things which were quite out of reach for . . . them." In that sense, "our parents did not give us only an education. By the way they lived their lives they developed in us a sense of responsibility—for our deeds and our behaviour. And perhaps the most important thing that my parents gave me was a capacity to share other people's needs and to enter into their grief, their pain: the quality of empathy. No, not a single generation lives in vain on this sinful earth."[76]

Raisa kept changing schools as her itinerant family kept moving. Like her future husband, she had to make do with scarce, often homemade school supplies—one textbook for five pupils, notebooks made out of newspaper paper, ink made from soot.[77] She remembered feeling "a sort of internal constraint, a feeling of diffidence, sometimes of isolation," the result, she thought, of continually changing schools. Then, like Mikhail, she came to love her lessons, along with activities like singing, acting, gymnastics, parties, even making solemn vows to fellow students—"to be faithful, always to stick together, to help each other and never conceal anything from each other. . . . We even mixed drops of our blood by making cuts in our fingers."[78] Like her future husband, Raisa studied so hard and so well that her parents didn't have to monitor her progress: "I can't recall an instance when my parents were summoned to school. And they never checked on my homework."

Like Mikhail, Raisa was an avid reader. "The happiest and brightest pages of my childhood . . . are of reading books in the family circle. I loved to read aloud. What wonderful evenings they were! The wood would be crackling in the fireplace or the stove. Mama would be cooking supper." Her sister, Ludmila (born in 1938), and her brother, Yevgeny (born in 1935), "would snuggle up to me side by side. And I would read." She graduated from high school in the Bashkir town of Sterlitamak in 1949 with a gold medal, one notch higher than her future husband's silver. That gave her the right to obtain a higher education without having to take university entrance exams. For her, as for Gorbachev, admission to Moscow University was a triumph, but her departure for the capital, at age seventeen, traveling alone in an overcrowded, overheated railroad car devoid of bedding and with no food except what her mother had packed for her, was an ordeal: "the sadness of parting from my family . . . from my school friends . . . from the world in which I was at home and understood. Sadness and anxiety. The beginning of the unknown. . . ."[79]

The study of philosophy enjoyed more prestige than the study of law at Moscow University, but not as much as fields like mathematics and the natural sciences, in which one could hope to rise without getting entangled in Stalinist political prohibitions. Furthermore, MGU students of law and philosophy generally fit different profiles. As Gorbachev's friend Rudolf Kolchanov put it, the philosophers were "just a little out of it."[80] Female philosophy students were considered particularly strange, "somewhere up in the clouds, far from life, and Raisa had some of that in her."[81]

Still, Raisa was very focused, according to her MGU friends Merab Mamardashvili, later a major neo-Kantian philosopher, and the future sociologist/pollster Yuri Levada. Attractive though she was, she wasn't coquettish.[82] "Everyone liked the fact that the sanitary inspector was such a babe," Gorbachev recalled proudly. "They couldn't take their eyes off her. They all wanted to hang out with her."[83] She was "a prestige object," Mlynář explained. When she spoke, "each word was a labor to which she had to give perfect birth."[84] Gorbachev remembered it was her "aristocratic bearing and sense of pride mixed with reserve that captivated me at our first meeting."[85]

She had arrived in Moscow a year ahead of Mikhail and already acquainted herself with enough of its culture to replace Nadezhda Mikhaleva as his guide. They bought the cheapest available tickets, with "top gallery, uncomfortable" stamped on them, for seats almost out of sight of the stage. "Whenever I enter a theatre I still look up to that gallery," Raisa wrote later, "because it was from there for the first time in my life that I heard an opera performed in the Bolshoi Theatre—Bizet's *Carmen*—and for the first time heard a performance of Tchaikovsky's First and Sixth Symphonies. It was from [there] that I saw my first ballet—Minkus's *Don Quixote*. And Chekhov's *Three Sisters* at the Moscow Arts Theatre."[86] Together, Raisa and Mikhail went to bookstores, museums, and exhibits of foreign art.[87] "By the third year, he knew as much about art, literature, culture and sports as anyone in the class," remembered Kolchanov. "Of course," Mikhaleva conceded, "Raisa Maksimovna played an early role in his cultural development."[88] She "had read more philosophy than I had," Gorbachev recalled, and "was always there alongside me. I didn't just learn historical facts, but tried to put them in a philosophical or conceptual framework."[89] At MGU, students studied the great philosophers in textbooks, outlines, and carefully selected translations. But Raisa insisted on trying to read Hegel, Fichte, and Kant in the original German, and recruited Mikhail to help her.[90] Raisa tried to read Western political theorists in primary sources—Thomas Jefferson, for example, whose vow of "eternal hostility to every form of tyranny over the mind of man" made a great impression on Gorbachev."[91]

"She read more political theory books than he did," Liberman recalled. Gorbachev's Komsomol duties required a lot work. "He couldn't study as much, and . . . sometimes missed classes. So she helped him . . . with his studying."[92]

Years later, Raisa would complain that the ideological constraints "deprived me . . . of a lot of knowledge relating to the history of Russian and world culture. We were obliged to learn off by heart Stalin's speech at the 19th Congress of the Party, but spent very little time studying the history of Russian thought: Solovyov, Karamzin, Berdyayev, Florensky." Not to mention "a real knowledge of a foreign language." Although "we studied German and Latin . . . we did not have any opportunity to practice foreign languages. . . . I have never in my life felt envious because someone was wearing a dress or other adornment that was more beautiful than what I was wearing. But I really do envy people who speak foreign languages fluently."[93]

At that stage of his life, Gorbachev still considered himself a "maximalist." But, he explained, she "remained that, whereas I, owing to the specifics of my education, and the multiple problems I later faced, had to turn into a man of compromise." Her "firmness of character" appealed to Gorbachev, speculates Grachev, firmness accompanied by a certain "methodicalness, a quality of being particularly organized that bordered on pedantic," an "unwillingness to be satisfied with half measures or surrogates, or pseudo-generalizations." That's why, Grachev continues, despite Gorbachev's own standing as the Communist party leader, he would jokingly refer to his wife as "the head of our family's party cell."[94] Nadezhda Mikhaleva, who knew both Gorbachevs well (and was perhaps still a bit jealous of Raisa), put it more sharply: Gorbachev was "softer" than his wife. He was in fact "henpecked."[95]

THE COUPLE DIDN'T MARRY until September 1953, but long before then they were inseparable. "We understood," he recounts, "that we could not and must not part."[96] "Our relationship and our feeling," she carefully told an interviewer in 1990, "were . . . perceived by us as a natural, inseparable part of our fate. We realized that our life would be unthinkable without each other. Our feelings were our very life itself. . . . All we had was ourselves. . . . *Omnia mea mecum porto*—'Everything I have I carry with me.'" Raisa remembered another Latin maxim, the same one Mikhail had cited to his high school girl friend, but which Yulia had rejected: "*Dum spiro, spero*—So long as I breathe, I hope."[97]

Before marrying, they had to worry about where to live and how to support themselves. Mikhail devoted part of the summer of 1953 to working, even harder than he had before, to bring in the Privolnoe harvest with his father. "That's what a new work incentive can do," laughed Sergei Gorbachev. Raisa loved beautiful clothes; in that sense, too, thought Gorbachev, "she was a real princess." Although they could barely make ends meet, they bought her a new skirt and blouse and material for an overcoat. Gorbachev particularly recalled "a waist-hugging coat made from bright green material with a little stand-up fur collar [that] she wore for the next eight years, turning it inside out when it got worn on one side." To Gorbachev she looked good in everything, she watched her weight, and, according to her husband, she "never used makeup until she was thirty." She had "an inner compulsion to look good on every occasion. In all our years together, she never appeared in the morning with a hair out of place."[98]

By selling nine centners of grain over and above the amount owed the state, Gorbachev and his father collected the then astronomical sum of one thousand rubles, which Mikhail used to finance the wedding. He had a "wedding dress" made out of light chiffon for Raisa, in which she "looked gorgeous" ("not a proper wedding dress," she remembered, "they didn't make special dresses in those days"); his wedding suit, which he also bought with his summer's earnings, was dark blue and made of a fancy, expensive fabric called "Shock Worker." They couldn't afford a ring, or a new pair of shoes for Raisa; she borrowed a pair from a girlfriend. They registered their marriage on September 25, 1953, at the Sokolniki registry office, in a large building near the Stromynka dorm, a date they always celebrated later, no matter where they were, as their wedding day. The wedding reception took place on November 7, no less, the anniversary of the Bolshevik Revolution, in the dorm's "dietetic" cafeteria. The food was mainly the student staple, "vinegret" (beet, potato, and pickle) salad, but with plenty of champagne and vodka, and toast after toast. Mlynář, Gorbachev recalls, "managed to adorn his

Gorbachev before
his marriage,
not later than
September 25, 1953.

Raisa Titarenko
before her
marriage to
Gorbachev,
not later than
September 25,
1953.

elegant, 'foreign' suit with a big greasy stain. The party was loud and high-spirited, and everyone danced a great deal. It was a real student wedding." As usual at Russian weddings, the guests shouted, "Bitter," which meant that the couple had to sweeten it with a kiss. But that "turned out to be a problem," Gorbachev remembered, since Raisa felt "kissing was something intimate that should be strictly between the two of us."[99]

The wedding night was a formality: they spent it in a Stromynka dormitory room along with thirty guests. Actually, Gorbachev later confessed, they had "become husband and wife" when they moved to the new skyscraper dormitory on Lenin Hills in early October. Even then, however, cohabiting wasn't easy, since parietal regulations required that they retreat to their separate rooms at night. Although Gorbachev was armed with a marriage certificate, the authorities did not relent until he protested and pasted up a huge cartoon depicting the rector as a giant, stomping on a marriage certificate with his boots.[100] After that, Raisa recalled, "we were always together. We wrote our theses [his on the topic 'Mass Participation in State Administration on the Local Level'] and prepared for the state examinations. We read a great deal. We studied the German language."[101]

They also conceived a child. "We were very inexperienced," Gorbachev recalled. "Nobody told us about these things at school or at the university or at medical institutions." So it came "like a bolt from the blue" that Raisa was pregnant. They badly wanted to have the baby. But at times her joints got so swollen she couldn't move; once, at Stromynka, Gorbachev and some friends had to carry her to the hospital, where she remained for nearly a month, sustained, as was usually the case in Soviet hospitals without reliable food service, by food brought by friends, especially, in this case, potatoes that Gorbachev fried in the Stromynka kitchen. And since her illness and the treatment for it affected her heart, doctors warned they might have to choose between saving the mother or the child. "We were at a loss for what to do," Gorbachev remembered. "Raisa was crying all the time." Eventually she decided to have an abortion at a maternity hospital on Shabolovka Street. When Gorbachev asked the physicians what they would recommend for the future, their answer was "contraceptives." What sort? They said the most effective method was abstinence.[102]

MIKHAIL'S PARENTS KNEW of the coming wedding only "vaguely." So in the summer of 1954, the couple traveled to Privolnoe to "restore our reputation," hitchhiking the rest of the way after they got off the train. First, they stopped to see Grandmother Vasilisa, who embraced Raisa, saying, "How thin you are! How beautiful!" Sergei Gorbachev, too, liked Raisa from the start and "treated her like a daughter." But Gorbachev's mother, who seemed jealous, did not.

"What kind of daughter-in-law have you brought us? She won't be any help."

Gorbachev said she had a university degree and planned to be a teacher.

"And who will help us? Why didn't you marry a local girl?"

Gorbachev got angry: "Mama, I'm going to tell you something you better remember: I love her. She's my wife. And I never want to hear anything like that from you ever again."

Once, when Gorbachev's mother ordered Raisa to water the garden, Sergei Gorbachev interrupted: "Let's do it together." His wife was furious, but she got over it, and later, she mellowed. In the meantime, however, on another tense occasion, Raisa left the house to avoid quarreling with her mother-in-law, and Gorbachev found her down by the river.

"What's the matter?" he asked her.

"Nothing."

"Fine. That's the spirit."[103]

Raisa's mother also reacted coolly to her son-in-law. Trying not to burden her parents with the sense they must help the newlyweds with money they didn't have, Raisa didn't inform them of the marriage until just before the event. But her attempt to be considerate backfired. When she and Mikhail traveled to Siberia the next summer to "atone for their sin" of previous inattention, her parents "greeted us accordingly, not exactly malevolently," according to Gorbachev, "but they didn't hide their sense of injury." Raisa's younger siblings quickly warmed to him, and her father did too, but her mother took longer. During a later visit, Gorbachev rose earlier than his wife and went into the kitchen where his mother-in-law was cooking. "Mama, how can I help you?" he asked. Startled, not used to men offering to help in the kitchen, Raisa's mother asked nervously, "Where's Raya?" "Quiet, quiet," he whispered putting a finger to his lips. "She's still sleeping." (Raisa suffered from insomnia.) Later that morning, Raisa's mother asked her, "What have you brought me, some kind of Jew?'" Gorbachev and his wife took that "not as criticism but as the highest praise, because Jewish men are known to be very good to their wives."[104]

From then on, Gorbachev and his mother-in-law got along fine. "I turned out to be their favorite son-in-law, in fact more like a son." But the warmest relationship of all was between the two fathers, not surprising, given their similar characters. "It didn't take more than two hours after they met for the first time in Privolnoe," Gorbachev recalled, "and they acted as if they'd been friends, almost brothers, for a hundred years. Both were veterans, both hard workers. Maksim Andreyevich was gentle and very humane, just like my father."[105]

MGU's law curriculum included internships in local government. While Zdeněk Mlynář was appalled by his exposure to the heartless Moscow bureaucracy, Gorbachev identified with procurators investigating a particularly bloody criminal case. He welcomed his role as an unofficial observer in court as "a way of testing my strength in practice."[106] But the pleasures of pursuing his own ambitions didn't overshadow the incompetence and arrogance he encountered on a summer internship in 1953, as a stunningly critical letter to Raisa makes clear.

Before helping with the Privolnoe harvest that summer, Gorbachev worked in the procurator's office of Molotovskoye district, where he had attended high school. On letterhead from that office, dated June 20, 1953, he wrote to his future wife in Moscow:

I am so depressed by the situation here. And I feel it especially keenly every time I receive a letter from you. It brings with it so much that is good, dear, close and understandable. And one feels all the more keenly how disgusting my surroundings are here. Especially the way of life of the local bosses. The acceptance of convention, subordination, with everything predetermined, the open impudence of officials and the arrogance. When you look at one of the local bosses you see nothing outstanding apart from his belly. But what aplomb, what self-assurance and the condescending, patronizing tone! The contempt for science. Consequently, a disparaging attitude to young specialists. I read recently in a newspaper a note from a livestock expert, . . . a graduate from the Stavropol agricultural institute. It is really shameful. . . . The man arrived here with great plans and set about his work with great enthusiasm, but he very soon began to feel that everyone was absolutely indifferent to it all. They all laughed at him and mocked him. Such passivity and conservatism! . . .

I have been chatting with a lot of young specialists. They are all very dissatisfied. As usual I have a great deal, a very great deal of work. I am normally at my desk till late. . . . I have been nowhere else in this place. But, to tell the truth, there's nowhere to go: it's all so boring.[107]

Ironically, the Stavropol region was precisely where Gorbachev would go to work after graduating from MGU. But not before he made every effort to stay in Moscow.

In the Soviet Union, the state decided what students did after graduation. In return for the education it provided them, they had to go where it "distributed" them. The state was represented by a "distribution commission" at the MGU law school on which, given his role in the Komsomol organization, Gorbachev himself sat; he was one of twelve members, of whom eleven were war veterans. This didn't hurt his chances to get the assignment he wanted, and in fact, he got it: he was to work in the USSR Procurator's Office. By 1955 that office was engaged in the sort of work that matched Gorbachev's "political and moral convictions," namely, the process of rehabilitating innocent victims of Stalin's repression. He hoped to work in newly formed departments devoted to monitoring the work of state security organs, making sure they fully observed legal norms. "When I found the notice of my assignment waiting for me on my bed in the dormitory, ooooh, I couldn't have been more satisfied! Not only was everything working out for me, but Raisa could continue her studies in Moscow."[108] Raisa, who graduated a year before Mikhail, was enrolled in a graduate program in philosophy at the Lenin Pedagogical Institute in Moscow.

Unfortunately for Gorbachev, the same considerations that demanded prosecutorial monitoring of the KGB led higher authorities to conclude that the monitoring ought to be done by experienced personnel rather than young people open to being intimidated by the secret policemen they were checking up on. As a result, when he reported to work at the procurator's office, Gorbachev learned there was no work for him there. "This was a blow to all my plans. In no more than a minute, they came crashing down. Of course, I could have sought out some cozy job at the university so as to stay in Moscow. Indeed, my friends were already weighing such options. But this was not my wish."[109]

Gorbachev was offered a slot in a MGU graduate program on collective farm law.[110] "As a matter of principle, I couldn't accept it," Gorbachev recalled. "My views on so-called 'kolkhoz law,' were crystal-clear: I considered this discipline absolutely spurious."[111] "I knew what collective farms were, what went on there, how the peasantry lived. I had already lived through that, and had no wish to go back. So I refused. What did interest me was legal and political theory. The other legal specialties didn't interest me."[112]

These events, along with Gorbachev's reaction to them, highlight elements of his character that would develop and endure: a burning desire to be in Moscow, not only where his wife wanted to be, but the only place in the USSR where a great career could be made; an ability to play the system (what for most people was a lottery initially produced just the assignment he wanted); and enough conscience to refuse a fall-back option that violated his sense of integrity. He refused other options as well—in the prosecutor's offices in Tomsk in far-off Siberia, in Blagoveshchensk, just across the border from the Chinese city of Heihi, in Tajikistan in Central Asia; or as assistant to the prosecutor in Stupino, a small city about sixty miles south of Moscow, which would have allowed Raisa to remain in her graduate program but require them to live apart much of the time.[113] Even to Westerners, who don't know the Soviet Union very well, the first three options must seem problematic. But the fourth seemed equally so to the Gorbachevs, who knew all too well that a small city that far from Moscow wasn't exactly the suburbs of New York, London, or Paris.

He and his wife didn't take these offers seriously. Why should they "go to some unknown place and try our luck in some foreign land?" After all, if they wanted Siberian frosts or Central Asian heat, Stavropol had plenty of both. "So the decision was made," he continues. "On the official directive, where it said, 'Assigned to the USSR Prosecutor's Office,' USSR was crossed out, and 'Stavropol Region' was inserted. And so, we were heading home, back to the Stavropol region."[114]

To Mikhail's home, that is. One can understand why, despite his unpleasant summer 1953 experience near Stavropol, the city itself would appeal to him. But it certainly didn't to Raisa's parents. They were horrified that he was ripping her out of graduate school in Moscow to take her off to "some sort of Stavropol 'hole.'"[115] In her memoirs, Raisa says little about the decision: "We decided to drop everything and go to work in Stavropol. . . . Yes, I gave up the idea of doing post-graduate work, although I had already passed the examination for it and had joined the course."[116] Later, however, she would resume working toward a candidate's degree in sociology.

Raisa's willingness to accompany her husband isn't surprising: that was expected of a Soviet wife. Doctors may have also influenced their decision when they recommended "a change of climate" for Raisa's health.[117] Beyond all this, the overriding factor in Raisa was love for her husband, which she recalled with characteristically overwrought emotion thirty-five years later: "What was Mikhail Sergeyevich like . . . when he came into my life?" she asked herself in 1990.

> An intelligent, reliable friend? Yes. A man who had his own opinion and defended it vigorously? Yes. . . . But that's not all. . . . I think of his love of his fellow-men. His respect for people. . . . Respect for their dignity as human beings. I think about his inability (my God, how many times have I thought about it!)

to assert himself at the expense of others, their dignity and rights. . . . I can see his face and his eyes. We have been together for thirty-seven years. Everything in this life changes. But a constant hope lives in my heart: that he, my husband, should remain just as he was when he came into my life in our youth. Manly and steadfast, strong and kind.[118]

A loving tribute, registering the hope with which Raisa Gorbacheva and her husband marched into their future. But she also had a premonition of very hard times to come. It came in a dream he remembers her having just after they decided to marry:

She and I are at the bottom of a very deep, dark well, a ray of light glimmering somewhere high up. We are climbing the wall, helping each other. Our hands are cut and bleeding. The pain is unbearable. Raya falls but I catch her, and we resume our slow upward climb. Finally, completely exhausted, we drag ourselves out of this black hole, and a straight, smooth, tree-lined alley opens before us. On the horizon we see an enormous bright sun, and the alley seems to flow into it, dissolving in its rays. We walk towards the sun. But suddenly out of nowhere terrifying black shadows loom over us on both sides of the road. What is that? We hear, "enemies, enemies, foes." Our hearts are filled with anguish. Holding hands, we continue walking on the road towards the sun . . .[119]

CHAPTER 3

CLIMBING THE LADDER

1955–1968

GORBACHEV REPORTED FOR WORK at the Stavropol regional procurator's office on August 5, 1955. But almost immediately he changed his mind. "Working in the procurator's office is not for me," he wrote to his wife, who was still in Moscow.[1] He claims he was greeted coldly on the first day and told to return a few days later for a specific assignment. But was that so unusual? Did he expect to be welcomed like a conquering hero? A less cocky neophyte might have been patient. Instead, he sought out local Komsomol functionaries "who remembered me from the old days." He figured they could help him win a better job with the party youth organization.[2] He was right: his Moscow University diploma and his Komsomol record at MGU "apparently did the trick."[3]

Nikolai Porotov, deputy director of the Komsomol cadres department, was favorably impressed by the young man with thinning hair, ruddy complexion and the beginnings of a paunch. Porotov was willing to take him on, but insisted Gorbachev clear the change with the procurator's office. "They won't accept me," Gorbachev complained. "They looked down on me over there." Porotov called ahead. This time, the procurator himself, Vasily Petukhov, received Gorbachev and agreed to release him. "We have plenty of jurists. We'll manage without him," Petukhov told Porotov. The two men shared the impression that Gorbachev was "not a bad fellow." But later that day Gorbachev wrote his wife that he'd had "a long unpleasant conversation with the procurator," adding, "They cursed me up and down, but agreed that I could work for the Komsomol." Naturally, Gorbachev remembers, "the conversation left an unpleasant taste in my mouth."[4]

Was this exchange really as hostile as Gorbachev portrays it? Or were Gorbachev's expectations too high, his job requirements too demanding? When Porotov offered him a position as secretary (i.e., head) of a rural district Komsomol committee, Gorbachev reportedly objected, "I'm from the countryside myself, so I'm not afraid of it. But you're not going to send me into the desert steppe, are you? I wouldn't object, except that my wife suffers from a thyroid condition. And she graduated in philosophy. With a specialty like that, it would be hard for her, too, out there. But the thyroid is the main thing. If we went there, it wouldn't be long before I'd be asking for a change, and you'd call me a 'deserter,' a 'whiner.'"[5]

Raisa Gorbachev's health problem wasn't thyroid (it may have been rheumatoid arthritis). Gorbachev's Stavropol critics charge him with distorting the truth to get special treatment, but it's entirely possible that Porotov misremembered the ailment. In any event, he called his boss, Viktor Mironenko, the first secretary of the regional Komsomol, who agreed to see Gorbachev. Gorbachev seemed nervous, but passed the test. "A Moscow University graduate," Mironenko reported to Porotov, "he's got a good grasp of things, knows the countryside, speaks well, what else do you need?"[6]

The task of the Komsomol, with millions of members between the ages of fourteen and twenty-seven (the leaders were older than that), was to mobilize Soviet youth to accomplish tasks set by the Communist party. Gorbachev's first appointment was to the lowly position of deputy director of the Komsomol's agitation and propaganda department for the Stavropol region. But over the next twelve years he rose steadily, first in the Komsomol and then in the Communist party apparatus itself: 1957— in charge of the Stavropol city Komsomol; 1958—number two man in the regional Komsomol and in 1961 its leader; 1962—party boss of a rural district; 1963—supervising appointments to all party posts in the Stavropol region; 1966—Stavropol city party chief; 1968—deputy party boss of the whole Stavropol region.

Looking back in 2007 at his Stavropol years, Gorbachev described them as "my little perestroika." Without them, he continued, "there would have been no Gorbachev. I would have found something else to keep me busy, something else to do; that's my nature. But my life would hardly have followed the same scenario." He had stood out in elementary and high school and at Moscow University, but his Stavropol experience further heightened his self-confidence. Comparing himself with the Komsomol propagandists he supervised in 1955, he could tell he was "so to speak, a head higher than they were." His university education gave him "indisputable advantages." In arguments with co-workers, he would draw on his MGU experience and "spring unexpected arguments" on them, "pulling the ground out from under them." He did it, he insists, solely to assert the truth and in the heat of the discussion. But at a regional Komsomol gathering he was publicly blamed for "taking unfair advantage of my university education," for making locals look like "ignoramuses or, even worse, fools." Was it their fault, he was asked, if they never went further than secondary night school? He "must treat colleagues with more understanding," he was told. He says he "took this remark to heart." He claims he was naturally "sociable" and "respectful," but "had to battle my own radicalism." What "radicalism" meant,

Gorbachev (middle row, fourth from right) among other
students in a course for "propagandists" conducted by the
Stavropol Komsomol's regional committee, 1955.

he insisted in 2007, was that he "was too principled." He had to learn "to use the power I had very carefully."[7]

The advantage that Gorbachev's education gave him over his peers is evident in this account. But so is the danger of appearing too full of himself. He was learning to play the system, to impress superiors while trying not to alienate those under him. One could call this "careerism," but there were plenty of careerists around, and Gorbachev was different. Almost every former Stavropol colleague, asked his first impression of Gorbachev, used the word "erudite." He was a moral straight arrow compared with peers who abused their power. And he was politically reliable. Powerful party bosses sent by the Kremlin to run Stavropol noticed Gorbachev early on and facilitated his rapid promotion. To them he seemed one of the best and brightest of the new generation of party officials, the kind of man on whom the future would depend.[8]

WHEN GORBACHEV ARRIVED in Stavropol in 1955, the city was, as Raisa Gorbachev later described it, "excessively provincial."[9] He felt as if he had journeyed back "several centuries." Stavropol was "the very image of a provincial city as depicted by Gogol."[10] Gogol's provinces were peopled by "dead souls" and hapless tsarist "inspector generals."

Stavropol's center is on the top of a hill. Until the 1960s, the large central square and the upper market, which attracted private-plot farmers from all over the region, were the city's most notable features. In 1955, several impressive prerevolutionary buildings surrounded the square: the former lycée (where, Gorbachev notes, the first Russian translator of Karl Marx's *Das Kapital* had studied), the institute for girls of noble families (later the Pedagogical Institute), the former headquarters of the imperial Caucasus army, the nobles' assembly building, the first theater in the Caucasus, and the tsarist governor's residence, later regional Communist party committee headquarters. In addition to the Lermontov Drama Theater, the city boasted a main cinema, called "Giant" as in every provincial Soviet town, two small movie houses, the "October" and the "Motherland," a regional library, an orchestra, a museum of local history, and, Raisa Gorbachev adds, "a few clubs and film-showing rooms." By the standards of a small American city in the mid-1950s, that was a lot of culture. Spoiled by five years in Moscow, Raisa had a different perspective: "That was all the cultural facilities there were."[11]

She remembered Stavropol's less-civilized aspects: only the central square and a few streets were paved. Just a few government buildings and apartment houses had central heating. Drinking water had to be carried from public faucets. "And in the very centre of town, opposite the teachers' college, there was an enormous sea of mud. All year round it stayed there and there was no way, on foot or on wheels, that you could get through it." But she was attracted to Stavropol's greenery: "It seemed as though the city had been decked out in luxurious green clothes. Lombardy poplars and such a lot of chestnuts. And willows and oaks and elms. And lilac. And flowers everywhere. In the autumn this apparel gives the city a beautiful, crimson-gold, touchingly gentle look." All this lent Stavropol "a certain . . . tranquillity."[12] The Gorbachevs took daily one- or two-hour walks regardless of the weather. The city was small enough that they could cover most of it, relaxing at the end of the day, seeing how people lived and worked. Besides their regular evening walks, they took more ambitious Sunday hikes in the countryside. The city is surrounded by broad rolling hills that offer a view of the steppe receding for miles to the east. About forty minutes south, on the way to the resort area of Piatigorsk, a nature preserve, Strizhament, atop a hill, was a favorite hiking spot.

Gorbachev arrived in Stavropol alone on August 5. "No one met me when I arrived," he recalled. Leaving his luggage at the station, he took a room at the Elbrus, a two-story structure described by a resident in 2008 as "the worst hotel in town." Gorbachev remembered it was near the "incredibly dirty lower market, where the fruit and vegetables were unbelievably cheap—you could buy a bundle of tomatoes for a few kopecks. But I was very careful with my money, saving it . . . to rent a room before Raisa arrived."[13] He spent several evenings roaming the streets, looking for a room to rent in the mostly one- and two-story buildings, but found nothing suitable. Someone at the procurator's office suggested he consult a "broker," a black market operator of the sort with whom procurator and police waged a continuing struggle. Fortunately, the woman quickly understood that her client had come for help rather than to arrest her, and for fifty rubles she gave him three addresses to

Gorbachev and his wife with her mother, Aleksandra Petrovna, and sister, Ludmila, 1955.

check out. One of them, on Kazansky Street, Gorbachev recalls, "became our home for the next few years."[14]

The house still stands. To get there, you leave Stavropol's central square, walk two long blocks north, about half a mile east along what is still called Soviet Street, then left again on Clara Zetkin Street (she was a German Marxist theorist and activist for women's rights), which curves steeply downhill. You can also get there (as Gorbachev himself often did) by plunging down a long, narrow, uneven stone staircase between ramshackle houses. Kazansky Street itself is uneven, deeply rutted, only partially paved. At its junction with Clara Zetkin Street sits house number 49, built toward the end of the nineteenth century by a landowner named Sergei Bibikov, nationalized and given over to an agricultural institute after the 1917 revolution, then traded in the early 1930s to a man named Grigory Dolinsky in return for his house, closer to the institute, on Tolstoy Street.

The two-story house has three windows facing the street. A gate to the right leads into a small courtyard, where the privy, now replaced

by indoor plumbing, stands crumbling in the corner. In back, a staircase leads up to the room that was the Gorbachevs' first home. It is tiny,
a mere 120 square feet. A large stove along the south wall for heating
the room took up more than 30 square feet. A bed under two east-facing
windows had only three legs when Gorbachev moved in; he replaced
it with a narrow four-footed frame with steel-mesh netting that settled almost to the floor when they lay down. The only other furnishing,
until Gorbachev built a clothes rack, was the plywood crate in which he
shipped the couple's books from Moscow; it served for a while as both a
bookcase and a table. Raisa cooked on a kerosene stove in the hall. There
was no telephone; the Gorbachevs had to run up to city hall in the center
of town to call anyone.[15]

Gorbachev rented the room from Dolinsky and his wife, retired
teachers who lived with their daughter, Liubov, son-in-law, and grandson. The owners were "good and kind," Raisa recalled, especially the
woman and her talkative daughter. The son-in-law, a local journalist,
was nice enough until he got drunk, at which point he was in the habit
of storming out and climbing a tree in the garden. Dolinsky himself
was mostly silent, except when he drank too much and began solemnly
instructing his tenants on the virtue of sobriety. In sharp contrast, the
next-door neighbor was a former White Guard captain, an elderly man
with the clipped mustache and aristocratic demeanor of an officer, who
particularly admired Raisa, perhaps, Gorbachev speculates, "because
she reminded him of his past and his dreams that never came true."[16]

Every morning Gorbachev shoveled a pail of coal from a shed behind
the house and lugged it up to their room, where Raisa mixed it with
embers left in the stove from the night before. In the evening he relit
the stove with wood from a pile in the yard. "By the time we woke up,"
he recalled, "our teeth were chattering." The northern window opened
onto a garden, with a lovely view (Raisa particularly cherished it) of distant hills, but the frames were warped and the windows wouldn't close
tightly. In typical Russian fashion, they wadded up the cracks with
cotton and paper and taped them tight, but some of the cold wind howling up from the valley got through. Gorbachev wouldn't allow his wife to
haul water from a pump that still stands on the corner, and he didn't like
her clambering up and down the narrow stone staircase to do her shop-

ping in the center of the city. Fortunately, his work left him enough time during their first years in Stavropol to help with shopping.

Raisa herself looked for a job, but "in the first few months I simply couldn't find any work. Then for a year and half I had a job I wasn't trained for [in the foreign literature department of the regional library]. Then I had two years of work in my specialty but with no real rights. Either I was paid by the hour or was on half-salary, with occasional dismissal when the staff was reduced. So there I was, a 'person with a university education from Moscow,' a rarity in Stavropol in those days—and I had no permanent job."[17]

Gorbachev and
wife, Raisa, in
Stavropol, 1955.

For a while, her husband recalled, his wife was the only MGU graduate in town and one of only two people in the whole region who had a university degree in philosophy, a subject taught in Stavropol by historians, he adds. But that made her almost a perfect nonfit for Stavropol—too refined, too educated, too Muscovite, unwilling to lower herself to the level of the provincial wives of her husband's colleagues. As Andrei

Grachev puts it, her "red diploma from Moscow State University acted like a red rag on a bull."[18] Trying to be polite, Raisa later recalled that many local college teachers, although graduates of correspondence courses or of the Stavropol teachers' college, were excellent professionals. But others didn't do any research, plagiarized their lectures, or hired others to teach their classes, and yet were kept on because an institute "regarded them as 'its own' people—people they knew, who knew its ways and were easy to manage."[19]

Raisa also dressed too well. When she was younger, she had worried that she would look too slender to be taken seriously (she weighed only ninety pounds at the time), so she began wearing "every piece of clothing I had. Mama would scold me: 'Now then, what on earth is that? Come on, unpack yourself!'" She did the same at college, wearing jackets and sweaters, "again in order to look more important." During her first years of teaching in Stavropol, she wanted "to look more adult and substantial."[20] Rumors spread that she had a fashion designer. In fact, her clothes were made by a female neighbor in a communal apartment into which the Gorbachevs moved in 1958.

"Raisa always wanted to be a teacher," Gorbachev reports, "beginning in childhood, when she would sit her younger brother and sister down and lead them through their lessons." During her first year or so on Kazansky Street, when she was unemployed, she took care of Liubov Dolinskaya's little boy when his mother was at work, taking him on walks in the neighborhood and reading him fairy tales whose sometimes sad endings she replaced with happy ones.[21] Raisa's didactic manner, typical of what Russians call an *uchilka*, or high school teacher/blue nose, alienated some people. But her husband, of course, defended her. "She was a teacher," Gorbachev adds, "and it affected how she spoke, it led people to suspect her of lecturing them."[22]

Eventually Raisa got regular teaching jobs in Stavropol, first at the medical institute, then in the economics department of the agricultural institute. But she constantly agonized about how well she was doing. Instead of reading her lectures, she memorized most of them "so as later to feel completely at ease ... before an audience." That self-torture, which must have conveyed something less than "complete ease" to her audiences, was provoked by the first lecture she ever gave, on the subject

"Sleep and Dreaming in the Teaching of I. P. Pavlov," at a factory club when she was still at Moscow University. She took fright at the sight of an old man with an enormous gray beard in the front row, read her lecture without looking up, and "then waited, terrified," for a reaction from the audience that never came—only "complete silence." Her first lecture at the Stavropol medical institute happened to be attended by a commission including heads of all academic departments and other well-known social scientists in Stavropol. Their presence was an error: they hadn't realized she was making her debut, but she discovered that only after staggering through a lengthy lecture and, to her horror, running out of things to say long before the bell.

No wonder "every lecture was an examination for me," Raisa admitted. "I was always nervous when I began a lecture, especially before a new audience." The subjects of her varied lectures were daunting: Hegel's *Science of Logic*, Kant on the antinomy of pure reason, Lenin's theory of reflection and of scientific perception, the role of the individual in history, the structure and forms of social consciousness, contemporary sociological concepts, philosophical trends in foreign countries. Explicating these themes to provincial audiences, even in oversimplified interpretations that were ideologically correct, was no easy task. And it didn't help that she hadn't yet joined the Communist party! At one point, Gorbachev challenged a local party official: "What's with you? Do you distrust my wife ideologically?" After the official reminded him that she wasn't a party member, she joined.[23]

THE GORBACHEVS DEARLY WANTED children, but Raisa's doctor warned them again that given her earlier illness, which might have weakened the heart, childbirth could seriously endanger her health.[24] Raisa bravely ignored the warning, and Irina Gorbachev was born on January 6, 1957, the day after her mother's twenty-fifth birthday. Gorbachev was delighted. His wife, he remembered, was "even happier." At last her fear that they would never have a "normal family" was behind them. He asked his mother to come and help for a few days, but Raisa, who hovered over the edge of the tub as her mother-in-law bathed the infant,

Raisa Gorbachev (first row, third from left) with colleagues in the
philosophy department at the Stavropol Agricultural Institute.

thought the older woman was too rough. So after staying for a week,
Gorbachev's mother went home.[25]

At the time, the Gorbachevs still lived on Kazansky Street. Since
Raisa had found temporary work, they hired a nanny from a nearby village, but Raisa had to hurry home during the day to feed the baby and
leave breast milk to be fed to her later. As soon as Irina was old enough,
her mother would rush her, "only half awake and dressed in a hurry,"
to the day care center. When she was old enough to speak, her mother
recalled, "Irina would keep saying: 'How far away we live! How far away
we live!' I shall not forget her little eyes, full of tears and despair, her
nose flattened against the glass of the door when, after I had been kept
late at work, I would rush into the nursery to collect her. She would cry
and keep saying: 'You didn't forget me? You won't leave me?' . . . I constantly had and still have the feeling that at some point in her childhood
I did not give her enough attention."

Raisa was too hard on herself, as usual. Most Soviet mothers worked.
With both spouses employed, some left their children in overnight nurseries for several days at a time. But that was small comfort to her. Gorbachev helped out not only by shopping at the local collective farm

**Raisa Gorbachev
with her daughter,
Irina, 1961.**

market (where produce was more plentiful than in state stores) but also
by washing the dishes and cleaning the house. His domestic contributions diminished, however, as his party workload rose.[26] Sometimes
Gorbachev found his wife weeping when he returned home late in the
evening: she had a lecture to deliver the next day, but Irina wouldn't go
to bed. Moreover, he was often away on business trips. Later, he recalled
with admiration that she never blamed him, "never complained" about
their living conditions. There was "never a whine out of her," he marveled, explaining her behavior by referring to how "powerfully connected we were to each other. It was unbelievable, almost pathological."
Even when tensions arose between them, "I could never bear to hurt
or offend her. Never! Rather, if something arose, I would interrupt and
leave the house. Or she would leave, and when she came back I would
be asleep." Unable to do anything else, even mentally process what had
just happened, he was so emotionally shaken that he simply shut down.
"That's how my nervous system worked, perhaps because I was so disturbed. She would come in and find me sleeping again."[27]

Gorbachev felt grateful and guilty at the same time. Clearly they needed better living conditions. In 1958 his Komsomol colleagues helped them obtain two rooms in a Soviet communal apartment, though that wasn't much of an improvement. Their new abode was in a four-story former "administrative" building not far from the city center on Dzerzhinzky Street (in 2008 the street still bore the name of the first Bolshevik secret police chief). Given the city's housing crunch, the two top floors had been turned into relatively spacious flats. On the ground floor, however, residents occupying one or two rooms each shared a common kitchen and a common toilet. *Kommunalki* were infamous in Soviet times; much depended on who happened to share them with you.[28] The Gorbachevs' neighbors included a retired lieutenant colonel (whose wife made clothes for Raisa), a welder, a worker in a garment factory, a hospital employee, an alcoholic bachelor, and four single women. It was, Raisa remembered, "a little sovereign state . . . with its own unwritten but universally understood laws. And in it people worked, loved, separated, drank like Russians, quarreled like Russians and made up again like Russians. In the evenings they played dominoes. We celebrated our birthdays together." Writing to his wife while traveling, he jokingly instructed her: "It's up to you to maintain diplomatic relations with the other sovereign units. I hope you will take pride in conducting our foreign policy. But don't forget the principle of mutual interest."[29]

For Raisa, as for so many Russians who had lived only in peasant huts, dormitories or a rented room, even a *kommunalka* was to be relished as "we . . . the first time in our lives had *our own* apartment."[30] Three years later, when Gorbachev was appointed regional Komsomol chief, they were finally assigned a separate 410-square-foot, two-room flat, including their own kitchen, bathroom, toilet, and corridor, in a prerevolutionary building on pleasant Morozov Street. Nine years after that, they moved into their small villa, renovated but still not in great shape, their daughter remembers, with a large garden and a little pond in the back.[31] By that time, Raisa had come to cherish "the measured pace of life and the patriarchal quiet" of Stavropol. "There was no transport problem, no 'rush hour.' . . . Wherever you were going—to work, to the shops, to the baths, the hairdresser, the polyclinic or the market—it was possible to get there on foot."[32]

TO UNDERSTAND GORBACHEV'S rise in Stavropol, one must understand the Khrushchev era, whose reformist spirit he embodied, and the early Brezhnev years, in which he also managed to find his place. On February 25, 1956, Soviet Communist party leader Nikita Khrushchev delivered a secret speech at the Twentieth Party Congress. Since this was the first congress since Stalin's death, his heirs felt obligated to evaluate the man who had dominated his country for a quarter of a century, terrorizing his people (including his Kremlin colleagues), even as he turned the USSR into an industrial power and led it to victory in World War II. Behind the Kremlin curtain, while Stalin's heirs debated what to say about their former master, Khrushchev was preparing to denounce him, a step that risked undermining the regime they had inherited. Khrushchev took this fateful step partly to steal a march on Kremlin rivals who had been closer to Stalin than he had been, but also as a grand gesture of repentance for his own complicity in Stalin's crimes. Reflecting his ambivalence about the man who had been both his mentor and his tormentor, Khrushchev's speech went only so far—denouncing Stalin but not the Soviet system itself—but far enough to create a political earthquake. Thousands of delegates in the Kremlin listened in shocked silence. So did millions around the country, who had the report read or summarized to them in the weeks following the congress. Khrushchev didn't want his "secret speech" to remain secret; he wanted to spread the word, but he didn't expect the reaction it provoked in the intelligentsia. Young people demanded to know how the older generation could have allowed the Stalinist terror to occur. MGU students ousted their Komsomol leaders and replaced them with new ones. Some students, including a number who later became champions of Gorbachev's glasnost, began to openly question the curriculum: "Marx and Lenin are banal." "Lenin is outdated." "The party Central Committee is not an icon." At the dorm where the Gorbachevs had lived, residents launched a boycott of the cafeteria. "If you do not want to be fed like cattle—support the boycott!"[33]

Many would-be reformers followed Khrushchev's lead in calling for a return to the Leninism that Stalin had supposedly betrayed. It was only in the late 1980s, on Gorbachev's watch, that Lenin himself would come under widespread attack for founding a repressive system that Stalin perfected. Those who dared voice that heresy in 1956 risked trouble, especially after the Hungarians mounted an October revolution against Soviet rule. MGU students and faculty continued to voice dissent until arrests of the most radical students in 1957 silenced all but the most daring.

From 1957 until his ouster in 1964, Khrushchev's de-Stalinization campaign followed a contradictory course. Encountering resistance from Communist conservatives, he alternated between encouraging freethinking writers and artists and berating them, between opening his country to fresh winds from the West and closing it down. But a generally optimistic mood endured—sustained by the sense that things were getting better, buoyed by Soviet successes in science and technology such as the launching of Sputnik, but rooted in Communist ideology itself. Many of Gorbachev's generation, "people of the sixties," as they were later called, still believed that with the spread of education and culture, human society could be perfected, that science and technology could transform nature.

This was the time of the "thaw" in Soviet culture: the rediscovery of the great poets Anna Akhmatova, Osip Mandelshtam, and Marina Tsvetaeva and the emergence of popular new ones: Andrei Voznesensky, Yevgeny Yevtushenko, Bella Akhmadullina. It was the heyday of "thick" journals, particularly Aleksandr Tvardovky's *Novyi mir*, which published Aleksandr Solzhenitsyn's *One Day in the Life of Ivan Denisovich* in 1962. Patriotic "village prose" writers had not yet become the fierce Russian nationalists who would condemn Gorbachev's reforms as treason. Soviet theater and cinema flourished as they turned from reiterating collectivist propaganda to illuminating individual lives. Soviet science emancipated itself from ideologically correct quacks like Trofim Lysenko. "Honest journalism" was born.

In this environment, reform-minded Communists could be found even in the party apparat. "Genuine Marxists" or "genuine Leninists," they dubbed themselves "children of the Twentieth Congress," including Gorbachev himself. Len Karpinsky, a graduate of MGU's philosophy department in 1952, applied what he called his "absolute faith in the correctness" of Marxist social and economic theory in writing for

Pravda. Under Gorbachev, he would edit the crusading daily *Moscow News*. Georgy Shakhnazarov, a 1949 graduate of Azerbaijan State University, moved from the Political Publishing House (1952–1961) to the Prague-based international Communist journal *Problems of Peace and Socialism*, to the Central Committee's international department, along the way quietly coming to consider himself a social democrat rather than a Communist.[34] In 1988 he joined Gorbachev's inner circle of advisers. Anatoly Chernyaev, who started MGU before the war, finished afterward, and taught there during the thaw, also worked at *Problems of Peace and Socialism*, and then in the Central Committee's international department before becoming Gorbachev's main foreign policy adviser in 1986.

Reformist thinking represented by men like this lived on for several years after Khrushchev's forced removal in October 1964. He himself had grown more erratic and unpredictable, alienating even those who supported his reforms. By the time he was unceremoniously ousted by his Kremlin colleagues, he had few defenders. The new regime, led by party General Secretary Leonid Brezhnev and Premier Aleksei Kosygin, promised to be steadier and more consistent. One of their first innovations, economic reforms designed to cut back on overcentralized planning, was welcomed by younger regional party leaders like Gorbachev. But the reform was soon gutted by the Moscow bureaucrats whose power it reduced. Meanwhile, Khrushchev's successors halted and then reversed his anti-Stalin campaign. They began a crackdown on liberal intellectuals, arresting the writers Andrei Sinyavsky and Yuli Daniel in 1966 and sentencing them to prison, and in August 1968 they crushed the Prague Spring.

Czechoslovakia's reform-minded Communists, led by Alexander Dubček, had sought to give Communism a "human face" by lifting restrictions on freedom of speech, press, and travel and by decentralizing the economy. As they did so, many in Moscow, both within and outside the party apparatus, welcomed the Prague reforms as the sort of change they hoped would eventually come in the USSR. By then the Soviet Central Committee's international department was a hotbed of liberal thinking. Instead of devoting themselves to recruiting foreign supporters for Soviet foreign policy, Andrei Grachev remembered, committee staffers convened meetings at which foreign left-wingers debated how to banish the legacy of Stalinism.[35] Nikolai Shmelyov, later an economic adviser to Gorbachev, recalled the mood in the summer of 1968: "Never before or since had I seen in the highest places such an outburst of liberalism. One could walk along the corridor inside the party Central Committee and shout at the top of one's lungs, 'We must not send tanks into Czechoslovakia!' Yet, in the same corridor, someone approaching from the other direction would shout back, 'It is time to send tanks into Czechoslovakia and finish off this whorehouse.'"[36] Aleksandr Bovin, another enlightened apparatchik, wrote in his diary just before Soviet tanks moved into Prague that the mood in Central Committee foreign affairs departments, and in the Foreign Ministry as well, was "sharply critical. [Intervention] is considered an unjustified step, or at least a premature one."[37] Bovin himself, who was assigned to write propaganda justifying the Soviet invasion, spent his days (according to Chernyaev) "wringing disgusting texts out of himself and his evenings in my kitchen drinking and weeping from shame and despair."[38] The fact that the same Bovin later served as a speechwriter for Brezhnev shows the degree to which liberal-minded apparatchiki led double lives.

Until the Soviet intervention in Prague, writes historian Vladislav Zubok, there was the possibility of a coalition among "enlightened apparatchiks, economic reformers, reformist scientists and the 'left' cultural vanguard." Could it have led to a Moscow Spring twenty years before Gorbachev created one? "We were too young when the 20th Party Congress took place," recalled Bovin. "Therefore we could not turn the Thaw into a spring." Adds Zubok, "There was still no person like Mikhail Gorbachev in the Kremlin leadership to initiate and guide such a coalition."[39]

IN FEBRUARY 1958, the Stavropol regional Komsomol held a seminar on the issue "What Qualities Should a Komsomol Leader Possess?" "A good family man," came one answer. "An excellent worker or student." "Someone who's knowledgeable about music and poetry, who can dance and sing, even better, play the accordion." "Extremely principled, demanding of oneself and of others." But not egocentric, not "always and everywhere putting the 'I' first." "Looks good" and is "meticulous." On time for meetings, of course. There was even discussion of the proper width for his trousers, and whether he had a right to lead others if he couldn't get along with his own wife.[40]

Gorbachev didn't play the accordion. But he sang well, particularly folk and popular songs. And he was just the sort of moral "paragon" the party wanted in order to inspire the young. Because he was so exemplary, he was particularly sensitive to the contradictions that plagued conscientious Communist officials. There was a huge gulf between utopian hopes and awful realities. The ideal of people caring for the collective as well as themselves was belied by the fact that so many officials cared for neither, drowning themselves in drink or engaging in crime. The image of collective leadership devoted to the common good clashed with frantic competition to climb the greased pole. The task of motivating workers mainly through moral exhortation seemed hopeless now that Stalinist fear had been reduced, especially since monetary incentives that promoted inequality were ideologically incorrect. Stavropol party and Komsomol archives reveal examples of social progress—extending education (however politicized) and health care (however minimal), and industrializing (with all its dismal ecological effects) a mostly agricultural province. But most of the documents mirror promises unfilled and disasters in the making—with the result that leaders like Gorbachev were forever open to being accused of dereliction of duty. In an economy built on corruption, nearly every official could be charged with violating one law or another. Most responded to this dilemma by hewing rigidly to the ritual formula: Everything was going wonderfully—except for a few allegedly isolated, entirely corrigible instances in which they were not. The most that a conscientious functionary could do was admit that there were more than a few shortcomings in his bailiwick.

Gorbachev's first speech as head of the Stavropol city Komsomol, in November 1956, reflected these cross-pressures. "For us, Komsomol members," he boasted, the party's exhortations "constitute our ticket to the future, our summons to go where the work is hardest of all, where our youthful energy is most needed. . . . In the battle for the harvest, our Soviet young people have marched in the first ranks." However, he admitted, in the construction industry, workers regularly ran out of construction materials, carpenters who had no wood to work with ended up digging holes, and the resulting chaos led young people to abandon their posts and their jobs. Yet no Komsomol meetings were held for months at a time, and no one attempted to organize Komsomol members or even collect Komsomol dues.[41]

Gorbachev's speeches contained no examples of heresy. On the surface, he was a cautious and capable junior apparatchik. Yet, his exposure, or, rather, reexposure after five years in the capital, to real life as lived by poor peasants in the deeply depressed provinces, reminded him of how bad conditions were, and he tried to make the system work better.

Overflowing with energy, but lacking an automobile (whether governmental or private), he raced around the region on trains, hitched truck rides, and tramped through villages on foot, seeing for himself how people lived, trying to rouse them to greater efforts on their own behalf. On one of these trips, he visited the remote village of Gorkaya Balka, spread out along both sides of a river with the same grim name, Bitter Hollow. From the top of a nearby hill he saw "low, smoke-belching huts, blackened dilapidated fences. . . . Down there, in those miserable dwellings, people led some kind of life. But the streets (if you could call them streets) were deserted. As if the plague had ravaged the entire village: no communication between the huts of this shantytown, just the everlasting barking of dogs. I thought to myself, 'This is why young people flee from this god-forsaken village. They flee from desolation and horror, from the fear of being buried alive.' I wondered, 'How is it possible, how can anyone live like that?'"[42]

How could he help Gorkaya Balka? Moscow University graduate that he was, Gorbachev consulted "some specialists, mainly young professionals like myself," almost certainly including his wife, who said the young people of Gorkaya Balka needed social contacts. So Gorbachev opted "to organize discussion groups for political and other education—to fling open a window on the outside world, as we say." Political indoctrination was of course standard in the USSR, but Gorbachev's version reflected his own fondness for a more meaningful exchange of views. The people who showed up for the first meeting were skeptical: when Gorbachev told them his Moscow University–trained wife couldn't find a job in Stavropol, one young woman retorted, "And you're telling us we should study? What's the point of studying?" But they indicated they'd like to meet on a regular basis. Later, in Stavropol, Gorbachev was confronted by a complaint from the party boss of the district in which Gorkaya Balka was located: "A certain Gorbachev from the Komsomol regional committee arrived and started organizing some kind of group, instead of restoring order, reinforcing work discipline and propagating advanced production methods." This was, Gorbachev realized, a "preemptive strike" by an official who feared he would be blamed for the "misery" of the villagers and his own failure to help them improve their lives.[43]

Wanting to share his impressions with someone close to him, he wrote his wife almost every evening. Conditions in his own village of Privolnoe weren't much better than those in Gorkaya Balka: "How many times, when I come to Privolnoe, does the talk concern how to come up with twenty rubles, although my father works all year round. I'm just filled with pain. Honestly, I can't keep from crying. Yet, at the same time, I know that they don't live so badly. But what about others? There's so much still to be done. Our parents, along with thousands of others like them, deserve a better life."[44]

Khrushchev's Twentieth Congress speech offered hope that the party would lead the effort to reform itself. Gorbachev read it at regional party headquarters in an informational letter sent out by the Central Committee. "Many of us simply could not believe that such things could be true. For me it was easier. My family had itself been one of the victims of the repression. . . ."[45] He welcomed the speech as a courageous step, but immediately encountered those who did not. Stalin's godlike authority, which had helped to legitimize party rule for decades, had suddenly been shattered by his successor. The party's iron discipline demanded that its minions accept their leader's new line, but, Gorbachev recalls, "many were simply unable to comprehend and accept it. A great number of them concealed their views, waiting for further developments. . . ."[46]

In the countryside, ordinary people were dismayed—but less by Stalin's crimes than by the fact that Khrushchev had revealed them. Assigned by the Komsomol to explain Khrushchev's speech to young people, Gorbachev visited the Novo-Aleksandrovsky district. There the party secretary for ideology looked at him sympathetically, as if Gorbachev had been set up. "I'll be frank with you," he said, "the people just refuse to accept the condemnation of the personality cult."[47] Was that because the message was sugar-coated at meetings to brief the rank and file? In one district a lecture titled "Why the Cult of Personality Is Foreign to the Spirit of Marxism-Leninism" was immediately followed by a concert. In another, where a Komsomol lecturer drew his main lesson from shortcomings not of Stalin but of local officials, one "concrete, practical task" to which young people were assigned afterwards was to plant four hundred trees in a new "friendship alley." Reports to Stavropol Komsomol authorities on postcongress activities in rural districts varied in degree of specificity, quality of written Russian, and even typewriters used (many of them were missing letters and printed unevenly) with little or nothing in them to suggest a careful, thorough weighing of Stalin's crimes.[48]

Knowing how party officials arrogated to themselves the right to speak "for the people," Gorbachev spent two weeks in the district, talking mostly to Komsomol and party members, but also to ordinary citizens. Some Communists, especially those younger and better educated, and those who had suffered from Stalin's repression, shared Gorbachev's views. Others either refused to credit Khrushchev's indictment of Stalin or granted that it was accurate but asked, "Why do we need it? Why wash dirty linen in public?" More disturbing to Gorbachev was the reaction of peasants who were grateful to Stalin for purging local leaders who had oppressed them. "Serves them right," one woman declared. "They were the ones who herded us into collective farms and oppressed people. Stalin had nothing to do with it." Added another, "They paid for our tears." "And this," Gorbachev commented in his memoirs, "in a region that had gone through the bloody meat grinder of the terrible 1930s!"[49]

Returning to Stavropol, Gorbachev asked himself more questions than ever, without finding answers to many of them. It dawned on him that one problem was Khrushchev's speech itself. It blamed Stalin for the crimes of his era. In that sense, he concluded, it lacked "an analytic or reasoned approach, and was rather a personal, emotional utterance." It reduced the causes of "a series of highly complicated political, socio-economic and socio-psychological processes to various evil traits in the leader's character."[50] Gorbachev's reaction contained the germ of a radical critique of Stalinism—that the Soviet system itself, rather than the man, was responsible. His resistance to Khrushchev's habit of reducing complex causes to simple explanations reflected pride in his own analytical skills. But he recognized the danger of pressing his analysis too far. At the time, he recalls, "people at the top realized immediately . . . that to criticize Stalin was tantamount to criticizing the system as whole," and hence was "a threat to its very survival." He wasn't intellectually ready, let alone politically prepared, to challenge his superiors.

Five years later, Khrushchev resumed his attack on Stalinism at the Twenty-Second Party Congress. In Moscow, Stalin's remains were hauled from the mausoleum on Red Square and buried late at night, under armed guard, next to the Kremlin wall. Stavropol authorities, mimicking their Moscow masters, brought in tractors to tear down their own Stalin statue, only to be confronted by a crowd of protesters. The authorities persisted, the statue came down, Stalin Prospekt was renamed Karl Marx Prospekt, and Gorbachev, as a Komsomol propaganda specialist, added his voice to the renewed anti-Stalin campaign, using language notable for its outrage. He lamented the "terrible harm" done by Stalin and condemned the "blood of innocent people" on the hands of Stalin's associates (Molotov, Malenkov, and Kaganovich) whom Khrushchev had just purged from the party. Following the party line, he added that the "consequences of the cult of personality have been eliminated once and for all."[51] But he knew quite well that the Stalin question wasn't resolved and continued to agonize over it. One of his wife's academic colleagues, whose mother had been arrested in 1937, was one of the comparatively few people who condemned Stalin. What brought Raisa's colleague and Gorbachev closer, the colleague recalled, were "the long discussions we had with Mikhail about Stalin."[52]

GORBACHEV'S PROMOTION to head the Stavropol city Komsomol in September 1956 gave him his first taste of quasi-independent authority. He was still subordinate to both city party and regional Komsomol authorities, but had some scope to promote his own ideas. His first speech as city Komsomol leader in November 1956 addressed education: "What does it mean," he asked, "that many Komsomol members attending the [Stavropol] Teachers College have C averages? It means that mediocre students will become mediocre specialists and that the results where they work will be mediocre, too." What good did Komsomol lecturers do, he asked, when their primitive message to their young charges amounted to: "This is good. This is bad."[53]

Gorbachev focused his attention on high school and college graduates without satisfying jobs who faced a grim future. Again, he settled on the idea of establishing a discussion club to inspire young people to join in reforming their country. It was, he recalled proudly, "an unheard of novelty" at the time, although similar clubs later appeared in other cities. For the first meeting in the House of Teachers, he chose a politically safe subject, "Let's Talk about Taste," but even so, ideological vigilantes warned city party bosses about an event "taking place right in the center of town . . . under some sort of camouflage . . . obviously a provocation." Apparently, the first discussion went well and was followed by others with more participants, in a bigger hall belonging to the local police, no less. Gorbachev chaired the meetings and made sure his innovation didn't get out of hand. On one occasion, which he would "remember all my life," an "apparently well-read and educated" young man accused Gorbachev and others of reducing culture to Communist ideology, whereas it should be understood to reflect "mankind's whole history." Together with the teachers' college dean, who helped organize the club, Gorbachev counterattacked, insisting that "only socialism had inherited and assimilated all the richness of mankind's spiritual heritage, and only socialism made culture available to the masses." Better schooled in ideological debate and armed with the power of the chair, Gorbachev smashed his "ideological enemy." All the student had done was what Gorbachev prided himself on doing, that is, "reasoning about problems," but at the time, Gorbachev later confessed, "I was only worried lest our popular discussion club be closed down."[54]

Gorbachev promoted another experiment that began idealistically but soon ran into trouble. To cope with rampant alcoholism, hooliganism, and crime, local police had used "forceful methods only," with little or no effect. Instead, he introduced slightly more gentle mobile Komsomol units of volunteers. But thugs themselves began taking over these units, using them to arrest people, and beating them up in the process.[55] Other activities Gorbachev encouraged were more prosaic: "academic-production brigades" in Stavropol high schools; construction of the first municipal camp for Young Pioneers (the Soviet equivalent of Boy Scouts, which children joined as a stepping stone to Komsomol); Komsomol brigades to plant trees along roads leading to the city.[56] After his 1958 promotion as deputy head of the regional Komsomol, he mobilized young people for Khrushchev's mass campaigns: building a huge nitrogen fertilizer plant near Nevinnomyssk, encouraging the cultivation of corn and raising of sheep, rabbits, and ducks. Khrushchev himself had hailed the tastiness of duck, and the Stavropol Komsomol newspaper issued an ominous challenge to its readers: "Komsomol members! What have you done lately for ducks?"[57]

Stavropol journalist Boris Kuchmaev described a springtime meeting where Gorbachev addressed award-winning young "poultry-women" from collective farms in the region. Outside the hall, lilacs were blooming. Gorbachev's stocky figure more than filled out a gray suit on which his Moscow University pin was prominently displayed. His bright tie was loosened, his eyes blazed, his cheeks were flushed. He glowed, Kuchmaev remembered, with the "unshakable self-confidence" of a man who could "lay down the law on matters which one would have thought only specialists had mastered."[58] Similar enthusiasm radiates from a letter Gorbachev sent Raisa after hearing Khrushchev address the Thirteenth Komsomol Congress in Moscow in April 1958: "The Congress left a very powerful impression . . . conclusions that one does not always reach at home . . . vindication for all my worries, striving and stress." The same letter contained this personal note: "I'm trying to carry out your requests. . . . I won't tell you what I bought. . . . I'm only sorry that I've run out of money. . . . I subscribed to a World History for you, ten volumes, the Smaller Soviet Encyclopedia and Plekhanov's [Georgy Plekhanov was an early Russian Marxist] philosophical works. . . . I'll be back soon, maybe before this letter, because it's not impossible that I'll catch a plane."[59]

Gorbachev admitted in his memoirs that the pressure of work, especially the bombardment of instructions from the Komsomol Central Committee in Moscow, was wearing. It was as if "those at the top were firmly convinced that without their bureaucratic directives no grass could grow and no cows could calve, as if the economy could function

**The Gorbachevs with their daughter, Irina, after a May Day
demonstration, Stavropol, 1964.**

only under a regime of 'permanent mobilization,' completely deprived of
any capacity for self-development."[60] But that didn't prevent him from
projecting during these years the image of a man fully in control of himself, his job, and his future.

Nikolai Yeriomin first encountered Gorbachev in the fall of 1956 while
working as a tractor driver in Novo-Aleksandrovsky district, northeast
of Stavropol. By 1958, he had become a Komsomol instructor and frequently saw Gorbachev in Stavropol. "He was a strongly built, inspiring man," Yeriomin remembered, "courageous, with a penetrating gaze,
and very accessible." Yeriomin's admiration, still strong in 2005, must
owe something to Gorbachev's having promoted and supported him. But
the string of admiring adjectives he applied to his former mentor, who
was no longer in a position to assist his career, was stunning: "capable, tenacious, responsible, innovative, focused, strict, principled, decent,
organized, smart, cultured, refined, determined, consistent, particularly

good at involving both scholars and practitioners in seminars and conferences devoted to developing long-term programs for the economy."[61]

Raisa Bazikova, a teacher of Russian language and literature, first
met Gorbachev in 1958, when she was Komsomol leader of the Budyenny
district. He appointed her regional Komsomol secretary for children,
schools, and other social organizations, and later tapped her as deputy
party boss of the October district. She got to know Raisa Gorbachev, Raisa's sister, Ludmila, the Gorbachevs' daughter, Irina, and Irina's husband. Like Yeriomin, Bazikova doesn't stint on praise. A meticulous
manager, Gorbachev insisted on keeping control, checking up on everyone and everything, frequently visiting farms and enterprises. He took
his time before deciding, but even when he had doubts, he was "firm and
decisive." "He was vain," admits Bazikova, "but aren't we all?" Of course
he wanted to rise, but most of all, "he wanted to grow."

Provincial party and government officials were notoriously dissolute.
(Two functionaries the author encountered in Soviet times in Donetsk,
having downed several hundred grams of vodka at breakfast, literally
chased a comely waitress around the restaurant and into the kitchen.)
When they weren't drinking or womanizing, they spent a lot of their
time with their colleagues on hunting and fishing trips in which as
much time was devoted to strong liquor as to fish and game. According to Bazikova, Gorbachev was virtually unique among Stavropol functionaries. Many of them were "show-offs and extremists," not nearly as
"smart and solid" as he. Many were "crude and arrogant, and took liberties with women," whereas he "treated them with respect." In addition,
Gorbachev went out of his way to appoint women as city and district
leaders.

Gorbachev wasn't a feminist in the Western sense. That sort of feminism was in bad odor under the Communists because Soviet "liberation" of women had supposedly given them political rights, along with
the "privilege" of doing the heavy labor of men, like cleaning streets.
Gorbachev's virtue was that, living with Raisa, he understood and
appreciated women's burdens, treated women respectfully, and promoted them when he could. His closest adviser, said Bazikova, was his
wife. They were wonderfully "open and sincere" with each other. She
was "very smart," and he "knew that and listened to her. He didn't trust

many party workers, but he did trust her—in everything." Even when the advice she gave him wasn't good, at least it was "sincere." His aides "just weren't on his level." That's why she influenced him on everything, including personnel issues.[62]

Viktor Kalyagin, trained as a veterinarian but serving as a state farm director and then a rural district party boss, first met the Gorbachevs in 1961–1962. They seemed an exemplary couple: "What a good guy! He treated his wife with such respect and love! As for the rest of us, our wives would criticize us, saying, 'Look how Gorbachev treats his wife! You should treat us the same way!'"[63]

Given how different Gorbachev was from his peers, how much more cultured, sophisticated, and successful, it's no wonder that some resented him. Aleksei Gonochenko, a Komsomol colleague beginning in 1955, said Gorbachev moved up too fast for his own good, failing to get the sort of basic experience that he would need in the long run. He was also too "soft," Gonochenko contended. "You could convince him to change his mind." The idea that such openness is a failing reflects the traditional Russian attachment to firm, even authoritarian leadership.[64] Even Kalyagin, a seemingly more tolerant soul who had a higher overall opinion of Gorbachev, agreed: "Even when he doubted advice his aides were giving him, they could always get him to listen before he made up his mind." In that sense, continued Kalyagin, who got to know Gorbachev's parents well, "he had his father's character. If he had resembled his mother, he would have said, 'You heard what I said. That's it!' But in fact, you could always get him to come to an agreement."[65]

No former colleague has been a fiercer critic of Gorbachev than Viktor Kaznacheyev. Like Gorbachev, Kaznacheyev rose from a humble background with the help of a higher education, but he had to settle for the Stavropol teachers' college rather than Moscow State University. By his third year, he chaired the student trade union and sat on the city Komsomol committee, where he met and became friendly with Gorbachev. Kaznacheyev's first impression was that Gorbachev was "energetic and resourceful" and "knew how to size things up," but Kaznacheyev insists that's because of Gorbachev's "pose"—his "seeming erudition," his "frequent quoting of Lenin, Stalin, and other Marxist classics," the way "he never missed a chance to remind you that he had led the Komsomol in his rural school, had worked on a combine, and been awarded the Red Labor Banner." Kaznacheyev confessed, "I was a prisoner of his charm for many years." But he eventually concluded that his friend was a veritable "Stavropol Narcissus," who was avid to become the top man in the region, fawned on his superiors, and was "envious and vengeful" toward rivals he couldn't stand and whom he "denounced" when necessary, a man who "loved to get close to brilliant people, but didn't like it when such people got too close to him" and threatened to outshine him.[66]

Kaznacheyev's virulent indictment extends to Gorbachev's wife, who, Kaznacheyev insisted, arranged her life so as to "do almost nothing at home." Unlike the wives of Kaznachaeyev and other colleagues, Raisa supposedly found women to clean her apartment, wash her family's clothes and prepare their meals; one helper's payoff was that Gorbachev allegedly arranged her husband's promotion. During their early days in Stavropol, Kaznacheyev recalled, the Gorbachevs formed a cozy social circle with him and his wife and two other couples, who regularly gathered on each other's birthdays and on holidays, and took vacations together in the countryside. Later, he said, since Raisa didn't like to cook, the Gorbachevs preferred to be entertained by others, and after a while, they became aloof and distant.[67]

What to make of Kaznacheyev's *j'accuse?* In 2005 he was president of the State Technical University in Piatigorsk, a resort town in the mountainous south of the Stavropol region. He readily agreed to be interviewed about Gorbachev, about whom he has written several extremely negative books, but managed to spend more time talking about himself. A short, squat, balding man with what seemed a permanently frozen face, he had to break away for a ceremony at which he received the key to the city. But he invited his American guests to a luncheon in his honor following the ceremony. At the luncheon, his faculty, administration, and students took turns toasting him. A young woman in charge of public relations declared him "a truly remarkable man, a man who rises at the break of dawn to conduct planning meetings by 6 a.m., a man who has 10,000 wives [i.e., the university's women students]. We are all his wives." Kaznacheyev badgered one reluctant woman student at the table to perform a song dedicated to him: "Long Live the King!"

If Gorbachev was a "Stavropol Narcissus," Kaznacheyev was a Piatigorsk Narcissus on steroids. Instead of advancing Kaznacheyev in the party hierarchy, Gorbachev twice passed over him for promotion. Asked about Kaznacheyev in an interview, Gorbachev at first said, "I don't react to what he says and writes." But he then demonstrated that his capacity to curse matched his ability to theorize: "He's the sort who will crawl into an asshole without using soap."[68]

Actually, relations between the Gorbachevs and Kaznacheyevs weren't so cozy to begin with. A photograph from that time shows the two couples together with two others, apparently during one of the "warm" social gatherings that Kaznacheyev describes. The other couples seem happily engaged in the drinking and smoking typical when Russian friends get together. Both Gorbachevs look distracted and pained.

SOME OF THE CRITICISM of Gorbachev by his Stavropol underlings is of traits and practices characteristic of virtually all ambitious Soviet party functionaries: determination to rise, plus an ability to flatter superiors, dominate underlings, and outmaneuver rivals to get ahead. And some of the praise seems exaggerated because his best qualities were so rare among provincial functionaries. In the long run, however, Gorbachev's fate depended not on his provincial peers but on his bosses in Stavropol and Moscow, and the impression he made on most of them was stellar.

Fyodor Kulakov, who took over in Stavropol in mid-1960, was decisive in Gorbachev's rise. Kulakov was only forty-two himself when he assumed command of the Stavropol party organization, after serving as the Russian Republic's minister of bread products. "Tall, handsome, willful, and energetic" (the words of a former colleague), and with a full head of dark hair, Kulakov had a smattering of culture, but was as crude as his name (based on the word *kulak*, or fist). Raised, like Gorbachev, in a peasant family, he had a correspondence course degree from the elite Timiryazov Agricultural Academy in Moscow. When Stavropol's output of eggs fell short of planned targets, he invoked the Russian slang for testicles to chastise malingering party officials: "If you don't fulfill the plan for eggs, you'll have to give up your own."[69] Others in Stavropol remembered his "cold-damp hands with knuckles he loved to crack," his "rumbling, metallic voice," his "enigmatic smile and sharp odor of cologne," his "capacity to down endless glasses of vodka," "his habit of flailing his arms around as if they didn't belong to him," and his particular respect for those who would "walk through walls" for him.[70] According to Gorbachev, Kulakov was as adept at conversing with ordinary people as he was with experts, and he had a "thorough" analytical mind. But his "weaknesses" included a tendency to "carouse" with his top associates, sometimes descending into "extended drinking bouts."[71]

Gorbachev knew his fate depended on Kulakov. He set out to learn what he could from Kulakov's best qualities—his decisiveness, "openness of character and human charm," his way of "working with feeling and giving all for the cause"—while eschewing drunken skirt chasing. Fortunately, Gorbachev recalled, Kulakov "never asked me to do anything untoward, although I know that he demanded others do whatever came into his head or his heart desired."[72]

Gorbachev became Kulakov's pet project. He often gave him special assignments that went well beyond Gorbachev's official role, inviting him to travel with him around the region. "It was a real education," Gorbachev remembered, "without any lecturing."[73] But Kulakov also set out to prevent his cocky younger colleague from getting a swelled head. True, he promoted him in March 1961 to lead the Stavropol regional Komsomol, and a year later to be party boss of a large agricultural area, but in the midst of this ascent, Kulakov chastised Gorbachev at a Komsomol conference in January 1962.

The conference was held in response to sharp criticism of Stavropol authorities by the Central Committee in Moscow in December 1961. Their sin was having failed to report fully to local party members on decisions of the recently ended Twenty-Second Party Congress. In standard, self-abasing fashion, Kulakov pled guilty as charged. But he singled out Gorbachev for special blame. Gorbachev had hailed the congress's call to make corn cultivation a particular Komsomol priority, but had done so "in words not deeds." Some eighteen thousand young people had been dispatched to the countryside to help with the harvest, Gorbachev had claimed, but that produced no effect because during the same period almost as many had fled from the farms. "Not to get married, Comrade Gorbachev," Kulakov sneered, but because "callous" Komsomol authorities had done nothing to improve "elementary conditions of everyday life for young people." Housing was awful. Milkmaids slept in unheated barns. There were no newspapers, magazines, or radios. Comrade Gorbachev blamed the farm managements, Kulakov noted, but "it would have been more honest and worthy of a Communist to blame the regional Komsomol itself."

This last line brought applause from the assembled delegates, doubtless relieved that Kulakov's wrath had not landed on them, but also glad to see a rising star get put down. Then Kulakov reduced the sting. "It would be a waste of time, my friends, to criticize those who are hopeless." Rather, his targets were those capable of "taking proper account of the criticism and working to make the Komsomol more 'battle-ready.'"[74]

During the summer of 1962, at a meeting of the Stavropol party bureau, the ranking party body in the region, Kulakov struck again. By this time the Central Committee had sent down a delegation to put the Stavropol party's house in order, which required another round of self-criticism from Kulakov and company. The regional propaganda chief, a man whom Gorbachev remembers as "wise like a brick that lands on your head," blasted him for failing to encourage "socialist competition," the practice of trying to motivate workers, in the absence of meaningful monetary incentives, by displaying their faces on "boards of honor." Gorbachev dared to talk back, sparking what he recalls as a hot "skirmish." Kulakov appointed a commission to scrutinize Gorbachev's work. That led to an August meeting, Gorbachev remembers, at which Kulakov himself "gave it to me full force," accusing him of "irresponsibility," and in general delivered remarks that were "unjust, sharp, and crude."

Gorbachev was bursting to reply on the spot but wasn't recognized. He confessed his anger to an old, much-decorated agronomist, who set him straight. Who would support him against Kulakov? Kulakov would never forgive him. "The very best speech," he continued, "is the one that goes ungiven." Excellent advice! Gorbachev didn't follow it often enough when he was Soviet leader. But he did this time, and was rewarded with his January 1963 promotion to personnel chief for the regional party organization's agriculture committee. (The formerly unitary regional committee had been divided into two parts, industrial and agricultural, at Khrushchev's insistence.) After this, the two men grew closer. Kulakov "had oversight of my department, we met almost daily, we gradually began interacting at work as equals," and when Kulakov was appointed to head the Central Committee's agricultural department in Moscow, "we parted as friends and remained close all the succeeding years."[75]

When Khrushchev was ousted from power in 1964 in what amounted to a palace coup by his closest Kremlin associates, Kulakov supported the conspirators. That ingratiated him with Khrushchev's successors, which strengthened his hand in supporting Gorbachev. But Kulakov's patronage came at a price. Before leaving for Moscow, he went out of his way to attend to the Gorbachev family's needs. In the fall of 1961, Raisa Gorbachev was sent to Kiev to attend retraining courses for social science teachers. She didn't want to leave her four-year-old daughter, but reluctantly agreed to have her stay with Gorbachev's parents in Privolnoe (where Irina managed to come down with chicken pox and her grandparents secretly baptized her). Having not seen his wife for several months, Gorbachev asked Kulakov's permission to visit her in Kiev en route to Moscow for the Twenty-Second Party Congress in October 1961. His plan to have her move into a Kiev hotel with him was at first thwarted by hotel administrators fishing for a bribe, but eventually they spent "three happy days together. It was as if we hadn't seen each other for half a lifetime."[76]

But Kulakov had his own agenda for Gorbachev's wife. Once, when Gorbachev returned from a two-week trip in the Stavropol hinterlands and was recounting his trip, Raisa suddenly said, "We have some news, too."

"Who is we?" Gorbachev responded.

"Me."

"What news?"

It was summer and she wasn't working.

"Fyodor Kulakov called me the other day."

"Interesting. What did you talk about?"

"He asked me out."

"You don't say."

"Yes, indeed. I said, 'Fyodor Davidovich, you know what my relationship with Mikhail is.'"

"'I do,' Kulakov replied. 'You can carry on with that relationship.' I said, 'That's not our idea of family life,' and then I hung up."

"An interesting conversation, indeed," Gorbachev said. "I'll have to ask him what it means."

"Don't," Raisa retorted. "I gave him my answer and now I've told you. So this is no longer news to you."

Gorbachev asked Kulakov anyway: "Did you call Raisa?"

Kulakov hesitated for moment, Gorbachev recalled, "and then wriggled out of it," saying, "I was looking for you. I thought you'd returned. I wanted to ask about your impressions of the trip."[77]

KULAKOV'S SUCCESSOR IN STAVROPOL, Leonid Yefremov, was a casualty of Khrushchev's ouster. He had been Khrushchev's first deputy chairman of the Central Committee's Russian Republic bureau, and he wasn't happy to be exiled to Stavropol. But he cut an impressive figure in a provincial capital.[78] Local observers remember him as "powerful," "intelligent," and, although his higher education extended only to the Voronezh Institute on the Mechanization of Agriculture, "unusually cultured." His wife was an accomplished actress, who continued to live in Moscow except for a brief stint when she performed in the Stavropol theater, and his son was a composer. Yefremov had a "deep, rich voice that sounded like a bell tolling in his chest," but, unlike Kulakov, he generally didn't raise it to berate his lieutenants, even in response to what he regarded as their "slovenly or unscrupulous" behavior. Instead, he managed to "convince them"—not that difficult since he totally controlled their fate.[79]

A boss like that would seem a better fit for Gorbachev than Kulakov had been. With what Gorbachev describes as his "broad political horizon, erudition, and general level of education and culture," Yefremov was equipped to appreciate Gorbachev's similar virtues, while as a "refined product" of the system and of the party's "apparatus school," he "taught" Gorbachev a lot. But despite this fit, tensions developed between the two men. It may be that Yefremov, with his cultural and intellectual pretensions, felt more challenged by Gorbachev than Kulakov had. Or that since his own career was declining, he resented a hotshot on the rise. Gorbachev probably also saw Yefremov as a loser who couldn't help him advance his career. At one point, having learned that Gorbachev and

Kulakov often talked on a secure government telephone line, Yefremov tried to find out what they had discussed and why Gorbachev had kept it from him. Gorbachev's insistence that the conversations were "purely personal" and had nothing to do with Yefremov, only made the latter "more angry." On another occasion, when Gorbachev dared question Yefremov's nomination of candidates for city and district party leaders, Yefremov shot back that Gorbachev was "getting too big for his boots." To which Gorbachev responded angrily, "almost at the top of my voice," and in the presence of the entire regional bureau, that he rejected that charge, and that if Yefremov and other bureau members didn't care to consider his opinion, then there was "no point inviting me to these meetings in order to publicly humiliate me."

Yefremov subsided, Gorbachev remembered, but not before "all the toadies in the room got the signal and, as if on command, attacked." Gorbachev wasn't intimidated. It wasn't, he recalled, that he himself was "devoid of diplomatic skills and flexibility, but when someone insulted my dignity, I would never tolerate it."[80]

BY 1966 GORBACHEV FOUND many things about his work gratifying. The header for the portion of his memoirs devoted to the period between 1962 and 1966 is "My Main Task." It was to find and support talented leaders who could make the system work, to "defend capable, often obstinate cadres, and to move decisively to replace those who were incompetent, uneducated, and didn't know how, didn't even try, to deal respectfully with people." Gorkaya Balka, the godforsaken village whose plight so stirred Gorbachev when he first returned to Stavropol, became Exhibit A in his attempt. The new collective farm chairman there, a wounded war veteran with deep scars furrowing his face, turned the place into a model not only of agricultural production but of beautification as well. Another young chairman, Nikolai Tereshchenko, confronting peasants stealing from kolkhoz fields at night, grabbed a shotgun and opened fire at the donkeys being used to cart away the grain. Gorbachev convinced Kulakov that instead of firing Tereshchenko, they should hold a region-wide seminar on his farm to celebrate his successes in growing corn.[81]

Meanwhile, Gorbachev's personal life was also more satisfying. At

last, his family had a "normal flat," as he put it. After ten years on the job
ladder, he earned a good salary (300 rubles a month), and his wife, after
obtaining a candidate of science degree in 1967 and a more prestigious
teaching job, earned 320 rubles. Now they could begin buying furniture
and better clothes. Moreover, they had a small circle of close friends—
not, to be sure, his crude party colleagues and their beaten-down wives,
but two couples who were much more to the Gorbachevs' liking. Aleksandr and Lydia Budyka hailed from the Don River basin, Mikhail and
Inna Varshavsky from Odessa. Both men were engineers who had
been sent to the Stavropol area as part of Khrushchev's post-1953 push
to modernize agriculture. Their wives were physicians, Lydia Budyka
a pediatrician who, Raisa said later, "helped me raise Irisha [short for
Irina]." Lydia became Raisa's closest friend. The Gorbachevs spent most
of their free time in Stavropol with the Budykas and Varshavskys, Gorbachev remembered, and "we supported each other in everything."[82]

Raisa Gorbachev's higher degree rewarded her work on a candidate's

The Gorbachevs with friends in the foothills near Stavropol, 1960s.

dissertation (roughly equivalent to a Ph.D., although the Russian doctoral degree is even higher) in the controversial field of sociology. Sociology, she would later explain, had "ceased to exist as a science" in the
1930s because it was "dangerous" to the system Stalin was construct-
ing. That system rejected the kind of "feedback" that sociological studies
could provide. The system was "organically alien to it, just as it is alien
to the system."

Sociology revived as part of the Khrushchev thaw and continued to
grow in the 1960s and 1970s, even though it still faced strong resistance
from guardians of ideological orthodoxy.[83] The fact that Raisa opted to
pursue it showed her independence of mind. The title of her dissertation, "The Formation of New Features of Everyday Life of the Collective
Farm Peasantry: Sociological Researches in Stavropol Region," doesn't
sound radical, but her approach to researching it was. Rather than rely
on approved texts, she resorted to fieldwork. Her husband recruited
friends in the party and Komsomol apparatus to make sure she was welcome in the villages she visited. Even so, she covered hundreds of miles
on dirt roads, sometimes in a GAZ jeep or truck or on a motorcycle, but
often slogging along on foot in rubber boots. She interviewed hundreds
of people, particularly women, collected documents and statistics, and
administered some three thousand questionnaires. The presence of
a philosopher/sociologist being unheard of in villages she visited, she
offered to give lectures and run discussion evenings. Back in Stavropol,
she spoke at conferences, seminars, and other meetings, reporting her
findings and recommending improvements in rural living conditions.

Raisa Gorbachev's "sociology with a human face," as she called it, deepened her understanding of "real life," particularly that of the old women
she found living in every fourth or fifth peasant hut. These women had
lost everything in the war. They "had never known the happiness of love
or the joy of motherhood," and now they were "living out their lives alone
in old, tumbledown houses that were also at the end of their days." Yet, the
majority of them "had not become bitter, did not hate the whole world and
had not withdrawn into themselves, but had preserved the selflessness and
sympathy for the misfortunes and sorrows of others that have always animated the Russian woman's heart."

Sounds sentimental? Well, she was. Late one evening she knocked on the door of an old woman. After answering Raisa's questions, the woman sighed and asked, "How it is, daughter, that you're so painfully thin?"

"Oh no, [that's] just my usual weight," Raisa answered.

"I suppose you haven't got a husband," the woman persisted.

"Yes, I have."

"I suppose he drinks?" she sighed.

"No."

"He beats you up?"

"Certainly not."

"Come on, daughter, why try to deceive me? I've lived a long time and I know people don't go round from door to door unless they're driven to it."[84]

On another occasion, when interviewing a lively, spirited Cossack woman, Raisa asked what held her family together: love, friendship, love of children, or—another possibility—sex?

"What's that?

Raisa explained: "It's your intimate relations with your husband." And when that, too, drew a blank, she further elaborated: "Well, you know, a husband and wife have a personal relationship. Well, never mind." Raisa added, intending to leave the conversation right there.

"No," said the woman. "Write it down: What the hell use is a man if not for that?"[85]

Neither conversations like this nor the sympathy that Raisa felt so strongly when encountering poor, lonely old women is on display in her dissertation, which she defended at the Moscow Pedagogical Institute in 1967. Her work is a classic example of how not to express, but only barely allude to, the critical views she by then held. The dissertation praised certain real Soviet achievements like the rise in rural literacy, but did so, in standard Soviet academic fashion, by comparing woebegone villages to even worse pre-1917 conditions. Phrases like "the socialist restructuring of the kolkhoz village has not entirely eliminated inequality" only hint at the gross inequality between town and country, which official ideology pledged to reduce. Reading between the lines, one can detect the Potemkin-village nature of libraries, clinics, nurseries, and old-age homes that barely deserved their names.[86]

Raisa Gorbachev had made herself into an accomplished social scientist. Particularly in her third chapter ("Change in the Character of Interrelations in Family Life: Affirmation of Socialist Norms and Customs in the Sphere of Nonproductive Life of the Collective Farm Peasantry"), which underlined the benighted position of women, she verged toward Western-style feminism, without using the label. She tried to help those she had met by recounting to her husband what she saw and heard in their villages. Working the system, using his privileges, he got a former colleague based in Moscow to help find a leading sociologist, G. V. Osipov, to direct her dissertation. And her husband was proud of the result: "What she produced had almost all the makings of a doctoral dissertation. All it lacked were general conclusions based on her research, but the time wasn't ripe for that. The sorts of serious conclusions that flowed from her work became possible to reach only much, much later."[87]

Raisa's work on her dissertation required her to make four trips to Moscow—to consult with her thesis supervisor, to submit the dissertation summary, to prepare for and then to undertake her thesis defense. By this time Irina, who was ten years old, was busy at school most of the day, but her father made sure he was home (if only briefly) when she returned. They cooked meals together; he recruited her for domestic chores; on weekends, when he ran out of other ideas for entertaining her, he took her to the cinema to see two or three films in a row. Like her mother and mother-in-law, Raisa wanted everything in her home to be just right, and she trained her daughter in the same spirit. Irina helped her mother sort through her sociological questionnaires, which Raisa spread out on the floor. According to Lydia Budyka, Raisa didn't worship order for its own sake, but loved her home and wanted it to be warm and welcoming. But some of her efforts went beyond that. For example, Raisa asked her daughter to prepare a card file for the hundreds, if not thousands, of books the Gorbachevs had collected, many of them philosophical tomes reflecting Raisa's academic specialty. By the 1960s, with her husband's help, she had managed to obtain copies of the Bible, the Gospels, and the Koran, none easily available in an atheistic state. In addition, there were the complete works of Marx and Lenin, plus a two-hundred-volume set of translated great works of world literature, which

Gorbachev ordered while on missions to Moscow. "We were a family of readers," he recalls, pointing proudly to his daughter as a "passionate" reader. She began to read at the age of four. He had deliberately set out to "cultivate her taste for reading" but couldn't believe she was reading as much as she claimed to be. "What do you mean you've read all that?" he demanded to know when she was still a schoolgirl. She remembers long periods of silence in the house when she and her parents were all reading, but answering her father's question, she explained that she did a lot of reading at night when they were asleep. Television didn't tempt her because her parents deliberately hadn't bought one.[88]

Propelled by his own intellectual ambitions, as well as his wife's, Gorbachev decided to get himself a second academic degree. Such an achievement would also advance his party career, as Kulakov reminded him in 1960. "He insisted I do it," Gorbachev remembered. "'Listen,' he said, 'your work involves the economy, but you know too little about it.' So you see, my guardian angel insisted."

Gorbachev enrolled in 1961 as an extension student at the same agricultural institute where his wife was teaching. (She said she avoided any connection with the administration of his exams.) He chose correspondence courses in the agro-economics department, which had recently been formed by combining agricultural and economics faculties. He chose for his thesis topic "Concentration and Specialization in Agricultural Production in the Stavropol Region."[89] "I threw myself into my studies," he recalled. "I had to pass higher math again, but I got up everyday at five and studied for two hours while the 'female component' of the family was still asleep."

Kulakov gave Gorbachev his own notes from the courses he had taken and then quizzed his protégé to make sure he was applying himself.

"What are you taking?" Kulakov asked.

"Soil science," Gorbachev replied.

"What grade did you get?"

"Straight A."

"That's because you used your party influence," Kulakov teased him, and then administered a quick quiz of his own, demanding that Gorbachev name the elements characteristic of salty soil.[90]

Gorbachev passed that test as well as those of the institute, and received his second bachelor's degree in 1967, about the same time Raisa Maksimovna defended her candidate's dissertation.

A YEAR LATER, Gorbachev considered giving up his party career and becoming an academic. Part of the problem was that he was exhausted. His regular routine (including Saturdays) during these years was to arise at five to do his homework on agricultural economics, awakening his women at seven. He was too busy at work to have lunch, so when he finally got home at nine or ten in the evening he overate and began putting on weight. (He later dieted and lost forty pounds over the course of three years.) He had gotten used to skipping regular meals at Moscow University, where he subsisted mostly on *pirozhki* (tarts stuffed with meat or cabbage), which led to gastritis and eventually a stomach ulcer. He switched to a healthier diet in Stavropol, and reserved time for stays at Caucasus health resorts, but it wasn't until 1971, when he was forty, that he "was back to normal."[91]

Another reason Gorbachev was tempted to shift careers was the tension with Yefremov. Still another was that the seeming promise of the post-Khrushchev era was waning. In particular, economic reforms introduced in 1965 by the new prime minister, Aleksei Kosygin, which Gorbachev welcomed, foundered because of just the sort of resistance that he witnessed in Stavropol. "They're beating their gums in Moscow," local bureaucrats grumbled, "but our job is to fulfill the plan." In January 1967, a Stavropol official whom Gorbachev admired for taking the reforms seriously was fired. Innokenty Barakov had gone so far as to stop transmitting central plans that were impossible to fulfill to collective farms under his supervision, so that they could develop their initiative and independence. Barakov had been inspired by a reform-minded economist in Moscow, Gennady Lisichkin, who was still pressing the case for change in the liberal journal *Novyi mir*. That September, several Stavropol functionaries led by Yefremov denounced Lisichkin in an angry piece in the Central Committee's newspaper, *Rural Life*.[92]

In the summer of 1967, Zdeněk Mlynář, Gorbachev's freethinking Czech friend from Moscow University, reappeared in his life. He had worked in the chief prosecutor's office in Prague after MGU and then moved to the Academy of Sciences. There, he told Gorbachev, he read the very "classics" that their MGU teacher Professor Kechekyan "told us about in his lectures, but not only those books; also polemical works by Marxists, including so-called revisionists and renegades, like Trotsky." Mlynář had twice visited Yugoslavia, where Tito was developing a non-Soviet model of "socialist self-management." He had been to Italy and Belgium twice, and to the Brussels World's Fair of 1958, an experience that, he said much later, "was for me literally the opening of a 'window on the world.'"[93] Mlynář came to Moscow in 1967 to sound out Soviet receptivity to the sorts of political reforms liberal Czechs were contemplating, but he didn't find much support. He visited the Gorbachevs in Stavropol in their two-room, fourth-floor apartment and pronounced it modest compared with what the Czech Communist leader of a provincial capital would inhabit. He and Gorbachev spent two days hiking in the mountains around the resort of Mineral'nye vody, ate and drank heartily, and talked frankly and at length.

Mlynář said big changes were coming in Czechoslovakia, and "made no secret," Gorbachev recalls, "of the fact that he thought the political system in Czechoslovakia had to be democratized." When his friend asked what was happening in the Soviet Union, Gorbachev expressed a view that he would later change—"In your country all that might be possible, but in our country it simply could not be done."[94]

Gorbachev still believed that the key to overcoming "deformations" in Soviet socialism was to find and promote enterprising new "cadres." But by 1967 it was clear to him that Brezhnev was not in the mood to change cadres in any "fundamental way." Instead, personnel changes were designed to promote clans of loyal underlings in a "war among different groupings going on in the leadership itself."[95]

If these were among the doubts that led Gorbachev to contemplate a career change, yet another consideration may have influenced him, whether consciously or not. In an evaluation written in April 1961, a Komsomol official lamented, "Comrade Gorbachev does not always finish tasks that he begins, and sometimes is not sufficiently demanding" of Komsomol cadres.[96] One could dismiss this complaint as coming from someone with a political or personal ax to grind, but during perestroika and afterward, it was echoed by former allies and friends. Did

Gorbachev sense his own weakness as an administrator and wonder whether he might be cut out more for intellectual reflection than for political administration?

Gorbachev's temperament wasn't suited for solitary contemplation in an ivory tower (the USSR didn't have such things, anyway). But he wasn't the kind of hail-comrade-well-met fellow who thrived in the party apparatus, either. Gorbachev was quite capable of throwing loud parties on state occasions—but not the sort most of his male colleagues preferred. On one occasion, Lydia Budyka remembered, Gorbachev reserved a large guesthouse, invited his colleagues for a sort of potluck supper, locked the door to the billiard room, and demanded that the men ask their wives to dance.[97]

Another pattern observable in 1960s Stavropol party documents seems to reflect Gorbachev's disenchantment with party work in Stavropol. At party meetings he was surprisingly reticent, rarely engaging with other speakers in the ritualized give-and-take that passed for debate. His more radical views weren't safe to proclaim, and he probably tried to keep the necessary fawning and flattering to a minimum. But his preference for making short comments, usually supporting someone in higher authority, may also have reflected an awareness of his tendency to talk too much for his own good. His choice of subjects for his longer, more critical perorations—education, on the one hand, and drunkenness and criminality, on the other—betrayed pride at his own accomplishments and disdain for others who fell short.

Gorbachev himself has another explanation for having almost turned away from party work: "I didn't like being bossed around. My nature is to be independent. I can adapt myself to almost anything, I'm not a troublemaker or conceited. Not at all, but I'm the sort of person who can do ten times more when I'm not pushed and pestered, but rather given the chance to think."[98] So "I actually made an internal decision to turn in the direction of scholarship. I passed the exam for a candidate's degree, I had chosen a topic for my dissertation, and I had begun to collect research materials." "I was ready to go."[99]

BY THE SPRING OF 1968, Zdeněk Mlynář was working for the Czech Central Committee; he had been one of the main authors of the Prague "Action Program," calling for democratic reforms, and was a close adviser to reformist leader Alexander Dubček. At a time when Moscow was increasingly alarmed about developments in Prague, Gorbachev sent him a telegram saying, "Zdenek, in a difficult time, we must maintain relations," but received no answer. Instead, the KGB's top man in Stavropol let Gorbachev know by a wink and a nod that his message had been "rerouted to another destination," that is, the Soviet security police.[100]

By July 1968, Brezhnev and the other leaders in Moscow were preparing to crush the Prague Spring. To prepare the Soviet people for this probability, party organizations across the country began warning of the danger Czech reforms posed to the Soviet camp. Stavropol party boss Yefremov condemned Czech heresies. Gorbachev joined in the assault (without mentioning Mlynář's name) on what his Czech friend was doing: "ignoring our [Soviet] party's vast experience in the battle for the victory and consolidation of socialism and the construction of Communism," calling upon the Czechoslovak people to join in "strikes, riots, and anarchy." Gorbachev urged the Soviet Union to do its duty and "come to the defense of socialism in Czechoslovakia."[101]

Did Gorbachev's conscience bother him about declarations like this? Was that another reason he would feel "more comfortable in the academic world, where I would able to use my energy, my bent for analysis, and my curiosity in a way that would benefit myself and everyone else"? Not to mention that professors "enjoyed more freedom, if freedom could be used to describe those times."[102] But less than a month later, on August 5, 1968, Gorbachev was named Yefremov's deputy, the number two man in the Stavropol region. So much for a change of career! Instead of abandoning the party apparatus, he recommitted himself to it. Even after that, he insisted, "we remained closer to the world of scholarship and culture" and to the "intelligentsia," but it was in the Communist party that he was now a rising star.[103]

CHAPTER 4

REGIONAL
PARTY BOSS
1969–1978

O N APRIL 10, 1970, THE STAVROPOL regional party committee held a plenary session. First secretary Leonid Yefremov had
been recalled to Moscow to be first deputy chairman of the USSR State
Committee on Science and Technology. It was hardly the promotion he
craved, into the Politburo itself, but at least he could return to the capital. The plenum released Yefremov from his Stavropol post and unanimously ratified the selection, made in Moscow, of Mikhail Gorbachev as
his successor.

The USSR consisted of fifteen republics. Russia, by far the largest, contained eighty-three regions or provinces, dominated by regional party
first secretaries. Unlike American governors, or even French prefects,
they were responsible for everything and everyone in their domains.
That included the economy, since in the absence of any meaningful private sector almost all economic activity was in state hands. The same
went for all social organizations, such as trade unions, which were also
subordinate to party and state. Regional party bosses were answerable
to their Central Committee overseers in Moscow, but that actually added
to their local power and authority. Neither the local procurator, nor the
regional KGB, nor even the Party Control Committee in Moscow, which
collected complaints and denunciations against high party officials, was
authorized to move against regional bosses without the permission of
the party general secretary himself.[1]

Along with other party and state bigwigs, regional first secretaries were members of the Central Committee, and as such they "elected" the party's general secretary. For much of Soviet history that "choice" was a rubber-stamp ratification. But as recently as 1957 the Central Committee rebuffed an attempt by Khrushchev's Kremlin colleagues to oust him, and in 1964 Brezhnev and company dumped Khrushchev only after obtaining the support of most Central Committee members. According to Vitaly Mikhailenko, a former member of Gorbachev's Stavropol administration, "The first secretary was God or at least a demigod. He was free to do anything he wished. For him all was forgiven."[2]

Gorbachev was only thirty-nine in 1970. The fact that all the other Stavropol regional party leaders were significantly older made, he says, for a "unique situation."[3] In 1969 he had almost been named to head the national Young Communist League; he was young enough, but his bald pate was held against him.[4] From Moscow, Gorbachev's mentor Kulakov pushed his candidacy for Stavropol party boss. Gorbachev had also been noticed by Yuri Andropov, a close ally of Brezhnev and head of the KGB, who himself hailed from the Stavropol area and in April 1969 vacationed in the resort town of Zheleznovodsk. Protocol called for the Stavropol party boss to greet him, but Andropov politely declined Yefremov's hospitality, at which point second secretary Gorbachev was dispatched instead. Their first meeting, at the Dubovaya Roshcha (Oak Grove) sanatorium, where Andropov and his wife were staying in a deluxe three-room suite, was brief, but it would lead to more and longer get-togethers in the years ahead.[5]

Regional party chiefs were personally vetted by Kremlin leaders. Gorbachev's record was scrutinized by Central Committee secretaries Ivan Kapitonov and Konstantin Chernenko, later Gorbachev's predecessor as general secretary. He was interviewed by Kapitonov, Kulakov, and Politburo members Andrei Kirilenko and Mikhail Suslov; Suslov was variously known by Westerners as the party's "gray cardinal" or "ideologist in chief." In none of these awkward conversations, marked mostly by small talk, did anyone mention why Gorbachev was being interviewed. That remained for Brezhnev himself, when he received Gorbachev in his party office on Old Square, several blocks from the Kremlin.

In early 1970, the black-haired, beetle-browed Brezhnev was sev-

eral years away from succumbing to the illnesses that would transform the leader of one of the world's two superpowers into a nearly dead
man walking. He was still sharp, lively, and cheerful, with a military
bearing, a pleasant smile, and a sense of humor, a man who radiated
benevolence and went out of his way, as Gorbachev learned on this and
later occasions, to "win over his interlocutors and create a free and
open atmosphere for conversation."[6] Brezhnev confided to Gorbachev
that the Central Committee would be recommending his appointment.
"Until now," he added, Stavropol's leaders had come from other regions,
whereas in Gorbachev it would be getting "one of its own." When
Brezhnev genially reminisced about his role in the war, emphasizing
how unbearably hot it had been in the summer of 1942 as the Red Army
retreated toward the Black Sea port of Novorossiisk, the complaisant, yet
confident Gorbachev, drawing on his own boyhood experience that same
summer, "confirmed the accuracy of [Brezhnev's] observations."

Gorbachev then dared lobby him for help in rescuing the Stavropol
region from the results of an extremely tough winter, complete with
bitter cold, drought, and dust storms. Brezhnev burst out laughing,
called Kulakov on the phone, and complained, "Listen, Fyodor, what
sort of guy have we picked for first secretary? He hasn't been elected yet,
and he's already beating us over the head for mixed fodder." Joining the
fun, Kulakov replied over the loud speaker on Brezhnev's desk, "Well,
Leonid Ilich, it's not too late to withdraw his candidacy." Brezhnev went
on to talk for several hours, according to Gorbachev, about matters foreign and domestic, as if confiding his "innermost thoughts" to a trusted
confidant.

NINETEEN SIXTY-EIGHT, the year of the Prague Spring, had been a turning point for many liberally inclined members of the Soviet intelligentsia.
That same year physicist Andrei Sakharov's manifesto, *Progress, Coexistence, and Intellectual Freedom*, came out in secret circulation. Future
Gorbachev aide Andrei Grachev, traveling in Western Europe on official
business, bought a copy, hid it at the bottom of his suitcase, and got it
past Soviet customs, feeling, as he did so, like a narco-courier. Several
years later, Gorbachev himself smuggled the Sakharov brochure home

so that his wife could read it.[7] Aleksandr Tvardovsky, editor of the liberal journal *Novyi mir*, admitted that he himself would have signed the Prague Spring manifesto, "Two Thousand Words." After Soviet tanks smashed the Prague Spring, some Soviet dissidents emigrated to the West. The Brezhnev regime arrested the handful who gathered in Red Square to protest the invasion, and adopted "prophylactic measures" against other potential dissenters: KGB warnings, firing and blacklisting, forcible commitment to psychiatric hospitals. But people who were outwardly obedient were free to think their own heretical thoughts. Enlightened apparatchiki who would become key Gorbachev aides after 1985—Anatoly Chernyaev, Georgy Shakhnazarov, Ivan Frolov, Vadim Zagladin, Oleg Bogomolov, Georgy Arbatov—stayed on their jobs in or near the Central Committee. Several of them, such as Chernyaev and Arbatov, actually worked as foreign policy aides and speechwriters for Brezhnev himself. Open dissidents didn't entirely trust such "party reformers." The latter, believing that reform could only come from the top, hoped that Brezhnev's pursuit of détente with the West, including U.S.-Soviet summits and arms control agreements, would pave the way for another round of reform, in which they might play a leading role.

One of the key rules of Gorbachev's game was to maintain General Secretary Brezhnev's trust. He and other regional party leaders all knew that if Brezhnev turned against them they were finished.[8] But Brezhnev had various levels of trust, and Gorbachev began at the highest level. On the eve of his elevation to Stavropol party boss, Kulakov told Gorbachev he'd be joining a hard core of Brezhnev supporters in the Central Committee, a kind of "rapid reaction force" ready to defend him against any attempt, for example, by Prime Minister Kosygin, to criticize the party leader. The existence of the "support group" wasn't a secret (a fact that itself deterred the actions it was sworn to resist), and its members were even initiated by being required to down in one gulp a tall champagne glass of vodka. When Gorbachev refused to do so, his new colleagues were dismayed. But when he recounted his long conversation with Brezhnev, the kind obviously reserved for a liege man in whom the boss had great trust, that reassured them.[9]

Had Brezhnev's team known of Gorbachev's private feelings, they would not have been so trusting. In the summer of 1968, he had, as required, condemned the Czech reformers and hailed the Soviet intervention. On July 19, he warned that the Prague leadership was ignoring "our comradely advice, based on the vast experience of our party," that by adopting a "reactionary political platform" and "losing control over events," it had made it necessary for Moscow to "defend socialist achievements" in Czechoslovakia.[10] On August 21, the day Soviet troops moved into Prague, he chaired a Stavropol regional party bureau session that "fully and entirely approve[d] the decisive and timely measures" taken by the Politburo.[11] But "my conscience bothered me," Gorbachev recalled. "I kept wondering whether the action made any sense and whether it hadn't been excessive."[12] In September 1969, he was sent to Czechoslovakia with a delegation of young party and Komsomol officials. Only a year after the Soviet invasion, Czechs and Slovaks were still bitter: demonstrations had recently occurred in Brno and Bratislava, so armed guards protected the Soviet "guests" around the clock. The Soviet delegation leader ominously informed Gorbachev that he would be unable see his old friend Zdeněk Mlynář, who had resigned from his official posts three months after the invasion and would soon be expelled from the Communist party. Even the new, Soviet-imposed Czech government showed its disdain: only the minister of higher education showed up to meet the Soviet visitors. In Bratislava, no one at all officially welcomed the delegation. In Brno, where Soviet troops still watched over the process of "normalization," delegation members tried to engage workers in conversation, only to have their "hosts" ostentatiously turn their backs. Before the very eyes of the Soviet visitors, a Czech worker tore down a portrait of Lenin that had hung on the wall. The only even lukewarm welcome they got was from farmers in a Slovak agricultural region near Košice where, Gorbachev remembered, his father had been wounded in the war. This visit confirmed Gorbachev's view of the invasion: "The people of Czechoslovakia had rejected our action."[13]

Gorbachev's qualms extended to the post-1968 "tightening of the screws in the ideological sphere," which the Kremlin required of all lower-level Soviet party officials.[14] In the period before August 1968, encouraged by the Prague Spring as well as by what remained of reformist spirit in the Soviet Union, the head of the Stavropol agricultural institute's philosophy department finished a book called *The Unity of the*

People and the Contradictions of Socialism. That sounds innocuous enough, but under the heading "contradictions," a phrase beloved by Marxist theoreticians but applied very gingerly to the Soviet Union by Soviet ideologues, Fagim B. Sadykov considered reforms prefiguring those Gorbachev would carry out two decades later. Sadykov's manuscript was discussed by his academic colleagues, and one of them, Raisa Gorbachev herself, wrote a favorable review.[15] Sadykov lugged his text to Moscow to have it vetted in the Central Committee apparatus, and a Stavropol publishing house brought the book out late in 1968.

None of this protected Sadykov. Soon, Gorbachev recalls, word came down from Moscow to give him a good "working over." On May 13, 1969, the regional party bureau considered Sadykov's book. "We tore him to pieces," Gorbachev remembered. "It was a real execution." Gorbachev himself gave what he calls a "sharply critical speech." Actually, Gorbachev's conscience slightly softened his own public indictment of Sadykov. He began calmly and respectfully, noting that Sadykov had a long list of publications, which, Gorbachev pointedly mentioned, he himself had made a point of reading. Sadykov's latest book was ten years in the writing, Gorbachev added, praiseworthy except that this meant its mistaken views were deliberate and calculated. The book contained certain conceptions that were quite "correct," but it was "distorted" and "undocumented," based on "little analysis," and contained no "statistical or serious sociological materials." Gorbachev ended without stating "general conclusions: I think there's no need to spend time on that since other comrades have spoken. Everything's been discussed in detail." He did, though, insist that Sadykov's views were "foreign to our ideology," and he condemned Raisa Gorbachev's institute colleagues (without of course mentioning her name) for evaluating the book in a "nonparty" manner and thus helping to promote its publication.[16]

Sadykov could have been expelled from the Communist party, or worse. But as he later admitted, thanks to Gorbachev he got away with being reprimanded and fired from his teaching job in Stavropol. Shortly thereafter he moved away to try to build a new life in Bashkiria, but later he corresponded with both Gorbachevs, and he greeted Gorbachev's reforms in the late 1980s with great enthusiasm. Although Sadykov's was a relatively soft landing, Gorbachev was "deeply affected" by what happened to Sadykov: "I knew him . . . as an intelligent, original thinker. My conscience tormented me that we had meted out such cruel and undeserved punishment to him."[17]

The party bureau's ruling on the case attacked Sadykov's contention that one of the main causes of the Stalin personality cult was "the absence among the masses of a democratic tradition" and the "underdevelopment of democratic institutions"—precisely what Gorbachev himself would contend two decades later. Meanwhile, he himself was already wondering about a system that depended on "the big boss." How was it, he asked himself, that "any initiative that patently served the interests of society was immediately viewed with suspicion and even overt hostility? Was our system really so unresponsive to renewal and innovation?"

During the next nine years, Brezhnev and his Kremlin colleagues cracked down on what was left of the Khrushchev thaw. Yet, at the end of that period, Gorbachev was named a Central Committee secretary in Moscow, where he soon joined the Politburo, just a few steps from the top spot. What happened between 1970 and 1978 to propel him upward? What happened to the doubts that nearly deflected him from his party path in 1968? Did he repress them entirely for the next decade? Was there any way to work within the system for the ideals he had nourished in the fifties and sixties? If his earlier reservations were visible at all, how could he have been allowed to continue his rise? At one point in 1975, his former girlfriend from Privolnoe, Yulia Karagodina, who was pursuing a higher degree in anatomy and physiology, arranged to bump into Gorbachev on a street in Stavropol. Her aim was to enlist his help in getting a pension for her ill mother, but she couldn't resist bemoaning the general stagnation of society.

"Don't you see what's happening all around us?" she asked.

"I see everything," he replied, "but I can't do everything."[18]

According to Gorbachev's longtime Kremlin aide Georgy Shakhnazarov, keeping one's thoughts to oneself was a regional party boss's ticket to rise even higher. That made it particularly easy for those, unlike Gorbachev, who "had no thoughts to hide."[19] Gorbachev put it this way: "The system carefully skimmed the cream." Those chosen knew they had to "play by the rules of the game," to pass through a "'party separator' that transformed the cream into butter." Those who made it to the top were for the most part "the thick-skinned ones," those who "didn't worry too much about the moral meaning of their actions, those whose consciences were buried very deep."[20] Was Gorbachev himself an exception to this rule? "No, I myself was undoubtedly a product of the system." But the various "products" differed. Most of those he knew were "so self-satisfied, not very democratic or open. Still, if I and the few people like me had been alone, perestroika would never have happened."[21]

During his first few years as Stavropol party boss, Gorbachev attributed economic and other failures to "the inefficiency and incompetence of cadres, flaws in management structure or gaps in legislation," but gradually he concluded that "the roots of inefficiency lay much deeper." What "deeper" meant to Gorbachev during these years was the severe overcentralization of the economy, in which all key decisions were made at the top. As a result, he and other regional leaders had to make "endless trips to the capital," where they had to cajole the big bosses and "endure abusive language and rudeness from officials." "The supercentralized attempt to control every single detail of life in an immense state sapped the vital energies of society."[22] Much later, after he became Soviet leader, Gorbachev would dig deeper still, tracing the problems he saw in Stavropol to the very essence of Soviet state socialism, that is, to the Communist party's monopoly of political and economic power.

In so doing, he would be informed by a series of heretical books by leftist Western authors, translated and issued in extremely limited editions by Moscow's Progress Publishing House, that he was able to obtain in his capacity as regional party boss. Many years later, Gorbachev proudly asserted that he still kept some of these volumes on his shelves: Louis Aragon's *The Parallel History of the USSR*, Roger Garaudy's *The French Model of Socialism*, Giuseppe Boffa's *History of the Soviet Union* and *The History of Marxism*, as well as books about the Italian Communist leader Palmiro Togliatti, and the famous prison notebooks of Antonio Gramsci.[23]

Although the French poet and novelist Aragon supported the Communist party, he was critical of the Soviet Union, especially after Khrushchev unmasked Stalin in 1956. The French philosopher Garaudy later converted from Communism to Catholicism and from there, in 1982, to Islam. Boffa was an independent-minded Italian Communist expert on the USSR. Gramsci, a founding member of the Italian Communist party who was later arrested by Mussolini, was one of the major Marxist thinkers of the twentieth century. His notion of "cultural hegemony" replaced cruder conceptions of how capitalism maintained its hold over society. His stress on the need for workers to become intellectuals described the path Gorbachev felt he himself had taken, and Gramsci's distinction between political society (the state) and civil society (social organizations and institutions) foreshadowed Gorbachev's later efforts to democratize the first by building up the other.

None of these readings transformed Gorbachev overnight into the gravedigger of Communism. But the fact that he turned to them in response to his growing doubts signaled the dilemma he faced as his career prospered. He remained, he says, a "man of the sixties," infected by the atmosphere of Moscow University and the Khrushchev thaw, and hence oddly out of place among the provincial bureaucrats he commanded. But in order to survive and prosper, he had to conform to the world in which he was a rising star.

GORBACHEV'S FIRST SPEECH as Stavropol party boss, in October 1970, like many of the policies he promoted there, demonstrated his capacity to conform. Summarizing a Brezhnev report on agriculture, Gorbachev hailed it as based on "profound analysis" that "illuminated" the road ahead.[24] One of his last speeches in Stavropol characterized Brezhnev as "the outstanding statesman of our time."[25] Compared with other up-and-coming leaders' boilerplate prose, Gorbachev's was relatively sophisticated. He could combine bombast against ideological enemies ("Bourgeois propaganda goes all out to cast suspicion on the great conquests of our party and state, such as the friendship that unites our peoples into one people marching to Communism.") with witty invective against corrupt local officials, such as an alcoholic instructor at a district cooperative who got married four times in three years, rarely showed up for work, and then, when expelled from the party, complained that during his twelve years of employment he had never once been reprimanded. "No comment necessary," concluded

Gorbachev.[26] But in a speech that was so retrospectively embarrassing that it didn't make it into Gorbachev's collected works, he hailed a volume of Brezhnev's memoirs, ghostwritten and shamelessly glorifying his undistinguished wartime experience, for "the profundity of its ideological content, the breadth of its generalizations"—"a major event in public life."[27]

Stavropol was one of the USSR's prime farming areas. Gorbachev's main task as its party boss was to raise its agricultural output to the very top rank and to keep it there. Was it his extraordinary skill in doing so that explains his later promotions? Not necessarily. He was good at the job, but not sensationally so. Although the land around Stavropol was fertile, it lacked water. Severe droughts struck in 1975 and 1976. When Gorbachev flew over the region in a small plane in May 1976, he saw mostly barren fields. Many peasants fled their homes and moved to other areas. He contemplated suspending work at 127 collective farms, one-third of the region's total. The Russian Republic's deputy minister of agriculture urged him to have cattle slaughtered immediately, but Gorbachev rejected the advice, whereupon Kulakov called from Moscow, angrily demanding to know why. Gorbachev suspected his former boss was still hurting because the previous year Kulakov himself had prematurely ordered the slaughter of millions of pigs throughout the country in the face of drought. So Gorbachev calmly promised to take the consequences of his own policy. "If you are sure of what you are doing, go ahead," Kulakov replied. "But watch out, the responsibility is yours."[28]

Disdaining Kulakov's tutelage took courage. But the approach he employed to meet the challenge was the thoroughly traditional Soviet method of mobilizing the region's population. He ordered peasants to drive their cattle to mountain pastures, and workers to collect fodder of every kind (including tree branches) in ditches, forests, and urban parks. He demanded that cities take responsibility for rural districts, and factories for collective farms, spawning corruption of the usual kind: a textile factory, for example, with no way to come up with fodder, provided textiles at a discount in return for the farm's testifying falsely that extra fodder had in fact been collected.[29] He also resorted to another traditional technique—flying to Moscow to beg help from Brezhnev, who fortunately came through, ordering that some sixty thousand tons of concentrated fodder be shipped to Stavropol. But what really saved the situation were the rains that finally came.[30]

Given the chronic water shortage (fifty-two years between 1870 and 1970 were afflicted by drought), Gorbachev set out to expand an already elaborate irrigation system. The idea for a canal initially arose at the end of the nineteenth century, in the 1930s two water supply systems were constructed, and by 1969 the system had been named the Great Stavropol Canal, but it was far from finished. Gorbachev proposed adding a 300-mile extension from the Kuban River to the Kalmyk Steppe so as to irrigate an additional 800,000 hectares of land, and again went about getting his way in the usual top-down Soviet fashion. While vacationing in Kislovodsk in the fall of 1970, he recruited a fellow vacationer, the country's minister of land reclamation, who not only agreed to help but suggested a five-year crash program. Next, Gorbachev won over Brezhnev, whom he was lucky enough to corner in Baku at a fiftieth-anniversary celebration of Azerbaijan's joining the Soviet Union. When Brezhnev presented the project to the Politburo, "I was not invited," Gorbachev recalled with a grimace, but Brezhnev more than made up for that by boasting at the meeting about "new young leaders who have big, statesman-like ideas about issues of national importance" and "who deserve our support."[31]

On January 7, 1971, the party Central Committee and the USSR Council of Ministers declared the Great Stavropol Canal an "All-Union Komsomol Project." That meant all-out allocation of equipment, plus the arrival of thousands of young people from all over the country to lend a hand. In 1974 a major tunnel was completed, and another section begun. Brezhnev tried to keep track of progress; every time he encountered Gorbachev, he asked about "the canal." He seemed to think it was the biggest such project in the world, and when Gorbachev admitted it wasn't, Brezhnev asked, "Then why are you building it endlessly with no end in sight?" This was a mild reprimand, but Gorbachev turned it to his advantage by prodding those building the canal to work faster.[32] In 1978, before Gorbachev left Stavropol for Moscow, he presided over a triumphal meeting to celebrate completion of a key section of the canal. On a wooden platform above the running water, surrounded by leaders from Stavropol and adjoining provinces and dignitaries from

Moscow, and with a banner overhead boasting, "The Kuban River Will Flow Wherever the Bolsheviks Tell It To," stood Gorbachev, described by a local journalist as "wearing a workman's helmet that particularly became him, looking as if he had just put down his own miner's pick, animated, talkative, smiling." One source of Gorbachev's pleasure was that the just-completed section of the canal ran close to, and would provide irrigation for, the village where Yuri Andropov was born.[33]

In addition to continually nudging Gorbachev about "the canal," Brezhnev kept asking how his "Sheep Empire" was doing. The Stavropol region's nearly ten million sheep produced about 27 percent of the total Soviet output of fine-fleece wool.[34] But fulfilling its annual quotas wasn't easy. "People looked at sheep raising," Gorbachev recalled, as an activity in which "everything takes care of itself: You put the sheep out to pasture and that's it. Not at all! As someone once said, to raise sheep you need a professor's erudition."[35] Proud of his own, he proposed transferring the breeding ewes from pastures to mechanized sheep farms and then sending young stock to mechanized fattening farms. But it turned out that sheep that roamed freely in pastures were much more productive than those jammed together in pens. His next hope was to make a model of a particularly gifted sheep farmer whose operation broke all records for output, but there weren't enough others who could produce more miracles. A local newsman recalled occasions when Gorbachev blew up at those who could not meet goals, and at journalists who reported as much. The amount of wool shorn yearly didn't rise at all as a result of Gorbachev's innovations. But meanwhile he managed to get more money from Moscow.[36] Again, he looked like a winner.

Stavropol's Ipatovsky district became the setting for more Soviet-style "miracle making."[37] Soviet leaders ran unopposed for the USSR Supreme Soviet from various electoral districts around the country. Ipatovsky was Kulakov's constituency, and he was determined, with Gorbachev's help, to have it break records for harvesting grain. "We've got to win," Gorbachev told Viktor Kalyagin, the Ipatovsky party boss. "Will you help me do it?"

"We barely had enough time to prepare," Kalyagin recalled. "He came down from Stavropol, and we worked day and night for two weeks."[38] Instead of using small groups of people and machinery (a combine and a couple of trucks) to do the harvesting, they divided the district into fifty-four zones, each with a harvesting-transport complex consisting of fifteen combine-harvesters, fifteen trucks, plus teams responsible for delivering fuel, repair of machinery, catering, medical assistance, and "ideological support"—i.e., providing newspapers, special postal service, and a daily newsletter touting the triumphs to come. Two professional and eight part-time party agitators were attached to each team, as were four political "informants" and one lecturer, all parts of a "temporary mobile party organization," and a "temporary mobile Komsomol group," which held meetings in the field. With the sixtieth anniversary of the Bolshevik Revolution coming up that fall, the whole enterprise resembled war mobilization, and the results seemed stunning. Whereas previous harvests had taken as much as three or four weeks, the Ipatovsky finished in nine days. The two hundred thousand tons of grain promised to the state were actually delivered. The Central Committee hailed the feat and called on other districts to equal it. The same July day *Pravda* featured a front-page article on Stavropol farmers that included an interview with Gorbachev, an honor never previously granted to a Stavropol leader.[39] In February, Kulakov was awarded one of the nation's highest awards—Hero of Socialist Labor. On March 1, Gorbachev received the Order of the October Revolution. In the meantime, a Moscow-based filmmaker had been preparing a film about the Ipatovsky triumph, but by the time it was finished in 1978, Gorbachev had been named Central Committee secretary in charge of agriculture, and he thought a film glorifying his exploits would be "unsuitable."[40]

Fortunately for posterity, Brezhnev's presentation of the October Revolution medal to Gorbachev in Moscow was recorded on film. Members of the leadership are seated at a large square table. An aide reminds Brezhnev of the honoree's name, whispering in his ear but loud enough for the microphone to pick up: "Gorbachev, Mikhail Sergeyevich," Gorbachev approaches, dressed in a well-fitting dark suit with a white shirt and striped tie, managing to radiate deep deference and irrepressible vitality at the same time. Brezhnev repeats the prompt: "Gorbachev, Mikhail Sergeyevich," then fumbles: "What we started over there . . ." Gorbachev provides the missing word: "The canal." Brezhnev: ". . . we'll finish from here." Gorbachev: "Certainly, Leonid Ilich." Brezhnev stares vacantly ahead. Gorbachev solemnly acknowledges the medal he holds in his hands: "You were right, Leonid Ilich, when you said this award was for our work in Stavropol."[41]

Gorbachev hadn't lost the actor's touch. Nor was all the celebrating entirely unfounded. Although the total Soviet harvest in 1977 (195 million tons) was lower than planned, it might have been worse if the "Ipatovsky method" hadn't been adopted elsewhere. And the Ipatovsky district broke its own record the next year. But the method worked best in a "flat, purely grain-producing district," and it wasn't nearly as effective in northern and eastern parts of the country.[42] Not to mention the campaigns' mammoth costs, which, naturally, weren't mentioned.[43] When Stavropol got its medal, Mikhail Suslov, second secretary to Brezhnev, presented it himself, and a day later he and Gorbachev set off together on an inspection tour of the region.

Gorbachev did endorse some practices that were more innovative than those just described, such as "the team system," which allowed small teams, including family groups, to farm given plots of land, and in a nearly unprecedented move, he encouraged a Privolnoe chicken farmer to open a retail outlet in Stavropol.[44] Just before being promoted to Moscow in 1978, Gorbachev sent a radical memorandum to the Central Committee, in which he dared to characterize the countryside as "an internal colony." Collective farms received less for their output than it cost them to produce it, he wrote. The lack of rural schools and other social services (the focus of Raisa Gorbachev's dissertation) explained why capable cadres were fleeing the countryside. Gorbachev noted a "vicious circle" in which shortages of animal feed and modern equipment reduced output, leading to fewer deliveries of the feed and equipment needed to increase output.[45] Some of his colleagues warned Gorbachev not to stick his neck out, but he ignored them. According to Prime Minister Kosygin, Gorbachev's memo went off like a "bombshell" in a commission preparing the 1978 Central Committee plenum on agriculture. But the only result of the plenum, Gorbachev remembered, was to propose higher output of agricultural machinery. In other words, "a mountain had brought forth a mouse."[46]

———————

GORBACHEV'S AMBIVALENCE—mouthing the party line while inwardly recoiling from much of it—led to a dilemma that Andrei Grachev describes poignantly: "What could he do, how remain true to his past and to the views he shared with Raisa," how could he "avoid being corrupted like other provincial bosses?" How could he "resist being fully assimilated—while at the same time not setting himself against his colleagues and isolating himself from them?"[47]

The answer is that Gorbachev couldn't do both, and that, in fact, he didn't fully do either. He *did* set himself against, or at least apart from, many of his colleagues, and he *did* isolate himself from some of them—not so much by remaining true to his and Raisa's values, as by maneuvering to ensure a bright future for himself and his ideas. This helps explain why his former subordinates' impressions of him as regional party boss, conveyed in memoirs and interviews, are so strikingly bimodal. Another explanation is that those who aspired to rise as high, or to equal him intellectually, envied him, whereas those content with lesser status were grateful for his noblesse oblige. Gorbachev's intellect and high moral standards evoked special respect from some, to whom he in turn showed special solicitousness. But his sense of self-importance and self-righteousness, and his need for attention and admiration, grated on others, especially those who suffered from the same cravings.

Some former colleagues admired him then and do so to this day. Others hate him now and claim to have done so since the beginning. His former speechwriter Ivan Zubenko bitterly recalls, "The better you knew him, the more you disliked him."[48] But according to Viktor Kalyagin, who also knew Gorbachev well, "He was a great guy: inspiring, loved to joke and laugh, didn't get drunk, a good, progressive thinker."[49] Viktor Kaznacheyev's indictment extends right up to 1978 and beyond: Gorbachev didn't listen; he made policy unilaterally; he divided and conquered; he was vengeful and supersensitive to slight; he avoided difficult decisions; he feigned feverish activity; he didn't follow through; he was under his wife's thumb; he was pathologically greedy; he lived the good life at a luxurious dacha; he was "limitlessly envious of others"; he "strangled foes in his own embrace."[50] Kaznacheyev was not only envious but apparently also corrupt. While Stavropol city party boss, he allegedly built a magnificent movie palace as a monument to his stewardship, transferred upscale apartments to bigwigs from whom he wanted favors, and pressured more than one enterprise to supply him with gifts—including fashionable, durable boots, shoes, and slippers—which he presented to Moscow big shots vacationing in North Caucasus resorts. Gorbachev would surely have liked to fire Kaznacheyev, but with Kulakov's protection, Kaznacheyev had not only survived but even become Gorbachev's deputy.[51]

Porotov, the Komsomol official who gave Gorbachev his first job in 1955, depicts his protégé as "vain and easily offended," "two-faced" in his habit of saying "different things to different people," a man with "no real friends," who was convinced of his own exceptional virtues, and with a craving for power that led him to fawn on those who could give it to him.[52] Anatoly Korobeinikov worked for Gorbachev as a speechwriter. Himself a graduate of the party's Academy of Social Sciences in Moscow, he prided himself on the high-quality work he did for his boss. It was all the more galling then, he recalled, that Gorbachev not only drove his aides mercilessly but belittled what they produced: "There are at least two pricks in the regional committee," Gorbachev allegedly said, "[Ivan] Zubenko [the other speechwriter] and Korobeinikov. The only way to squeeze something out of them is to drive them hard enough." He "purported to disdain flattery, but he actually couldn't get enough of it," adds Korobeinikov. Gorbachev had "two higher degrees, but in reality he acted as if he had none." He was proud of his "philosophical" approach, but he actually "distrusted" the "scholarly insights" that "we speechwriters tried to insert into his speeches and reports." He knew that in order to rise he had to shine, but being a "loner" without "friends or true comrades-in-arms," he had to do it on his own. Of course, he had his wife, admits Korobeinikov, but she was often "incompetent," and Gorbachev aides who showed they knew that were "doomed."[53] According to Zubenko, Gorbachev "picked your brain and then kept you at a distance. In the years I worked for him, he never invited me to drink tea with him. Whereas [Gorbachev's successor] Murakhovsky often invited me to do so and often asked about my family." Gorbachev was a "perfectionist," Zubenko insists, and a mean one, at that. "He insisted that everything had to be done just right. For example, you couldn't say the time was 3:15 p.m.; you had to say 15:15. He was also emotional: He would curse you out if you didn't do things his way. And he never thanked you. Say someone had been accused of drunkenness, Murakhovsky would check out the accusations, whereas Gorbachev would fire the guy without checking."[54]

To another colleague, on the other hand, Glkorbachev wasn't just a "quick study," and equally "quick to make decisions," but a man who "lifted people up."[55] Nikolai Paltsev, who ran the Komsomol under Gorbachev, recalled, "We all loved him, worshipped him even. His way of dealing with us was so free and open. He was young, energetic, thoughtful, full of new ideas. He was direct and accessible. Once, when my five-year-old son and I were walking by Gorbachev's house, he happened to come out, and he crossed the street to greet us.

"'Hi, Nikolai,' he said to me. 'Who's this?'

"'My son,' I answered.

"'Hi. What's your name? What do you like to do? Can you read this?' he asked, pointing to a sign that said Department of Internal Affairs.

"My son read it. 'Attaboy!' Gorbachev said. 'Listen, when you grow up you're going to head the regional party committee.' Things like that inspired us to work hard for him."[56]

Vitaly Mikhailenko was a young district party secretary when he was invited to attend a holiday gathering of regional officials and their wives. Mikhailenko's qualification was his winning personality and his ability to play the accordion. "I was always the life of a party," recalled Mikhailenko, a jolly, rotund man who during a 2005 interview broke out his accordion and invited his American guests to join him in singing Russian folk songs, "but so was Mikhail Sergeyevich: He organized it. He chose the songs, knew all the words, and sang them with great gusto, especially his favorite, a tango: 'Inhaling the rose's aroma, remembering the garden shade, I recall the tender "I love you," that you said to me that day.' He loved to dance, too."[57] That doesn't sound like a man with no friends, but Mikhailenko confirms that Gorbachev much preferred smaller, more-private gatherings where the talk was about philosophy and art, among other things, just the sort of subjects most of his colleagues weren't equipped to discuss. What he particularly didn't like, according to Mikhailenko, were the long, drunken feasts so many province officials relished. Gorbachev had no hobbies, Mikhailenko added; his favorite leisure-time activity was taking long nature walks with his wife. Mikhailenko remembered that Gorbachev, in contrast to Kaznacheyev, worked very hard—"like a machine with colossal capacity, with all his energy concentrated on the task at hand. When he had to write a report, he would collect material from aides, summon the stenographers, and then dictate whole reams of material that they would type up and give back to him for further editing." Not only did he write his own speeches; he once went so far as to prepare one for a Stavropol area teacher, who was invited to address the Twenty-Fifth Party Congress in 1976, an extremely high honor that would reflect well on her mentor.[58]

Mikhailenko also contradicted Gorbachev's Stavropol critics on other points. The Gorbachevs did *not* build a luxurious private dacha. Rather, they made use of one of two small houses specifically reserved for the Stavropol party and government bosses.[59] As for Raisa Gorbachev, who taught Mikhailenko in the agricultural institute's extension program, she was quite wonderful: "beautiful, charming, highly intelligent, seemingly serene and calm, never raised her voice. The students adored her, and would have even if her husband hadn't been the party leader."[60] But Mikhailenko also recalled how Gorbachev maneuvered to get and keep the attention of higher-ups in Moscow, perfecting in the process ploys that would serve him when he himself reached the Kremlin. After the harvest, Gorbachev would organize mass celebrations in Stavropol's central square, complete with flags, banners, and large portraits of top Soviet leaders carried by marchers from all across the region. Who decided exactly where the faces of Brezhnev, Kosygin, Kirilenko, and others on whose goodwill Gorbachev's fate and that of his region depended should be displayed? Gorbachev himself. He kept up avidly with the latest doings in the Kremlin; he seemed to know Brezhnev's daily schedule. After talking on the phone with a Politburo member, he would immediately summon his chief Stavropol aides, even on a weekend, to report on his conversation. Why? Because, says Mikhailenko, "he knew that his doing so would be reported to the top."[61]

According to Mikhailenko, Gorbachev was a "subtle psychologist." When the deputy head of the Stavropol regional government married his own secretary, the young woman turned out to be "psychologically unprepared" to join the Stavropol elite. At that point, Gorbachev "showed great patience and great tact, providing support in smoothing over sharp moments" until things could be worked out. "The way he behaved was quite remarkable." But so was the time Gorbachev phoned Mikhailenko at nine in the evening to deliver a fifteen-minute "tirade" for neglecting to take care of a city park named in honor of the Komsomol. Kaznacheyev, it seems, had denounced Mikhailenko. "It was so painful," the latter recalls, "that to this day it still hurts." But the next day, Gorbachev landed on Kaznacheyev. At the time, Mikhailenko continues, "I didn't understand that 'the great stage director' was playing us off against each other. He had to do that sort of thing—to set people against each other. It was an 'art' that he later used in the Politburo so that they couldn't gang up against him."[62]

IT WAS DURING THESE YEARS that Gorbachev befriended and was befriended by Yuri Andropov, another son of the Stavropol region, who was heading the KGB. While on vacation in the Caucasus, Andropov and his wife, Tatyana Filipovna, generally kept to themselves, but of the ten to twelve days the Andropovs were in residence, Gorbachev usually spent two or three with them.[63] Twice they all vacationed at the same time at the Krasnye kamni sanatorium, took joint family excursions near Kislovodsk, and drove up into the mountains. Sometimes they stayed up late, grilling shashlik and sitting around a bonfire. "Like me," Gorbachev recalled, "Andropov didn't like the kind of long, noisy, drunken dinners that Kulakov couldn't get enough of. The summer night was magnificent, it was quiet, and we talked openly." Sometimes Andropov brought along a tape recorder, on which he played the music of leading bards of the 1960s, such as Vladimir Vysotsky and Yury Visbor, whose politically incorrect songs were suspect to ideological guardians. Not all their songs were forbidden; indeed some were recorded, and Vysotsky was a star actor at the Taganka Theater in Moscow. But many songs were available only on tapes passed from hand to hand by admirers who told the next in line not to reveal where they came from. Andropov not only liked these songs; he and his wife sang them themselves. Once, Andropov challenged Gorbachev to see who knew more Cossack songs.

"I flippantly agreed," Gorbachev remembered, "and suffered a crushing defeat. After all, Andropov's father was of Don Cossack origin and he spent his childhood among Terek (River) Cossacks."[64]

Yuri Andropov photographing Mikhail and Raisa Gorbachev on vacation in the Caucasus, 1976.

How friendly did Gorbachev really get with Andropov, then in his fifties, with thinning hair and glasses that gave him a somewhat intellectual mien? Gorbachev himself wasn't sure. As he found out later, there was "little room for simple human emotions at the top."[65] Andropov "never opened up completely," Gorbachev remembered; "his trust and frankness stayed within established limits," but with Gorbachev, and especially with Raisa, he felt comfortable enough to speak fairly candidly. "She and Yury Vladimirovich would sit and talk while I was busy, sometimes for as long as three hours. He would ask her about students and young people in general, about their mood. She had a lot to tell him." Once, in 1975, with the Soviet system beginning to run down and its elderly leaders weakening apace, Gorbachev dared to ask Andropov whether he and his Kremlin colleagues "were really thinking about the good of the country."

"What did you say?" Andropov responded sharply. "Are you talking nonsense?"

"Just look at photos taken during the Red Square parade on the anniversary of the revolution," Gorbachev replied. "Who's going to take the place of your generation of leaders?"

"So you've decided to bury us all, have you?" Andropov snapped.

"I'm just thinking about the picture, the men in the coats and hats [on the Lenin Mausoleum]. All I'm saying is there can be no forest without undergrowth."

Andropov didn't hold Gorbachev's cheekiness against him. He countered that both older and younger leaders were needed, the elders guarding against the young men's careerism, the young pushing their elders to work harder and better. Several years later, after Gorbachev had been promoted to Central Committee secretary in Moscow, Andropov greeted him with a smile: "Congratulations, Mr. Undergrowth. Now you're part of the forest."[66]

What sort of secret police chief sang along with Vysotsky tapes while dispatching dissidents into mental hospitals? Andropov's paternal

Gorbachev with KGB police chief Yuri Andropov, Stavropol, 1970s.

ancestors were indeed Cossacks, but his parents were not. In fact, his mother was Jewish: Evgenia Fainshtein. After his father died in 1916 and his mother in 1923, Andropov lived with his stepfather's family, starting work as a child laborer in 1922, when he was eight, then becoming a movie projectionist, and then, at age eighteen, a sailor on a riverboat. Later, he would often repeat advice given to him by a boatswain, clearly applicable in the dog-eat-dog world of the Kremlin: "Life, Yura, is like the ship's deck when it's wet: If you don't want to slip, you must move carefully and find a place to plant your feet."[67]

The apogee of Andropov's formal education was at a water transport technical school, from which he graduated in 1936. After serving as a Komsomol official in Yaroslavl and Karelia, and graduating to party work in Petrozavodsk in 1944, he took courses at Petrozavodsk State University and then at the Central Committee's Higher Party School, but never graduated from either. He was an avid reader who tried to learn English and German on his own. Georgy Arbatov, head of the Academy of Sciences' Institute on the USA and Canada, was a close adviser from the 1960s until Andropov's death in 1984. "Compared with other leaders," he recalled, "even those 'rigged out' with higher educational diplomas and scholarly titles, Andropov was absolutely brilliant."[68] Another liberal-minded Andropov adviser, economist Oleg Bogomolov, recalled seeing copies of books by Montaigne and Machiavelli on Andropov's desk in the 1960s. "Why are you reading those books?" Bogomolov asked. "So as to be able to speak with you and your colleagues as equals," Andropov replied.[69]

Arbatov and Bogomolov were members of a group of "consultants" formed by Andropov when he headed the Central Committee department in charge of Soviet relations with foreign Communist countries and parties, from 1957 to 1967. During the last five of those years, Andropov held the high rank of Central Committee secretary. But his department was an oasis of relatively free thinking, and his consultants were nothing less than "Team Gorbachev" in training. Besides Arbatov and Bogomolov, they included Georgy Shakhnazarov (later Gorbachev's chief adviser on politics and law), Fyodor Burlatsky (later editor of *Literaturnaya gazeta*), Aleksandr Bovin (journalist/generalist extraordinaire), Lev Deliusin (China specialist), and Gennady Gerasimov (later Foreign

Ministry press spokesman). Andropov made clear that he expected his consultants to level with him: "In this room we talk openly and frankly. No one should conceal his real views. It's another matter when you go through that door. Outside, you of course conduct yourselves according to generally accepted rules."[70]

Like Andropov, Gorbachev was polite and tactful, didn't smoke, and limited his alcohol intake. Both men knew how to make others feel comfortable in their presence. Both could carry a tune and each tried to write his own speeches, or at least rewrote draft after draft. (Andropov actually wrote poetry as well.) Neither knew enough about economics.[71] It's not surprising, then, that Andropov took a liking to Gorbachev, such a strong one that in the spring of 1977, he singled him out, in a conversation with Arbatov, as the kind of young leader who represented the hope of the nation. By that time Brezhnev was in severe physical and mental decline. A heart attack in the early 1950s and another in 1957 hadn't slowed him down, nor did a seizure during the 1968 Soviet invasion of Czechoslovakia. But by 1973 Brezhnev was using sedatives and anti-anxiety medications that produced sluggishness and depression.[72] As KGB chief since 1967, Andropov was better informed than anyone else about Brezhnev's deterioration, and was particularly sensitive when Arbatov (like Gorbachev in Stavropol) dared to warn that too many leaders were too old and too many younger ones mediocre.

Andropov got angry, Arbatov remembered, "perhaps because deep down he agreed with this assessment. He sharply objected that I didn't know these people and yet I was ready to damn them up and down."

"Have you heard the name Gorbachev?" Andropov asked.

"No," replied Arbatov.

"So, you see: Completely new people have come along, people on whom we can link our hopes for the future."

If Gorbachev gave Andropov hope, Andropov gave the same to Gorbachev. If he could complain about the system's shortcomings to Andropov, confiding in one of the top men in the Kremlin what he couldn't say in public, then the system's top ranks might still be open to him. And yet, clambering up the party ladder under Stalin had taught Andropov extreme caution: according to one report, he himself feared arrest after the war.[73] Serving as Soviet ambassador to Hungary from

1954 to 1957 extended that lesson. At first he stood out among Moscow's East European viceroys for wanting to understand the nation to which he was accredited, even trying to learn Hungarian, an extremely difficult, non-Slavic language. But he watched with growing alarm in the fall of 1956 as the Hungarian revolution began to unfold—protests by intellectuals against what remained, even after Stalin's death, a rigidly Stalinist regime; massive marches joined by workers and students; attempts by liberal Communists like Imre Nagy to reform the regime and thus contain the upheaval; an initial intervention by Soviet troops that seemed to end the turmoil, leaving the troops to withdraw. Khrushchev and the rest of the Soviet leadership hesitated at first to crush the rebellion. Andropov urged them to act, buttressing his case by sending them photos of Hungarian Communist corpses hanging from lampposts and trees. Delivered directly to Khrushchev, these helped persuade him to return troops to Budapest on November 4, 1956.[74] As Soviet tanks crushed the uprising, firefights raged near the Soviet embassy, and rebels fired upon Andropov's embassy limousine. Fearing for her life and her husband's, Andropov's wife fell ill—a malady from which she never fully recovered.[75]

Andropov developed what Arbatov and Soviet dissident historian Roy Medvedev called a "Hungarian complex," namely, the fear that attempts to reform "from below" were fated to morph into mob rule (the same sort of complex, one might add, that seemed to animate Russian President Vladimir Putin half a century later).[76] The official Soviet version of what happened in Hungary was that Western imperialist machinations sparked a right-wing "counterrevolution." Andropov knew the truth—that a majority of Hungarians, many proletarians themselves, rose against the regime—and that prompted him to favor a controlled process of reform "from above" so as to defuse the potential for upheaval. That's why he recommended that János Kádár, a relative moderate, assume control of Hungary after the rising was put down, why Andropov surrounded himself with smart, open-minded consultants in the Central Committee, and why he favored promoting Gorbachev. But that's also why in 1968 he was one of the first Soviet leaders to press for Soviet military intervention against the Prague Spring, warning as early as March, "The situation is very serious. . . . This is how it began in Hungary."[77] And why, as KGB chief, he cruelly cracked down on dissidents, many of whom dreamed of getting the USSR to follow the high ideals proclaimed in its own Constitution.

Of course, Andropov's crackdown wasn't unilateral. It was regime policy. And before he began to crush dissent, Andropov tried to talk dissidents out of it, going so far as to meet with some of them and talk on the phone with the father of the Soviet H-bomb turned dissident Andrei Sakharov.[78] But Andropov's instinctive caution prevailed. Back in the early 1960s, Shakhnazarov had watched him undergo an almost physical transformation upon receiving a phone call from Khrushchev: "Before my very eyes, this lively, brilliant, interesting man turned into a soldier ready to carry out any order of his commander. His tone suddenly became submissive and obedient. I saw similar reincarnations many times. It was as if he had a dual personality—on the one hand, he was a member of the Russian intelligentsia, on the other, a functionary whose life's mission was to serve the party."[79]

Andropov's top KGB deputies included two Brezhnev cronies who watched Andropov's every move, Semyon Tsvigun and Georgy Tsinev. In Politburo discussions, Andropov reportedly resisted harsh methods against certain reform-minded cultural figures, including his favorite bard, Vladimir Vysotsky. But for the foreseeable future he was dead set against just the sort of radical change that Gorbachev eventually promoted. In 1975, Andropov helped persuade Brezhnev to sign the Helsinki accords on security and cooperation in Europe, even though Basket Three required signatory states to pledge their support for human rights and political freedoms that were routinely denied in the USSR. "In 15 to 20 years we'll be able to allow ourselves what the West allows itself now," Andropov told diplomat Anatoly Kovalev, "freedom of opinion and information, diversity in society and in art. But only in 15 to 20 years, after we're able to raise the population's living standards."[80] After he took power in 1985, Gorbachev reversed the sequence, pushing political reforms even when the Soviet economy had not been fixed. But if Andropov dreaded the prospect that freedom could get out of hand, Gorbachev wasn't entirely comfortable with pluralism either, for in pushing glasnost and democratization as hard as he did, he was violating Andropov's injunctions.

ALEKSEI KOSYGIN, THE VETERAN prime minister, also vacationed in Gorbachev's fiefdom. To use a distinction familiar to Communists—between reds (ideologues and party apparatchiki) and experts (those with training as engineers who initially made their careers in industry)—Kosygin was an expert. Born in 1904 and educated at the Leningrad Textile Institute, he became the USSR people's commissar for the textile industry in 1939. As early as 1946, he was a candidate member of the ruling Politburo, of which he became a full member in 1948. The infamous 1949 Leningrad Affair, in which Stalin arrested and liquidated Politburo members with ties to the city (including heir-apparent Aleksei Kuznetsov), almost carried away Kosygin. When Khrushchev was ousted in 1964, Kosygin took over his role as prime minister. The next year he pushed through the program of limited economic reform, and for a while seemed capable of challenging Brezhnev.

**Gorbachev with Soviet Premier Aleksei Kosygin
at the Caucasus resort of Arkhyz, 1975.**

Like Andropov, and unlike most of their Politburo colleagues, Kosygin was a thoughtful man with a serious mind. Craggy-faced and with a habitual crewcut, he was, according to chief Kremlin doctor Yevgeny Chazov, who observed him closely over many years, straightforward, knowledgeable, firm, and endowed with a stupendous memory.[81] But he was less open than even the self-contained Andropov. On vacation in the North Caucasus, Gorbachev recalls, Kosygin was "cautious and reserved. Even when the two of us talked in private he remained wrapped in his shell. . . ." Kosygin didn't like to talk about the Stalin era, but once he confided, "Let me tell you—life was difficult. Most of all, morally or, rather, psychologically. We were constantly under surveillance. Wherever I went, I was never, ever left alone." Unlike Brezhnev, who reveled in luxury, and Andropov, who tolerated it, Kosygin had tastes that were modest, even "ascetic," according to Gorbachev. Rather than commandeer a special dacha, he stayed in the main sanatorium building at Krasnye kamni, although, Gorbachev noted, "it was a strange sort of modesty since he and his staff occupied a whole floor."[82] Kosygin couldn't stand to be "fawned on by local bosses," remembered Gorbachev; he shunned "formal meetings and dinner parties" and "frowned on idle table talk." He did, however, go out of his way to inspect the countryside around Stavropol and meet with farm leaders, perhaps because, Gorbachev added, "he didn't know much about agriculture" and was "trying to understand why the agrarian sector was lagging behind."

It is a testament to Gorbachev's combination of seriousness and charm that the reserved Kosygin invited him to a small birthday gathering with his adult daughter, Ludmila, a girlfriend of Ludmila's, and several others. When Kosygin turned on music and asked his daughter's friend to dance, Gorbachev gallantly invited Ludmila. He and Kosygin took long walks in the countryside, during which Gorbachev couldn't resist complaining. As Stavropol leader, he was so hamstrung by Moscow's endless directives that he had "neither the right nor the financial means to make even the most ordinary decisions." In the absence of meaningful work incentives, farmers didn't farm properly, workers didn't work well, and local hospitals and clinics lacked doctors and nurses. Kosygin's silence seemed to indicate agreement. Part of the problem, Gorbachev told him on another occasion, was that the economic reforms Kosygin had championed had died: "So let me ask you, why did you yield, why did you let them bury it?" Usually Kosygin took Gorbachev's "cockiness" (to use Gorbachev's own self-description) in stride, sometimes smiling silently to indicate that he shared Gorbachev's opinion. But this time he shot back: "You are a member of the Central Committee? Why didn't you fight for it?"[83]

By the mid-1970s, a chastened Kosygin took up rowing. On one occasion, he lost his balance and capsized along with his boat. The cause of the accident was a minor stroke, from which he recovered enough to resume his duties as prime minister, but according to Chazov, "he wasn't the same Kosygin." Real power in the government gravitated to his first deputy, Nikolai Tikhonov, a longtime bureaucrat and Brezhnev loyalist, who would later resist Gorbachev's ascent to the top.

Mikhail Suslov, too, vacationed near Stavropol. Born in 1902, a Politburo member since 1952, he himself was Stavropol regional party chief from 1943 to 1944. His hands were not clean: as chairman of the Central Committee commission for Lithuania from 1944 to 1946, he supervised its reoccupation, complete with bloody repression and the arrest and exile of thousands. But his heart and mind were ideologically pure. Famously ascetic, he was, Gorbachev remembered, "absolutely, 100 percent non-moneygrubbing. He was entirely upright and without sin. He always wore the same long gray overcoat and old rubbers over his shoes, even in good weather; he would take off the rubbers when he got on an elevator. He made sure that his limousine driver never exceeded thirty miles an hour, not one more than that. When he was on the road there would be a long line of cars following him. No one dared to pass him, except perhaps [the Politburo member in charge of the military, Dmitry] Ustinov. If anyone did pass, Suslov would tell his bodyguard to note down the license plate."

Suslov was so intimidating that even Brezhnev, who addressed all his Kremlin colleagues except Kosygin in the second person singular (*ty*), addressed Suslov formally by his name and patronymic (Mikhail Andreyevich). Gorbachev cultivated Suslov, whose approbation was as important as Andropov's, and Suslov, too, took a liking to him. The fact that Gorbachev actually read Marx and Lenin (unlike most leaders),

Gorbachev (first row, second from right) with Central
Committee secretary Mikhail Suslov (extreme left), 1976.

and asked Suslov to help him interpret their texts, confirmed that the
founding fathers in whom Suslov placed such stock were in fact still rele-
vant. According to the ever envious Kaznacheyev, it was Gorbachev who
pressed Suslov personally to honor Stavropol's two hundredth birthday
with his presence. When Suslov arrived with his daughter Maya, on
Maya's birthday, no less, Gorbachev's wife "wouldn't let anyone else get
near her. That's why the wives of other regional secretaries [including
Kaznacheyev's] weren't invited to the jubilee celebration that evening."[84]

Taking advantage of his location near the mountain resorts, Gorbachev got to know other Soviet leaders, too. Viktor Grishin, the veteran Moscow party boss (whose clumsy attempt to promote himself as
a candidate to succeed Chernenko as party leader would constitute the
Brezhnevite old guard's last stand against Gorbachev), recalled liking
him and Raisa when they met in Zheleznovodsk in the early seventies.
"He was young, energetic, relaxed, cordial, and hospitable. I remember
that one Sunday we and our families drove to Dombai in the mountains
and stayed overnight. We went fishing and dined together. Our host was
kind and attentive. We got together other times, too. We liked each other
a lot."[85]

FOREIGN TRAVEL, ESPECIALLY to capitalist countries, was ironically one of the greatest gifts Soviet Communism could bestow on its own faithful servants. Only the politically reliable were allowed to visit the West; the very best candidates were those who were particularly attractive and articulate and would impress their hosts. Gorbachev and his wife were Exhibit A: as he put it, "The Central Committee's international department could see—how shall I put it?—both a certain level of interest on my part in traveling, and a certain ability to conduct conversations with foreigners."[86] Prior to 1970, Gorbachev's foreign travel was limited to the Soviet bloc: East Germany, Czechoslovakia, and Bulgaria. Between 1970 and 1977, he made no fewer than five visits to Western Europe.

His first exposure to West Europeans had come during the 1961 World Youth Festival in Moscow when he served as the Italian delegation's host. Being appointed a delegation host, especially for the Italians, whose Communist party was so important to the Kremlin, was a high honor. Spending long hours with the free and easy Italians was eye-opening. Besides meeting Achille Occhetto, who was to lead the Italian Communist party from 1988 to 1994, Gorbachev discovered differences in national character ("There wasn't one occasion throughout the forum when the Italians arrived at a meeting on time."), as well as portents of the sort of "Eurocommunism" that would later plague the Kremlin until Gorbachev, as Soviet leader, adopted its freewheeling principles himself. A young Soviet editor told the Italians how he had once asked a French abstract artist whether he would want to sleep with the woman whose human form could barely be discerned in his portrait of her. But instead of laughing, an Italian delegate reprimanded the Soviet editor: "The Soviet comrade's remark was reminiscent of the Nazis, who also condemned abstract artists, many of whom had been active opponents of fascism."[87]

Fittingly, the Gorbachevs' first trip to the West together, in September–October 1971, was to Italy with a Soviet delegation. The trip included standard "fraternal" meetings with Italian Communist officials and participation in a tribute to the Italian Communist party's newspaper, *L'Unità*. But there was also the embarrassing moment when Khrushchev died, on September 11, after living as a "nonperson" under what amounted to house arrest ever since his ouster. The Italians thought very highly of him, especially of his anti-Stalin campaign, and asked Gorbachev's view. He had to scramble to say something that would betray neither the Soviet party line nor his own admiration for Khrushchev's contribution.[88]

The Gorbachevs noticed what they regarded as "capitalist contradictions" in Italy: the forbiddingly high price of shoes, the dismaying sight of houses standing empty because poor people couldn't afford the rent, the gap in Sicily (where the group spent four days) between stylish neighborhoods with luxurious villas and filthy streets swarming with beggars. But they were stunned at how relaxed Italians seemed to be with one another and how straightforward, open, and friendly with their Soviet guests, so different from the way Soviets behaved back home, berating each other in overcrowded, undersupplied food stores, fearing to get too close to Westerners lest the authorities become suspicious.

More than anything else, what Gorbachev remembered from the trip was falling in love with the country and its culture. Throughout their stay, which included visits to Rome, Turin, and Florence, his wife filled her diary with impressions, particularly noting that a monument to Giuseppe Garibaldi, the great unifier of Italy, depicted him together with his wife![89] Gorbachev remembered Michelangelo's frescoes and sculptures, the vista of Roman hills in the setting sun, the Uffizi Gallery in Florence, the view from the bus as it drove past olive and almond trees and lemon and orange groves, and leading his comrades in Russian songs as the bus rolled along "under the Sicilian sky." What comes through in these recollections is not so much political as personal, not so much Gorbachev's dawning realization that the Western way of life was in some ways superior to the Soviet, but that, to his surprise, he felt entirely comfortable in the West.

In 1972 it was Belgium (including Liège, the Ardennes, Antwerp, Ghent, and Bruges) and the Netherlands, with another Soviet delegation having to confront criticisms from fellow Communists, who lamented the lack of democracy in the USSR. "It wasn't easy to assuage their doubts," Gorbachev recalled, especially since all he had to counter them was "the usual collection of ideological prejudices zealously banged into our heads by Agitprop." Instead, he discovered the extent to which "we shared common problems," especially the ethnic, linguistic, and political barriers that divided Belgians as well as Soviets. There was the scene at the border where Gorbachev dug out his passport, expecting it to be scrutinized, only to learn that no one wanted to check it, that, in fact, there was hardly anyone around to police the border at all. In Amsterdam, a tour took Gorbachev's group through the "red light" district with its profusion of sex shops and pornographic movies. "We dragged him to one of those," Chernyaev recalled. "He was embarrassed by what he saw, perhaps even revolted. But he didn't say anything."[90]

In 1975 Gorbachev visited West Germany, where he helped celebrate the thirtieth anniversary of the victory over fascism. His delegation traveled by car from Frankfurt to Nuremberg. Stopping for gasoline near Mannheim, he fell into a conversation with a German who lamented the postwar division of his homeland. Gorbachev answered with Soviet clichés about German war guilt, but remembered the exchange twenty-five years later, when he blessed German unification.

In 1976: France. As leader of a delegation from Stavropol, he spent a "stunningly interesting" day on a farm near Toulouse,[91] where he learned at least three lessons: how farmers benefited from participating in cooperatives that supplied them with up-to-date technology and advice about processing and marketing; how their practice of contracting directly with processors increased their incentive to do high-quality work; how their own self-interest led them to organize their stock raising in a way that suited climatic conditions.

France, again, in 1977, with his wife, as part of a delegation taking part in an exchange with the French Communist party. According to Vitaly Gusenkov, a Soviet embassy official assigned to accompany the delegation, the Gorbachevs stood out in the group for their "youth, their education, and the skillful, open way" they conversed with French Communists, ranging from rank-and-file party members to top officials."[92] For twenty-one days in September, the Gorbachevs and two other Soviet couples toured France by car, with French drivers. They were accompanied by an official from the French Communist party, but were free to choose their itinerary. Some of their choices were predictable: a demonstration organized by the French Communist newspaper, L'Humanité; the museums and churches of Paris; an evening cruise on the Seine; fine dining in the capital, including memorable onion soup, frog legs, and marvelous wine; the fountain in the center of Lyon; the bustling, multiethnic port of Marseille; the gloomy island fortress where the Count of Monte Cristo languished; the azure sea filled with yachts on the Riviera; Cannes, Nice, and Monaco; then a return to Paris through Arles, Avignon, Dijon. But other destinations were not so standard: the kind of modern art that was anathema to Soviet ideological watchdogs, plus a detour to see an apartment near Nice that their French Communist host had bought for himself. "What a place!" Gorbachev exclaimed later. "He bought it himself! He lived in Paris and yet had a place like that here. By that time I was already first secretary of Stavropol and a Central Committee member, but for me this was—well, damn it, what can I say? The way they lived! Was it ever dissolute!"[93]

Gorbachev was enchanted by France—enough to repeat a parable told by a French interpreter on the highway from Paris to Lyon: Having finished distributing the peoples of the earth, the Almighty pronounced himself satisfied until He heard sudden sobbing.

"Who's that?" He asked.

"It's the French," an angel answered, "they're complaining they've been forgotten."

"Well, do we have any place left?"

"Nothing except your dacha."

"Okay, give it to them."[94]

Gorbachev's trips provided him with the kind of information that, even for someone of his rank, was "extremely scarce and, on top of that, subject to careful reworking at home." What particularly struck him was the willingness of West Europeans to talk freely about everything, including their own governments and political leaders. "Often they disagreed among themselves about these matters, whereas we had to demonstrate complete unity of opinion on all questions—just as we did at home, except for private conversations at kitchen tables."[95] The Gorbachevs didn't conceal their impressions from close friends and colleagues. Viktor Kalyagin recalls his boss marveling at the high quality and low prices of food in the West.[96] "They were absolutely delighted with what they saw," remembered Raisa's friend Lydia Budyka, "and they didn't hide that from us. Other Russians saved their money to spend on things to buy, Misha and Raya to spend on vacations abroad."[97]

What Gorbachev *did* hide was the way these trips "shook our a priori belief in the superiority of socialist over bourgeois democracy." He and his wife concluded, "People lived better there. Why did our people live worse than in other developed countries? I never could get that question out of my mind." Nor could he rid himself of the determination, if he ever had the opportunity, to press for Soviet reforms. "I understood that changes needed in our country could only come from the top. That helped to determine my reaction when it was suggested that I move on to work in the Central Committee."[98]

THE HIGHER GORBACHEV ROSE in the party hierarchy, the more often he had to preside over public occasions, and the more he and his wife had to socialize with their colleagues. But they drew the line at the border of their family. Raisa never invited any of her students to her home, lest they see how well the local party boss lived. But the Gorbachev's obsession with privacy was personal as well as political. "We never invited anyone [into our home]," recalled Gorbachev. "That was our own world." For his wife, especially, family took precedence over almost everything. "Nothing can replace the emotional, loving relationship between the child and its parents," she later wrote in her memoirs. "It is essential!" According to Lydia Budyka, Gorbachev's wife "had a stronger character than he did. Out of love she almost always gave way when they differed," but on the importance of family they agreed. Their daughter, Irina, remembers how they constantly informed each other of what they were doing: "I'm leaving." "Is everything alright?" "Have you returned?" Later, in Moscow, when Irina and her family lived separately, her mother couldn't fall asleep at night until Irina called to say all members of her family were home.[99]

Gorbachev's parents, still living in Privolnoe, continued to play an important role in his life. When he was named first secretary of the Stavropol region, his father wrote, "We congratulate you on your new job. There is no limit to your mother's and father's joy and pride. May that joy never fade! We wish you good health and great strength for your work for the country's well-being." Raisa Gorbachev, who cited these words in her own memoir, added, "That very simple letter can still bring tears to my eyes." The director of Gorbachev's school also sent congratulations: "If it were possible, as it was then in the school, when it was announced that the schoolboy Mikhail had been decorated with a medal, to call a meeting, I would like to say to people: 'May our region be prosperous! It is now headed by a "homegrown" secretary of the region who even as little boy in Privolnoe made the work of a farmer famous throughout the land.'"[100]

Sergei and Maria Gorbachev came down from Privolnoe to visit their son and his family. More often, Mikhail, Raisa, and Irina, with access to a car, drove up to visit his parents. Aleksei Gonochenko, the Gorbachev underling who thought Mikhail Gorbachev moved up too fast for his own and the country's good, contends that Gorbachev's father, whom he got to know, shared this view.[101] But Raisa remembered that her father-in-law "would shower his son with a stream of pointed and vital questions. And his son had not only to answer, but to give an account to his father. Sergei Andreyevich would listen long and respectfully to what his son had to say."[102]

Gorbachev's parents helped to care for Irina. When she was young, they would take her to Privolnoe for several months at a time, especially in the summer. As she got older, she helped with chores—digging potatoes, weeding the garden, feeding chicken, geese, and pigs, washing the floors in the large house to which they had moved from the one near the river. Irina remembers her grandmother as a "battler" with a strong character, and her grandfather as quieter, softer, calmer, a man who loved to listen to classical music.[103]

In 1976, when Mikhail Gorbachev was in Moscow attending the Communist party's Twenty-Fifth Congress, he learned that his father was dying and returned home. He spent two days at Sergei Gorbachev's bedside, even though his father never regained consciousness.[104]

The Gorbachevs were lucky with their daughter, but the way they raised her helps to explain how well she turned out. They trusted her to do well at school without parental guidance, and she did. Remembering how his father hadn't interfered in his education, Gorbachev accompanied Irina to school exactly twice: once to her first first-grade class and then when she finished school with highest honors. From an early age, Irina helped with house cleaning. Later, she did some of the shopping and cooking and helped her mother wash and iron Gorbachev's shirts. In a still totalitarian society where unguarded words could get someone into trouble, especially a rising party official with unorthodox views, the Gorbachevs shared their thoughts with Irina. During evening meals in Stavropol (which they tried to have at home as often as possible), they reviewed what each of them had done that day and discussed what each was reading, including books that weren't available to ordinary Soviet readers. "They never asked me to leave the room," Irina recalls, never said, "This isn't your affair." From an early age, "I would sit there and listen to everything. Absolutely everything."[105]

Rather than sending their daughter to special schools for the party elite, the Gorbachevs enrolled her in a regular school. Some of Irina's fellow students were tough kids from a poor section of town, but although she got straight A's and became a teacher's pet, Irina remembers winning over her less dutiful peers by summarizing for them the books that they didn't read. And it must have helped that her parents rejected the usual elite practice of having papa's chauffeur drive her to class.[106] After high school, when Irina wanted to apply to MGU's philosophy department, where her mother had studied, her parents wanted to keep the family together in Stavropol. They didn't forbid her to apply, but kept saying, "How can you do that? You're our only child, but you want to go away?"[107] Irina applied to the Stavropol medical school (which in the Soviet Union was an undergraduate program) and was readily admitted; with a gold-medal transcript (all A's except for one B in drawing), she didn't need her father's clout to get in. Once she enrolled, the institute's director hesitated to subject her to uncomfortable parts of the regular routine. Why should she have to work as a hospital orderly like all other first-year students? Or take long trips on rickety, sweltering buses to help gather the harvest? The daughters of two other local pooh-bahs were driven to the fields in their father's cars, and spent most of their time there loafing. But when the deputy head of the party education department offered a similar arrangement to Gorbachev, he retorted, "What do you mean? Irina chose her profession. Let her do everything everyone else has to do."[108]

While in medical school, Irina met and fell in love with a fellow student, Anatoly Virgansky, whom she married on April 15, 1978. Her parents closely monitored their first dates.[109] Gorbachev's emotional nature, which he ordinarily kept contained, burst through at Irina's wedding. "He wept," recalls Lydia Budyka. "He cried, 'I'm losing my daughter!'"[110]

According to Irina, her mother mostly avoided special elite food and clothing stores in Stavropol, which like most Soviet provinces suffered from severe shortages. But Gorbachev, while traveling to better-stocked places at home and abroad, was not so abstemious. Every time he left on a business trip, his wife recalled, "we would draw up a list of our own and our friends' needs. The list would include everything—books, overcoats, blinds, underwear, shoes, tights, saucepans, detergents, medicines. . . . I can show you a dozen letters from Mikhail Sergeyevich written, say, from Sochi or Moscow, saying he had managed to buy some shoes."[111] When Raisa did buy groceries in the regional party committee's special store, she always paid cash (so as not to run up any debt), and she kept all the receipts, so as to demonstrate her frugality. She even brought all those receipts to Moscow when they moved there in 1978 to testify to her rectitude.[112]

"Lysistrata," she later wrote (the eponymous heroine of the Aristophanes play who withholds sex from her husband to end the Peloponnesian War), "is needed in every home. And in every family as a means of preserving it. Because devastating wars can break out in families. But Lysistrata is herself in need of protection and help." The trouble, she continued, was that "the problematic and complicated balancing of a job and family obligations in our life" held down "the level of women's professional qualifications and slowed their advancement in employment."[113] Raisa's own scholarly and teaching career prospered partly because of her husband's rank. "People don't just greet me; they bow down to me," she complained to one of Gorbachev's colleagues. "It's disgusting! What can I do?" He answered, "Don't pay attention to it. You'll get used to it." Did she? the colleague was later asked. "Yes," was his reply.[114]

When it came to socializing outside the family, Gorbachev's wife kept him on a short leash. Once, after taking part in a Komsomol-sponsored "voluntary" clean-up day in the local botanical garden, he stayed afterward for a celebratory, largely liquid lunch. That was unusual for him—

another habit that alienated his colleagues and subordinates. "That's it, fellas," he announced, after a while. "Gotta go." "Just one for the road, Mikhail Sergeyevich!" his colleagues begged. "Please." "No. That's it. Raisa Maksimovna will let me have it. She's the boss."[115]

A joke, but with far more than a grain of truth. In addition to a "feminine kindness and courteousness," Raisa's colleagues noticed a certain "dryness" that seemed to stem from her "consciousness of her position," and a kind of "imperiousness." It was easy to take this as arrogance, of course, but it reflected her uneasiness. Despite her high position as the boss's wife, or perhaps just because of it, she struck people as having a "heightened sense of vulnerability," an intense sort of "sensitivity combined with an ability to control herself." Not only did she have to be careful how she behaved; she was extremely protective of her husband, and she agonized more than he did. Several times Gorbachev mentioned to close aides that, owing to her worry about one sort of issue or another, his wife "was so upset that she didn't sleep at all last night."[116]

Raisa remembered "never-ending alarms and worries connected with my husband's work in addition to my regular professional and family cares." His exalted status ensured that the family's financial state improved, that they got better medical treatment, and that they took wonderful vacations at North Caucasus resorts, in Moscow or Leningrad, and once in Uzbekistan, where they toured Tashkent, Samarkand, Bukhara, and the Kyzyl Kum Desert, not to mention the trips to Italy and France. But with power came burdens. The years before 1970 "had not been easy," she recalled, but the next eight or nine "were especially tense for us."

Late one evening in November 1978, Gorbachev called from Moscow to say he was being promoted to the capital to serve as a Central Committee secretary. Irina rejoiced at the prospect of moving to the capital. But she couldn't tell from her mother's first reaction whether Raisa did or not. "Was there regret," Raisa asked in her memoirs, "or was there joy at having at last escaped from the provinces? You know, it's not so simple." For her, the return to Moscow meant "the completion of a huge diversion in our lives." Yet it was "there, in Stavropol, that we were given the opportunity to realize ourselves. I was worried once again by that feeling of facing the unknown. I felt rather anxious."[117]

CHAPTER 5

RETURN TO MOSCOW

1978–1985

GORBACHEV FLEW TO MOSCOW on Saturday, September 25, 1978, to attend a Central Committee plenum. His rank entitled him to stay at the Stalin-era Moskva Hotel, a hulking gray concrete behemoth built in the 1930s just outside the Kremlin. The odd asymmetry of its façade was a monument to Stalin's terror. When presented with two alternative designs, he misunderstood and signed off on both, and the architects were too scared to ask which he preferred, so they built each half of the façade differently. Gorbachev chose to stay at the more modern white-marble Rossiya Hotel, covering a megablock on the bank of the Moscow River. Finished in 1967, it was the largest hotel in Europe until it was demolished in 2006 to make way for a five-star successor. The Rossiya offered breathtaking views of the Kremlin, especially from the tenth-floor rooms, one of which Gorbachev occupied. When colleagues asked why he preferred the Rossiya, Gorbachev would say he "somehow got used to it." His choice distinguished him as a man of special tastes, who kept a certain distance from other provincial officials visiting the capital.

On Sunday at noon, Gorbachev arrived at the apartment of a friend from Stavropol who was celebrating his fiftieth birthday. Six hours later, sated and lubricated in traditional Russian fashion, host and guests were still celebrating. Much of the conversation concerned who was likely to be appointed Central Committee secretary in charge of agriculture at the Monday plenum. "As a rule," Gorbachev recalls, regional party leaders like him knew who was "coming up," and sometimes were even consulted in advance, but there were "no preliminary consultations this time." Meanwhile, Brezhnev's top aide, Konstantin Chernenko, had been trying to contact Gorbachev. Chernenko's office called the friend's apartment several times but got no answer, until the friend's son picked up and informed them they had the "wrong number." Finally, another guest, arriving just before 6 p.m. from where Central Committee members were gathering, urged Gorbachev to call Chernenko's office. "The General Secretary wants to see you. We'll lose our jobs," Gorbachev was told. "OK, I'll be right over."

Chernenko was waiting. The usually sober Gorbachev explained his slightly tipsy state by citing his "countryman's" celebration, but Chernenko had more serious things in mind: "At tomorrow's plenum Leonid Ilich intends to propose your election as a secretary of the Central Committee. That's what he wanted to see you about." By now Brezhnev had left for the day. Gorbachev expected Chernenko to elaborate on his new assignment, but he did not. Chernenko was known in the Kremlin as "the silent one," Gorbachev recalled, "the sort of person often thought to be discreet and even modest, while men of a different character and temperament like me may appear overambitious by comparison." Being overambitious was bad form even though, or perhaps because, so many Soviet leaders were just that. So Gorbachev quickly expressed "doubts as to whether the decision about my election had been thoroughly considered." He wasn't sure whether he was "up to the job," he said. To which Chernenko replied, "Whether you're up to it or not isn't the issue now. The point is that Leonid Ilich [Brezhnev] trusts you. Do you understand?"

Gorbachev returned to his Rossiya room and gazed at the brightly illuminated Kremlin. "I had a sleepless night. I pushed the armchair to the window without turning on the light: before me the domes of St. Basil's Cathedral were outlined against the night sky and the majestic silhouette of the Kremlin. God knows, I had not expected such an important appointment!"[1]

Surely Gorbachev knew he was in the running. Three months earlier, his mentor Fyodor Kulakov had died unexpectedly of heart failure at the age of sixty. Before that, Gorbachev had been considered for other big jobs in Moscow: head of the Central Committee propaganda department, USSR minister of agriculture, and USSR procurator general. Gorbachev turned away these feelers. He'd heard that "some people" in the Kremlin "did not particularly approve of the independent-minded secretary from Stavropol." But he'd also been told that others were holding him in reserve, "an axe under the bench," as one of them put it, for bigger things.[2]

The competition wasn't steep. Sergei Medunov, party boss of the Krasnodar region, Stavropol's neighbor to the west, was another candidate for Central Committee secretary in charge of agriculture. Although the same size as Stavropol, Krasnodar had a larger population and produced twice as much grain. Moreover, Medunov was a trained agronomist with a candidate's degree in economics, and he was close to Brezhnev, who often vacationed in Krasnodar. But Medunov was so corrupt that a year after Brezhnev's death he would be fired from his Krasnodar post and expelled from the Central Committee. And Gorbachev himself had a powerful patron. What made them choose him? "The Andropov factor."[3]

In August 1978, Andropov made sure he and Gorbachev would vacation at the same time in Kislovodsk. Andropov talked less about Stavropol, Gorbachev remembered, than about "the general situation in the country," including foreign policy. The next month, Brezhnev stopped in the North Caucasus resort town of Mineralnye Vody on his way to award the Order of Lenin to Baku, the capital of Azerbaijan. Accompanied on his special train by Chernenko, he was greeted at the station by Andropov and Gorbachev. In retrospect the scene is remarkable in that it featured four successive Soviet leaders strolling together on the same platform. At the time it was a trial by fitful conversation. As they drove to the station, Andropov told Gorbachev, "Listen, you're the host here, so you take the initiative in leading the conversation." That didn't require much effort, Gorbachev says, since Brezhnev "was not quite there and didn't notice us as we walked alongside him." As usual, the ailing Soviet leader managed to mumble something about Gorbachev's "sheep empire," and then topped that by asking how the irrigation canal was "getting on." Gorbachev dutifully answered, but realized Brezhnev wasn't listening. Andropov, however, was looking at his protégé expectantly, while the faithful Chernenko, "dumb as a fish," seemed to be func tioning as some sort of "walking tape recorder." After several false starts, the general secretary suddenly asked Andropov, "How's my speech?" Gorbachev wondered which oration he meant. Andropov later explained that Brezhnev was having trouble speaking, which probably accounted for his silence on the platform.[4]

Another "test" followed, administered by Politburo member Andrei Kirilenko, age seventy-two, who wasn't much healthier than his boss. In 1981, when Kirilenko read out the names of new Central Committee members at the Twenty-Sixth Party Congress, he mispronounced most of them, even though his text listed them in huge letters. Only when he wasn't able to conduct a conversation or even recognize his colleagues, did Andropov insist that Kirilenko resign. Meanwhile, in 1978, Kirilenko took Gorbachev on an inspection tour of the Stavropol region. In charge of the nation's machine-building industry, Kirilenko kept complaining that agriculture was taking too much machinery, and his "overbearing, hectoring tone got on one's nerves," Gorbachev recalled. "His inarticulate manner of speaking turned every conversation into an ordeal; it was impossible to understand what he was trying to say."[5]

Tests like these weren't that hard for a gifted student like Gorbachev. The Central Committee plenum on September 27 approved his new appointment unanimously. With Andropov standing beside him, Gorbachev accepted congratulations from other leaders, but Brezhnev, having trouble coping with a teacup, only nodded. Gorbachev expected Brezhnev to summon him to the Kremlin for instructions. When that didn't happen, he requested an audience himself. "I don't know how I will manage," he told the boss in one more burst of false modesty, "but I can assure you I will do my best." Brezhnev "showed no response at all, either to my words or to myself. I had the impression he was completely indifferent to my presence." He uttered but one sentence: "It's a pity about Kulakov, he was a good man . . ."[6]

Taken together, these events not only mark Gorbachev's entry into the Kremlin's higher circles; they set the tone for the next seven years and for his time in power after that. Brezhnev's debility personified the "stagnation" (as it was later called) into which Soviet society had descended. His successors, Andropov and Chernenko, were both gravely ill and died quickly. The social and political disasters they left behind, at home and in foreign policy, constituted a daunting agenda for change. But their personal examples were less intimidating. Far from being hard acts to follow, Brezhnev, Andropov, and Chernenko were too easy. Predecessors like these help to explain why Gorbachev's expectations for himself were so high, why he drastically underestimated the obstacles he would face, and why his troubles, once they landed on him, were so devastating.

Looking back, Gorbachev wrote that his "long-term plans began to take shape after I arrived in Moscow and saw how things were with my own eyes." Only a year later, he and Eduard Shevardnadze (then Georgian party boss, later Gorbachev's foreign minister) were strolling along the Black Sea shore, when Shevardnadze suddenly remarked, "You know, everything is rotten." Gorbachev agreed.[7] But for the time being, Gorbachev played the Kremlin game: watching and waiting, listening and learning rather than speaking out, concealing his unorthodox views, cultivating bosses who could move him ahead, getting around those who stood in his way. In retrospect, it's clear he was playing the game in order to change it. Ironically, though, he was better at old-style Kremlin infighting than at the new game of open, mass politics that he himself would later introduce.

Gorbachev's self-proclaimed modesty wasn't entirely false. His promotion to Moscow was the latest in his long string of successes—in school, at the university, and again in Stavropol. But each victory led to new challenges that demanded he prove himself yet again. When Andropov died in February 1984, it looked for a moment as if Gorbachev would succeed him. When Chernenko was chosen instead, Gorbachev told aides he wasn't ready "psychologically," anyway.[8] Was this just for show? Or a flash of fear that his latest successes, on top of all those that preceded them, would put him in position to fail?

GORBACHEV DESCRIBES HIS PARTING with Stavropol colleagues as heartfelt, stressing his cordial relations with his successor, Vsevolod Murakhovsky, while not mentioning his bitter second-in-command, Kaznacheyev. Gorbachev regretted not touring the region to bid farewell to people with whom he had "shared and endured so much," but that would have looked "immodest." But many of his associates already viewed him that way, and his aide turned biographer Grachev doesn't disagree: "He took his promotion to Moscow not as an unexpected gift for which he had fate and the Politburo to thank, but as logical. The fact that he would become the youngest Central Committee secretary didn't so much disturb him as confirm that he had chosen the right path and managed in optimal fashion the possibilities that opened up for him."[9]

Reflecting on his Stavropol years, Gorbachev recalled that he had "tasted politics," and "the political world had fully captivated me." Besides thriving in their chosen professions, he and his wife had raised a talented, dutiful daughter. Mikhail and Raisa had earned further academic degrees and read forbidden books by authors of whom his local colleagues had never heard. Proud of such accomplishments, Gorbachev declared in his memoirs, "We ourselves made our own fate. We ourselves became who we were. We used to the fullest all the possibilities that the country opened up to its citizens."[10]

Does the claim that they had accomplished so much imply some others hadn't? Grachev's assessment is suggestive: "Despite all the years they had spent in the Russian provinces, the Gorbachevs had trouble taking to provincials."[11] Moreover, their strivings and achievements, balanced by tense relations with less accomplished colleagues, were stressful. At such moments, Gorbachev recalls, "nature was my saving shelter. . . . I retreated to the forest or the steppe. . . . I could always feel my anxiety ebbing away, my irritation and fatigue passing, my spiritual balance returning." After prairie fires blackened vast swaths of steppe, he felt uplifted by the first abundant rains: "Suddenly the earth began to breathe, to come back to life, to be reborn. Where did it get the strength? Gazing at its luxuriant flowering, a man couldn't help being inspired by hope." His wife shared his passion for nature. "Together," he recalls, "we strode countless kilometers, in summer and winter, in all kinds of weather, even in blizzards." Most of all they loved the end of June. "We would drive way out from the city, to where the softly waving grain stretched to the horizon, or to the forest, where you could dissolve into the silence and the beauty. Toward evening the heat would die down, and at night in the wheat fields you could hear quail singing. It was then that you felt an incomparable kind of happiness that all of this existed—

the steppe, the grain, the smell of the grasses, the birdsong, the stars in the lofty sky—that you yourself existed."

On December 5, their last day in Stavropol, the Gorbachevs drove to the edge of the forest, then got out and walked. "The forest wasn't as lovely and well-dressed as it is in the fall. The thickening shadows made it look sad, as if at parting with us. Our hearts ached. The next day, lifting its heavy chassis from the Stavropol earth, our plane set sail for Moscow."[12] This last passage is obviously overblown, but Gorbachev's poetic descriptions of nature suggest how different he and his wife were from the Kremlin elite he was about to join.

According to her friend Lydia Budyka, Gorbachev's wife went to great lengths to make their home "a place it was a pleasure just to enter."[13] That was harder to do in Moscow, where they were moved from house to house as Gorbachev was made Politburo candidate member (November 27, 1979) and then full member (October 21, 1980). First, they were assigned a large musty dacha outside the city. It was as if "we were marooned on a desert island after a shipwreck," Gorbachev remembered, and it didn't help that during the winter of 1978–1979 the temperature plummeted as low as minus forty degrees Celsius. Despite the cold, the Gorbachevs continued their practice of going on long evening walks to share impressions "in private." He thought he already knew "the ways of the Tsar's Court," but it took time to understand "all the subtleties and nuances." For all his innate optimism, he wasn't in an upbeat mood— partly because his wife certainly wasn't. "How will it all work out for us here?" she kept asking. It was bound to be better than their first ten years in Stavropol, he assured her, and she seemed to agree. But she worried about her work. Should she continue preparing her doctoral dissertation? He hadn't thought much about that, he admitted, adding that they would have a new home, which would "take a lot of work to make comfortable."[14]

That wasn't exactly an enthusiastic endorsement for her continuing her academic career. Moreover, while she was contemplating resuming work on her dissertation, they made another move—into an old wooden house in a picturesque, wooded spot on the banks of the Moscow River about twenty miles from Moscow. Stalin's Georgian henchman Sergo Ordzhonikidze had lived there before he committed suicide; Chernenko had recently resided there. This dacha was at Sosnovka, not far from the Krylatskie Hills, and across the river from Serebryany Bor, where there was a pine forest when the Gorbachevs moved in. (The forest later gave way to a high-rise residential district.) However, this villa, too, they found "oppressive like a barracks."[15] Later they would move into a more modern brick house built in the 1970s, where Kulakov had resided before his untimely death. In addition, they were assigned an apartment on Shchusev Street in a downtown Moscow building known, with a nod to Turgenev's novel, as the "nest of gentlefolk," but they turned that over to Irina and her husband once she finished her studies in Stavropol.[16]

The furnishings in all Kremlin-assigned homes were standard issue: hefty sofas, chairs and tables, heavy curtains and many carpets. But Raisa preferred modern furniture and hated carpets because they "collected dust." She, her daughter, and son-in-law returned to Stavropol in December to collect their things, but all she brought back were two chairs that her husband had bought in 1955, plus a bright-colored mat, a gift from her mother.[17] Cooks and servants, bodyguards, secretaries, and other aides came with the Gorbachevs' Moscow residences, as did access to the exclusive Kremlin polyclinic, hospital, and sanatorium, and to the equally elite Kremlin cafeteria and food store overflowing with fantastic edibles unobtainable by ordinary citizens or lesser elites. Not to mention a massive ZIL limousine with driver.[18] But the "helpers" who served and protected also kept watch for the KGB. The Gorbachevs felt lonely, he recalled, and "mentally uncomfortable because we had no privacy." Since the Ordzhonikidze dacha had no outbuildings, all service personnel worked in the house itself. The only place the Gorbachevs could talk privately was outside, during strolls around the grounds, especially in the evening when he came home from work, while the guards following them politely kept their distance.[19]

Gorbachev soon began working twelve- to sixteen-hour days. At first, his wife busied herself with fixing up their home, reconnecting with her best friend from Moscow University, Nina Lyakisheva, from whom she had borrowed lovely white shoes for her wedding, and visiting the university's philosophy department, where some of her teachers still taught. She still "felt drawn to research work," according to her husband. "Perhaps I should work on my doctorate," she told him. "Everybody here knows me and my work in sociology." He describes his reaction as "prag-matic." "Time will tell."[20] What time (and her husband's lukewarm response) told her was that she should abandon her academic career. "That was very hard for her," remembered Lydia Budyka. "Very, very hard. She loved her work so much. She often talked about how much it meant to her. But she sacrificed it for his career."

The Gorbachevs kept to themselves much of the time in Moscow, as they had done in Stavropol. Compared with most Soviet leaders, who brought a "tail" of former associates with them to the capital (from Ukraine in Khrushchev's and Brezhnev's cases), Gorbachev brought few from Stavropol—mostly because he didn't think much of them in the first place.[21] And members of the super-elite had to be careful about whom they befriended. According to Budyka, that intensified Raisa Gor-bacheva's innate caution: "She didn't settle on friendships easily. She was kind, she was sweet, but she didn't trust people. I was amazed, when we were first becoming friends, that she kept asking me if I knew a cer-tain doctor. I racked my brain and said, no, I didn't. Well, it turned out some rumor was circulating about the Gorbachev family, and she kept testing me to make sure I wasn't the source. Finally, I said to her, 'Raisa Maksimovna, please: Either you trust me, or you don't.' Only then did she stop."[22]

By now Irina Gorbachev and her husband, Anatoly, were building their own careers at the Second Medical Institute in Moscow. Irina grad-uated with honors, finished a graduate program, and started teaching there. Her dissertation topic, mixing medical and social themes, was "The Causes of Death among Working-Age Men in the City of Moscow." The subject was so sensitive that her dissertation was classified and remained so more than thirty years later, according to her father.[23]

To keep busy, Raisa attended academic conferences and other meet-ings and began studying English. She and her husband frequented high-culture venues: the Bolshoi, the Main Concert Hall of the Conservatory, the Tretyakov and Pushkin Museums, and many theaters: the Moscow Art Theater, the Malyi, the Vakhtangov, the Satire, the Contempo-rary, the Moscow Soviet, the Mayakovsky, and especially the Taganka, whose daring, innovative productions, like *Ten Days That Shook the*

World, and poet Andrei Voznesensky's *Antiworlds*, the Gorbachevs had admired in earlier years. She and her husband also undertook sight-seeing excursions, beginning with places they had known and shared in the early fifties, then proceeding, in her typically meticulous way, chronologically—Moscow of the fourteenth to sixteenth centuries, then the seventeenth, eighteenth, and nineteenth—and guided by experts on the periods in question whom she recruited to accompany them.[24]

Raisa still felt isolated, however, and her exposure to other Polit-buro wives only made things worse. Much younger, far better educated, more attractive and energetic, she couldn't but constitute a challenge to dowdy Kremlin matrons. They responded, Grachev says, by "putting her in her place, quite literally." At an official reception for foreign guests in March 1979, the elegantly attired Mrs. Gorbachev, unaware that Krem-lin wives were expected to occupy the same rank order as their husbands, occupied the first free place she saw, which happened to be next to Mrs. Kirilenko. "Your place is over there," her neighbor coldly informed her, pointing with her finger: "At the end of the line."[25]

"What sort of people are they?" Raisa later exclaimed to her husband. Her own answer: they were "estranged from one another." "You were seen and somehow not noticed. Even the usual greetings were not exchanged. There was surprise if you addressed someone politely, by his or her first name and patronymic. What? You actually remember them?" People had "pretensions to superiority, to being one of the chosen. Judgments were pronounced categorically and without tact." Even Krem-lin children were ranked according to their fathers' status. When Raisa wondered aloud about the rude behavior of some Kremlin offspring, she was chided: "What are you saying—those are Brezhnev's grandchildren!" When Kremlin wives met (mainly at official receptions and only seldom privately), there were "endless toasts to the health of those higher up, nasty talk about those lower down, discussion of food and their children's and grandchildren's 'unique' abilities. And card games." Not to mention "indifference and lack of concern," a kind of "consumerism." Once Raisa warned children gathered with their families at a state dacha to be careful lest they break a chandelier. "Don't worry!" she was told, "It's government property."[26]

WHAT WAS LIFE LIKE for more-ordinary people in the stagnant period of the late 1970s? Anatoly Chernyaev, then in the Central Committee's international department, remembers that food shortages were bad enough in Moscow, but far worse in the provinces. A niece of his, visiting from Volgograd, where food was rationed, complained that five of the ten kilos of meat she was entitled to per month were invariably rotten.

"Tolya," she continued, "when are they going to remove him?"

"Whom?"

"You know, your guy, the top man. The people don't like him.'

"Why?" Chernyaev asked.

"Because there's no order anywhere. People say that under Stalin, prices were cut every year. There was hope that things would get better. But now prices keep going up, not just every year, but every month with no end in sight, despite all your assurances, all your party congresses."

Privately, Chernyaev was no less critical. His diary recorded complaints from people around the country, collected for the Politburo by the Central Committee's general department. From Yaroslavl: "Butter's not for sale anywhere, milk only occasionally, and the supply of meat and vegetables is irregular." From Uglich: "All there is in stores is bread, salt, margarine, and jars of compote. We don't know what to feed the children. Milk is available only by coupons, and only for kids younger than three." Well informed though he was, Chernyaev was "stunned": "all this against a background of self-congratulation at the top, an insane conflation of loud declarations with vulgar, high-flown claims of success, of lying plain and simple."[27]

Otto Latsis, then working at the Institute of the Economy of the World Socialist System, later a Central Committee member, felt "suffocated." "Everything began to fall apart physically; accidents started to happen all over the place." At the end of 1978, a steam plant supplying heat to several Moscow districts failed. When thousands of residents resorted to electric heaters, they blew out an electric power plant, so that many people greeted the New Year in candlelit bathrooms warmed by hot water. The regime tried to pretend that "everything was wonderful," but the propaganda backfired. When the main TV news program showed the obviously ill Brezhnev decorating his aged Kremlin colleagues with medals and awards, "one could see that these people could hardly move. All these decrepit people congratulating each other, putting medals on each other's chests—they could hardly talk. All these old guys . . . in opulent rooms with brocade and gilt and chandeliers, while people all over the country had a very hard life."[28]

An American expert on the Soviet economy, Ed A. Hewett, listed "evidence of an economy in deep difficulty": "The service sector is incredibly primitive by Western standards, indeed by world standards. Consumer durables are scarce. The underlying technology dates from the early postwar years, and the quality is frequently poor. This economy seems unable to produce a cheap, reliable, automatic washing machine, radio or phonograph, and cheap powerful hand calculators and personal computers are still no more than a distant hope. Decent fruits and vegetables . . . are seemingly out of reach even though twenty percent of the labor force works in agriculture."[29]

The Soviet Union mined eight times as much iron ore as the United States but produced only twice as much steel.[30] On average, an industrial plant took ten years to build, compared with two in the United States. The USSR manufactured sixteen times more grain harvesters than America, but, humiliatingly, had to buy grain abroad. Years of forced-draft industrialization had created an ecological crisis. Alcoholism had grown both quantitatively (per capita consumption of alcohol more than doubling over twenty years, while the number of alcohol-related crimes jumped 5.7 times) and spatially; villages had long since transitioned from episodic holiday drinking bouts to daily, urban-style binges. The effect on labor discipline and productivity was devastating, yet another reason why overall economic growth was slowing.

One possible response to the food crisis was to raise prices, so as to provide more incentive to collective and state farmers, but the regime didn't dare. Better to preserve a kind of tacit social contract according to which the state kept the cost of consumer goods and social programs low, and in return people accepted or at least tolerated the regime. Instead, purchases of grain abroad rose from 2.2 million tons in 1970 to 29.4 million in 1982, and to 46 million in 1984. In the past, shortages and price rises had triggered riots.

A few years earlier, rising Soviet oil exports and oil prices financed purchases of foreign grain, machinery, and consumer goods. As oil production dropped and the price of oil did, too, the regime's margin for error narrowed. Meanwhile, the country's political position in the world was deteriorating. Brezhnev, in particular, had put great stock in détente, first with European powers like France and West Germany, then with the United States, particularly in a series of summit meetings and arms control agreements with Presidents Richard Nixon and Gerald Ford. But by the beginning of the 1980s, détente was dead. Seeming Soviet gains in the Third World (particularly in Angola, the Horn of Africa, and Nicaragua) alarmed the Americans, as did events in Poland, where Solidarity-led strikes threatened to provoke Soviet armed intervention. Equally unnerving was a massive buildup in Soviet nuclear forces, especially the deployment of new SS-20 rockets capable of obliterating Western Europe. In response, President Carter played "the China card," going so far as to discuss military security ties when Moscow was still deeply at odds with Beijing. And when Soviet troops invaded Afghanistan at the end of 1979, the Americans responded with harsh sanctions. The newly elected Ronald Reagan damned the USSR as an "evil empire," "the focus of evil in the modern world," and provided lethal aid to mujahideen fighting the Red Army in Afghanistan. He also launched the Star Wars missile defense program that threatened Moscow's capacity for nuclear deterrence and deployed Europe-based Pershing II missiles, whose firing would give the Soviet leadership only five minutes before they were obliterated.[31]

Cold War II was on. The Soviets were isolated and defensive. In February 1980, Andropov outlined to visiting East German foreign intelligence chief Markus Wolf "a gloomy scenario in which nuclear war was a real threat," and East German Foreign Minister Oskar Fischer got "similar impressions" at meetings with Gromyko.[32] In May 1981, at a secret KGB conference in Moscow, Andropov declared, "The United States is preparing for nuclear war," an assessment buttressed later that year when more than eighty NATO warships observing radio silence moved through the Greenland-Iceland-UK gap and approached Soviet territory before being detected. In another provocative exercise, four American surface ships penetrated the Barents Sea, where Soviet nuclear subma-

rines were supposedly safe, and then to within twelve miles of the huge
naval base at Murmansk, before switching on their electronic equipment. The message to Moscow, says former member of the British Joint
Intelligence Committee Gordon Barrass, was "We can run rings around
you."[33] In response to this challenge, KGB agents overseas kept their
eyes peeled for signs of an impending attack, such as lights on late at
night in Western defense ministries, or hospitals collecting more than
the usual amounts of blood. Then, on the night of September 26, 1983,
in a secret underground bunker outside Moscow, alarms indicated that
American missiles were speeding toward Moscow. The duty officer had
seven minutes to alert Andropov, who was on a dialysis machine in a
suburban sanatorium. Fortunately, Lieutenant Colonel Stanislav Petrov
concluded that the alarm was false. Meanwhile, however, the Americans and British were preparing to conduct the "Able Archer 83" war
game, in which NATO's supreme commander would request permission to use nuclear weapons and receive it. When Able Archer began in
early November, the chief of the Soviet General Staff took cover in his
command bunker under Moscow and ordered a "heightened alert" for
some land-based Soviet forces. Luckily, in the end, Soviet monitoring of
Able Archer 83 confirmed that this was just an exercise, not cover for
an actual attack.[34]

The last thing the USSR needed under these circumstances was
decrepit political leaders. By now the aging Brezhnev, who had suffered
several minor strokes and a heart attack in 1975 but continued to smoke
and drink compulsively, was exhibiting wild mood swings. One day he
was depressed, the next day he was wearing a massive gold signet ring
("Don't you think it becomes me?" he asked his doctor) and boasting
he should have shared the 1971 Nobel Peace Prize with West German
Chancellor Willy Brandt. Trying to avoid work, Brezhnev often escaped
to Zavidovo, a hunting preserve about 75 miles northwest of Moscow.[35]
There he begged aides to regale him with stories of his own "heroics"
during World War II or as party leader in Dnepropetrovsk, the Virgin
Lands, and Moldavia. They begged him to declaim poetry and rejoiced
when he did: "Leonid Ilich, you could have had a career onstage!" They
feigned admiration as he flirted with stenographers and waitresses, and
joined him in what passed for impromptu choral singing and dancing

to the tune of tangos, fox-trots, and waltzes played on a Japanese record player in a summer house on the edge of a lake.[36]

Before Brezhnev's condition deteriorated, he had an ironic sense of his own limitations. Instructing his speechwriters to minimize quotations from Marx and Lenin in his speeches, he added, "No one will believe that Lyonya Brezhnev read them all anyway."[37] But his illness turned Politburo sessions into a joke. Dozens of important policy questions were "decided" without any discussion in a mere fifteen or twenty minutes. Brezhnev wasn't too far gone to raise the possibility of his own retirement. But whenever he did so, his colleagues insisted he was indispensable. What they actually feared was that his departure would reduce their own power to govern in his name, while triggering a dangerous succession struggle.[38]

Gorbachev's future aide Anatoly Chernyaev was then deputy head of the Central Committee's international department. "I practiced a regime of doublethink," he later admitted. "I was no longer disappointed when Brezhnev treated me coldly; in fact, in my soul I congratulated myself on that." Chernyaev justified his continued service by hoping Brezhnev would revive détente, but he felt a "growing enmity" for his boss, which "later, when he began to decay, turned to physical and moral aversion."[39] Another international department official, Karen Brutents, remembered, "I didn't sincerely agree with anything in the official ideology and behavior of the leadership, with the exception, perhaps, of certain of its foreign policy actions." In the case of the Czechoslovak intervention, he confessed, he had "passionately wanted my own government to fail."[40]

Other future Gorbachevites then working for Brezhnev fell by the wayside. Aleksandr Bovin, a rotund, witty bon vivant and raconteur who dubbed absurd Brezhnev episodes "moments musicaux," was fired for complaining to a friend about wasting his talent on a nonentity like Brezhnev. Shakhnazarov, a high-ranking Central Committee functionary, was demoted for writing science fiction with heretical implications, for privately translating George Orwell's *1984*, and for supporting Vladimir Vysotsky, whose songs Andropov had sung around Kislovodsk campfires with Gorbachev.[41]

BETWEEN HIS 1978 ARRIVAL in Moscow and Brezhnev's death on November 10, 1982, Gorbachev was a Kremlin backbencher while a gang of six ran the country: Brezhnev (who still had the last word when he was able to utter it), Suslov (an exceptional number two man, until his death on January 25, 1982, in that he didn't aspire to be number one), Gromyko (Politburo member since 1973 as well as foreign minister since 1957), Andropov (promoted from the KGB to Central Committee secretary after Suslov's death), Defense Minister Marshal Dmitry Ustinov and Chernenko. In the beginning, Gorbachev was mostly silent at Secretariat and Politburo meetings, and what he did say was unexceptional. He wasn't specially informed about the Soviet invasion of Afghanistan in December 1979, let alone consulted about it in advance.[42] A small Politburo subgroup made the decision: Ustinov, supported by Andropov and Gromyko, persuaded Brezhnev to strike, partly by saying, "The Americans have done it over and over in Latin America. What are we, worse then they are?"[43] According to Eduard Shevardnadze, later to become Gorbachev's foreign minister, they both considered the invasion a "fateful mistake."[44] Gorbachev's November 20, 1979, memorandum on agriculture hailed a recent Brezhnev speech as a "major, broad-based statement," in which Leonid Ilich spoke with "the depth, breadth, and detail that is characteristic of him."[45] On October 29, 1980, he echoed other Politburo members' calls for Polish Communist authorities to crack down on their domestic opposition.[46] According to a Westerner who has read records of all Politburo meetings on the Polish question, "Gorbachev is present at all of them, but almost never speaks, except to say that whatever Brezhnev just said was just right."[47] Gorbachev followed Suslov's lead on June 2, 1981, about the need to be stricter in deciding which Soviet citizens should be allowed to travel abroad.[48] On August 19, 1982, he praised Brezhnev for the "great tact" he showed in talks with East German leader Erich Honecker.[49]

Naturally, Gorbachev doesn't stress his own passivity either in his memoirs or in interviews. He says only that it took him quite a while "to catch on to all the subtleties and nuances at the top." And that, in the meantime, he had to watch out for veteran leaders who "looked on me as an upstart."[50] He tried to build on his relationship with Andropov; from time to time, they talked on the telephone, but that was all. After becoming a full Politburo member, Gorbachev invited Andropov and his wife, who lived next door, to a picnic, "as in the good old days" near Stavropol.

"Yes, those were the days, but now I have to decline your invitation, Mikhail," Andropov replied coolly.

"Why?" Gorbachev asked.

"Because, tomorrow, even before then, there would be all kinds of loose talk—who, where, why, what was said?"

"What do you mean, Yuri Vladimirovich?"

"Just what I said. Even before we get to your house, Leonid Ilich would hear about it. I'm telling you this, Mikhail, first and foremost for your own sake."[51]

Gorbachev should have known better. When Kulakov died, none of his Kremlin colleagues interrupted their summer holidays to pay last respects. "That's how incredibly remote these people at the top levels of power were from each other!" Gorbachev recalled. He had to get Moscow's permission to speak at the funeral and submitted his text beforehand to the Central Committee "so as to avoid repetition and divergence of opinion with the other speakers"—as if, one might add, repetition of hackneyed phrases wasn't the norm in Kremlin speeches and a public divergence of opinion wasn't unheard of.[52] The one, odd exception to the rule that Kremlin leaders didn't socialize was Suslov, cold and remote, but exalted enough to take liberties. In the summer of 1979, he invited the entire Gorbachev family to spend all day strolling the grounds of a deserted dacha that formerly belonged to Stalin—not quite a sunlit romp, even though Suslov brought along his daughter, son-in-law, and grandchildren. The ascetic Suslov did, however, draw the line at lunch, offering his guests only tea.[53]

On his very first day in Moscow, Gorbachev learned something about Kremlin infighting. By then Brezhnev's rise to full power was complete. The next to last of his former rivals, titular head of state Nikolai Porgorny, had been retired in 1977, as Prime Minister Kosygin would be two years later. But Andropov noticed Kosygin congratulating Gorbachev on his promotion with particular warmth. "Aleksei Nikolayevich has already started to court you," Andropov warned. "Hold your ground."[54]

Kosygin did Gorbachev the favor of arguing with him in Brezhnev's presence. At a September 7, 1979, Kremlin reception for cosmonauts who had spent a record-breaking 175 days in space, Kosygin complained that Gorbachev wanted to hoard scarce machinery for the harvest in Kazakhstan and central Russian provinces. Brezhnev, apparently having one of his better days, came to Gorbachev's defense, but Kosygin added that Gorbachev was being too "tolerant" of those who didn't fulfill the plan. Gorbachev couldn't contain himself and talked back to the prime minister, triggering a hushed silence in the room. He later berated himself for not "keeping his composure," and soberly assessed whether he had "made some mistake or not." But Brezhnev congratulated him on standing up to Kosygin. Gorbachev was emotional enough to have erupted spontaneously, but clever enough to sense that his outburst might prove productive, and a good enough actor to make the most of his own anger. Kosygin soon called to make peace, and Gorbachev's appointment as Politburo candidate member quickly followed.[55]

Gorbachev was inwardly appalled by what passed for the Kremlin decision-making process. One day, when Brezhnev fell asleep in the middle of a meeting, other members acted as if nothing had happened. When Gorbachev complained to Andropov, he was reminded that the "stability of party, country and even the world" demanded that everyone "support Leonid Ilich." That required that everyone "know his place and no one aspire to more than his own roost." Those roosts were set in stone at Politburo meetings: to Brezhnev's right at the long table sat Suslov, to his left, Kosygin, until replaced as prime minister by Nikolai Tikhonov, with other members always occupying the same seats. The table was so long and Brezhnev's diction so slurred that Gorbachev, seated farthest from the general secretary, could hardly make out what he was saying. Someone "kept jumping up and running over to Brezhnev, shuffling the papers in front of him and telling him what issues had already been decided, which had been tabled, and which papers he now needed to address." All of this "was done openly, without any inhibition. I was ashamed and thought to myself that others must be as well. But everyone sat there, not batting an eye."[56]

Gorbachev concentrated on his own job—agriculture. The 1978 harvest seemed a fine one, record-breaking, in fact, at 237 million

Gorbachev with other Politburo members, whose average age was
over seventy, November 7, 1980. Left to right: Mikhail Solomentsev,
Vladimir Dolgikh, Viktor Grishin, Pyotr Demichev, Mikhail Suslov,
Konstantin Chernenko, Leonid Brezhnev, Mikhail Gorbachev,
Nikolai Tikhonov, Yuri Andropov, Andrei Kirilenko,
Andrei Gromyko.

tons of grain.[57] But the yield was deceptive—much of it was wet when
gathered, and when dry it weighed 25 million tons less. Moreover, the
seeming success required so much effort that preparations for 1979
(providing winter fodder for livestock, autumn fertilizing of fields)
lagged badly. The winter of 1979 was particularly severe, May and June
turned out drier than usual, and an early summer drought followed.
The 1979 harvest was 179 million metric tons, requiring the state to buy
31 million abroad. The year 1980 looked even worse, partly because of
the grain embargo President Jimmy Carter imposed as punishment for
the Soviet invasion of Afghanistan. Unprecedented rain followed a cold,
late spring, bringing bad floods in some regions. The result (189.1 million tons) was a bit better than 1979, but the potato harvest, 40 million
tons less than planned, was the lowest since the 1930s, milk and meat
fell short of 1979, and foreign imports rose to 35 million tons of grain
and a million tons of meat. The 1981 harvest was so disappointing that
it was never reported, and after that, agricultural output figures were
kept secret—a mere 160 million tons in 1981, it turned out, so low that

grain imports rose to 46 million tons, while the 1982 harvest rose only to about 175 million tons.

Soviet agriculture was usually "the political graveyard" of the man in charge.[58] Gorbachev himself often fired lower-level officials ("without pity," he admits) who failed to achieve the planned results.[59] Yet not only was he not blamed for disastrous shortfalls beginning in 1979; he was promoted. A higher rank would give him more clout in dealing with lower-level functionaries. Andropov knew that more than one man was to blame for the troubles of Soviet agriculture, and that Gorbachev was better than most. No harvest was "normal," Gorbachev recalled. Each one required a "national battle for grain," a "bitter struggle to wring it, rake it, and shake it out of every collective and state farm." Rather than being rewarded, the most efficient farms had their "above-plan" harvest "torn away" to cover other farms' losses. "Sheer stupidity" compounded the problem: To coax wheat out of unfavorable northern regions, the state paid a higher price per ton than in fertile southern areas. Local leaders madly chased after results that could win them awards and promotions, sometimes by stealing grain from state reserves to add to their regions' totals. Much of the harvest rotted in the absence of facilities for storage and transport. "I myself took part in this procurement hullabaloo for many years," Gorbachev admits, "both in Stavropol and in Moscow." In the capital "the flow of petitioners crashed down on me from my first days in office," functionaries at all levels requesting more resources and assistance. Corruption ranged from "outright bribes to presents and gifts, to more 'subtle' measures like mutual back-scratching, petty personal services, and joint drinking bouts in the guise of hunting or fishing trips."

He doubted the "rationality" of current policies, but his public speeches and articles between 1978 and 1982 are empty and uninspired, full of requisite quotations from Marx, Lenin, and Brezhnev, hailing the very policies about which he had inner doubts. He worked mightily to produce Brezhnev's much-heralded ten-year Food Program (for 1981 to 1990), which promised to make the USSR fully self-sufficient in agricultural products. But the program, which included increased investment in agricultural machinery and technology and a rise in rural manpower and services, was dead on arrival. According to Zhores Medvedev, thousands of experts spent thousands of hours producing the program, but although huge investments were made, "it was obvious that these enormous funds would be wasted because there was to be no liberalization of the decision-making process at the bottom level and no freedom of choice for collective and state farms. Once again, everything was prescribed from the top."[60]

IN MAY 1981, Valery Boldin arrived in Gorbachev's Central Committee office, a relatively small room with a low ceiling and venetian blinds where the air smelled of the synthetic carpet. Gorbachev would soon make Boldin, a former *Pravda* newsman, his chief staff aide, a fateful decision that, in retrospect, almost none of Gorbachev's other close aides and associates could understand. Born in 1935, a graduate of the Timiryazov Agricultural Academy with a candidate of sciences degree in economics, Boldin was a lean man of medium height who, according to Shakhnazarov, "never smiled" and "never opened his mouth except to convey something confidential in a conspiratorial whisper," a "consummate bureaucrat who could deaden any living issue and strike fear into his subordinates with his ominous silence." Shakhnazarov found it "incomprehensible" that Gorbachev kept promoting Boldin (in 1987 to head the Central Committee's general department, and in 1991 to be presidential chief of staff), refusing to heed those who warned him that Boldin would bury important intelligence in a "bureaucratic cemetery" and supply Gorbachev instead with "unreliable information." After former ambassador to the United States Anatoly Dobrynin returned to Moscow to become a Central Committee secretary himself, he found Boldin to be a "haughty, narrow-minded Mandarin," yet it was Boldin who had daily access to Gorbachev, who filled him in on the latest rumors about top officials, and who helped him set the agenda for Politburo meetings.[61]

Boldin's memoirs are obviously biased, but his description of Gorbachev in May 1981, especially of small sartorial signs that distinguished Gorbachev from his unfashionable peers, has the ring of truth. Gorbachev was "a good-looking man of medium height with a fine set of teeth and hazel eyes with a kind of inner sparkle." Boldin was particularly struck by Gorbachev's brownish suit, made by a high-class tailor, and an expensive cream-colored shirt, matched by a brown tie and shoes. Later on, Boldin was "often astonished" by "how such an immensely busy man would find time to focus every day on his large tie collection," always "matching each day's tie with his suit and shirt," actually "knotting each tie when putting it on, rather than simply slipping it, already assembled, over his head, the way many other men did." Gorbachev always tried to be fashionable, even before he met Raisa: witness the photos at Moscow University in which he looks like a French movie star. Raisa, who was fastidious in choosing her own stylish clothes, helped him select his and saw to it that he wore them to good effect.

In 1981 Gorbachev slowly began expanding his portfolio beyond agriculture. Late one evening he asked Boldin to help prepare a list of experts on a wide range of economic issues. Boldin claims to have warned him that such an initiative would raise Politburo eyebrows (as if his boss didn't already know that), but Gorbachev proceeded anyway, meeting with experts from government agencies, directors of economic research institutes, academicians, and university scholars.[62] Even before he became party leader, Gorbachev recalled to a group of party officials in 1990, the office safe in which he kept confidential documents was loaded with proposals from academics and others for all sorts of reforms— "heart-felt cries" he called them, that "we couldn't go on living as we had in the past."[63]

Gorbachev's real breakthrough came when Andropov succeeded Brezhnev. Chernenko aspired to the promotion, but his main qualification, or, rather, nonqualification, was his long tenure as Brezhnev's chief paper pusher. Chernenko's main strategy, Gorbachev recalls, was "to isolate Brezhnev from any direct contact [with others], claiming that only he could understand . . . what Leonid Ilich wanted." But it didn't work.[64] In July 1982, during one of his lucid moments, Brezhnev pushed Andropov to seize the reins, telephoning him to say, "Why do you think I transferred you from the KGB to the Central Committee apparatus? I put you there to lead the Secretariat. . . . Why don't you act?" What happened next reminded Gorbachev of "a scene from Gogol." As Central Committee secretaries gathered for a formal session, Andropov suddenly declared, "It's time to start," and grabbed the chair. "At the sight of Andropov sitting there," Gorbachev continues, "Chernenko seemed to slump; he collapsed into the armchair [and] almost disappeared from view. An internal *coup d'état* had taken place before our eyes."[65]

Andropov turned Politburo sessions into lengthy confrontations with corrupt or incompetent officials—"his anger throwing such a scare into them," Gorbachev says, "that despite the fact they were guilty, one couldn't help feeling sorry for them." He demoted Gorbachev's former competitor, corrupt Krasnodar party chief Medunov, to deputy minister of fruit and vegetable procurement. By striking at a Brezhnev favorite, hitherto deemed untouchable, Andropov deterred anyone who might think of challenging him.[66] When Brezhnev finally died, on November 10, 1982, it was Andropov who called Gorbachev to inform him. Politburo members quickly named Andropov their new leader. "I support your candidacy with all my strength," Gorbachev told him. He remained by Andropov's side, he says, in the days that followed, convinced that the new leader was determined "to dissociate himself from many features of the 'Brezhnev era.'"[67]

Andropov's former aides had high hopes for him. During Brezhnev's funeral, Arbatov whispered to Chernyaev and Bovin his "program for Andropov." It would begin by replacing Prime Minister Tikhonov with Gorbachev, firing other Brezhnev favorites, and replacing them with liberals like themselves. Chernyaev's "Andropov program" included pulling out of Afghanistan, ceasing to dictate to East European allies, curbing the military-industrial complex, freeing dissidents from prison, and allowing free emigration. Chernyaev's dream was just that, a dream, he concedes in retrospect. What Andropov wanted most of all was power, Chernyaev later admitted. Even if he aimed "to make the people happy," there was no way he could do so under the current regime.[68]

According to former East German spy chief Markus Wolf, Andropov talked frankly about the "decline" of the Soviet Union, tracing its beginning to the Czech intervention in 1968.[69] Arbatov told Brutents that Andropov mocked Brezhnev's boast that the USSR was now practicing "developed socialism," insisting it was a long way from any socialism at all.[70] But during his fifteen months in office, Andropov's program emphasized style more than substance, and personnel shifts, far from all of them for the better, rather than structural reforms. He quickly fired the minister of the interior, Nikolai Shchelokov, whose personal servants included an architect, a tailor, and a dentist, who had in effect privatized two huge dachas and one large apartment, and who possessed a stunning array of accessories confiscated from underground economic criminals and sent directly to his homes: "Mercedes cars, furniture ensembles, crystal chandeliers, facial powder cases for household staff, a small bed for his grandson, as well as antiques, paintings, gold, and silver."[71] But Andropov also made Azerbaijan party leader Geidar Aliev a full Politburo member, mainly, Gorbachev says, because of Aliev's personal loyalty; he promoted Leningrad party boss Grigory Romanov, despite his being "limited, perfidious and with dictatorial ambitions"; and he left in place two Chernenko supporters, Moscow party chief Viktor Grishin and Prime Minister Tikhonov, because they hadn't opposed Andropov's selection.[72] Gorbachev mocked these moves in retrospect, but only after he later followed the same pattern himself—purging corrupt bureaucrats but avoiding confrontation with potential rivals as long as possible. And Andropov may well have anticipated that his protégé would do just that, pushing him ahead not because Gorbachev was liberal but because, as Grachev puts it, he was "a fresh face not linked with interests and habits of corrupt Moscow clans," a man who would "clean up after the elephants."[73]

Andropov's idea of economic reform was to crack down on idlers and malingerers, to have police detain people found at stores, public baths, and beauty parlors when they should have been working. Given shortages of nearly everything, citizens had no choice but to search for scarce goods during working hours. Gorbachev expressed doubts about this approach, but Andropov waved them off, insisting that ordinary people craved order and discipline: "Just you wait," he said, "when you get to be my age, you'll understand."[74]

Near the end of 1982, Andropov told Gorbachev, "Mikhail, don't limit yourself to just agriculture. Try to get involved in all policy areas. Act as if there may come a time when you'll have to take on full responsibility yourself. I'm serious."[75] Gorbachev got the hint.[76] So did his Kremlin colleagues when he occasionally chaired Politburo meetings. A much broader audience noticed when Gorbachev delivered the annual Lenin's birthday speech on April 22, 1983, just as Andropov had the year before. On the other hand, according to Grachev, the remarkable fact that the youngest man in the Politburo was now second or third in the line of succession antagonized Chernenko and the old guard, and fostered "Hamlet-like doubts" in Gorbachev himself. Was he really ready to lead the country?[77]

Perhaps not yet, but he was getting there, inspired by rereading Lenin while preparing his Lenin Day oration. Rather than assign speechwriters to collect standard citations, he himself pored through Lenin's works, concentrating on late articles and letters in which Lenin recognized that the Bolshevik Revolution was running aground, called for reforms to set it right, warned against overly harsh methods that would make matters worse, even warned about Stalin himself. Of course, Gorbachev couldn't say such things in his speech, which he later admitted had little redeeming social value, but his determination to work for reform was strengthened by the fact that Lenin himself had sought to do so before his early death.[78]

On Monday, May 16, 1983, at 4 p.m., Gorbachev arrived at the Ottawa airport for a weeklong visit to Canada. The man behind the visit was the Soviet ambassador to Canada, Aleksandr Yakovlev, short, thickset, with two clumps of dark hair on either side of his bald head framing his round face. Born in 1923, Yakovlev was eight years older than Gorbachev, with longer experience in the central party apparatus. Like Gorbachev, he had been raised in the countryside, near Yaroslavl, and his family resembled Gorbachev's: a grandfather who didn't drink, smoke, or curse and served as a kind of village elder, a father who never beat his son, and an illiterate but "limitlessly, even excessively, conscientious mother." The visit to Canada and the Gorbachev-Yakovlev friendship that began there reinforced Gorbachev's sense of mission and provided him with a key ally, a man who soon became a key collaborator in Gorbachev's perestroika project.

Yakovlev was severely wounded in the war (from which he emerged with a lifelong limp) and was revolted by its horrors, including the arrest and imprisonment of Soviet soldiers whose only sin was to have been captured by the Germans. After attending the Yaroslavl Pedagogical Institute and the Higher Party School in Moscow, he worked for the Yaroslavl party committee, where, he admits, he wrote "hack" articles, but managed to develop a "happy, healthy cynicism." Next stop: in charge of education in the province, and then, just after Stalin's death in March 1953, Central Committee assignments in Moscow: instructor in the schools department (1953–1956); at the party's Academy of Social Sciences (1956–1960), where he wrote a doctoral dissertation on "the historiography of U.S. foreign policy"; section head in the Central Committee's propaganda and agitation department (1960–1965); and then first deputy chief and de facto head of that department until his exile to Canada in 1973. Yakovlev attended Khrushchev's 1956 secret speech, which sent "chills through my brain," and his exposure to liberal poets during the thaw opened up a "new and beautiful world." But Yakovlev, too, maintained a "dual consciousness," still a "slave of torturous pretense," but trying not to "lose myself in filth."[79]

While at the Academy of Social Sciences, Yakovlev concentrated on international relations. He spent the 1958–1959 academic year in the United States as an exchange student at Columbia University. That was the first year of the exchange program. The FBI assumed all Soviet students were spies (as Yakovlev's three fellow Soviets at Columbia apparently were), and suspected Americans who tried to befriend them. Yakovlev mostly kept to himself, concentrating on his research on FDR and the New Deal, attending classes on American history and politics taught by distinguished scholars Richard Hofstadter and David B. Truman, even sitting in on Alexander Dallin's course on Soviet foreign policy. The one American graduate student with whom he became friendly was Loren R. Graham, later to become a leading historian of Soviet science and technology. Once, when the two encountered each other in Butler Library stacks, Yakovlev exclaimed, "Loren, I've been reading FDR's right-wing critics. They all said that Roosevelt was a traitor to his class, that he was destroying capitalism in America. But it's obvious to me that Roosevelt was not destroying capitalism at all. He was saving capitalism when it was on its knees." At the height of perestroika, Graham asked Yakovlev if he and Gorbachev were "trying to save communism the way Roosevelt saved capitalism." Yakovlev smiled: "Yes, you are right."

At Columbia, according to Graham, Yakovlev was "an ardent defender of Communism." After returning to Moscow, he wrote angrily anti-American books containing statements like "Vampires are insatiable for blood, and [capitalist] exploiters are insatiable for money." But by the late 1960s and early 1970s he was tormented by doubts, both about the system he served and about himself for doing so. He was disgusted when his department head curried favor with Khrushchev's successors by boasting that Khrushchev had called him a "shit," and equally disgusted because the speeches he helped write for Brezhnev weren't much better than "shit" themselves.[80]

By 1972, Yakovlev was riding herd on the Soviet media. In that capacity, he defended Marxist internationalism against the right-wing Russian nationalists who were dominating journals like *October* and *Young Guard* (*Molodaya gvardiya*). The journals' Kremlin supporters arranged for Yakovlev to be dumped in Canada, which they considered a backwater compared with its mammoth southern neighbor. Only once in the ten years he spent there was Yakovlev asked by his superiors to report on Canadian farming, which, with a climate similar to the USSR's, could be productively compared with Soviet agriculture. Soviet farm delegations did arrive from time to time, but mostly they went shopping for goods that couldn't be obtained at home. For Yakovlev, Canada provided a long, close-up view of democratic capitalism and plenty of time to think about its lessons for the USSR. Canadian Prime Minister Pierre Elliott Trudeau, a great fan of Tolstoy and Dostoevsky, treated the sophisticated Soviet ambassador like a friend of his family. But by the end of the 1970s, bored by composing memos and reports about which Moscow couldn't have cared less, Yakovlev was eager for visits to Canada by enlightened Communists like himself.

Gorbachev had planned a ten-day trip to Canada. Andropov vetoed that ("To Canada? Are you out of your mind? Now's not the time to go abroad."), but accepted what turned out to be a jam-packed seven days. Although Gorbachev took a predictably hard line on foreign affairs at a meeting with Canadian parliamentarians, he struck his hosts as "charming. He was witty; people were genuinely impressed; they were witnessing the performance of a new type of Soviet politician."[81] Gorbachev called it "a circus" when Trudeau's opposition attacked the prime minister during the parliament's question period, but it wasn't long before he was allowing his own Soviet opponents to criticize him.

After an official meeting with Gorbachev, Trudeau showed up unexpectedly at a dinner Yakovlev threw for his visitor, plopped himself down next to the guest of honor, and invited him to have two more long, informal conversations. Next came a cross-country tour accompanied by the jovial, heavyset, green Stetson–wearing Canadian minister of agriculture, Eugene Whelan: an experimental farm near Ottawa; greenhouses, a vegetable-packing plant, and an automated Heinz ketchup-processing facility near Leamington; a meatpacking plant in Toronto; a winery on the Niagara peninsula; and a supermarket—to show Gorbachev that Canadian agriculture produced abundance for ordinary people. Gorbachev countered by pointing out that bread was much cheaper, as well as a whole lot tastier, in the USSR. At a 5,000-acre family-run beef and dairy ranch in Alberta, Gorbachev seemed stunned (he repeated his question three times) to learn that the rancher and his wife, along with two or three others, ran the ranch themselves, taking turns operating the combine around the clock during the harvest.[82]

The most fateful event was a private tête-à-tête with Yakovlev on Whelan's farm near Amherstburg, Ontario. The eighteen-member Soviet delegation arrived before their host at his unpretentious, split-level house across the street from the Detroit River. While they and a dozen local Canadian politicians struggled to make small talk before dinner in a low-ceilinged basement crowded with card tables and folding chairs, Gorbachev and Yakovlev strolled around a nearby field bordered by woods. It was here, Yakovlev recalled, at seven thirty on a lovely evening, with Gorbachev's guards standing a safe distance away at the edge of the forest, that the talk "suddenly broke from a conventional conversation into one that threw caution to the winds. [Gorbachev] talked about sore points back home . . . about the country's backwardness and the lack of vision in the way it approached serious political and economic problems, about dogmatism, about the need for fundamental changes. I, too, broke free from my chain and talked frankly about how primitive and shameful Soviet foreign policy seemed from Canada." Dissidents like Solzhenitsyn, whom Yakovlev had been ordered to unmask, were guilty only of thinking differently, he said. Canadian trials showed that the Soviet judiciary should be independent. "The laws should be changed first," Gorbachev replied. "They should become real laws, not weapons in the hands of individuals or the party." For the rest of the trip, Yakov-lev continues, "We talked to our hearts' content. It was as if these con-versations sketched the contours of the reforms to come in the USSR."[83]

Yakovlev's tendency to claim credit for himself later annoyed the prideful Gorbachev, whose resulting coldness alienated the supersensi-tive Yakovlev. But in 1983 they established a bond that Gorbachev soon reinforced. In July, he summoned Yakovlev back to Moscow to direct the Academy of Sciences' Institute for World Economy and International Relations. After that, according to Yakovlev, "he continually telephoned me, sometimes just to chat, more often on business." The institute sent Gorbachev memoranda that Yakovlev somewhat condescendingly char-acterizes as "educational. You could tell [Gorbachev] was preparing him-self for the future, but he carefully concealed that. People in his inner circle knew there was a taboo about talking about that."[84]

YAKOVLEV WASN'T THE ONLY one who got a startling glimpse of what Gorbachev was thinking. In early 1982, while preparing Brezhnev's Food Program, Gorbachev convened a group of academic experts: sev-eral economists and Tatyana Zaslavskaya, an economist turned sociolo-gist from the Siberian branch of the Academy of Sciences. Zaslavskaya had never met a Politburo member before; she had seen them at confer-ences, but "security was always very tight; you could never speak to any of them, and outside they were always in their great, big, armed cars." Gorbachev was "young" and "radiated energy." Compared with other agricultural officials, who were "amazingly ignorant and incompetent," Gorbachev "understood the economy and the substance of every issue." He was "candid, his manner was open and friendly," and "we could talk about everything." It was as if "he was our seventh, like-minded associ-ate." He spoke to them "as equals."

Gorbachev's easy openness emboldened his guests. They told him the Food Program consisted of "half-measures that would change nothing." When the group suggested abolishing all existing agro-industrial min-istries and replacing them with a single, new agency, Gorbachev turned to his assistant and asked, "If I were to include that suggestion in my proposal, do you think I'd still be allowed to sit in this chair?" In fact, the experts' recommendation (a version of which Gorbachev adopted once he became party leader) wasn't very radical, since it preserved top-down agricultural administration. But Zaslavskaya's diagnosis of the main source of economic stagnation was daring. As she put it later, people had "no reason to work well, do not want to work well, and do not know how to work well"—even when they were specifically trained to do so. "The quality of the people is deteriorating," Zaslavskaya added, "horrible though that may sound." In Marxist terms, which particularly appealed to Gorbachev: "The working people are alienated from the means of production and from the result of their work."

Encouraged by Gorbachev's receptivity, Zaslavskaya's institute sponsored a meeting in 1983, at which more than sixty experts prepared a summary of similar views in more general terms. The institute, directed by economist Abel Aganbegyan, another future Gorbachev adviser, wanted to publish the summary, but the censor refused: "They never said why; they never asked or answered any questions; they never spoke to authors, only to directors of institutes," Zaslavskaya later explained. Aganbegyan distributed the report as an unofficial document to be returned after the conference, but when two copies disappeared, the KGB launched a countrywide search for them. The institute itself was "turned upside down," Zaslavskaya remembered, and after the paper reached the West and was published there, the regional party committee formally reprimanded her and Aganbegyan for serious "ideological errors." Zaslavskaya broke down and wept in Aganbegyan's office. "I gave her tea and wiped her tears," Aganbegyan recalled. "What could one do? It is a terrible thing when women cry."[85]

Did Gorbachev have any allies besides Andropov at the highest levels? He first met the Tomsk province party boss, Yegor Ligachev, on the delegation to Czechoslovakia in 1969. After that they often saw each other at Central Committee meetings. Born in 1920, the white-haired, square-faced Ligachev also had relatives who suffered during the Great Terror of the 1930s: his father was expelled from the party (although later readmitted), and his wife's father was arrested on false charges and executed.[86] As a province party chieftain, Ligachev was vigorous and incorruptible, a kind of Communist Puritan. Gorbachev persuaded Andropov to summon him to Moscow as a Central Committee secretary. A fellow workaholic, Ligachev was delighted to find Gorbachev in his office late at night after other Politburo members had departed. As authoritarian as he was energetic, Ligachev later broke with Gorbachev and became for a while his foremost antagonist. But in 1983, Ligachev, too, feared that "the country was headed for social and economic disaster." After he took command of the Central Committee department in charge of party personnel on December 26, 1983, and began replacing geriatric party officials with would-be reformers, he and Gorbachev grew even closer. "Our relationship had reached the point where we could understand each other with a single word."[87] Sometimes, in fact, one spoken word was all they could allow themselves; since they assumed their offices were bugged, they communicated about sensitive subjects by exchanging written notes.[88]

Nikolai Ryzhkov, only two years older than Gorbachev, rose from a worker's family in Ukraine to direct a vast heavy machinery factory in the Urals and then serve as first deputy head of the State Planning Commission from 1979 to 1982. An engineer by training, he shared Gorbachev's sense that the system was rotten. The atmosphere in the country was "stifling," Ryzhkov recalled, "the next step would be death itself."[89] By 1983, when Andropov appointed him to head the Central Committee's new economic department, Ryzhkov had noticed Gorbachev's "vigorous and determined efforts to extend his range of interests" beyond agriculture, and also how senior leaders, jealous of their prerogatives, tried to "flick him away." Gorbachev "knew the regions and their internal economic structure . . . whereas I knew production and planning." Together they commissioned reform-minded experts (including Aganbegyan, Arbatov, Bogomolov, and Zaslavskaya) to do studies, and welcomed the conclusion that it was past time to "end the rigid centralization of economic administration" and to "rely instead on incentives—to pay well for good work." When Andropov asked the two men to work on budgetary matters, they naturally asked to scrutinize the budget itself. To which Andropov replied angrily, "Don't try to poke your noses in there. That's none of your business." Gorbachev later explained why: "It wasn't a real budget, but the devil knows what."[90]

Ryzhkov, too, would eventually break with Gorbachev, and he traces at least some of the bad blood between them back to 1984: "His self-confidence was such that it didn't let him admit that there was something he didn't know or understand." If the two men nonetheless worked together "splendidly," that was because "I accepted [Gorbachev's] rules of the game. I didn't flaunt what I knew and simply said whatever had to be said at the moment."[91] Ryzhkov, like Yakovlev, was highly sensitive and even more emotional, but his psychological assessment of Gorbachev was slightly off the mark. If Gorbachev had truly been so self-confident, he could have confessed there were some things he didn't know. If Ryzhkov is telling the truth, then Gorbachev's self-assurance was somewhat more fragile than it seemed.

Gorbachev also considered his staff aide, Boldin, to be loyal and indispensible. To reward him after three years of faithful service, Gorbachev and his wife invited Boldin into their cabin on a flight from Stavropol to Moscow in the spring of 1984, offered him a cup of tea, and informed him that "since I had lived up to their expectations, they had decided to keep me on as their assistant." Rather than being pleased, Boldin says he was quietly enraged. Because "the attempt to impose on me a three-year period of probation, followed by the magnanimous announcement that I would be allowed to continue working sixteen hours a day, seemed utterly ludicrous."[92] The scene rankled all the more because Boldin already resented the way Gorbachev treated other aides, for example, speechwriters who, after marathon work on a Gorbachev address, indicated that they wouldn't mind being thanked. According to Boldin, Gorbachev declined to do so, agreeing only to sign four copies of the speech with the laconic inscription "To Comrade so and so. With respect, M. Gorbachev."[93]

Ryzhkov and Boldin may have transmuted their later animus into recollections of these earlier episodes. The male chauvinist Boldin almost certainly felt that Raisa Gorbachev's presence during his "promotion," whether or not she actually co-announced it, detracted from its value. But there must be something to the charge that Gorbachev lorded it over some of his aides since it echoes accusations made in Stavropol.

DURING THE ANDROPOV interregnum, when Gorbachev was spreading his wings and honing his reformist views, he continued to play it safe at

Kremlin meetings. At a January 18, 1983, conference of Central Committee secretaries, he complimented Andropov ("Yuri Vladimirovich, you have raised a series of extraordinarily important questions," and "I fully support your approach."), echoed Andropov's call for greater labor "discipline," and only hinted at the need for structural reform by condemning excessive centralization.[94] On April 20, while chairing a Secretariat session, he blasted cultural officials for not closing down Ludmila Razumovskaya's *Dear Elena Sergeyevna*, just the sort of critical play he would champion several years later.[95] The Politburo had reinstated the party membership of Vyacheslav Molotov, Stalin's longtime henchman, whom Khrushchev had ousted in 1962, and on June 12, 1983, it considered readmitting two other surviving colleagues, Lazar Kaganovich and Georgy Malenkov. "If it hadn't been for Khrushchev," Ustinov sneered, "they never would have been expelled and there never would have been these outrageous actions regarding Stalin. . . . Not a single one of our enemies has inflicted so much misfortune on us as Khrushchev did [in his] policies and attitude toward Stalin." Gorbachev supported reinstating Kaganovich and Malenkov ("Yes, these are elderly people."), but he wasn't so sure about Ustinov's proposal to rename Volgograd back to Stalingrad: "Well, there are pluses and minuses to this," he commented delicately.[96]

On the night of August 31–September 1, 1983, Soviet jet fighters shot down Korean Airlines flight 007, which had blundered into Soviet airspace en route from Alaska to Seoul. The death of 269 innocent people horrified the world and sharply intensified the new cold war. According to Soviet ambassador to Washington Dobrynin, Andropov privately raged at the "gross blunder" of his "blockheads of generals," but not at a Kremlin meeting on September 2. Gorbachev probably shared Andropov's disgust, but all he said at the Kremlin session was, "The plane remained over our territory for a long time. If it strayed off course, the Americans could have informed us, but they didn't."[97]

Meanwhile, Andropov's health had worsened. As early as February 1983, his kidneys ceased functioning on their own. By summer, he was spending most of his time in bed at his dacha. His face had turned pale and his voice hoarse; and instead of getting up to greet visitors to his office, he merely extended his hand from his seat. As a result of undergoing dialysis treatment twice a week, the IV tubes remained on his arms, covered by bandages from the wrist up. The last Politburo session he attended was on September 1.[98] Visiting him in the hospital in December, Gorbachev saw a "totally different person." He was "puffy-faced and haggard." His skin was "gray-green, even blue-green." His eyes were "dim; he barely looked up. . . . I exerted every effort to look away, to somehow disguise my shock."[99] According to Andropov aide Arkady Volsky, Andropov tried to name Gorbachev his successor from his hospital bed. Andropov was too sick to address the Central Committee at the end of December, but when Volsky picked up Andropov's final text at the hospital, he found that his boss had scribbled the following instruction—that "during my forced absence from the Politburo Mikhail Sergeyevich Gorbachev be charged with chairing its sessions." This was a clear signal—so clear that Chernenko and his backers, particularly Prime Minister Tikhonov, arranged to excise it from the speech read to the plenum. Volsky was about to telephone Andropov when a conservative Central Committee official, Klavdy Bogolyubov, warned him, "If so, that will be the last phone call you ever make." Andropov found out anyway and cursed Volsky up and down, but was too weak to do anything about it. Volsky wasn't surprised at the outcome, having previously overheard Ustinov whisper to Tikhonov, "Kostya [Chernenko] is an easier person to deal with than Misha [Gorbachev]."[100]

Andropov died on February 9, 1984, after a mere fifteen months in office. His death was "hard on me," Gorbachev recalled. "There wasn't a single person in the leadership to whom I was so closely attached." Several years later, when Raisa Gorbachev was visiting Pamela Harriman in Washington, she noticed a photo of Andropov with Averell Harriman. "We owe everything to him [Andropov]," she said.[101] Gorbachev could get quite sentimental about his mentor-not-quite-friend. He often recalled their times together in the North Caucasus foothills: "A star-speckled sky, a blazing campfire, and Yuri Andropov gazing at the flames in a moment of dreamy revelation, a tape recorder at his side playing an irreverent song by Yuri Vizbor that Andropov particularly liked: '*Who needs it? Nobody needs it. / Who cares? Nobody cares.*'"

Perhaps Andropov himself didn't care. Or perhaps, Gorbachev concluded, Andropov, with his Stalinist training and his long stint in the

KGB, didn't dare "embark on radical change, any more than Khrush-chev." Perhaps "fate ordained" that he would die before people became "disillusioned with him." Gorbachev, for his part, cared and would dare.[102]

CHERNENKO SUCCEEDED ANDROPOV. According to Volsky, who told Gorbachev about Andropov's abortive attempt to advance his candidacy, Gorbachev took it philosophically. The fact that Chernenko took over, writes Grachev, "only played into [Gorbachev's] hands." As Gorbachev put it to Grachev, again referring to himself in the third person, "After Chernenko's death, Gorbachev's election [as general secretary] became inevitable."[103]

It wasn't that easy, as Gorbachev well knew. "I'm not a simpleton," he said in a 2007 interview. "I could see what was happening, I ana-lyzed everything."[104] At Andropov's funeral, Gorbachev's wife saw "some openly happy faces" among the "mourners."[105] After Chernenko's elec-tion, he gallantly proposed that Gorbachev chair the Secretariat, but Prime Minister Tikhonov objected: "Gorbachev's job is agriculture. If he [becomes second secretary] that might bias the work of the Secretariat in that direction." Ustinov reminded Tikhonov that Gorbachev had pre-viously chaired the Secretariat. But the real issue, according to Vadim Medvedev, who was present, was that Tikhonov and others didn't want Gorbachev to dominate the weakened Chernenko, or potentially to suc-ceed him. Moscow party boss Grishin suggested tabling the motion, equivalent to killing it. Foreign Minister Gromyko agreed. Gorbachev sat silently. He continued to the chair the Secretariat, but without a formal mandate to do so.[106]

Chernenko was barely able to function. As observed by British For-eign Secretary Sir Geoffrey Howe's interpreter, K. A. ("Tony") Bishop, at a meeting on July 3, 1984, Chernenko exhibited "shortness of breath" and had a "ten-second coughing fit." "An air of abstraction and bewil-derment" clung to him, and his "reading of his prepared text was disas-trously bad," not to mention "the high-speed gabble, the stumblings, the breaking of sentences off in mid-phrase in order to breathe," as well as "the apparent lack of conviction and even, at times, of comprehension."[107] But the Soviet leader's illness led to humiliations for Gorbachev. Chernenko was so sick that sometimes he had to be carried into the Politburo's meeting room before his colleagues were invited in. When he was too ill even for that, Gorbachev was asked to chair the sessions, but only at the very last minute.[108] "Every Thursday morning," Ryzhkov recalled, Gorbachev "would sit in his office like a little orphan . . . nervously awaiting a telephone call from the sick Chernenko: Would he come to the Politburo himself, or would he ask Gorbachev to stand in for him again?"[109] According to Gorbachev, Tikhonov tried and failed to turn Ligachev and another secretary, Vladimir Dolgikh, against him, the latter by hinting that Dolgikh would someday make a fine prime minister.[110] *Pravda* didn't mention Gorbachev's speech at the February 13, 1984, Central Committee plenum that anointed Chernenko. A plenum on science and technology, which Gorbachev and Ryzhkov were preparing, was delayed. A similar fate loomed for a conference on ideology at which Gorbachev was to be the main speaker.[111]

Gorbachev later claimed that he still felt "confident," that he followed his "long-standing principle: life will sort everything out."[112] But his frustration could be seen in the way he treated bumbling province party bosses at a meeting in August 1984. "He really gave them a hard time," Chernyaev recorded in his diary. "He knows the problem inside out, better than they do. The smallest mistake, the slightest indication of incompetence or an attempt to mislead, provoked his fury. And then he made the speaker look really stupid. It was especially difficult for them because Gorbachev can't stand people reading from their notes something they should know like their ABCs."[113] Gorbachev was as demanding of himself as he was of others. By now he was in a hurry to expand his support in the Kremlin and outside it. In 1984 Vitaly Vorotnikov was prime minister of the Russian Republic and a full Politburo member. Gorbachev cultivated him, Vorotnikov recalls, by inviting "confidential conversations as you would with a real comrade" conveying the impression of "candor, a wish to get your advice, to learn your opinion." Vorotnikov was "delighted with Gorbachev's ability to befriend people, to win them over with his charm." Vorotnikov, too, would later turn against him, at which point he concluded that all Gorbachev had offered was "the appearance of comradeship and friendship" to "secure [my] support," that he had thrown out "hints and half-hints" only to declare later, "Well, it seems you misunderstood me."[114] If so, how was Gorbachev's conduct different from that of most politicians?

Gorbachev could be more direct. His boldest move in 1984 was to insist that the ideological conference be held and to use it to project the image of a dynamic, young leader with fresh, new ideas. Protocol required that the Central Committee's propaganda department draft his speech, but Gorbachev knew, recalled Yakovlev, that they would produce "nothing sensible." So Gorbachev instructed his own team—Yakovlev, Vadim Medvedev, and others—to prepare a parallel text that would address such hot topics as "property, the character of production relations in our society, the role of interests, social justice, the relationship between money and goods, etc."[115] To post-Soviet ears these don't sound so controversial. But Gorbachev was implying that state property might not be the only approved kind, that diverse social interests should be recognized rather than repressed, that social injustice existed under socialism, even that a market of some sort wasn't beyond the pale. None of this could be said straight out. Even if it could, Gorbachev and his speechwriters hadn't clarified in their own minds what they believed. "Our task," Yakovlev remembered, "was beyond our strength. Gorbachev wanted to say something new, but just what and how, he himself didn't know. We didn't know either. It was as if we were blind men trying to trade a mirror to deaf people in exchange for a balalaika."

Despite Gorbachev's cautious locutions, his draft speech alarmed party hard-liners. When they suggested changes, Yakovlev recalls, Gorbachev "boiled over." The propaganda department wanted to make him "look like a fool." When Chernenko asked Gorbachev to call off the conference the day before it was to convene, Gorbachev turned red in the face and exploded that the conference "must not be postponed," that doing so would only fuel "false rumors," that Chernenko's criticisms of the speech were "simply far-fetched."[116]

Chernenko backed off. The conference was held. Gorbachev's speech reads like a state-of-the-union address, presented with the authority of an heir apparent, touching on ideas that would be become his trademarks after 1985, even using, although without developing them, terms like "perestroika" and "glasnost."[117] According to Yakovlev, some of

the denser ideologues in the hall didn't understand what he was driving at, while others pretended they didn't.[118] The functionary whose job
was to collect notes and questions from the hall and pass them to the
speaker recalled how different Gorbachev seemed from previous leaders: his speech was "very literate"; he improvised; he actually smiled; the
audience neither "slept or nor read newspapers."[119] *Kommunist*, the party's ideological journal, did not publish Gorbachev's speech. Yakovlev,
known to be close to him, wasn't allowed into the hall until the second
day of the conference. "You see how far they'll go!" Gorbachev growled
to Yakovlev. "What shits!"[120]

"There's a big game going on," Gorbachev told Yakovlev. In that game,
he now made two moves involving foreign affairs. Foreign policy wasn't
his strong suit, but he wanted to make it one. According to Chernyaev,
Gorbachev wanted "to associate with new people who were capable of
independent thinking, he really wanted to know what was going on in
the world."[121] By traveling to Italy and Great Britain, he could also prove
that he was a match for foreign leaders.

The occasion for the Italian trip was the June funeral of Communist party leader Enrico Berlinguer. The Italian Communists, founding fathers of "Eurocommunism," were fierce critics of Soviet actions,
ranging from domestic repression to the invasions of Czechoslovakia
and Afghanistan and the December 1980 declaration of martial law in
Poland. Initially, the Politburo didn't want to send Gorbachev, Chernyaev
says, because of his "democratic leanings," but decided to do so because
he "could speak like a normal human being—non-confrontationally."
He prepared for the trip by rereading works he had previously read in
Stavropol—by the late Italian Communist leader Palmiro Togliatti,
and by the Marxist philosopher Antonio Gramsci. Gorbachev admitted
to Berlinguer's successor, Alessandro Natta, that Italian Communists
"had good reason to criticize us." Upon returning to Moscow, he told the
Politburo, "We can't disregard a party like that. We have to treat it with
respect."[122] Not only did he do so; he was overwhelmed by what he saw
in Rome—hundreds of thousands of ordinary citizens paying tribute to
a Communist leader, leaders of all political parties attending the funeral,
President Sandro Pertini bowing his head before the coffin. Gorbachev
knew all too well that "this way of thinking and political culture was

not characteristic of us."[123] Soon he would try to bring this vision to life in the USSR—of a genuinely popular Communist party leading a willing people in a crusade to reform Communism—only to discover that the difference between Italian and Soviet political culture made all the difference in the world.

Gorbachev and his wife flew to London on December 15, 1984. With the new cold war on, Prime Minister Margaret Thatcher was reaching out to Communist leaders. She was "unusually curious intellectually," recalls Rodric Braithwaite, who four years later would become British ambassador to the USSR, and "she made a particular study of the Soviet Union, calling officials to seminars to discuss issues of foreign and defense policy, interviewing many dissidents, and reading a great deal."[124] Her decision to invite Gorbachev stemmed partly from a session on the Soviet Union she had convened at Chequers, her country retreat, fifteen months before. "This is NOT the way I want it," she tartly wrote on a list of seminar participants proposed by the Foreign Office. "I am not interested in gathering every junior minister . . . who has ever dealt with the subject. . . . I want also some people who have really studied Russia—the Russian mind—and who have had some experience of living there. More than half the people on the list know less than I do."[125] At the seminar, she focused on scholars such as Oxford don Archie Brown, who suggested that "a movement for democratizing change [words underlined by Mrs. Thatcher on her copy of Brown's paper] can come from within a ruling Communist party as well as through societal pressure." Brown knew Zdeněk Mlynář (by now living in Vienna), who in June 1979 described Gorbachev to him as "open-minded, intelligent and anti-Stalinist." Brown didn't cite Mlynář, but characterized Gorbachev at Chequers as not only a contender for Kremlin power but also "the best-educated" Politburo member and "probably the most open-minded." At this point, Thatcher turned to Foreign Secretary Geoffrey Howe and said, "Should we not invite Mr. Gorbachev to Britain?"[126]

In April 1984, Gorbachev had been appointed chairman of the Foreign Affairs Committee of the Soviet legislature, an honorific post that traditionally went to the party's second secretary. That gave the House of Commons Foreign Affairs Committee an excuse to propose that Gorbachev lead a Soviet "parliamentary" delegation to London, after which the British ambassador to Moscow made clear that "if Gorbachev comes he will be received at the highest political level (i.e., by the Prime Minister)" for discussion of "a wide range of questions" as a step toward "a broad dialogue with the Soviet Union."[127]

Gorbachev hesitated. He seemed concerned, says Chernyaev, whom he consulted on British politics, not to rile Kremlin colleagues "who didn't approve of his international exposure." But Gorbachev also seemed unsure of himself. Meeting in September 1984 with a British Communist party delegation visiting Moscow, he handled the meeting "intelligently, openly, with good humor," Chernyaev recalls, "nothing like the old [Boris] Ponomarev or Suslov style." But a couple of days later he phoned Chernyaev to ask, "How did it go?" Quickly, however, Gorbachev regained his confidence. By going to London, he told Chernyaev, "we'll erode the monopoly," obviously referring to Gromyko's hammerlock on foreign policy, although he didn't mention him by name. "That means he has big plans," Chernyaev wrote in his diary. "God help him!"[128]

Another reason for the trip was to signal Washington that Gorbachev was interested in improving Soviet-American relations. For that, Thatcher, an arch-conservative and close to President Ronald Reagan, was the perfect intermediary.[129] Gorbachev brought with him high-powered experts who were already his unofficial advisers (Yakovlev, physicist Yevgeny Velikhov, diplomat Anatoly Kovalev, and deputy chief of the Soviet General Staff General Nikolai Chervov), as well as Raisa Gorbachev—glamorous, educated, so different from the wives of previous leaders who, with the exception of Nina Khrushchev and Viktoria Brezhnev, never accompanied their husbands on foreign trips. According to Martin Nicholson, the British Foreign Office official who interpreted for Raisa, "she wanted all of us to know that she wasn't just another dumpy, head-scarved wife." When a guide pointed out Russia on an ancient globe in a library, Mrs. Gorbachev snapped, "I know where my own country is."[130]

The eight-day itinerary included a speech in the British Parliament on December 18, meetings with government, party, and business leaders, visits to factories, plus a tour of the British Museum. The centerpiece was a day at Chequers, where Mrs. Thatcher, her husband, Denis, and cabinet ministers and aides awaited the Gorbachevs in the Great Hall on

Sunday morning, December 16. Gorbachev "had a broad grin" when he walked in at 12:25 p.m., recalled Thatcher's personal secretary, Charles Powell. "He bounced on the balls of his feet."[131] Mrs. Gorbachev, Thatcher remembered, "was dressed in a smart, western-style outfit, a well-tailored grey suit with a white stripe—just the sort I could have worn myself."[132] "They came off as an extraordinary, self-confident couple," Powell said, "who had no difficulty inserting themselves promptly into the very different ambiance of a senior Western leader."

Mikhail and Raisa Gorbachev with British Prime Minister Margaret Thatcher, at her country retreat, Chequers, December 16, 1984.

After cocktails, lunch commenced in the sixteenth-century dining room. According to Powell, the two leaders "talked throughout the whole lunch. Neither of them ate very much because they were so busy." Neither seemed to be "a particularly good listener, but they certainly loved talking." Actually, the conversation was quite polemical. According to the British interpreter, Tony Bishop, Mrs. Thatcher "deliberately and breathtakingly . . . set about serially cross-examining [Gorbachev] about the inferiority of the Soviet centralized command system and the merits of free enterprise and competition." Gorbachev replied that if Mrs. Thatcher came and took a look for herself, she would see that the Soviet people lived "joyfully." If so, she countered, why was the Soviet government afraid to let them leave the country "as easily as they could leave Britain?" "They were clearly intrigued with each other from the very first moment," Powell noted. "I think they both thought, 'This is not quite what I expected.'" "In a sense," Thatcher later recalled, her "argument" with Gorbachev "has continued ever since and is taken up whenever we meet. I never tire of it."

After lunch the leaders retired to a drawing room, while Mrs. Gorbachev went upstairs with Denis Thatcher to examine a collection of ancient books and letters, including Napoleon's from exile. In the talks that stretched on for hours, Gorbachev was attended by Yakovlev and Leonid Zamyatin, chief of the Central Committee's international information department, and Thatcher by Foreign Secretary Howe and Powell, plus interpreters. But "nobody spoke, except the principals," recalled Powell. Unlike previous Soviet leaders, whose aides whispered in their ears and passed them papers, Gorbachev consulted only what he had scribbled in green ink in a little notebook he kept in his pocket. His reference to Chernenko was respectful but clearly pro forma. He stunned his hosts by quoting Victorian British statesman Lord Palmerston's famous dictum, clearly at odds with official Soviet ideology, that, in Mrs. Thatcher's words, Britain had "no eternal friends or eternal enemies, but only eternal interests." With what Thatcher describes as a "touch of theater," he pulled out a full-page diagram from the *New York Times*, which showed that the terrible destruction that nuclear weapons could wreak far exceeded that of all of World War II.[133]

In the drawing room after lunch, sitting in front of a fire to which the prime minister herself would occasionally add a new log, Thatcher focused on Gorbachev's style: "He smiled, laughed, used his hands for emphasis, modulated his voice, followed an argument through, and was a sharp debater. He did not seem in the least uneasy." She found herself "liking him."[134]

Meanwhile, upstairs, Mrs. Gorbachev pulled volume after volume down from the shelves and commented on them at length. "She displayed an extraordinary knowledge of British history and philosophy," then British ambassador to Moscow Bryan Cartledge remembered. "When she came across a portrait of David Hume, she knew all about him."[135] Mrs. Thatcher remembered "how erudite she was with her degree in philosophy." Raisa's "sound knowledge and sharp comments" stunned Mr. Thatcher, his wife continued.[136] But Powell had a rather different impression: "Poor old Denis was longing to get out and practice his golf on the lawn. Instead he was stuck with this quite opinionated, highly intelligent, slightly didactic lady." As were several of Mrs. Thatcher's government ministers during other formal talks in which they did not participate. "To their utter surprise," recalled Raisa's proud husband, "she engaged them in a conversation about English literature and philosophy, which had always been one of her major interests."[137] Geoffrey Howe's wife, Elspeth, assigned to keep Mrs. Gorbachev company at points of interest like Hampton Court, was struck by Raisa's determination to show off what she knew. But, Howe recalled, "My wife is a very extroverted, campaigning feminist. That makes her sound unattractive, but she certainly isn't. She enthuses about things and responded to finding Raisa the same kind, I think."[138]

Throughout Gorbachev's visit he was accompanied by British interpreter Bishop, whose impressions of Gorbachev proved particularly revealing: Gorbachev "proved not just equal to but much bigger than his task. . . . There was about his movements and his utterances an unaffected, self-assured and un-self-conscious air of competence and confidence. One was conscious of the great resources of energy in him, well-harnessed." He "never flagged or faltered. He spoke as a rule in generally short and clear sentences." He "would listen, immobile, with concentration and great attentiveness." He had a knack of answering questions "in a disarmingly straightforward, unpolemical manner and of finding apt, often humorous, turns of phrase to register his point or defuse unwanted tension." A "roguish twinkle was never far from his eye." While "not an intellectual," he had a "very good memory and a disciplined head," and was "quick on the uptake," much "quicker than his more 'intellectual' wife" to get the point of the unfamiliar plot of Mozart's *Così Fan Tutte* and to "appreciate the spirit and humor of the production."

Whether addressing British or Soviets, he seemed extraordinarily "natural." But he could be tough, even brutal. When Labour party leader Neil Kinnock privately pressed him on human rights, particularly on the case of dissident Natan Sharansky, who had then been in a Soviet prison for seven years, Gorbachev responded with a volley of obscenities and threats against "turds" and spies like Sharansky. Prison was "where he would stay," Gorbachev warned (although he himself would release Sharansky as part of a larger exchange of detainees in 1986), and Britain would "get it right in the teeth" in a "merciless" denunciation of its own human rights violations if that was the game it wanted to play.[139]

At the end of the visit, Mrs. Thatcher famously declared, "I like Mr. Gorbachev. We can do business together," and soon flew off to Washington to tell this to Reagan in person. British and Western media covered the Gorbachevs' visit in lavish detail, calling them "the new Gucci comrades" and wrongly reporting that Mrs. Gorbachev used an American Express card to make expensive purchases in posh stores. Actually, she paid "in cash" provided by a Soviet embassy aide for jeweled drop earrings costing several hundred pounds that she bought at Mappion and Webb.[140] As for the Soviet press, whose editors were aware that some Kremlin colleagues were jealous of the attention Gorbachev was getting, it was less fulsome. Soviet ambassador to Washington Dobrynin sent two long telegrams to Moscow reporting on American reactions to the Gorbachevs' British success. Ordinarily, such information would have been circulated among Politburo members, but not this time. When Gromyko saw Dobrynin, he chided him, "You're a wise, veteran diplomat with vast experience, yet you sent off two telegrams about the visit of a parliamentary delegation of less than overwhelming significance?"[141]

WHILE THE GORBACHEVS were in London on December 20, Ustinov died in Moscow. Gorbachev cut short his trip and rushed home. During the next two and half months, Chernenko's health crumbled. Gorbachev kept calling the main Kremlin doctor to find out how Chernenko was doing. Given what he knew about the tensions between Chernenko and Gorbachev, Dr. Chazov was somewhat amazed that Gorbachev kept pressing him to bend every effort to keep Chernenko alive.[142] The Stalin-

**Mikhail and Raisa Gorbachev flying back to Moscow from London,
December 21, 1984.**

ist practice of hastening the death of political enemies was long gone.
But skirmishing in a milder form continued. Gorbachev's opponents in
the Politburo, backed by Chernenko aides, seemingly settled on Moscow
party chief Grishin as their candidate to succeed Chernenko—a long
shot, given his record. Seventy years old and with an utterly undistinguished career, Grishin would mean more of the same—witness the way
he tried to wrap himself in Chernenko's threadbare mantle. "Elections"
to the Russian Republic's Supreme Soviet were scheduled for February
25, 1985. Since Chernenko was too sick to read a trite speech to a ritual
gathering of voters in his Moscow district, Grishin read it for him. Listening with other Politburo members at a long table on the stage behind the
podium, Gorbachev felt like a "participant in a farce." Grishin was rat-
tling on "in his tedious monotone, trying to combine pathos, uplift and
inspiration. It was surreal." Grishin's next two moves were even more
pathetic. On election day, Chernenko aides disguised his hospital room
as a voting place, lifted him from bed, dressed him in a business suit,
and propped him up as he voted in front of television cameras. Four days
later the same room became Chernenko's "office," where he was con-

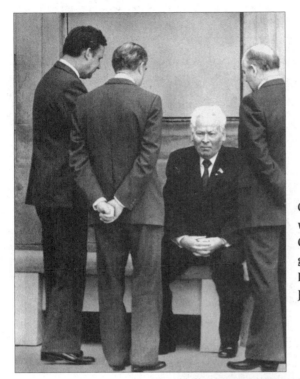

Gorbachev (far right) with gravely ill Soviet Communist party general secretary Konstantin Chernenko, January 1985.

Gorbachev voting in elections for the RSFSR Supreme Soviet and local soviets, with granddaughter Ksenia, February 24, 1985.

gratulated by Grishin and a couple of other party stalwarts. Somehow Chernenko managed to deliver a short speech. "To this very day," says Gorbachev, "I can still see his stooped figure, his hands trembling, his voice cracked . . . the pages of his text falling from his hands. He himself began to fall and was caught by Dr. Chazov, who had categorically opposed the whole thing but was overruled by Chernenko himself at the insistence of his aides and of Grishin."[143]

On March 7, 1985, Chernenko reportedly asked Gromyko, "Don't you think it's time for me to retire?" To which the unflappable Gromyko replied, "No need to hurry events, Konstantin Ustinovich."[144] Three days later, Chernenko died.

CHAPTER 6

—

WHAT IS
TO BE DONE?
1985–1986[1]

MARCH 10, 1985, WAS A SUNDAY, but Gorbachev didn't return home from work until midevening. Shortly after that, Dr. Chazov called him (as the number two man in the Kremlin) to report that Chernenko had died at 7:20 p.m. Chazov had also informed KGB chief Viktor Chebrikov. Gorbachev contacted two senior colleagues, Prime Minister Tikhonov and Foreign Minister Gromyko, as well as Klavdy Bogolyubov, head of the Central Committee's general department, and called an emergency meeting of the Politburo for ten o'clock that night.[2]

Gorbachev was sure several Politburo colleagues hoped to succeed Chernenko. Besides Grishin (age seventy-one) and Grigory Romanov (sixty-two), he thought the eighty-year-old Tikhonov probably did, too, and that the "hugely vain" Gromyko, although seventy-six, suffered from "an irrepressible desire for power."[3] According to Gromyko's deputy at the Foreign Ministry, Georgy Kornienko, his boss didn't consider Gorbachev a "serious" statesman, and had therefore joined with Grishin and Tikhonov to try to keep him from chairing Politburo meetings during Chernenko's illness.[4] Later, in 1989, by which time Gorbachev's ally Yegor Ligachev had turned against him, Ligachev would claim that the choice of Gorbachev to succeed Chernenko had been hotly contested.[5] In fact, however, the succession could not have gone more smoothly; all the other contenders not only fell in line behind Gorbachev but fawned over the new leader who would now have their fate in his hands.

The Politburo's meeting room was on the third floor of the old tsarist Senate Building, the yellow-walled triangular structure just inside the Kremlin wall from the Lenin Mausoleum in Red Square. A door at one end of the chamber led to the Walnut Room (so called because of its walnut paneling and furniture, including a large round table), which in turn opened into the general secretary's office. Full members of the Politburo traditionally gathered in the Walnut Room to compare notes prior to formal sessions next door. At the other end of the meeting room was the Politburo's official reception area, known to its members as the "dressing room" because candidate members and Central Committee secretaries gathered there, waiting for their senior colleagues, led by the general secretary, to arrive. At that point, the two groups would greet each other, each man shaking hands with every other, as Nikolai Ryzhkov remembered it, "like two soccer teams before a game."[6]

Gorbachev convened the meeting on March 10, but demonstratively did not seat himself in the chairman's place. Three full Politburo members were absent. One of them, Ukrainian party boss Vladimir Shcherbitsky, may also have been a contender, but he was stuck in Los Angeles with a Soviet "parliamentary" delegation; he set out for home immediately but did not get back until Chernenko's successor had been chosen. Kazakhstan party leader Dinmukhamed Kunayev arrived from Alma-Ata on March 11, as did Russian Republic Prime Minister Vitaly Vorotnikov, who had been in Yugoslavia. Gorbachev briefed his senior colleagues on Chernenko's death; many of them learned for the first time details of his illness (emphysema, aggravated by pleurisy and pneumonia, and heart failure), previously vouchsafed only to the inner circle.[7] When their junior colleagues joined them, Gorbachev repeated the sad news. All rose and stood silently. Now it was necessary to summon Central Committee members to Moscow to choose the new party leader: Ligachev, Bogolyubov, and Defense Minister Marshal Sergei Sokolov would make the necessary arrangements. The next order of business was to appoint a funeral commission. In the past, its chairman had always been named the new general secretary. A long silence followed.[8] It was Moscow party leader Grishin who said, "Why should we delay?

Everything is clear. Let Mikhail Sergeyevich do it." Thus did Grishin concede defeat in a struggle he had hardly begun to wage.[9]

So did Gromyko. Gromyko's reservations about Gorbachev, coming
from a Kremlin titan who had been a member of Andropov's inner circle,
made it crucial for Gorbachev to win him over. Fortunately, Gromyko's
health was declining—to the point, recalled Kornienko, that he fainted
several times at meetings of the Politburo, at the Foreign Ministry, even
at the United Nations. For that reason, he had given up the dream of
becoming party leader and had been angling since Brezhnev's death to
become titular head of state, i.e., chairman of the USSR's rubber-stamp
legislature, the Supreme Soviet. Andropov didn't grant Gromyko that
status, nor did Chernenko, probably because Defense Minister Ustinov
had also aspired to it. That meant that Gromyko had a special stake in
cultivating Gorbachev.

Gorbachev encouraged Yakovlev to explore a deal with Gromyko.
Even before Chernenko died, Yevgeny Primakov, then director of the
Academy of Sciences Institute of Oriental Studies and later to become a
trusted Gorbachev adviser, approached Gromyko's son, Anatoly, director
of the Institute of African Studies, and not so delicately asked whether
his father wanted to be general secretary. The senior Gromyko confessed
to his son he was too old and ill. His first choice for party leader was
actually the tough Azerbaijani party boss, Geidar Aliev, but, he said,
"One Stalin [who, like Aliev, was from the Caucasus] was enough." Gromyko thought Gorbachev had "too little experience," but he was ready
to nominate him as the next leader when the time came. Anatoly Gromyko conveyed that to Yakovlev, adding as tactfully as he could that his
father wouldn't mind being head of state. Gorbachev's response, delivered through Yakovlev, was cautious but clear: "I've always been pleased
to work with Andrei Andreyevich, and I will gladly do so in the future
in whatever positions he and I occupy. Tell him also that I know how to
keep my promises."[10]

On the evening of March 10, Gorbachev wanted to talk to Gromyko
before the Politburo convened. He reached him by phone, told him
Chernenko had died, and arranged to meet him thirty minutes before
the Politburo session. "I think we need to unite our efforts," he told Gromyko. Gromyko said he agreed. "So it's a deal," Gorbachev said.[11]

After Grishin's concession, Gorbachev cut off further discussion of who the new leader would be. He suggested that the Politburo not hurry, that it schedule a Central Committee plenum for five o'clock the next day, with a Politburo meeting to precede it at two. "That way everyone would have all night and half of the next day to think it over and weigh everything."[12] That was a bold move. If there were still doubters about his candidacy, it would give them time to organize. To make sure that didn't happen, Gorbachev and his aides worked feverishly throughout most of the night. He remained in the Kremlin after his Politburo colleagues went home. Anatoly Lukyanov, Central Committee official and Gorbachev's fellow Moscow University alumnus, labored nonstop (pausing in the morning only to shave) on an acceptance speech for delivery at the Central Committee plenum. Other pro-Gorbachev Central Committee officials reported for duty during the night, as did Gorbachev's aide Boldin, and Aleksandr Yakovlev, early the next morning.[13] Ligachev caucused with regional party secretaries as they arrived from around the country. Since he and Gorbachev had appointed most of them in the last three years (replacing veteran Brezhnevites), Ligachev didn't need to do much convincing. Nor did Ryzhkov, who lobbied high government officials who were also members of the Central Committee. They were already convinced that, as one of them told Ryzhkov, "twice was enough. We won't support another old guy."[14]

All these preparations raise questions about a conversation Gorbachev had with his wife when he returned to their villa outside Moscow at about four in the morning. She was waiting up for him. As usual, they began walking the garden paths surrounding the house. Snow still lay on the ground. "There was something oppressive in the late night air," Raisa remembered. "Mikhail Sergeyevich was very tired. At first he remained silent." Then he told her of the next day's Central Committee session at which "the question may arise of my taking over the leadership." This, she recalled, "was completely unexpected news for me. It was . . . a shock." It was also, she insists, "a surprise for my husband. We had never previously discussed this subject together." But by the end of their conversation, he told his wife, "I worked so many years in Stavropol. This is my seventh year in Moscow. I came to Moscow hoping and believing that I would be able do something, but so far I haven't accomplished much. It's impossible to achieve anything substantial, the things the country is waiting for. It's like coming up against a wall. So if I really want to change anything, I have to accept the position—assuming, of course, they offer it to me. We just can't go on living like this."[15]

Some of this—a lot, in fact—seems odd. Had Gorbachev never discussed the possibility of becoming Soviet leader with his wife, with whom he discussed everything? If not, as he insisted in an interview, if he hadn't previously told her that Andropov had encouraged him to prepare for just that eventuality, was that because she would fear he wouldn't make it to the very top—or that he would? Indeed, he admitted in a later interview, she was not keen on the idea at all. "Do we really need this?" she asked.[16] "I don't even know if that's a good or bad thing," she said.[17]

Five years later, Gorbachev confided to a reunion of his Moscow University classmates that at first he had been "against" taking the job because he "still wasn't ready."[18] But if so, why was he wheeling and dealing so aggressively to get the job? His harshest critics contend Gorbachev's self-proclaimed modesty concealed a lust for power. Not exactly. True, he wanted the top spot and had been maneuvering to get it. But he didn't want power for its own sake; if power had been his goal, he often insisted in later years, he would have presided happily ever after over the status quo, as Brezhnev had. He wanted to change the country, but was the country ready to be changed? Gorbachev insists that up to the moment the Politburo met at 2 p.m. on March 11, he refused to commit himself to take the top job, even to his primary backers Ligachev and Ryzhkov. He wanted "everything to be clear." Given the terrible condition of the country, the need for a wholesale change of personnel, the need, in short, "to go very far," he had to know that more than "fifty percent plus one" would support him. If there had been any resistance at all in the Politburo, "I would have withdrawn my candidacy."[19]

There was no resistance. In fact, Gorbachev told Vorotnikov early on March 11 that several Politburo members had just called to say they supported him. "What about you?" Gorbachev asked. "Of course," Vorotnikov replied. Gromyko kept his word. In fact, he spoke first when the Politburo assembled: Gorbachev possessed "boundless creative energy plus a determination to do more and to do it better." He "never gives priority to personal interests. He always holds the interests of the party, the interests of society, the interests of the people above all." Gorbachev has "great experience," "knowledge," and "stamina." "Without doubt we will not be mistaken if we elect him General Secretary." Tikhonov seconded the motion: You can "communicate with [Gorbachev], one can discuss issues with him, discuss them at the highest level." Grishin confirmed his concession: "We do not, we cannot, nominate anyone but M. S. Gorbachev to the post of General Secretary." Other Politburo members competed to praise him. Mikhail Solomentsev (chairman of the party control commission): "Boundless energy," "broad perspective," "spirit of innovation," "demanding character" but "very tactful." Aliev: "Humble, modest and approachable." Romanov: "Erudite." Vorotnikov: "Knows how to listen," "wants to help," but "not just a kind leader," "knows how to be demanding." Boris Ponomarev (veteran ideologue, Central Committee secretary and head of its international department, and Politburo candidate member): "Deep understanding of Marxist-Leninist theory." KGB chief Chebrikov, speaking for the KGB, whose voice, he insisted, "is the voice of our people": Gorbachev was "sociable," "knows how to listen to others," "great ability to work and great erudition." Vladimir Dolgikh (Central Committee secretary): "Sincere, courageous, and demanding." Shevardnadze: "Humble, modest, and responsible." Ligachev: "Intellectual and physical power," "great passion in his work." Ryzhkov: "Has been growing as a political figure before our eyes," "always tries to move forward rather than stopping at what has been achieved." Konstantin Rusakov (Central Committee secretary): "This is a man with a capital M."

There was no dissent. Then Gorbachev spoke. What was most important was that the Politburo was united. He had listened to its members "with a feeling of great excitement and anxiety." He would be unable to lead, he said, without their support. Soviet society needed more "dynamism," but "we should not change our policy. It is the right, correct, genuinely Leninist policy. We should pick up the tempo, move forward, identify shortcomings and overcome them, and behold the sight of our bright future even more clearly. I assure you that I will do everything to live up to the great trust of the party and your trust, comrades."[20]

The Central Committee convened at five o'clock. Long before then, its members arrived and were milling around the beautiful marble lobby, gobbling down free food from overloaded buffet tables, whispering anxiously about what might or might not happen next. Most hoped Gorbachev, not another aged contender, would be presented to them as the Politburo's choice. Bells rang to mark the start of the session. Members took their seats. Lukyanov had to walk in front of the assembled titans to get to his desk near the stage. "When I entered," he recalled, "I felt the hall go silent as one man. They all knew where I worked; they knew I knew who was going to be nominated. The death-like silence of everyone watching me was terrifying."[21]

On the way up in the elevator, Central Committee secretary Dolgikh teasingly inquired whether Gorbachev had prepared his "speech from the throne." Gorbachev laughed and replied that aides had done so "just in case."[22] At last, the door on the left of the stage opened. In walked Gorbachev, his eyes modestly downcast, followed by other members of the leadership in order of seniority. Central Committee members stood. Gorbachev walked to the center of the presidium table, stood silently for a few moments, and then pronounced the requisite tribute to Chernenko, "a true Leninist, an outstanding leader of the Communist Party and the Soviet state, a man with a sensitive soul and vast organizational talent."[23] But "there wasn't a drop of sadness or distress in the air," recalled Chernyaev, "as if the audience was thinking, 'You suffered, you poor bastard for accidently ending up in a job you didn't deserve.' If not joy, then a suppressed sense of satisfaction reigned in the hall—as if the era of uncertainty had come to an end and the time had come for [the USSR] to have a real leader."[24]

Gorbachev introduced Gromyko. Speaking without notes in a rasping voice, he nominated Gorbachev to be general secretary. Gorbachev had "vast experience." The way he had chaired the Secretariat and Politburo during Chernenko's illness was "brilliant." He "always knows his opinions and expresses them directly, whether his interlocutors like them or not." His "profound mind . . . can analyze the most complicated domestic and international issues, can see all their facets, not only the black and the white." He "quickly and accurately grasps the essence of foreign policy processes." His "broad erudition" and "analytical approach" enabled him to "break questions down into their component parts" and "to think broadly." He "knows how to approach people, to organize them, to find a common language—a natural gift, but the product of social and political experience as well." He was bound and determined "to keep our powder dry"; for him "the holiest of holies was to maintain the national defense and conduct an active foreign policy." "In a word, this is a broad-gauged, outstanding statesman who will serve with distinction as General Secretary."[25]

Listening to Gromyko, Gorbachev "felt agitated: Never before had I heard such words about myself, such high praise."[26] But what did he expect? What else could Gromyko have said on such an occasion? Especially since the part he was playing, vouching for the new leader on behalf of the old guard, was part of the deal that would make him head of state. Ritual kowtowing was de rigueur for everyone. Even Tikhonov, Grishin, and Romanov had done it, and Gorbachev's own homage to Chernenko was thoroughly disingenuous. What made Gromyko "seem sincere," Gorbachev explains, was that he spoke without a text. Chernyaev confirms that Gromyko's tone "wasn't customary": it sounded "more relaxed and less hackneyed" than usual. But there was more to it than that. Gromyko cleverly emphasized virtues that Gorbachev most esteemed in himself. In the excitement of the moment, with his improbable dream about to come true, Gorbachev suspended disbelief, allowing himself to believe that Gromyko believed in him, or at least that what Gromyko said was true. When Gromyko first mentioned Gorbachev's name, Chernyaev remembered, "the hall exploded in an ovation, comparable to the one that greeted Andropov's election, nothing like the sour applause that followed Chernenko's. The ovation rose in waves and did not abate for a long time."[27] During this time, remembers Boldin, all eyes were on Gorbachev, who "sat for a while with head bowed, then looked up and tried to halt the applause. His gesture, however, had the opposite effect."[28]

Elected unanimously, Gorbachev made his maiden speech as Soviet leader. True, he uttered the words "democratization" and "glasnost" and pledged to seek better relations with the West. But nothing even hinted at the broad, new meaning he would later give these terms, and the only applause registered in the official transcript came after an old-fashioned cold war warning: "Everyone should know that we will never forgo the interests of our Motherland and of its allies." Gorbachev also reaffirmed the Brezhnev "strategy" proclaimed at the Twenty-Sixth Party Congress, in March 1981: "acceleration of the country's socioeconomic development and the perfecting of all sides of social life," "transformation of the material-technical base of production," and "development of man himself, plus qualitative improvement of his material circumstances and his spiritual life."[29] Standard Soviet rhetoric that could as easily have been uttered by his predecessors.

ABOUT TWO MONTHS after he became Soviet leader, Gorbachev traveled to Leningrad in May, his first trip outside Moscow as general secretary. Surrounded on the street by a crowd of several hundred, he cheerfully announced, "I'm listening to you. What do you want to say?"

"Continue as you've begun," someone shouted. "Just get close to the people," a woman added. "We won't let you down."

"I can't get any closer," joked Gorbachev who was standing a few feet away.[30]

Gorbachev's speech to Leningrad party activists was hardly revolutionary; he called on people to work harder and be more disciplined, summoning the country to "a vast mobilization of all creative forces."[31]

Gorbachev meeting the people, Leningrad, May 15, 1985.

But his presentation of self was astounding. TV viewers were used to feeble leaders stumbling through stilted lines. Reading his prepared texts, Brezhnev often muffed letters and sounds, for example, when the Russian word for "systematically" (*sistematicheski*) emerged from his mouth as "tits" (*siskimasiski*). To avoid such total disasters, Brezhnev's orations were taped and doctored before they were broadcast; TV editors replaced words he misspoke or failed to utter with similar phrases found in previous speeches. Gorbachev, however, spoke without a prepared text. (That, according to a Soviet joke, led a simple citizen to conclude that Gorbachev was actually in worse shape than his pathetic predecessors: he couldn't even read.) Leonid Kravchenko, deputy head of the State Committee on Television and Radio, didn't broadcast the Leningrad address live, but recorded it without Gorbachev's knowledge and then begged to televise it so the world could see "the USSR finally had a great leader." Gorbachev told Kravchenko not to flatter him, but took the tape home and showed it to his family on Sunday at their dacha. All were "excited," his wife especially. She thought "everyone must hear this." So did Ligachev and Central Committee secretary Mikhail Zimyanin.[32]

The result, after the speech was indeed shown on television, exceeded Raisa Gorbachev's expectations: "People are literally dumbfounded by yesterday's television broadcast," marveled Chernyaev. "All one hears is, 'Did you see it?' Finally we have a leader who knows what he's talking about, who is interested in his work, who knows how to talk to people, who's not afraid to engage with them, who's not afraid to appear less than majestic, who gives the impression of wanting to move the load out of the mud, to rouse people, to make them be themselves, to get them to act boldly, to take courage, to take risks, to rely on common sense, to think and to act."[33] Videotapes of Gorbachev's Leningrad address were soon selling for five hundred rubles on the black market, an outlet normally reserved for bearded bards singing dissident ballads.

The image Gorbachev presented in Leningrad as a bold, charismatic, accessible new leader, along with people's reaction to it, showed his potential to change the face of his country and to carry the people with him. Which raises the enormous question of just what he wanted to accomplish. Gorbachev insists his thinking gradually evolved, a process that his wife described as "agonizing."[34] He admits that he dissembled for tactical reasons, "consciously stretching a point" in his March 11 speech so as "to "abide by the rules of the game."[35] But his obeisance to traditional Bolshevik goals was sincere as well as tactical. He was in fact a true believer—not in the Soviet system as it functioned (or didn't) in 1985 but in its potential to live up to what he deemed its original ideals.

Gorbachev believed in socialism, the faith of his beloved father and grandfather. (Although the Soviet Union was known at home and abroad as a Communist country, Communism, based on the Marxist principle "From each according to ability, to each according to need," was actually its ultimate goal. In the meantime, it claimed to be practicing socialism.) Stalin's crimes and Brezhnev's "stagnation" mocked Marxist ideals, but Gorbachev thought Soviet socialism could be saved by being "reformed." It was "only after 1985," he recalls, "and not immediately then, that I ceased to believe this."[36]

Gorbachev believed in Lenin long after that. "I trusted him then and I still do," he wrote in 2006. Gorbachev's speeches in 1985, filled with tributes to and lessons from Lenin, seem to confirm this, but to what extent were they tactical, too? Lydia Budyka, the Gorbachevs' longtime friend, swears he was sincere. She and her husband frequently took Sunday hikes with the Gorbachevs near Stavropol. Once "Misha" remarked that he was rereading Lenin, all fifty-five volumes of the great man's collected works. Budyka was amazed, all the more so since she and Raisa were then entranced by the English novels of John Galsworthy. "Can it really be," she asked Gorbachev, "that at night, instead of reading some interesting novel, you're reading Lenin?"

"Lida," he replied, "if you were to read Lenin's disputes with [Czech-German Marxist theoretician] Karl Kautsky, you would understand that they're far more interesting than a novel."[37] "The essence of Lenin," as Gorbachev understood him, was his desire to develop "the living creative activity of the masses." That sounds like a stock Marxist phrase, but what Gorbachev read into it was an endorsement of democracy, for how could the people play a creative role "without the expression of differing views and the clash of those views, that is, pluralism and freedom of choice"?[38] Many scholars would say Gorbachev was actually misreading Lenin, who was never a democrat in the way that Gorbachev proved to be. By now most historians, inside the former Soviet Union and out, blame Lenin for founding the totalitarian system that Stalin perfected and personally placing Stalin at its helm. By contrast, Gorbachev points out that just before his death, Lenin broke with Stalin, called for his removal as party general secretary, and proposed reforms that inspired Gorbachev's own. In fact, Lenin's proposal—to tame the powerful party bureaucracy by adding more proletarians to the Central Committee— fell far short of the real democratization Gorbachev eventually carried out.[39] If Gorbachev blurred that distinction, in his own mind as well as publicly, that was because his oft-proclaimed Leninism was useful to him psychologically as well as politically.

The political payoff came from seeming more faithful to the founder than were Gorbachev's immediate predecessors and current Politburo colleagues. They, his aide Boldin reports, "had not read Marx at all and merely quoted suitable passages from Lenin as the occasion required." Gorbachev, however, kept bookmark-filled volumes from Lenin's collected works on his desk and "would often pick one up in my presence and read aloud, comparing it to the present situation and extolling Lenin's perspicacity."[40]

Gorbachev also identified personally with Lenin. "Catastrophe for the country was banging at the doors and windows," he says, when Lenin seized power in October 1917. So he thought it was in 1985. After Bolshevik excesses and civil war nearly ruined the revolution, Lenin reversed course in 1921, "putting himself at odds with his own and others' outdated views." That's why Gorbachev saw "much in common between that time and my own, when I, too, had to go against generally accepted party precepts." To compare himself to Lenin, "a great man who played a huge role in the history of humanity," took some doing.[41] It also gave him the courage to attempt great things, the stamina to plow on when the going got very rough, and the self-assurance to maintain his self-control throughout most, but not all, of his travails.

In 1985 "reform" was a dirty word to guardians of ideological orthodoxy. Why should the "most advanced" society in the world need to change? Where had efforts at "so-called reform" gotten Hungary in 1956 and Czechoslovakia in 1968? Of course, the USSR had its own reformers: Khrushchev, the prime example, and Kosygin, who tried to decentralize the economy in 1965. But Khrushchev was still in posthumous disgrace in 1985, and Kosygin's Kremlin reputation wasn't much better. For Gorbachev, however, the lesson of Khrushchev and Kosygin wasn't to shun reform but to do a better job of it. But what sort of reforms should he promote, and would any of them work?

One possibility, which Gorbachev initially adopted, was to revive the campaign for law and order and discipline that Andropov had begun. But that hadn't helped much then and it wouldn't now. Another option, which several former Gorbachev aides retrospectively wish he'd endorsed, was a crash program to provide the consumer goods and services the population had long been denied and desperately craved. That could have boosted Gorbachev's popularity, while soaking up all the inflationary cash that people hid under mattresses waiting for something worth spending it on. But the Soviet economy wasn't set up to produce abundance, partly because military spending (which equaled or exceeded U.S. levels, though the Soviet economy was one-quarter the size of its American counterpart) disposed of so much of the gross domestic product. Reducing such spending would require proving that the capitalist threat, which Moscow had used for so long to justify one-party rule, had substantially abated. When Gorbachev aide Shakhnazarov later asked Chief of the General Staff Sergei Akhromeyev why the country needed so many weapons, Akhromeyev answered, "Because through enormous sacrifice we have created first-class plants that are no worse than what the Americans have. What are we going to do, tell them to stop working and make pots and pans instead? That's simply utopian."[42]

What about economic reforms of the sort the Chinese carried out after Mao Zedong died in 1976? Deng Xiaoping's reforms freed peasants from collectives and spurred them to produce for the market as well as for themselves. The result was an agricultural boom that in turn fueled miraculous economic growth. The Chinese postponed political reforms and to this day are still resisting democratization and glasnost. Could Gorbachev have tried the Chinese road? He, too, began with the economy. But Soviet farmers, brutalized by Stalin's decades-long war against the peasantry, couldn't have matched the Chinese agricultural revival. When Soviet economist Oleg Bogomolov returned from a 1987 visit to China recommending the Chinese model, Gorbachev dismissed the advice out of hand, partly, Bogomolov thought, because Central Committee officials, long accustomed to dismissing anything Chinese (especially reforms that might threaten their power), provided misleading information; they told Gorbachev that Chinese output of rice had fallen, when, in fact, that was a temporary result of farmers' being encouraged to produce crops like cotton.[43]

One other model of reform was the Prague Spring of 1968. Alexander Dubček and Gorbachev's MGU friend Zdeněk Mlynář (among others) had tried to give socialism a "human face"—not by creating a multiparty political system (which they knew Moscow wouldn't allow), but by allowing pluralism within the party and freedom outside it. Something like that is probably what Gorbachev meant when he said he was prepared to "go very far." But he couldn't admit that openly and maybe not even to himself—especially since no one knew how the Czech experiment would have turned out if it hadn't been crushed by Soviet tanks.

One thing Gorbachev rejected from the start was any attempt to recast the Soviet system by means of force and violence. Whatever changes he introduced had to be "gradual," he wrote later, since "revolutionism leads to chaos, destruction and often to a new kind of unfreedom."[44] This was Gorbachev's sharpest break of all with tradition—not only with the Bolsheviks' bloody way of doing things but with other Russians' belief, both before 1917 and after 1991, that glorious ends justify the most repugnant means. His great insight was to realize that means that don't prefigure admirable ends will all too often compromise and contaminate those ends.[45] Gorbachev himself eventually abandoned incremental change and attempted to transform almost everything—the political system, the economy, ideology, ethnic relations, foreign policy, even Soviet identity itself. And that not only sounds revolutionary—it is. How, then, could he call himself a gradualist? Because he was less radical than his predecessors (Lenin and Stalin) and his successor, Boris Yeltsin, who tried to create capitalism almost overnight via economic "shock therapy." According to Gorbachev, his was a "revolution by evolutionary means."[46]

This was an abstract formula rather than a practical guideline for everyday action. But that, too, was typical of Gorbachev. Grachev refers to Gorbachev's "unwillingness, bordering on an aversion, to spend too much time on routine, everyday, ongoing matters." He preferred "matters of great moment, vast ideas, fateful decisions and projects that transcended mundane horizons." He loved to converse with people "who distracted him from boring, everyday details, who invited him into the rarefied air of profound ideas. His Politburo colleagues clearly weren't equipped for Athenian-style philosophical debates. . . ."[47] These qualities, too, help to explain Gorbachev's cast of mind as he took office in March 1985. Many years later, in a conversation with Mlynář, Gorbachev summarized his "original plan" this way: he wanted to "combine socialism with the scientific and technical revolution." By "using the advantages we believed were inherent in the planned economy, and making use of the concentration of governmental power, and so forth, things would be changed." But that wasn't a plan. It was a hope.[48]

THE GREAT QUESTION Gorbachev faced, which Lenin famously formulated as "What is to be done?," concerned not just policy but also politics. As the leader of a supercentralized regime, Gorbachev had tremendous power, but not to do what he pleased. Although almost all his Politburo colleagues agreed that change was needed, most preferred the minimum consistent with retaining their own power and privileges. In the beginning, Gorbachev later told economist Abel Aganbegyan, "they had me surrounded."[49] Removing them was crucial, but dumping them precipitately would look like an old-style purge. So Gorbachev proceeded cautiously, even though that limited his freedom of action.

Gorbachev's most hidebound Politburo colleagues were in no shape politically or physically to resist. Romanov was not only dim but a drinker, too. He was affronted, of course, when Gorbachev told him his choice was to step down voluntarily or have his habit discussed by his colleagues. Romanov "shed a few tears," Gorbachev recalls, but "in the end he accepted my proposal."[50]

Romanov was gone by July. Removing Tikhonov took until September. Even at age eighty, says Gorbachev, Tikhonov "was sure we couldn't do without his services." Gorbachev explained that "we could," and when he added that Tikhonov could preserve all the perks of power while in retirement, he, too, went quietly and was replaced as prime minister by Ryzhkov.[51] Only in December did Grishin depart. He was so "excessively self-assured and morbidly power-loving," says Gorbachev, that "he couldn't stand to have anyone near him who was outstanding and capable of independent thought." Grishin yielded the Moscow party helm to someone who eventually couldn't stand Gorbachev either— Boris Yeltsin.

Foreign Minister Andrei Gromyko was the most delicate case— because he had helped Gorbachev become general secretary. Gorbachev kept his promise; Gromyko became head of state in July, but otherwise, Gorbachev treated him roughly. Gromyko expected to keep control of foreign policy by having his longtime deputy, Kornienko, succeed him. Instead, Gorbachev selected Politburo candidate member Eduard Shevardnadze, whom he had known and trusted since their days in neighboring Stavropol and Georgia, and whom he valued as a "fully formed politician, educated and erudite."[52] That left Gromyko, who wasn't exactly voluble to begin with, speechless, but the veteran diplomat recovered enough to say, "I'm not against it since I assume, Mikhail Sergeyevich, that you've thought this through."[53] Gromyko was bitter, but he remained in the Politburo until 1988.

Reviewing the May Day parade, Red Square, May 1, 1986.
Left to right: Gorbachev, Andrei Gromyko, Nikolai Ryzhkov.

Shevardnadze was one of only three Politburo colleagues who backed Gorbachev to the very end, despite periods of tension and separation. (Shevardnadze resigned as foreign minister in 1990, only to resume the post in late 1991.) Another, Yakovlev, worked closely with Gorbachev from March 1985 onward, but, given that he wasn't even a Central Committee candidate member in 1985, he could not become a Central Committee secretary until March 1986, a Politburo candidate member until January 1987, and full member until July of that year—a remarkably rapid rise, owing to Gorbachev's patronage. The third, Vadim Medvedev, with a background that blended academic administration with service in the Central Committee apparatus, became a Central Committee secretary in 1986 and full member of the Politburo in 1988. Ligachev, Ryzhkov, and KGB chief Viktor Chebrikov all made full Politburo members in April 1985, seemed staunch allies in the early going, but not after Gorbachev endorsed more radical change. No other Politburo member Gorbachev inherited was remotely ready for an assault on the status quo. Boris Ponomarev had been a Central Committee secretary since 1961! He was so set in his ways that when asked to edit a draft of Gorbachev's report to the Twenty-Seventh Party Congress, in February 1986, he instinctively but unknowingly deleted Gorbachev's own words. By this time, Ponomarev's international department deputy, Chernyaev, was bold enough to tell his boss, "Ninety-five percent of what you've so carefully cut from the text came directly from Gorbachev. . . ."

"But I didn't do it on purpose," Ponomarev whimpered.

"Of course, you didn't," Chernyaev replied soothingly.[54]

Kazakhstan party boss Kunayev had held a full Politburo seat since 1971, and was a past master of corruption until he was fired in January 1987. Pyotr Demichev, Politburo candidate member since 1964, and minister of culture since 1974, had hounded the artists and writers who later became Gorbachev's champions. He wasn't retired until September 1988. Ukrainian party leader Shcherbitsky, whose late arrival from California on March 11 spared him the need to hold his nose and vote for Gorbachev, lasted until September 1989. Other Politburo members appointed in the early 1980s (such as Aliev, Vorotnikov, and Mikhail Solomentsev) were only marginally more progressive. Lev Zaikov, whom Gorbachev picked to join the Politburo in 1985, played a useful role as

buffer between Gorbachev and the military-industrial complex. Viktor
Nikonov, chosen to oversee agriculture, failed (like most of his predecessors) to galvanize the countryside.

This roster underlines again how different Gorbachev was from his
peers. That absence of like-minded leaders was a fact of Soviet political
life. But his capacity to take the measure of those he favored left a lot
to be desired. Boris Yeltsin and Gorbachev were almost exact contem-
poraries and initially political allies; Yeltsin, too, stood out from party
peers as energetic and innovative. In March 1985, Yeltsin was still party
boss in Sverdlovsk and going nowhere fast—partly because he was as
explosive as Gorbachev was self-controlled. That's why Ryzhkov warned
Gorbachev not to promote Yeltsin, saying, "He'll bring you grief. I know
him and I don't recommend him." But Ligachev, a hard-hitting Siberian
administrator himself, recognized a fellow pile driver in Yeltsin. After
checking in Sverdlovsk, he telephoned Gorbachev in the middle of the
night and said, Yeltsin is "the very man we need. He's got everything:
he's knowledgeable, he's got a strong character, he thinks big and knows
how to get things done."[55] Whereupon Gorbachev put him in charge of
the Central Committee's construction department, a slot Yeltsin considered too modest for someone of his talents and experience. Elevations
to Central Committee secretary in July 1985 and to Moscow party boss,
replacing Grishin, soon followed, perfectly positioning Yeltsin to eventually challenge his benefactor.

With Kremlin colleagues like these, Gorbachev hardly needed adversaries. It was all the more important, therefore, to gather a team of
close personal aides whom he could trust. But that, too, took a long
time, and, in fact, he never fully succeeded. Boldin, his chief aide since
1982, whom he later promoted to presidential chief of staff, eventually
betrayed him. So did Lukyanov, whom Gorbachev had made chairman of the new Soviet parliament elected in 1989. Andrei Aleksandrov-
Agentov, age seventy-seven, was Brezhnev's chief foreign policy aide
from start to finish, yet Gorbachev didn't replace him for almost a full
year. Aleksandrov-Agentov later complained that Gorbachev "is utterly
unable to listen to (or rather to hear) what his interlocutor says, so
enamored is he of his own words." That may simply mean, as Archie
Brown contends, that Gorbachev was not "particularly interested" in

Aleksandrov-Agentov's views, but it says something that Gorbachev kept around someone who thought his boss's "surface openness and benevolent politeness were a habitual mask covering not warmth and goodwill but nothing but cold calculation."[56]

Chernyaev, who replaced Aleksandrov-Agentov in February 1986, was a real soul mate—in the sense that he had long ago arrived at the radically reformist ideas that Gorbachev eventually adopted. An enlightened apparatchik, Chernyaev was the kind of intellectual whom Mikhail and Raisa Gorbachev respected, one who found time amid his Central Committee duties to read Byron, Strindberg, Ibsen, Nietzsche, and Carlyle.[57] Grachev describes Chernyaev as Gorbachev's "most faithful and reliable" assistant. Gorbachev himself once introduced Chernyaev to Spanish Prime Minister Felipe González as his "alter ego."[58]

Like Chernyaev, Georgy Shakhnazarov was a radical reformer.[59] Like Gorbachev, Shakhnazarov studied law at Moscow University in the early 1950s, taking courses as a graduate student from some of the same professors. Besides having a doctorate in law, and having helped found the discipline of political science in the Soviet Union, Shakhnazarov wrote poetry and science fiction. He was "thunderstruck" when, upon meet-

Gorbachev with two of his closest aides, Georgy Shakhnazarov and Anatoly Chernyaev.

ing Gorbachev for the first time, Gorbachev told him he had read Shakhnazarov's books *Socialist Democracy* and *The Coming World Order*. "For
the first time in my quarter of a century of working in the party apparatus, I could speak with one of Russia's bosses as a colleague-political
scientist."[60]

Shakhnazarov became Gorbachev's chief adviser on the socialist
countries and on political reforms in the USSR in 1988. Even before that,
he frequently traveled abroad with Gorbachev. Often, on the flight home,
Gorbachev invited aides to join him and Raisa for a relaxed supper in
their section of the plane. She was always a charming hostess, and on
the way back from Belgrade in March 1988, she suddenly announced to
her husband, "Misha, it seems to me that these are comrades you can
rely upon. They are Gorbachev's team."

Gorbachev remained silent, Shakhnazarov recalls, the expression
on his face indicating her remark had "stung him." Not because her
comment was so clearly political, since she often participated in policy
discussions. Rather, Shakhnazarov thought, because "it wasn't in his
nature to express goodwill to someone." That habit was deepened by the
traditional Bolshevik preference for keeping emotion out of politics, but
Shakhnazarov felt Gorbachev's wife's remark somehow "wounded his
self-esteem." Shakhnazarov didn't elaborate, but the implication was
that Gorbachev didn't like to admit that he had to depend on anyone.[61]

Except for his wife. Gorbachev had other loyal and knowledgeable
aides: Vadim Medvedev had a doctorate in economics. Ivan Frolov had
known Raisa Gorbacheva at Moscow University and had a doctorate in
philosophy. But Gorbachev's wife was his closest adviser. By this time,
after "agonizing" over the decision, she had given up her own career. For
a while, she had continued to "gather material for a doctoral thesis" and
attend "philosophical seminars and conferences that interested me." She
also "followed the philosophical and sociological literature" and "maintained active contact with my colleagues. But the circumstances of my
daily life faced me with a choice and I made that choice. Other people can
write doctoral theses."[62]

Giving up her career to help her high-ranking husband was an
acceptable wifely choice. Joining his inner circle of advisers was not, particularly in the USSR, where political wives were to be neither seen nor

heard. When Nancy Reagan appeared by President Reagan's side, Raisa later commented, that was perfectly normal, but "when Gorbachev appeared with his wife," that violated the tradition that "wives didn't exist."[63] But, given the Gorbachevs' long-standing habit of discussing almost everything, the real surprise would have been if Gorbachev had *not* included her. Gorbachev admitted that he consulted his wife. Once asked by NBC television newsman Tom Brokaw about what, he replied, "About everything." But when this interview was telecast and published in the Soviet Union, Gorbachev's answer was considered too sensitive to be transmitted by the Soviet media.[64] As for Raisa, she carefully played down her role: "Never did I interfere in government or political affairs. My role was only to be supportive and helpful. . . . Of course, I had my own views. And like any normal people, we discussed things, argued, and sometimes quarreled. What's so special about that?"[65]

Gorbachev's wife certainly didn't dictate to her husband, insists Chernyaev. His impression was that in their regular late-evening walks, Gorbachev recounted details of his day to his wife, tried ideas out on her, heard out her reactions, and paid particular attention to her views of people, especially his close aides.[66] Raisa's presence had some salutary effects. It toned down the kind of swearing at which he was as skilled as his male colleagues. Her chief aide, Vitaly Gusenkov, says she couldn't stand "incompetence and irresponsibility," of which Russia had more than its share.[67] But she was so strict with household staff, so prone to upbraid them and tell on them to her husband, that many came to fear and hate her. Gorbachev's chief bodyguard, Vladimir Medvedev, thought a leader who promised democratic reforms would treat his own staff democratically. It turned out, he insists, that "it is much easier to respect 'the people' than to respect a concrete individual. It's easier to declare yourself a democrat than to be one."[68]

Gusenkov praises Gorbachev's wife as "tougher" than her husband, who was more likely to "maneuver and compromise." Shakhnazarov, who once contended that Gorbachev could have avoided many mistakes if he had heeded his advisers at least 5 percent of the time, believed that Gorbachev listened to his wife not too much, but too little.[69] Another Gorbachev aide, Aleksandr Likhotal, remembered times when Gorbachev brushed off advisers' criticism of his speeches—only to have Mrs.

Gorbachev quietly declare, "No, Misha. You listen to what they're telling you." After that, Likhotal adds, "he listened."[70] But if Raisa's participation in policy discussions was welcomed by some of Gorbachev's aides, it was never accepted by most of his countrymen, and especially not by his countrywomen. She was the first Soviet "first lady"—the first to play that role, to dress for it elegantly, and to accompany her husband on virtually all of his official travel. Her teacher-like tone irritated Russians who thought women should know their place. One of the less biting jokes that circulated about her in Moscow had it that Gorbachev was once stopped as he was about to enter some government building by a guard who demanded to see his official pass. "What do you mean?" Gorbachev objected. "I'm Gorbachev—the General Secretary." "Excuse me, Comrade Gorbachev. I didn't recognize you without Raisa Maksimovna."[71]

According to her sister, Ludmila, who described herself as shy and retiring, Raisa wasn't entirely adverse to the self-display that came with being first lady. Despite her obsession with her family's privacy, "she wanted to be seen. It was in her blood. She knew how to approach people. She was very ambitious, even, I'd say, too much so."[72]

The resentment against Raisa reached into the Politburo, of course. On one occasion in Kiev, an aide informed her that the next stop on her husband's schedule was a meeting with the Ukrainian party leadership.

"I accompany Mikhail Sergeyevich everywhere," Raisa is said to have retorted. "So I'll be going to the Politburo meeting, too." Ukrainian leader Shcherbitsky contained himself until the Gorbachevs had departed, but then sneered sarcastically to his wife, "Perhaps you should accompany me to Politburo meetings from now on."[73]

Gorbachev's Moscow University classmate Dmitry Golovanov, who was now a television producer, warned him, "Listen, Misha, you should tell Raya not to get so close to you in front of television cameras," only to be told off in no uncertain terms.[74]

Golovanov and other Moscow University classmates resented the fact that Gorbachev didn't invite them to work with him in the Kremlin, but since none of them (except Lukyanov, who graduated two years earlier) was a professional party politician, that wasn't surprising. What was stunning was that Gorbachev brought with him almost no political advisers or colleagues from Stavropol. The only one he promoted to a major Moscow post was his Stavropol successor, Vsevolod Murakhovsky, whose record in charge of the agro-industrial complex proved no better than Gorbachev's had been. One could say that none of Gorbachev's former associates deserved such promotions. But that hadn't stopped his predecessors, who surrounded themselves with loyal henchmen from previous postings. The obvious shortcomings of Gorbachev's former colleagues reinforced his sense that the system needed change, but his lack of trusted associates was an obstacle to reforming it.

The political atmosphere in March 1985 was more favorable to change outside the Politburo than within it. Liberal intellectuals— artists, writers, scientists, and engineers—were particularly impressed by the young and vigorous Gorbachev, even before they realized how much his convictions resembled their own. It wasn't just enlightened apparatchiki like Chernyaev and Shakhnazarov who welcomed Gorbachev's ascension; party and government functionaries at all levels hoped to move up as he cleaned out their longtime superiors. The Soviet military had exploited the country's feeble leaders to build up their weaponry and their authority, but they, too, craved a more decisive commander in chief. General Valentin Varennikov, who took part in an abortive 1991 coup against Gorbachev, was "full of sympathy" for Gorbachev in 1985.[75] Top KGB officials also favored Gorbachev, whom they provided with information that compromised Romanov and Grishin. But their regard also reflected the personal ambitions of secret policemen like Vladimir Kriuchkov, whom Gorbachev made KGB chief in 1988, three years before he led the August 1991 coup attempt. Gorbachev trusted Kriuchkov because Andropov had done so, and also because, as he told aides on several occasions, Kriuchkov's position in the KGB had been in foreign intelligence and therefore he was not associated with domestic repression.[76] Kriuchkov and Yakovlev had been together on March 11, 1985, when they learned Gorbachev was to be the new leader. Kriuchkov "breathed a sigh of relief," Yakovlev remembered; "we congratulated each other and drank a toast to the new *Gensek*." Yakovlev later chastised himself for mistaking Kriuchkov's careerist ambitions for sincere political convictions. Kriuchkov later lamented, "The KGB's biggest mistake in its whole history was to misunderstand Gorbachev."[77]

SINCE HE DIDN'T BEGIN with a clear strategy for radical reform, and probably couldn't have rammed one through the Politburo anyway, Gorbachev's most drastic early innovation was a stunning change in leadership style. The new general secretary refused to have his portrait displayed during holiday demonstrations in Red Square at the end of 1985. He would strike up conversations in the street with ordinary citizens, Chernyaev noted in his dairy, "something that hadn't happened since the 1920s." He made sure issues were really "discussed" at Politburo and other meetings, rather than being "obediently approved." He "encouraged, even required, everyone to say what he thought." He dropped the "grand manner" of the "unapproachable divine leader . . . and appeared before the people as a person like everyone else," as a "real leader, the kind people really wanted and had missed for a long time." And he did all this "not intentionally, not so as to invent a new style, but according to the inner motives of his own nature, and 'for the sake of liberating minds,' as he would say."[78]

Hyperbole from an ardent admirer? Gorbachev's March 13 oration at Chernenko's funeral contained the obligatory tributes, but also declared war on "ostentation, idle talk, arrogance, and irresponsibility."[79] At a meeting of Central Committee secretaries on March 15, Grishin suggested that province party committees convene to discuss the new leader's directives. "More plenums?" Gorbachev replied sharply. "What for? We have too much to do as it is without more meetings. And what is there to discuss? That I was elected General Secretary? What's there to say about that?"[80] At the same session, Gorbachev repeated what he had told a deputy prime minister who wanted to ceremoniously convey the new leader's "greetings" to a rally in Tallinn celebrating an award to the Estonian Soviet Republic, "There's no need for that. People are sick and tired of these 'greetings.'"[81]

Gorbachev was a natural politician. But what came naturally could still be improved. Gorbachev worked to perfect his "spontaneity." He was initially cautious about appearing on TV; he wanted to avoid "self-advertising," he said. He rejected teleprompters that made him look mechanical, and big cue cards placed near his desk in his Kremlin office. "We just counted on his phenomenal memory," remembered Kravchenko. Gorbachev occasionally referred to sheets of paper, but when he addressed the nation "he would conduct a conversation with TV viewers." To achieve that effect, he would have an "interlocutor" other than the cameraman seated across from him, "so I can see your eyes," he told him, "so I can assess your reaction and read from it whether I'm getting you interested." Gorbachev never read the text "exactly as it was written," Kravchenko added, "even when he wrote it himself."[82]

Gorbachev set a new democratic tone in the way he conducted Politburo meetings. Introducing topics for discussion, he kept his own remarks brief before inviting others to speak. But he showed his colleagues a selection of letters from ordinary citizens containing rave reviews of his appearances around the country. The reactions were "very moving," Chernyaev noted in his diary. "Tongues have been loosened. People are writing candidly, powerfully, without looking over their shoulders. . . . People are unbosoming themselves of everything they've stored up during the Brezhnev and Chernenko eras."[83]

During a Central Committee plenum on October 15, 1985, a province party boss from Kazakhstan began to rave about "Comrade Gorbachev's Bolshevik style and Leninist approach," about "how fortunate we are to have such dynamic leadership." Gorbachev blew up. "Why do we need this here? Gorbachev this, Gorbachev that, Gorbachev's style? Why should we keep picking at this?" The speaker hurried on to the end of his speech. Central Committee members who had applauded his praise of their leader erupted in an ovation when Gorbachev rejected it.[84]

Gorbachev worked very hard, not just compared with his frail predecessors, but by any standard. According to his bodyguard Vladimir Medvedev, Gorbachev didn't go to bed until one or two in the morning, as late as four when preparing for particularly important events. He arose at seven or eight and worked while being driven to his office in a huge ZIL limousine, reading papers, making notes, placing calls on two telephones. During the short walk from car to office, he relayed instructions to three or four aides, in the elevator to his office, to still more—"whom to talk to, what to say, what to pay attention to, what to insist on, what to ignore." At this early stage, Medvedev still admired him, and wasn't

above flattering him as well. "It's as if you were born to be General Secretary," he told his boss. Gorbachev smiled but didn't reply.[85]

Communist party congresses were grand occasions when several
thousand delegates converged to hear their leader define the party's policies for the next five years. Gorbachev's immediate predecessors merely
presided over congress preparations (to the extent that their ill health
allowed), and then droned through the long, dull orations (amounting
to interminable exegeses of whatever slogan had been devised to summarize the next five-year plan, e.g., "The Economy Must Be Economi-
cal")[86] provided by speechwriters. In contrast, Gorbachev dominated the
preparations, immersing himself in every phase, delegating responsibility from time to time but then grabbing it back—a perfectionist pattern
that proved gratifying when he and his handiwork were highly popular, but much less so when his reforms were under assault from all sides.

Twenty-Seventh Party Congress preparations began toward the end
of 1985 when he invited Boldin, Yakovlev, Lukyanov, and Nail Bikkenin,
a longtime Central Committee staffer, to his office for initial brainstorm-
ing. As stenographers scrambled to keep up, Gorbachev laid out his general approach, after which the group subdivided the labor of drafting
the report's various sections. Next, the scene shifted to Volynskoe-2,
a retreat located in a forest near the Minsk highway outside Moscow.
There the drafters, isolated from their daily responsibilities, started writing, summoning party and government specialists to provide them with
data, and began to meld their sections into a unified whole. Several times
during this process, Gorbachev drove out to take part in drafting and
redrafting, repeatedly urging his aides to "be clear, avoid bookishness
and artificial prettiness." He not only tolerated debate; he encouraged it.
By the time a complete draft was ready, he and his family were taking a
brief winter vacation in Pitsunda, an opulent government retreat located
in a pine grove in Abkhazia, by the Black Sea. Boldin and Yakovlev flew
there for another round of revising along with Gorbachev and his wife.
The wind was damp and penetrating. Wrapped in blankets in a gazebo
on the beach about fifty yards from the surf, they took turns reading
the text aloud. Boldin recorded everyone's comments on a portable tape
recorder so that some could be inserted into the speech. Toward evening,
the foursome, including Raisa, would reconvene in the Gorbachevs'

dacha, a large two-story house with spacious rooms and wood-paneled walls, until the Gorbachevs set out on their nightly walk.

From Pitsunda, Boldin and Yakovlev returned to Volynskoe and continued revising until the end of January. At that point, they and Vadim Medvedev joined the Gorbachevs for yet more collective editing, at yet another government retreat, in Zavidovo, the game preserve north of Moscow on the Leningrad highway. Khrushchev and Brezhnev had loved to hunt here, often hosting foreign leaders. The Gorbachevs stayed in a magnificent villa with the requisite wood paneling and heavy chandeliers, with his aides nearby in a five-story apartment house equipped with a large pool and sauna, as well as hunting trophies that Brezhnev had awarded to himself and his guests. At ten every morning, collective editing commenced in the Gorbachevs' villa, in large armchairs covered with boar and bear hides around a small unpainted table. The group discussed the latest draft "section by section, page by page, line by line," recalled Medvedev, with those who had not drafted particular passages serving as critics, and drafters defending their work. At noon, Raisa Gorbachev called for refreshments—warm milk, coffee, candy, whipped-cream fruit mousse, cakes, and coffee from a special recipe, which she and her husband drank in Turkish glasses. The workday lasted ten to twelve hours. Finally the job was done. At a farewell dinner, Gorbachev recalled his Kremlin rivals' attempts to keep him from coming to power. The next morning, the Gorbachevs accompanied their guests to waiting cars. "We were saying thank you," remembered Boldin, nursing his sense of grievance at being taken for granted, "although we were not the ones who should have been expressing gratitude."[87]

ALTHOUGH GORBACHEV'S STYLE was unprecedented, the substance of his policies during his first year in office was not—beginning with the fateful anti-alcohol campaign that the Politburo launched barely a month after he took power.

Drunkenness has long plagued Russia, and the toll only rose under the Soviets. In 1914, when the tsarist government instituted prohibition, the average amount of alcohol consumed annually per capita was 1.8 liters. The Bolsheviks, too, legislated abstinence for a while, but by 1985 the amount per capita was 10.6 liters, counting "babes in arms" in the total population. Khrushchev raised the price and limited the supply of vodka. Brezhnev formed a commission, but quickly lost interest, partly because, as he once put it to Gromyko, "a Russian can't get by without a drink."[88] Andropov revived the commission, and on April 4, 1985, its chair, Solomentsev, briefed the Politburo: 9.3 million drunks picked off the streets in 1984, 12 million drunks arrested, and 13 thousand rapes attributable to alcohol, along with 29 thousand robberies. In public opinion surveys, as many as 75 percent of respondents named "drunkenness" as the nation's number one problem. "There's nothing worse," complained one citizen. "Vodka is rotting our youth," moaned another. Economic losses attributable to alcohol totaled 50–60 billion rubles. Solomentsev proposed to cut the production of vodka, fortified wines, and wine from berries. He rejected a proposal from Shevardnadze to go easy on regions (like Georgia) that produced wine rather than vodka, and not to crack down on popular production of moonshine.[89]

Gorbachev considered a campaign against drunkenness a moral imperative. He also thought improving health and work efficiency would pay economic dividends. He paid too little attention to warnings about other costs. First Deputy Finance Minister Viktor Dementsev predicted overall retail trade would decline by 5 billion rubles in 1986 and as much as 18–20 billion in 1990, while losses to the state budget would rise from 4 billion in 1986 to 15–16 billion in 1990. To provide the population with something to buy other than alcohol, the chronically short supply of consumer goods would miraculously have to balloon by some 21 billion rubles' worth. Otherwise, warned the State Planning Commission's Lev Voronin, "we literally will have nothing to sell to people who have money to spend."

Gorbachev's response on April 4 was to blame the messenger. Dementsev had said "nothing new. We all know that people have nothing to buy with their money. But what you're proposing is forcing people to drink. So keep your remarks shorter. This isn't the Finance Ministry. You're talking to the Politburo." To Voronin: "We can no longer tolerate a 'drunken' budget."

The anti-alcohol campaign did some good: life expectancy and the birthrate rose slightly in 1986 and 1987, and the crime rate fell. But as the first great initiative of Gorbachev's administration, it was a disaster. Economic and budgetary losses amounted to as much as $100 billion between 1985 and 1990.[90] Soviet imports of foreign liquor plummeted, damaging allied countries' wine-making industries. Vineyards that had been a source of great pride as well as profit for regions including Stavropol were laid waste. Beer factories built around expensive new equipment purchased in the West were abandoned (although the huge plant that produces Baltika beer was later bought from Denmark and installed during Gorbachev's time in office). People used to lubricating everything from national holidays to birthdays and weddings felt humiliated when forced to make do with soft drinks. Supplies of sugar, carted away for making moonshine, had to be rationed. At liquor stores long lines of customers passed the time coining new titles for their new leader: instead of *gensek*, *gensok* (*sok* is Russian for "juice"); and instead of *general'nyi sekretar'* ("general secretary") *mineral'nyi sekretar'* ("mineral water secretary"). A widespread anecdote had it that a disgruntled citizen left a long liquor line to go and kill Gorbachev, but returned from the Kremlin complaining that the queue of would-be assassins was even longer. Central Committee secretary Dolgikh drove past a liquor store on his way back from visiting a hydroelectric station outside Moscow: "People raised their fists at my car. They were cursing me and all of us for having created this situation."[91]

Gorbachev aide Shakhnazarov found the anti-alcohol campaign "incomprehensible."[92] Grachev calls it "an utter fiasco."[93] According to another Gorbachev aide and admirer, economist Nikolai Shmelyov, it was "a fundamental error, just plain stupidity."[94] Gorbachev didn't dream up the campaign, but he supported it as a kind of continuation of Andropov's push for order and discipline. In retrospect he blamed Ligachev and Solomentsev as well as local functionaries who turned a moderate program into an indiscriminate crusade.[95] But he also accepted "a big part of the blame." It was, he later admitted, a classic example of a policy based on "inertia and administrative thinking."[96] Several Politburo members (Aliev, Dolgikh, Ryzhkov, Vorotnikov) doubted the campaign from the start, but if they said so at the time, at the risk of incurring Gorbachev's wrath, it was none too forcefully. Ligachev and Solomentsev were passionate prohibitionists (the former a teetotaler, the latter a first-class tippler), and at this early stage Gorbachev was relying heavily on Ligachev. Gorbachev himself had no love of liquor, even though two Moscow University classmates remember his helping "kill" a liter now and then. Furthermore, he and his wife carried what she termed "the family cross" for brothers who were alcoholics. Raisa's younger brother, Zhenya, who was particularly dear to her, attended a military academy in Ufa, but dropped out when confronted by the hazing that is still omnipresent in the Russian army. After enrolling in a Moscow literary institute, he wrote several children's books, but then descended into drink. One of his (and Raisa's) grandfathers and a great-grandfather had been alcoholics, too. Raisa tried to save her brother, their sister, Ludmila, said, but he refused to be saved, insisting, "I'm not an alcoholic." He lived for a while with the Gorbachevs and then with his mother, and spent time in various clinics, but he couldn't stop drinking. Of course, the Gorbachevs didn't publicize this fact; whenever word came that Zhenya had disappeared, they quietly dispatched their physician son-in-law, Anatoly, to search for him in grim sobering-up stations, or among drunks sleeping in railroad terminals. Raisa could hardly bear to watch as her brother disintegrated. In addition, her sister, Ludmila, was an indirect victim of alcohol. She graduated from a medical institute, worked as an ophthalmologist for a local draft board in Bashkiria, and married a successful aviator/inventor who died in 1999 after falling down a flight of stairs while drunk.[97]

Raisa Gorbachev backed the anti-alcohol campaign with special enthusiasm. But Gorbachev's mother, resuming her old role as his disciplinarian, did not. When he visited her in Privolnoe, she as usual "covered" the table with all sorts of food and drink, but without anything alcoholic. "Mama," she remembered her son chiding her, "couldn't you have put out a bottle of wine?"

"You know, Misha," she replied, "someone in this country dreamt up a law against that. Well, I must tell you: That was a bad thing to do. People curse at you during weddings. So does everybody on birthdays. If I set out a bottle, tomorrow everyone will say, 'That's alright for him and his mother, but we're not allowed.' So I'm not putting out any bottle."[98]

IF THE ANTI-ALCOHOL CAMPAIGN got Gorbachev off to a bad start, other early innovations didn't fare much better, largely because, like that campaign, they weren't really new at all.

On April 5, Gorbachev summoned close aides to help him define a new course for party and country. What they offered was a series of vague clichés: Lukyanov—"a qualitatively new level of party work"; Boldin—"raising the authority of party members." Gorbachev—"opening a new and responsible stage in the country's development." Vadim Medvedev used the term that became the watchword for the first two years of Gorbachev's administration: "acceleration."

Acceleration of "social-economic development," said Medvedev.[99] "Acceleration of scientific-technological progress," Gorbachev proclaimed three days later at a meeting with leaders of industry, agriculture, and construction.[100] Soon afterward he took his message to the proletarian district of Moscow, where he spent two days meeting local party leaders, touring industrial enterprises, and inspecting housing, schools, and hospitals. At the jewel in the district's crown, the Likhachev Automobile Factory, he warned workers on the factory floor, "We're using up raw materials, we're using up energy, we're expending labor and work time, but we're not getting what we want. But there's no one to complain to, comrades. You've got to take responsibility yourselves, to get down to work, in everything."[101] The comrades applauded and may even have meant it, but they also devoted a lot of time to concealing the full extent of the mess around the plant. As Chernyaev put it, "They had already set up 'Potemkin villages' before he arrived."[102] Visiting the home of an "ordinary worker," Gorbachev was served lavish hors d'oeuvres, candies, and other delicacies. Boldin recalls that the road to a hospital's main entrance got a new coat of asphalt from which "steam and the smell of hot tar were still rising." Patients in the wards that Gorbachev visited were impersonated by "healthy, well-fed security officers with closely cropped hair, who warmly welcomed the medical staff and the hospital food, while finding it difficult to be precise about their ailments."[103]

The Central Committee's plenum on April 23 was a big deal, a "breakthrough," Gorbachev proclaimed it later, the moment when he officially embraced "acceleration of social and economic development." In June, he boasted that the whole nation welcomed the new course.[104] Science and technology, especially in the key area of machine building, were the first to be "accelerated." Gorbachev and Ryzhkov had sponsored the 1984 plenum on this subject that Chernenko canceled. Preparing for a new conclave on June 11, 1985, Ryzhkov remembers, the two men "wore ourselves out, locking ourselves in his office, not breaking for lunch, sitting there from morning 'til night, or rather pacing back and forth, in fact, crawling" around the floor, "which we covered with papers instead of a carpet."[105] But Gorbachev's speech to the gathering didn't break much ground either, with its less than clarion call to "mobilize our massive reserves and concentrate them so as to produce scientific-technological progress."[106]

What Gorbachev's speeches showed, Chernyaev confided to his diary, was that "he has not yet developed even a more or less clear conception of how to raise the country to level of world standards," that all he'd come up with so far were "fragments of a methodology."[107] Nor did his painstakingly prepared and much-heralded address to the Twenty-Seventh Party Congress in February 1986 do much better. His admission that the wider world was "complex, multifaceted, dynamic, full of contradictions and clashing tendencies" foreshadowed his later break with the Bolshevik bipolar image of "class-based" cold war conflict. And he had very sharp things to say about the system he inherited. But his recipe for the future still boiled down to "acceleration."[108] He was also beginning to use the term "perestroika," which literally means "restructuring," but it was a while before it became the new watchword for wholesale change.

The promised pace of acceleration was fantastic. Not only would the current Five-Year Plan, extending from 1986 to 1990, be fulfilled; it would grow national income by 20–22 percent and industrial production by 21–24 percent, while agricultural output doubled. By 2000, Soviet industrial output would match that of the United States.[109] Shades of Khrushchev—who promised to "catch up and overtake" the United States by 1960. Other moves recalled Khrushchev's effort to energize the economy by reshuffling bureaucrats. Seeking to galvanize agriculture, the Politburo decided to merge five ministries and a state committee into a super, agro-industrial committee (Agroprom), headed by Gorbachev's Stavropol protégé, Murakhovsky. But adding a new layer of bureaucracy on top of all the others was hardly a cure for stagnation caused by too much centralization. By the end of 1986, Gorbachev judged Agroprom a failure.[110] Another new agency, the State Acceptance Commission, applied quality-control methods that worked in military procurement to high-priority civilian output: output had to be approved by the commission before it could be sold and shipped. But the main result was to create a new layer of inspectors who were bribed or otherwise convinced that the same old low-quality output passed muster. All we succeeded in doing, Gorbachev recalled, was to "move the lump."[111]

The most important lever for galvanizing the country, Gorbachev still thought, was the Communist party and its officials at all levels of society. The party had been the backbone of the Soviet system since Lenin; its apparatchiki at every level (republics, provinces, cities, towns, and villages) were responsible not only for ideological orthodoxy and social conformity but for economic output. Gorbachev himself personified what he regarded as the party's still untapped potential. Just as he had restlessly roamed the Stavropol region, pushing and prodding people to work harder and better, now he barnstormed the country in search of failures to fix and people to fix them. He traveled to Ukraine in June 1985 and Siberia in September. In both places he combined sharp attacks on shortages of all sorts (The Siberian city of Nizhnevartovsk, with a population of 200,000, "doesn't have a single movie theater! What are [city] leaders thinking?") with calls for restructuring "not just of the way people work but of the psychological makeup of people. Without a perestroika of minds, there will be no restructuring of practical behavior."[112]

He didn't directly urge party leaders to model themselves on himself. On the contrary, when Vasily Demidenko, a province party boss in Kazakhstan, exhorted his colleagues to adopt "the Gorbachev style," Gorbachev rejected "eulogies that no one needs." But his specific advice amounted to his own credo: Get closer to the people! Engage with them more actively! Learn how to lead them! Hear them out, analyze their situation! Don't immediately start lecturing them and giving them instructions![113]

For a while, Gorbachev thought the new course was working, or at least said he did. "We know what we have to do, and we're going to do it," he told visiting American Communist party chief Gus Hall, on March 4, 1986.[114] He celebrated the Twenty-Seventh Congress's "creative" and "open" new atmosphere—in sharp contrast to "tightly choreographed" past conclaves in which people "feared to say something wrong," and "applause was carefully allocated."[115] He extended the term "perestroika" to encompass almost everything: "We must seriously restructure economic management, social policy, and political and ideological work. The Congress completely confirmed this."[116] The West wasn't nearly as worried about Soviet rockets, he boasted, as it was that the "new team" in the Kremlin would succeed.[117]

In fact, however, the notion that acceleration could jump-start the nation was itself a nonstarter. The trouble was that it relied on what had caused economic stagnation in the first place. The rigid central planning process, along with pervasive secrecy, stifled scientific and technical innovation. The machine-building enterprises Gorbachev wanted to encourage struggled to find customers for their low-quality production. Agricultural output lagged even as state subsidies designed to boost it ballooned. Shortages, which once had been largely limited to imported luxury items and then spread to ordinary consumer goods, now extended to necessities, including food; shoppers talked not of "buying" them but about "obtaining" them—by hook or crook or connections. The most ominous development involved oil. In the seventies and early eighties, the high price of oil and gas had sustained the economy by supporting the Soviet budget, fueling foreign trade, and helping to service the foreign debt. Now the global price of oil plummeted, from $31.75 a barrel in November 1985 to $10 in the spring of 1986.[118] Soviet oil production dropped, too, by as much as 12 million tons in 1985—just when Moscow needed to export more oil than ever in order to import grain.[119]

Another reason Gorbachev couldn't devise effective solutions to economic problems is that, even after he became Soviet leader, he didn't know exactly how bad the situation really was. Until then he wasn't privy to dire statistics that had been closely held by his predecessors. According to Nikolai Petrakov, the economist who later served as Gorbachev's chief economic adviser, most Soviet leaders didn't really want to know the truth. Their ideological motto was "If the facts contradict theory, so much the worse for the facts." Gorbachev did want the truth, but it wasn't easy to glean it from functionaries at all levels, who concealed it to avoid being punished. "Socialist language" itself, recalled Petrakov, whitewashed reality since its lexicon boasted plenty of synonyms for success while regularly affixing the adjectives "partial" and "temporary" to failures.[120]

It is no wonder, then, that "acceleration" didn't accelerate. By the end of November 1985, only 51 percent of construction projects planned for that year, and only one-third of the most crucial ones, had come online. Agricultural output, too, was less than expected, partly because up to 30 percent of the fodder was allowed to rot. During the last four days of October, factories engaged in the usual mad dash to turn out production planned for the whole month—40 percent of the freight cars and machine tools, and 22 percent of the televisions. "You can imagine the quality of these products!" groaned Gorbachev. Because of delays in bringing new plants online, overall output fell short by 15 to 17 billion rubles, while output of steel lagged by 9 million tons because of underuse of existing plants.[121]

Increasingly in early 1986, Gorbachev's speeches conveyed anxiety and dire warnings. March 10: "The country is filled with problems and disorder!"[122] March 12: "If we don't fulfill the 12th five-year plan, all will be lost."[123] When Solomentsev admonished the Politburo on March 20 that collective farmers' individual plots "threatened" socialist agriculture, Gorbachev exploded: "What are you saying? There's nothing to buy in the stores. Yet we're still afraid of individuals working on their own? Can't you see that socialism itself is in danger?"[124] March 24: "Our pollution is such that if we were to reveal the numbers, they'd nail us to the post of shame and say, 'See what socialism does to nature!'"[125] In Kuibyshev, which Gorbachev visited in early April, he found the textile industry backward, housing scarce, food rationed, one movie theater for 600,000 people, 17,000 children without places in kindergartens, and despite all this, "any manifestation of initiative is punished."[126] In Togliatti, home to the country's largest car-manufacturing plant, Gorbachev felt as if "a time machine" had taken him backward before March

1985.[127] "Keep in mind, Mikhail," a former Moscow University classmate of his, now the head of a Gorky university philosophy department, wrote him, "Nothing is happening in Gorky—NO-THING!"[128]

And that was before Chernobyl.

AT 1:23 A.M. ON APRIL 26, 1986, nuclear reactor number four at the atomic power station near the town of Pripyat in Ukraine exploded. The explosion and the fire that followed blasted radioactive fallout into the sky, many times more than was released by the atomic bomb that destroyed Hiroshima. The cloud spread over vast areas of the western USSR and eastern and northern Europe. More than 336,000 residents would eventually be evacuated from the area near the plant and resettled. Many died from cancers they would otherwise not have developed. Yet the initial report Gorbachev received on April 26, from the first deputy minister of energy and electrification, concluded, "No special measures, including evacuation of the population, are needed."[129] That helps explain why the Kremlin did not broadcast an immediate alarm to the country and the world, but not why the Soviet Union didn't acknowledge the explosion until April 28, why Gorbachev himself remained silent about the disaster for more than two weeks, or why, although he dispatched his prime minister to the disaster site, he never visited Chernobyl himself.[130]

Chernobyl officials who feared blame offered inaccurate information. Notified on April 26 that the fire had been contained and that the power station had survived, the Politburo merely formed a high-level commission to investigate. On April 27, nuclear engineers in Sweden detected heightened levels of radiation that did not come from their own reactors, and asked whether they originated in the USSR. So on April 28 Gorbachev pressed for a minimal public announcement that an explosion had taken place and that "necessary measures to localize its consequences are being undertaken."[131] But it wasn't until May 14 that he addressed the nation on television about the disaster. In the meantime, troops were mobilized and evacuation began of people living within six, and then twenty, miles of Chernobyl. But as late as May 1, by which time the Politburo was much better informed, traditional May Day celebrations were allowed to proceed in Kiev and other cities within range of

Chernobyl, with thousands of citizens, including children, marching innocently past statues of Lenin in public squares.

The chain reaction at Chernobyl and the Kremlin's nonreaction to it marked a turning point for Gorbachev and the Soviet regime. Atomic energy had been perhaps the regime's highest priority, especially for its military, but for civilian uses as well. Its nuclear prowess was proof, when so much else was going wrong, that the system still worked. The top scientists and engineers in charge of atomic development were virtually beyond criticism, even by the Politburo. That even the untouchable nuclear realm turned out to be rotten suggested that the whole system was, too. For the flaws revealed at Chernobyl and afterward were characteristic of the system as a whole: rampant incompetence, cover-ups at all levels, and self-destructive secrecy at the top. "Chernobyl really opened my eyes," Gorbachev recalled. In a sense, he continued, his life could be "divided into two parts: before Chernobyl and after it."[132]

Chernobyl resulted from "stunning irresponsibility," Gorbachev told the Politburo on May 22, from the ingrained habit of "not looking beyond one's narrow, technical obligations," from the near monopoly of information and control over atomic energy by untouchable, senior scientist-bureaucrats.[133] Anatoly Aleksandrov, president of the Academy of Sciences, and Efim Slavsky, the government minister in charge of atomic energy, sounded, Gorbachev later recalled, "like philistines; they told us nothing really terrible had happened, that such things take place at civilian reactors, that all you had to do was drink a glass or two of vodka, have a bite to eat, and sleep it off, and everything would be fine."[134]

"No one was prepared," Gorbachev thundered at a Politburo meeting on July 3. "Not civil defense, not the medical services, not those who measure radiation, not the firemen, who had no idea of how to cope. They all fucked up. The day after the explosion weddings were still being held nearby. Children were playing on the streets. Did anyone try to gauge where the cloud of radiation was going? Did they take measures? No. The director of the nuclear power station assured us that nothing like this could happen. Didn't the fact that 104 accidents occurred over the last five years worry you? And now Slavsky's deputy still assures us that reactors like this are reliable."

For thirty minutes, Gorbachev told Slavsky, "we've been listening to you tell us that everything is reliable. You've been counting on us to regard you as gods." "Where we're supposed to have centralization it doesn't exist. But when all that's needed is to hammer in a nail, thousands of agencies have to approve."

The whole atomic energy establishment, Gorbachev concluded, "is dominated by servility, bootlicking, cliquishness, and persecution of those who think differently, by putting on a good show, by personal connections and clans."[135] What Chernobyl revealed, he realized, was that "the old system had exhausted its possibilities." Raisa Gorbachev long remembered the shock of getting the news about Chernobyl. It was the "first and therefore particularly ominous sign" of troubles ahead, "an evil augury of what was to come."[136] At the time, however, the damage Chernobyl did to Gorbachev's new course was more concrete: the time, energy, and resources it took to recover from the catastrophe made it all the more difficult to produce the kinds of results that Soviet people wanted and expected.[137]

Gorbachev also crossed "a psychological barrier" after Chernobyl, contends Grachev, a step that "freed him to take more decisive action."[138] But first came a dual process of convincing himself and trying to convince his Kremlin colleagues that their initial strategy, or lack of strategy, had failed. From April 1986 until the end of the year, his complaints about virtually every aspect of Soviet life rose in an astonishing crescendo.

May 29: Vegetables in Moscow. Only 4,000 tons on sale every day, instead of the needed 7,000. Between 1981 and 1985, 3.3 million tons out of a total of 13 million rotted in storehouses. In Italy 90 percent of storage places were modern and ventilated. "What about us? Zero percent."[139]

June 5: The military draft. Every other draftee was a Muslim. Many didn't speak Russian. One hundred thousand draftees had served time in prison. Pacifists who refused to take the oath or bear arms were being drafted. And "the situation is getting worse every year."[140]

June 13: Anonymous denunciations. "We'll never get rid of them unless we eradicate the habit. When someone requests that some problem be investigated, they investigate him instead of the problem. We've gotten out of the habits of democracy—or rather, we never got into them in the first place."[141]

June 23: Bureaucracy. Government ministers were too old. Party officials were preserved in "mothballs." "We're sitting in a swamp. That's
where we are." "We talk about embarking on a 'Five-Year Plan of Efficiency and Quality,' but we haven't had either and we don't now." "Some
developing countries have already overtaken us." "We're all sitting in
the same crap."[142]

July 24: Theory and philosophy (Gorbachev's old favorites). "Our
task of tasks. But . . . we're unequipped. Almost all the economists favor
change, but when we ask them for suggestions they have nothing to
offer."[143]

August 14 (after a trip to far eastern provinces): "People attacked me
on streets and in factories, especially women; they just let me have it.
Defense industries are in great shape. But people wait ten to fifteen years
for housing. A city right next to a lake has no drinking water. There's no
children's clothing. They've never seen ice cream. Not even apples are
available."[144]

September 25: Agriculture, and prisoners. The Soviet Union produces
more harvester combines than any other country, "but they don't work."
In tsarist Russia's last years, the average number of people in prison was
108,000. In 1986, ten times more. "And we call that socialism!?"[145]

October 23: Universities. Lazy professors reading from yellowed old
notes. Some students write dissertations, but most just have fun or
simply drink. "When I lived in Stromynka, twenty-two students shared
one room. Was that so horrible? Now they have single rooms on Lenin
Hills."[146]

October 30: Governance. "We misfired a long time ago. We only think
that we govern. It just seems that way."[147]

Gorbachev's outrage and frustration mounted. During an August
vacation on the Black Sea near Yalta, his "concerns and anxieties" were
such, he recalls, that he "felt low" and "tense." He spent his time planning a drastic overhaul in party personnel, but kept worrying that new
cadres would be crippled by the old system. "What was really needed
was a real change in the system," he thought, surprised that "such a
conclusion no longer seemed seditious to me."[148]

By this time, Chernyaev had officially become Gorbachev's chief
foreign policy aide, but he sat in on discussions of all subjects, taking

notes when the Politburo met, meeting with his boss and other close aides, often talking with Gorbachev one on one, or with Yakovlev the only other person present. Chernyaev marveled at "the things that [Gorbachev] says at Politburo sessions and with close aides!" But "only I (and perhaps Yakovlev) hear him talk completely frankly and openly." Gorbachev was "relentless in criticizing what we have done and what we are doing." But Chernyaev concluded his diary for 1986 this way: "Exceptionally daring in words and how he evaluates the situation, but cautious in actions."[149]

ACCELERATION HAD FAILED, but what could replace it? And how could he get support in the Politburo for an alternative? Opting for acceleration had helped to bridge Kremlin differences: Ligachev, Solomentsev, and, to a lesser degree, Chebrikov and Vorotnikov had wanted to emphasize restoring order; Ryzhkov and others championed scientific-technological advance; Medvedev and Yakovlev called for economic reforms. Gorbachev's compromise, he says, had been to put off more-radical reforms until the beginning of the 1990s, by which time he counted on accelerating the economy.[150]

Yet even this timid approach seemed too radical for some. "Some people wonder whether we risk shattering the system," Vorotnikov warned at a Politburo session on June 20, "whether it wouldn't be better to move gradually, taking small steps."[151] Others, Chernyaev noted in his diary on July 29, "are beginning to grumble.[152] A further sign of disagreement was that two new laws passed in 1986, one in May on "unearned income," the other in November on "individual labor activity," were contradictory. The first law targeted corruption but ended up punishing the sort of small private tradesmen whom the second law tried to encourage. That's because not all of Gorbachev's colleagues wanted to encourage them in the first place. "One or two kids are learning some sort of trade," he said sarcastically in response to Politburo objections, "and we call that 'exploitation' . . . as if socialism itself were being undermined!"[153]

Aleksandr Yakovlev believed the desperate times called for truly radical measures. At a meeting of the Central Committee's propaganda department in August 1985, he erupted: "We've slept through a decade and half. The country is growing weaker. By the year 2000 we're going to be a second-rate power."[154] At the end of December, he sent Gorbachev a set of startling recommendations. The party itself must give up its "leading role" in the state. It must govern itself democratically. The state's legislative and executive branches must be separated. The legislature must become a working parliament with members chosen in competitive elections. The judiciary must be independent in guaranteeing individual rights, including the right to property and freedom of personal communications. Workers must have a real voice in running their enterprises. The country should have a president elected by the people from nominees presented by two (count 'em) two political parties—Socialist and National-Democratic parties—both associated with a renamed League of Communists.[155]

These weren't just reforms; they would revolutionize the Soviet political system. Moreover, they would have climaxed an alternative plan of action that Yakovlev wished Gorbachev had pursued throughout 1985 and 1986. He should have "created a social base" for such radical change, Yakovlev explained in a 2005 interview. He should have "reformed the army"; he should have "created a new, renovated KGB"; he should have disbanded collective farms and promoted private farming; he should have spurred small business. Instead, he let hard-liners lead him into misbegotten ventures like the anti-alcohol crusade and the campaigns against "unearned income" and "individual labor activity." According to Yakovlev, Gorbachev feared that the party elite would rein him in or kick him out if he took such drastic action; indeed, hard-liners were already sabotaging even lesser reforms. But Gorbachev underestimated his own power, Yakovlev contended. The old guard was scared of him. "They were wretched cowards; they'd been shaking in fear since Stalin's time." They would have acquiesced if Gorbachev had brought entirely new people into the leadership, not just slightly more enlightened party apparatchiki, but real liberals like Anatoly Sobchak and Gavriil Popov, Leningrad law professor and Moscow economist, respectively, who would later become their cities' mayors.

Gorbachev didn't reject Yakovlev's December 1985 recommendations as unthinkable. He merely said, "It's too early, too soon."[156] And he didn't think the country was ready for the rest of Yakovlev's alternative program either. Gorbachev was convinced his Politburo colleagues would move to oust him, just as Khrushchev had been deposed in 1964. And he was probably right. Indeed, Yakovlev himself made the case for caution on another occasion: "Any leader who wanted to make major changes had to be extremely crafty," to "dose out the acid that would corrode the dogmas of the existing punitive system," to be "a virtuoso, a master of the calculated compromise, for otherwise the very first missteps could bring disaster."[157]

YAKOVLEV'S SCHEME WOULD have to wait. Meanwhile, however, Gorbachev's campaign for glasnost was already underway. In theory, the Bolsheviks had always welcomed "criticism and self-criticism," while punishing those who practiced the wrong kind. Glasnost (derived from the Russian word for "voice") means something broader—openness and transparency. In the beginning Gorbachev limited its range and scope. Gradually, he allowed it to expand—partly to help mobilize support (especially from the intelligentsia) for other reforms, but also for its own sake as a halting Soviet version of freedom of speech.

Gorbachev called for more glasnost in "party, state, and social organizations" in his acceptance speech on March 11, 1985.[158] Until then defense-related matters had been off-limits even to Politburo members, who, as Gorbachev later put it, "didn't dare take an interest in or even ask for information" before they had to sign off on decisions. KGB-related materials, foreign trade data, especially information concerning weapons sales, but also trade in grain, oil, gas, and metals, were kept secret, even when such information was available abroad. Statistics of all sorts—economic, social, cultural, demographic, especially the standard of living and levels of health and crime—were strictly censored and even kept from the leadership. No one knew, Gorbachev later revealed, the "full extent of the ecological calamity" which resulted from our "wild, barbaric treatment of nature."[159]

Gorbachev complained about the information blockade in a special memorandum to the Politburo on November 26, 1985: "half-truths" fed to the leadership; successes hyped and mistakes concealed or blamed on others; diplomats abroad reporting what they thought Moscow wanted to hear; factories pretending that a single, solitary handmade product had just been mass-produced on the assembly line.[160] Such practices weren't new; they were as Russian as the vodka that comforted those who engaged in them. What was new was Gorbachev's conviction that he could change all this by extending glasnost to society at large.

"The people should know well what is happening in the country," he admonished province party leaders on October 16, 1985. "Only if they understand will they support us, will they come forward with their ideas and contribute to the common cause."[161] How to get the truth to the people? In the beginning, he relied on the media and the intelligentsia—not on the main party newspaper, *Pravda*, whose conservative editor, Viktor Afanasyev, remained in his post until 1989, but on magazines and journals with new editors, and on writers and filmmakers to whom Gorbachev reached out early on. Soviet leaders since Khrushchev had rarely met with this constituency. Gorbachev's sessions with them lasted as long as six hours. Other Politburo members who accompanied Gorbachev "started to snooze," recalled Grigory Baklanov, editor of *Znamya*, one of the country's "thick" journals containing prose, poetry, and social commentary, but Gorbachev's "eyes were alive, he spoke without notes, with ease." Baklanov watched Gorbachev's face—"the face of a clever man . . . interested in hearing everything, in learning everything, while keeping to his own opinion."[162]

Lenin had viewed film, with its vivid mass appeal, as a prime means of propaganda. "For us," he reportedly told People's Commissar of Culture Lunacharsky, "cinema is the most important of all the arts."[163] Like writers, artists, and composers, filmmakers had been herded into a "union," the better to tame them with a mixture of perks and threats. The union's leaders were only nominally "elected." In fact, the party apparatus prepared a slate of candidates (one candidate for each office) who were "unanimously" approved at periodic union congresses. In the spring of 1986, however, filmmakers revolted. Instead of accepting the slate, the union's nominating committee expanded it, voted down the party-approved nominees, and put forward their own. Asked later whether this upheaval wasn't stage-managed from above by liberals around Gorbachev, film and theater critic Maya Turovskaya said the rebels were as "flabbergasted" as the former leaders themselves. "We hadn't agreed in advance on what to do, we hadn't prepared. It happened quietly, spontaneously, and drastically."[164]

Decades of discontent by filmmakers whose films had been cut or shelved exploded at the union congress between May 13 and 15. "Critical speech after critical speech, very sincere, very harsh, very strident," recalled film director Elem Klimov, who was elected the union's leader after the officially approved candidate was voted down and twelve others were rejected for the union board.[165]

What followed after the congress was even more striking. Klimov made it a priority to release "arrested films," although "none of us knew how many had been shelved."[166] The union formed a conflicts committee, which started viewing and "rehabilitating" banned films. It eventually released more than a hundred of them. *Repentance* had been completed in 1984 by the Georgian master Tengiz Abuladze, with the help of Shevardnadze, then Georgian party boss, but hadn't been released. The film is a powerful allegory in which Varlam, the mayor of a small Georgian town, is a composite of Hitler, Mussolini, and Stalin: a man with a small mustache, a black shirt, and thick dark hair. Varlam dies and is buried with honor at the beginning of the film, but his corpse keeps reappearing until it, too, is "arrested." In flashbacks, the film describes how Varlam imprisoned and destroyed countless victims. *Repentance* is complicated and difficult to follow, but, at a time when it was still unclear whether Stalin could be criticized, the film was a revelation. Realizing that, Klimov took the issue directly to Yakovlev. Yakovlev, despite his commitment to radical reform, hesitated, asking Klimov, "What will comrades in other socialist countries say? The release of this film will change our social system."[167] Gorbachev, to whom Yakovlev took the film, recognized it was a "bombshell"; he promised Shevardnadze, who also lobbied him for the film, that it would eventually get a "green light." Some in the Politburo wanted to decide whether the film could be released, but Gorbachev insisted on letting the filmmakers' union decide, an unprecedented move. First, there were showings in Georgia, then selected ones in Moscow, finally, general release, but the reaction was spectacular. Soviet viewers immediately took it as a sign that truly radical change was indeed underway.[168]

The Soviet Writers' Union had been even more hidebound than the filmmakers'. Long led by cultural watchdog Georgy Markov, it too "elected" its leaders from a single slate, under conditions that precluded even crossing out names on the ballot. Delegates to writers' congresses in the Kremlin were ushered into a narrow corridor where there was no place to sit and read the names on the huge ballot sheets. All you could do, recalled Byelorussian writer Ales Adamovich, was "put the sheet in the ballot box, nothing else."[169] Gorbachev considered the old-guard leaders to be "talentless old fools," who "praise themselves and give themselves awards." But he didn't order their ouster, because they had supporters in the Politburo like Ligachev, and because the practice of dictating to the intelligentsia was what he was trying to change. At the writers' congress in June 1986, Adamovich and other liberals managed to get a few of their own elected to the union's governing board, but the old guard got on, too, and maintained its sway.[170]

About the same time, Anatoly Rybakov's novel *Children of the Arbat*, a literary counterpart to *Repentance*, was making its own way through the ideological obstacle course. Born in 1911 to a Jewish family in the Ukrainian city of Chernigov, Rybakov was arrested in 1934 and exiled to Siberia. After his release and service as a tank commander in World War II, his early, politically orthodox writing won two Stalin prizes. But the semi-autobiographical *Children of the Arbat* recounts the story of a sincere young Communist, Sasha Pankratov, who is exiled in the 1930s as Stalinist terror crushes young and old idealists alike, and includes a searing portrait of the bitter, paranoid Stalin, portraying him as guilty of ordering the 1934 assassination of his fair-haired young lieutenant, Leningrad party boss Sergei Kirov. The novel had circulated in samizdat in the 1960s, but after Yakovlev was made head of the Central Committee propaganda department in July 1985, Chernyaev sent him Rybakov's manuscript. Again Yakovlev hesitated, worried both about the portrait of Stalin and that there was "too much sex."[171] So Rybakov sent the manuscript directly to Gorbachev. He and his wife both liked it, although, according to Gorbachev, "it did not make a great impression on us from an artistic standpoint." Gorbachev felt "the book had to be published," and in 1987 it was. In retrospect he thought "the novel helped to conquer the fear that many still had of . . . unmasking totalitarianism."[172]

Even in limited form, glasnost galvanized the intelligentsia. But it stirred up the Politburo, too. Some members were dead set against *Repentance* and *Children of the Arbat*. The novel, Ligachev grumbled on October 27, 1986, "amounts to a denunciation of Stalin and all our prewar policies," "distorts the murder of Kirov," and "must not be published."[173] At the same Politburo session, KGB chief Chebrikov condemned "thick journals that spit on Soviet power" and writers who "settle accounts for the harm done to their parents."[174] More ominous was the special report Chebrikov prepared several weeks before the writers' congress. Its gist was that Western intelligence agencies had been "working on" certain Soviet writers known for "deviating" from class principles, for questioning collectivization of agriculture and the party line on literature, for holding "oppositionist and revisionist" views.

"Opposition to whom?" Chernyaev growled in his diary. "To Gorbachev? To the April plenum guidelines? To the Twenty-Seventh Congress?" Rybakov was among "oppositionists" singled out. "It looked like a regular denunciation from Stalin's time," Chernyaev continued, "as if nothing in the country had changed."

The most puzzling thing to Chernyaev was that Gorbachev himself had forwarded Chebrikov's denunciation to the Politburo. One might say that he had no alternative, since Chebrikov himself was a member. But when Yakovlev asked Gorbachev, "We've already forced fifteen or twenty talented writers to leave the country, do we want to lose more?," the latter "didn't seem to react" and then told him "to go talk to Ligachev"— whose only objection was that it was the KGB that was still hounding writers. Ligachev's idea of reform was to reserve that punitive function "exclusively to the Central Committee."[175]

In 1985 Andrei Sakharov, the father of the Soviet H-bomb turned persecuted dissident, was still in exile in Gorky with his wife, Elena Bonner, who had herself been convicted of "slandering the Soviet system." In April and again in July, Sakharov engaged in hunger strikes, demanding that Bonner be allowed to go abroad to visit her mother, children, and grandchildren in Boston and receive medical treatment for a bad heart. In July, begging Gorbachev again to let her travel, Sakharov pledged to "discontinue" his political activities (which had shrunk to very few in the face of the KGB's all-out efforts to smother them) except for "exceptional circumstances."[176]

A month later, on August 29, Gorbachev got the Politburo to agree— keeping the franchise with hard-liners by sneering that Sakharov's Jewish wife's influence on him showed "what Zionism is."[177] Bonner traveled to Boston and then returned to her exile in the couple's Gorky apartment. It was there, at ten o'clock on the evening of December 25, 1986, that the doorbell rang, "too late for the postman," Sakharov remembered, "and no one else ever came to see us." Two electricians accompanied by a KGB agent wanted to install a phone. "You'll get a call around ten tomorrow morning," said the agent.

The call came around three in the afternoon. "Mikhail Sergeyevich will speak to you," said a woman's voice.

"Hello, I'm listening," Sakharov replied.

"I received your letter," Gorbachev said, referring to another one Sakharov had sent in October 1986 demanding that all "prisoners of conscience" be released. "We've reviewed and discussed it. You can return to Moscow. . . . A decision has also been made about Elena Bonnaire [mispronouncing her name]. . . . You can return to Moscow together. . . . Go back to your patriotic work."[178]

Sakharov's release was a milestone, but it portended polarization. Sakharov himself, together with intellectuals who regarded him as a saint, would support Gorbachev, while pressing him to go further and faster in liberating the country. Hard-line Communists inside the Politburo and out would resist. As tensions rose, glasnost would cut several ways. It boosted Gorbachev's popularity. It alarmed most of his colleagues. It allowed the failure of Gorbachev's policies to be widely publicized, eventually prompting critics on both sides (those who feared he was going too far, and those who wanted to go further) to aim their fire directly at him.

CHAPTER 7

ONTO THE
WORLD STAGE

March 1985–December 1986

W HAT GORBACHEV CALLED his "new thinking" about foreign affairs developed further and faster than his reforms at home. He had a better idea of what he wanted to do abroad when he took power, and by the fall of 1986 some of his ideas were stunning, like the need not just to limit but to abolish nuclear weapons. Still, it took a while to put together a new foreign policy team. In foreign affairs, too, he faced the inertia of old ideas, so his earliest innovations, like those domestically, were more stylistic than substantive. He also confronted resistance from foreign leaders, especially U.S. President Ronald Reagan. But foreign leaders proved easier to handle than forces that frustrated him at home—political rivals, entrenched bureaucracies, persistent economic and social stagnation. Foreign affairs offered the satisfaction of performing on the world stage, jousting with the likes of Reagan, Thatcher, and French President François Mitterrand, being accepted into their club, and coming to feel he was not only their equal but in some ways superior. Despite all this, by the end of 1986, Gorbachev's foreign policies, like his domestic programs, had stalled and needed drastic renovation.

GORBACHEV'S PRE-1985 experience in foreign affairs wasn't negligible, but it wasn't extensive either. Valery Boldin, his longtime aide turned bitter enemy, sneers that "foreign policy issues were not [Gorbachev's] forte," since "he did not have any training in this area."[1] True, his early travels in the West were more tourism than diplomacy, but he won over Mrs. Thatcher in England in 1984, and in the summer of that year he impressed President Mitterrand in France. "It was on the morning of our departure from Moscow," recalled former French foreign minister Roland Dumas, who persuaded his boss to see Gorbachev for an hour-and-a-half conversation. "You were right to insist that I meet him," said Mitterrand afterward. Gorbachev's sense of humor was part of his appeal. According to Claude Estier, a French legislator traveling with Mitterrand, when Gorbachev arrived late at an official Kremlin reception, "he apologized, saying he had been busy trying to solve some urgent problem of the agricultural sector. I asked when the problem had arisen, and he replied with a sly smile: 'In 1917.'"[2]

After his promotion to Moscow, Gorbachev was exposed to diplomatic issues that came before the entire leadership. Under Brezhnev, recalled senior diplomat Yuli Vorontsov, who occasionally attended Politburo meetings, Gorbachev "always listened attentively" but "didn't pronounce himself one way or another," since "Gromyko was the big Tsar on foreign policy matters."[3] Andropov encouraged Gorbachev to familiarize himself with foreign affairs, but cut him off during at least one Politburo discussion, lest Gromyko take offense.[4]

Progress Publishers issued "white books"—Russian translations of foreign political literature that were available only to a restricted readership. Authors ranged from West European Communists to social democrats like Willy Brandt and Mitterrand. Future foreign minister Aleksandr Bessmertnykh read them while serving as Gromyko's duty officer in the Foreign Ministry. Gorbachev, too, had been an avid reader, and as far as Bessmertnykh could tell, "no other Politburo members read them."[5] In addition, Gorbachev regularly invited reform-minded foreign policy experts to his Central Committee office to brief him on the world economy and the overall strategic balance: Arbatov, Yevgeny Primakov (Institute of Eastern Studies), atomic energy expert Yevgeny Velikhov, space scientist Roald Sagdeyev, economist Abel Aganbegyan, and sociologist Tatyana Zaslavskaya.[6] Sagdeyev discovered that "all of my friends, and a few other acquaintances, had been invited to be members of different parallel working groups chaired by Gorbachev."[7] Besides these conversations and others with Yakovlev (after he returned from Canada to direct the Institute of the World Economy and International Relations) and Yakovlev's predecessor, Nikolai Inozemtsev, Gorbachev commissioned some 110 papers on foreign as well as domestic policy.[8]

Gorbachev's consultants included other "enlightened" bureaucrats: Chernyaev, Shakhnazarov, and Brutents from the Central Committee's international departments; Nikolai Detinov and Vitaly Katayev from its defense department, and veteran diplomats Valentin Falin and Anatoly Kovalev. Referring only to liberal-minded colleagues whose task was to handle freethinking Eurocommunist parties, Chernyaev recalled, "there were many of us, if not dozens, in our two international departments." It wasn't the Eurocommunists who liberated our thinking, adds Shakhnazarov; "we were ripe for new thinking, and came to it on our own."[9]

All these constituted, as Grachev puts it, "a kind of professional army awaiting its leader," along with scientists who wanted more access to foreign colleagues, economic managers, and local party officials jealous of resources gobbled up by the defense budget, even high KGB officials like Nikolai Leonov, who thought, "The people from the military-industrial complex . . . didn't take economics into account at all. They thought our resources were unlimited—as if they had not been informed as to the country's real situation." "We could write a lot of memos," recalled Shakhnazarov, "but it didn't matter until a [new] leader appeared in the General Secretary's chair. . . ."[10]

However, some of Gorbachev's early pronouncements after taking office sounded as if they had been prepared under Brezhnev. Chernyaev believed that a quick exit from Afghanistan would give the new leader "a moral-political platform from which he could later move mountains. It would be the equivalent of Khrushchev's anti-Stalin speech to the 20th Party Congress. Not to mention the great start it would get us off to in foreign policy." He was horrified to discover Gorbachev had said to Raúl Castro, "We will not abandon our brothers in need."[11] Gorbachev's much-ballyhooed speech to the Central Committee plenum on April 19 struck Chernyaev as at least "energetic" on domestic policy, but "on foreign policy it was flat, ordinary, standard." Arbatov, who was sitting next to Chernyaev at the plenum, grumbled that Gorbachev had not included anything from "what I submitted to him at his request."[12]

Brutents considered Gorbachev's speech on the fortieth anniversary of victory in World War II to be "entirely Brezhnevite," and lamented that the new leader had harangued Willy Brandt about Washington's "aggressive expansionism."[13]

Chernyaev explains the pattern this way: "He wanted to change things, abroad as well as at home, but he didn't yet know how."[14] Gorbachev admits he had "no detailed plan of action," but insists he had "a sufficiently clear aim and a rough draft of first steps."[15] But if what he called his "new thinking" seemed underdeveloped at this point, that was because he still shared in the old thinking. According to Grachev, Gorbachev "continued to believe that the basic orientation of the Soviet foreign policy in the postwar period was correct, justified by the prevailing interests of national security and concerns for the historic destiny of world socialism."[16]

Tactical considerations also accounted for Gorbachev's caution. "He had to watch his step in the beginning," recalled Dobrynin, then Soviet ambassador to Washington, "and needed time to consolidate his power, especially in the Politburo and among the top military proponents of continued confrontation" with the West. Moreover, "he was never sure what Reagan would do next."[17]

Gorbachev's earliest innovation was that he gave detailed instructions to Gromyko, "not simply a scrap of paper with his signature," Chernyaev recalled, "but notes explaining how he saw the questions at hand." Chernyaev didn't like everything Gorbachev said to Raúl Castro, but found his approach to the Cuban leader "fresh, broad, lively, unconstrained by clichés or dogma," in short, "genuine political realism." Likewise, his conversations with Brandt: "Strikingly skillful and crafty." When he received U.S. Speaker of the House "Tip" O'Neill in the Kremlin in May, Gorbachev was "brilliant, vivid, powerful, lively, and confident, speaking with competence and conviction."[18]

DURING GORBACHEV'S FIRST YEARS in power, the Politburo had a large say in his foreign policy. It discussed major diplomatic moves, approving instructions for high-level negotiations, even details such as the makeup of Soviet delegations to summit meetings. So the fact that it took so long for Gorbachev to alter the Politburo's membership was an important constraint. A commission known as the Big Five—the heads of the Foreign and Defense Ministries, the KGB, the Military-Industrial Commission, and the party's international department—coordinated Soviet bargaining positions on disarmament. Under Gromyko and Defense Minister Ustinov, the Big Five's reports had been mostly joint products of the Foreign and Defense Ministries. Under Gorbachev, and with a new chairman, former Leningrad party leader Lev Zaikov, the commission's recommendations reflected a broader consensus. Still, Gorbachev recalls, national security agencies were "at least as conservative and ideologically 'drilled' as the bureaucrats in our domestic administration."[19]

Unlike American presidents and other Western leaders, who have large national security staffs to coordinate (and sometimes supersede) their foreign and defense ministries and intelligence agencies, Soviet leaders did not have substantial foreign policy staffs of their own. Instead, they were served by Central Committee departments specializing on foreign affairs. But in the beginning, Gorbachev didn't trust his own staff. Since his foreign policy assistant, Andrei Aleksandrov-Agentov, known as "the sparrow" among his Central Committee colleagues because of his slight build, was a Brezhnev holdover, Gorbachev didn't bother to discuss key matters with him, a fact Aleksandrov-Agentov deeply resented.[20]

Likewise, international department chief Boris Ponomarev. With Gromyko monopolizing East-West relations, Ponomarev's domain consisted of East European allies and other Communist parties in and out of power. According to Chernyaev, the elderly Ponomarev (born in 1905) was "far from the worst" of the high-level aides with whom Gorbachev had to begin perestroika. He was quietly anti-Stalinist, but he dismissed "new thinking" that Chernyaev tried to insert into the text of a Gorbachev speech, assuming Gorbachev shared his perspective. "What new thinking?" Ponomarev asked. "We [already] have the right thinking. Let the Americans change their thinking."

Chernyaev pointed out places in the text where Gorbachev referred to "*our* new thinking."

"I don't know, I don't know," Ponomarev sighed. "He said that in Paris, in Geneva, for them, for the West."

"You mean you think that's just demagogy?"

"One needs to know how to conduct the fight. . . ."

It was only by reforming Soviet society, Chernyaev continued, that Moscow could win the competition with the West. Ponomarev grumbled, "Are you talking about peaceful coexistence? I wrote about that in materials for the Nineteenth Party Congress [in 1952]. What's new about that?"[21]

Until Shevardnadze took over in the summer of 1985, Gorbachev still relied on Foreign Minister Gromyko.[22] But Gromyko was soon seething at Gorbachev's approach; he was energetic alright, Gromyko told his son, but he "tries to do too much at once, he doesn't succeed in finishing one thing before he latches onto another. He talks incessantly, can't pick out what's most important, and often repeats himself."[23] There was some truth to this, especially later on in his administration, but, of course, Gromyko himself was hardly without sin. Gorbachev "did not hide his displeasure at Gromyko's conservative, dogmatic approach," remembered Dobrynin; he "had not forgotten Gromyko's criticisms of his trip to Britain."[24] Aleksandrov-Agentov also picked up on Gorbachev's disdain for Gromyko. When he reported that a paragraph about to be included in a Gorbachev speech was "not admired" in the Foreign Ministry, Gorbachev snorted, "Include the whole text as it is."

Gorbachev kicked Gromyko upstairs on June 29, 1985. Gorbachev's speech nominating him as titular head of state was pro forma: Gromyko had been a party member for a long time, he said, and had consistently followed the party line. Stinting on praise for a man who was no longer a threat was politically maladroit, but it was characteristic of Gorbachev. It "showed once again," Chernyaev confided to his diary, "that the 'personal' aspect does not matter to him."[25]

The consensus in Moscow was that a veteran diplomat would replace Gromyko. First Deputy Foreign Minister Georgy Kornienko was Gromyko's first choice, but that helped to disqualify him in Gorbachev's eyes. In an interview, Kornienko recalled how Gorbachev proposed he accompany him to London in December 1984. Kornienko replied he had to get his boss's permission, which he doubted would be granted since preparations were underway for talks between Gromyko and U.S. Secretary of State George Shultz in January in Geneva. Three times Gorbachev asked whether, Gromyko's views notwithstanding, Kornienko "would like to come with me." Each time Kornienko answered that the question was "abstract" since Gromyko, not he, would decide the matter. Gorbachev then asked Gromyko's permission for Kornienko to go to London, and Gromyko said no. A short time later, when Gorbachev arrived at the airport to depart for England, he was bid farewell, as was Soviet custom, by a phalanx of government ministers. Gorbachev introduced his wife to each of them, including Kornienko, who was standing in for Gromyko that day. "This is my old friend," said Gorbachev after a long pause. He's "Gromyko's right-hand man."[26]

Kornienko took that as a sarcastic rebuke, and it was. Kornienko later said it "showed" Gorbachev's "insincerity" and his insistence on having aides "who served not the cause, but him and only him." That was unfair; Gorbachev later appointed Kornienko first deputy director of the international department. Even if Kornienko was correct, however, the key point isn't that Gorbachev chose loyalists to serve him but that so many of them ended up betraying him.

Dobrynin himself was another logical possibility as foreign minister. He had been ambassador to Washington since 1962, which confirmed not only his expertise but, as Gorbachev put it, that Gromyko did not want him around, "realizing that in many ways Dobrynin was his equal and perhaps even his superior."[27] Before appointing Shevardnadze, Gorbachev went through the motions of asking Gromyko's opinion of another candidate, Yuli Vorontsov, ambassador to India between 1977 and 1983 and to France since 1983. But Gromyko's objections to Vorontsov, which counted as praise in Gorbachev's eyes, weren't quite enough to push Dobrynin or Vorontsov over the top.[28]

Gorbachev's choice of Shevardnadze, announced to the Politburo on June 29, was totally unexpected. When Gromyko informed his senior staff, "his face was flushed with rage and Kornienko's was white as a sheet."[29] Shevardnadze himself was shocked. "I might have expected anything but this," he blurted out when Gorbachev telephoned him with the news. . . . I am not a professional [diplomat]. . . . I'm a Georgian. . . . People may start asking questions." Gorbachev cites several reasons for his choice: Shevardnadze was a "major political figure," he was "capable of deliberation and persuasion," and he was "graced with Eastern affability." Most important, Shevardnadze's appointment "assured [me] of a free hand in foreign policy by bringing in a close friend and associate."[30] Their careers overlapped in Stavropol and Georgia, and their early lives had much in common: both were born in rural villages; both had relatives arrested and then released during the purges; both were student leaders in high school and college who pursued their political ambitions in the Komsomol and Communist party; both were outraged by what Khrushchev revealed about Stalin's crimes.[31]

As foreign minister, Shevardnadze did not disappoint Gorbachev. According to Deputy Foreign Minister Anatoly Kovalev, Gromyko, in his last years, usually arrived at the ministry after nine in the morning, left work between six and seven, and with rare exceptions, didn't appear on weekends. Shevardnadze's workday, on the other hand, lasted fourteen or fifteen hours (he rarely left before eleven at night, lugging piles of documents with him), he sometimes slept in his office, and on Saturdays he worked "only" seven or eight hours. He devoted hours to debriefing Soviet negotiators, pressing them for information and taking notes, so that, like Gorbachev, he need not rely on experts while negotiating with foreign leaders. He replaced Gromyko's men with his own, promoted smart, young diplomats to top posts, and created new departments on disarmament and on humanitarian problems, in preparation for engaging, rather than stonewalling, the West on human rights issues. One thing Shevardnadze didn't or couldn't change was his ministry's adversarial relationship with the Central Committee's international department, though it, too, soon got a new leader, Anatoly Dobrynin.[32]

Dobrynin replaced Ponomarev in March 1986, simultaneously becoming a high-ranking Central Committee secretary. One of Gorbachev's aims was to end the Foreign Ministry's monopoly over foreign policy, but the international department's focus, Dobrynin discovered, was only "Communist and other left-wing parties as well as radical international organizations and mass movements in the West and in the Third World."[33] Dobrynin extended his department's brief to Soviet-American relations and hired Kornienko and Vitaly Churkin (who later became deputy foreign minister), as well as arms control experts.[34] He accompanied Gorbachev to several summits, but bureaucratic turf warfare, Gorbachev's determination to conduct his own policy, and what

Gorbachev later described as Shevardnadze's "Georgian self-respect and pride" combined to limit Dobrynin's overall role.[35]

Chernyaev became Gorbachev's chief foreign policy aide on February 1, 1986. Having emancipated himself from Soviet dogma earlier and more completely than his boss, he acted as Gorbachev's conscience, not only in foreign affairs, but on domestic matters, about which Gorbachev kept consulting him. According to Grachev, they were "practically inseparable." He was at Gorbachev's side during virtually all of his foreign travels and most of his meetings with foreign leaders in Moscow; he wrote memos, drafted speeches, and edited all press releases on Gorbachev's talks with foreigners; he even accompanied his boss on vacations, during which Gorbachev tried out his thinking about matters foreign and domestic. Moreover, Chernyaev's personal modesty and lack of ambition for higher office allowed him to preserve good relations with Shevardnadze and Dobrynin.[36]

Chernyaev was ten years older than Gorbachev, born in 1921 into the kind of family the Bolsheviks had made the revolution to destroy. His paternal grandfather served Tsar Alexander II as a general. Chernyaev's father was a tsarist officer in the First World War, and his mother, too, was from an aristocratic family. Somehow they survived and even managed to live fairly well in the 1920s. By no means all aristocrats and tsarist officers were admirable people, but Chernyaev's family was particularly cultivated; he received music lessons, learned French and German from private teachers, and fell in love with Gogol and Shakespeare in school. He studied history at Moscow University in the late thirties, fought heroically in World War II (part of the time on skis in an alpine battalion), then got a candidate's degree (roughly equivalent to an American Ph.D.), writing his dissertation on the topic "Britain's Role during the First Years after World War I." Unlike so many of his generation, he never worshipped Stalin. It wasn't the repressions, "about which we didn't know much and which we thought might have been mistakes or even justified," he recalled, or the "terrible losses early in World War II," or inner revulsion against policies like the 1939 Hitler-Stalin pact. It was the sense that "a crude, ignorant, completely alien force" was ruling over a culture that cherished Tolstoy and Chekhov and admired foreign writers like Shakespeare and Anatole France.[37]

The very image of a former officer—ramrod straight, with brush-backed gray hair and small mustache—Chernyaev came almost to worship Gorbachev, "the one who dared to raise Russia and make it rear up," he wrote in his diary on June 6, 1986, alluding to the symbolism of the equestrian monument to Peter the Great christened the Bronze Horseman by Pushkin. Yet he had "all the traits of an intelligent, normal, sensible, and practical person," a man "who can process a colossal amount of information (I can't understand how he manages to do so) and emerge with deductions, analysis, conclusions, decisions." He was a leader with "a great wealth of intelligence, character, awareness, knowledge, and precision, with the ability to grasp the essence of a matter and decisively reject anything even resembling demagogy, as well as attempts to cover up a lack of talent."[38] So little did his admiration blind Chernyaev to his boss's real flaws as a man and a politician that his criticisms, which mounted up as the years passed, are far more telling than wild charges of treason by Gorbachev's fiercest adversaries. It also should be noted, however, that Chernyaev was a very emotional man who blew hot and cold about Gorbachev.

Gorbachev's wife was much less equipped by knowledge and experience to advise him on foreign, as opposed to domestic, affairs. She had traveled abroad with him, but that was before he took power. If she had found her debut as a teacher daunting, representing her country abroad as its "first lady" was even more intimidating. She was aware she had no "special diplomatic knowledge and certainly no experience of 'high society.'" She learned for the first time that "there are strict rules governing diplomatic ceremonies and protocol," that "even such occasions as a 'lunch,' 'tea,' or 'fourchette [cocktail buffet]' have their own 'individual' elements of diplomatic etiquette," that dinner, "which has to take place in the evening after seven o'clock or later" had "a strict and well-defined order of 'seating' at the table and, as a rule, [required] formal or evening attire."[39]

Despite her inexperience, or rather, because of it, she bent every effort to master her new role, especially after Margaret Thatcher went out of her way to "nudge her into playing the part of first lady more boldly."[40] According to the Kremlin's chief of protocol, Vladimir Shevchenko, Mrs. Gorbachev prepared meticulously for foreign trips, requesting exhaustive advance information on the country, its culture, its leaders, and the specific places she would be visiting. She didn't just "picture the upcoming program," English-interpreter Pavel Palazhchenko recalled, "she mastered it," peppering Gorbachev aides and embassy officials so insistently for concrete answers that they often grew weary and annoyed. During foreign trips, she entered her impressions in little notebooks, Palazhchenko observed, in her "precise, legible script," so as to be able to recall them later on. Much of what she recalled, often painfully according to Grachev, were commentaries about the visits in the local press that she took to reflect "misconceptions, superficial and primitive judgments, and frequently gossip and obvious slander."[41]

While Gorbachev engaged in diplomacy, his wife followed special "first lady's programs"—sightseeing, meeting with women's groups, visiting schools, kindergartens, and especially museums, for which she prepared by acquainting herself in advance with their holdings.[42] She also "managed to slip away 'incognito'" to "wander the streets of Helsinki" or visit a "family grocer's shop" in San Francisco.[43] She had always paid particular, tasteful attention to her dress, but even more so now, on state visits. It was not easy, given the limited resources of textiles and design in the USSR, so later she began to shop abroad. All this made her an international celebrity, who personified the way her husband was modernizing his country. She also made sure that the gifts she and her husband received during their official trips were deposited in Soviet state archives, and that they received receipts in return, lest it be claimed that they had appropriated them for their own personal use.[44]

EVER SINCE LENIN, the Bolsheviks had viewed world politics as class struggle projected onto the global stage. Soviet Russia represented the exploited of the earth. The capitalist, imperialist powers were Moscow's sworn enemies. Stalin saw the world as divided into two camps with conflict between them inevitable and enduring peace impossible. In Stalin's time, the imperialist camp seemed more powerful, but the Soviet camp had important advantages. It could play on "contradictions" among imperialist powers, attempting to divide if not conquer them. It could urge on the working class in capitalist countries, if not to seize power, then to resist anti-Soviet aggression by their rulers.[45] After Stalin's death, his dog-eat-dog view of the world underwent important, but limited, modifications. Khrushchev transformed "peaceful coexistence" from a short-term tactic into a long-run strategy. But his attempt to ease the cold war helped to trigger its two most dangerous crises, in Berlin and Cuba.[46] Brezhnev succeeded where Khrushchev had not by negotiating East-West détente in the 1970s. But absent a fundamental rethinking of Soviet goals and a corresponding reduction in Western alarm about "the Soviet threat," détente soon gave way to the renewed high tension that Gorbachev inherited.

Even before March 1985, Gorbachev arrived at two new postulates, which Grachev formulates as follows—that the Soviet Union was "clearly losing the competition with its historic capitalist rivals," economically, technologically, and in living standards, and that, contrary to Soviet propaganda's image of a monolithic, aggressive West, "the so-called 'imperialist world' represented a complex reality of different states and societies" and "apparently was in no way preparing to attack or invade the Soviet Union."[47] Chernyaev identifies a "moral foundation," also in place by 1985, that underlay Gorbachev's future policies—"the conviction that it was possible to unite politics with morality," plus Gorbachev's "aversion to violence."[48] What followed from this, Gorbachev believed, was the need for a sharp improvement of relations with the United States. If the arms race continued, especially if Reagan's Strategic Defense Initiative, known as Star Wars, extended it into space, Gorbachev feared, the USSR would lose the battle, along with any chance to mobilize resources for a domestic renaissance. Not to mention the rising risk of a war that could destroy civilization. In addition to all its other lessons, Chernobyl showed him how devastating a nuclear strike would be. "How can anyone think after Chernobyl that life would continue after a nuclear war?" he exclaimed on November 3, 1989. "After all, that was only one reactor that blew up."[49]

If these were cornerstones of the new thinking, the old thinking wasn't entirely alien to it. Moscow's many "peace offensives," cynically turned on and off over the decades, had been designed to achieve only temporary "breathing spells." But they provided ideological cover for Gorbachev's effort to bring about a more permanent peace. Even before

1985, Dobrynin recalled, Soviet leaders knew that "nuclear war was to be avoided at all costs" and that the interests of the Soviet Union and the United States were served by "at least a minimum of cooperation."[50] That allowed Gorbachev eventually to seek maximum cooperation of the kind his predecessors had deemed neither possible nor desirable. A traditional Soviet tactic for undermining NATO was to propose an alternative security structure built around the Conference on European Security and Cooperation. Gorbachev eventually transformed that propaganda mirage into a vision, which sounded phony but wasn't, of a "common European home."

In retrospect, Gorbachev's drift is obvious in statements he made early on. "We must live and let live," he told *Time* magazine in August 1985. "Any thought at all about starting a nuclear war is madness," he informed visiting U.S. senators in early September. To French parliamentarians he damned "the infernal train of the arms race." Not just "national interests, but world interests" must guide humanity, he informed Nobel laureates in November. At a press conference following the U.S.-Soviet summit in Geneva that same month: "The interconnections and interdependence of nations demand new policies." From a New Year's address to the Soviet people: "In the nuclear age, all the peoples of the earth are in one boat." In an interview with the French Communist newspaper, *L'Humanité*, on February 4, 1986: "It won't even take unprecedented stupidity or criminality for civilization to destroy itself. All it would take is to continue acting as mankind has acted for thousands of years—to keep relying on arms and force to settle international disputes. It is this tradition that we must ruthlessly demolish."

Because these were all public pronouncements buried in heaps of old-style rhetoric, Western observers could, and often did, dismiss them as propaganda. The world didn't know that Gorbachev told the Politburo on May 8, 1985, that Brezhnev's détente hadn't gone nearly far enough. Nor that he recognized (in a January 28, 1986, conversation with Italian Communist party leader, Alessandro Natta) a universal right that, if taken seriously in Eastern Europe, would explode the Soviet empire: "the right of every people to choose their own political and social-economic path."[51]

The Twenty-Seventh Party Congress, in February 1986, provided a platform for a definitive statement on foreign affairs. Work on it, which began the previous summer, elicited old-style contributions from the Foreign and Defense Ministries and Central Committee departments. Chernyaev, who saw Central Committee submissions in August 1985, described them in his diary as "primitive and traditional." One draft portrayed the socialist camp as a "besieged fortress" and summoned "all hands on deck to resist the imperialist threats." There wasn't a word about Soviet allies' "sovereignty and independence." The whole text had a "lecturing" tone. "Almost every phrase contains the words, 'must,' 'necessary,' 'ought to,' 'should,' 'requires.'"[52]

In response, Gorbachev turned the drafting over to Yakovlev, who by then headed the Central Committee's propaganda department. Hating collective drafting and priding himself on his own craftsmanship, Yakovlev recruited only two aides to help him prepare a final version. He told one of them, Valentin Falin, that Gorbachev wanted "a fresh vision of the international scene along with the constructive role the Soviet Union was prepared to play in it," adding, "Try to put the best of yourself into it." The other speechwriter remembers Yakovlev's saying "it was time to include in the text most of the ideas we had dreamt of and talked about among ourselves in the past, that we had to use the chance we were offered."[53]

Yakovlev's draft was "the only section" of the draft report that Gorbachev accepted without major changes.[54] In addition to the nuclear danger, it warned of ecological disasters that threatened both sides: "Never before has our earth been subject to such political and physical overloads. Never has man extracted so much tribute from nature while becoming so vulnerable to the powers that he himself has created." Yet the very next paragraph veered back to the past: "Global developments confirm the fundamental conclusion of Marxism-Leninism—that social history is not random . . . but a natural forward-moving process" in which "progress will inevitably unfold in the midst of struggle as long as exploitation and exploiting classes exist."[55]

Despite such passages, Gorbachev's former associates consider his Twenty-Seventh Congress report a turning point. "It resounded with a categorical 'no' to the system of prevailing views," recalls Shevardnadze.[56] "It radically changed the direction of Soviet foreign policy," remembered Dobrynin.[57] The "foundation for changes," Chernyaev says, was the idea that "we must leave our isolation and join the general flow of civilization." What remained to be done, Chernyaev continues, was to turn the new thinking into "practical policy," to get the national security bureaucracy to implement it, and to get the world to admit that Gorbachev's new thinking was not just "pretty words."[58]

Gorbachev addressed the first two of these tasks in a remarkable talk at the Foreign Ministry on May 23. No previous leader had taken his case directly to the nation's diplomats, let alone talked to them in the way he did. Foreign policy needed a "radical restructuring." Peace was the "highest of high priorities." The main task was "to stop the nuclear arms race." The United States wanted to keep that going in order to prevent Moscow from shifting military resources to civilian needs. Soviet diplomacy must aim to reduce the burden of defense spending. As for dealing with Moscow's East European allies, "we must not think that we are omnipotent and can teach everyone." Even if national experiments by other socialist countries were not in the Soviet interest, they must be allowed. Soviet diplomats must also take "human rights" out of quotation marks, as if they weren't real, must stop being afraid of them, must cease being so defensive.[59]

Talk like this, revolutionary though it was, didn't persuade all of Gorbachev's listeners. Nor, if it had been made public, would it have convinced the outside world. The assembled diplomats, like functionaries throughout the Soviet bureaucracy, had witnessed plenty of previous "campaigns" that hadn't changed anything. Western cold warriors didn't believe Gorbachev meant what he said. Even East European allies, with their longtime, inside exposure to Soviet cynicism, thought his call for change was just more of the same. The real test was his concrete policies and actions in key parts of the world.

THE COLD WAR BEGAN in Eastern Europe. Stalin seized it after World War II as a buffer zone and erected a series of satellite states. Khrushchev and then Brezhnev tried to give their allies more autonomy, but intervened to crush uprisings in East Germany (1953), Hungary (1956), and Czechoslovakia (1968). When the movement of workers and intellectuals known as Solidarity threatened a similar upheaval in Poland, a fourth Soviet intervention loomed in 1980. But Poland was bigger and tougher than its neighbors, Soviet troops were bogged down in Afghanistan, and Soviet leaders were older and, at least in one respect, wiser. "Poland is not Czechoslovakia or Afghanistan," Brezhnev lamented. Andropov said to a trusted subordinate, "The quota of interventions has been exhausted."[60] Even the ideologically pure Suslov was prepared to let a few social democrats join Poland's government rather than send in troops. Instead of invading, Moscow pushed Polish General Wojciech Jaruzelski to declare martial law and provided him with funds, food, and other supplies to pacify Poland, at least for the time being.[61] Between 1981 and the time Gorbachev took office, Soviet leaders paid virtually no visits to Eastern Europe, while avoiding sharp issues when allied leaders came to Moscow.[62] That signaled not the region's declining importance but their own physical and mental deterioration.

Gorbachev insists Eastern Europe remained all-important for him. He knew, he says, that an internal crisis was coming, the same sort that faced the USSR, but worse because aged East European leaders had been in power for decades and refused to recognize the need to change. Moreover, the "socialist camp" (including Vietnam, Cuba, and North Korea as well as East European allies) had become a drag on the Soviet economy, receiving as much as $17 billion worth of raw materials and other goods from Moscow while providing only $3.5–5 billion in return. "From the very start," Gorbachev remembered, "we made it our rule" that Soviet allies would be "independent in their decisions and that what happened with the Prague Spring should never be repeated—when the people wanted to build socialism 'with a human face' . . . and we responded with tanks."[63]

In fact, however, the most striking thing about Gorbachev's approach to Eastern Europe is how little attention he paid to it early on. Upon becoming Soviet leader, he drew up a list of his ten most important priorities in foreign policy. Neither Eastern Europe nor the Warsaw Pact (the Eastern bloc version of NATO) was on it.[64] "As regards the 'socialist community,'" recalled Chernyaev, "I don't think it held much interest for Gorbachev." Chernyaev wasn't directly involved in dealing with foreign Communist leaders (Shakhnazarov was), but "watching Gorbachev and listening to his opinions I sensed—and I was not alone in this—that he was unenthusiastic about contacts with socialist leaders, that he had trouble agreeing to visits and apparently didn't want to emphasize his 'leading role.'"[65] Adds Shakhnazarov: It wasn't that Gorbachev's attitude toward East European states was "You can go now, we do not need you anymore." He wanted to see them reformed so as to continue to provide "a belt of friendly states along [Soviet] borders." But the area "was not his main priority, he did not want to hold it together by violent means, just as he did not want to hold the Soviet Union together by violent means."[66] Shevardnadze's assistant Tarasenko remembers urging reforms in the Warsaw Pact that would "scale down our presence and make it less visible, and less provocative" to East European allies. Shevardnadze took the memo to Gorbachev and came back saying such moves were premature. "They probably decided," says Tarasenko, "that that was not a priority."[67]

Given that Communism crumbled in Eastern Europe just four years later, and that Gorbachev's critics roundly condemn him for letting that happen, his top aides' assessment seems particularly damning. It wasn't, however, that Eastern Europe was a low priority for Gorbachev, but that other areas—domestic reform, East-West relations, and Afghanistan— were higher. It wasn't that he closed his eyes to the coming Communist collapse, but that he and his colleagues, even hard-liners, thought the region was stable enough ("apparently tranquil," in Grachev's phrase) for the foreseeable future.[68] It wasn't that he couldn't be bothered with interfering in his neighbors' affairs; it was that he was opposed in principle to doing so.

But there was also this, according to Chernyaev—that with the exception of Jaruzelski (and Hungarian leader János Kádár, whose health was failing), Gorbachev "did not feel that other East European leaders were his equals. He did not think they were at the level of modern international relations. He could not allow himself to speak openly with them because . . . they were locked in ideologically" and would "misunderstand him even worse if he was to speak with them as he spoke with Western leaders." But not leveling with them led to a crucial misunderstanding. Since Gorbachev addressed allied leaders mostly in their own ideological language (which also had the tactical virtue of reassuring conservatives in Moscow), they went away convinced that he would not abandon them, but rather rescue them from the holes they were digging for themselves.[69]

Gorbachev's priorities were visible in the foreign leaders he chose to meet with individually on the day of Chernenko's funeral—Westerners including U.S. Vice President George H. W. Bush and Prime Minister Thatcher. The only Communist leader was Natta of the Italian party. "What's the matter with [Gorbachev]?" Ponomarev complained to Chernyaev. "So many leaders of 'good' communist parties are here, but he only received the Italians, the 'bad' ones."[70] After the funeral, East European leaders trooped to the Kremlin for a group session with the new Soviet leader. Gorbachev opened the session by endorsing "equality among allies and respect for their sovereignty and independence," in other words, he later recalled, "a repudiation of the so-called Brezhnev Doctrine" that had justified Soviet interventions in East Germany, Hungary, and Czechoslovakia.[71] But he admits that his listeners "didn't take it seriously." They had heard sweet words before; their attitude was "We'll wait and see."

A public renunciation of the Brezhnev Doctrine would have convinced them. But "to say so publicly," recalled Shakhnazarov, "to say, 'You know, friends, beginning tomorrow, if you wanted to leave us, and to join NATO, do not be afraid'— . . . one would have had to be a complete idiot to say that."[72] Indeed, Gorbachev's only harsh words to his East European colleagues, directed against the uppity Romanian dictator, Nicolae Ceaușescu, who wanted to renew the Warsaw Pact for only ten years instead of twenty, were in support of tighter ties within the alliance. In general, Gorbachev told the Politburo the next day, the meeting was marked by "an exceptionally warm, comradely, and business-like atmosphere."[73]

Gorbachev could have clarified his policy on Eastern Europe at the April 1985 Central Committee plenum. But the plenum did not deal with the region at all.[74] And his address to alliance leaders later that month at a meeting in Warsaw was mostly old-style oratory. One might have thought he was buttressing the Brezhnev Doctrine, not dropping it, and in fact, one of his top aides believed that was Gorbachev's general aim. Oleg Rakhmanin, first deputy head of the Central Committee's socialist countries department, was "very conservative," says Shakhnazarov, a "very strong fundamentalist." Rakhmanin thought Gorbachev would "discipline" the "disorderly" socialist camp in which Hungarian leader Kádár "was doing whatever he wanted," the East German Honecker was "hiding some things from us, making deals with West Germany, . . . accepting loans, letting people travel," Ceauşescu was "doing nobody-knew-what," and the Poles "flirted with the Americans and planned to purchase Boeings instead of our airplanes."[75] Rakhmanin therefore published an article in *Pravda*, under the pseudonym of "Vladimirov," blasting Soviet allies for nationalism and even Russophobia, condemning "unnecessary reforms," and demanding greater obedience in the camp.[76]

The Western press pounced on the article, asking whether it reflected Gorbachev's actual policies or opposition to them.[77] Liberals like Shakhnazarov got calls from like-minded East European friends, while allied officials demanded to know, "Is this really the official point of view of the new leadership? If so, it is a scandal. Where are we going?" Gorbachev saw the article as insubordination, if not outright subversion of his policy. He was so outraged, Shakhnazarov recalled, that he started "throwing papers around" and demanding to know why the East Europeans were "portraying me as some kind of monster."[78] He'd had to display maximum flexibility and tact, Gorbachev told the Politburo on June 29. He made up excuses to call Kádár and Honecker and then, as if by the way, reassured them that the "Vladimirov" article didn't reflect his views. "I really had to sweat," he complained and then interrogated Rakhmanin's boss, Central Committee secretary Konstantin Rusakov: "Did you know that this article was being written in your department?" How about veteran secretary Mikhail Zimyanin: "Did you?" And *Pravda* editor Viktor Afanasyev: "And you? Didn't you know what you were doing?" None of them took responsibility. None was immediately dismissed, although it wasn't long before close Gorbachev adviser Vadim Medvedev replaced Rusakov, and Shakhnazrov replaced Rakhmanin.[79]

Even after this embarrassment, Gorbachev failed fully to clarify his East European policy. He still didn't have "a full picture of what was going on in the region," he later admitted, "much less a thought-through system of [new] measures to suggest to our allies."[80] Gorbachev's formula for dealing with socialist allies was stern but vague: "Instructions, directives, sermonizing—all this should disappear into the past."[81] His comments to the Politburo after another Warsaw Pact meeting blended unjustified optimism ("Our friends . . . are still drawn to us.") with a diatribe against his favorite punching bag, Ceauşescu: "He is always trying to steal the march [on us], as if he has already done everything before us. Well, to hell with him! . . . It's a mess in his head, a jumble."[82]

Gorbachev went so far as to prepare a special memorandum to the Politburo in June 1986 on relations with Communist allies, but its injunctions, too, were imprecise: "eliminate everything that impedes the development of interactions with our friends [so as] to provide a new impetus . . . and release socialism's potential on an international scale." His insistence that "relations with our allies must occupy first place" implied, quite correctly, that this wasn't currently the case. The memo pressed the Central Committee apparatus, along with the Foreign Ministry and the KGB, to "overcome negative phenomena and provide necessary acceleration [that dread word, again!] in our relations with socialist countries." On July 3 he even told the Politburo, "The methods that were used in Czechoslovakia and Hungary are now no good; they will not work!"[83] This was his first declaration that military force would not be used to hold on to East Europe. But as historian Svetlana Savranskaya notes, "no concrete steps" toward "a new coordinated strategy" toward the region were taken "until early 1989, when by all measures it was already too late."[84]

THE WAR IN AFGHANISTAN had been raging for more than five years when Gorbachev became party leader. By the time the last Soviet troops departed, in February 1989, more than thirteen thousand Soviet soldiers had died, with thousands more wounded. Thousands of Afghans perished, and millions fled to Pakistan and Iran. The Soviet military had been against the Politburo decision to invade. Even before March 1985, Soviet leaders had searched for an exit. By 1982, they accepted a UN attempt to resolve the conflict. By 1984, a draft agreement was nearly complete, except for the intractable, intertwined issues of the timing of a Soviet withdrawal and an end to interference by outside forces, primarily the United States and Pakistan, which had been supporting the mujahideen.[85]

Gorbachev himself seemed intent on ending the war. Near the top of his urgent "to-do" list were the words "Exit from Afghanistan."[86] He understood, recalled Arbatov, "we had to get out of this mess."[87] In June 1985, according to Kornienko, Gorbachev assigned him to prepare a proposal for "settling the Afghan question." Sensing the new mood at the top, and at the same time reinforcing it, ordinary citizens flooded the Central Committee and leading newspapers with letters: "Why do we need this? When will it end?" Women grieved for husbands and sons suffering and dying. Soldiers had no idea why they were fighting. Officers, even one general, couldn't explain to their men "why they are here." Two letters, from a tank and a helicopter crew, condemned *Pravda* for its depiction of heroic Afghan soldiers. In reality, "we are the ones doing the fighting; everything is utterly different [from your report]." What was most stunning to Chernyaev was that, unlike in the past, this time there were very few anonymous letters. "Almost all of them were signed."[88]

Afghan Communist leader Babrak Karmal was one of the first foreigners Gorbachev received after becoming general secretary. Karmal assured him on March 14 that the Soviet-Afghan friendship was "unique in the history of humanity."[89] By October, however, when Gorbachev summoned Karmal again, the material Chernyaev helped prepare for the meeting was somber in the extreme: "Every day ten of our boys die. There is no hope that the Afghan people will ever defend their revolution." And the recommendations were equally stark—"a swift return to free elections and to Afghan-Islamic values, and power sharing with the opposition—even with the rebels." Gorbachev conveyed that message to Karmal "very gently," but "didn't meet with understanding," a result reflected in what he told the Politburo on October 17. Although Gorbachev had decided "to end it," Karmal, he said, "thinks we need Afghanistan more than he does and clearly expects we will stay for a long time, if not forever." That's why he had to be told "with the utmost clarity: by the summer of 1986 you will have to learn how to defend your own revolution. We'll help you for a while longer, but not with troops, just with aviation, artillery, equipment. If you want to survive, you'll have to broaden the regime's social base, forget about socialism, and share power." With or without Karmal's consent, Gorbachev told his colleagues, "We'll firmly carry out our policy of an extremely rapid withdrawal from Afghanistan." The defense minister, Marshal Sergei Sokolov, agreed it was time to get out. Gromyko did not. "You had to see the ironic expressions on his colleagues' faces, including Gorbachev's," Chernyaev continues. "Their looks said it all: 'What are you babbling about, you prick? You got us into this mess and now, according to you, we're all responsible.'"[90]

The Politburo approved withdrawal in principle at the same session.[91] At the Twenty-Seventh Party Congress, Gorbachev called the Afghan war "a bleeding wound."[92] But the troops stayed. In fact, some of the most ferocious fighting of the war took place during Gorbachev's first years in office, and the number of Soviet troops, which had risen from 100,000 to 120,000 under Chernenko, remained at that level through the first half of 1986.[93] Moscow reorganized the Afghan leadership by replacing Karmal with Mohammad Najibullah, and launched a campaign for "national reconciliation," while conducting four-party talks (with the United States, Pakistan, and Afghanistan) on terms to end war. But the last Soviet combat soldier did not leave Afghanistan until February 15, 1989.

"It was not [Gorbachev's] war," recalls former American ambassador to Moscow Jack Matlock Jr., "but by not ending it he was making it his own."[94] According to Artemy Kalinovsky, author of a full Western account of the withdrawal, Gorbachev "feared undermining Moscow's status as a defender of Third World countries" against Western imperialism.[95] Even though, by that time, he had soured on Third World entanglements established by his predecessors. Libyan dictator Muammar al-Gadhafi portrayed himself as "world revolutionary," Gorbachev said, but he acts as if "he's dealing with representatives of kindergartens, as if he who shouts louder makes the better revolution."[96] Syria "is beginning to dictate to us . . . while taking our money. It turns out we're carrying out not our policy, but theirs."[97] (Was this not also the case thirty years later?) Foreign aid was fine, but "huge amounts are now senseless."[98] Revealingly, Gorbachev's favorite Third World partner wasn't some radical anti-imperialist firebrand, but India's moderate, cultivated prime minister, Rajiv Gandhi. Pavel Palazhchenko, who interpreted their conversations, recalls, "Gorbachev trusted Rajiv Gandhi. He shared with him his plans, his ideas . . . even his doubts." "Their rapport was total."[99]

Despite all this, Gorbachev still believed, or felt he had to seem to believe, what he said at an April 1986 Politburo meeting: "We can under no circumstances just clear out of Afghanistan, or we'll spoil our relations with a great many foreign friends," such as Cuba, East Germany, and Iraq.[100] He also believed, or said he did, that Moscow could not just abandon its Afghan allies. "We'll be out in two or three years," he told the Politburo on June 26, 1986, but "the result must not look like a shameful defeat, as if after losing so many young men we just gave up."[101] Many years later Gorbachev admitted he should have moved faster, that, alas, he hadn't learned the lesson of Vietnam.[102] The United States fought on in Vietnam to avoid seeming, in President Nixon's words, "a pitiful helpless giant." The parallels between Soviet problems in Afghanistan in 1985 and the American dilemma there thirty years later are legion: corrupt Afghan leaders; unreliable Afghan army; population increasingly alienated; enemy sanctuaries across the Pakistan border; national reconciliation not working; deadlines for departing seemingly fungible.

Domestic politics also explain Gorbachev's behavior. Until he changed its membership, the Politburo contained an "Afghan lobby" led by Gromyko. The Soviet military and the KGB supported different factions in the Afghan Communist party, which cultivated their Soviet sponsors and played them off against each other. In addition, Moscow needed Washington's assistance to leave on tolerable terms, but the Americans wouldn't oblige. The Soviets wouldn't set a firm date for withdrawal until Pakistan stopped supplying the mujahideen. Pakistan wouldn't do so until Moscow set a date for its departure. The United States was Pakistan's paymaster and supplier of arms for the Afghan rebels, and the Reagan administration was still engaged, or so it seemed, in all-out cold war with the USSR.

"WE CANNOT DO ANYTHING without them and they cannot do anything without us," Gorbachev told the Politburo on April 3, 1986.[103] He was referring to the United States. He had in mind not only the reduction he sought in cold war tensions but also the reordering of Soviet priorities (from defense spending to civilian needs) that depended on better relations with Washington. But President Reagan seemed intent on ruining relations with Moscow rather than improving them.

From his vantage point in Washington, Dobrynin compiled a long list of Reagan's sins: détente scrapped, arms control abandoned, rapid military buildup, attempts to separate Eastern Europe from Moscow, military cooperation with China, resistance to Soviet influence in the Middle East, intimidation of Cuba, no interest in an Afghan settlement. Not to mention blasting the USSR as an "evil empire" whose leaders "reserve unto themselves the right to commit any crime, to lie, to cheat to promote world revolution." Or the Strategic Defense Initiative (SDI), which Moscow thought was designed to deprive the Soviet Union of a chance to retaliate in case of nuclear war. Never before during Dobrynin's long career as ambassador had he seen the Soviet leadership "so deeply set against an American president. It was a catastrophe in personal relations at the highest level."[104]

But there was another side to Reagan: personal, almost mawkish, handwritten letters to Brezhnev proclaiming peaceful intentions; a visit to the Soviet embassy in Washington offering condolences after Brezhnev's death; a prediction to Dobrynin by a close colleague of Reagan's, Nevada Senator Paul Laxalt, that Reagan would eventually prove to be "a partner ready for agreement." Reagan himself assured Dobrynin that "although people in the Soviet Union probably regard me as a crazy warmonger, I don't want war between us, because I know it would bring countless disasters. We should make a fresh start." Dobrynin was puzzled by these contradictions. His bosses in Moscow regarded them as "a sign of deliberate duplicity and hostility."[105]

The Kremlin's view was not altered by a "thaw" that Reagan seemed to promote before the 1984 election. Now that American economic and military might had been rebuilt, he declared on January 16, 1984, he was ready to start settling differences with the Soviet Union. Reagan not only received Foreign Minister Gromyko in the White House in September but confided to him ("as if this was a big secret," noted Dobrynin) that his personal dream was "a world without nuclear arms."[106]

Reagan's thinking about the USSR was genuinely inconsistent. He knew of "no Soviet leader since the revolution" who was not determined to promote "world revolution and a one-world Socialist or Communist

State." They had spoken, he contended, "as plainly as Hitler did in *Mein Kampf.*" Yet the same Reagan had "a gut feeling" that if he could just talk to Chernenko "man to man," he might "convince him there would be a material benefit to the Soviets if they'd join the family of nations." Reagan considered the Soviets "paranoid about being attacked," but thought the cure for that could be "a meeting to see if we can't make them understand we have no designs on them but think they have designs on us. If we could once clear the air, maybe reducing arms wouldn't look so impossible to them."[107] But if the Soviets really were paranoid, wouldn't they take such assurance as a trick?

Reagan's stand on nuclear weapons was also unusual. The fact that he favored elimination of them was no secret; he said so more than 150 times during his two administrations.[108] But what made him think abolition was both desirable and possible, if almost none of his advisers or allied leaders agreed? They were convinced that nuclear deterrence had kept the peace. He thought SDI could make offensive nuclear missiles obsolete, and that, in the meantime, the very prospect of it could persuade the Soviets to give up the missiles they had. But most defense experts didn't believe Star Wars was realistic either.

Reagan's hopes for nuclear disarmament looked wildly utopian. Frances FitzGerald portrays them as wares of a master pitchman, an actor turned salesman who resembled Arthur Miller's Willy Loman—"a man way out there in the blue, riding on a smile and a shoeshine."[109] But what made his pitch more powerful was that he apparently believed it. And in the fall of 1986 he almost achieved his goal! Because in Gorbachev, Reagan found the perfect partner—he, too, convinced that a U.S.-Soviet settlement was possible, with his own vision of nuclear abolition, and his own conviction that personal chemistry could produce miracles.

In the beginning, however, it didn't seem likely to work out that way. On March 12, 1985, the day after he was named Soviet leader, Gorbachev had Yakovlev prepare a memorandum on a possible summit with Reagan. The memo forecast no major changes in Reagan's hardline course, recommending a meeting only as a way to begin to ease tensions.[110] On the day of Chernenko's funeral, Gorbachev received Vice President Bush at 10 p.m. in the Kremlin, accompanied by Gromyko and Secretary of State George Shultz. In an important departure, Bush delivered a letter from Reagan inviting Gorbachev to visit the United States. But Gorbachev's answer would have to await a Politburo discussion, he said. And although he swore to his guests that the USSR "has never intended to fight the United States," adding, "there have never been such madmen within the Soviet leadership, and there are none now," he also asked bluntly, "Is the United States really interested in achieving results at the talks or does it need them to implement its rearmament program?"

What was new and different was the way Gorbachev conducted the conversation. He had a full set of typed notes, but put them aside. He was, reports Shultz, "articulate and spontaneous. He seemed to be thinking out loud." His performance "showed a mind working at high intensity, even at the end of a long, hard day. He displayed a breadth of view and vigor." Shultz compared Gorbachev with other Soviet leaders he had met: He was "quicker, fresher, more engaging, and more wide-ranging in his interests and knowledge." He was "comfortable with himself and with others, joking with Gromyko in a way that emerged from genuine confidence in his . . . knowledge and in his political abilities. He performs like a man who has been in charge for a while, not [one] who is just taking charge." Shultz told the press afterward, "Gorbachev is radically different from any Soviet leaders I have ever met." Back in Washington he praised Gorbachev highly to Reagan. Ambassador Dobrynin heard more praise from Bush on March 19, along with a mild put-down of the president. Dobrynin complained that after inviting Gorbachev to Washington, Reagan lashed out again at "Marxist-Leninists." Bush admitted Reagan's rhetoric was sometimes "careless." "Reagan is still Reagan," he said.[111]

And Gorbachev was still Gorbachev—initially perhaps in awe of the world leaders he was meeting for the first time, but quick to feel himself on a higher plane. "Gorbachev impressed everyone," Shultz recalled. But not everyone impressed Gorbachev. Mitterrand shared the Soviet stance against an arms race in space, Gorbachev told other Central Committee secretaries, but he "looked ill and had trouble speaking." West German Chancellor Helmut Kohl was anxious to talk, but seemed fearful that England, France, Italy, and other NATO allies were trying to "circumvent Bonn in repairing relations with Moscow." As for Bush and Shultz, with whom he conversed for almost two hours, they struck him as "mediocre. Not a very serious team." Whenever Gorbachev tried to take the conversation beyond what Bush expected, "he became flustered." Although the Americans stressed that Reagan wanted a meeting, his letter was "diffuse and not concrete."[112]

Reagan and Gorbachev both wanted a summit, but there were doubters in their capitals. The Kremlin traditionally insisted that summits be crowned with a major agreement. Gorbachev's view, expressed in his March 24 reply to Reagan, was that a summit "should not necessarily be concluded by signing some major documents,"[113] but that concession had to be pried out of his Politburo colleagues. If they insisted on precooked agreements, Gorbachev told them, "the summit will not be held earlier than in two or three years. Probably it will not take place at all. Now time is short."[114] But while pushing for a meeting, Gorbachev stuck to Gromyko's line that Washington would have to end its Star Wars program if it wanted a deal. And the trouble with that, Chernyaev thought, was that Gorbachev would now "have to back down *from his own*, not Gromyko's, conditions" (emphasis in original). In brief, Chernyaev wrote in his diary on May 5, "Things haven't begun well in foreign policy. All because we're even further from a revolutionary approach here than we are in domestic affairs."[115]

Meanwhile, Reagan "was getting clobbered by Defense Secretary Caspar Weinberger and the hard-liners for wanting to meet with Gorbachev."[116] Or so he told Shultz. Shultz was prepared to schedule a summit when he met Gromyko in Vienna in early May, but feared Gromyko would "try to extract some concession from me as the price." As a result, the two talked for six hours without mentioning a summit and agreed on one only as they walked out the door.

"President Reagan would be welcome in Moscow," Gromyko said.

"It's your turn to come to Washington," replied Shultz.

Gromyko insisted on Europe. Shultz suggested Geneva.

"If you say Geneva, I'll have to say Helsinki," growled Gromyko, who was not without an extremely dry sense of humor.[117]

THE TWO SIDES agreed in June on a November 19–20 summit in Geneva. To prepare the way, Gorbachev resorted to another old Soviet tactic— "softening up" Washington by cultivating NATO allies more eager than

the Americans for East-West agreements. He chose to make his first official visit abroad to France, with its Gaullist tradition of distancing itself
from the United States.[118]

Western Europe shared a continent with the USSR; it traded more
with the Soviets than the United States did; its Communist parties had
long-standing ties with the CPSU; even its non-Communist parties
were better disposed toward Russia than Reagan and his Republicans
were. And Mitterrand had important reasons to invite the new Soviet
leader. His grand strategic goals, phrased in the kind of lofty language
that appealed to Gorbachev, were "the gradual affirmation of Western
Europe's autonomous personality, the promotion of its complementar-
ities with Eastern Europe, the obligation of the USSR to re-establish a
more trusting climate with [European] Community countries . . . and the
assurance that it [Moscow] should obtain from these countries in return
that the independence of Europe will not become a war machine against
the USSR."[119] But when Gorbachev and his wife flew into Paris on October 2, 1985, his immediate aims were more limited, and so were Mitterrand's. If Gorbachev wanted to renew détente, Mitterrand would require
him to abandon the aggressive practices that had led to its demise. Gorbachev wanted Mitterrand to join him in denouncing SDI and in direct
negotiations about nuclear weapons, but Mitterrand rejected joint declarations on both these subjects.[120]

In some ways, the visit was a throwback to the bad old days. Gorbachev's public speeches weren't scintillating. His call for a moratorium
on the deployment of Euromissiles (those that could reach and devas-
tate Moscow in just a few minutes) echoed Brezhnev-era propaganda.
His mention of a "common European home" got a lukewarm reception
from a group of legislators. He was not invited to speak to the National
Assembly.[121] Soviet Ambassador Yuli Vorontsov thought Gorbachev
did a "brilliant" job at a joint press conference with Mitterrand at the
Elysée Palace, leaving the French president "sitting there unemployed,"
but "wise enough to smile and say, 'No, no, it's his press conference, ask
him your questions and I'll sit here waiting.'"[122] Chernyaev thought
Mitterrand's face looked "mean and haughty," an "ironic, cold, politely
condescending response" to "yet another sally in Russia's centuries-
long attempt at a brotherly embrace of Europe."[123] Gorbachev literally

**Gorbachev press conference with French President
François Mitterrand, Paris, October 4, 1985.**

sweated through his debut news conference with a Western leader. "My whole back is wet," he told Grachev afterward, "the way it used be after I worked on the harvesting combine."[124]

Gorbachev and Raisa were delighted with the warm public welcome they received. French TV interviewers challenged Gorbachev on Soviet human rights violations (to which he responded angrily), but they also inquired flatteringly about "the Gorbachev style"—to which he replied that there was no such thing, that all he did was keep working the way he'd worked all his life, and that many of his colleagues did likewise.[125] Mrs. Gorbachev visited the Rodin Museum, which she remembered from a previous trip, addressed the Society for Friendship with the Soviet Union, and met with a group of Frenchwomen at the Soviet embassy. Crowds followed her everywhere. Danielle Mitterrand invited her to dine at the Elysée Palace with the cream of the intelligentsia.

Vitaly Gusenkov, who served eight years as a diplomat in Paris before joining the Central Committee's international department in 1979, helped Mrs. Gorbachev prepare for her trip. In 1977 Gusenkov and his wife, Ludmila, had shown the Gorbachevs around Paris, and in 1985 Gorbachev telephoned to ask Gusenkov's help again. Raisa wanted to minimize protocol and formalities and to maximize "human contacts," Gusenkov remembered. She also "prepared very carefully. If anything wasn't clear to her, she called up and asked. She dug down to the tiniest details. She was always prepared. She could answer any question. It was amazing, colossal really, simply colossal. She almost never read a speech. She had notes, which I helped her prepare beforehand, but she decided which ones to use, and she didn't read from them."[126]

When Mrs. Mitterrand mentioned that she had her own staff, consisting of several aides and secretaries who prepared briefings for her and handled her correspondence, Mrs. Gorbachev was amazed. Later she learned that American first ladies, too, had their own office staff, as did the West German chancellor's wife.[127] As for Gorbachev's wife, Gusenkov recalled, "She had no such thing. Just me. I helped her when she asked for help, and accompanied her on some foreign trips. And there was one other man, a writer, who helped her write her book. But beyond that there was no one. Not even a secretary."

ON THE EVE of the Geneva summit, Gorbachev struck Arbatov as "nervous, although he tried not to show it."[128] Dobrynin remembered him in state of "high anxiety."[129] Some of the excitement went with the territory—the first summit after five years of high cold war tension. But Gorbachev went into it with an uneasy mixture of great need and low expectations. If he were to ease the cold war and restructure Soviet society, he required Reagan's cooperation. But he certainly couldn't count on getting it.

A meeting in Moscow with Shultz on November 3 showed what Gorbachev was up against. Before this session, too, Dobrynin recalled, Gorbachev was "agitated." He needed "to convince skeptical members of the Politburo that the meeting was worthwhile." But, Gorbachev complained to Shevardnadze and Dobrynin, "we hear nothing from the Americans but generalities." Shultz, too, was hopeful. Unlike most of Reagan's advisers, he thought Gorbachev might be contemplating major moves. To encourage him, Shultz planned to talk to him about "the information age," the way it was "transforming the worlds of finance, manufacturing, politics, scientific research, diplomacy," the fact that the

Soviet Union "would fall hopelessly and permanently behind the rest of the world in this new era unless it changed its economic and political system." State Department colleagues warned Shultz against conducting "a classroom in the Kremlin; it's condescending. The Soviets will resent your presentation deeply."[130]

But Shultz was right. His message was just the sort of social-scientific theorizing in which Gorbachev liked to engage—even when Shultz told him directly that "closed" societies cannot "take advantage of the information age," and that the Soviet system would "have to be radically changed to adapt to the new era." Rather than being offended, Gorbachev responded "with a twinkle in his eyes: 'You should take over the state planning office here in Moscow . . . because you have more ideas than they have!'"[131]

Other elements of the meeting encouraged Shultz: Gorbachev didn't flare up when interrupted, but seemed to relish sharp exchanges, and although "he talked a lot, he also listened." But on the whole, according to Dobrynin, the conversation was "long and difficult." Gorbachev complained heatedly about SDI. Shultz gave as good as he got. Dobrynin thought Gorbachev was "overdoing [SDI] because that would merely reinforce Reagan's belief in its importance."[132] Shultz felt Gorbachev was "acting, posturing, trying to show how tough he was."[133] Gorbachev came away disappointed that Shultz "did not have serious baggage for the summit."[134]

In preparation for Geneva, Gorbachev received the traditional joint memorandum from the Foreign Ministry, the Defense Ministry, and the KGB (none of them expected much from the meeting), which became the basis for formal negotiating instructions from the Politburo. On the other hand, the official delegation to Geneva included "new thinkers": Yakovlev, Arbatov, and scientists Velikhov and Sagdeyev. The last three were part of an intellectual advance team ("the political call girls of the Soviet delegation," as one of them put it) that arrived early so as to answer questions from the assembled world press.[135]

Reagan's summit preparations were "so unusually extensive," according to his Russia adviser Jack Matlock Jr., that "they are probably unique in the annals of the American presidency." Beginning the previous summer, Matlock and others put him through "the equivalent of a college course," including more than twenty papers followed by discussion with their authors, meetings with other academics from outside the bureaucracy, and video presentations on Gorbachev put together by the CIA from broadcast material. At one point, Matlock recalls, "we could get two or three two-hour sessions with him a week! (Try to get 15 minutes with any other president.)" Reagan's attention waned when confronted with too many details, but "never flagged when we were talking about Gorbachev as a person."[136] One of the experts he consulted was Suzanne Massie, author of *Land of the Firebird: The Beauty of Old Russia* and of *Pavlovsk*, with whom he had eighteen meetings throughout his presidency.[137] This exposure to Russian history was doubtless instructive, even though it didn't seem so to Reagan's advisers during a last-minute review of the American negotiating position on arms. At one point, there was a long silence and Reagan seemed far away. "I'm in the year 1830," he explained. "What happened to all those small shopkeepers in St. Petersburg in the year 1830 and to all that entrepreneurial talent in Russia? How can it have just disappeared?"[138]

The summit itself, to judge by its transcripts and results, didn't constitute a breakthrough, yet both its leading actors were convinced that it did. It began on the morning of November 19 in the elegant nineteenth-century Château Fleur d'Eau on the shore of Lake Geneva. Despite a cold wind whipping off the lake, the seventy-four-year-old Reagan emerged from the house without an overcoat and jauntily descended the front steps to greet his guest. Gorbachev, in a gray overcoat, plaid wool scarf, and signature fedora, was twenty years younger, but didn't look it. Gorbachev made light of the contrast, telling Reagan, "You're lightly dressed. Don't catch cold, or I won't have anyone to hold talks with."[139] In fact, this move was planned by Reagan's handlers, and it worked.[140] "Gorbachev made a mental note," Dobrynin remembered, so "when it was our turn and Reagan came to our residence, Gorbachev also came out coatless to meet him."[141] Mrs. Gorbachev, as usual, did her best to appear quietly elegant in the Western manner, but her outfits still revealed the limitations of what was possible in the USSR, even for the wife of the general secretary. At least one beige blouse with a pussycat bow appeared on two occasions. Nancy Reagan, by contrast, appeared at the two dinner parties in stunning designer outfits and elegant jewelry. Raisa's dress for dinner was floor-length, though the men were in dark suits, in deference to the traditional Soviet disdain for formal wear as "bourgeois."

The first session began at ten o'clock: just Reagan, Gorbachev, and their two interpreters in a pale-blue sitting room. Although scheduled to last fifteen minutes, it went on for more than an hour, leaving half a dozen advisers on each side to wait in an ornate salon, uncomfortably seated on either side of a long table.[142] Reagan's contributions to the tête-à-tête featured pieties lifted from election stump speeches: Countries didn't mistrust each other because of their arms; they armed themselves because they mistrusted each other. It wasn't "people but governments that created arms." He accused the Soviet Union of using force to advance "socialist revolutions throughout the world," but hoped that the summit might "eliminate suspicions each side had of the other." Gorbachev was more realistic; he wondered whether "changing relations for the better" wasn't "perhaps too simplistic, bearing in mind the tremendous differences between the two countries." At the press meeting and photo op, Gorbachev looked tense, holding tightly to the arms of his chair, blinking frequently, and looking to Reagan for cues. Reagan sat

Gorbachev and Reagan synchronize their watches at Geneva summit, November 18, 1985.

**Gorbachev and U.S. President Ronald Reagan's fireside chat
during Geneva summit, November 19, 1985.**

casually, one leg crossed over the other, a pose Gorbachev had adopted by the end of the summit, when he was visibly more self-confident, relaxed, and affable.[143]

The first plenary session, with advisers from both sides present, was a cold war set piece, "a repetition," says Dobrynin, "of the private correspondence between Reagan and the Soviet leaders during the past five years of his administration." The only improvement was "a businesslike atmosphere without mutual irritation."[144] Gorbachev saved his irritation for his advisers after the session. Reagan, he told them, "does not seem to hear what I am trying to say. He's deep in his memos prepared by the advisers. He's a real dinosaur."[145]

The second plenary, after lunch, was no better. The two leaders argued at length about SDI. The atmosphere, according to Dobrynin, became "heated and emotional." At this point, Reagan suggested they walk down to a pool house by the lake. He and his wife had inspected it the day before, and ordered it prepared with a blazing fire in an oversized hearth. Many commentators, including Grachev, say the seventy-five-minute conversation there, attended only by interpreters, broke the ice.[146] But it's hard to tell that from its transcript, which shows the two men continuing to clash over SDI, Reagan offering yet again to share space defense weapons, Gorbachev demanding to know why he should believe the president.[147]

The rest of the summit went a bit more smoothly. From SDI the crossfire shifted to Afghanistan, Nicaragua, and human rights. At one point, when Reagan repeated for the umpteenth time that SDI was defensive, not offensive, Gorbachev's face flushed with anger: "Do you take us for idiots?"[148] Reagan's awkward toast at dinner that evening—that if aliens astride Halley's Comet were coming to attack Earth, "that knowledge would unite all peoples of the world"—didn't help much. But the two men did agree that "a nuclear war cannot be won and must never be fought," a very important statement since both sides had long feared that the other didn't believe that. Moreover, while walking back from the pool house, they also agreed to two more meetings, in Washington in 1986 and Moscow in 1987.

According to White House Chief of Staff Donald Regan, his boss "glowed with pride and a sense of accomplishment" about this "masterstroke of personal diplomacy," which he had carried off on his own without his advisers. The episode seemed to confirm his view that "two men of good will could move the world together if they only spoke as one human being to another."[149] Reagan thought enough of the summit to devote the prologue of his memoirs to it: "The world was approaching the threshold of a new day. We had a chance to make it a safer and better place. . . . There was much more to be done, but we laid a foundation in Geneva."[150]

Gorbachev, too, considered the summit a "breakthrough."[151] "A fundamental thing has happened," Chernyaev wrote in his diary on November 24. "A turning point in international relations" was taking shape.[152] After Geneva, recalled Dobrynin, Gorbachev staked more "on a direct dialogue with the Americans at the highest level."[153] Grachev remembered encountering Gorbachev at the summit, being struck by the confident look in his eyes, and recalling Tolstoy's description of a similar face: "radiant, the look of someone who is enjoying success and is sure that success is recognized by all others."[154]

Something big happened at Geneva, but what? It wasn't that the two leaders outdid themselves in their performances. Reagan took particular care to be in good physical condition: he and his wife arrived a day early to ease the jet lag; he spent four days on a feast/famine/feast regime to get his meal times adjusted. "The answer is to set my clock to his time," he confided to his advisers. Before the summit, Reagan rehearsed carefully, with his Russian affairs adviser, Jack Matlock, playing the role of Gorbachev. But the president nonetheless overflowed with what Gorbachev called "banalities," and he got his facts wrong, for example, when he claimed Moscow had refused to let American bombers refuel at Soviet bases after bombing Nazi targets in World War II. "Your president was totally *wrong*," Kornienko burst out to Shultz. "I know because I was stationed at a base where your bombers came in to refuel." Adds Shultz in his memoirs, "Many times I would try to correct the President on the particular facts of a favorite story. It rarely worked. Once a certain arrangement of facts was in his head, I could hardly ever get them out."[155]

Gorbachev worked feverishly throughout the summit, conferring with advisers until four o'clock in the morning, then arising at seven, but he didn't do brilliantly either.[156] By arguing for increased trade, says Matlock, he "reinforced Reagan's determination to withhold any trade concessions" until Moscow provided more of its own on emigration and human rights. By accusing the Americans of harboring delusions about Soviet economic and technological troubles, he drew attention to just those weaknesses.[157] Gorbachev got so "fixated" on SDI, recalled Dobrynin, as to make an American retreat from it "a precondition for summit success," thus letting the president "[drive] us into a deadlock" from which "we ourselves had to search for an exit."[158]

What happened at Geneva was partly political. Each man sensed the other was willing to contemplate not just limited arms control but far-reaching nuclear disarmament as well. At the pool house, Gorbachev accepted Reagan's proposal for "50 percent reductions in strategic offensive arms," although he quickly demanded limits on SDI, which Reagan wasn't about to accept. But the personal chemistry between them was more important. Gorbachev came across as natural, informal, charming, and with a real sense of humor. He "laughed appreciatively" at Reagan's anecdotes, the president's chief of staff Donald Regan recalled, and at some he "guffawed in outright pleasure." Gorbachev, the schoolboy actor, "seemed spellbound" when the president described the Hollywood studio system and the movie stars (like Jimmy Stewart, John Wayne, and Humphrey Bogart) he had known.[159] On the way to the pool house, he said he'd watched the president's most celebrated film, *Kings Row*, and "liked it very much."[160]

Gorbachev was also thoughtful and gracious. During their morning tête-à-tête on November 19, he said he "would like to talk quietly, with respect for the United States and for the President." Later, he said he could "understand the President on a human level; he could understand that the idea of strategic defenses had captivated the President's imagination." When he first greeted Gorbachev at the Château Fleur d'Eau, Reagan felt a "surge of optimism" as he "looked into Gorbachev's smile." Even during their acrimonious exchanges, he recalls, "Gorbachev was willing to listen."[161] At one point, while their advisers were poring over a document, the two leaders sat next to each other in matching overstuffed chairs, drinking Russian tea, deep in conversation. When Regan advised them it was time to reconvene, Reagan joked, "Who cares? Mikhail and I are having a good time sitting here talking."[162]

They looked, according to Regan, "like a couple of fellows who had run into each other at the club and discovered they had a lot in common." And in fact they did. In their first one-on-one meeting, Reagan said he and the general secretary "had come from similar beginnings." Both began life in "small farming communities," yet here they were "with the fate of the world in their hands, so to speak." Actually, this understates their similarities. Both had mostly happy childhoods in harsh times. Both preferred to reminisce about only one of their parents: Gorbachev, about his father; Reagan, whose father was an alcoholic, about his mother. Each was an optimist who believed, as Reagan's biographer Lou Cannon put it, that "success was there for the finding and that it would surely come his way." Neither was a teetotaler, but neither loved to drink. Both were readers as youths. Each was a big man on campus in secondary school (Reagan was the student body president), each won the lead in school plays (Reagan in Philip Barry's *You and I*), and each wooed and for a time won his leading lady (Mugs Cleaver was the young actress in Reagan's case). Both had the kind of small-town feeling (described by *Washington Post* reporter Dan Balz, who grew up not far from Reagan in Illinois) that "people are basically good and will treat you right if you're good to them." For both leaders, college was a defining experience. Gorbachev might have echoed what Reagan said at his alma mater, Eureka College, in October 1982: "Yes, this place is deep in my heart. Everything that has been good in my life began here."[163]

Even the two men's marriages (Reagan's with his second wife, Nancy) resembled each other, to the point that both are captured in Frances FitzGerald's description of Reagan's: "Nancy devoted herself to her husband . . . and the marriage became an extremely happy one. Temperamentally the two were as different as people could be. He was optimistic and confident, she was high-strung and insecure. He sailed through life while she worried, fretted and feared the worst. He trusted those around him; she suspected people's motives and stood watchful guard against the slightest sign of disloyalty to her husband. Many people found her trying, but Reagan, unfailingly upbeat, sunny-tempered and distant, did not seem to notice how 'difficult' she was."[164]

Of course, there were also differences. Reagan dealt in generalities; Gorbachev paid more attention to details. Gorbachev seemed "more flamboyant" to Reagan's chief of staff Regan: he "struck the table with the edge of his hand, raised his voice, demanded answers. Reagan controlled his voice, his expressions, his gestures" in a "calm, understated performance." Both were former actors, but as Regan correctly sensed, one was "a stage actor," the other a screen actor. Gorbachev, the former high school thespian, took charge of the stage, projecting to the audience. Reagan underplayed his part, as if letting the camera provide the drama. Moreover, similarities don't always produce affinities between people, especially when one or both are insecure about the features they share and irritated with the other for manifesting them—witness the way Raisa Gorbachev and Nancy Reagan grated on each other from the moment they met in Geneva.

True, they came from different backgrounds. Mrs. Reagan's mother was an actress and her stepfather, whom she "always considered my true father," a famous Chicago neurosurgeon.[165] And Mrs. Reagan clearly lacked Mrs. Gorbachev's academic credentials. But it's not quite the case, as Mrs. Reagan remembers, that "we had little in common and completely different outlooks on the world."[166] Both were sticklers who made sure everything went just right. Mrs. Reagan consulted a San Francisco astrologer to make sure the summit was held on favorable dates, and insisted that she and her husband stay not at the Prince Sadruddin Aga Khan's Château de Bellerive, selected by the advance team, but at Prince Karim Aga Khan IV's Maison de Saussure, which did indeed turn out to be more conveniently located.[167] Both women were nervous about meeting each other. But, recalls Mrs. Reagan, "I needn't have worried. From the moment we met, she talked and talked and *talked*—so much that I couldn't get a word in, edgewise or otherwise." Mrs. Gorbachev talked about Marxism and Leninism and remarked on the flaws of the American political system. Mrs. Reagan remembered, "I wasn't prepared for this, and I didn't like it." At a tea Mrs. Reagan hosted on the afternoon of November 19, Mrs. Gorbachev acted like "a woman who expected to be deferred to." When she didn't like the chair she was seated in she summoned her KGB detail to provide another one, and still another when the substitute didn't suit her either. "I couldn't believe it," Mrs. Reagan recalls. "I had met first ladies, princesses and queens, but I had never seen anybody act in this way." The next day at the Soviet mission, she felt "condescended to" when her hostess analyzed the meaning behind every children's painting on the wall, and Nancy "couldn't possibly try everything" when Mrs. Gorbachev offered what she called a "typical Russia tea": "blinis with caviar, cabbage rolls, blueberry pie, cookies, chocolates, honey and jam." "If that was an ordinary housewife's tea," thought Mrs. Reagan, who prided herself on her superslim figure, "then I'm Catherine the Great."[168]

Even when Mrs. Reagan was the hostess for dinner on November 20, Mrs. Gorbachev, says Donald Regan, "was the chief orchestrator of the dinner party—changing the subject when her husband had been on it long enough, introducing new subjects, entering in on conversations down the table," certainly not confining herself, "as most other wives of heads of state and government did in such meetings, to cross-chat with Mrs. Reagan on palace housewifery and other harmless subjects." At the end of the evening, after the Gorbachevs had departed, Mrs. Reagan commented, "Who does that dame think she is?"[169]

For her part, Mrs. Gorbachev rejected rumors spread in the American press about "'friction' between Nancy Reagan and myself," adding in her 1991 memoir, "I did not take, and I still don't take [them] seriously." Perhaps she didn't pick up on Mrs. Reagan's feelings and hadn't read Mrs. Reagan's memoir, which was published a year earlier. Or she felt it wasn't proper to distract attention from her husband's achievements, which she described in typically exalted language: "Nancy Reagan and I were lucky" to be present at "the greatest and most important historic meetings between leaders of our two countries. All our feelings, worries and anxieties were just a drop in the ocean of the hope born of these meetings and felt by people throughout the world: the hope of peace and a future for the whole of mankind."[170]

REAGAN WAS EAGER to follow up on Geneva. A week later, while vacationing at his California ranch, he prepared a long, handwritten letter to Gorbachev expressing his pleasure with Geneva, trying again to allay Gorbachev's concerns about SDI, and offering to try to facilitate a Soviet withdrawal from Afghanistan in a way that "does not damage Soviet security."[171] Shortly after that, Shultz proposed to Dobrynin that Gorbachev come to Washington in June 1986.

Gorbachev was even more eager, but determined not to seem so— neither to Reagan nor to his own Politburo, whose instructions for the summit had been "not to leave Geneva without obtaining sizable results."[172] So he took nearly a month to answer Reagan (with a letter devoted mostly to rebutting the president's arguments about SDI), and he didn't respond at all to the invitation to visit Washington in June. True, he was busy preparing for the Twenty-Seventh Party Congress, in February 1986. But Gorbachev was also using the old Soviet device of increasing political and propaganda pressure designed to push Washington back to the negotiating table.[173] Reversing his pre-Geneva course, he now conditioned agreement to hold another meeting on certainty that it would produce concrete results. Meanwhile, on January 15, 1986, he publicly proposed a three-stage program for abolishing nuclear weapons by the end of the twentieth century, with 50 percent of strategic nuclear weapons to be eliminated in the first five to eight years.[174]

In the past, Soviet plans for "general and complete disarmament" had been propaganda. This time, too, Gromyko's former deputy Kornienko and Chief of the General Staff Sergei Akhromeyev, who recommended the proposal, presumed the United States would reject it.[175] Gorbachev not only welcomed it as a bold initiative that would appeal to Reagan but took it seriously. "I can pinpoint the exact time when Gorbachev placed his stake on a direct dialogue with the American leadership," Chernyaev recalled. "It was at the very beginning of 1986," with the "declaration about a nuclear-free world by the year 2000."[176] Dobrynin thought the plan was actually "adequate and realistic," covering "a broad range of weapons" outlining "a concrete schedule," taking "into account the latest American proposals," and providing "a visible and practical basis for compromise, although negotiations would certainly be needed."[177] In that sense, adds Grachev, "traditional Soviet form represented the obligatory price that had to be paid for the insertion of new content."[178]

Gorbachev presented his proposal as a stand-alone initiative, rather than making it at the party congress in the usual fashion. But by announcing it to the whole world, rather than conveying it privately to the Americans, he confirmed to many in Washington (and Moscow, too) that it was propaganda. Shultz, however, regarded the proposal as "our first indication that the Soviets are interested in a staged program toward zero," and Reagan not only agreed but wanted to go faster: "Why wait until the end of the century for a world without nuclear weapons?" he asked Shultz. "Of course," he confided to his diary that night, "he has a couple of zingers in there which we'll have to work around. But at the very least it is a h—l of a propaganda move."[179]

Meanwhile, however, a series of developments—Soviet troops still in Afghanistan, Cubans in Nicaragua, the Libya-assisted bombing on April 5, 1986, of a discotheque in West Berlin frequented by American servicemen, Gorbachev's disdain for further Reagan proposals to share strategic defenses—sapped the president's enthusiasm for another summit, and if there was no summit on the horizon, Matlock adds, "Reagan just lost interest."[180] As for Gorbachev, he feared that Reagan was "recoiling" from Geneva.[181] Washington sent two U.S. warships to within a few miles of Crimea just when Gorbachev was vacationing nearby, it demanded that fifty Soviet diplomats in the United States be withdrawn as intelligence agents, and it bombed Tripoli in retaliation for the West Berlin bombing.[182] Had the military-industrial complex "landed on Reagan?" Gorbachev wondered. Was the president brooding about criticism that he had fallen for the Soviet leader's magnetism? (That thought, in particular, probably appealed to Gorbachev.) Or had he frightened himself by making "too many concessions to the Soviets"?[183]

Gorbachev was partly projecting his own consternation onto his American counterpart. For in a very real sense the Soviet leader was trapped. If, as he suspected, Reagan was using SDI to intimidate him, Moscow's all-out opposition to it only validated the president's scheme. Gorbachev sounded defensive at a Politburo meeting on May 8: "What have we conceded? Not a thing!"[184] He comforted himself with the illusion that what Washington feared most was Soviet economic success; that's why they were trying to force Moscow into a costly arms race.[185] He blamed Soviet negotiators, rather than himself, for "sticking to old ways."[186] He warned his associates against what he himself was doing: "fussing, twitching, getting agitated. There's no justification for any of this. Our task is to stay the course."[187]

In the end it was Gorbachev, not Reagan, who couldn't wait any longer—but only after his nerves were soothed by Mitterrand and none other than Richard Nixon. The French president paid a return visit to Moscow in July 1986. Mitterrand said he'd asked the Americans some of the questions that most worried Gorbachev: Did they want Moscow to cut its military budget and spend more on civilian economic development? Or "does the United States want to exhaust the Soviet Union via the arms race?" Mitterrand told Reagan that the first choice meant "peace" and the second "war." He came away convinced that Reagan was "intuitively striving to find a way out of this dilemma," that "unlike many other American politicians, Reagan is not an automaton. He is a human being." "This is extremely important," Gorbachev replied, "and I'm taking special note of it."[188]

Nixon met with Gorbachev in Moscow on July 18. "I have known President Reagan for a long time, over thirty years," he said. "And I have the strong impression that he views the American-Soviet relationship as his personal responsibility." Moreover, Reagan had been stirred by Geneva. "He has been very impressed by your conversations as well as your personal commitment to the cause of peace between our countries. He also thinks he made a certain personal connection with you and, based on that, he believes an agreement is possible if you work together."[189]

In late August, while vacationing in Crimea, Gorbachev often called in Chernyaev, who was acting as virtually "his whole secretarial staff, as well as his policy aide in every policy area." Chernyaev joined Gorbachev just before lunch, on the veranda or in his office. Together they looked through the mail and coded messages from abroad. Chernyaev remained with his boss as he spoke on the phone with Moscow, made decisions, and assigned tasks. At one of these sessions, Gorbachev instructed the Foreign Ministry to prepare a reply to a letter from Reagan. When the outline arrived, Gorbachev rejected it as "simply crap" and told Chernyaev, "Write this down. Urgently prepare a draft of my letter to the president of the United States of America with a suggestion to meet in late September or early October either in London, or [he paused for a moment] in Reykjavik."

"Why Reykjavik?" asked a surprised Chernyaev.

"It's a good idea. Halfway between us and them, and none of the big powers will be offended."[190]

GORBACHEV'S LETTER TO REAGAN, dated September 15, proposed "a quick one-one-one meeting" to last "maybe just one day," not for "a detailed discussion," but to prepare "draft agreements on two or three very specific questions which you and I could sign during my visit to the United States."[191] Shevardnadze delivered it on September 19. Reagan would have accepted immediately, but waited until yet another cold war obstacle could be cleared away.[192] The KGB had arrested American journalist Nicholas Daniloff in response to the FBI's nabbing Soviet spy Gennady Zakharov, who worked for the UN Secretariat. Once they were exchanged (and Soviet dissident physicist Yuri Orlov was released from prison), the two leaders announced on September 30 that they would meet in Reykjavik on Saturday, October 11.

"It's a joke," scoffed President Jimmy Carter's former national security adviser, Zbigniew Brzezinski, "a summit on two weeks notice? Without an agenda?" Henry Kissinger intoned that tensions between the two superpowers "cannot be removed by the personal relationship between two leaders, and it is not in our interest to create the impression that they can be."[193]

One reason Reagan agreed to meet so soon was that he, too, hoped for just a couple of agreements that would allow Gorbachev to come to Washington for a full-dress summit. His best chance, he thought, was a deal to reduce intermediate-range missiles in Europe and Asia.[194] But Gorbachev's notion of a merely preparatory get-together was a trap. What he really wanted to do was to "sweep Reagan off his feet," to confront him with a "completely new approach" and "an offer he cannot refuse."[195] He was prepared to make "concessions," he told the Politburo, even though KGB chief Chebrikov objected to the very term. Gorbachev's "ultimate goal" was the liquidation of nuclear weapons. To move toward it, he would have to "give Reagan something [of] breakthrough potential." Specifically, he would cut long-range nuclear missiles by 50 percent, including the massive SS-18 missiles with their huge warheads that Washington regarded as the most dangerous threat in the Soviet arsenal. He would accept the "zero option" for Euromissiles that Reagan had proposed, and would limit the number of intermediate-range missiles based in Asia. He would drop the long-standing Soviet demand that British and French missiles be included along with American rockets in an intermediate-range nuclear forces (INF) deal. He would even agree that Reagan could continue to work on his beloved SDI as long as research and development remained within "laboratories" for the next ten years. If Reagan did not agree, Gorbachev assured the Politburo, he would unmask him before "the whole world" as a fraud who did not want peace, and inform him "there will be no Gorbachev visit to the United States." That, too, Gorbachev said, was "a hook on which we will hold Reagan."[196]

Gorbachev knew his demand to limit SDI testing to laboratories could be a deal breaker. Back in February, he wondered aloud to assistants whether "it is time to stop being afraid of SDI." He feared the Americans actually wanted Moscow to match SDI, hoping that the task would prove technologically impossible while crippling the Soviet economy. But his own scientists told him that Moscow could "destroy or neutralize" SDI by spending only 10 percent of what Washington was spending.[197] If all else failed, the Soviets could simply build and deploy enough offensive missiles and warheads to overwhelm any American defense.

Why, then, did Gorbachev continue to hold everything hostage to SDI? Because of pressure from "our military-industrial complex," according to Dobrynin. Many years later two leading representatives of that complex specifically denied that they had been as alarmed about SDI as Gorbachev seemed to be. Said former KGB chief Vladimir Kriuchkov, "We concluded that SDI was unrealizable and that the U.S. was bluffing." Oleg Baklanov, in charge of the atomic energy industry in 1986, recalled "no particular anxiety [being] expressed about it at Defense Council sessions."[198] But Roald Sagdeyev, then head of the Soviet space program, remembers Soviet military thinkers' "worst-case scenario" in which "the real intention of SDI was to deploy hydrogen bombs in space, masquerading as innocent SDI assets."[199] Did Gorbachev lack the nerve to resist such paranoia in October 1986? Was he spooked by American technological prowess? Whatever his reasoning, he remained as determined to block SDI as Reagan was to protect it. Yet, despite that, they came very close at Reykjavik to the most sensational agreement imaginable—to eliminate all nuclear weapons within ten years.

The summit took place in Hofdi House, a small, square, two-story building on the edge of the bay. The first session convened at ten forty on a raw, windy morning in a small room on the first floor, the two leaders sitting in brown leather armchairs at opposite ends of a table barely big enough to accommodate them, their interpreters, and notetakers. When Shultz and Shevardnadze joined them midway through the session, the foreign ministers wedged themselves in diagonally across from each other, close enough to their bosses to whisper or pass notes. On one side of the table was a long horizontal window opening onto the turbulent gray water, an image echoed in an oil painting, on the other side of the room, of waves cascading onto the shore. Advisers to both leaders worked in equally cramped quarters on the second floor, two small rooms for each side, the Americans to the left at top of the stairs, the Soviets on the right, with a shared meeting room in between. At one point the next day, the American delegation hurriedly drafted a crucial proposal on a board placed over a bathtub. Meanwhile, Soviet and American technical personnel shared the basement, in such close proximity as to simultaneously gladden and freeze the hearts of both KGB and FBI. When the summit wasn't in session, Reagan stayed at the U.S. ambassador's residence in town, while Gorbachev and his advisers resided on a Soviet ship moored in the harbor.

Gorbachev and Reagan during Reykjavik summit, 1986.

Both leaders began cautiously, neither wanting to seem too eager. Reagan hoped the summit would "make sure their next meeting would be a productive one." The very fact that they were meeting, Gorbachev said, showed that "cooperation" between the two countries "was continuing." Yet, almost immediately the notion of nuclear abolition passed their lips. "A world without nuclear missiles," was how Reagan put it. "The total elimination of nuclear arms" was Gorbachev's formulation.

When Shultz entered the room, Gorbachev struck him as "brisk, impatient and confident, with the air of a man who is setting the agenda and taking charge of the meeting," while Reagan "was relaxed, disarming in a pensive way, and with an easy manner."[200] Gorbachev insisted that his willingness to cut Soviet heavy missiles was a "concession," that not cutting British and French missiles was a big step, and that his proposal on SDI was "a compromise taking into consideration the US approach." Reagan found the Soviet approach "encouraging," but before long he again was trying to equate SDI with gas masks and blithely promising that its fruits would be available to both sides.[201]

After the first session, the American team assembled in the U.S. embassy's small, secure, soundproof vault that was invulnerable to listening devices. "Everyone was surprised," Shultz recalls, Gorbachev "was laying gifts at our feet." Veteran arms negotiator Paul Nitze, famous for doubting Soviet motives, added, "This is the best Soviet proposal we have received in twenty-five years." Reagan looked at the transparent walls, floor, and ceiling of the vault, which made it resemble a bubble, and asked, "If there was water in here, could we keep goldfish?"[202]

Reagan began the afternoon session by praising Gorbachev's concessions, but his response to Gorbachev's "concerns" was laughable. If the Soviet leader was afraid SDI might be used to attack the Soviet Union, he could "assure" him "it is not being developed for that purpose." Gorbachev apparently feared the United States might launch a first strike and then use the new defenses to prevent retaliation. Well, "we don't have that capability and that is not our objective." Reagan was correct, of course: the United States did not have such a capability. But how could Gorbachev be expected to trust Reagan's amiable personal assurances to bind not just himself but his successors as well?

"Believe it or not," said Reagan charmingly after addressing points Gorbachev made at the first session, he had "come to the end." At which point Gorbachev began to boil. When Reagan urged that difficult issues be handed over to the two sides' experts, Gorbachev complained this was "the kind of porridge we've eaten for years." If the U.S. side was trying somehow to "outsmart him, it would be the end of the negotiation." If Reagan's maneuvering meant "the U.S. just didn't want to remove its missiles from Europe," the president "should just say so." If the Soviets themselves had a "better solution" than SDI, Reagan countered, then perhaps "they can give us theirs."

At this point, Gorbachev could have challenged Reagan to sign a treaty requiring the United States to share SDI. If Reagan had agreed, a firestorm would have exploded in Washington and allied capitals, leaving Reagan to cope with the consequences. Instead, it was Gorbachev who exploded: he "could not take the President seriously." The United States "was unwilling to give the Soviets oil drilling equipment, automatic machinery, even milk factories." So for the United States to hand over SDI "would be a second American revolution, and it would not happen." Reagan had said, "If I thought the benefits would not be given to others, I would give up the project myself." Gorbachev doubted the president even "knew what the project contained."[203]

On this grim note, the second session ended. From preparatory reconnoitering, the summit had turned into a full-fledged negotiation. The two leaders agreed that their senior advisers would reconvene at eight that evening to try to reconcile differences. Gorbachev surprised the Americans by designating a military man, Chief of the General Staff Akhromeyev, as his main negotiator. Akhromeyev surprised them by being more engaging and flexible than his civilian predecessors. "I'm the last of the Mohicans," he later told Shultz, meaning the last active commander who had fought the Nazis in World War II. When Shultz asked where he got that phrase, Akhromeyev replied, "I was raised on the adventure tales of James Fenimore Cooper." "Akhromeyev is a first-class negotiator," Nitze informed Shultz whom he awakened at 2:00 a.m. to report on progress. The seventy-five-year-old Nitze was positively giddy the next morning: "I haven't had so much fun in years," he informed Shultz. "Akhromeyev is very sound. Great guy. We had a good exchange."[204]

The advisers agreed on a draft including a 50 percent cut in long-range missiles, plus a reduction of Euromissiles to one hundred on each side. "We were getting amazing agreements," Reagan remembered. "As the day went on I felt something momentous was occurring."[205] But Gorbachev wasn't convinced. He still wanted a ban on SDI. That would be "the test of American readiness to meet the Soviets half way." But Reagan said he'd "made a pledge to the American people that SDI would contribute to disarmament and peace," and he could not "retreat from that pledge." By now, Reagan, too, was showing his anger. Why was Gorbachev so opposed to SDI, which had the potential to render nuclear weapons obsolete? "What the hell!" the president exclaimed. "Why the hell should the world have to live for another ten years under the threat of nuclear weapons?"[206]

The Sunday morning session produced no agreement. The summit was slated to end at that point, but the two leaders agreed to meet one last time that afternoon. Each thought he might yet persuade the other.

At 3:25 p.m., Gorbachev laid out his final offer: no withdrawal from the ABM Treaty for ten years, no SDI testing outside laboratories, a 50 percent cut in "strategic offensive weapons" by the end of 1991, liquidation of the remaining such weapons by 1996. "This seems only slightly different from the U.S. position," Reagan responded. "There are important differences," Shultz corrected him.[207] Reagan then outlined his offer: a 50 percent cut in "strategic offensive arsenals" in five years, the remaining "offensive ballistic missiles" eliminated in ten years, no laboratory limit on SDI testing, after ten years either side "free to introduce defenses."

The two sides' proposed reductions of offensive arms (Washington wanting to reduce ballistic missiles, in which the USSR was particularly strong, Moscow seeking to include bombers and cruise missiles, in which the United States was ahead) were negotiable. Everything hinged on Gorbachev's demand that SDI testing be confined to laboratories. Then, suddenly, according to American minutes of the meeting: "The President asked whether Gorbachev was saying that beginning in the first five-year period and then going on in the second we would be reducing *all nuclear weapons*—cruise missiles, battlefield weapons, sub-launched and the like. It would be fine with him if we eliminated all nuclear weapons" (emphasis added).

Gorbachev said, "We can do that. We can eliminate them."

"Then, let's do it," added Secretary Shultz.[208]

THIS WAS THE CLIMAX at Reykjavik. For those who believe in abolishing nuclear weapons, it was a miracle. For those who don't, it was bizarre. After decades of empty talk of eliminating all nuclear weapons and convoluted agreements to modestly limit their number, after leaders and experts on both sides reluctantly concluded they were actually a good way to keep the peace, and many around the world sadly reconciled themselves to their permanent existence, Gorbachev and Reagan suddenly agreed to eliminate them in ten years. This showed how far Gorbachev's "new thinking," and Reagan's as well, had come.

It was not to be. The prospect of SDI, like a science-fiction phantom with magical powers, brought the agreement within reach and then vaporized it. For Reagan, it was SDI that rendered nuclear weapons obsolete. For Gorbachev, SDI rendered an agreement to abolish them impossible.[209] The rest of the discussion, which centered on SDI, was passionate but unproductive. Gorbachev took "a principled" stand. Reagan said he could not "give in." Reagan said the American right-wing was "kicking his brains out." Gorbachev said Reagan was "three steps away from becoming a great President," that if the two of them could just settle their differences, all of Reagan's critics "would not open their mouths" and "the whole world would cheer." Reagan said it was "just a question of one word," that is, "laboratories." Gorbachev said he "could not return to Moscow" if he allowed the testing of weapons in space; he would be called a "fool and not a leader." Reagan asked Gorbachev to drop that word, "laboratories," as a personal "favor." "If they could agree to ban research in space," Gorbachev responded, "he would sign in two minutes." He had "tried." His "conscience" was "clear before the president and his people." What had "depended" on him he had "done."[210]

It was now six thirty. The two delegations were waiting in the next room. "The tension was growing," Chernyaev remembers. "We didn't want to talk about anything anymore. We stood by the windows, looking out at the dark ocean. Waiting, waiting, hoping."[211] Both leaders stood up and gathered their papers. Both understood, Gorbachev recalls, that this was "a political and moral defeat." The mood was "foul" when the front doors of Hofdi House opened and they emerged, Reagan in light-colored raincoat without a hat, Gorbachev in a dark coat and a fedora.[212] Both men looked stricken.

"I still feel we can find a deal," Reagan said as they parted.

"I don't think you wanted a deal," Gorbachev replied. "I don't know what more I could have done."

"You could have said yes," said Reagan.[213]

Settling himself in his car, Reagan held his thumb and forefinger less than half an inch apart. "We were *that* close to an agreement," he told Chief of Staff Regan.[214] Back at the U.S. ambassador's residence, he slumped into a chair in the solarium. "Bad news," he said. "One lousy word." Reagan chose not to have a press conference, but headed for the American airbase in Keflavik to fly home. Shultz, who spoke to reporters, recalls, "I looked worn and exhausted and I was."[215]

Gorbachev, too, seemed crushed. Thomas Simons, the American

notetaker at the last session, was struck by Gorbachev's "impatience and urgency" as it became clear he wasn't going to get what he wanted. "You could feel the gridlock. Everything was dancing on the head of SDI."[216] According to Shultz's close aide, Charles Hill, Gorbachev seemed "rattled," even "losing his confidence" and his "command of himself."[217] And now that it was over, he was going to face thousands of correspondents waiting downtown. It felt, recalled his bodyguard Medvedev, as if Gorbachev were going to face the "guillotine."[218] "He was very angry," remembered Dobrynin, who was riding with him, "eager to denounce Reagan at his press conference. We who were with him were trying to calm him down."[219] Gorbachev had promised the Politburo that if Reagan rejected his offers he would condemn the president as the main obstacle to world peace.[220] But that would only further delay the kind of U.S.-Soviet settlement on which Gorbachev's whole program depended, while hardly excusing his own miscalculation since, in most Soviet eyes, Reagan's intransigence was all too predictable.

What happened next was classic Gorbachev. When he entered the opera house, he recalls, "thousands of journalists," usually "merciless, often cynical, even brazen," rose and stood silently and anxiously. Gorbachev was "gripped by excitement, maybe even more than that, I was stunned. It was as if they represented the whole human race, waiting for their fate to be decided." It was then "that I understood what had happened at Reykjavik and how I had to act."[221]

Gorbachev outlined his proposals to Reagan and reported Reagan's rejection. But he hailed the result, the fact that they had almost reached agreement, failing only to "put them into final form."[222] His message, he recalls, was: "For all its drama, Reykjavik wasn't a defeat but a breakthrough." To which the audience reacted with "thunderous applause. Everyone jumped up in their seats." In his memoirs, Gorbachev quotes a correspondent who was looking at Mrs. Gorbachev during the ovation: "As the General Secretary characterized the defeat at Reykjavik as a triumph, Raisa Gorbachev gazed upon her husband with joy and tears streaming down her face."[223]

Mrs. Gorbachev's presence in Reykjavik, along with Nancy Reagan's absence, not only further strained their relationship, but may have affected their husbands' negotiations. Mrs. Reagan assumed from

Mikhail and Raisa Gorbachev, 1980s.

the outset that this would be "a business meeting and wives were not invited." (But that did not stop her from consulting her astrologer about the most auspicious date for her husband's departure for Iceland, October 9, which Donald Regan thereupon "wrote into the schedule.")[224] When Mrs. Gorbachev decided at the last minute to accompany her husband, Mrs. Reagan regarded that as "one-upmanship" or, as her son, Ron, put it, "being jerked around." Mrs. Gorbachev was "testing me, to see if I would cave in and change my mind," just as Gorbachev was "testing Ronnie" at Reykjavik. Watching summit coverage on television, Mrs. Reagan saw Mrs. Gorbachev meeting with children—"the first time I had seen her do anything with children"—handing out pins of Lenin—"which I thought was a bit much." When an interviewer asked the Soviet first lady why her American counterpart wasn't there, Mrs. Gorbachev answered, "Perhaps she had something else to do. Or maybe she isn't feeling well." Mrs. Reagan's reaction to that: "Oh, please!"[225]

This may seem a sideshow to the main event, but Reagan's Russia expert, Jack Matlock, wasn't so sure. During a break in the summit's last, decisive session, someone suggested that since both principals were weary, the meeting could be extended for another day to allow advisers to work further on language overnight.

"Oh shit!" Reagan blurted out. If he had been pressed to stay, Matlock thinks he would have agreed, but nobody dared to insist. If Nancy Reagan had been in Reykjavik, "he probably would have been content to continue the meeting another day. Gorbachev was not the only leader who seemed lost without his wife."[226]

FOR THE REST OF THE YEAR, Gorbachev tried to stay upbeat. On the plane heading home from Iceland, he urged his aides "not to despair." The summit showed "an accord is possible." That's why "after Reykjavik I am still a great optimist."[227] Two days later he lambasted Reagan to the Politburo as "extraordinarily primitive, troglodyte, and intellectually feeble," as someone who "couldn't even look me in the eye at the end" of the summit. But he also assured the Politburo that "success was near and it would have had vast significance." "There's no need for haste. Time is working for us," he told them two weeks later.[228]

But time wasn't. Too much depended on what hadn't been achieved at Reykjavik. His veteran aide Boldin wasn't the only one who thought Gorbachev had let the Americans "play with him as a cat does with a mouse." What else could be expected, the sour Boldin asked much later, from "a man with a peasant upbringing who wanted to become a great diplomat?"[229]

During the remaining months of 1986, Reagan retreated further from Reykjavik. As it became clear that he had contemplated eliminating ballistic missiles, perhaps even all nuclear weapons, he had some answering to do in Washington and elsewhere. Chairman of the Joint Chiefs of Staff Admiral William J. Crowe Jr., who hadn't been consulted, told the president, at an October 27 White House National Security Planning Group meeting, that zero ballistic missiles "would pose high risks to the security of the nation."[230] Margaret Thatcher, such a true believer in nuclear deterrence that she was "totally appalled" by the prospect of eliminating nuclear weapons, told Reagan as much in Washington in November.[231] Meanwhile, the Republican party lost control of the Senate in congressional elections, and the Iran-Contra scandal broke (the United States had secretly been buying Iranian arms for Nicaraguan rebels to use against the existing leftist regime), distracting Reagan and leading to the resignation of his national security adviser, John Poindexter, who had backed the radical notions Reagan entertained at Reykjavik. When Poindexter was replaced by Frank Carlucci, Matlock recalls, "there was no longer any interest in moving on arms reduction, only in containing the political fallout of Iran-Contra."[232] The president went so far as to request a study of what would be involved in sharing SDI with the Soviets, but it went nowhere in the bureaucracy.

"What does America want?" Gorbachev seethed at a Politburo meeting on October 30. "They're perverting, revising Reykjavik, backing away from it." What they were saying at ongoing disarmament talks in Geneva was "garbage in mothballs."[233] Confronting a dead end, Gorbachev was finally ready to let SDI testing take place outside laboratories, "in the air, at test-sites on the ground, but not in space." But when Shevardnadze tried to get Shultz to talk further about "what is allowed and what is not allowed," the latter, according to Shevardnadze, "did not want to talk about it."[234] "Let's not chase after shit," Gorbachev told his colleagues after the Shultz-Shevardnadze meeting in Vienna.[235] "We musn't allow it to appear as if we're not getting anywhere," he told Chernyaev on November 17.[236] But he was increasingly alarmed. The Soviet people wanted progress. Soviet generals were sputtering that the leadership was "disarming the country."[237]

And so 1986 came to an end. Gorbachev was revolutionizing Soviet thinking about the world, but not changing the world itself. He favored a new relationship with Eastern Europe, but had barely begun to construct one. He wanted to end the Afghan war, but it was still on. He couldn't change his country unless he could drastically lower its defense burden, but the United States wouldn't cooperate. He realized too well that domestic and foreign affairs depended on each other, but after twenty-one months in power he wasn't getting anywhere fast enough in either realm.[238]

CHAPTER 8

TWO SCORPIONS
IN A BOTTLE
1987

I F GORBACHEV FELT STYMIED at the end of 1986, the next year
brought three seeming breakthroughs on the home front. In January 1987, he proclaimed a new course toward democratization. Six
months later, he proposed deeper economic reforms; he even dared use
the word "reform," which had been anathema for decades. In November 1987, on the seventieth anniversary of the sacred Bolshevik Revolution, he delivered a long, candid speech on Soviet history, condemning
Stalin's crimes. In effect, he was picking up where Khrushchev's secret
speech had left off in 1956, this time denouncing the dictator for all the
world to hear.

Each of these innovations required months of painstaking preparation. Each was difficult and delicate, demanding that Gorbachev
simultaneously celebrate past Soviet achievements and challenge old
orthodoxies while gauging what the political climate would bear. Each
change required compromises with Kremlin colleagues, but in the end
they seemed to support them all. At the time, Gorbachev regarded each
occasion as a critical turning point ("Everyone started saying, 'Perestroika will take hold after all,'" he recalled), but none of them fully
turned.[1] He failed to lay out a concrete plan for democratization. His
economic reforms turned out to be half measures. His anniversary
address "called things by their real names," but still left a great deal
unsaid.

Then, right on the eve of the anniversary, as the celebration was about to begin, Boris Yeltsin unexpectedly challenged him. Yeltsin had been sniping, but his main target seemed to be Ligachev, about whom Gorbachev, too, had growing reservations. Suddenly, instead of pushing the reforms he announced earlier, Gorbachev pushed back against Yeltsin. Gorbachev's Yeltsin problem was in large part of his own making. He had promoted Yeltsin. His cavalier treatment of him egged Yeltsin on. And the way Gorbachev punished him virtually guaranteed that Yeltsin would turn from an awkward critic in 1987 into a devastating rival in the years ahead. Why did Gorbachev help to create his own arch antagonist? This, too, is "hard to understand."

Taking stock at the end of the year, Anatoly Chernyaev registered in his diary a roller coaster of emotions in his boss. On the surface, 1987 seemed "the peak of perestroika," with Gorbachev "still full of optimism." But this was also the year when "his first doubts emerged about the possibility of success," doubts he conveyed "only to the people closest to him," doubts about "where unknown forces are leading us."[2]

THE JANUARY 1987 Central Committee plenum was supposed to prepare for extensive personnel changes, reflecting the long-standing Soviet pattern of blaming system failures on incompetent cadres. Gorbachev's decision to shift the focus to democratization twice delayed the start of the session. Central Committee departments preparing materials for the meeting interpreted their mandate narrowly. But by the time Gorbachev summoned close aides (Yakovlev, Medvedev, Lukyanov, Boldin, and others) on November 19, 1986, his aim was a "political turning point," a "decisive change," a "transformation of the totality of social relations," changes that "capture all sides of our life," that "restructure consciousness" and help people, at long last, to "feel themselves to be fully human." Yakovlev and Lukyanov hinted gently that this was too abstract. Gorbachev's response: "What are we afraid of—the people? If so, that's not socialism."[3]

It was precisely the people whom Gorbachev's predecessors had feared, and quite a few of his colleagues still did. That's why his conversations with aides preparing for the plenum are so stunning. During numerous sessions at Volynskoe, the site of Stalin's former dacha on the outskirts of Moscow, they discussed the possibility of choosing party officials by secret ballots in competitive elections—the only way, they agreed, to rein in "all-powerful, everything-is-permitted, out-of-control party grandees." When the scene shifted to Zavidovo, the hunting retreat farther away from Moscow, Gorbachev and his wife settled in for sustained work on his draft report. It was here, Medvedev recalled, that the planning group actually discussed transforming the ruling Communist party into an ordinary one that would compete with others for power.[4] Gorbachev remembers the discussions getting so hot that even the presence of his wife didn't "restrain the passions." Instead, the session had to be halted, to be resumed only the following day.

The Zavidovo draft dropped the notion of requiring the party to compete for power. But even so, when the Politburo met on January 19, 1987, Gorbachev was anxious about how his colleagues would react. He counted on Prime Minister Ryzhkov and Foreign Minister Shevardnadze to support him, but on no one else (Yakovlev was not yet a full member), so it was a pleasant surprise when all of them did.

Yeltsin did not voice an opinion until Gorbachev invited him to do so. The result was a twenty-point critique. Yeltsin warned against overoptimism, about comparing perestroika to the world-changing revolution of 1917, about lack of "self-criticism" in the party leadership, about limits on glasnost and social justice. At first, Gorbachev listened patiently, but as Yeltsin rolled on, Gorbachev ordered him (using the curt second-person singular) to "finish up." Gorbachev rejected Yeltsin's "loud, empty, ultra-leftist words." The draft report wasn't too optimistic; there was plenty of self-criticism in it. As for "failures of the leadership": "What do you want, Boris Nikolayevich?" Gorbachev demanded to know. Yeltsin himself, Gorbachev implied, could do with the kind of criticism he said his colleagues needed.

Gorbachev's outburst seemed to work. Yeltsin retreated: "I'm still new in the Politburo. This has been a good lesson for me. I don't think it has come too late." Gorbachev accepted the apology: "You and I have talked about this before. Such conversations were needed. But you're an emotional man. I don't think your remarks today change our attitude toward you. We value your work highly. But remember, we have to work together. And you have to get used to being criticized, as do I. . . . So let's not take offense. We'll work together. We'll help you in the future."[5]

The plenum itself was held a week later. In the language of journalism, Gorbachev's long speech "buried his lede." He began with a litany of past Soviet sins that made perestroika an "objective necessity"; he tried for the umpteenth time to define it (as "the deep renewal of all aspects of national life"); he guaranteed its success. Many pages later, he declared that the Soviet electoral system needed "more effective and genuine participation by voters at all stages of the electoral process." The Soviet people needed democracy "like air itself." Without it, perestroika would "choke and suffocate."[6]

The plenum unanimously approved Gorbachev's speech. Soviet politicians weren't idiots. They could see where Gorbachev was going, but he hadn't gotten there yet, and they doubted he ever would. "The majority of the Central Committee didn't support him," was the way one Gorbachev aide put it, "but they were afraid of him and so sabotaged him in silence."[7] Glasnost, on the other hand, defined as openness to criticism, could itself be criticized. Ivan Polozkov, seemingly a Gorbachev protégé, condemned the press for "picking at scabs" and thus "ravaging the soul." A female textile worker complained that the "fixation on shortcomings has gone on too long." Famed actor Mikhail Ulyanov leaped to Gorbachev's defense, but this was the first time such a crossfire had occurred at a Central Committee session.[8]

Gorbachev soon realized that the "new phase" marked by the plenum was stillborn. But when the plenum ended, he was elated. He had remained calm in the face of criticism. His extensive concluding remarks, delivered without notes, struck the editor of the newspaper *Sovetskaya kultura* as particularly inspired.[9] Politburo member Vorotnikov, increasingly disillusioned but not yet a sworn enemy, thought the plenum "raised Gorbachev's authority," a conclusion confirmed early in February when a mass of letters supporting Gorbachev poured into the Central Committee.[10] The plenum ratified the demotion of two Brezhnev holdovers (Kazakhstan party boss Dinmukhamed Kunayev and Central Committee secretary Mikhail Zimyanin) and the elevation of Gorbachev allies Yakovlev (to Politburo candidate member) and Lukyanov (Central Committee secretary). The Central Committee also agreed to convene a full party conference as soon as possible to ratify the new course toward democracy. To celebrate these successes, Gorbachev and his wife took the unusual step of inviting Yakovlev, Medvedev, and Boldin to join them for dinner in the Kremlin. The conversation was "warm and relaxed," Medvedev recalled, the mood "euphoric."[11]

PLANNING FOR ECONOMIC REFORM began as soon as the January plenum was over. In mid-February, Gorbachev spent several days in Latvia and Estonia. He had no inkling yet of the Baltic upheaval to come, but he knew quite well that the region, incorporated by force into the USSR in 1939 and then again after the war, was potentially restive. That may have prompted him to make the kind of promise that would come back to plague him: after two or three more hard years, the Soviet economy would gain momentum and then "come around once and for all."[12] But before that could happen, radical reforms would be needed.

Despite all of Gorbachev's complaints in 1986 about poor economic performance, the final numbers for the year weren't bad—especially in comparison with those of future years. According to Ryzhkov, national income grew by 4 percent, productivity of labor by 4.9 percent, and industrial production by 4.9 percent.[13] The totals for January 1987, however, were abysmal. The heads of the State Planning and Supply Commissions brought the bad news to the Politburo on February 12: only 67 percent of machine-building industry output was "acceptable"; 3 billion rubles' worth of light industrial goods found no buyers; twenty-nine of thirty-two railroad networks failed to fulfill the plan; half of the nation's metal output was lost as the result of accidents.[14] Numbers like these, Gorbachev recalled, posed a real danger that the 1987 economic plan could "collapse like a house of cards."[15]

Before leaving for a Black Sea holiday at Pitsunda on March 9, Gorbachev decided to convene a plenum on the economy and asked several colleagues to start preparing for it.[16] While on "vacation," he pored over piles of documents and huddled with government officials and academic economists. Back in Moscow, he summoned Ryzhkov, Yakovlev, Medvedev, Boldin, and economists Aganbegyan and Abalkin, among others. At a freewheeling, four-hour meeting, all seemed to agree on the need for radical reforms. But they disagreed on what those changes should be. For decades state planners had set output targets, regulated supplies, and rewarded or punished enterprises according to the quantity of output they produced. Whether they actually sold what they produced was irrelevant. Ryzhkov wanted to maintain "quantitative indicators," along with controls over supplies and prices, lest the government lose its grip on the economy. The economists wanted drastically to reduce ministerial controls, allowing enterprises to set their own output targets, obtain their own supplies, and be rewarded according to their sales and profits. Abalkin warned against "entrusting the reforms to those [i.e., government planners] who will be affected by them."[17]

This division persisted. Economists could hardly conceal their disdain. Nikolai Petrakov, Gorbachev's future economic adviser, later remarked, "We *do* have competition—but it's of consumers for goods. Absurd! Producers should compete with each other and run after consumers, not the other way round."[18] Meanwhile, Ryzhkov stressed the danger of hollowing out central state (and party) institutions that, for better or worse, still held the system together. He and his ministers remained responsible for overall economic welfare, he complained, but the proposed reforms would deprive them of the capacity to ensure it.

The two opposed camps divided the labor of preparing for the Central Committee plenum in June. The economists concentrated on the overall conception of the reforms, while government officials drafted concrete proposals and decrees for implementing them. The economists secluded themselves (along with speechwriters, typists, and technicians) at Volynskoe, where they were often joined by Yakovlev, Medvedev, and other Gorbachev aides. He himself joined them "practically everyday," or he summoned them to his office.[19] The Ryzhkov team championed new devices (such as "state orders" requiring enterprises to produce what ministries wanted) to take the place of old controls. Ryhzkov also lobbied for gradual implementation of changes. Gorbachev wanted to move faster.[20]

Tensions rose as the plenum approached. Ryzhkov warned against "exceeding the boundaries of socialism," boundaries, Gorbachev retorted, which had "stifled society and smothered initiative and incentive."[21] Ryzhkov's and Finance Minister Gostev's reports were bleak on

April 23 (budget deficit deepening, inflation rising, economic growth slowing), but Gorbachev was bleaker: "economic illiteracy" all around; Moscow buying grain from the Americans and French for five times what it cost to produce in the USSR; Soviet-made "junk and trash" costing more than high-quality goods.[22] Politburo colleagues seemed deferential on May 14 when Gorbachev summarized his upcoming plenum speech, although Yeltsin couldn't resist suggesting that Prime Minister Ryzhkov, rather than Gorbachev, present the report to the Central Committee. But on May 21 the heat rose when Ryzhkov "didn't hide his intention to defend the interests of central state ministries." Asked by Gorbachev which functions those ministries would agree to relinquish, Ryzhkov responded, "None."[23]

In June, Gorbachev spent ten days rewriting and editing the final version. The final showdown at Volynskoe, attended only by Gorbachev, Ryzhkov, and a few aides, came on June 20. Ryzhkov was wavering, Gorbachev remembered, between accepting and rejecting Gorbachev's final version. But Gorbachev wasn't so sure of himself either. At ten that evening, he called Chernyaev on the secure telephone line that served high party and government officials and summoned him to Volynskoe. Chernyaev wasn't an economist; he was his boss's liberal conscience. Gorbachev sat him down next to him, passed him the report, and kept asking him, "How is it?" Yakovlev, who wasn't an economist either, was sitting across the table. "You see, Anatoly," he joked, "this is how the country's fate is decided." Gorbachev laughed, but asked again, "How is it?" When Chernyaev tried to avoid answering directly, Gorbachev said bitterly, "So, there's nothing new for you in this?"[24]

For most of the meeting Gorbachev argued against Ryzhkov's attempt to preserve ministries' controls over their enterprises, but according to Chernyaev, he "tried not to hurt anyone's feelings," especially not Ryzhkov's, and in the end they compromised.[25] The output targets that ministries assigned to their enterprises would remain, but should no longer be "binding." But this unstable compromise only guaranteed a struggle between the two sides. The tortured process reminded the former actor Gorbachev of a "play" with "a beginning, several story lines, unexpected twists, open skirmishes between the heroes, climax, and denouement." If the play was incoherent, that was because "all the participants were

both authors and actors," with Gorbachev himself an uncertain performer.[26] He once told Petrakov that he "loves economics, that it fasci-
nates him." Shortly before the plenum, however, he admitted anxiously
to Chernyaev, "I myself don't fully understand all of it."[27] According
to Petrakov, Gorbachev was "the kind of person who needs to absorb
an idea, to learn to live with it. He doesn't believe things immediately,
doesn't accept words at their face value, even though he may have profound respect for the . . . economist that he's talking to." Even when he
likes an idea, "he never shows it immediately."[28] The same blend of pride
and insecurity helps to explain why Gorbachev didn't hire an economist
adviser, Petrakov, until it was virtually too late, in December 1989.

The plenum, held on June 25 and 26, unanimously adopted Gorbachev's recommendations. Then the Supreme Soviet passed a "law on
enterprises" to implement the changes. Chernyaev thought the plenum
"a more significant event" than the adoption of the "New Economic
Policy" in 1921, which saved the revolution after the destruction of civil
war.[29] Gorbachev aides toasted their success at Volynskoe, and the next
day, as he had in January, he invited Yakovlev, Medvedev, and Boldin to a
celebratory dinner in the Kremlin.[30] Gorbachev told the Politburo on July
1, and boasted to editors and journalists ten days later, that the January
and June plenums had created the basis for a new political and economic
order and had launched perestroika into a "new phase."[31]

In fact, Gorbachev was putting the best possible face on a very mixed
result. He himself found the June plenum discussion too general to be
interesting. Central Committee members' endorsement of the reforms
was mostly dutiful. Yeltsin had used the occasion to say that perestroika
"hasn't accomplished much in two years."[32] The plenum elevated Yakovlev to Politburo voting member, but soured Gorbachev's close relationship with Ryzhkov. The new economic reforms gave rights to enterprises
without taking them away from ministries. Enterprises used those rights
to benefit themselves rather than the consumer: they pursued profits by
turning out more expensive products (rather than more high-quality
ones), leaving all except well-off buyers without choice, as usual. The
new enterprise law gave workers a greater voice in management, but
they used it to push for higher wages, which in turn aggravated inflation.

Gorbachev sensed troubles like these ahead. On one occasion after the plenum, when ministers had to admit they had not met their output targets, Gorbachev blew up at them: "I'm warning you—this is our last conversation about such issues. If nothing changes, next time I'll be talking to different people." But he continued talking to the same people with the same result.[33] The most important thing, he later recalled, was "to grab hold and begin, and then let life itself show which way to go and what changes were needed."[34] Chernyaev noticed the personal strain. "I am terribly tired," Gorbachev told him. "I work late every night. I'm not myself anymore. The work keeps piling up. But it has to be done, Anatoly. What a great cause, we've begun! We have nowhere to retreat. . . . The main thing is not to waver, not to show that you're hesitant, that you're tired, uncertain. . . . And you know what pains me: they don't want to believe that I'm doing it for the cause. They're envious. Envy, you see, is a terrible thing."[35]

WHILE POLITICAL AND ECONOMIC reforms were just being proclaimed in 1987, glasnost was already spreading like a wildfire on the steppe. Journalists were "actually writing what they are thinking, without glancing over their shoulders or being afraid of anyone," Chernyaev noted in his diary in January. By now "the vices, the failures, the outrages have been named; everyday there are plenty of them in the newspapers." Not to mention "a storm in literature, film, and theater."[36] Gorbachev didn't just welcome this explosion; he saw it as "the crucial, irreplaceable weapon of perestroika." Since the rest of perestroika wasn't yet working out, "glasnost alone is supporting the process," he told Chernyaev in mid-June.[37] It recruited and mobilized perestroika's supporters. It appealed to people over the heads of the hidebound party apparatus. It encouraged the birth of "free Russian men and women." Yet, at the same time, he recalled, "due to the very nature of 'Russian freedom,' it greatly harmed perestroika."[38]

"Russian freedom"—Gorbachev's contradictory conception of it captures the dilemma he, like so many Russian reformers before him, faced. Russia's long-standing lack of freedom explained why it was so difficult to come by. Could the very people who had so long been denied freedom handle it responsibly? Historically, their tendency had been to go

too far, to take arguments to extremes, to demand too much too soon—
precisely what Gorbachev feared some practitioners of glasnost were
doing. That's why his defense of glasnost at Politburo meetings in 1987
was almost bipolar. The people needed glasnost, he said on January 29,
because "we haven't given them anything [else] yet."[39] The lack of any
organized political "opposition" also made glasnost necessary, he told his
colleagues on February 5—as if regretting the monolithic party dictatorship that his predecessors had bent every effort to build and preserve.[40]
But he simultaneously insisted that glasnost avoid "sensationalism" and
be "completely objective."[41] "We've made a mess of socialism, nothing is
left of it," he muttered to close aides.[42] But he also warned against seeming to blaspheme the sacred cause in whose name countless Soviet citizens sacrificed and died, and in which many of them still believed.[43]

If Gorbachev was trying to demarcate the boundary between acceptable and nonacceptable glasnost, some of his Kremlin colleagues—in
fact most of them—were zealously policing those borders. Ligachev, still
the number two man in the leadership, with a portfolio that included
ideology, was the primary enforcer. In his view, "distortion and slander"
filled the "radical press."[44] But Yakovlev, officially in charge of propaganda and thus co-responsible for the mass media and culture, was glasnost's greatest champion. By 1987, Ligachev sensed that Gorbachev "was
gradually being surrounded by people who were personally dependent
on Yakovlev." But Yakovlev wished Gorbachev would be more supportive
of him; Yakovlev couldn't understand, recalled Boldin, why Gorbachev
never allowed him to give any of the ceremonial addresses that preceded
Lenin's birthday and the anniversary of the revolution, so he kept asking
Boldin to intercede for him with Gorbachev.[45]

When Politburo members met with the media, "Gorbachev was the
only one who spoke, while we were relegated to the odd role of extras,"
Ligachev recalled. The sessions turned "into long hours of Gorbachev
yakking away, criticizing, instructing, and exhorting . . . , while no
one paid any attention," and in the meantime, "the extremist press . . .
tore apart our whole past."[46] According to Yakovlev, Gorbachev was
deliberately defending glasnost in "small doses" because of the party
apparatus's opposition. As a result, Yakovlev had to maneuver, sometimes secretly, to defend liberal writers and filmmakers. Once, after he

approved an investigation of a conservative editor accused of drunkenness, Gorbachev bawled him out. "I know you," he warned Yakovlev. "I know you're biased. Call off the investigation!" Gorbachev issued this reprimand, Yakovlev later learned, to impress Vorotnikov, a harder-line colleague who was sitting in his office.

When Politburo members criticized glasnost, Gorbachev too often "agreed reluctantly or remained silent," according to Yakovlev.[47] Ligachev later griped that although Gorbachev "would express outrage at certain articles or [television] programs," it was "all words and no action."[48] Meanwhile, the jousting between Ligachev and Yakovlev caused confusion among lower-level officials accustomed to following one party line, not two.[49] Did Gorbachev want Ligachev and Yakovlev to quarrel, Boldin wondered, was he dividing in order to conquer? Or did the conflict result from Gorbachev's "lack of guile"?[50] Lukyanov thought Gorbachev wanted access to both men's views so he could "compare them and work out the right solutions."[51] But a free marketplace of ideas, which allowed the truth to emerge from the exchange, was foreign to the Russian, especially the Soviet, tradition. It wasn't that Gorbachev was wavering between the two points of view (he clearly favored Yakovlev's) but rather that by hearing out both of them, he could gauge their political weight and keep both camps with him. Gorbachev was aware that he seemed erratic, but that was the price he had to pay for the balancing game he was playing.

Gorbachev prepared a memo on "the range and pace of perestroika" while on vacation in September 1987. Typically, he asked Ligachev and Yakovlev jointly to prepare a Politburo resolution on the subject. As usual, they disagreed and maneuvered to get rival formulations into the final version. Ligachev complained to Gorbachev that Yakovlev cut out "everything that condemns the press's sensationalism or attempts at blackening everything achieved by our society." Gorbachev's handwritten reply asked Ligachev and Yakovlev to "meet once more and discuss it calmly." But their ninety-minute session in Ligachev's office went badly. "We had different positions," Ligachev recalled. "We disagreed on history, the Party, and the processes of democratization." Yakovlev "couldn't affect me; however, his scythe kept hitting stone, as the saying goes."[52]

Of all the issues glasnost illuminated, Soviet history was potentially the most explosive. Gorbachev himself had hammered away at
the Brezhnev era, the better to justify his reforms, and the press followed his lead. But that left unaddressed his and his Kremlin colleagues'
own responsibility for the period of "stagnation." Gorbachev had not
yet confronted Stalin's crimes, let alone their roots in the system Lenin
founded, but others, particularly intellectuals, were eager to do so. Not
most Soviet historians, who had been trained and disciplined to avoid
precisely such issues. Initially, the task fell to literary works focused on
historical blank spots: collectivization (Boris Mozhaev's *Peasant Men and
Women*), the purges (Rybakov's *Children of the Arbat*), wartime deporta-
tion of ethnic minority nations (Anatoly Pristavkin's *A Little Cloud Spent
the Night*), the Stalinist bureaucracy (Aleksandr Bek's *A New Assignment*),
the destruction of Soviet genetics (Vladimir Dudintsev's *White Garments*
and Daniil Granin's *Zubr*), not to mention two long-suppressed narra-
tive poems by beloved poets—Anna Akhmatova's *Requiem* and Aleksandr Tvardovsky's *By Right of Memory*, both of which treated the terror
from the point of view of relatives (mother and son) of victims. With the
exception of Akhmatova's poem and perhaps Mikhail Bulgakov's short
novel *Heart of a Dog*, which ridiculed early Bolshevik hopes to create a
"new Soviet man," none of these works is a literary masterpiece, but each
became the subject of analysis and argument in newspapers and journals, generating masses of readers' letters, which were published in turn
as part of the ongoing debate.[53]

Gorbachev started planning his November address on the seventieth birthday of the Bolshevik Revolution in January 1987. As always, he
"began at the beginning," by thinking about the first years after 1917.
"I'm devoted to a systematic approach," he later declared proudly, "I
can't analyze, or speak or write until I understand a subject's internal
logic." He reread Lenin (yet again), especially the last articles in which
the founder worried about the fate of the revolution he had begun.[54]
When Gorbachev and close aides started outlining the speech in April,
the volatile nature of his subject had already been on display at two
Politburo meetings. KGB chief Chebrikov warned that unnamed hostile
forces were "using glasnost against perestroika," and that the study of
history, in particular, should be left to the party's Institute of Marxism-

Leninism, lest "any and every author" have the right to pronounce personal judgments on it.[55] But Gorbachev complained, "We still haven't
even touched on Stalin. We have to talk about many others, too, especially about Khrushchev. Wherever you go in the West, they talk about
a whole gallery of historical figures, including very recent ones. But here
we don't talk about anyone. Twenty to thirty years went by, people lived
and worked, but as to who were our leaders—that's off limits."[56]

In June, Gorbachev complained again to Chernyaev about envious critics. Chernyaev considered their cynicism a legacy of Stalinism.
"You're at it again," Gorbachev chided him, "but you're right. Stalin is
not just [the terror of] 1937. It is a system that touches everything—from
economics to people's consciousness. . . . [A]nd it still exists today. Everything stems from that, everything that we need to overcome."

But Gorbachev was "not very consistent," Chernyaev noted in his
diary. "He's afraid that they'll accuse him of blackening the past. . . ." At
the Politburo meeting on the June 22 anniversary of Hitler's attack on
Russia, Ligachev, seconded by Vorotnikov, Solomontsev, and Gromyko,
again condemned "vilifiers" of the past. Gorbachev agreed on the need to
respect ordinary people who "built the country, defended it against fascism, and fought for an idea," all the while "hungry and tattered, with
only the shirt on their backs, with heads shaved against lice, without
leaving anything for themselves, without reserving for themselves the
fruit of their hellish labors. . . . Are we so smart now that we can tar all
of that, that we can say, 'You did it all wrong?' No, we must be careful.
We must respect the people."

Chernyaev "listened, steaming." Back in his office, he dictated five outraged pages about how Stalin "respected" the people, how he destroyed
the most diligent part of the peasantry, how he sacrificed millions of
Soviet soldiers by trying to appease Hitler, how he "liquidated everyone
who made the revolution and started socialism in Russia." Chernyaev
sent his memo to Gorbachev. Gorbachev didn't reply.[57] But Chernyaev
was asking too much. The long-suffering people Gorbachev described
included his own parents and grandparents. How could he blame them
and others like them? To be sure, Chernyaev didn't either; rather, he
blamed Stalin and the merciless system that so victimized so many
people. But the fact was that many of them identified with the history

they had suffered through, especially with the triumphs (the industrialization of the country, its victory in the war) they had achieved under
Stalin. To demean the past (or to seem to do so) thus not only degraded
their sacrifice but risked their wrath at a time when perestroika had as
yet delivered very little.

Gorbachev went on vacation for nearly a month beginning in late
August, staying at a Black Sea dacha at Nizhniaia Oreanda, near Yalta
in the Crimea. He didn't rest much, of course. All sorts of business, routine and otherwise, crowded in on him, but he did find time to condemn
others for not working as hard as he did: "Our society is so lazy!" he
complained to Chernyaev. "The bosses, too: Once they're in power, they
spend time at the trough, drinking tea (and not just tea), and cursing
out their own bosses." With his anniversary speech two months away,
Gorbachev was still exploring what he regarded as the fine line between
smearing the past and criticizing it constructively, still hoping to "regu-
late" the debate about history in his upcoming address. He read Marx's
1844 *Economic and Philosophical Manuscripts*, noting to Chernyaev that
the great man himself had not entirely rejected private property, then
dictated his thoughts on "alienation" (societies should be judged not
according to the level of consumption but according to the degree of people's self-development) for an article to be published in the party theoretical journal, *Kommunist*.[58]

Gorbachev's intellectual bent was also reflected in the way he devoted
most of his "vacation" to writing a book, *Perestroika: New Thinking for Our
Country and the World*. American publishers had suggested Gorbachev
do so, and although Yakovlev and Dobrynin proposed a collection of
his speeches, Gorbachev opted for a book. That spring a team headed
by Chernyaev had gathered material, not only from speeches, but from
notes on Politburo meetings and private conversations. According to
Chernyaev, who worked with him that summer, Gorbachev attacked the
project "with passion," dictating whole drafts two or three times, sitting
for hours on the terrace (Gorbachev in the sun, Chernyaev in the shade)
discussing the major segments and how the book "moved" through
them, extending his Crimean stay for more than a week to finish the
manuscript. Although the book is a broad survey of Gorbachev's thinking on domestic and foreign affairs, it broke no new ground at home. But

its appearance in the West, in 1987–1988 in millions of copies, caused a sensation—which not only advanced his foreign policy but tickled his ego. He foresaw that the book would create "a new image for him and his changing country; it would help win the West's trust," which in turn would help him to "transform international relations."[59] Gorbachev worried about how his Politburo colleagues would react to such a personal project. So he showed the manuscript to some of them. He received almost no critical comments (except for minor corrections from Ryzhkov), but no "enthusiastic approval" either.[60]

After returning from the Black Sea, Gorbachev and aides huddled at Zavidovo to finish his anniversary speech. The Politburo considered the 120-page draft on October 15. All members praised it, some fawning shamelessly on its author (Aliev: "philosophically, politically and ideologically profound, extremely objective, balanced and clear, innovative and nontraditional"), but others wanted changes. Ligachev: more emphasis on Stalin's battle against "Trotskyism." Gromyko: How, in the absence of collectivization, could the country have survived World War II? "We must never forget that we have class enemies." Chebrikov asked sarcastically how anti-Stalinist literary works had managed to become "the basic texts of Marxism-Leninism." Solomentsev: more coverage for wartime heroism, not to mention the glorious postwar "renewal: Wasn't that heroic as well?!" As for "dekulakization" (that abstract euphemism for the murder of millions of peasants), yes, there had been some excesses, but not uniformly in every district. Gorbachev replied with some heat: "I remember how my grandmother assessed collectivization." "What enmity! Brother against brother, son against father, whole families torn apart. Quotas sent down from above: how many kulaks to exile. They rushed to fulfill the quotas; it didn't matter whether you were a kulak or not. The same thing happened in 1937, except this time each district, each village, had a quota for the number to be executed."[61]

Interestingly enough, given his later radicalism, Yeltsin's critique also sounded conservative: too much focus in the draft on the "bourgeois-democratic" February 1917 revolution rather than the glorious Bolshevik Revolution of October; warmer tributes to Lenin needed; more attention to the "smashing of Trotskyism." Yeltsin got in a needle about Gorbachev's habit of delineating "stages" of perestroika and indicating how long they would take. "Better not talk about stages," said Yeltsin sensibly, lest people be disappointed when they failed to bear fruit. "Just say simply [his strength, not Gorbachev's] what the next task is and the one after that."[62]

Gorbachev delivered his much-anticipated speech on November 2, 1987, to a ceremonial joint session of the party Central Committee and the USSR and Russian Republic Supreme Soviets in the marble and glass Kremlin Palace of Congresses. The festive session lasted for two days, including speeches by leaders of allied countries and their Communist parties. The huge celebration in Red Square occurred on November 7, complete with a mammoth demonstration of military might and a parade of citizens past their leaders atop the Lenin Mausoleum. That evening there was a gala reception in the Palace of Congresses.

Gorbachev's address was titled "October and Perestroika: The Revolution Continues." Compared with what he had been saying at Politburo meetings, and especially in private to Chernyaev, the speech was cautious. A mixed characterization of Trotsky was removed at the last moment. So were incriminating, personal details about Stalin, statistics on the number of people liquidated under Stalin, and a formal endorsement of the new "pluralism."[63] Gorbachev hailed the revolution itself and Lenin, of course. Stalin, however, was now fair game. Gorbachev condemned Stalin-era lawlessness as "vast and unforgivable," and, as if rebutting his grandfather's faith that Stalin didn't know what was done in his name, proclaimed the truth so many Soviet citizens still refused to admit: "Stalin knew."[64]

Gorbachev's speech struck hard-liners as going too far, liberals as not far enough. It didn't satisfy him either, he admits in his memoirs. "We had to remain silent about some things." "There was much we still had to comprehend. We had to overcome psychological barriers. More research was needed on 'blank spots.' As the saying goes, in such cases, you can't jump higher than you are."[65] This admission is partly disingenuous. Gorbachev's own thinking had gone further than he cared to admit, lest his equivocations in the speech seem too calculated. Yet he still had a lot to celebrate. He had finally opened the way, after decades of repression and evasion, to a full accounting of Stalinist crimes. Despite all the sniping in the Politburo about glasnost, and especially about Soviet history, he had managed to preserve at least the public appearance of Kremlin unity.

IN FACT, THAT UNITY was shattered twelve days before the speech. At a Central Committee plenum that approved the main outlines of Gorbachev's upcoming address, Yeltsin disrupted the meeting, ruined his relationship with Gorbachev, and began the fateful process that culminated in Gorbachev's fall from power four years later.

Yeltsin's rise in 1985 had been rapid: from party leader in Sverdlovsk to head of the Central Committee's construction department in April, to Central Committee secretary three months later, to Moscow city party boss in December. But not rapid enough for Yeltsin. Stavropol and Tomsk provinces (Gorbachev's and Ligachev's launching pads) were smaller and less important than Sverdlovsk, and two of Yeltsin's three Sverdlovsk predecessors had leaped directly to Central Committee secretary status (Andrei Kirilenko in 1962 and Yakov Ryabov in 1976), while a third, Nikolai Ryzhkov, was the country's prime minister.

When Yeltsin returned to Sverdlovsk from Moscow in April 1985 with his new promotion in hand, his colleagues could see he was bitterly disappointed. He arrived late for a meeting (untypical for him), broke a pencil into three parts (typical when irked), and complained about those running the country, explicitly about "doddering [Brezhnev-era] halfwits," but implicitly about Gorbachev's new team. "We all froze and blanched," a Yeltsin colleague recalled. "We could see what it was about"—the fact that Yeltsin had been made only the "head of a department. . . . He said it right out."[66]

Yeltsin's resentments began even earlier. He and Gorbachev got along well enough when they were both province party bosses, but once Gorbachev was in Moscow as a Central Committee secretary, Yeltsin found him "controlling and patronizing," reports biographer Timothy Colton. Gorbachev's habit of addressing subordinates in the second-person singular, *ty*, particularly grated on Yeltsin, who, though more direct and outspoken than Gorbachev, always used the more formal *vy*. According to a Sverdlovsk colleague, "notes of disrespect for Gorbachev" continually appeared in Yeltsin's comments at the party bureau.[67]

Yegor Ligachev standing to Gorbachev's right at a Communist party conclave. Andrei Gromyko stands to Gorbachev's left. Yeltsin is visible in the second row behind Ligachev.

Ligachev had pushed to bring Yeltsin to Moscow, but Gorbachev was also impressed by his early exploits there. After Yeltsin attacked the previous city administration as corrupt at a Moscow party conference, Gorbachev thanked him for providing "a strong and welcome gust of fresh air" for the party, but "without an approving smile and with an impassive expression," Yeltsin recalled.[68] A month later, at the Twenty-Seventh Party Congress, Yeltsin called for far-reaching political changes (such as "periodic accountability" of the top political leaders), raised the delicate question of why he himself had not been more outspoken at past congresses, and then answered his own question: "I did not then have enough courage and political experience."[69]

Yeltsin took Moscow by storm. He rode the metro, trams, and buses in solidarity with ordinary citizens and as well-rehearsed populist advertisements for himself. He descended on stores, cafeterias, and dormitories, bantering with crowds, berating miscreants or firing them on the spot, occasionally giving away his own wristwatch to a particularly virtuous Muscovite. (Yeltsin's bodyguard, Aleksandr Korzhakov, kept spares in his coat pocket.) As the new Moscow party boss, he purged all his predecessor Grishin's deputies, two-thirds of district party bosses, and 90 percent of leading figures in the city administration. Yeltsin canned the Moscow city mayor, who had been on the job for twenty-three years, giving him a day and half to get out. At Yeltsin's urging, the Moscow party newspaper exposed elite privileges: special stores to which wives of leaders were ferried in chauffeured limos, special restaurants and dachas, preferential admission to universities and institutes. Meanwhile, Yeltsin badgered the Politburo and Secretariat for support, including special provisioning of the city with extra foodstuffs, and complained when he didn't get it. On top of that, he began meeting with foreign journalists. He was interviewed in May 1987 by Diane Sawyer of CBS television.[70]

All this looked like self-promotion to Yeltsin's Kremlin comrades. Their reaction to it seemed to him like disrespect. Ligachev, whose chairing of the Secretariat didn't satisfy Yeltsin, turned against him, all the more bitterly since he had regarded Yeltsin as his protégé.[71] Gorbachev also had growing reservations. When Yeltsin became Moscow party boss, he and everyone else expected him to gain full Politburo voting rights, as his predecessors had before him. But Gorbachev made him only a candidate member. In mid-1986, Gorbachev ordered coverage of Yeltsin in *Pravda* toned down. According to Vitaly Tretyakov, a sharp journalistic observer, Yeltsin started out trying "to do what it seemed to him Gorbachev expected, and to do it better and faster than others," but once he sensed that Gorbachev "did not view Yeltsin's zeal and shock-tactics with gratitude," his "constructive aggressiveness" turned into the "destructive" kind.[72]

Yeltsin's sniping at Gorbachev during Politburo meetings in the first months of 1987 must be understood against this background. So should Yeltsin's growing sense of grievance and isolation. Several witnesses recall (without using the term) his "passive aggressiveness" at Kremlin meetings, including scowls and long, stony silences. Meanwhile, his physical condition deteriorated: "Tough as I am," he recalled, he had reached "the limit of my capacity." He was working "from 7:00 a.m. until midnight, sometimes to one or two o'clock in the morning, with Saturday a full working day," with Sundays devoted to inspecting his domain and writing speeches and letters. "There were times when I would drive home, my bodyguard would open the door, and I just didn't have the strength to get out of the car. I would sit for five to ten minutes gathering my senses, as my wife stood on the porch looking anxiously at me. I was so worn out I lacked even the strength to raise my hand."[73]

Late in 1986, Yeltsin entered a clinic with symptoms of hypertension and anxiety. The doctors diagnosed his condition as the result of over-work and concluded he "had begun to abuse sedatives and sleeping pills and to be enamored of alcohol." Yeltsin refused to slow down and told them that he had "no need of moral lectures."[74] Yet in October 1987 he delivered just such a lecture to Gorbachev, with dire consequences.

GORBACHEV WAS STILL IN CRIMEA when the Politburo met on September 10, so Ligachev was in the chair. He lambasted Yeltsin for the way he handled Moscow street demonstrations by Russian nationalists and Crimean Tatars, whom Stalin had exiled to Central Asia and who now wanted to return to their homeland. Yeltsin had decided to allow meetings in Izmailovo Park, east of the city center, but had not cleared his plan with the Kremlin. That night Yeltsin began writing a letter to Gorbachev, which opened by charging "several Politburo members and some Central Committee secretaries" with "personal coldness" and "indifference" to his work. Ligachev, in particular, was guilty of "systematic persecution." Yeltsin partly blamed himself—his own style, his candor, his inexperience on the Politburo: "I am an awkward person, and I know it." But he also blamed Gorbachev for welcoming as sincere some of his colleagues' obviously false commitment to perestroika: "This suits them and, if you will forgive me for saying so, I believe it also suits you." Yeltsin regretted that his tense relations with other Politburo members were likely to cause trouble for Gorbachev and "hamper you in your work." The letter closed with a request to resign as Moscow party boss and Politburo candidate member. "I want you to release me," he wrote, followed by what seemed a not-so-veiled threat to take his case to the Central Committee itself: "I do not think it should be necessary for me to submit my request directly to a plenum of the Central Committee."[75]

Gorbachev was sufficiently concerned when he received Yeltsin's September 12 missive to phone him back. Chernyaev happened to be there at the time and heard Gorbachev "complimenting [Yeltsin], persuading, begging: 'Wait, Boris, don't fly off the handle, we'll work this out.'" With the seventieth anniversary of the revolution coming up in two months, Gorbachev asked Yeltsin to hold off until afterward. After putting down the phone, Gorbachev told Chernyaev, "I managed to talk him into it; we agreed that he won't have an attack of nerves and rush around until after the celebrations."[76]

Gorbachev considered the matter closed for the time being. Yeltsin did not. His recollection is that Gorbachev said, "Let's meet later," which Yeltsin understood to mean before the next Central Committee plenum on October 21. So "I waited," Yeltsin continues. "A week passed, two weeks, and there was still no invitation to talk. I decided he had changed his mind about meeting me and would take the matter of my dismissal to the Central Committee." As he waited, Yeltsin brooded, fearing that Gorbachev would denounce and purge him at the plenum. He had always felt, he insists, like "an outsider, or rather an alien, among these people." So instead of waiting for Gorbachev's ax to fall, he planned a speech to the plenum, while "preparing myself psychologically for the worst," which he assumed would follow. Instead of writing and rewriting his speech many times, his usual habit, he scribbled "seven headings on a piece of paper," a sign, he thought later, that a possible retreat was "lurking somewhere in my subconscious."[77]

The plenum convened in the Kremlin's Sverdlov Hall, with its splendid rotunda ninety feet high supported by Corinthian pillars and crowned with a narrow gallery. The Politburo's voting members were seated as a presidium behind the speaker's platform, looking down at Central Committee members and guests. Politburo candidate members, Yeltsin included, sat in the first row below the stage. The main business of the day was Gorbachev's preview of his anniversary report. Since it had been distributed in advance, with recipients invited to respond in writing, no comments from the floor were anticipated. For the sake of formality, however, Ligachev, chairing the meeting, asked, "Shall we open the floor for discussion?" "Not necessary," came shouts from the hall. "Let's approve it!"[78]

At this point, Yeltsin tentatively raised his hand and then lowered it. But Gorbachev noticed. "Look," he said, "Yeltsin wants to say something." "So," said Ligachev, "let's decide: Shall we open the floor for discussion?" More shouts in the hall: "No." Ligachev: "No." Yeltsin half rose, then subsided. Gorbachev again: "Comrade Yeltsin has some sort of statement." Ligachev invited Yeltsin to speak. Yeltsin climbed the stairs to the stage, moving slowly, looking agitated. At first, he stood silently at the podium, then he began to speak, trying to restrain his emotions, gradually gaining in assurance.[79]

Yeltsin attacked Ligachev for his "bullying reprimands," then moved on to Gorbachev without mentioning his name. All those boasts about what perestroika would achieve in its first two to three years had proved empty, yet more promises were now being made. All that time had been spent drafting documents, "which never got to the people," who were now upset because they had gotten "nothing" out of perestroika so far. Meanwhile, however, certain full members of the Politburo had been "glorifying" the general secretary, all the more impermissible with democratization the watchword of the day. Gorbachev himself had rightly attacked the past abuses of leaders who were "totally immune to criticism." Yet, now "a cult of personality" was arising again. Yeltsin's remarks lasted four to five minutes. He closed this way: "Things haven't worked out for me in the Politburo. For various reasons. One is my lack of experience, but another is lack of support, especially from Comrade Ligachev. . . . I have already handed in my resignation. As for my future as Moscow first secretary, that will be decided by the Moscow party committee."[80]

At this point, Gorbachev took back the chair from Ligachev. Containing his emotions, he characterized Yeltsin's remarks as "serious" and summarized them. Then he mocked Yeltsin's last sentence. The idea of the Moscow party committee's deciding his future as Moscow leader was "something new." Was Yeltsin planning to set the Moscow committee against the Central Committee, which everyone knew was a higher authority? Was he intending to fight the Central Committee? Yeltsin leaped to his feet to protest. Gorbachev slapped him down: "Sit down, sit down!" Second-person singular again, particularly crude and dismissive in the imperative form, used mostly when ordering dogs and small children to stay put. "Let's hear your opinions, comrades," he invited the others to speak.[81]

What happened next, recalled Central Committee official Karen Brutents, who witnessed it, was a "five-hour Bacchanalia."[82] "Eyes ablaze," recalled Yeltsin, people "who had long worked beside me, who were my friends . . . hurled invective at me." It all added up to: "Yeltsin is an expletive, a four-letter word. . . . How I endured it I don't know."[83] Nine Politburo members, fifteen other officials, and two token blue-collar members of the Central Committee mixed tirades at Yeltsin with just the sort of fawning at Gorbachev that Yeltsin had condemned.

Ligachev: Yeltsin was "an ultra-leftist," a "provocateur," "political and intellectually hopeless," a "political nihilist," guilty of "the purest slander."

Leonid Borodin (Astrakhan province party boss): "I respect Mikhail Sergeyevich with my whole heart. Am I not allowed to say good things about him?"

Stepan Shalayev (head of the tame Soviet trade unions): "We should rejoice that Mikhail Sergeyevich heads the Politburo. [*Stormy applause*] He would never permit people to 'glorify' him."

Yakov Ryabov (ambassador to France) on his former Sverdlovsk underling: "arrogant, malevolent, a megalomaniac."

Ryzhkov: "We spend seven to eight hours in Politburo meetings. We come out covered with sweat. Does Yeltsin mean to tell us we spend all this time telling Comrade Gorbachev what a great guy he is? No way!" Yeltsin "loves being quoted in the foreign press." "Why is he silent at Politburo meetings?"

Aleksandr Kolesnikov (miner): "We believe you, Mikhail Sergeyevich. We love you."

KGB chief Chebrikov: "The holiday is upon us. The country is celebrating." But all Yeltsin "thinks about is himself." He talks about "bullying in the Secretariat. It's in the Moscow party bureau that there's bullying. People there feel as if they're walking the scaffold."

Some speakers tried to defend Yeltsin, but only up to a point. Yeltsin's dissent was a "normal" product of perestroika, said Poltava province party chief Fyodor Morgun, but his failure to feed Moscow was not. Arbatov: The very fact of Yeltsin's speech testified to what glasnost had accomplished. "None of us is an angel," Yakovlev admitted, but for Yeltsin, "personal ambition is primary." Shevardnadze warned against "dramatizing and oversimplifying" the situation, but then did so himself, condemning Yeltsin's "treason."[84]

Gorbachev didn't try to halt the discussion. "It would have been impossible to stop it," he later recalled, "and there was no reason to try to." As the assault rolled on, he watched Yeltsin and tried to understand what was going through his mind. "I couldn't figure him out," Gorbachev recalled much later. "He was all over the map."[85] "His face displayed an odd mixture of exasperation, uncertainty, and regret— everything characteristic of an unbalanced man. Speakers who only yesterday had curried favor with him were now berating him mercilessly—we are all too good at this."[86] Finally, Gorbachev asked Yeltsin whether he had anything further to say. Yeltsin tried to defend himself. Gorbachev himself then attacked. How could Yeltsin talk about "a cult of personality"? Didn't he know that was a thing of the past? Apparently not—he couldn't tell "God's gift from an omelette." He was so "politically illiterate" he needed an "elementary primer." All Yeltsin cared about was himself. Perestroika was at a delicate stage. But because of Yeltsin's "escapade," because of his "hypertrophied pride and high opinion of himself," the Central Committee hadn't gotten to discuss Gorbachev's "crucial" report.

Gorbachev pressed Yeltsin again to reply. Yeltsin mumbled that he had "let down" the Central Committee, that his speech today had been "a mistake."

Gorbachev then threw Yeltsin a lifeline: "Do you have the strength to continue your work?" he asked, as if taking pity on Yeltsin. Shouts in the hall: "No he doesn't. Fire him!" Gorbachev: "Wait, wait, I've asked him a question. Let's be democratic. Let's hear him out before any decision is made." Yeltsin: "I repeat my request—to be relieved of my duties as a Politburo candidate member and as Moscow party leader."

Yeltsin had conceded. If Gorbachev really wanted his report to be discussed, now was the time. Instead, he quickly called for a vote (his report was approved unanimously) and returned to berating Yeltsin. Gorbachev had never expected "such disloyalty," such "egotism." Yeltsin was "irresponsible," "thoughtless," "immature." He "carped" about everything so as to "make himself stand out." Gorbachev proposed that the Central Committee censure Yeltsin and that the Politburo and the

Moscow committee proceed to scrutinize his status. Yeltsin voted for the resolution along with everyone else.[87]

THE OCTOBER 21 SHOWDOWN was almost as damaging to Gorbachev as it was to Yeltsin. For those in the know (Yeltsin's speech wasn't published until two years later, but word quickly spread throughout the elite), it overshadowed Gorbachev's anniversary report. It revealed that glasnost ended at the Kremlin's edge. It turned tensions between the two men into a deep, mutual hatred.[88]

There may have been a chance to make peace. The Moscow party bureau, meeting shortly after the plenum, condemned Yeltsin for not consulting them about his resignation, but urged him to remain as their leader. Moscow's new mayor, appointed by Yeltsin, was dispatched to make the case to the Kremlin, but Gorbachev refused to see him. Yeltsin apologized at a Politburo session on October 31, confessing that "self-love" had led him astray, and asking to stay on as Moscow party leader. Gorbachev responded that he did not consider Yeltsin "an opponent of perestroika." But he didn't forgive Yeltsin either.[89] Yeltsin reiterated his request in a letter of November 3, but Gorbachev turned it down, telling aides, "He thinks of himself as a popular hero." On November 10, Chernyaev urged Gorbachev to reach out to Yeltsin so as to preserve him as a reform-minded ally. If Yeltsin had been allowed to remain as Moscow party leader, his biographer Timothy Colton thinks, he could have been persuaded to accept demotion from the Politburo, "something he had wanted since September, with eligibility for a return."[90]

By November 10, however, events had taken a bizarre turn. The day before that, Yeltsin was found covered with blood in his office. He had slashed his chest and stomach with a pair of office scissors. The fact that the injury was too superficial to require stitches leads Colton to conclude it was "a howl of anger, frustration, and perhaps self-hate" rather than a real attempt at suicide. Yeltsin himself later described it merely as a "breakdown." But his wife removed hunting knives, guns, and glass objects from their home before he returned from the hospital, and took steps to prevent his overdosing on prescription drugs.[91]

"What a bastard!" Gorbachev thought to himself. "He bloodied his

own room."[92] Gorbachev and Ligachev had scheduled a city party committee plenum for the evening of November 11, when it would officially
fire Yeltsin as Moscow party leader. According to Gorbachev, doctors
assured him that Yeltsin's condition had stabilized, so he called Yeltsin
in the hospital and urged him to attend. But Dr. Chazov remembered
cautioning that attendance could endanger Yeltsin's health, and Yeltsin
told Gorbachev that he couldn't even get to the toilet without assistance.
Gorbachev sweetened his "invitation" by saying he was prepared to let
Yeltsin serve in the government with the rank of minister, but added a
warning that Yeltsin would never let him forget—that he would never
allow Yeltsin back into high-level politics.[93]

Yeltsin agreed to go. When KGB officers arrived to take him to the
plenum, his wife tried in vain to stop them. Yeltsin arrived bandaged,
his face purplish blue. Doctors had administered an analgesic and anti-
spasm medication. "I was barely conscious," Yeltsin recalled. Gorbachev
later claimed he was determined to avoid a "row," to handle "the Yeltsin
affair" in the new spirit of the time. He went out of his way, in his own
remarks to the gathering, to praise Yeltsin's "good side" and to defend
his right to criticize the Politburo, the Secretariat, and "individual comrades." Under glasnost, that was entirely "normal." What was unacceptable was to do so at a "critical moment," when "principled questions of
theory and practice relating to our development" were being decided.
But when weren't they? What did glasnost protect if it didn't protect that?
Moreover, Gorbachev couldn't resist several more slams at Yeltsin in his
speech: "not one constructive idea," "theoretically and politically helpless," "inordinate vanity."[94] After that, other speakers felt free to have at
Yeltsin without restraint.

KGB agents had reserved the first three rows of the hall for preselected
orators. Yeltsin describes them as "flushed, quaking," like wolfhounds
"before the hunt." "You have ground everything into dust and ashes,"
snarled a former district party boss. "A party crime" and "blasphemy"
was the way another district chief characterized Yeltsin's behavior. Anti-
Communists, another speaker charged, were trying to turn Yeltsin into
"a Jesus Christ who has been tortured for his frightfully revolutionary
love of social renewal and democracy."[95]

When it was over, Yeltsin dragged himself up to the platform, with

Gorbachev supporting his elbow. This time he was utterly abject before "Mikhail Sergeyevich Gorbachev, whose authority is so high in our organization, in our country, and in the entire world." Yeltsin had tried to "struggle with ambition," but, he admitted, "without success." The city committee replaced Yeltsin as its leader with Lev Zaikov. Since shrouding the October 21 Central Committee plenum in mystery had only fueled rumors about Yeltsin's martyrdom, *Pravda* printed an edited transcript of the city plenum. On November 17, the Soviet news agency, TASS, announced that Yeltsin had been demoted to first deputy chairman of Gosstroi, the State Construction Committee. Three months later Zaikov boasted, "The Yeltsin era is over."[96]

IT WASN'T, OF COURSE. But what had already happened raises key questions about Gorbachev. Why did he keep Yeltsin down even after making him Moscow party leader? Why didn't he respond immediately and fully to Yeltsin's September 12 letter? Why didn't he just thank Yeltsin for his services and let him resign? Why did he insist on inviting him to speak at the October 21 plenum? Why did he react so allergically to Yeltsin's remarks? Why didn't he accept a cease-fire and nonaggression pact after the plenum? Why did he cruelly drag Yeltsin to the city party session? Why did his treatment of Yeltsin guarantee that if and when Yeltsin recovered, he would never forgive or forget? Why didn't he exile him, as Khrushchev and Brezhnev had done with their adversaries, to some very small, very faraway country?

Even if Gorbachev had made Yeltsin his full partner in perestroika, even if he had replaced Ligachev with him, Yeltsin probably would have challenged Gorbachev in the end. After all, they differed drastically on how fast and how far to carry out change. But more than politics was involved. There were deep and corrosive differences of character and style. His enemies may have exaggerated the charges against him, but Yeltsin himself admitted he was almost impossible to deal with. Still, there was something blindly venomous about Gorbachev's reaction to him. Gorbachev "didn't see or refused to see," recalled Brutents, that "all the steps taken against Yeltsin, even those evoked by Yeltsin's unseemly behavior, lowered Gorbachev's prestige and increased Yeltsin's popularity." In that sense, Gorbachev "created" Yeltsin as his own "political gravedigger."[97] So striking, so Shakespearean is this sequence that it raises questions about its psychological wellsprings, so apparently out of character for Gorbachev as to make one wonder whether it wasn't in character, after all.

Gorbachev recalls being "apprehensive" about Yeltsin before 1985. After a Central Committee investigation of agriculture in Sverdlovsk province, Yeltsin asked him not to forward the report's critical conclusions to the Central Committee, but rather let Sverdlovsk authorities correct their own mistakes. Gorbachev agreed, but Yeltsin then buried the report, prompting a Moscow emissary to rebuke Yeltsin, and Yeltsin to rebuke his critic in turn. Yeltsin "did not react adequately to the comments addressed to him," Gorbachev wrote, using the sort of delicate language at which Yeltsin would have sneered. Nor did the abstemious Gorbachev like it when he heard Yeltsin had appeared drunk at a session of the Supreme Soviet.[98]

Gorbachev took his cue partly from Andropov. Just weeks before his death, Andropov approved Ligachev's recommendation that Yeltsin head the Central Committee construction department, although the appointment was delayed during the Chernenko interregnum. But Andropov wasn't wild about Yeltsin, praising him not as a great province party boss and a future leader but only as "a good builder." Even though Yeltsin impressed Gorbachev early on as Moscow leader by hiring "active, decisive, and innovative" subordinates, and by the way he cleaned up the mess Grishin had left behind, according to Grachev, Gorbachev "didn't consider Yeltsin an important political figure on his chessboard." How did Grachev know Gorbachev felt so superior? Because Gorbachev's daughter, Irina, told him Yeltsin's name rarely came up in the Gorbachev family's nightly discussions of his Kremlin colleagues.[99]

Gorbachev was cautious and calculating, Yeltsin an impulsive risk taker. Gorbachev worked at being or seeming even tempered; Yeltsin either loved or hated you, and it showed. Gorbachev was instinctively democratic, Yeltsin an authoritarian populist. Gorbachev was highly educated in the humanities and married a philosopher; Yeltsin, trained in construction, married an engineer. Gorbachev was smooth, Yeltsin rough; Gorbachev, a persuader; Yeltsin a brawler. Gorbachev was garrulous and long-winded, circling his subject and repeating himself, as if trying to clarify his thoughts as he spoke. Yeltsin used fewer words, often presenting them as "points one, two, and three." Gorbachev's favorite exercise was long walks with his wife. Yeltsin was a champion volleyball player as a youth and played tennis even after his first heart attack. Even their tastes in music differed: Gorbachev favored symphonies and opera, although he loved to sing folk songs and was good at it; Yeltsin's taste ran to pop tunes.[100]

Differences like these made for mutual nonunderstanding. But so did some similarities. Both men came from provincial backgrounds, but so did almost all Soviet leaders (apparently, Muscovites knew enough to avoid political careers). Grandparents of both were victims of Stalin's terror.[101] Both Gorbachev and Yeltsin raised their hands at about the same age to stop a parent (Gorbachev's mother, Yeltsin's father) from beating them ever again. But rather than creating a bond between them, these parallels may have exacerbated their mutual antipathy: neither had raised himself up from almost nothing just to take guff from the other.

Why didn't Gorbachev respond more urgently to Yeltsin's September 12 letter? Yeltsin fantasized that it would spur Gorbachev into action: "Would he call me down to see him? Or would he telephone me to ask me to stay working steadily at my job . . . ?" Or perhaps the letter would prompt Gorbachev to take "immediate steps" (such as replacing Ligachev with Yeltsin?) to "ensure a healthy, constructive attitude in the Politburo."[102] Instead, reflecting his sense of superiority, Gorbachev took the letter to reflect (as Grachev puts it) a "banal tiff" between Yeltsin and Ligachev, hardly something he needed when faced with "the important and politically delicate task of preparing for the 70th anniversary of the revolution"[103]

In contrast to Yeltsin's daydreams of glory, some have attributed more Machiavellian motives to Gorbachev in September. One theory is that he wanted to keep Yeltsin around as a radical counterpoise to Ligachev— so that Gorbachev could play the role of a reasonable centrist between them. Gorbachev later admitted that Yakovlev recommended just such a scheme.[104] Another theory is that he wanted to kick Yeltsin out publicly later, rather than let him quietly resign now, so as to curry favor with conservatives.[105] In fact, Gorbachev simply couldn't be bothered dealing with the irascible, obstreperous Yeltsin until it was too late to do so without inflicting a mortal wound to himself.

Why did Gorbachev press for Yeltsin to speak on October 21? Again one can (some Gorbachev colleagues did) imagine a devious design—to lure Yeltsin into undermining Ligachev while at the same time incriminating himself. Thinking like that certainly wasn't beyond Gorbachev, but why should Yeltsin be denied the right to speak to the Central Committee, especially since Gorbachev thought he wasn't capable of doing much damage even if he wanted to?

What caused Gorbachev's agitated reaction to Yeltsin's October 21 remarks and to virtually all his actions, whether aggressive or appeasing, from then on? Although Gorbachev struggled to contain his anger on October 21, his face turned "purple with rage." He tried for a while to "preserve decorum," Boldin remembered, but then allowed "the feeding frenzy" full rein.[106] Grachev confirms that "emotions" drove Gorbachev when he swore to Yeltsin that he'd never allow him back into "high-level politics."[107]

By now Gorbachev hated Yeltsin. Yeltsin had tried to steal Gorbachev's banner by presenting himself as the real champion of change. Yeltsin dared to point out Gorbachev's shortcomings: the failure to develop a clear strategy and explain things clearly, the tendency to talk too long and to promise too much. Yeltsin reminded Gorbachev of the crude colleagues in Stavropol he despised. Moreover, Gorbachev shared some of the very failings he condemned in Yeltsin. Arrogance, vanity, pride—to the extent he was aware of these shortcomings in himself, Gorbachev tried to contain them. So when Yeltsin flaunted them all, in what Gorbachev regarded as a wild, erratic attempt to damage the great cause of perestroika, Gorbachev's anger may have been aimed at least partly at himself.

Yeltsin's attitude to Raisa Gorbachev, and hers to him, did not help. When Yeltsin, as Moscow party leader, rebuffed her proposal to turn the GUM department store on Red Square into an art museum, and then complained about her to her husband, Gorbachev was furious.[108] Her own anger at Yeltsin reinforced her husband's.

Gorbachev was a very emotional man, who even wept in response to sentimental movies. But he was determined to keep emotion out of politics, not to let it affect his calculations. So he tried to contain his anger against Yeltsin and even to make up for it with small gestures: inviting Yeltsin to speak on October 21, holding back, if only briefly, the onslaught that followed, supporting Yeltsin's arm on November 11, regretting in his memoirs the most vicious attacks on Yeltsin that day, and praising Yeltsin for conducting himself in the face of adversity like a real man."[109]

Why did Gorbachev let Yeltsin remain at large rather than exile him? That decision, more than almost anything else Gorbachev did, baffled (and still baffles) Russians, who are all too accustomed to rough, cynical leaders. Even Gorbachev himself later conceded that he should have banished Yeltsin. But at the time he told Grachev and other aides who urged Yeltsin's exile, "No, fellows. That's out. He's a politician, after all. I can't just throw him out." And he later warned KGB chief Kriuchkov, "Look out, if as much as a hair falls from his head, you'll have to answer for it."[110] It is probably true, as Brutents sensed, that Gorbachev was so confident of his control over Yeltsin that he was blind to the danger his rival posed. But it was also the case that Gorbachev was trying to live up to what was best in his own nature.

CHAPTER 9

WHO'S AFRAID OF NINA ANDREYEVA?

1988

Boris Yeltsin's October 1987 attack on Gorbachev, calling for more rapid reforms, had the redeeming feature (from Gorbachev's point of view) that Yeltsin was a lone voice in the Politburo, who did not yet have a political and social base and could be quickly shoved aside. In March 1988, Gorbachev was ambushed by hard-liners, who accused him of going too far too fast. This time, as well, his critics were Kremlin colleagues, but theirs was a far broader assault—an article in a national newspaper, apparently penned by a rank-and-file Communist named Nina Andreyeva but secretly staged by Ligachev, with backing by a majority of the Politburo and wide support throughout the party apparatus and much of society as well.

Gorbachev's response wasn't as fierce as it had been to Yeltsin; he allowed Ligachev and company to remain in the Politburo. But their broadside helped prompt Gorbachev to take a great leap toward democracy. Until then, his own hesitations and the balancing act required by working within the system to change the system had held him back. Now he embarked on truly radical reforms that ended Communism as the Soviets had known it for decades. Looking back, he and his supporters said the "real" perestroika began only in 1988 at the historic Nineteenth Party Conference in June, which decreed a drastically reduced role for the Communist party, and in later decisions to partially purge the Politburo and prepare the way for mostly free elections to a new national legislature the next spring.

These were great victories in the liberalization and democratization of the country. But the task he took on was overwhelming. Trying to bring an entire country back from fear, he sharpened challenges that would eventually undo him—from hard-liners increasingly convinced of his betrayal, from Yeltsin, whose bizarre reappearance at the Nineteenth Conference further exacerbated (if that was possible) his relationship with Gorbachev, and from separatist nationalism that should have been quite predictable but that nonetheless blindsided Gorbachev and eventually helped destroy not just perestroika but the Soviet Union itself.

A FREER AND LESS AFRAID press had always been essential to Gorbachev's plan for democratization and change. By the end of 1987, glasnost was already flourishing, but early 1988 amounted to a full-fledged Moscow Spring; not just a hundred, but thousands of free-speech flowers were blooming.[1] Gorbachev's 1987 November anniversary speech, limited though it was, prompted a burst of revelations. *Argumenty i fakty*, once a dull magazine for party activists but now boasting a circulation of several million, estimated that more than ten million had died in the course of Stalinist collectivization. *Moscow News*, which had transformed itself from a broadsheet for tourists into a tribune of the people, contended (granted, in an interview with Zbigniew Brzezinski, rather than in its own voice) that 20 percent of the Soviet gross domestic product was spent on defense, as compared with 6 percent in the United States. Former Brezhnev adviser Aleksandr Bovin disclosed in the journal *New Times* that the Soviet Union was referred to by some foreign critics as "Upper Volta with rockets." (Today Upper Volta, a small land-locked nation in West Africa, is known as Burkina Faso.) Yevgeny Chazov, Soviet minister of health (and personal physician to Soviet leaders), revealed that 30 percent of Soviet hospitals lacked indoor plumbing. Seminars at the Historical Archives Institute in Moscow leveled charges that in past years could have been made only in private kitchen conversations, the telephone covered with a pillow: Stalinism was a species of totalitarianism on a par with Hitler's; Nikolai Bukharin, Stalin's comrade turned victim whom Gorbachev rehabilitated in his anniversary speech, had in fact helped Stalin to power, then betrayed others by confessing to crimes he never committed; Marxist-Leninist philosophy was neither Marxist nor Leninist nor philosophy.

To judge by the long early-morning lines at newsstands, Moscow itself had become a seminar in which, miraculously, everyone had done the required reading. So-called thick journals, two hundred or more pages of prose, poetry, literary criticism, and *publitsistika* (essays and opinion pieces on social, economic, and political themes), had astonishing circulations: *Novyi mir*, the liberal journal that began the year by publishing Boris Pasternak's *Dr. Zhivago*, had 1,150,000 subscribers. At *Druzhba narodov*, which published Anatoly Rybakov's *Children of the Arbat* in 1987, circulation was up an astonishing 443 percent. *Ogonyok*, a *Life* magazine look-alike with several million readers, recounted how Stalin's favorite charlatan, Trofim Lysenko, trashed Soviet biology by destroying its most distinguished geneticists. It also revealed the full story of rocket scientist Sergei Korolyov, who was imprisoned under Stalin before going on to direct Khrushchev's successful effort to put the first man into space. The actual number of readers was four or five times higher; since few families could afford to subscribe to all these journals, households divided up subscriptions and circulated issues among themselves and their friends. Conservative journals, like *Moskva* and *Molodaya gvardiya*, scored smaller circulation gains. *Pravda* was one of the few periodicals that actually lost readers.

Until the advent of glasnost, dissident literature circulated in samizdat (self-publishing) or was published abroad (*tamizdat*) and then smuggled into the Soviet Union. Readers with the desire and the connections (admittedly a small portion of the overall Soviet population) could get access to almost anything. Given a book or manuscript for twenty-four hours, they would think nothing of staying up all night to read it. A joke circulated about the mother who typed out all of *War and Peace* in a carbon copy on onionskin, so that her daughter, thinking it was samizdat, would read it. But by 1988 most of the "forbidden" classics had been published in Soviet journals: Evgeny Zamiatin's *We*, Vasily Grossman's *Life and Fate*, Vladimir Nabokov, even, incredibly, George Orwell's long-taboo *1984* and *Animal Farm*, and Arthur Koestler's *Darkness at Noon*.

Previously unmentionable names of émigré writers like Joseph Brodsky, Vladimir Voinovich, and Vasily Aksyonov were spoken aloud from public stages as their works found their way into print. Could even Aleksandr Solzhenitsyn be far behind? *Gulag Archipelago*, his devastating indictment of Communism and all of Soviet history, would have to wait another year. Vladimir Vysotsky, whose bitter, satirical ballads not only circulated in crude, homemade recordings (*magnitizdat*) among the intelligentsia and the working class, but were sung by Yuri Andropov at North Caucasus campfires in the seventies, had died in 1980 of a heart attack at the age of forty-two. Early in 1988 the mass media launched an all-out observance of his fiftieth birthday that nearly rivaled the 1987 sesquicentennial of Pushkin's death.

Religion was also making a comeback. When celebration of the millennium of the Russian Orthodox Church began in June, media treatment of religion changed dramatically. For the first time, part of the Easter service was broadcast on Soviet television. In late April, the nightly television news and central newspapers featured pictures of Gorbachev meeting cordially with the patriarch and other church leaders. A feature-length documentary on the Kiev Cave Monastery was released in honor of the occasion, and the media gave extensive coverage to millennium festivities.

Soviet theater, limited over the years to muffled expressions of dissent phrased in Aesopian language, was now more explicit. Mikhail Shatrov's docudrama *The Brest Peace*, written in 1967, but first staged in early 1987, treats the Bolsheviks' agonizing decision in early 1918 to pull out of World War I by signing the punitive Treaty of Brest-Litovsk with Germany. Bukharin and Trotsky appeared on stage for the first time since Stalin ordered them murdered, Bukharin as a sympathetic figure, Trotsky, since he hadn't been rehabilitated, looking like Dracula in a diabolic cape accompanied by ominous organ music. Shatrov's *Further, Further, Further*, published in January 1988, depicted Lenin wrestling with his conscience about making it possible for Stalin to take control, while other characters, ranging from Marxist theoretician Georgy Plekhanov to liberal politician Pavel Miliukov to White general Anton Denikin, all charged that the fundamental error from which so many horrors followed was Lenin's decision to seize power in October 1917.

By 1988 most of the nearly two hundred films "shelved" before 1985 had been released. Meanwhile, ebullient Soviet citizens were lining up to see a wide range of Western movies: *One Flew over the Cuckoo's Nest*, *Amadeus*, *A Chorus Line*, *Crocodile Dundee*, *Purple Rose of Cairo*. During an unprecedented festival of American films, thirty were shown in one week; none had previously been screened in the Soviet Union.

WHILE MUCH OF THE SOVIET INTELLIGENTSIA thrilled to the new openness, Yegor Ligachev did not. His memoirs recall how Ligachev viewed the flood of free speech: "some writers . . . talk about the past caustically, gloatingly . . . narrow-mindedly relishing the misfortunes that had befallen earlier generations," as if "the social system was guilty of everything, and therefore had to be changed." Self-proclaimed experts were rushing ahead like "beasts of prey, tearing our society to shreds, destroying the historical memory of the nation, spitting on such sacred concepts as patriotism, and discrediting the feeling of pride in our Motherland," lowering "our great state to the status of a second-rate country."[2] Ligachev didn't lay out these views openly at the time, but he came close in a February 1988 speech attacking "certain people" who depicted all of Soviet history as "a chain of nothing but errors." At a Central Committee plenum later that month, he demanded "vigilance against the ideological enemy."[3]

Gorbachev still admired Ligachev, regarding him as "one tough cookie," as "open and frank," as "a man of culture" and "a good husband," as a "one-woman man," which, Gorbachev adds, "said a lot about him."[4] Gorbachev also sympathized with him, according to Chernyaev. Having struggled to overcome his own past as a party apparatchik, Gorbachev was reluctant to come down hard on colleagues who hadn't managed to do the same. In addition, Chernyaev continues, Gorbachev "overestimated the power of his own 'charm,' convinced that all reasonable politicians would follow and none would dare to cross him."[5] Gorbachev was spoiled, adds Grachev, by perestroika's still soaring popularity, still so sure of his ability to reconcile rival camps that he underestimated the first open clashes between his colleagues. Gorbachev told Chernyaev that Ligachev should "express his views more politely," but that he "is honestly concerned about the future of perestroika." He assured Yegor Yakovlev, the liberal editor of *Moscow News*, that Ligachev "doesn't see everything in the same dark colors." Back in August 1987, Gorbachev received letters from what he called the "three Yegors" (Ligachev, Yakovlev, and USA Institute Director Arbatov). By then Ligachev, on the one hand, and Yakovlev and Arbatov, on the other, were practically sworn enemies. Yet Gorbachev told Chernyaev, "All three Yegors are worried about the same thing. All fear that perestroika, God forbid, will go under." True, their positions differed, but that's what pluralism was all about. "So let's not panic, Anatoly," Gorbachev told his closest aide. "Let's unite them all."[6]

Gorbachev's own stance on glasnost remained carefully balanced. "Conservatism is now the main obstacle," he told Chernyaev on January 19, but added, "Beware as well the "ultra-leftist loudmouths!" At a January 8 meeting with writers, artists, and media representatives, he simultaneously embraced and restrained them, urging them to "rethink history, but without any hullabaloo," not only to "unmask errors" but to "recognize achievements," to publish not just pieces they agreed with but to welcome many points of view.[7] In a passage more reminiscent of John Stuart Mill than of Marx or Lenin, he advised his listeners to listen to and "respect each other" so that from their principled exchanges of opinion the common good might emerge.[8]

ON SUNDAY, MARCH 13, *Sovetskaya Rossiia* published an open letter titled "Why I Cannot Forsake My Principles," a phrase Gorbachev had used the month before in an address to the Central Committee. Its author, Nina Andreyeva, was identified as a Leningrad chemistry teacher. Gorbachev left for a four-day visit in Yugoslavia the next morning, without reading the article. His chief ally, Aleksandr Yakovlev, was out of the country in Mongolia.

"I decided to write this letter after lengthy deliberation," Andreyeva began. She claimed to be pleased by her students' new perestroika-prompted political activism. Strolling together amid the gold statues at Peter the Great's magnificent Peterhof palace by the Baltic Sea, "We argue. We do argue! The young souls are eager to investigate all the complexities and to define their path into the future. I look at my loquacious young interlocutors and I think to myself how important it is to help them find the truth."

Andreyeva first named the issues they were discussing in neutral fashion: "a multiparty system, freedom of religious propaganda, emigration, the right to wide discussion of sexual problems in the press, the need to decentralize the leadership of culture, abolition of compulsory military service." But her students' "verbiage" about other topics, which Andreyeva ironically identified in quotation marks, outraged her: "terrorism," "the people's political servility," "our spiritual slavery," "universal fear," "domination by boors in power." The extent of political repression, she insisted, had been "blown out of all proportion in some people's minds and overwhelms any objective interpretation of the past." Students were being indoctrinated with so-called "revelations about a counter-revolution" under Stalin, and about his "guilt for the rise of fascism and Hitler in Germany."

Andreyeva portrayed herself as an ordinary person whose relatives had suffered under Stalin, who "shared all Soviet people's anger and indignation over the mass repressions in the thirties and forties for which the party-state leader was to blame." But the "obsession with critical attacks" on Stalin was a travesty of "an epoch linked with unprecedented feats by a whole generation of Soviet people." Andreyeva implied Jews and other ethnic and social groups were responsible for "anti-Stalinist" excesses. She condemned "spiritual heirs" of Trotsky, who was widely known to have been Jewish. She accused "neo-liberal intellectual socialists" of glorifying something as unsocialist as the "intrinsic value of the individual," while dismissing the slightest expressions of Great Russian nationalism as "great-power chauvinism."[9]

Did Nina Andreyeva really exist? During the turmoil following the appearance of her letter, liberals speculated she was the pseudonym of some troglodyte in the Kremlin. A Gorbachev associate later remarked, with more than a whiff of male chauvinism, that she simply couldn't have written it.[10] In fact, she did exist: a tall, strongly built woman in her forties with dark hair severely framing a round face. She had submitted longer versions of her letter to Leningrad newspapers, which rejected them. She wrote this version with "a little help" from her husband, a doctor of philosophical science and author of eight monographs on Soviet society with whom, as she put it, she agreed "on practically everything."[11] According to Aleksandr Yakovlev, the couple had once been expelled from the Communist party for submitting "slanderous, anonymous denunciations," but later were reinstated under pressure from the KGB.[12]

After her letter was rejected in Leningrad, Andreyeva sent it to several central newspapers. *Sovetskaya Rossiia* had a reputation for publishing hard-line pieces, chief editor Valentin Chikin's way of currying favor with Ligachev. According to Vladimir Pankov, the paper's managing editor, and Vladimir Dolmatov, its propaganda editor, Chikin was looking for a piece warning that socialism was under attack. "It was as if God had created Andreyeva," recalled Pankov. "Chikin understood immediately that this is what we needed."

Bypassing Pankov and Dolmatov, who didn't entirely share his views, Chikin sent another editor to Leningrad, where he spent four days helping Andreyeva polish her piece. ("The only thing he added," she later bristled, was the bit about admiring the statues, "although everyone who has visited Peterhof at that time of year knows perfectly well that the statues are all covered up in the winter for their protection.") The piece was secretly typeset and revealed to the editorial board at twelve noon, just six hours before the paper's first edition appeared on Sunday evening. Chikin told his staff that Ligachev had phoned to say the piece was splendid, that he supported and approved of it. Soon, telegrams flooded in from delighted readers: "At last our press has found room for a real Marxist," said one.[13]

Chikin was a cautious person, said Dolmatov; he always consulted Ligachev. A Ligachev assistant confirmed that Chikin and Ligachev had a long conversation shortly before Andreyeva's letter appeared. Did Ligachev actually read the piece before it was published? "The odds are about 70% yes," the assistant answered. "It was the normal practice. And I know [Ligachev] liked it."[14]

The next morning the heads of the country's mass media gathered around a large table at the Central Committee Secretariat. According to *Argumenty i fakty* editor Vladislav Starkov, Ligachev hailed Andreyeva's piece as "a very important article"; it was "the powerful voice of the party" and should be read "very attentively."[15] "I would ask you, comrade editors," *Izvestia*'s editor Ivan Laptev remembered Ligachev saying, "to be guided by the ideas of this article in your work."[16]

Once Ligachev endorsed the article, the Central Committee propaganda machine roared into action. TASS distributed the text. Soviet republics where *Sovetskaya Rossiia* wasn't sold bought up copies wholesale for local distribution. Province party papers reprinted the piece, a practice reserved for extremely important party documents, and organized mass writing of the letters in support of Andreyeva that soon inundated the *Sovetskaya Rossiia* and the Central Committee.[17] All told, recalled Andreyeva herself, who was apparently keeping score, her open letter was reprinted in some 936 papers.

The Foreign Ministry, the Communist party's Academy of Social Sciences, and other lesser institutions held study sessions about the article. At one factory, older workers who had been criticizing perestroika suddenly cheered up and began telling co-workers that they had "told you so" all along. The training academy of the Ministry of Internal Affairs (MVD) devoted a party meeting to the Andreyeva article. When it quickly became clear that few participants had seen the piece, the instructor asked, "What's the matter, doesn't anybody read here?" An older man insisted that the people had lived well under Stalin. "Those were happy days. We won the war thanks to Stalin." A few younger faculty and graduate students dared recall the millions who were shot under Stalin or died of starvation in the camps. "That wasn't Stalin's fault," they were told; "that was history, a tragic moment of history." Afterward, recalled a MVD major, "we went off to smoke, and as usual, people said what they really thought."[18] At a Moscow high school, a young Moscow University graduate student who was interning as a teacher had been ignoring standard textbooks and assigning instead the latest revelations of glasnost. Now suddenly, she was reprimanded and threatened with not being allowed to receive her degree.[19]

Well-known reformers panicked. "I'm a man of old times, I have old fears and habits," remembered Grigory Baklanov, editor of *Znamya*. "I knew no articles of this kind were published accidentally in our press."[20] Novelist Daniil Granin felt as if he were "on a train that suddenly came to a halt and then began moving backwards."[21] "Everyone shut up, fell silent," actor Mikhail Ulyanov remembered.[22] The playwright Mikhail Shatrov, who was traveling in Japan, found Soviet embassy personnel there "terrified," because they assumed the Andreyeva broadside came from the very top.[23] According to Tatyana Zaslavskaya, the sociologist with whom Gorbachev had begun consulting in the early 1980s, she and her colleagues feared that "the thaw was finally over" and that now they would have to become an "underground opposition."[24]

Fear itself was the hard-liners' best weapon. Even in the Central Committee, roughly half the apparatchiki opposed the Andreyeva line, but they kept their mouths shut.[25] Andrei Grachev, along with two other international department staffers, secretly prepared a rebuttal to the Andreyeva article, but showed it to no one until Aleksandr Yakovlev returned to the capital. Of all the artistic unions that had been struggling to emancipate themselves from Kremlin control, only the film-makers' protested.[26] Journalists at *Literaturnaya gazeta* were "in despair"; when Aleksandr Levikov proposed writing a rejoinder to Andreyeva, hard-line editor Aleksandr Chakovsky shot back, "I have just told you in plain Russian that this was approved by Ligachev. What's wrong with you? Didn't you hear me?" *Moscow News* dared to publish Levikov's rebuttal, creating a sensation, but editor Yegor Yakovlev hesitated long and hard before approving it.[27] When Andrei Grachev asked Ivan Laptev, liberal editor of *Izvestiia*, to come out against Andreyeva, Laptev replied, "We're powerless against Ligachev." The only paper powerful enough to challenge what seemed the new party line was *Pravda*, the party paper itself, but that would require a decision by the Politburo.[28] Shatrov lamented his and other liberals' reaction: "That we waited for authorization from above is a gigantic reproach to us all. . . . The fate of each of us is at stake and yet we once again require permission to act." If perestroika were to fail in the end, "Andreyeva and her ilk won't be to blame. We'll be the guilty ones, we who today pledge allegiance to per-estroika but yesterday were silent."[29]

WHEN GORBACHEV BOARDED his plane to Yugoslavia on Sunday, March 13, he invited aides into his compartment to prepare for meetings, nego-tiations, and speeches in Belgrade. Once that was done, Shakhnazarov gave him the day's newpapers, pointing out Andreyeva's article. After they arrived in Belgrade, according to Shakhnazarov, there wasn't a single free moment, and it was only on the way back, when they boarded the plane, that Gorbachev said, "I read the article. It's terrible, a direct attack against the Central Committee line."[30]

Aleksandr Yakovlev learned about the Andreyeva letter on the morning of March 14 in Mongolia. "Something was up in Moscow," he remembered thinking, "but what?" Worried because Gorbachev was also out of the capital, Yakovlev ordered an aide to phone Moscow. All he could learn was that Ligachev would be holding a meeting that morning with media bigwigs. Yakovlev put two and two together: "It was clear that this was a very serious attack against perestroika. It wasn't just Andreyeva's letter." She wouldn't have known how to write "Soviet-speak" with such mastery, "so someone was behind it."[31]

Yakovlev got back to Moscow before Gorbachev. There he found the pro-Andreyeva campaign in full swing, with hard-liners celebrating, "their faces shining." "It was precisely the fact that the press took fright and fell silent that made me realize we had to react. At the time it was still possible that glasnost might be smothered."[32] Liberal editors telephoned Yakovlev, but he advised them to delay any "small" responses to Andreyeva until a "big" one could be organized.[33] When Gorbachev returned on the eighteenth, he hesitated to confront his pro-Andreyeva colleagues immediately. Before he could do so, they confronted him.

On March 23, the Fourth All-Union Congress of Collective Farms was held in the Kremlin. Politburo members were drinking tea in a private room during a break when Ligachev commented, as if by the by, "The press has started to give it to them. . . . There was an article in *Sovetskaya Rossiia*. A very good article. Our party line."

"Yes," Vorotnikov said. "The real thing. A sound article. Just what was needed."

"Yes, indeed," added Gromyko, who had privately complained to his son that the Gorbachev he nominated as general secretary in 1985 and the current Gorbachev were "two entirely different people."[34] "A very good article. It put everything just right."

Solomentsev seemed about to agree, and Chebrikov had opened his mouth to join in, when Gorbachev spoke out: "I glanced through the piece before taking off for Yugoslavia." Before he could continue, others added their praise for the piece: "Very worthwhile." "Pay particular attention to . . ."

Gorbachev broke in: "I finished reading later on, on the way back . . . I have a different opinion."

"Uh-oh!" exclaimed Vorotnikov.

"What do you mean, 'Uh-oh'?" Gorbachev snapped. The others looked at each other. "So that's how it is," Gorbachev continued. "Let's talk about this at a Politburo meeting. This smells of a split. The article is against perestroika. . . . [It's] the result of a directive. It's being discussed in party organizations as if it were law. The press has been forbidden to print rebuttals. . . . I'm not clinging to the [general secretary's] chair, but while I'm in it, I will defend the idea of perestroika. No, this will not pass. We will discuss it in the Politburo."[35]

The Politburo met all the next day and the day after that. Ligachev later called it a "witch hunt." The discussion was "punitive." "They wanted to turn Andreyeva into the symbol of Stalinist excesses, and then tie Ligachev to her. . . ."[36] Grachev's characterization is only somewhat milder: a Chinese-style self-criticism session in which Ligachev and others were forced to confess and repent.[37] Actually, to judge by Chernyaev's notes on the sessions, Gorbachev did counterattack, but not to the point of a break; he demanded to know who had authorized the article, but seemed to settle for evasions and lies. Ligachev and company retreated, but only so far. They claimed glasnost allowed the Andreyeva article, but not all the liberal heresies that had appeared in print. Whiffs of Stalinism were in the air on both sides. Gorbachev detected treason against perestroika. Fawning and kowtowing to protect himself, at least one hard-liner called for a KGB investigation to unmask the traitor. What did *not* happen during the two-day meeting was a candid thrashing out of the issues.

"Have you read the article?" Gorbachev asked at the start of the March 24 meeting. Some said they hadn't, at least not carefully. How had it gotten into *Sovetskaya Rossiia*? Had anyone in the Central Committee approved it in advance? Yes, Ligachev responded, Central Committee officials had seen Andreyeva's article before it was published. But *Sovets-*

kaya Rossiia editor Chikin had been told to decide for himself whether to publish it. Nor had party organizations been ordered to discuss the piece. Whether you agreed with Andreyeva or not, her article paled in comparison with other articles that were filled with "provocations, lies, and slander."[38]

On March 25, Yakovlev (supported by Shevardnadze and Medvedev) presented a lengthy, point-by-point indictment of the Andreyeva article. Premier Ryzhkov implied that Ligachev should be demoted, wondering why it took two Politburo members (Ligachev and Yakovlev) to superintend ideology when one (presumably Yakovlev) would do.[39]

In the face of this offensive, conservatives scrambled for cover. Ligachev insisted perestroika was necessary as "air itself," and that for all this, "the country had Mikhail Sergeyevich Gorbachev to thank."[40] Moscow party boss Zaikov echoed Yakovlev's critique.[41] It was Ukrainian leader Shcherbitsky who suggested a KGB investigation.[42] Agricultural chief Nikonov praised Gorbachev's intellect as the "core around which the Politburo's work revolves," but chastised Yakovlev for allowing far worse than Andreyeva to appear in the press. Since agriculture was in such great shape, Yakovlev shot back sarcastically, with store shelves groaning from an abundance of foodstuffs, perhaps Nikonov "would like to take over ideology and bring it into equally good order."[43]

Concluding the two-day marathon, Gorbachev charged that Andreyeva's "deviation" from perestroika was "the greatest possible betrayal." But he complimented his critics on a conversation that bespoke their "unity on the main issues," and apologized to Vorotnikov for exploding at him.[44] The Politburo unanimously "disapproved" of the Andreyeva article, ordered *Pravda* to rebut it, and decided to send regional party committees a memo summarizing the Politburo's discussion.[45] But Gorbachev refrained from punishing Ligachev and company. He wasn't just merciful, Yakovlev complained to Chernyaev; he helped Ligachev cover his own tracks. Why? Gorbachev was in effect following Machiavelli's maxim: Keep your friends close, but your enemies closer. But his abiding sense of personal superiority helped to stay his hand. "You must understand," he told Chernyaev several days later, Ligachev and company were "simply limited people. . . . I don't think there's any malicious intent, factionalism, or principled disagreement. They just have their limitations. Although that's a problem too."[46] Or, as he put it to Yakovlev on another occasion, "Let's let sleeping dogs lie."

Should Gorbachev have purged Ligachev and company at this point? "The Central Committee would probably have approved it," Chernyaev recalled. "But what then? The system would have remained the same"— even if Gorbachev had "filled the Politburo with Yakovlevs."[47]

While the Politburo deliberated (if that is the word for it) in secret, the country waited in suspense. Then suddenly, on April 5, the fog lifted. *Pravda* published a full-page blockbuster article that made several things clear. There had indeed been a Kremlin crisis. It was now over. For the time being, at least, the reformers had won.

The *Pravda* broadside, which Yakovlev prepared and Gorbachev edited, characterized Stalin's "guilt for massive repressions and lawlessness" as "enormous and unforgiveable." Those "who look everywhere for internal enemies" were "not patriots." But the same article was a reminder of how far reform had to go. As usual, *Pravda* arrogated to itself the right to speak for all Soviet citizens: "We have changed over the past three years. We have raised our heads and straightened up, we look facts honestly in the face, we speak aloud and openly of painful things. . . ." Nothing wrong with those sentiments, but if everyone was indeed of one mind, what was *Pravda* tilting against anyway?[48]

Even the boldest reformers had not dared to take on Andreyeva publicly until *Pravda* did, but after that, radicalized by their own temporary impotence, they began to fire at will, not just in *Moscow News* and *Ogonyok* but in *Pravda* and *Izvestiia*, even in *Sotsialisticheskaya industriya* (Socialist Industry). One long article in *Novyi mir*'s May issue challenged the sacred authority of Lenin himself, contending that his brutal policies had set the mold for Stalin. A television program called *Public Opinion*, which originated in Leningrad, invited citizens to come down to the studio to question panels of experts. One such citizen, long-haired, bearded, and with intense staring eyes, accused a party official of firing him for no good reason. Would the official like to answer the charge on the screen? the moderator asked. Of course not, but he had no choice but to try. "Dear Ivan Ivanovich," he began in his most unctuous official manner. "Surely you remember the unfortunate circumstances that required that you be released." Strong men usually trembled in this official's presence, but here he was having to answer on television to a wild-eyed nonconformist.

The next person in the street demanded the Communist party's monopoly of power be replaced by a multiparty system. Immediately several homemade signs popped into view on television: "Down with the One-Party System!" "Let's Have More Than One Party!" Strangely, the show's moderator seemed unperturbed by the spectacle, as if the USSR had a tradition of free speech and assembly dating back more than five minutes.[49]

IT WASN'T NINA ANDREYEVA who prompted Gorbachev to convene the Nineteenth Party Conference. He had first proposed it in January 1987 as a way to promote democratization, and in June of that year the Central Committee decided the conference would open on June 28, 1988. But the Andreyeva affair raised the stakes and helped radicalize Gorbachev. He had her to thank for clarifying the real balance of opinion in the Politburo. Unable to sleep on March 25, the night after the Politburo finished discussing her article, he lay awake thinking: "A split is inevitable. The only question is, when?"[50] Having gone to great lengths to avoid just that, he now took steps that had contradictory consequences: on the one hand, they would broaden his support when the bigger split came; on the other, they would exacerbate that split itself. What he proceeded to do was invite into the political process masses of voters who could be counted on (or so he thought) to support him against the conservatives, who were all the more alarmed by the democratic change that Gorbachev had accelerated.

Ordinarily, it was party congresses that set overall foreign and domestic policy and "elected" Central Committee members. But the next congress wasn't due until 1991. In the early years after 1917, party conferences were called to address extraordinary matters between congresses, but none had been held since 1941. Gorbachev was now in a hurry, however, to reduce the power of the Communist party—by instituting mostly free elections, by transferring party power to elected soviets, by drastically reducing the size of the party apparatus, and by trying to introduce a real rule of law that would insulate the judicial process from party interference.

Another reason for this political upheaval, recalled Gorbachev aide Brutents, was that economic reforms weren't working.[51] Yakovlev documented their failure in a March 3, 1988, memorandum: no effect whatsoever in many workplaces, no much-touted boost to "self-management and independence." Only 21 percent of workers saw any connection between how hard and well they worked and how much they were paid. Popular trust in economic administration was even lower; a mere 7.3 percent evaluated economic managers positively; 13 percent, local soviet officials; and 14 percent, party officials.[52] Central ministries were "trampling" on the new enterprise law, Gorbachev told the Politburo that same day. In the West the service sphere had grown to nearly 80 percent of economic activity; "here it's still the same—12 percent," with a dreadful effect on everyday life and people's mood.[53]

Gorbachev still publicly endorsed the party's "leading role" in the economy, but his private view was closer to Yakovlev's—that instead of promoting economic self-management, party bureaucrats "fiercely protected their own power."[54] The answer therefore was to cut back the party's supervision of the economy and focus its attention instead on more general matters like ideology. Beyond all this, however, Gorbachev championed democracy for its own sake. Reversing seventy years of Bolshevik tradition, he wanted to make the party answerable to the people. True, many people were apathetic and alienated, but self-government, he too optimistically believed, could help cure those ills.[55] Gorbachev himself had doubts about whether Soviet citizens were ready for more democracy, but not enough doubts. He once referred to the population's "slave psychology," but he attributed it to Stalin's tyranny.[56] In fact, centuries of tsarist autocracy, too, had bred a sense of fatalism, while decades of totalitarianism, by forcing Soviet citizens to denounce each other, had gravely damaged the mutual trust among citizens on which democracy depends.[57]

For all these reasons, Gorbachev's first task was to convince *himself* he was doing the right thing.[58] But, if so, how could he hope conservatives would agree? He counted on his still vast authority as the party's general secretary to compel their compliance, and on his intellectual prowess, as well. Reformers were still a minority in the Central Committee, and even in the fourteen-member Politburo—just he himself, he admitted in his memoirs, plus "Yakovlev, Medvedev, Shevardnadze, Ryzhkov, for the most part, [Central Committee secretary Nikolai] Slyunkov."[59] Most of his colleagues, he characteristically told Chernyaev, were "philosophically impoverished" and "lacking in culture." The Russian Republic that Vorotnikov headed was "the worst" of any republic. Premier Ryzhkov spent more time blaming the Politburo for usurping his work than doing it himself. As for Ligachev, who hated Ryzhkov and was hated in return, "for eighteen years he led a province committee [as Gorbachev himself had for eight years!] and he knows no other way." So what was needed at the party conference was not just a political breakthrough but "a new intellectual breakthrough."[60]

Gorbachev began preparing for the Nineteenth Conference late in 1987 by soliciting ideas from officials and scholars. In January 1988, Medvedev and Shakhnazarov distilled initial suggestions into a tentative outline. Next, Gorbachev prepared "theses" summarizing (but not yet detailing) his plans, his purpose, Medevdev recalls, being to "wear down" party resistance by overwhelming doubters with "discussions, interpretations, and explanations." Later, Gorbachev settled in with aides at villas in Volynskoe and Novo-Ogaryovo to draft and redraft his speech to the conference. By now Gorbachev knew what he wanted: to turn rubber-stamp, rarely-in-session soviets at each level of government into year-round legislatures. The idea of building on existing structures rather than importing Western institutions wholesale was a good one— except that given the soviets' long history of impotence, it was overly ambitious. Moreover, Gorbachev and his advisers had another idea that was almost too clever—to have party leaders at each level chair the soviets, with himself leading the national legislature. To liberals that seemed like a way of perpetuating party power. But party leaders had little appetite for chairing popular assemblies, especially since before they could do so, they would have to be elected, and if not, they would have to vacate their party post. The elections for a new institution, a 2,250-member Congress of People's Deputies in Moscow, would be partially free and open, although with a certain number of seats reserved for "public organizations" like the party itself. The Congress would elect a smaller USSR

Supreme Soviet, which would do the ongoing work of legislating.[61] In the long run, Gorbachev told Chernyaev in January, his plan was to add "President of the USSR" to his title of party general secretary.[62]

During the spring Gorbachev campaigned for the new plan in three long sessions with some 150 republic and province party leaders, one-third of them brought to Moscow on each of three days in April. By then he had replaced a great many of those he inherited in 1985, but that made little difference: he was as wary of them as they were of him. In the past, their support at the Nineteenth Conference would have been automatic, but no longer. So he put on a dazzling performance, flattering and chastising them, begging, badgering and bullying, repledging his allegiance to socialism, but going so far as to cite Western examples to prove that the existing Soviet system was outmoded.

"You and I are the vanguard," he assured them. The vanguard's job was to reshape "political power, the political system, the system of property—all with the aim of revealing the full potential of socialism."[63] Western critics were right to ask, "How can you justify having twenty million [Communist party members] rule over two hundred million people?" The answer, Gorbachev said sarcastically, was "We elect ourselves to rule over the people."[64] The country groaned under a mountain of problems, but "where is the party?" Some party officials were "shocked" by what he was doing. He could understand their "anxiety," but must tell them "over and over again: We must not lag behind."[65] "Don't be afraid of . . . 'socialist pluralism," he urged. "Go back and read Lenin's resolution on party unity!"—which actually was designed to severely limit real pluralism. Let there be democracy within the party as well as out of it; let there be term limits even for top leaders: two five-year terms, absent a two-thirds vote for a third term.[66] What is the role of law in our country? Gorbachev asked. "'What law?' You'll reply." The truth was that party officials' word was the real law: "Do as I tell you, that's the law."[67] In fact, province party organizations were the "biggest law violators, officials who ought to be the first to observe the law and morality." No other regime in the world, even "the cruelest, has as much power as we do. Private property limits them. All that limits us is our conscience and sense of party responsibility."[68]

This was extremely strong stuff. Having browbeaten his audience,

Gorbachev offered a loftier role for party officials, the kind, he insisted, that Lenin had originally intended. Not to get bogged down micromanaging the country's everyday affairs, not to have the Central Committee rule on "roosters and chickens" and tell farmers "how to feed and milk cows," but to think big about overall policy: "international affairs, organizing the masses, ideology, defense."[69] Not to consider themselves "smarter than everyone else."[70] Not to assume that the people are there "to serve us, but to remember that our job is to serve them."[71]

Serving the people was *not* Lenin's idea of the vanguard party's role (except insofar as the party itself defined what the people needed), but no one dared say so to Gorbachev. On the whole, objections were mild. Local soviets weren't up to managing the economy, the Volgograd province boss insisted with justification. "Life itself" demanded that party officials do so.[72] What would the Central Committee do with itself, whined the Kirghiz Republic first secretary, if its functions were transferred to the government's Council of Ministers?[73] One official tried to ingratiate himself with Gorbachev by calling for a party purge, for "getting rid of deadweight." For the time being, Gorbachev rejected the idea, lest he further alienate his audience, but in the long run the deadweight would have to go if his reforms were to succeed. It was as if the tsar had turned Bolshevik and decided to overturn his own regime.[74]

Surprisingly, the specter of Nina Andreyeva and her article still hung in the air. (Is there any Western counterpart to a single published polemic having such an enduring effect?) She was, as Chernyaev put it, "the subtext" of the three meetings.[75] Most of Gorbachev's listeners had reprinted her article and were in no mood to discuss it. But he himself seemed unable to drop the subject. He asked hopefully whether some of them had not agreed with it and ordered it reprinted only because they thought it was the party line. "We reprinted it," replied Sverdlovsk's first secretary, Yuri Petrov. "What of it? I liked the article. . . . Enough apologizing for the mistakes of the past. Workers collectives are wondering: How long will this be tolerated?"

"So you're still not convinced that *Pravda*'s criticism is correct," said Gorbachev.

"People reacted positively to Andreyeva," Petrov retorted. "In the beginning everyone was for her."

Gorbachev turned purple, but Petrov continued, "You always demand that we speak our minds, so I am speaking mine."

"On Sakhalin, we regarded [the Andreyeva piece] as a routine example of glasnost," commented the island's party boss.

"The older generation approved of it," remarked the Yakutsk party leader. "We have to point out Stalin's achievements. This was an important period in our country's history."[76]

Throughout most of the three meetings, Gorbachev held his fire. On April 14, when his aide Ivan Frolov charged that Andreyeva's piece was prepared "right here, within these [Central Committee] walls," Gorbachev rhetorically demanded to know: "Where? By whom?" But he quickly changed the subject before Frolov could directly incriminate Ligachev and smash the crumbling façade of Politburo unity. Gorbachev seemed inclined to let Chikin, the *Sovetskaya Rossiia* editor, off the hook. "He's a decent man." "All this has been hard on him. He has repented. I believe him. In general, I believe people."[77] But on April 18 Gorbachev again lashed out. What Andreyeva was saying was, "Don't touch Stalin! Don't touch bribe-takers! Don't touch party organizations that have long since rotted!" People who demand this "don't love their country or socialism. All they want is to make their little nest a little warmer." Stalin was "a criminal, devoid of any morality. Let me tell you on your own behalf: one million party activists were shot, three million sent to the camps to rot." "That's who Stalin was." Why had Khrushchev, who began to tell the truth about the terror, backed off? "Because his own hands were covered with blood." Gorbachev pointed at Petrov, the Sverdlovsk chief who had defended Andreyeva. "You honestly said what you think. I admire that. But clean the chaos out of your head."[78] Petrov was soon dispatched as ambassador to Cuba—"closer to his spiritual brothers-in-arms," recalled Chernyaev.[79]

AT THE END of these meetings, Gorbachev declared himself satisfied. His critics were not, of course, but they were cowed. Ligachev, as Chernyaev observed him at the April 14 meeting, didn't "have the same aplomb anymore. He spends more time being quiet; he looks kind of pathetic." Ligachev was slated as usual to lead a Secretariat meeting on April 23, but Gorbachev seized the chair himself. It was important, he said, that delegates to the coming party conference be not only "pro-perestroika" but able to operate at a "high, conceptual level."[80] To his aides, Gorbachev sounded almost giddy on April 25: the country and the world were "waiting for the conference," which was "fated to have central significance."[81] The Soviet people were so committed to him, he told them the next day, that when he took three days off from work the previous week for a medical checkup, traffic police stopped his son-in-law's car (whose license plate they not surprisingly knew) and demanded to know where Gorbachev was. When his son-in-law didn't give them a straight answer, they said, "Don't try to play around. Tell us, where is he? We know his car hasn't entered the city in three days. There are rumors he's been removed. . . . If that's true, the people will arm themselves and take to the street."[82]

Gorbachev was euphoric. For the time being, he had beaten back conservative resistance. But the pace was taking a toll. He telephoned Chernyaev on the twenty-fourth to talk about Secretary of State George Shultz, who had just visited Moscow, but began by complaining: "I'm sitting surrounded by journals and articles. Raisa Maksimovna came in and scolded me: Why are you sitting around! The air is so fresh! You haven't moved all day. Let's go for a walk."[83] Gorbachev was in a hurry. He was determined, he told the Politburo on April 28, to cut the party bureaucracy by 40 to 60 percent, maybe even 80. But where would those newly unemployed apparatchiki go? Wasn't he aware that they would become his sworn enemies? "We've got to act like revolutionaries," he said, "to set the process in motion and then we'll see."[84] The same rule applied to soviets about to be entrusted with new authority, and party committees asked to surrender previous powers. Would they be able to cope? "We'll see . . . ," he told editors, writers, and other cultural figures on May 7.[85]

Gorbachev was convinced that transforming a complex society in accordance with a preconceived plan (vide 1917) was not only impossible but dangerous. But doing so without more planning than he did was dangerous as well. His critics would eventually pounce on this failing. They merely grumbled, however, on May 19 when the Politburo discussed his "draft theses" for the conference. Party leaders chairing soviets was "undemocratic," complained Ligachev, not previously known for his devotion to democracy. Gromyko wanted greater stress on the party's "leading role" and on the "class [i.e., proletarian] basis of our policies and society." By now Gorbachev had tolerated Gromyko in high office for three more years than he wanted to. That, plus perhaps his annoyance at himself for doing so, helps explain why he lashed out at the man who had helped make him general secretary. Did Gromyko want "incantations"? If so, then "let's take a vow!"

"No," Gromyko retreated.

"I asked you a question," Gorbachev insisted. "You said we should make [the text] stronger. How should we make it stronger?"

"I said, 'Perhaps' we should make it stronger."

"The minute we don't repeat certain [formulaic] words, suspicions arise. Is it a matter of who shouts louder? Well, we've had a lot of shouting. The task now is to develop socialism in the interest of the people . . ."

Gromyko: "No suspicions, Mikhail Sergeyevich."

Gorbachev: "You leveled a serious accusation. Don't you see that? I'm simply amazed."

"It wasn't an accusation. . . . Perhaps I expressed myself poorly."

"I understood exactly what you were saying. That's why I couldn't ignore it. This is a very serious matter."[86]

The Politburo formally approved Gorbachev's theses. The Central Committee followed suit on May 23. In the middle of June, Gorbachev spent twelve or thirteen hours a day revising his report to the conference. He wanted a report so authoritative it would resemble "the Bible."[87] Chernyaev thought the report would "shock" and "stun" Politburo members because "the majority of them will not have high-level positions in the new system."[88] Gorbachev's colleagues did indeed have serious complaints on June 20: Ligachev about party bosses chairing soviets; Chebrikov about the party's reduced role; Dolgikh about the danger of opposition political parties; Vorotnikov that reforms were being pushed through too fast. But Gorbachev brushed them aside. He would take colleagues' concerns into account before the conference opened on June 28. "Rework it in a week?!" Vorotnikov complained—not, however, to Gorbachev, but in the privacy of his diary.[89]

Despite all these preparations, the conference outcome was far from certain. For the first time in decades, delegate elections were contested, but leading reformers, including sociologist Zaslavskaya, playwright Shatrov, and economist Nikolai Shmelyov, were defeated. Yuri Afanasyev, liberal director of the Historical Archives Institute, was nominated by the institute's party cell, only to be vetoed by party officials and then rise again with Gorbachev's personal support. Afanasyev (who would later become one of Gorbachev's fiercest radical critics) squeaked by with 83 out of 155 votes at a Moscow city party plenum. The lesson: liberals could lobby and protest, but it took old-style party pressure to put them over the top. In most cases, however, especially in the provinces, conservatives pushed through their own people. So the vast majority of delegates were in fact opposed to the proposed reforms.[90] In the past, delegates' own opinions meant nothing since they were subject to strict party discipline. Paradoxically, Gorbachev still counted on that discipline while trying his best to undermine it.

FIVE THOUSAND DELEGATES gathered for the Nineteenth Party Conference in the Kremlin Palace of Congresses from June 28 through July 1, 1988. The formal agenda was familiar: a long report by the general secretary followed by four days of "discussion." But the nature and tone of the proceedings was unprecedented, and so was the role of television. Delegates didn't rise when Gorbachev led the Politburo into the hall. Instead of endorsing the party line, speakers acted as if there wasn't one. Some backed Gorbachev, but others condemned him (although not yet by name) and his program. Hard-liners silenced reformers by drowning them out with rhythmic clapping. Liberals fought back. For the first time since the 1920s, voting wasn't unanimous. To top it all, much of the proceedings were televised. The party bosses hadn't realized, *Ogonyok* editor Vitaly Korotich recalled, that "the delegates would be speaking not to them but over their heads to the country as a whole." Once they woke up to the danger, "they wanted to stop the transmissions, but that was impossible because the delegates liked being TV stars, and people on the streets got a taste for it." "It was summer," a Gorbachev aide remembered, "so you could hear the broadcasts coming out of practically every window in Moscow."[91]

Gorbachev's report bowed several times to conservatives, and they reacted accordingly. His warning that "democracy is incompatible with willfulness, irresponsibility, and lack of discipline" prompted "applause." His rejection of opposition parties as "an abuse of democracy" produced "prolonged applause." "Perestroika demands the directing hand of the party" triggered "stormy applause." But these were spoonfuls of sugar to make his harsh medicine go down. His notion that a one-party system required "a constant confrontation of opinions" evoked no applause at all.[92]

Other speakers were stunningly outspoken. Leonid Abalkin, liberal director of the Institute of Economics, contended that political reforms weren't enough: "So, we'll elect deputies in competitive elections. . . . So what?" That wouldn't solve economic problems. Since the latter were the product of "the economic system itself," what was needed was "an entirely different system." Gorbachev had invited candor, but he didn't like its results. He accused Abalkin of "economic determinism" (an odd charge for a follower of Marx), after which Abalkin found himself ostracized. Usually, he recalled, during conference smoking breaks, "people gathered together to discuss political news, cultural life, etc. This time, all of a sudden, I found I was alone, nobody around me, nobody came up to say hello, to tap me on my shoulder."[93]

Yuri Bondarev, novelist and deputy chairman of the conservative Russian Republic Writers' Union, compared perestroika to "an airplane that takes off without knowing where it will land." It made no sense, he said, "to destroy the old order down to its foundation," to "trample down millet that someone sowed, flooding the field with his sweat." He accused perestroika of a sin often attributed to Communism: "treating mankind like an experimental guinea pig" with "the scalpel of history." He blasted the liberal journalists for proving that "a man, like a fly," could be "crushed with a newspaper."[94]

Bondarev's philippic was interrupted several times by applause. So was an attempt to rebut him by Grigory Baklanov, liberal editor of *Znamya*, but in his case the hand clapping and foot stamping were meant to drown out the speaker. It was as if party functionaries "possessed a dog's sense of smell," noted writer Daniil Granin: They knew what Baklanov was going to say, and they weren't going to allow him to say it.[95] Gorbachev intervened: "Let him speak. Let's listen. Democracy presupposes the ability to listen to each other."[96] Chernyaev thought Baklanov should have stalked off the stage ("that would have been a defiant action"), but instead he kept giving a talk that, in its sophistication, "would have been more fitting at a literary symposium." Moreover, Chernyaev was sure that the hostile reaction to Baklanov, born Grigory Friedman, "had an anti-Semitic air."[97] Conservatives also tried to silence Mikhail Ulyanov, the renowned actor turned reformer, until, "channeling" the voice of famed World War II hero Marshal Gyorgy Zhukov, whom he had portrayed on film, he ordered them to shut up.[98]

Not to be outdone, Boris Yeltsin reemerged from hibernation to cause another explosion. After enduring Gorbachev's November 1987 onslaught at the Moscow party plenum, Yeltsin had returned to the hospital. Early in December, he was moved to the Barvikha sanatorium in the woods west of Moscow. Even after returning home in February, he struggled "to lift myself out of the personal crisis I was in. I looked inside, and there was no one there. . . . I was only nominally alive. Politically I didn't exist."[99] Yeltsin felt well enough to start work at the State Construction Committee on February 8, 1988, but sitting in his vast office in front of a silent white telephone with a red-and-gold Soviet state seal, he "felt like pulling the telephone right out of the wall." Gorbachev had seemed "gracious" in demoting rather than banishing him, but "few people know what torture it is to sit in the dread silence," waiting for "the telephone with the state seal to ring. Or not."[100] Later that month, he attended a Central Committee meeting that formally dropped him from the Politburo. Moscow media were now off-limits to him. KGB agents tapped his phone and monitored the entrance to his apartment house, but he broke through the blackout at the Nineteenth Conference.

"I had to attend the conference and speak there," Yeltsin wrote later, "to explain what had happened at the October [1987] plenum." Still a Central Committee member, he had a right to attend the conference, but that wasn't enough: "It would be a crushing blow not to be elected as a delegate." Supporters in Moscow and Sverdlovsk tried to nominate him but were blocked by the party apparatus. At the last minute, he was chosen one of thirteen delegates from Karelia, near the Russian border with Finland. Members of the Karelian delegation were seated at the top of the balcony with their heads nearly touching the ceiling, and the presidium chaired by Gorbachev barely visible far below. Yeltsin had prepared "a fighting speech," but to deliver it he would have to be recognized by the chair, and his repeated written requests to speak, passed down to Gorbachev, were ignored.

"Comrades," he informed the Karelian delegation on the conference's last day, "I must take the rostrum by storm." He descended from the balcony, strode through double doors opening onto the center aisle, and marched straight toward the stage, brandishing his red delegate's card above his head and looking Gorbachev straight in the eye. "Every step reverberated within my soul," Yeltsin recalled. "I could feel the breathing of five thousand people, every one of them staring at me." Climbing the three steps to the stage, he approached Gorbachev and demanded to be allowed to speak.

"Take a seat in the first row," Gorbachev commanded. Yeltsin reluctantly complied, until an assistant approached and asked him to leave the hall to consult with a higher official. Yeltsin refused, but he did retreat toward the double doors, where Gorbachev's aide promised that he would be given the floor if he returned to his delegation. Yeltsin balked again, tramped back down the aisle, and planted himself in the first row, right in front of Gorbachev.

Gorbachev gave in, lest he be accused of violating glasnost. Yeltsin spoke for more than fifteen minutes. He supported some of Gorbachev's proposed reforms, but attacked him for failing to provide precisely what Gorbachev prided himself on—"a profound historical analysis" of the past, and not "adequately analyzing the current state of society." As a result, Yeltsin continued, three years of perestroika had "not solved any of the real problems experienced by ordinary people."

Yeltsin asked to be politically rehabilitated. "While I am still alive," he added pointedly. Loud noise in the hall drowned him out. Gorbachev rescued him: "Speak on, Boris Nikolayevich!"[101] Yeltsin did. Then, as in the fall of 1987, the barrage began. "As if with his sleeves rolled up," Granin recalled, Ligachev "signaled all the jackals to tear Yeltsin apart."[102] Gorbachev joined them—not bloodthirsty like the others, noting with satisfaction that Yeltsin praised many of the proposed reforms, but devoting a third of his final remarks to recounting yet again Yeltsin's sins in the fall of 1987 and zeroing in on Yeltsin's charge that Gorbachev's report lacked "profound analysis."[103]

"M. S. should have been above the Ligachev-Yeltsin conflict," Chernyaev wrote in his diary. "Instead, he practically joined Ligachev, in effect, swallowing his platform and his insults." Not because Yeltsin posed a political threat (as his biographer Colton puts it, "Yeltsin was in a nether world, politically, until the spring of 1989."), but because, Chernyaev rightly believed, Gorbachev "has a [Yeltsin] complex." Moreover, Chernyaev added, Gorbachev's wife egged him on. "M. S. didn't want to talk about Yeltsin," but suddenly in the back room during a break after Yeltsin's speech, Raisa "came in and started to berate Yeltsin, saying, 'We can't leave it like this.' That settled the question." In addition, Yakovlev told Chernyaev, Gorbachev feared that Yeltsin (or some other speaker) would criticize Gorbachev's wife and "get a round of applause." Although Raisa was widely unpopular, she had not yet been the target of a direct political attack. But Yeltsin was capable of anything. Gorbachev was protective of his wife and, according to Chernyaev, afraid to offend her authority.[104]

After all the Sturm und Drang, conference delegates reverted to their old obedient selves and approved Gorbachev's program. They ordered that the party apparatus be reorganized by autumn; they commissioned new legislation and constitutional amendments to alter the government structure. Gorbachev shocked them by proposing that the new Congress of People's Deputies, which delegates regarded as a matter for the distant future, be elected the next spring and new local soviets in the fall of 1989, but they acquiesced in that, too. Even the contested scheme to have party bosses chair the soviets prompted a mere handful of negative votes. As a result, marveled Gorbachev ally Vadim Medvedev, the whole political system would be transformed "in no more than one year."[105]

Gorbachev had prevailed. During the most hostile speeches at the conference, Politburo member Dolgikh noticed him "sitting there with a black look on his face; not many people could take such criticism."[106] But Gorbachev recalled feeling like "the captain of a ship in a raging ocean," the vessel "listing so perilously, first to the left and then to right, that the helm seemed about to be ripped from my hands. I won't deny it: keeping it on course was a source of satisfaction."[107]

As usual, Gorbachev downplayed his personal pride. But others could see it. On the eve of the conference's final day, he was "bubbling over," Chernyaev recalls. Several days later, he spontaneously decided to walk (rather than take his limousine) from the Kremlin to the Central Committee—through a courtyard crowded with tourists and sightseers, then through the streets to Old Square. The result, wrote Chernyaev, who accompanied him, was "total consternation." Women "rush to hug him. He tries to talk to them, but people have been struck speechless." Foreigners wanted to "introduce themselves, shake Gorbachev's hand, touch his jacket." A Russian woman cried, "What about me? What about me?" Gorbachev hugged her. A Russian man put his hand on Gorbachev's arm: "Mikhail Sergeyevich, you should work less, take care of yourself. I can see you're tired." "It's all right, my friend," replied Gorbachev patting him on the shoulder. "I'll be fine. Now is the time to work. We'll rest later." Soaking up the adoration, Gorbachev remembered how far he had come. He wanted to walk past the Rossiya Hotel, he told Chernyaev. "I always used to stay there when I came to visit from Stavropol."[108]

He was "so cheerful and confident" after the conference that

Gorbachev with advisers and aides at Novo-Ogaryovo.
Left to right: Gorbachev, Aleksandr Yakovlev, Valery Boldin, Ivan Frolov,
Nail Bikkenin, Nikolai Petrakov, Georgy Shakhnazarov.

Chernyaev forbore to mention his own reservations. He, too, celebrated Gorbachev as "a politician with enormous self-confidence, master of the art of leading, winning over and subduing." The conference was "a turning point like never before." But Chernyaev, like most of the liberal intelligentsia, was still worried, even "depressed" by all the antiperestroika anger among the delegates, by the sense that without Gorbachev to restrain them, they would have sunk the listing ship. In that sense, Gorbachev's unique, driving role was cause for concern as well as celebration. His strengths made everything possible, but his weaknesses undermined his whole project. By focusing so obsessively on Yeltsin, Brutents recalled, "he guaranteed Yeltsin's revival and took another step on the path to his Canossa at Yeltsin's hand."[109]

Gorbachev himself realized that the conference would energize "the right-conservative opposition." Before the conference, he had "wavered, fearful of tearing myself away" from old ideas and institutions, wary of "a mutiny on board." Now he was determined to go all out: "We didn't have much time. We didn't have a day, even an hour, to lose."[110]

FAR MORE THAN A DAY or an hour or even a year would be lost, however; ultimately, the Soviet Union itself would be lost, owing in large part to an issue that first emerged in 1986 and became a major drain on Gorbachev's attention in 1988. The Soviets called it the "nationality" question—relations among the many nationalities that composed the Union of Soviet Socialist Republics, especially between Russians and non-Russians, but between others, such as Armenians and Azerbaijanis, as well. Before the 1917 revolution, non-Russians had been inmates of what Lenin called the Russian Empire's "prison house of nations." Ahead of his time in recognizing the appeal of ethnic nationalism, Lenin exploited it to make the revolution and then tried to tame it by providing non-Russians with their own accoutrements of authority: Soviet republics of their own complete with legislatures, academies of science, flags, anthems, even foreign ministers. In theory the USSR was a federal union, but in fact it was a supercentralized state. Its component republics even had the "right to secede," but Lenin vitiated that right by stipulating that it could be exercised only by the proletariat guided by the Communist party. Stalin, whom Lenin had named his commissar of nationalities, smashed the last remnants of real nationalism with his totalitarian fist. Khrushchev loosened the reins by appointing local ethnic leaders to head republic Communist parties. Brezhnev bought them off by ignoring their corruption as long as they kept their bailiwicks stable and quiet. But by repressing non-Russians while at the same time equipping them with formally national institutions, the Kremlin prepared them to rise again, embittered by their trials and determined to turn the trappings of authority into real power. At which point it was only a matter of time, along with a push by Yeltsin and assorted other Russian politicians until Russians, too, although dominant in the allegedly federal union, rose up and demanded their own autonomous state.

How did Gorbachev fail to foresee the rise of nationalist unrest? Few if any Soviet leaders read the extensive Western literature on nationalism, not even Gorbachev, who reached out to acquaint himself with left-wing European political thought.[111] Gorbachev wasn't the only Soviet leader who missed what was coming. Ironically, however, his special mix of idealism and optimism rendered him particularly blind. His faith in reformed socialism extended to thinking it could satisfy non-Russians and Russians alike. He assumed, though he was a confirmed internationalist, that he could speak for Russia himself. He knew from growing up just north of the Caucasus that nationalist passions could flare up when "incited for the sake of selfish interests and ambitions." But he was convinced "there was only one way to handle this problem, through cooperation." His celebration in May 1985 of the "united family of the Soviet people" was, according to Grachev, "entirely sincere."[112] Gorbachev sensed possible trouble, but was in no hurry to address it. Only in August 1988 did he call for a special Central Committee plenum on nationalities to be held "sometime around June 1989."[113]

It was Gorbachev himself, actually, who ignited the first ethnic explosion, in late 1986 in Kazakhstan. The republic's then leader, Dinmukhamed Kunayev, was as corrupt as they came. Brezhnev had tolerated him, but Gorbachev wasn't about to. Kazakhs had plenty of grievances: the use of republic territory for Soviet nuclear testing, the steady shrinkage of the Aral Sea (once one of the four largest lakes in the world) excessively diverted for irrigation, the dominance of Russians in the developed north of the republic. But instead of addressing these problems, Gorbachev decided to replace Kunayev, not with another Kazakh, but with a Russian, Gennady Kolbin. Kolbin once served as deputy party leader in Georgia, but had never set foot in Kazakhstan. Not only that, but Moscow rammed Kolbin's candidacy through the Kazakhstan Central Committee without debate, producing the obligatory unanimous consent in about fifteen minutes.[114]

Gorbachev later admitted that Kolbin's appointment was a mistake.[115] But in the meantime, protest demonstrations began that evening in the capital, Alma-Ata, starting with students from theater arts and foreign-languages institutes and swelling the next day to several thousand people, many of them carrying nationalist placards and banners. When local police and KGB units tried to disperse the crowd, they were met with a shower of sticks, rocks, and iron bars. At least two people were killed and more than a thousand, both demonstrators and police, wounded in skirmishes over the course of the next two days.[116] According to Kolbin, Gorbachev followed the situation closely, sometimes calling every twenty to thirty minutes, stressing that "no force should be used" and rebuking Kolbin for employing water-cannons.[117]

A second warning came from Crimean Tatars in the summer of 1987. The entire nation had been deported to Central Asia during World War II by Stalin, who accused them of collaboration with the Germans. Now thousands were demonstrating in Moscow, demanding the restoration of their territory in Crimea. Gorbachev's less than decisive response, with the whole world watching, was "I suggest we form a commission." The commission was headed by none other than Andrei Gromyko, who had plenty of experience stonewalling foreign leaders, but none negotiating with Soviet citizens. The Politburo's instructions to Gromyko tried to have it both ways. He was to "recognize the right of people to assemble with their demands and slogans," but not to "confuse glasnost with license." When Gromyko asked for more concrete guidance, all the Politburo could suggest was the status quo. If the Tatars were allowed to go back to the Crimea, then other exiled groups would demand return from Central Asia banishment—Meskhetian Turks from Uzbekistan to Georgia, Volga Germans to the Volga, and so on. Fortunately for Gorbachev, the Tatar demonstrators settled for vague promises and dispersed.[118]

A third and more enduring conflict, one that preceded Gorbachev and still burns in the twenty-first century, flared in Nagorno-Karabakh in February 1988. Located in the South Caucasus and long an object of contention between Christian Armenians and Muslim Azerbaijanis, Nagorno-Karabakh has a predominantly Armenian population (more than 75 percent in 1979), but was awarded to Azerbaijan by the Bolsheviks after the two republics gained independence from the Russian Empire. Many Armenians and Azeris lived in each other's countries, for the most part peacefully, but with tensions occasionally driving refugees back into their ethnic homelands. Armenians in Nagorno-Karabakh experienced discrimination at the hand of Azerbaijani authorities. But until the advent of perestroika and glasnost they (and their compatriots in Armenia itself) had no choice but to accept their fate. Nagorno-Karabakh Armenians began to petition for reunification with Armenia in 1987. Demonstrators took to the streets early the next year, carrying portraits of Gorbachev, and on February 21 the Nagorno-Karabakh soviet formally asked Azerbaijan and Armenia to transfer the region to Armenia. This provoked Azerbaijani counterdemonstrations insisting that the disputed region was "an inalienable part" of that republic.[119]

Gorbachev called an emergency session of the Politburo on Sunday, February 21. The issue was not just clashing street demonstrations, Ligachev warned, but a collision between two constituent Soviet republics. Once again, Gorbachev's response was to seek a political compromise: he issued an appeal to the "working people" of Azerbaijan and Armenia in which he promised to convene a Central Committee plenum on the nationality question;[120] and he invited two leading Armenian intellectuals who had been prime movers of the Nagorno-Karabakh movement, journalist Zori Balayan and poet Silva Kaputikyan, to a meeting with him on February 26.

This last move was especially characteristic—even more so, notes Grachev, of Gorbachev's wife. Both still "believed almost religiously in the intelligentsia, its noble mission and its political potential," both considered intellectuals to be their "loyal allies in pushing democratic reforms." But, as Grachev says, that faith was "romantic and naïve," especially when it came up against the siren calls of nationality and ethnicity.[121]

Gorbachev took a hard line with his two guests. What was happening in and around Nagorno-Karabkah was a "knife in our back." The country had "tens of such potential ethnic flashpoints," to which the spark could spread. Fourteen million Russians lived in Ukraine, not to mention Germans, Poles, and Hungarians. More reckless action "will put an end to all reforms." Gorbachev acknowledged Nagorno-Karabakh's grievances, pledged material assistance, and promised to bolster its rights as an "autonomous" region within Azerbaijan. What he couldn't do was endorse its transfer to Armenia, for that would "dislodge the rock from the mountain and thereby let loose an avalanche."[122]

Gorbachev spoke passionately. As often happened, his guests succumbed to his powers of persuasion, reiterating their faith in perestroika and promising not to exacerbate the situation. "Just don't raise the territorial issue," Gorbachev pleaded as they departed, and, for a while, they did not.[123] They thought, Balayan recalled, that Gorbachev was going "to do everything that needed to be done. And we believed him, the way we believed in perestroika from its inception." When Balayan returned to Armenia the next day and reported on the meeting to a rally of several hundred thousand, "the people believed me and then went home, the rally dispersed. It was but an hour later that Sumgait happened."[124]

Sumgait is an industrial city of some 200,000 in Azerbaijan, fifteen miles north of the capital, Baku. Many Azerbaijani refugees from Armenia resided there, but so did many Armenians. Some tension between the groups had always been present, but it had now been exacerbated by the clash over Nagorno-Karabakh. What began in Sumgait on February 27 was a pitiless pogrom that lasted three days. Gangs roamed the city beating and killing Armenians. In one case, eight who barricaded themselves on the eighth floor of an apartment house were reached with the help of a fire engine ladder, then dragged down and murdered. Armenian women were stripped naked and marched through the streets. Two had their breasts cut off, one was decapitated, and a little girl was skinned alive. Estimates of the number of those slaughtered range from thirty-two up to one hundred.[125]

The Politburo in Moscow didn't meet until February 29. By then, Ministry of Interior troops had tried to stop the violence in Sumgait, but they were ill prepared and were themselves attacked by mobs with Molotov cocktails. The Politburo ordered in professional army units. Ligachev favored a massive use of force, but Gorbachev insisted they hold their fire. In retrospect, some contend that use of force in Sumgait could have deterred national separatists in other areas like the Baltics later on. "They should have hanged twenty or so murderers from lampposts, without any trial," recalled economist Nikolai Shmelyov, who generally admired Gorbachev. "If so, [nationalists in Georgia, Lithuania, and elsewhere] would have taken him more seriously instead of regarding him as weak."[126] But Gorbachev, as always, was reluctant to use force. He feared, "They'll start shooting anyone wandering around the streets." "We have a stake in a political solution." He counted on rational citizens, especially members of the working class, to help restore order. He urged Armenian and Azerbaijani party leaders, who amazingly had not been in contact with each other, to act. He demanded that the party Secretariat in Moscow study the roots of the problem. Not to mention the Academy of Sciences, in which, he told the Politburo, "no one is working on the problem." Perhaps, he added, that Central Committee plenum on the nationality question should be held even before the Nineteenth Conference.[127]

The nationality plenum wasn't moved up. For the rest of the year, in fact, Gorbachev tried to convince his colleagues, and himself as well, that nationalism was under control. "The integrity of the Soviet state isn't being questioned," he declared on March 3. People were still loyal to the Soviet Union and to its Communist party. Why else were both Armenians and Azerbaijanis appealing to Moscow for help? He denied that greater democracy would make things more difficult. On the contrary, he was convinced that nationalist excesses arose from the lack of democracy.[128] He believed that tyranny had bottled up ethnic grievances until they exploded, and that in the long run democracy could prevent genocide. Troubles in Nagorno-Karabakh were the product not of perestroika but of the stagnation to which perestroika itself was the antidote. Speaking of nationality unrest in other places as well, he assured the Politburo on October 13, "This isn't a crisis situation."[129]

Despite these declarations, Gorbachev was alarmed. What was at stake, he warned on March 21, three days before the Nina Andreyeva affair exploded in the Kremlin, was "the fate of our multinational state." It would take just "one spark to ignite a fire."[130] "The situation [in Nagorno-Karabakh] is getting out of control," he said on July 4. "You and I, are guilty, too," he told the USSR Supreme Soviet on July 18, "because we didn't see what was happening and resolve it in time."[131] "The intellectuals have gone bankrupt," Gorbachev confessed to Chernyaev and Shakhnazarov in early October. "They can't offer anything that would lead to a solution." But he didn't have one himself. He wanted a "humane solution." He did not want "blood." He wanted "for us to start talking to each other." But, he added, "if I knew what the solution was, nothing could stop me, I would break all conventions to get it done. But I don't know it!"[132]

BETWEEN THE END of the Nineteenth Party Conference and the end of the year, Gorbachev pushed political transformation harder than he ever had economic reforms. He devoted a grand total of two days of his August-long Crimean vacation to swimming and daydreaming on the beach, and reserved time for writing a short new treatise, "On Socialism," but almost immediately began redesigning the party apparatus.[133] The Central Committee staff consisted of about 3,000 people; it would be cut by more than a half. Multiple Central Committee departments supervising all aspects of society and the economy would be reduced to just two: a socioeconomic department with no administrative responsibilities (its mandate would be to concentrate on social theory), and an agricultural department. Two international departments (one covering relations with capitalist and Third World countries, with particular attention to nonruling Communist parties, the other, attending to socialist countries) would become one. Three ideological departments would amalgamate. Later, Gorbachev added defense and legal departments to the newly configured Central Committee apparatus. As for local party organizations, in provinces, cities, town and rural districts around the country, he hoped for a massive reduction of 800,000 to 900,000 of local apparatchiki.[134]

Meanwhile, the Politburo would be purged. Gromyko, Solomontsev, Demichev, and Dolgikh, all veteran hard-liners, would "retire at their own request." Vorotnikov would be made titular head of the Russian Republic, where, as Gorbachev put it to Chernyaev in August, "he can continue to grumble." Ligachev, cocurator of ideology, along with Yakovlev, would now handle agriculture, the graveyard of aspiring leaders, which Gorbachev himself had escaped only with Andropov's assistance. But since leaving Yakovlev in charge of ideology would provoke conservatives, he would head the international department, with Vadim Medevev in control of ideology. "Oh, is [Gorbachev] clever!" Chernyaev marveled in his diary.[135] But yet another move turned out to be disastrous. KGB chief Chebrikov was kicked upstairs as a Central Committee secretary. At Aleksandr Yakovlev's urging, Chebrikov was replaced by Vladimir Kriuchkov, who would lead an attempted coup against Gorbachev in August 1991.

All these changes were approved by the Central Committee. In December, the USSR Supreme Soviet passed a new electoral law and constitutional amendments allowing elections to be held in the spring. This added up to what Gorbachev called "the dawn of a new era."[136] At the time, he even bragged to Chernyaev about "another victory," adding, "praising yourself gives you moral support." But according to Chernyaev, the party apparatus, "realizing that it was living its last days," either "just stopped working," thus crippling the old system of administration, or used the many means still at its disposal to "demonstrate that it was all an adventure of Gorbachev."

Intellectuals who complained about economic and social conditions also "increasingly annoyed" Gorbachev, adds Chernyaev. So did "the people" themselves who, instead of taking up his challenge to improve their own lives, still blamed him for not doing so. "What do you think I am, a tsar?" he chided residents during an early September walking tour of Sevastopol in Crimea. "Or Stalin?" What did they expect him to dole out: "an apartment to you, a pension to him, a fair salary to her"? Hadn't they figured out in three years "who can do what, who can be a leader, organize others"? If they still expected him to "solve everything," then they had "missed the point completely."[137]

Blaming ungrateful beneficiaries of his own largesse wasn't a good sign. Even the Politburo purge had its drawbacks: Gorbachev didn't want to seem to be settling personal scores, and he found it extremely painful to dismiss people with whom he had worked for so long. Moreover, by keeping them on board, he had compelled them to share responsibility with him. Now, with their departure, the responsibility for what happened next was his and his alone. Most important, by gutting the party's ability to run the country, he was undermining his own power.

Was there an alternative? Looking back, sympathizers like Chernyaev wish Gorbachev had moved even faster, quitting as party leader before the new Congress of People's Deputies was elected, and then running to become "the people's president" in another general election. But Gorbachev wasn't ready to do so; had he done so, he feared, his opponents could have used the party he abandoned to destroy him.

Meanwhile, Gorbachev's mood was darkening. Familiar failings of perestroika seemed more frustrating than ever: "The whole country is standing in lines," he told the Politburo on July 4. "The lines are tormenting people." "And we call that perestroika!"[138] Early campaigns, like the one against alcoholism, had foundered: "As always," he lamented on September 8, "we overdid it."[139] Nationalism wasn't confined to the Caucasus; it was spreading in the Baltics. Did the Balts "really want to leave" the USSR? Gorbachev asked Chernyaev, Yakovlev, and Shakhnazarov in December. Chernyaev thought they did.[140]

The strain Gorbachev was feeling took a toll on his family as well. His wife's way of reducing it was to treat her home not just as her castle but as her world, her galaxy. But the outside world kept intruding—press coverage, of course, but also stepped-up monitoring, medical and otherwise, of everything and everyone who came in contact with family members. From the start of his administration, Gorbachev's daughter and son-in-law had been targets of petitioners complaining about abuses by authorities at all levels. Gorbachev and his wife drew even closer, he remembered, "sharing our common cares and helping each other always and in everything." She accompanied him on trips at home and abroad, attended official ceremonies, and went with him to the theater and artistic exhibitions. Recalling Dostoevsky's words "Beauty saves the world," she helped found and maintain the Soviet Culture Foundation, which fostered local arts and crafts in small cities and towns around the country, assisted young writers and artists, and helped found a historical-cultural journal called *Our Heritage*. She also tried to promote philanthropy, which had been (and still is) underdeveloped in Russia,

and particularly supported the opening of a center for treating leukemia at the Children's Hospital in Moscow. Some of Gorbachev's advisers
looked so askance at his wife's press coverage that they dared to suggest
curbing it. When Western media played up Soviet citizens' negative reactions to her, he detected an attempt by "Western centers of psychological
warfare" to discredit him. "These were unbelievably difficult years," he
recalled, in which she "courageously bore her burden, carried her cross
and did so much to support me."[141]

How did Gorbachev himself cope? By throwing himself even more
into his work, which was the source of so much stress in the first place.
"To avoid falling into grudges or hypochondria," he wrote in his memoirs, "one must not allow oneself to rest. I know from many years of
experience that work can cure everything. You have to throw everything into your work. If you do that, then your own worries will fade into
the background."[142]

But they didn't. Gorbachev developed a twitch in one eye in October
and got sick in December, shivering with chills, feeling dizzy, not going
to work for a week.[143] During the winter of 1987, Yakovlev and other
aides had urged him to shorten his speeches and make them more concrete. But Gorbachev insisted the people wanted answers to complex
questions, which could be provided only in "big speeches." Gorbachev
was enamored with "theoretical formulations," according to Yakovlev,
particularly "fresh" ones, which, in fact, left his listeners cold. It was as
if, Yakovlev recalled, he were "attached to verbosity" as a way "to escape
from concrete problems into a dense, almost impenetrable thicket of
words."[144] According to his wife (and to his aide and English-language
interpreter Palazhchenko), Gorbachev's verbosity stemmed from (as she
put it) "wanting to be understood."[145] Whatever its source, in October
1988 Chernyaev urged his boss to "stop constantly appearing on the TV
screen . . . and filling newspaper pages while the shelves in the stores are
empty."[146]

Gorbachev's attitude toward Chernyaev and other aides also was
changing. He was still eager to share his excitement at reading records
of early Bolshevik party congresses, still "animated like a young student,
reading excerpts out loud, commenting, drawing lessons for the present day, philosophizing" about "the basic problems of existence." But he

no longer talked to his assistants in what Chernyaev called "a simple, straightforward fashion." Instead, when he disagreed with Chernyaev, he quickly interrupted him and "stated his position in a way that let me know that the discussion was closed."

Chernyaev felt hurt and worried that he shouldn't. His boss had "turned the country upside down, given it back a human face, saved humanity from a catastrophe. . . . And who am I? Nobody in particular." But this new way of treating aides, this "instrumental approach" ("Let the person do his work, I'll take what I need and discard what I don't. I don't have time to explain things to him, and why should I? He'll get over it!"), portended trouble outside Gorbachev's inner circle as well—the "growing danger of inconsistency and outright blunders" as a result of ignoring people "who are ready to speak their minds and tell him what they really know."[147]

None of the flaws that emerged by the end of 1988 was fatal in itself. But they didn't help as Gorbachev's situation deteriorated. In 1999 Chernyaev wrote an afterword to his diary entries for 1988. "If it is fair to speak of Gorbachev's fate as tragic (in the grand Shakespearean sense), then it was during 1988 that not only Gorbachev's adviser but Gorbachev himself first sensed this possibility."[148]

CHAPTER 10

BEFORE
THE STORM
1987–1988

"WE HAVE TO GET OUT OF THERE," Gorbachev told the Politburo on June 2, 1986. "I'm afraid we are losing time," he declared on November 13. "We need to end the war and pull our troops out." Just back from Afghanistan, Shevardnadze told the Politburo on January 21, 1987, "We've been waging war against the peasantry." "We've known absolutely nothing about the psychology of the people or the real situation. . . . What we're doing there is totally inconsistent with the moral face of our country." Even Ligachev agreed: "We can't bring them freedom with our arms. We've been defeated." So did Defense Minister Marshal Sokolov: "We can't win this war militarily." Gromyko himself joined the chorus on February 23: there was no way to close the Afghanistan-Pakistan border, so Moscow needed to end the war.[1]

No way to win, but no will to lose either, no way for Soviet troops to prevail, but the Kabul government couldn't cope on its own. Gromyko "wouldn't bet a kopeck" the Afghans could create an effective army of their own, "no matter how many resources we pour in there." And yet, he insisted on February 26, 1987, "we have no alternative but to supply them." Vladimir Kriuchkov, the KGB's highest authority on Afghanistan (soon to be its chief), refused to "leave, to run away, to throw away everything," to allow the country to become "a beachhead for Iran, Turkey and the fundamentalists." Despite the chaos he had witnessed in Afghanistan—just because of it, in fact—Shevardnadze felt duty-bound, he said on June 11, to "help" President Najibullah and determined to "believe in him." Meeting with Najibullah in Moscow in July, Gorbachev sounded as if all was lost. But he himself had an eight-point plan for avoiding a "shameful" exit leading to a further bloodbath: UN-sponsored negotiations, getting Washington to help, better advice to Kabul, carefully targeted military operations, offering rebels a share in governing, reshaping the country's ruling party, talks with Afghans in emigration, all guided by the Politburo's Commission on Afghanistan headed by the two men most resistant to abandoning Afghanistan, Shevardnadze and Kriuchkov.[2]

"Fuck it all!" Chernyaev wrote in his diary on August 28. "We got dragged in and now we don't know how to crawl out." (He didn't have much use, either, for "the shitload" of Marxists in Africa whom Moscow had been supporting since Brezhnev.) It is to Gorbachev's credit that Chernyaev felt free to argue (somewhat more decorously, one presumes, than in his diary) against new offensives supporting the Kabul government. But when he did so in the fall of 1988, Gorbachev complained about "some people who want to throw Najibullah on the mercy of fate." When Yakovlev echoed Chernyaev's objections at a Politburo meeting, Chernyaev noted, Gorbachev "completely flew off the handle, as he always does when he knows he's wrong," for example, when "the subject of Yeltsin or Nagorno-Karabakh comes up."[3]

Beginning in the fall of 1987, Moscow tried urgently to obtain Washington's help in leaving Afghanistan. In September, Shevardnadze privately told Shultz that the Soviets would soon be pulling out. What Gorbachev needed most in return was for the Americans to stop supplying arms to the mujahideen when Moscow withdrew. If he had proposed such a deal at the end of 1985, says Ambassador Matlock, "he almost certainly could have secured from the United States what he sought in 1988."[4] But by now Reagan was committed to all-out aid for the rebels.[5] Denied that concession, Gorbachev nonetheless announced on February 8, 1988, that Soviet troops would begin their withdrawal on May 15, 1988, and complete it within ten months.[6] An international agreement signed in Geneva on April 14 (between Afghanistan and Pakistan, with the United States and the Soviet Union as guarantors) gave Gorbachev only minimal diplomatic cover. Since the mujahideen weren't party to the accord, Soviet troops would have to pull out under hostile fire, and the civil war would rage on with the Najibullah regime at the mercy of the rebels. In several speeches that spring, Gorbachev put the best possible face on what he had once described as a humiliating defeat. "They say we lost Afghanistan," he told a gathering of editors, writers, and other cultural figures on May 7, "as if we had previously 'found' it." Some 13,000 Soviet soldiers had died; 43,000 were injured; more than a million passed through the "nightmare"; six billion rubles a year had been spent on the war. "From every point of view—human and economic—we had to get out."[7]

Not doing so sooner was a terrible mistake. But even at this late date, it took courage to leave—the first time the Soviet Union had pulled back from territories it had "liberated" for Communism. Not only that, Gorbachev was at last able to pursue his highest-priority foreign policy goal—cooperating with the United States to end the cold war—free of the burden of Afghanistan.

EASTERN EUROPE WAS STILL a second-order priority, even though Gorbachev and his colleagues realized that storm clouds were gathering there. Following a visit in the summer of 1987, Shevardnadze recounted troubling signs: "the possibility of social turmoil" in Hungary and "indecision and uncertainty" in Bulgaria, where "outwardly everything looks good."[8] Several months later, Gorbachev warned the economic situation was "worsening," leading to "socio-political aggravation." Even Yugoslavia was "on the brink of collapse." In Poland, Ligachev added, "everything" was moving toward "renunciation of the [Communist] party."[9] Two weeks later, Shevardnadze complained that "primitivism and narrow-mindedness" were leading Soviet allies into "deadlock": take the old leadership of Poland; take "the current situation" in East Germany, in Romania. "Is that socialism?"[10]

Something had to be done. Shakhnazarov, who had become Gorbachev's chief adviser on Eastern Europe early in 1988, asked him in October, "How we will act if one or even several countries simultaneously become bankrupt?" What should be done if "social instability" in Hungary coincided with "another round of trouble-making" in Poland

and "demonstrations" in Czechoslovakia? It was "high time," Shakhnazarov urged his boss, "to discuss these issues at the Politburo in the presence of experts." It was no time "to bury our heads in the sand like an ostrich."[11] Gorbachev's Politburo critics, treading carefully after their setbacks earlier in the year, put the matter more delicately in December: Vorotnikov called for "clarifying our thinking" about the ominous situation in Eastern Europe.[12]

As these injunctions imply, little if anything had in fact been done. One might have thought, indeed many did think, that by 1987 Gorbachev would actively encourage reforms in Eastern Europe. In retrospect, his best chance to prevent Communism from collapsing, taking with it the whole Soviet alliance system in Europe, would have been to encourage reformers like himself to take command of their countries with the support of their people. Instead, he gave every appearance in his public meetings with the old guard (such as East Germany's Erich Honecker, Czechoslovakia's Gustáv Husák, and Bulgarian leader Todor Zhivkov) of backing them, never pressing them to adopt their own versions of perestroika or yield to others who would. "A few clear signs," concludes historian Jacques Lévesque, would have given reformers "strong encouragement," but instead Gorbachev seemed all too willing to continue with "business as usual."[13] Another choice that seems "hard to understand."

Czechoslovakia, as Lévesque points out, was a classic "missed opportunity." At the beginning of 1987, Husák, who was ill, wanted to retire. Lubomír Štrougal, prime minister during the Prague Spring, had turned against it after the Soviet invasion, but then pressed for reforms when Brezhnev died. Now he asked Moscow's support to succeed Husák. Chernyaev, Shakhnazarov, and Foreign Ministry spokesman Gennady Gerasimov, informally known as the "Czechoslovak lobby" or "Prague club" since they had all been stationed there in the mid-1960s, wanted to provide that help. When Gorbachev visited Prague in April, Chernyaev suggested he revise Moscow's view of the Prague Spring. When Western journalists asked Gerasimov to explain the difference between 1968 and 1987, he answered pointedly: "Nineteen years"—saying, in effect, there was no difference at all.[14] According to Central Committee official Valery Musatov, "Gorbachev listened attentively to Chernyaev's suggestion without saying anything, which was often his habit, but several of us had the impression that he would say something along these lines in Prague."[15] If Gorbachev wanted to promote reform in Prague, renouncing the 1968 invasion was the place to begin.

Gorbachev received what he called a "stupendous" welcome there. The electric atmosphere was reminiscent of May 1945, he told the Politburo afterward, when the country celebrated victory over Hitler. Thousands of people lined the streets and cheered from rooftops and balconies, partly in response to party summonses, but mostly in a spontaneous outpouring of respect. Many, Gorbachev reported, chanted, "Gorbachev, Gorbachev," as if "Husák, who was standing beside me, wasn't there." People "cried out to me, 'Stay with us, if only for a year!'" He himself wasn't the issue, he insisted; people were sending a message to the Czechoslovak party leadership. And the leadership knew it: "They feel they're lagging behind their own people and losing their trust." Especially since the Czechs kept "comparing perestroika with their own 1968."

The situation was "dangerous," Gorbachev told his Moscow colleagues. Half a million Communists, one-third of the Czech party, had been "expunged" from its ranks in 1968. "What is to be their role now?" The Czech party line on Alexander Dubček, leader of the Prague spring, remained the same: "a traitor to socialism." "How," Gorbachev asked, "is 1968 to be assessed?" How were all the Communists ousted in 1968 to be treated? He had given his answer to the Czech leadership in Prague: "I told them, 'It's your business.'"[16]

Their business? If it had been their business in 1968, Soviet troops wouldn't have invaded. Having cut Czech reform off at the knees then, wasn't it Moscow's business to encourage it now? Gorbachev's Moscow State University friend Zdeněk Mlynář, interviewed in exile, said Moscow "is doing what we did in Prague in 1968, but even more radically." Dubček, who had worked in an obscure forestry administration job in Slovakia and been tailed by the secret police for years, wrote to the Soviet Central Committee in support of perestroika. "I swear on my heart I knew they were right," Gorbachev recalled in his memoirs. "What was 1968 in the light of 1987–1988? It was when we should have begun perestroika, twenty years ago, in the Soviet Union." Nonetheless, he kept silent. Being asked about 1968 in Prague was "the hardest of all." "Never" had he experienced "such internal discord [in himself] as at that moment."[17]

Who would replace Husák—Štrougal, the would-be reformer, or Vasil Bilak, or Miloš Jakeš, who had suppressed Czech reform in 1968 and opposed Soviet perestroika? No—that wasn't Gorbachev's business either. Even after Husák himself praised Štrougal in Moscow in November 1987, the Soviet leader remained neutral. As the succession struggle dragged on in Prague, Husák asked Gorbachev to phone him, but Gorbachev refused. According to Lévesque, "even a hint of support from Gorbachev" might have swung the outcome. Absent such a hint, Jakeš was appointed party leader.[18]

A similar struggle in Hungary had a proreform outcome, but not thanks to Gorbachev. Party leader János Kádár, in power since Soviet troops crushed the Hungarian revolution in 1956, had himself become a reformer, but at the age of seventy-six he was considering retirement. Štrougal's Hungarian counterpart, Prime Minister Károly Grósz, also expected at least minimal backing from Moscow. Vadim Medvedev, Soviet Politburo member responsible for Eastern Europe, recommended supporting him, but again, Gorbachev refused to get involved. Grósz won out and was named general secretary, but more, Lévesque concludes, as the result of the "Gorbachev effect," that is, the carryover influence on Hungary of perestroika in the USSR, than of any "direct action" by Gorbachev.[19]

Gorbachev didn't press either for the replacement of Honecker, Zhivkov, or Ceauçescu, although all of them, he later complained, led their countries "to the brink of catastrophe." Because, he insisted in his memoirs, he had no "right to interfere shamelessly in the affairs of our 'satellites.'" Because he and his Communist allies had so often proclaimed that relations among them were to be based on "equality, independence, non-interference in internal affairs."[20] Because, as he explained to Politburo members on February 12, 1987, they could and would defend perestroika ("a hundred times over if necessary") to the whole world, but direct "pressure will not help." Because the world had changed, he said in Yugoslavia in March 1988, to the point that "no one can impose anything on anyone. . . . Today neither the USSR nor the U.S.

can impose its will on any country."[21] In that sense, he later argued, critics who charged him with "betrayal" of friends and allies, like those who said he'd been too "patient" with Communist troglodytes, assumed "an outmoded notion" of international relations. In the new world, the best way to lead was "by the power of example"[22] or, as he told the Politburo on February 12, 1987, by letting "natural processes" take their course in Eastern Europe, for "in them is our hope."[23]

By the start of 1987, Gorbachev had begun referring to "freedom of choice" as a basic principle of his "new thinking" about world affairs. As he wrote in *Perestroika: New Thinking for Our Country and the World*, "Universal security in our time rests upon the recognition of the right of every nation to choose its own path of social development. A nation may choose either capitalism or socialism. This is its sovereign right."[24] Put that way, the principle allowed for a Communist party and its leader to speak for a nation—just as they had been doing for decades. But Gorbachev would soon grant that right to the people themselves, a total reversal of Leninism. In the meantime, at the Nineteenth Party Conference in June 1988, he declared, "The imposition from outside, by any means, let alone military force, of a social system, or a way of life, is a dangerous trapping of the past."[25]

That seemed to mean that East European countries had a sovereign right to throw off Communist rule, as they did the very next year with Gorbachev's acquiescence. Did he not see that coming? Was he prepared to accept the loss of a region long deemed of vital strategic importance to the USSR? Or, as his aide and biographer Grachev puts it, "had he fallen into the trap of abstract political formulas, a prisoner of his ambition to offer the world a new utopian ideology?" This last interpretation is all too plausible. For even if, as is likely, he neither foresaw nor wished the collapse of East European Communism, what he was counting on to avoid it was utopian—the triumph of perestroika in Eastern Europe without his intervening directly to promote that outcome.[26]

Gorbachev's thinking was so extraordinarily high-minded as to suggest that something else lay behind or beside it. Lévesque can't believe "it was only or mainly 'the beauty of the principle'" that guided Gorbachev in 1987 and 1988, thus harming his cause "at the very moment" when it was "reaching a fundamental turning point."[27] Grachev thinks Gorbachev's certainty that success was guaranteed served as "an alibi for inaction in Eastern Europe," allowing him to "escape the necessity" of elaborating and applying a "concrete program" to promote reform in the area.[28] But, if so, why did he want to escape that necessity? One reason was economic: the cost of sustaining East European regimes had become prohibitive. The Soviet Union couldn't keep providing cheap oil to its allies (as much as 100 million tons in one five-year period, at prices four or five times less than on the world market), especially when world prices themselves had plummeted. "We must take care of our own people first of all," Gorbachev told the Politburo on March 18, 1988. Even though, as Shakhnazarov later noted, "ideology and Soviet military forces stationed in those countries notwithstanding, our influence was based 90 percent on economic ties."[29]

Another motive for "nonintervention" in Eastern Europe involved Kremlin politics. As long as Ligachev and other Politburo conservatives were resisting Gorbachev, whether covertly or openly, as in the Nina Andreyeva affair, why further antagonize them by pressing on Eastern Europe the reforms they opposed at home? When Musatov and Central Committee officials wanted to promote reform there in 1987, they were told this wasn't the time "for opening a new front in the battle with conservatives" at home.[30]

Beyond economic and political reasons were more personal motives. One was that Gorbachev's seeming certainty that all would go well without his direct intervention concealed growing uncertainty—about Eastern Europe as well as developments in the USSR itself. Of course, he never confessed that openly to his Politburo colleagues. But his seemingly jocular explanation for not pressing the Czechs to follow Moscow's example gave him away: "God forbid we go to them with our own jumble of thoughts on the theme of their *perestroika*. It could destroy everything."[31]

Personal antipathy between Gorbachev and conservative East European leaders also explains Gorbachev's not-so-benign neglect. It was not just that he felt superior to them, that in fact he regarded them as nearly hopeless, but that several of them (all much more senior than he) felt superior to him, which irritated him all the more. Todor Zhivkov, Bulgaria's party leader since 1954, stolid, paunchy, and balding at seventy-six, acted as if he had invented perestroika. His trick was regularly to host close Gorbachev aides like Arbatov and Aganbegyan in Sofia or by the Black Sea at Varna, quiz them about upcoming innovations in Moscow, and then beat Gorbachev to the punch by introducing the same in Bulgaria. "We can be bolder than Moscow," he boasted, "because in a small country it's easier to experiment."[32] In fact, his experiments were as phony as his pretense of being the Soviet Union's most loyal friend in Eastern Europe. Gorbachev confessed later that it took him a while to "see through" another Zhivkov "game," which was to meet with Gorbachev one-on-one without any aides, interpret their conversations "selectively and to his own advantage," and then act as if he had Moscow's "agreement and support in everything."[33]

East Germany's Honecker, seventy-five, short, ramrod straight and just as inflexible politically, had led East Germany since 1971. He had the gall, in Gorbachev's eyes, to consider himself not just the most senior Communist leader but the wisest.[34] He claimed to have introduced reforms long ago, particularly crowing about his country's prowess in science and technology. In all his talks with Gorbachev, recalls Medvedev, Honecker carried with him a thick folder of documents, as if "implying" that whatever ridiculous claims he made "far from exhausted the facts at his disposal." Gorbachev's January 1987 speech supporting democratization in the USSR was banned in East Germany, with the "absurd" result, says Medvedev, that East Germans had to learn about it from West German media. Honecker's chief ideologist, Kurt Hager, remarked, "Just because your neighbor decides to change the wallpaper doesn't mean you have to change it in your apartment."[35] Honecker was, Gorbachev concluded, "more Catholic than the pope."[36]

Ceauşescu, Romanian party boss since 1965, shorter and slighter than the others, but even more tyrannical, was the most appalling. Gorbachev recoiled in horror from a May 1987 visit to Romania. There were shortages of everything, he told the Politburo on his return, but "he kept telling me everything was fine," as if they had already established "democracy, free elections, cooperatives and workers' rights." "I look and listen to him and feel like a fool." Crowds on the street, bused in for the occasion, kept shouting, "Ceauşescu—Gorbachev!" Gorbachev went up to them, he later recalled. "I approach. I try to speak, but they just keep yelling. I grab one by the arm, 'Wait a minute. Stop,' I say. I try to talk to them, but all I get is more, 'Ceauşescu—Gorbachev!'" with an occasional "Gorbachev—Ceauşescu" thrown in for good measure. "It made one's head burst," Gorbachev told his colleagues. "Human dignity has absolutely no value." Ceauşescu was "terribly offended" when Gorbachev talked about glasnost and perestroika. "He is unbelievably brazen. His self-assurance and self-praise are simply monumental. He attempts to teach and edify everybody." His thinking about international relations was "chaotic and confused."

If it hadn't been so repulsive, it would have been pitiful. A steamy early summer day was sweltering enough, but Ceauşescu insisted on a fireside chat made even hotter by television lights. "He probably wanted to match the Reagan-Gorbachev" fireside chat in Geneva, Gorbachev continued, even though it had been late autumn and unusually cold in Geneva.

There is little or no sign in the public record, or even in minutes of official talks in Bucharest, of the tensions barely below the surface. But Gorbachev finally exploded at a private dinner for the two leaders and their wives. Another blazing fire on a stifling night. Again, the host's "mentoring tone," this time complaining that his guest was too actively courting the West. Again, Ceauşescu reacting badly to Gorbachev on glasnost and democratization. Elena Ceauşescu tried to change the subject, but Raisa Gorbachev wouldn't let her, informing her host that Mikhail Sergeyevich received three or four thousand letters each day pressing him to push reforms faster and more boldly. If he were a Soviet citizen, Ceauşescu retorted, he would urge Gorbachev to go slow. Finally, Gorbachev blew up: "What you pass off as a prosperous and humane society isn't either, let alone democratic. You're holding the whole country in fear and isolating it from the world."

By this point, the shouting had gotten so loud that open windows providing the hot night's only "air-conditioning" had to be closed, and bodyguards in the courtyard were ordered deeper into the grounds where they couldn't hear the yelling. The evening was "ruined," Gorbachev later recalled, but that didn't prevent Ceauşescu and his wife from taking the Gorbachevs sightseeing around Bucharest the next day. The policy of nonintervention, though tattered, was still intact.[37]

Until the summer of 1988, despite all Gorbachev's talk about nonintervention, hard-line East European leaders probably assumed Soviet troops would rescue them from potential revolts of their own people.[38] Only then did Gorbachev's hands-off approach begin to change. Not, Lévesque emphasizes, that Moscow adopted "direct intervention and pressure to modify the composition of regimes," but rather that their leaders were treated "less tactfully" to broad hints that if they didn't reform they would face dire consequences. Gorbachev's speech at the United Nations in December, stressing every nation's sovereign "right to choose" its own fate, and announcing the unilateral withdrawal of 500,000 troops from Eastern Europe was a thunder clap. But even then, Shakhnazarov later confirmed to Grachev, there was never "practical analysis," or a "tactical program," let alone a "strategic plan" for dealing with Eastern Europe.[39]

Leaders of Communist bloc countries at a meeting of the
Warsaw Pact's Standing Consultative Committee, June 11–16, 1988.
Left to right clockwise around the table: Erich Honecker,
Wojciech Jaruzelski, Nicolae Ceauşescu, Mikhail Gorbachev,
Gustáv Husák, Todor Zhivkov.

EARLY ON, GORBACHEV'S West European strategy didn't seem much clearer. His predecessors had hoped to drive a wedge between it and the United States and eventually oust Washington from the continent. And on February 27, 1987, Gorbachev confirmed that goal to the Politburo—"to force the United States out of Europe. Will we succeed? I don't know. But that must be our aim." But a month later he denied this aim to Italian Foreign Minister Giulio Andreotti, insisting, "We are realists." And two weeks after that, in Prague, he proclaimed a vision of a "common European home," which eventually led to a brave but unsuccessful attempt to transcend East-West barriers in Europe, dissolve both NATO and the Warsaw Pact, and tie together the whole continent with the United States.[40]

For the time being, however, Gorbachev was practicing traditional diplomacy, trying to improve relations with Paris, Bonn, and London for their own sake, but also to facilitate his continuing courtship of Washington. Unfortunately, however, France was distracted by its domestic politics, and West German Chancellor Kohl had compared Gorbachev to Nazi propaganda chief Josef Goebbels in a *Newsweek* interview published on October 27, 1986. Mrs. Thatcher did indeed "do business" with Gorbachev, just as she predicted in 1984, but they remained far apart ideologically. And yet, by the end of 1988 Gorbachev felt as comfortable with West European leaders as he was uncomfortable with his East European peers, in part because they felt so comfortable with him. Chernyaev observed in July 1987 that "whoever sits opposite M. S. (with the possible exception of Gadhafi's representative) trusts him. . . . They believe he wants to do exactly what he tells them, [even if] he cannot do all, or even the most part, of what he says. It is impossible to be cunning and play games with him. He is open and disarms any 'class' opponent because he invites him to be first and foremost a normal human being."[41]

Chernyaev doubtless exaggerated. But if Gorbachev had anything like the same sense of his own virtuosity and its effect on his interlocutors (which he almost certainly did), it is no wonder that he felt himself more in tune with his adversaries than with his allies.

After the March 1986 French elections, Mitterrand had to "cohabit" (the French technical term) with a conservative prime minister, Jacques Chirac, who distrusted Gorbachev. And it was Chirac who conducted the next Franco-Soviet summit, in Moscow in May 1987. Chirac spent much of the time rehearsing the sins of Soviet foreign policy prior to 1985.

In some ways, Gorbachev told the Politburo afterward, Chirac's positions, especially on military matters, were "worse than Thatcher's."[42] Fortunately for Gorbachev, Mitterrand maintained direct contact with Moscow, and in November 1988 his own talks in Moscow went much better. Mitterrand shared Gorbachev's opposition to Washington's Star Wars program and was open to the general idea of a "common European home." But Gorbachev also stressed Mitterrand's personal qualities. Of all the leaders with whom he negotiated, Mitterrand was "the most interesting and substantive." "Such a vast range of interests and so highly educated!"[43] As Gorbachev put it later, Mitterrand "not only understood but subtly sensed everything."

In his *Newsweek* interview, Kohl said Gorbachev seemed more promising than his predecessors, but he remained a Communist leader with a "flair for propaganda." Goebbels, too, Kohl added, had been a "propaganda specialist." The remark mortified Gorbachev, and it took him more than a year to get past it. West Germany's economic and political weight was undeniable, but he wanted, according to Chernyaev, to "teach Kohl a lesson" by ignoring him.[44] As early as February 26, 1987, Gorbachev stressed to the Politburo the need to "find the key to Kohl."[45] But for the time being he would receive only Richard von Weizsäcker, the titular president of the Federal Republic in July 1987.

Weizsäcker, like so many other foreign leaders, was wowed by Gorbachev's demeanor—radiating "concentrated energy" without conveying "any tension at all," his "welcoming gaze even more open than his ears," a man of "exceptional intelligence and emotional as well." The meeting was notable for Gorbachev's seeming hint that the long-stalled issue of German reunification might someday be reopened. When the German president ritually raised it, Gorbachev insisted on "the reality of the two German states," but added, "Where they'll be a hundred years from now only history can decide." That allowed Weizsäcker to announce publicly, "For the Soviet leader the German question is not closed." And, according to Chernyaev, he was correct: "I would say that deep down [Gorbachev] realized—then if not even earlier—that without solving the German problem . . . we could not expect any major improvement in international relations."[46]

Gromyko certainly did not realize that, deep down or otherwise, so he ordered that Weizsäcker's speech at a formal dinner in Moscow be cut in half before publication in *Izvestiia*. It turned out that Gorbachev had approved this, probably to keep the franchise with Gromyko, and he refused to reverse himself. But, reporting to the Politburo on July 16, he stressed not only the importance of cultivating West Germany but of meeting with Kohl himself.[47] Kohl's apology for the Goebbels comparison, delivered informally by Weizsäcker, paved the way, but it was only in October 1988 that Kohl came to Moscow. The old issues still divided them. But the tone of the talks was striking. Gorbachev talked about a "strategic turning point" in Soviet–West German relations, about disarmament and the eventual disbanding of both NATO and the Warsaw Pact. Kohl reached out personally: "You and I are roughly the same age." (Kohl was eleven months older.) Their families "lived through the war with all its horrors." "Your father was gravely wounded. My brother perished at the age of eighteen."[48]

Gorbachev was touched. He felt he and Kohl had "crossed the Rubicon," that after a cozy dinner for the two men and their wives, they parted, "or so it seemed to me, as well disposed toward each other as we could possibly be."[49] Chernyaev marveled at the result: he had "a

Gorbachev with West German Chancellor Helmut Kohl and their wives, Hannelore Kohl (left) and Raisa Gorbachev, at a concert during Kohl's official visit to Moscow, October 24–27, 1988.

physical sensation of entering a new world defined not by class struggle, ideology or hostility, but by a shared humanity," plus an even greater appreciation of how "brave and far-sighted" Gorbachev was. What had taken place between the two leaders was "an amazing metamorphosis," a Russian and a German, inheritors of the "long, dramatic, interwoven histories of the two great nations" talking to each other like "ordinary people," without "a hint of hostility or distrust."[50]

Besides Mitterrand and Kohl, Gorbachev had particularly gratifying talks with Italian Prime Minister Amintore Fanfani, Italian Foreign Minister Giulio Andreotti, even with the Vatican secretary of state (an expert on the persecution of the church in the Soviet bloc), Cardinal Agostino Casaroli, with whom the conversation was so rewardingly "philosophical" that Gorbachev decided not to circulate the transcript, as was usually done, to the Politburo. "He doesn't want to tease the geese," Chernyaev noted in his diary, an expression that his boss had used a lot lately about his colleagues, because, "of course, they would not 'understand' it."[51] Gorbachev found only one Communist leader in Western Europe he enjoyed talking to—not Georges Marchais or Álvaro Cunhal of the still hard-line French and Portuguese parties, but Alessandro Natta, leader of the freethinking Italian party.

Most stimulating of all was Mrs. Thatcher, whom Gorbachev found to be a brilliant sparring partner. During her visit to Moscow from March 28 to April 1, 1987, they clashed continually, producing little or no progress on diplomatic issues, but they enormously enjoyed doing so. Their afternoon-long talk in the Kremlin's St. Catherine's Hall on March 30, attended only by Chernyaev and Charles Powell, struck the latter as astonishingly tough. "No quarter asked or given," recalled Powell. "Thunderstorms, squally, bright periods in between." "Pretty cracking form: Mrs. Thatcher going on about what a lousy system Communism was and how it needed to be changed, attacking . . . everything you could think of, Gorbachev firing back equally and strongly: the absence of democracy in Northern Ireland, the terrible oppression of Catholics there. If ever two people spoke frankly to each other in a diplomatic exchange, this was it."[52] At times the tension was so high that Powell "thought we'd be thrown out at once."[53] Thatcher's advice about perestroika, which she found extremely promising, challenged the way Gorbachev was implementing it; he had to push reforms much more boldly, she insisted.

What made this so satisfying to Gorbachev? Partly that she cared enough to engage with him at a time when the French were still deciding what to think about perestroika, Kohl was only beginning to realize how "stupid" his invocation of Goebbels had been, and the Americans hadn't moved beyond Reykjavik, but had actually fallen back. Gorbachev also used something Thatcher said to teach the Politburo a lesson on April 2. "We're afraid of you," she had told him. "We don't believe you." Moscow had invaded Hungary, then Czechoslovakia, then Afghanistan. "We warned you what would happen to European trust in you if you deployed SS-20 rockets, but you went ahead and deployed them."[54] Gorbachev's point, a revolutionary break with his predecessors' thinking, was that the Soviet Union's security depended on its adversaries' also feeling secure.

On top of all this, the legendary "iron lady" wasn't always so steely. When Gorbachev accused her of being ready to go to war (why else was she so resistant to nuclear disarmament?), Chernyaev recalled, "she got very tense, blushed, and her expression hardened. She reached out and, touching Gorbachev's sleeve, began to talk without letting him get in a word." She became "so excited that the conversation got completely out of hand."[55] Gorbachev boasted to his male chauvinist colleagues about his success. When she and he had come close to a "fight," she got "agitated." She put on a powerful performance—strong arguments, skills of an experienced debater—of the sort "you'd never see in a theater." She "never looked at a note," and knew the numbers of missiles each side had by heart. But unlike Mitterrand, she "couldn't hide her thoughts and schemes." She was a "raging anti-Communist," who agreed in the end to "live and let live." She set out to "unmask" Soviet sins, then "panicked" at the prospect that the summit would seem to "fail."[56]

A cozy dinner with the Gorbachevs at a prerevolutionary villa in the country, obviously meant to echo their luncheon at the prime minister's Chequers estate, also went swimmingly. In addition to Prime Minister Ryzhkov and his wife, neither of whom said much, only Chernyaev, Powell, and two interpreters were present. The company sipped cognac in front of the requisite fire in the hearth. Mrs. Thatcher's question about just who constituted the Soviet "working class" sparked a friendly debate between the Gorbachevs: Raisa ("in very chirpy form" according to Thatcher's interpreter Richard Pollack) contending that anyone who worked, whatever his job or profession, was a worker; her husband trying to restrict the term to blue-collar workers, but then, characteristically, elaborating at some length that (in Thatcher's paraphrase) "working class" was "largely an historical or 'scientific' term which did not do justice to the diversity of today's society."[57] Mrs. Gorbachev challenged Mrs. Thatcher's notion that it was moral "to preserve nuclear weapons on this earth." To which the prime minister replied, "You are an idealist, Mrs. Gorbachev." To which Gorbachev's wife retorted, "There are many idealists like me and I'm sure there will be a lot more."[58]

Thatcher was greatly impressed with Gorbachev's intellect, according to her foreign secretary, Sir Geoffrey Howe. She also greatly admired Reagan and Jordan's King Hussein, the latter because he was "so courteous and formal." But she "didn't believe Reagan was a man of great intellect, and she did believe Gorbachev was." Gorbachev sensed that, which helps to explain his pleasure in her company. Sir Geoffrey's own opinion wasn't quite as exalted: "I thought he was an intelligent man—an able all-rounder."[59]

GORBACHEV'S TALKFESTS with West European leaders, strikingly warmer than his frigid encounters with the East Europeans, counted as diplomatic successes at home. By the end of 1988, he felt himself entirely comfortable with Western leaders—not hidebound Communist party chieftains, and not just socialists like Mitterrand—but thoughtful, card-carrying capitalist statesmen like Thatcher and Kohl. Reagan, transformed though he was, didn't make the cut on intellectual grounds, but following Reykjavik, he became not just a former adversary but a real friend.

CHAPTER 11

SUMMITS
GALORE
1987–1988

AFTER THE STALEMATE AT REYKJAVIK in October 1986 and the bad feeling that followed it in Washington and Moscow, who would have predicted that the next two years would see three extraordinary U.S.-Soviet summits? Early in 1987, Gorbachev found himself in a quandary: How should he respond to Reagan's rigid commitment to SDI? Matching it was impossible, given the high cost and lagging Soviet technology. The military proposed an "asymmetrical" response, a massive buildup of offensive nuclear weapons that could overwhelm any American attempt to shoot them down; specifically they suggested 117 scientific and 86 research projects and 165 experimental programs at the cost of up to 50 billion rubles over ten years.[1] But that expense would gut reforms at home, while returning to the worst of the cold war. So instead, Gorbachev broke up the disarmament package he had insisted on at Reykjavik (a slowing of SDI in return for massive cuts in intercontinental and intermediate-range nuclear weapons), put SDI and ICBMs aside, and mounted a campaign to reduce only intermediate nuclear forces (INF). His efforts and Reagan's produced the first summit by the end of the year, but it wasn't easy.

The Kremlin climate was favorable. Yakovlev proposed the move, in a memo. Ligachev supported it: "By agreeing immediately to cut medium-range missiles, we'll win over public opinion without weakening our defenses."[2] With Republicans losing the Senate in the November 1986 elections, the Iran-Contra scandal raging, and the president's personal popularity plummeting, Reagan was receptive, too. Soviet Defense Minister Sokolov privately damned the notion of destroying a whole class of weapons as "a state crime."[3] But he got a consolation prize: Moscow set off its first nuclear blast since 1985 at the Semipalatinsk testing range in Kazakhstan.[4]

Why focus on intermediate-range rockets? Because the most deadly threat Moscow faced was from Pershing II missiles positioned in Western Europe, with a five-minute flight time to the Kremlin, and because Reagan himself had once suggested eliminating INF. But Reagan administration hard-liners endorsed the proposal because they were certain the Soviets would never accept it. And before Secretary of State Shultz came to Moscow in April 1987 to explore it, a series of spy scandals set a bad tone: Soviet recruitment of Americans working for the CIA, FBI, and the National Security Agency; U.S. Marines apparently allowing Soviet agents into top-secret areas of the U.S. embassy in Moscow; eavesdropping devices found in the beams of the new embassy chancery (under construction precisely because there were so many bugs in the old building on Tchaikovsky Street). Shevardnadze thought some in the U.S. administration welcomed the scandals as a way to scuttle the talks.[5] Gorbachev seemed so discouraged that at one point he told the Politburo, "Apparently normalizing U.S.-Soviet relations will be the work of future generations."[6]

When Gorbachev and Shultz sat down to talk in St. Catherine's Hall in the Great Kremlin Palace, new issues arose: Shultz further hardened Reagan's stance on SDI.[7] His position on Afghanistan, Gorbachev said, put a "stick in the spokes." Shultz stalled on the main issue of INF cuts, insisting that before Washington could negotiate, it would have to build enough short-range missiles (those with a range of less than 500 miles) to match Soviet levels.[8] Gorbachev attacked the Reagan administration for acting as if all it had to do was "put out a basket and collect concessions" from a weakened Soviet Union.[9] "I'm weeping for you," replied Shultz with a smile. The talks went nowhere, Gorbachev told the Politburo.[10]

Gorbachev had made striking concessions. He offered the most comprehensive regime of inspection and verification that Moscow had ever presented, going beyond what the United States itself was prepared to accept. Ignoring advice from Marshal Akhromeyev and former ambassador Dobrynin, he was ready to eliminate short-range SS-23 rockets (known as the Oka, after the Russian river). That infuriated Akhromeyev and Dobrynin but didn't sway Shultz. The military prided itself on the Oka—all 239 of them, recently deployed, single-stage, solid-fueled, easily mobile, and readily launched from truck-like launchers. The military listed the Oka's range as only 250 miles, but Washington claimed it could fly much farther.[11]

Akhromeyev wasn't present when Gorbachev offered up the Oka, and when he learned of Gorbachev's concession, he rushed into the general secretary's office to complain. Gorbachev said he had "forgotten" the "warning" from Akhromeyev and Dobrynin, so the marshal suggested that Shultz, who was still in Moscow, be informed. Gorbachev, enraged, shouted, "Are you suggesting that the secretary of state be told that I, the general secretary, am incompetent in military matters, and that after being corrected by Soviet generals, I am changing my position and going back on my word?"[12]

Shultz insisted on consulting West European allies before proceeding further with INF negotiations. Still, Gorbachev came away with the same rapport with Shultz that he had with his favorite West European leaders. "Shultz is special," Gorbachev told the Politburo afterward.[13] Who else would have unfurled two large four-color pie charts during a break in the talks, visual aids showing the distribution of world GNP, and projecting various nations' prospects to the year 2000? Who else would have explained to Gorbachev that the world was moving quickly from the industrial to the information age; that so-called less-developed countries were rapidly gaining on both the United States and the USSR; that manufacturing was now global in scope? (At this point Shultz displayed a shipping label for an integrated circuit that read, "Made in one or more of the following: Korea, Hong Kong, Malaysia, Singapore, Taiwan, Mauritius, Thailand, Indonesia, Mexico, Philippines.") The "philosophical implications" of all this, Shultz explained, were that scientists in any one country would have to be in constant touch with others around the world. The distinction between capital and labor (central to both Marxist and non-Marxist thought) was becoming obsolete because "we have entered a world in which the truly important capital is human capital—what people know, how freely they exchange information and knowledge."[14]

Shultz's own aides and associates doubted that this approach, that of a former professor rather than a diplomat, would work. "He was trying to get inside of Gorbachev's mind," said Assistant Secretary of State Rozanne Ridgeway.[15] "None of the rest of us took it seriously," recalled Ridgeway's deputy, Thomas Simons, "and I'm not sure Gorbachev did either."[16]

In fact, he did. He felt Shultz was not only "realistic" and "serious," but had potential as an "intellectual, a man of creative imagination, capable of taking the long view." In other words, he reminded Gorbachev of himself.[17] "We should have more of this kind of talk," he told Shultz.[18] Shultz agreed. He returned home "more convinced than ever," Ambassador Matlock recalled, that he was making progress and there was "a good chance" of a summit in Washington by the end of the year.[19]

Eliminating intermediate-range missiles wasn't popular in the Republican party or with West European governments, one reason for Shultz's relatively hard line in Moscow. Richard Nixon, Henry Kissinger, and Brent Scowcroft warned against breaking the nuclear chain— from tactical to short-range to intermediate-range to intercontinental missiles—that had allegedly deterred a Soviet attack, or nuclear threat, on the continent. The British and French agreed. "I think I'm the only person left in this government who wants to try to see the completion of an INF treaty with the Soviets," President Reagan told his new chief of staff, Howard Baker. Public opinion polls, however, especially in Britain, Italy, and West Germany, where American missiles were based, showed more trust and confidence in Gorbachev than in Reagan. In June, NATO approved the "double-zero" idea of banning both intermediate- and short-range missiles. A month later, Gorbachev offered "global double zero": eliminating such missiles in Asia as well. Previously, he had insisted on keeping at least a hundred, theoretically to match U.S. deployments, in Asia, but also, no doubt, to intimidate the Chinese.[20]

ON THE EVENING OF MAY 28, a small, one-engine airplane descended low over the Lenin Mausoleum in Red Square and, to the amazement of strollers, landed just south of St. Basil's Cathedral. The pilot was a nineteen-year-old West German, Mathias Rust. He had flown undisturbed across four hundred miles of Soviet territory. Rust had come on "a mission of peace" to present Gorbachev with a plan for a nuclear-weapons-free world—or so he tried to tell the crowd that gathered around him in Red Square. After some confusion, Rust was hustled off by police to Lefortovo Prison.[21] But his feat allowed Gorbachev to rein in top Soviet military men with doubts about an INF treaty, clearing the path toward another summit.

Gorbachev was in East Berlin when Rust dropped into Red Square. When he arrived at Vnukovo-2 Airport in Moscow the next day, he was angry. He hurried the Politburo and Central Committee welcoming delegation into a private reception room and emerged an hour and a half later "looking flushed and threatening." Grumbling, "Politburo meeting tomorrow at eleven," he stalked to his car. At the Politburo meeting, military commanders sounded incompetent. They hadn't learned of Rust's flight until he landed in Red Square. "Who informed you about it," Gorbachev sneered, "the local traffic police?" Air defense personnel had spotted something on radar, but couldn't tell whether it was a plane or a flock of birds. Jet interceptors fly too fast to bring a small plane down, reported Chief Air Marshal Aleksandr Koldunov. "Well then," Gorbachev retorted, "why didn't they send up a helicopter?" Because the air defense forces don't have any helicopters, Koldunov explained. Marshal Sokolov pleaded guilty to "criminal incompetence" and resigned on the spot. Other top officers were fired. Sokolov was replaced by Dmitry Yazov, a more obedient general, who was promoted over more-senior officers.[22]

Gorbachev called Chernyaev at home on the evening of May 30. "We discredited the country, humiliated our people. . . . But fine, at least everyone here, and in the West, will know where power lies. It is in the hands of the political leadership, the Politburo. This will put an end to gossip about the military's opposition to Gorbachev, that he's afraid of them, and they're close to ousting him."[23]

By September 1987, Moscow had ceased jamming broadcasts of Voice of America and the BBC, though not Radio Liberty. A U.S. congressional delegation led by Speaker Jim Wright was received in April 1987 not only by Gorbachev and Shevardnadze but by Ligachev as well; Wright addressed the Soviet people on television. Soviet and U.S. government experts were now meeting regularly on regional trouble spots such as Nicaragua, Angola, and Cambodia, preparing agreements that would be reached later on. Matlock and the Soviet ambassador to Washington Yuri Dubinin began lecturing at each other's military academies. Gorbachev accepted human rights as a legitimate topic for U.S.-Soviet discussion, Shevardnadze set up an office on human rights in the Foreign Ministry, and many more Soviet citizens were allowed to emigrate to Israel, Germany, and the United States.[24] When Shevardnadze came to Washington in mid-September, the two sides "agreed in principle" on an INF treaty. Reagan and Gorbachev would meet in the fall with "exact dates" to be set when Shultz returned to Moscow.

But the momentum reversed in October. Shultz's improvised train ride from Helsinki (the Moscow airport was fogged in) was positively festive, and it was matched by his reception at the train station in Moscow on October 21. His preliminary talks with Shevardnadze went well. So he wasn't prepared for what happened in St. Catherine's Hall. Gorbachev greeted him warmly and spoke positively about the INF treaty, but then suddenly turned cold. He waved a State Department document, "Soviet Intelligence Activities: A Report on Active Measures and Propaganda, 1986–87," published in October in conformity with a 1985 law. It was "shocking," he said. It alleged that a "Mississippi Peace Cruise" Gorbachev had hailed during his 1985 summit with Reagan was "being used by the Soviets to deceive Americans." "So it turns out," Gorbachev continued sarcastically, that "all social movements in the USSR are agents of the KGB" and "perestroika itself is only a means to deceive the West and insidiously prepare the ground for further Soviet expansion." Despite everything he had been doing to improve relations, the United States couldn't seem to exist without portraying the Soviet Union as the enemy. "What kind of society is it that requires such distortions?"

Shultz couldn't resist citing Afghanistan and the shooting down of the Korean airliner to explain U.S. "skepticism" about the USSR.

"How much did the U.S. pay for the death benefit of the pilot who flew KAL 007?" Gorbachev shot back, implying he was an American spy.

"I will not dignify that comment with a response," Shultz snapped.

But, determined to fight back whenever Gorbachev attacked, he accused Moscow of spreading rumors that the United States had invented AIDS.

Gorbachev subsided, but refused to set a date for the Washington summit. "I will report to the Soviet leadership," he told Shultz, "and I assume you will report to the President." If Gorbachev couldn't come to Washington to sign the INF treaty, Shultz retorted, another way to sign the treaty could be found. Gorbachev said he would write directly to the president about this. With that, the meeting was over.[25]

Shultz wasn't totally surprised. In all their meetings, Gorbachev "always precipitated at least one episode of tension and acrimony."[26] Still, Shultz felt something unusual had transpired, something he "couldn't quite place his finger on." Something had changed, he told his delegation when they returned to the embassy and crowded into its security vault. Until then he had viewed Gorbachev as "super-sure of himself." Now he remembered a line from Carl Sandburg's poem "Chicago"—"laughing even as an ignorant fighter laughs who has never lost a battle." "Today," Shultz told his colleagues, "he no longer looks to me like a boxer who has never been hit. This boxer has been hit."[27]

Gorbachev's own colleagues were troubled by his behavior. There was "a heavy silence," his interpreter Palazhchenko remembered, when the Soviet side (Shevardnadze, Dobrynin, Akhromeyev, Chernyaev, and others) repaired to a nearby room for tea. When Gorbachev finally spoke, it was only to summarize the meeting. Again silence, until Chernyaev spoke up: "So, did we try in vain? Did we bend over backward on INF and come so close to a treaty just to see the whole thing ruined now?"

"Don't boil over, Anatoly!" Gorbachev responded. "We'll have to think over what happened. I said I would write the president a letter. I'll do it soon." Ordinarily, one of Shevardnadze's deputies accompanied Shultz to the airport to say goodbye. This time the foreign minister did so himself.[28]

What happened in St. Catherine's Hall? Gorbachev had indeed been hit—by Boris Yeltsin. Yeltsin delivered his speech attacking Gorbachev to the Central Committee (treated in chapter 8) on the same October day that Shultz arrived in Moscow. That speech, along with the orgy of attacks on Yeltsin that followed, shocked Gorbachev into thinking that "things were not going right, that something yet to come was wrong.

It was a vague feeling, and Gorbachev does not like vague feelings," reflected Palazhchenko in 2007.

Beyond that, the KGB constantly told Gorbachev that, despite all he had done to reform his country and end the cold war, the Americans were still "at the old game of trying to undermine the Soviet leadership." The State Department document that Gorbachev waved at Shultz was less offensive than other documents with which the KGB plied him, including secret U.S. intelligence reports that dismissed Gorbachev and perestroika as either not significant or fated to fail. "Gorbachev still resents this and has hard feelings about it today," said Palazhchenko twenty years later.[29]

Palazhchenko didn't know or wouldn't say which purloined U.S. intelligence reports so agitated his boss. Could one of them have been "Gorbachev's Gameplan: The Long View," prepared at about this time by Robert Gates, then deputy director of central intelligence? Gorbachev was trying to modernize the Soviet economy, Gates granted, but not "to make Soviet citizens more prosperous, but to strengthen the USSR at home" and "further consolidate and expand Soviet power abroad." Gorbachev wanted "significant reductions in weapons, but only in ways that protect existing Soviet advantages." Gorbachev was still providing billions to clients in the Third World and seeking "to weaken ties between the U.S. and Western allies." Despite Gorbachev's reforms, the Communist party "certainly will retain its monopoly of power and the basic structures of the Stalinist economy will remain." Gorbachev intended to make the USSR "a more competitive and stronger adversary in the years ahead."[30]

Gates can't be blamed for not seeing the future, but he missed almost entirely the trajectory that would take Gorbachev there. If Gorbachev saw something like Gates's memorandum (classified "Super Sensitive"), he put hard feelings aside; he wrote to Reagan on October 28, describing his talks with Shultz as "business-like, constructive and, most importantly, productive," and suggesting the first ten days of December "would be the most preferable period for my trip to Washington."[31]

When Shultz and Shevardnadze met in Geneva on November 23, the atmosphere, Shultz recalls, was "entirely positive," and they resolved their last minor differences on the INF treaty. Shultz felt triumphant. An entire class of nuclear weapons was going to be eliminated. Gorbachev had agreed to destroy 1,500 deployed warheads, while the United States would eliminate only 350, all verified by measures including complete inventories of weapons, on-site and short-notice inspections, and continued monitoring of all sites where those weapons had been produced. On December 4, three days before Gorbachev was to arrive in Washington, Shultz reiterated the "information age" themes he had presented to Gorbachev in April. The media mostly ignored the speech, but Shultz had it translated into Russian and presented to Gorbachev, Shevardnadze, Akhromeyev, and others in the Soviet delegation.[32]

THE WASHINGTON SUMMIT of December 7–10, 1987, one of the highest points of Gorbachev's career, started quietly.[33] No music or military honors when his blue and white Ilyushin 62M jetliner touched down at Andrews Air Force Base at dusk on a clear but chilly Monday; the official ceremonial welcome would occur the next morning at the White House. Given tight security, no members of the public, or even Andrews personnel, were present when Gorbachev, wearing a dark suit, overcoat, and fedora, and his wife, in a knee-length silver fur coat, were greeted on the magenta carpet by Secretary of State Shultz and his wife, Helena, along with Ambassador Matlock and other officials. Descending from the plane with Gorbachev were Yakovlev, Marshal Akhromeyev, and former ambassador Dobrynin. The only audience for Gorbachev's brief, unexceptional arrival statement, expressing hope for "a constructive dialogue and for better relations," was a crowd of reporters and photographers.

Nor did Gorbachev's formal talks with Reagan break new ground. In fact, in some ways they went backward. Reagan began the first meeting on Tuesday morning with human rights, as was his habit, giving Gorbachev a list of Soviet citizens and asking they be granted exit visas. He further hardened his stance on SDI, wanting to "shorten a bit" the ten-year delay he had previously accepted before it could be deployed. He rolled out another of his Hollywood fantasies (that "confronted with a hostile threat from another planet, our differences would disappear and we'd be totally united") and then a personal plea—that Gorbachev "humor him a bit by letting him see the deployment of advanced strategic defenses in his lifetime." Gorbachev kept his temper, thanking Reagan at one point for the "tact" with which he had raised the "delicate and sensitive" issue of human rights.[34]

The second session, on Tuesday afternoon, was worse. This time, Gorbachev took the lead, impressing Reagan's new national security adviser, Colin Powell, who jotted down, "Bright. Fast. Quick turning radius. Vigorous. Solid. Feisty. Colorful speech . . . tossing off terms like 'MIRV' and 'depressed trajectories' and the throw weights of SS-12's 13's, 18's and 24's like a wonk in the U.S. Arms Control and Disarmament Agency."[35] Reagan's response was his familiar maxim: It wasn't arms that created distrust, but distrust that created armaments. Gorbachev was dissecting domestic Soviet politics (saying he didn't so much face "political opposition" as opposition in the mind of every Soviet citizen, all of whom were "children of their time") when Reagan suddenly told a joke: an American scholar on his way to the Soviet Union chatted with two young cabbies who drove him to and from the airports in New York and Moscow. He asked both, who had taken time out from their studies, what they would do when they finished their education. "I haven't decided yet," answered the American. "They haven't told me yet," was the Soviet cabbie's response.[36]

As Reagan finished the story, Powell recalled, "the Americans wanted to disappear under the table, while Gorbachev stared ahead expressionless." Shultz was disturbed and disappointed; if Gorbachev had been allowed to continue, the discussion "would have been revealing to us and possibly helpful to him." Shultz nudged the meeting to a close by saying that joint working groups were waiting for instructions. Afterward he dared tell his boss, "That was a disaster. That man is tough. He's prepared. You can't just sit there telling jokes." The unflappable Reagan didn't seem taken aback. "Well, what do we do now?" he asked.[37]

A brief Wednesday morning meeting, one-on-one in the Oval Office with only interpreters present, was better. The president started by handing Gorbachev an autographed baseball from Joe DiMaggio, who had attended the previous evening's state dinner and asked for Gorbachev's autograph. Far more important, Reagan committed himself to another summit in Moscow, perhaps in early summer. Gorbachev did not condition that meeting on a prior agreement on strategic arms limitations. But at longer session later that day, Reagan demanded that SDI testing in space be permitted and Gorbachev fought back. SDI was not acceptable politically, militarily, or economically. The United States was "simply squeezing more and more concessions out of its partner." "If you respect me," went a Russian proverb, "don't make a fool of me. Tell me what you want."[38]

Reagan seemed intransigent on Afghanistan on Thursday morning, refusing to stop aid to the mujahideen, and he didn't pick up on Gorbachev's hint that he was ready to pursue peace in Nicaragua. Gorbachev remembered saying at one point in the talks, "You, Mr. President, are not the judge and I am not on trial." But at Thursday's working luncheon, Gorbachev hailed the summit as "a landmark." It had witnessed "important agreements" and other questions had been "discussed intensively." Most important, the atmosphere had been "good" and there had been "mutual understanding." For all this, Gorbachev paid tribute to the president. Gorbachev even descended to Reagan's level, joining in an exchange of lame jokes. The president's was about a chicken with three legs who ran so fast the farmer who raised him couldn't catch him, Gorbachev's about Russian drunkards. After another Reagan joke (about an American who complains to the president about how he's running the country, and a Russian who boasts he, too, can complain to the general secretary about how Reagan is running his country), "Gorbachev howled," Reagan recalled. If so, Gorbachev hadn't lost his touch as an actor.[39]

If the formal talks were mostly sterile, why did Gorbachev celebrate the summit? Because almost everything else about it seemed extraordinary, both to Gorbachev and to Americans. The INF Treaty signing (scheduled at precisely 1:45 p.m. on Tuesday on the advice of Nancy Reagan's California astrologer) was, Gorbachev said, "a historic milestone in the chronicle of man's eternal quest for a world without wars." But the staging of the ceremony captivated him as well: the U.S. Marine Band playing American and Soviet marches in the foyer; congressional and military leaders, the chief of staff of the Soviet armed forces, and other Soviet and American officials waiting eagerly in the East Room; Reagan and Gorbachev striding together down the long red-carpeted corridor. The atmosphere was "triumphant," Gorbachev recalled. "The event was televised. The audience greeted us with a standing ovation." After the signing, "Reagan and I exchanged a firm, manly handshake and then addressed the American and Soviet peoples and the whole world." The friendly feeling between the two men was obvious, Shultz recalled. "*Doveryai, no proveryai*; trust, but verify"—Reagan again quoted his favorite Russian adage, mangling the pronunciation. "You repeat that at every meeting," Gorbachev chuckled. "I like it," said Reagan with his familiar smile and nod. *Washington Post* television critic Tom Shales compared the ceremony to "Christmas, Hanukah, the Fourth of July and your most fondly remembered birthday party all rolled into one."[40]

The full-honors arrival ceremony on the White House south lawn that morning had been stirring as well: a twenty-one-gun salute, a fanfare from U.S. Army Herald Trumpets, the U.S. Army Band playing the two national anthems, the Third U.S. Infantry Fife and Drum Corps marching before the two leaders as they stood side by side, even two remarkably similar speeches by the president and his guest. The formal, black-tie state dinner that night at the White House was magnificent: Gorbachev, the leader of an allegedly proletarian state, dressing down in a dark-blue business suit with a wine-and-dark-blue striped tie, his wife in a two-piece black-brocade gown with a long narrow skirt, pearl necklace, and earrings. They were greeted at the South Portico by the Reagans (he in black tie, she in a black beaded Galanos gown with diamond drop earrings) to the sound of "Ruffles and Flourishes" and "Hail to the Chief." The 126 A-list guests ranged from actor James Stewart to the Reverend Billy Graham to former Harlem Globetrotter Meadowlark Lemon; pianist Van Cliburn played Brahms, Rachmaninoff, and Debussy, followed by "Moscow Nights," with the Gorbachevs and the rest of the Soviet delegation singing along. The song took Gorbachev back to the 1957 Moscow Youth Festival for which it was written, a year before Cliburn electrified the world by winning the Tchaikovsky Piano Competition in Moscow. "We didn't hold back," recalled Gorbachev who prided himself on his strong singing voice. Afterward, walking past a portrait of Lincoln on a White House wall, his interpreter overheard two American generals saying something Gorbachev remembered when writing his memoirs: "What would old man Lincoln say? The White House draped with a red flag with a hammer and sickle, and inside they're singing 'Moscow Nights!'"[41]

A grand luncheon in the State Department's elegant diplomatic receptions rooms the next day. "Everyone wanted to come," Shultz recalled, "The crowd was the largest ever for such an event." "People came from all corners of America," Gorbachev remembered. "'The cream of society.'" Donald Trump supposedly fit that description; so did Ross Perot. Seated at Gorbachev's table were Pepsico chairman Donald Kendall, philanthropist Brooke Astor, and Senator Alan Simpson (R–Wyo.). "Gorbachev's strong, he's tough as hell, and he likes the reputation," Simpson said afterward. "He's not one of those guys with a 2,000-mile stare." Senator John Warner (R–Va.) found Gorbachev to be "an inspiring politician. It takes a politician to know a politician." Shultz opted for a short toast, but made sure it included yet another "information age" lesson: "openness to ideas, information and contacts is the key to future success." Gorbachev considered Shultz the perfect host, who "knew how to create a warm, friendly atmosphere." Gorbachev thought his own speech his best oration in Washington, and it probably was: "Two world wars, an exhausting cold war, plus small wars—all destroying millions of lives. Isn't this a high enough price to pay for adventurism, arrogance, contempt for the interests and rights of others . . . ? Humanity has been forced to put up with this for too long. We can no longer allow it."

"How far we had come from the days of tension with Brezhnev, Andropov and Gromyko," Shultz thought to himself. "A transformation had occurred."[42]

Gorbachev did extensive entertaining of his own, staging separate meetings at the Soviet embassy with intellectual, cultural, and political luminaries, media moguls and star reporters, congressmen, and business leaders; welcoming President and Mrs. Reagan for a formal dinner. He was animated and engaged on all these occasions, but seemed particularly pleased by the presence of George Kennan, Henry Kissinger, John Kenneth Galbraith, Gore Vidal, James Baldwin, John Denver, Robert De Niro, Arthur Miller, Paul Newman, Yoko Ono, Gregory Peck, and Meryl Streep, whose names he lists proudly in his memoirs. Speaking without notes, jabbing his fingers into the air, and leaning in toward his audience, he cited "something very profound," the "awareness that we cannot go on as we are, we cannot leave as it is the state of relations between our two peoples," and credited it to intellectuals, "the yeast of society as it were." The response was ecstatic: "The things he said were almost too good to be true," gushed Joyce Carol Oates, delighted that Raisa Gorbachev said she'd read her novel *Angel of Light*. "He's a very gifted performer," noted Paul Newman. "He'd make a good actor because he's loose and you don't see the machinery of that looseness."[43]

Congressmen and senators got their ninety-minute meeting on Wednesday at 9 a.m. in the ornate Gold Hall of the Soviet embassy. Actually, Gorbachev wanted to address a joint session of Congress; many years later he still resented being denied that honor. "Why else," he asked in his memoirs, would a visitor have been told no, except to deny him the chance to "score points"? Or was it that Democrats were trying to keep Reagan from reaping more credit? In this light, his self-effacing remarks to his audience ("When you look closely you will see that I am not exceptional. I am just like other people. I am a normal person.") implied a rebuke: just because he was normal, he should have been treated like other leaders who got to address Congress.

Gorbachev vigorously defended the Soviet human rights record, but also admitted he faced political opposition at home. "He's not a B.S.-er," said Senator Simpson afterward, "I'd rather sit in a room with a guy who comes at you like six headlights—like a Mack truck—instead of someone who just sits there and picks around the issues. He wasn't defensive at all. His neck muscles didn't stick out." Assistant House minority leader Trent Lott (R–Miss.) was "stunned by his candor." "It's obvious when you sit with him that he's a world leader," said California Democratic Congressman Tony Coelho. "He fills the room." "No notes whatsoever," marveled House minority leader Robert Michel (R–Ill.). "He never once turned to any of his advisers. He knew exactly what he was going to say."[44]

Some twenty publishing executives got the treatment several hours later, except that this time, perhaps weary from the frantic pace, Gorbachev seemed irritable. After a lengthy lecture, he allowed his guests to speak, but refused to answer direct questions. "I did not come here to be interviewed, but to have a conversation. If you want an interview, I will ask you questions." He seemed particularly touchy about human rights. Given America's "handling of the poor and the homeless, what right does it have to be the teacher? Who gave it the moral right?"

Thursday's breakfast with eighty leading business executives was more upbeat. After all, Gorbachev wanted their business, and they wanted his. Occidental Petroleum chief Armand Hammer, who had been buttering up Soviet leaders since Lenin, said, "I've never seen such enthusiasm" from businessmen about a Soviet leader. Alexander Trowbridge, president of the National Association of Manufacturers, was more realistic about his colleagues' reaction: they walked out "less afraid of trying than when they walked in." Jack Valenti, president of the Motion Picture Association, was wowed by the Soviet leader's "animal energy." "You're now running third in the Iowa primary," he told him. "But I already have a job," laughed Gorbachev.[45]

The Soviet embassy was a little less glittering for its formal dinner than the White House had been the night before. Large men in drab suits supplemented security provided by American police outside. But Raisa Gorbachev looked ravishing in a gold, two-piece evening gown, as did Nancy Reagan in a black dress with blue-gold design. Vodka and champagne flowed. Bolshoi Opera star Yelena Obraztsova sang. Reagan toasted in Russian: "*Za vashe zdorov'e*—To your health!" Gorbachev added, "Until we meet in Moscow!" Reagan followed Gorbachev's toast in a printed English translation. Mrs. Gorbachev helped Vice President George Bush do the same by telling him when to turn the page. Bush returned the favor with "a little levity" on "a rather somber evening." Finding the mezzo-soprano to be "very talented, but not very pretty," he leaned over to Mrs. Gorbachev as Obraztsova was starting her final song, and whispered, "I think I'm falling in love with her." "You better not," she replied sternly. "Remember what happened to Gary Hart," the Democratic senator who abandoned his presidential campaign after being caught in an extramarital adventure. Of course, Gorbachev's wife was joking, but Bush wasn't so sure: he looked in her eyes to "see if she was kidding; but no, I think she was serious."[46]

Then there was the famous walkabout. Gorbachev and Bush were driving from the Soviet embassy to the White House when Gorbachev's car screeched to a stop at the corner of Connecticut Avenue and L Street. Cars racing ahead of Gorbachev's in the Secret Service/KGB caravan jammed on the brakes and backed up. Security agents jumped onto newspaper vending machines trying to form a protective cordon. Crowds lining the sidewalk rushed forward. "The door opened and he got out," an account executive for Wang Laboratories said afterward. "He walked over and shook my hand. I'm still shaking. It was like the coming of the second Messiah or something." Customers and waiters at Duke Zeibert's popular restaurant rushed to the balcony overhead. By a stroke of luck (PR couldn't have arranged it, especially not Soviet PR), the offices of the *New York Times*, *Time* magazine, the *Wall Street Journal*, the *Washington Post*, and ABC News were a few blocks away, so reporters quickly swarmed the scene. Bush, who stood at the edge of the crowd, was mostly ignored. "It was an amazing sight," he recalled, "and it was like a shot of adrenaline to him. He got back into the car visibly uplifted by the warm reception." Gorbachev was an hour and half late to the White House. "I thought you'd gone home," cracked Reagan. Gorbachev smiled. "I had a chat with a group of Americans who stopped the car."[47]

It was raining on the South Lawn during the White House departure ceremony on Thursday afternoon, but Gorbachev, recalled Powell, was "sunny as a politician who had just won a primary." At his press conference three and a half hours later, Gorbachev droned on for seventy-five minutes (about progress made and still to be made) and then took questions for forty-five more. Losing his touch from exhaustion? Returning to his norm as the tension wound down? Overconfidence in his own oratory, certainly, but some self-doubt as well? "I understand you watched my press conference," he said to Shultz who joined him at the Soviet diplomatic compound afterward. How did it go? "You went on much too long," Shultz answered. "Well," Gorbachev replied, clapping Shultz on the back, "at least there's one guy around here who tells you what he thinks."[48]

Other unprecedented moments occurred during the summit. At one point, Reagan suggested to Gorbachev, "Why don't you call me Ronnie, and I, with your permission, will call you, Michael."[49] Marshal Akhromeyev huddled with his Joint Chiefs of Staff counterparts at the Pentagon. Vladimir Kriuchkov, head of all the KGB's foreign operations and soon to be its chief, dined with CIA Deputy Director Robert Gates and Colin Powell at Maison Blanche, a swish downtown restaurant. Offered Johnnie Walker Red scotch, Kriuchkov, looking like an elderly academic with thinning gray hair and a cardigan sweater under his suit jacket, ordered Chivas Regal instead. Did this imply he knew the difference and wanted to show he deserved the best? "How powerful the United States seems," he confessed. "You can feel the power." But "the Soviet Union is not a weak, poor country that can be pushed around," he insisted plaintively.[50]

Meanwhile, the saga of the first ladies continued. Well before December 7, Mrs. Reagan invited Mrs. Gorbachev to tea, or to lunch, or to "whatever she preferred," as Powell put it. When Mrs. Gorbachev didn't reply immediately (probably the result of Russian incompetence rather than arrogance on the part of Raisa), Mrs. Reagan was "offended." Mrs. Gorbachev had already accepted an invitation from Democratic fund-raiser Pamela Harriman to meet with a group of female power brokers: Supreme Court Justice Sandra Day O'Connor, Senators Barbara Mikulski and Nancy Kassebaum, *Washington Post* publisher Katharine Graham, and Hanna Gray, president of the University of Chicago. ("This is the first person I've ever met who talks more than I do," Mikulski said afterward.) Powell's complaint to Ambassador Dubinin produced Mrs. Gorbachev's RSVP twenty-four hours later, on December 5.

"Raisa and I hadn't seen each other in two years," Mrs. Reagan recalled, "but nothing had changed." The two women "barely looked at each other" during the summit's opening ceremony, noted a keen-eyed journalist. "Raisa never once mentioned my recent cancer surgery," remembered Mrs. Reagan, "or asked me how I was feeling," or offered "condolences on the death of my mother." Mrs. Reagan assumed "the Soviets know everything," so her guest must have known "what I had gone through a few weeks earlier." Another case of overestimating the adversary? Almost certainly.[51] Russians don't generally talk about illness and death in the family.

After her surgery and her mother's death, Mrs. Reagan was "wearing black and was not in a terribly good state," Ambassador Matlock's wife, Rebecca, recalled. But Mrs. Gorbachev arrived "looking like a snow maiden in all sorts of white fur." And the first thing Raisa said to Nancy was, "Oh, we missed you in Reykjavik," although Mrs. Reagan hadn't been invited to Reykjavik. Mrs. Gorbachev hadn't been invited either, but had gone anyway.[52]

When their husbands headed for the West Wing after the opening ceremony, Mrs. Reagan entertained Mrs. Gorbachev, along with Barbara

Bush, Rebecca Matlock, Helena Shultz, and Liana Dubinin. Mrs. Reagan had "a good idea of what to expect," she recalled, but her guests were shocked when "Raisa proceeded to lecture us for the entire hour" about Russian history, the Soviet political system, and the absence of homeless people in the USSR. "That was the rudest thing I've ever seen," a guest told the first lady afterward.

Mrs. Gorbachev returned the next morning for a private tour of the White House. Awaiting her guest's late arrival, Mrs. Reagan denied to reporters that the two first ladies didn't get along. "So silly," she said. "It's so silly." But it wasn't. When Mrs. Reagan tried to show Mrs. Gorbachev a portrait of Pat Nixon in the lower hall, Mrs. Gorbachev was obviously more interested in an abstract painting on the opposite wall, about which her hostess knew nothing. Mrs. Reagan tried to keep moving, but Mrs. Gorbachev kept wanting to talk to the press, and when Mrs. Reagan "tried to put my hand on her arm, she pulled away." Asked her impression of the White House, Mrs. Gorbachev replied, "It's an official house. A human being would like to live in a regular house. This is a museum." Not "a very polite answer," Mrs. Reagan remembered, "especially from someone who hadn't even seen the private living quarters!" To which she hadn't been invited, one might add, and whose existence she may not even have known about. It didn't help that after Mrs. Gorbachev lamented the Soviet Union's colossal wartime losses, and Mrs. Reagan countered with American Civil War losses, Mrs. Gorbachev gave a long lecture on the American Civil War.[53]

Mrs. Gorbachev had her own grievances. According to her husband, she planned to make several stops during her tour of Washington, only to have her car race past all of them, supposedly for security reasons. She was also distressed by journalists' obsession with the first ladies' allegedly strained relations.[54] She even tried to help her hostess deflect the endless questions: "I've answered this, I think, five times," snapped an exasperated Mrs. Reagan during the White House tour. "Everything is all right," added Mrs. Gorbachev. "It seems to me Mrs. Reagan gave the answer and that was her word."[55]

The trip left "an unforgettable emotional impression," Gorbachev wrote later. On the way to the airport, Bush, obviously the Republican front-runner to replace Reagan, hailed the summit's results, saying Gorbachev had "splendidly advanced" the prospects for a new era between Moscow and Washington, and that Gorbachev's press conference left "a powerful impression" on him. The reaction to Gorbachev in the Midwest (judging by comments Bush encountered on a televised Q and A he had conducted that morning) "literally borders on euphoria," he told Gorbachev. Most important, Bush seemed to sign on to Reagan's policies. "If elected, I will continue what has been begun." It might not always sound that way in the election campaign, when "things are said that we all regret afterward." But these "should be disregarded." There would be opposition to the INF Treaty's ratification, but it would surely pass since "no one in America is to the right of Reagan."[56]

The mood on the flight back to Moscow was "festive."[57] But not everyone back home was so pleased. Many in the military, and their allies in high party posts, felt betrayed. Oleg Baklanov, Central Committee secretary in charge of the military-industrial complex, warned Gorbachev that the INF Treaty would "fatally break" Soviet-American strategic parity. Generals particularly feared the new system of inspections would reveal well-kept military secrets—not sensational new weapons but rather, as Grachev puts it, "the miserable conditions and poor internal discipline" in the Soviet armed forces.[58]

With these doubters in mind, Gorbachev didn't hold back in his report to the Politburo. Washington "was no Geneva or Reykjavik." Its success was "weighty proof" that "our course" was succeeding. Negotiating the INF Treaty had been "a test for us and our partners." Passing that test opened the way to further nuclear, chemical, and conventional disarmament. Americans' "vast interest" in the summit, plus their "goodwill" and "enthusiasm" even in "smug" Washington, proved that the "image of the enemy" and the "myth" of a Soviet military threat were crumbling."[59]

THE NEXT SUMMIT was held in Moscow from May 29 to June 3, 1988. It was crucial "not to slow down," Gorbachev thought, lest we "fall back," to crown the coming summit in Moscow with deep cuts in strategic nuclear arms.[60]

On the whole, the Moscow summit preparations went more smoothly than in 1987. For the first time, Ambassador Matlock recalls, "there was no verbal wrestling" over whether it would take place. Nor did Gorbachev try, as he had in 1986 and 1987, "to place preconditions on the meeting." Despite his hope for a strategic arms agreement, or at least, on its general principles, he never held the summit "hostage to this or any other specific agreement."[61] Neither did Reagan. But although he still wanted to sign a START treaty in Moscow, Reagan was deterred by sharp Republican resistance to ratifying the INF Treaty, and by the U.S. Navy's refusal ("absurd," according to Matlock) to limit submarine-launched cruise missiles.[62]

"Time is too limited" to complete a START treaty before the Moscow summit, Reagan declared at the end of February.[63] But it took Gorbachev a while to realize and accept that, which helps explain why he blew hot and cold in talks with Shultz that winter. When the two men posed for a photo session in the Kremlin on February 22, American newsman Don Oberdorfer noticed Gorbachev was no longer interested in "banter with the press"; he was "plainly irritated by the need for even this brief delay of the business at hand." Although this time there were no surprises or temper tantrums, whether real or feigned, Deputy Assistant Secretary of State Simons found Gorbachev "subdued."[64]

By the time Shultz returned to Moscow in April, START's dim prospects had sunk in, the Nina Andreyeva affair had exploded, and the critical Nineteenth Party Conference was right around the corner. At first Gorbachev struck Shultz as "self-confident, behaving as if he had no rivals at all," but then, suddenly, he "flew into a tantrum." "Face grim," Colin Powell remembered, "voice tight, hand chopping the air," Gorbachev denounced a speech Reagan had given at the World Affairs Council in Springfield, Massachusetts, the day before. In the speech (which took credit for the Soviet retreat from Afghanistan, repledged aid to Afghan rebels, and called for resistance to Soviet aggression elsewhere), Reagan was appeasing conservatives opposed to INF Treaty ratification. But Gorbachev condemned yet another attempt "to preach to us, lecture us, admonish us." Was Reagan going to "bring this with him" to Moscow? How was Gorbachev going "to explain this? Is the summit going to be a catfight?"[65]

To Shultz, Gorbachev "seemed at a fever pitch." Or was the emotion mostly theatrical to impress his own conservatives? Shultz hadn't read Reagan's Springfield speech; he decided to ignore Gorbachev's outburst. At which point, Gorbachev calmed down. He even recalled Shultz's information-age tutorial in the same room the previous spring: "I welcomed that talk. I have thought about it a lot, and not just by myself. I have consulted experts. If the trends continue as you outlined, our two countries have a lot of reason to cooperate."[66]

Gorbachev seemed prepared to settle for a mostly symbolic summit. Reagan "will come to Moscow and get photographed, we'll give him a good welcome, and that will be that," he told Czech leader Husák in April.[67] It won't be "useless," he informed a visiting Japanese Communist leader.[68] Chernyaev's June 19 diary entry weighed the relative importance of the summit and the Nineteenth Party Conference this way: "We took a break from [conference preparations] due to Reagan's visit."[69]

Ideally, of course, Gorbachev wanted more, but he couldn't afford to have Reagan make the summit a platform for anti-Soviet propaganda. Fortunately, Reagan got the message. After Gorbachev's blowup with Shultz, the president moderated his tone, citing gains already made in relations with Moscow, emphasizing how different Gorbachev was from his predecessors, even telling Soviet interviewers he'd read the Soviet leader's book, *Perestroika*, which made him optimistic about the future.[70]

Like its predecessor in Washington, the Moscow summit was short on substance, long on style, and high on symbolism, enough so Gorbachev could hail it, with some justification, as a victory. The Reagans flew in to Vnukovo-2 Airport at two o'clock on a sunny Sunday afternoon after a two-day rest in Helsinki. While they were en route, Gorbachev's revolutionary "Theses" for the Nineteenth Conference were issued, leading Matlock to tell Reagan, "If Gorbachev means what he says—and he must mean it or he wouldn't present it to a Communist party conference—the Soviet Union will never be the same." All the more ironic, then, that waiting to greet the Reagans at Vnukovo was none other than Gromyko, still titular head of state, and that on arriving, Reagan rolled out another Russian proverb: *Rodilsya, ne toropilsya*, Everything in its own good time—meaning there would be no major agreements signed in Moscow.[71]

Even more than in Washington, the formal talks—four sessions over three days—managed to be both sterile and cordial. As always, Reagan began, on Sunday afternoon in St. Catherine's Hall, with human rights: if Gorbachev would just grant freedom of religion to his people, he would be "a hero, and much of the feeling against his country would disappear like water in hot sun." Gorbachev responded by citing poverty and racial discrimination in America, but then declared himself "very pleased" that the two leaders were "still on friendly terms" and "truly beginning to build trust between the two countries."[72]

The next morning, Gorbachev just as amiably offered "free advice" for which, he said, Henry Kissinger would have charged "millions"; namely, that the president had been deceived about SDI by his former defense secretary Caspar Weinberger. Gorbachev pressed his case on space weapons and seemed irritated when Reagan showed utterly no give, but, recalled Matlock, these exchanges were "not prolonged and were delivered without heat," as if the two were "actors wearily reciting a familiar script after it had been decided to postpone indefinitely the play's opening."[73]

Gift giving set the tone for a one-on-one session in Gorbachev's Kremlin office on Tuesday morning: a denim jacket from the American West for Gorbachev, a scale model of the Kremlin for Reagan. Gorbachev gave the president letters from ordinary Soviet citizens who had named their children Ronald and Nancy. Reagan said he would send photos of himself and his wife to the children named after them. He cited an American example that "fit what Gorbachev wanted to do with perestroika"—of a young pianist who, after developing arthritis, began baking brownies, which she sold to top restaurants and airlines, employing thirty-five people and earning herself more than a million dollars a year.[74]

Gorbachev's most serious démarche came at the first session: without warning, he proposed a joint statement rejecting military solutions to world problems, endorsing "peaceful coexistence as a universal principle of international relations," and recognizing "equality of all states, non-interference in internal affairs, and freedom of socio-political choice." The notion of "free socio-political choice" was very promising; when Gorbachev repeated it at the United Nations in December, many in Eastern Europe took it as an invitation to break from the Soviet bloc. But the term "peaceful coexistence" was anathema to American diplomats, who had long viewed it a cover for continuing cold war. The statement read,

Simons said later, as if it were written by Gromyko. "In fact," he added, "it probably *was* written by Gromyko."[75]

That didn't bother the president. "I like it," he said of Gorbachev's draft. No wonder the Soviet leader raised it again at their last session on Wednesday morning, but by then American diplomats had watered it down. What was wrong with it? Gorbachev demanded to know, leaning forward in his chair, eyes flashing, chin out. Reagan shrugged. Not wanting to admit he had forgotten it, recalled Matlock, the president called for a break to discuss the issue with his advisers. Reagan would have liked to humor Gorbachev, but was persuaded not to. Gorbachev pressed hard, taunting Reagan with his "reluctance to exercise the authority that was clearly his," but finally accepted wording the Americans preferred. Years later, Matlock asked Gorbachev why he had sprung his draft without going through the usual diplomatic preparation. Gorbachev said he done so in order to challenge Reagan to make a decision on his own.[76]

The summit wasn't without concrete achievements: the exchange by the two leaders of the INF Treaty instruments of ratification, an agreement on ballistic missile test launch notification, a vast expansion of cultural, educational, and scientific exchanges, and agreements on transportation, science and technology, maritime search and rescue, fishing, radio navigation, cooperation in space, and peaceful uses of atomic energy. Still, just as Gorbachev's "extracurricular" activities had conquered Washington, so Reagan's were the highlight of his Moscow visit.

The Reagans met with monks at Danilov Monastery, where Mrs. Reagan asked whether Soviet believers and nonbelievers would ever have equal opportunity for advancement in life, and Metropolitan Philaret hoped that after the summit "all such problems would go away." The president met at Spaso House (the American ambassador's residence) with a hundred or so dissidents and refuseniks, who had plagued the Soviet regime for years and been hounded and ostracized in return, but whom Gorbachev was now demonstratively tolerating. At a state dinner in the Kremlin's Chamber of Facets, Reagan summarized at length and gave Gorbachev a videotape of the 1956 film *Friendly Persuasion*, starring Gary Cooper, about a Quaker family during the American Civil War.

Reagan chose it to show "the tragedy of war, the problems of pacifism, the nobility of patriotism and the love of peace." (He either didn't know or had forgotten that its screenwriter, Michael Wilson, had been blacklisted and denied an Oscar nomination because he refused to cooperate with the House Un-American Activities Committee.) At a reciprocal dinner at Spaso House, Reagan aimed higher, quoting the voice of Jesus in Boris Pasternak's Doctor Zhivago poem "The Garden of Gethsemane," and the great poet Anna Akhmatova's "Requiem," about the purges and arrests of the 1930s, probably brought to his attention by Suzanne Massie or James Billington, librarian of Congress and Russian historian, whom Nancy Reagan had enlisted as an adviser. Even if Reagan didn't write his speech, it pleased many in his audience. "This feeling of responsibility before God," said novelist Daniil Granin, "created a feeling of sincerity. Hearing this from a politician is not something I'm used to."[77]

At Moscow State University, Gorbachev's alma mater, Reagan stood under a mammoth white marble bust of Lenin before an immense mosaic of billowing red flags, offering a civics lesson on the virtues of American democracy. He cited Michael Jackson and treated his young audience to old jokes, leaning casually over the lectern with the U.S. presidential seal while answering student questions, getting a standing ovation when he was done. The Reagans' attempt at a stroll down the Arbat, the long, vibrant pedestrian mall filled with street artists, matryoshka sellers, and musicians, quickly turned so chaotic that panicky Soviet security men charged eager onlookers, shoving them aside so the Reagans could return to their limousine. On Tuesday morning the two leaders walked from Gorbachev's Kremlin office in the Kremlin out through Spassky Gate onto the cobblestones of Red Square. The huge expanse had been cleared except for several small clusters of people. "I have great admiration for the women of Russia," Reagan told one group, mainly women. "Shake hands with dedushka [grandfather] Reagan," Gorbachev instructed a towhead he had taken from his mother and cradled in his arms. At one point, Gorbachev, in a light suit, and Reagan in a dark one, stood side by side with arms clasped around each other's waists. Back in the Kremlin, near the gigantic tsar cannon, built too heavy to be shot, a reporter asked Reagan, "Do you still consider this an evil empire?" "No," the president replied, "That was another time, another era." "Are you now old friends?" came another question. "Da, da!" Gorbachev said immediately. "Yes," added Reagan.[78]

By now "Michael" and "Ronnie" *were* "friends." So they could live with the fact that their wives still weren't. "It doesn't take much to make me nervous," Mrs. Reagan confessed in her memoirs, "but I was especially tense before going to Moscow." This was partly because "I was terrified that I might say or do the wrong thing and find myself accidentally starting World War III," but also because another first-lady showdown loomed. Even if Mrs. Gorbachev "hadn't intended to be rude" in Washington, Mrs. Reagan recalled, "now the shoe would be on the other foot." Embarrassed by her rival's seeming mastery of American culture, Mrs. Reagan asked Billington's help on Russian culture. Sure enough, the jousting resumed at the fifteenth-century Assumption Cathedral in the Kremlin, where Mrs. Reagan asked about the icons and whether religious services were held there, especially in 1988, the millennium of Christianity in Russia. (Mrs. Reagan's handlers should have warned her that this was a highly impolitic question.) "Nyet," Mrs. Gorbachev replied curtly. "I hadn't meant to be insulting," insists Mrs. Reagan in her memoirs, but apparently that was "how it was interpreted." Two days later an encounter in the Tretyakov Gallery reprised another scene in Washington, but with roles reversed—Mrs. Reagan resisting Mrs. Gorbachev's

Gorbachev and Reagan strolling in Red Square, Moscow, May 31, 1988.

attempt to get her away from the press: "Now wait a minute. I want to say something. I want to say something, OK?"[79]

What Nancy Reagan wanted to say was "Thank you." But it was hard to get a word in edgewise. As a result, when it turned out Mrs. Gromyko was to escort the first lady to Leningrad, that was quite fine with Mrs. Reagan. But she wasn't pleased at the Gorbachevs' suburban villa (to which they all repaired, along with the Shultzes and Shevardnadzes after a Bolshoi Ballet performance). When the Americans were tired and ready to leave, Mrs. Gorbachev jumped up, saying, "No, no, I want everyone to sit down. I have something to say"—kind things, Mrs. Reagan recalled, "but as usual she went on too long."[80]

On the summit's last day, Gorbachev held his first-ever Moscow press conference, televised live from the newly refurbished Foreign Ministry Press Center. After promising just a few words to the international press corps, he orated for almost an hour, mostly without notes, hailing the summit as "a huge international event," but being careful to avoid "euphoria and excessive optimism." To the Politburo four days later, he was less restrained: "Our prognosis was completely right." The president proved himself "a realist." "He was able to get in touch with the people." The Soviet people were "very friendly to him." The American people could see "our lives, the lives of regular Soviet people" on television. "Overall," a "new turn" had taken place in Soviet-American relations. Ambassador Matlock agreed: Reagan's personal praise for Gorbachev "probably did more than any other single event to build support in the Soviet Union for Gorbachev's reforms."

Much remained to be done, however. The strategic arms agreement, to which Gorbachev attached so much importance, remained as remote as ever. And Reagan's term was in its last half year. The summit's excitement couldn't erase irritating domestic issues; in fact, Gorbachev's press conference resurrected one of them. Yeltsin had held a press interview of his own during the summit, at which he called for Ligachev to be fired. When Gorbachev was asked about this at his news conference, Soviet officials on the dais went white. Reporter Don Oberdorfer "could almost see the wheels of [Gorbachev's] brain turning" until "he went at Yeltsin with sudden ferocity," condemning yet again the views Yeltsin had expressed in October 1987, warning that Yeltsin might be called before the Central Committee again to explain himself, dismissing the all-too-real problem of Ligachev: "The problem is simply nonexistent. That's all."[81]

THE THIRD SUMMIT was held in New York City in December. In the meantime, the Moscow meeting accelerated contacts between Soviet and American officials. Defense Ministers Frank Carlucci (who had replaced Weinberger) and Dmitry Yazov met in Switzerland, then Carlucci flew to Moscow in August. Deputy Secretary of State John Whitehead traveled to Moscow, and in talks on regional conflicts, according to Matlock, "Soviet officials began a serious search for solutions." But although Shultz and Shevardnadze continued strategic arms negotiations, they got nowhere. Given Soviet superiority in conventional weapons, Washington still counted on strategic weapons for deterrence, portending trouble in the Senate for any START agreement reached before the conventional imbalance was rectified. Moreover, Vice President Bush didn't want such an agreement while he was wooing hard-liners in his election campaign.[82]

The answer to this dilemma, Arbatov advised Gorbachev that summer, was a major "unilateral" initiative to command the West's attention. In mid-September, Dobrynin recommended an "extraordinary" early meeting with Reagan's successor before his January inauguration. Gorbachev huddled with his closest advisers (Yakovlev, Shevardnadze, Dobrynin, Chernyaev, Falin) at the Black Sea on October 31. He would speak at the United Nations. He would "present 'the new us.'" He would announce deep unilateral cuts in Soviet armed forces. He had just met with Young Communist League members, and they "overwhelmed me with questions: What do we need such an army for, Mikhail Sergeyevich?" He would describe the UN as an instrument of the new world. He would portray the Soviet Union's role in "the creation of the new world: We are not just calling for it, we are going to act." Churchill's 1946 "Iron Curtain" speech in Fulton, Missouri, marked the beginning of the cold war; Gorbachev's would be "an anti-Fulton—Fulton in reverse."[83]

Gorbachev took his case to the Politburo four days later. He was "clearly nervous," noted Chernyaev, and therefore "agitated and tough." The INF Treaty had been a "little step"; now a "major" one was imperative. He had announced a new military doctrine of "sufficiency" in the summer of 1987, a supposedly defensive stance giving the lie to Western charges that Moscow believed in offensive war. But, Gorbachev admitted, "powerful" Soviet armed forces in East Germany included "pontoon forces" poised to roll westward. So with "all this hanging over them," how could the West "believe our doctrine is defensive?" He had pressed the Americans for more data on their force levels and military spending and said he would provide the same. But if he admitted that "we spend more than twice as much as the U.S." and that "not one country in the world spends as much per capita as we do . . . all our new thinking and our new foreign policy will go to hell."

The next step, therefore, Gorbachev said, was to consider a range of arms-cut options. Did anyone in the Poliburo have any questions? No one did. Only Prime Minister Ryzhkov spoke, his voice "very tense." Without major cuts in military spending, he said, "we can forget about any increase in the standard of living." If the Politburo agreed, Gorbachev added, he would announce "major decisions" at the UN. "Yes, yes," came the chorus.[84]

Preparation of Gorbachev's UN speech, with domestic politics pressing in on all sides, with Kohl, Mitterrand, and other leaders visiting Moscow, and Gorbachev squeezing in a trip to India before he left for New York, was hectic, to say the least. As of November 27, one week after returning from India and another before departing for New York, Gorbachev was just drafting his UN speech. He dictated and redictated his text three times, the last time on the flight to New York. He was determined to present nothing less than "a comprehensive concept of a proper world order and a view of how to achieve it." In addition, he hoped "a positive international response . . . would strengthen my position and help overcome the growing resistance to change in the Soviet Union." Meeting this challenge would require "maximum self-discipline." Once on the plane, he blocked out anything else that might irritate him.[85]

What awaited Gorbachev in New York on December 6, besides the UN General Assembly and the president and vice president of the United

States, was the Big Apple's version of the December 1987 Washington circus. Following brief remarks at Kennedy Airport, Gorbachev set off for the Soviet UN mission in Manhattan in a black ZIL limousine, the forty-car motorcade making the journey in an astounding twenty-five minutes on highways closed to traffic. Hundreds of police blocked off East Sixty-Seventh Street, where the mission was located. Later in the visit, as Gorbachev's convoy of limousines and blue police motorcycles wheeled up Broadway past thousands of cheering fans, he staged a walk-about in front of the Winter Garden Theater, where the musical *Cats* was playing, and then another in front of Bloomingdale's on Third Avenue and Fifty-Ninth Street. UN Secretary-General Javier Pérez de Cuéllar hosted a splashy reception, something he hadn't done for other visiting heads of state during the General Assembly, and a magnificent luncheon (attended, said cosmetics executive Estée Lauder, by "all the people who run the country and New York") at the Pérez de Cuéllars' Sutton Place home. A Gorbachev imitator fooled the all-knowing Donald Trump into greeting him at the Trump Tower, where the Gorbachevs were to visit but never showed up.

Something else happened in Manhattan: the first ladies finally made peace. Their détente was visible at a chic lunch that Mrs. Pérez de Cuéllar gave for them after Gorbachev's UN speech. They smiled at each other and held hands. "Something had clearly changed," Mrs. Reagan recalled. Mrs. Gorbachev even confessed that the Soviets could have done a better job with day care by encouraging mothers to keep children at home for the first few years. She "talked but didn't lecture." She said she would miss Nancy and her husband. The two women exchanged invitations to visit each other's countries. "Believe it or not, I really meant it," remembered Mrs. Reagan, who had figured out a deeper reason for their "difficult" relationship: "We were both enormously self-conscious."[86] Asked many years later whether that was so, Gorbachev said, "I think that's correct."[87]

The pièce de résistance was the UN speech itself. Gorbachev was "anxious" at first. He started "hesitantly," he remembered, "sometimes pausing." But gradually he felt "growing contact with my audience, sensing as if with my very skin that my words and ideas were coming across." As a result, "I gained confidence and apparently in eloquence," for the speech ended to "a storm of applause, which was apparently more than a mere sign of courtesy."[88]

All the ideas Gorbachev had been gathering, pondering, nurturing, and positioning to replace Marxist-Leninist orthodoxy poured forth in their fullest statement yet. The cold war world had fundamentally changed. In the new, interdependent world of global mass communications (pace George Shultz), a "closed" society was impossible. In this world, neither force nor threat of force should be used, "freedom of choice" should have "no exceptions," ideology had no place in international relations, and no one had a monopoly on truth. Then came these dramatic announcements: The Soviet Union would unilaterally reduce its armed forces by 500,000 soldiers; 50,000 of these, along with six tank divisions including 5,000 tanks, assault troops, and all their weapons and combat equipment, would be withdrawn from Eastern Europe. In all, Soviet armed forces in the USSR's European region and on the territory of its East European allies would be reduced by 10,000 tanks, 8,500 artillery systems, and 800 combat aircraft, cuts that amounted (by U.S. calculations) to 10 percent of Soviet armed forces, and a much higher proportion of the forces in Eastern Europe, about which Western strategists had worried for so long.[89]

No wonder, as Matlock recalled, the applause was "more prolonged than any of the assembled delegates could remember."[90] Chernyaev recalled "an eruption of ovations," and that "they would not let M. S. go for a long time. He even had to take a bow as if he were on stage."[91] Gorbachev quotes two of the rave reviews in his memoirs: "Breathtaking," "Risky," "Bold," "Heroic," cheered a *New York Times* editorial. "Perhaps not since Woodrow Wilson presented his Fourteen Points in 1918 or since Franklin Roosevelt and Winston Churchill promulgated the Atlantic Charter in 1941 has a world figure demonstrated the vision of Mikhail Gorbachev." "A speech as remarkable as any ever delivered at the United Nations," proclaimed the *Washington Post*'s Robert Kaiser. "Mikhail Gorbachev today proposed to change the rules the world has lived by for four decades. . . ."[92] "You were a great success," boomed Richard Nixon when he shook hands with Gorbachev afterward. Retired general Andrew Goodpaster, former NATO supreme commander, called Gorbachev's troop reductions "the most significant step since NATO was founded" in 1949. The day after the speech, even the not-so-almighty dollar rose in appreciation, posting its biggest one-day gain since a steep plunge earlier that fall.[93]

Gorbachev understood, Chernyaev recorded in his diary, that the speech was "bigger than a sensation"; it was "a triumph." After that, the summit with Reagan and Bush was an anticlimax. Gorbachev took the ferry to Governors Island, bought by the Dutch from native Americans in 1637, set aside by the British for colonial governors, now a secluded Coast Guard preserve of 173 acres just south of the tip of Manhattan. The president greeted his guest at Quarters One, the Coast Guard commandant's residence, which was brimming with Christmas wreaths, poinsettias, and Soviet and American flags; President-elect Bush politely remained inside so as not to intrude and then quietly joined them; Gorbachev greeted him warmly, grabbing Bush's hand in both of his.[94]

Gorbachev assumed the meeting and lunch that followed would celebrate his UN speech, and that Bush would commit himself to finish the START treaty forthwith. Instead, Reagan merely said he'd had a brief report on Gorbachev's UN speech earlier that morning, but "it all sounded good." He was warm and jovial, of course, and proud, he said, of what he and Gorbachev had accomplished together. Bush, according to Shultz, was "a reluctant presence." He would like "to build on what President Reagan had done," Bush said when asked by Reagan to speak, but he would need "a little time to review the issues." He had no intention of "stalling things," he added, especially since he would have "the extra incentive of the President on the phone from California, getting on his case and telling him to get going." But he didn't commit himself to anything specific. The only bristly moment was when Reagan innocently asked Gorbachev about progress in perestroika. Bush could tell Gorbachev was annoyed: his eyes flashed, he turned red, and he shrugged with his mouth firmly set. But he quickly calmed down when Reagan and Bush said how much they wished to see perestroika succeed.[95]

Gorbachev had hoped to "relax and rest a bit" on Governors Island. But late the previous evening he had received a telegram from Margaret Thatcher mentioning an earthquake in Armenia. How big and damaging a quake wasn't clear until Gorbachev's limo reached the ferry slip, where his security chief, Yuri Plekhanov, called him over to a commu-

Gorbachev with Reagan and Bush on Governors Island, New York, November 30, 1988.

nications car for a phone call from Prime Minister Ryzhkov in Moscow. "It's bad, really bad," Gorbachev said after returning to his car and sitting silently for a moment. "Enormous destruction. I'll have to get in touch with them right after the meeting. It's bad."[96]

"You can imagine my mood" at the meeting, Gorbachev wrote in his memoirs. He had already decided to cut short his stay in New York, cancel his visit to Cuba, and head home the next day. "I tried to seem calm, I pronounced the appropriate phrases, I tried to hurry Reagan and Bush along." Reagan immediately offered American assistance, something Soviet authorities had always refused since World War II. Gorbachev thanked him, but didn't accept the help immediately, although later he did. Gorbachev returned to the Soviet mission, stopping at the World Trade Center to take in the view from the 107th floor, and halting the car to greet the crowd just past the Queensboro Bridge. "He was tired and prepared for bad news at the mission," his interpreter, Palazhchenko, recalled, "but the few minutes with the crowd seemed to recharge him with fresh energy." Raisa Gorbachev was "more somber," according to Palazhchenko, as if fixated on the earthquake and the interethnic strife in the region. "If this tragedy doesn't make them forget

Gorbachev and Bush wave to a crowd.

their quarrels," she said in a low voice, "then I don't know whether anything will."[97]

The next morning the Gorbachevs flew home, then went directly to
Armenia. The quake registered 6.9 on the Richter scale; the damage was
immense: 25,000 eventually perished, 500,000 were left homeless, on
top of 300,000 previous refugees from Azerbaijan. The Gorbachevs wept
at the sight of a boy desperately seeking his mother among the ruins,
unsure whether she was dead or alive. But when they tried to comfort
him, he demanded that Nagorno-Karabakh be returned to Armenia—as
did many other earthquake victims whom the Gorbachevs encountered.
Raisa Gorbacheva's worst fears had come true. She and her husband
were enraged. In a TV interview on their plane leaving Armenia, he
seemed to lose his self-control; his face was dark; he could not understand how people could think of Nagorno-Karabakh when tens of thousands had died.[98]

Back in the USSR, things looked a lot grimmer than at the General
Assembly. And, as Gorbachev would discover in 1989, the wider world,
too, was uglier than the vision of it proclaimed in his UN speech.

CHAPTER 12

1989:
TRIUMPH AND TROUBLE
AT HOME

NINETEEN EIGHTY-NINE WAS a pivotal year in the history of Communism and of the whole twentieth century. The liberation of Eastern Europe—a "velvet revolution" in Czechoslovakia, remarkably smooth transitions in Poland and Hungary, bloody in Romania—and the fall of the Berlin Wall led with startling swiftness to the unification of Germany and its accession to NATO the next year. By then, if not before, most observers would agree, the cold war was really over.

But the epochal events of 1989 abroad would not have occurred without the domestic developments that preceded and accompanied them in the Soviet Union. Gorbachev's innovations at home encouraged East Europeans to reform their own versions of Communist rule, or even to free themselves from Communism entirely. And when they did so, he was mightily distracted by his battle to democratize the USSR itself. Given his own pursuit of democracy, one might say he would never have tried to stop East Europeans from achieving their own. But in fact, he was so preoccupied with internal Soviet events that he barely had time to react to what was happening in Eastern Europe.

Within the USSR, 1989 saw the peak of perestroika and, according to the most reliable public opinion polling, the peak of Gorbachev's personal popularity.[1] The Soviet regime was transformed when mostly free elections were held for the first time in more than seven decades, and a genuine, functioning parliament replaced the rubber-stamp Supreme Soviet.

Yet the same year marked the beginning of the end of perestroika, since these same innovations crippled the institutions that had previously held Soviet society together, failed to replace them with effective new ones, and sharpened crises already undermining Gorbachev's authority and the Soviet system itself: economic decline, ethnic separatism, political polarization both within and outside the Kremlin.

Gorbachev's initial response to the elections and the new Congress of People's Deputies was ecstatic. As time went on, however, his mood darkened and his political skills, as judged by friends and foes alike, began to deteriorate. He was replacing the old political "game," at which he excelled, with a new one that he never really mastered. He had devised the new rules of electoral and parliamentary politics, but their effect was to liberate his radical critics (who proved to be more adept at the new game than he was) while further alienating hard-liners. Gorbachev continued to play the old game to rein in his hard-line critics, but they now attacked him with ferocity and impunity at party meetings previously characterized by at least the appearance of "monolith unanimity."

Taken together, the domestic and foreign pressures on Gorbachev in 1989 were nearly overwhelming, all the more so because of how they began to erode his own sense of himself. On the eve of 1989, in his New Year's address to the Soviet people, he hailed 1988 as a "critical year." A year later he lamented that 1989 had been "the most difficult year" since perestroika began in 1985.[2]

GORBACHEV LATER SUMMARIZED his 1989 strategy this way: "to shift power" from the Communist party to the soviets through free elections, compelling the party "to voluntarily give up its own dictatorship." The party apparatus, which still controlled "the main levers of power," would of course resist "at bayonet point," but they would be pressured by the newly aroused "majority of society," while he himself would engage in "tactical maneuvers" designed to "cut off" Kremlin conservatives and replace them with fresh forces from outside.[3]

But the rules governing elections didn't seem to reflect this strategy. Of the 2,250 legislators in the new Congress of People's Deputies, 750 were to be elected in territorial districts, 750 in districts chosen in ethnic territories (national republics and other smaller entities), and 750 by social organizations: 100 each by the Communist party and the Central Council of Trade Unions, 75 each by the Komsomol, the Soviet Women's Committee, and the War and Labor Veterans' Organization, and 325 by other organizations, such as the Academy of Sciences. Later, the 2,250 elected deputies would themselves select a 542-person Supreme Soviet, which would function as the country's working parliament.

That last twist would distance Supreme Soviet deputies from the electorate. Moreover, reserved seats for the party and other organizations it dominated did not bode well for democracy, since the party itself nominated exactly 100 candidates for its 100 seats. The liberal press dubbed them the "Red Hundred" (a reference to the ultranationalist, anti-Semitic "Black Hundreds," who supported the monarchy in the revolution of 1905). Party-led electoral commissions supervised selection of candidates in territorial districts. The result: 399 districts held uncontested elections; 953 districts ended up with two candidates each, and 163 with three or more.

The electoral process itself was even more complicated than it looked, and surprising in its results. Gorbachev wavered before including himself and his Politburo colleagues in the Red Hundred, rather than having them run in contested district races. His aide turned enemy Boldin insists Gorbachev feared he would lose in more open competition. According to Yakovlev, Gorbachev shrank from posing that sort of challenge to his colleagues. But even reserved party seats weren't entirely safe. Gorbachev ally Vadim Medvedev says his boss feared that if the Central Committee itself had a choice, it would defeat both Ligachev and Yakovlev and perhaps even Gorbachev himself.[4]

Gorbachev worked long and hard picking the Red Hundred. He wasn't pleased with the usual suspects, mostly high-level party officials, nominated by the Central Committee personnel department. He pored over the list for two days, sustained by coffee, tea, and sandwiches, crossing out names and substituting other ones—to the point, laments Boldin, that the list looked "as if it had been prepared by some organization of writers or artists."[5] Gorbachev selected such stars of glasnost as Tengiz Abuladze (director of the groundbreaking anti-Stalinist film *Repentance*), actor turned tribune of the people Mikhail Ulyanov, writers

Chingiz Aitmatov and Daniil Granin, economist Leonid Abalkin, and physicist Yevgeny Velikhov, who, in addition to serving as a wise counselor on disarmament, had been willing to expose himself to near-lethal amounts of radiation while supervising the recovery from Chernobyl. As a grand gesture of gratitude, which Gorbachev wasn't known for showing his close aides, he included Chernyaev, congratulating him twice, once while telling Raisa Gorbacheva on the phone, "We made Anatoly Sergeyevich a candidate today. He's standing right here in front of me." It never occurred to Chernyaev to "thank him back," Chernyaev admitted to his diary, "and I sincerely don't understand why I need this." He considered himself a "behind-the-scenes" person "unfit for an active role in public." Plus, the hundred handpicked deputies were "a vestige of the past, and my appointment even more so."[6]

When the Central Committee finally ratified the party's Red Hundred in March, the only suspense concerned which of them would receive the most "no" votes. Ligachev came in first with 78, Yakovlev was runner-up with 59, while Gorbachev himself garnered 12.

The Academy of Sciences also diverged from the electoral script. Members of its scientific and scholarly institutes met in December and January 1988 to nominate candidates for its twenty-five reserved seats. Leading the list were Andrei Sakharov (nominated by 55 institutes), space scientist Roald Sagdeyev (24), Old Russian literature expert, survivor of Stalinist labor camps, Dmitry Likhachev (19), and liberal economists Gavriil Popov (16) and Nikolai Shmelyov (11). But when the academy's presidium winnowed down the list, it excluded Sakharov as well as the other liberals. In response, other groups in Moscow and around the country (one as far away as Kamchatka on the Pacific coast) nominated Sakharov to run in their districts, while more than 3,000 academy members protested the presidium's decision at its Moscow headquarters on February 2, carrying banners and chanting slogans: "Shame on Presidium bureaucrats!" "Sakharov, Sagdeyev, Popov, Shmelyov for deputy!" When some 1,500 members of the academy gathered later for final selection of their deputies, they voted down twelve nominees of the presidium and voted in Sakharov, Sagdeyev, and Shmelyov.[7] Popov and Likhachev were elected from territorial districts.

In vast swaths of the country, particularly rural regions and the Central Asian republics, the party machine duly delivered deputies who could be counted on to follow their local leaders. But in Moscow, Leningrad, and other large cities, party apparatchiki failed to deliver, either because they couldn't play the new electoral game or because they were so confident they couldn't lose that they hardly tried to win. As a result, liberals came out of nowhere to win, while party bosses went down to demoralizing defeats.

Sergei Stankevich, a thirty-five-year-old historian specializing on the U.S. Congress and other Western parliamentary systems, had started giving talks on politics to informal political clubs in 1986 and then joined the Moscow Popular Front, a would-be grassroots organization much less imposing than its name. When he decided to run for deputy in 1989, he thought he had no chance against eleven opponents; they included the party-backed director of a defense plant, who campaigned by funding repair of local roads, as well as a medical center director and a surgeon. But Stankevich deployed an arsenal of Western techniques: leaflets aimed at diverse constituencies distributed where they lived and worked (women at food stores, students in dormitories), and at stations on a metro line that carried the bulk of his electorate to work in central Moscow; youthful volunteers with placards and loudspeakers who moved from place to place where voters were most likely to be—outside stores, at bus stops, at movie theaters when films ended. Stankevich himself tirelessly pressed the flesh throughout his district, something that more establishment candidates didn't deign to do. His volunteers even conducted opinion polls every day at all metro stations. In the first round of elections, Stankevich got 49 percent of the vote. In the second, during which his remaining opponents tried to beat him at his own game with clumsy campaign workers of their own, Stankevich won with 57 percent.[8]

When Leningrad law professor Anatoly Sobchak was nominated as one of ten possible candidates from his university, he, too, assumed he would lose, especially when district party officials supported two vanguard workers from local factories. Sobchak not only deployed the same sort of techniques as Stankevich but insisted on televised debates, in which he trounced the competition. The result: he won by a large margin, and went on to become one of the most visible liberals in the new parliament and later mayor of the newly renamed St. Petersburg.[9]

Boris Yeltsin ran in Moscow's vast at-large district, populated by nearly six million souls. After taking his latest lumps at the Nineteenth Party Conference in June 1988, Yeltsin had characteristically gone into a funk in which "a feeling of apathy washed over me. I did not want struggle, not explanations, not anything. All I wanted was to forget it all and be left in peace."[10] With time and encouragement from liberals, who were beginning to see him as an agent of faster change, he decided to run. Even then he was full of self-dramatizing self-pity: he had been "under a ban; I was alive but it was as if I didn't exist. So if I suddenly reemerge into the political area . . . then the whole of the party's immensely powerful propaganda machine will come down on me with a barrage of lies, slander and half-truths."[11]

Yeltsin took two months to decide where to run. Supporters filed papers on his behalf in fifty districts around the country. At first he focused on his native town in Siberia. But Moscow would make the biggest splash, and once aroused, he threw all his formidable energy into the race. Posters went up all over the city. Volunteers descended on factories and institutes. Yeltsin himself seemed to be everywhere, meeting voters, giving several talks a day, some at town meetings where he answered endless questions. By the end of his campaign, he was drawing tens of thousands to rallies in parks, hockey arenas, and stadiums, many of his fans wearing sandwich boards saying "Fight, Boris!" or carrying handmade signs: "Hands off Yeltsin!" But Yeltsin's greatest weapon, ironically, was party officials' all-out but ham-handed opposition to him. At the final nomination meeting on February 22, they arranged for Yeltsin to lose to Yevgeny Brakov, director of the ZIL auto factory, and Georgy Grechko, a popular cosmonaut. But Grechko withdrew at the last minute, allowing Yeltsin to come in second and gain a place on the ballot. Local authorities denied Moscow media to Yeltsin, but the Moscow Aviation Institute published his program in its student newspaper, and printers worked overtime to turn out thousands of extra copies.[12]

Yeltsin won with 89 percent of the vote—5,117,745 out of 5,736,470 cast. Well-known liberals like economist Oleg Bogomolov and historian

Yuri Afanasyev also prevailed over party-backed candidates in Moscow, as did hitherto unknowns like thirty-two-year-old physicist Arkady Murashev and Ilya Zaslavsky. Not yet thirty and with a physical handicap that prevented him from standing for any length of time or walking without crutches, Zaslavsky carried the capital's October district. Across the country, thirty-eight top party bosses were defeated, including twenty-nine province party chiefs. Moscow party first secretary Zaikov escaped that fate by being included in the party's Red Hundred, but his deputy did not. In Leningrad, not a single city or province party or government leader won, not even the top party boss, Yuri Solovyov, or the commander of the Leningrad military district. Solovyov, also a Politburo candidate member, managed to lose while running unopposed, garnering a mere 110,000 out of 240,000 votes while the majority crossed out his name. Gorbachev ally Vadim Medvedev estimated that 20 to 25 percent of deputies elected in territorial districts and a somewhat smaller percentage of those representing social organizations were "disposed to be sharply critical of the party."[13]

Gorbachev was elated by the election results: the elections were "a huge step in realizing political reform and democratizing our society," he informed the Politburo on March 28. "We achieved an enormous political victory under extraordinarily difficult circumstances." The results showed, he told mass media leaders the next day, that "the people have accepted perestroika with their hearts and minds." What they were saying when they voted down party officials was that they wanted perestroika to go faster and better. "There must be no talk of any defeat," Yakovlev said on March 28, stressing, as Gorbachev did, too, that 85 percent of the freely elected deputies were members of the party, compared with the Communist quota of 50 percent in the old rigged, rubber-stamp Supreme Soviet.[14]

Most of Gorbachev's Kremlin colleagues weren't buying his optimism. Politburo members usually fell silent when their leader called their meetings to order, but on March 28 they continued arguing about the election results. When Gorbachev hailed the fact that 85 percent of the elected were Communists, Ligachev and Vorotnikov retorted, "But what sort of Communists?"[15] Ligachev lamented "serious political losses." People "voted against perestroika," said the defeated Solovyov.

He blamed the opposition for out-organizing the party apparatus, and the press for egging them on. *Pravda* itself, he grumbled, was depicting province party organizations as "forces of evil." "The Balts went around the entire country, campaigning against party candidates," former KGB chief Chebrikov complained. "They made it as far as Irkutsk. Who gave them the right?" Even Moscow districts populated by high government officials voted overwhelmingly for Yeltsin, Zaikov added grimly: 74 percent where Supreme Soviet and Council of Ministers officials lived, and 90 where most Soviet diplomats resided.[16]

Solovyov and Ligachev went so far as to imply that Gorbachev had "set up" hard-line party officials to be defeated. And in a sense they were right. He wanted to subject them to the popular will, and he rejoiced when they were rejected. "It serves them right for treating the people as they do. The people are just cattle to them," he told Politburo colleagues. Thousands of petitioners "spend years in the waiting rooms of these big shots," but they "do nothing, not even to help supply the people with basic necessities." Let the losers "draw their own conclusions from the election, and we'll draw ours about them." As Chernyaev put it, "This was the way it would be in every election from now on, with the people having the opportunity to choose and get rid of the inept."[17]

Not so, alas. The elections turned out to be a defeat, recalled close Gorbachev aide Shakhnazarov, but that "came to light only gradually."[18]

THE BROADER MEANING of the elections was clarified when the new parliament convened on May 25. In the meantime, economic decline, ethnic discontent, and tensions in the Kremlin intensified, the last two exacerbated by the burst of political activism that accompanied the elections.

Prime Minister Ryzhkov recited the bleak economic statistics: government expenditures exceeding revenues by 133 billion rubles over the last three years, owing partly (44 billion) to the fall in oil prices and the reduction in vodka sales (34 billion); losses in agriculture over the same period totaling 15 billion; 11 billion rubles printed in 1988, the most in any year since the war; 40 billion surplus rubles chasing nonexistent goods, while 70–80 billion rubles' worth of shoddy goods languished unwanted on warehouse shelves. There were severe shortages, if not total unavailability, of goods, including meat, sugar and sweets, tooth paste, soap and detergent, school notebooks, batteries, shoes, fur hats and coats.[19] Gorbachev himself sounded almost as gloomy. Economic acceleration hadn't worked, but neither had reforms. He and his colleagues had underestimated the hole they were in and overestimated the possibility of getting out of it. [20]

Agriculture, as always, was the economy's Achilles' heel. "So many decades, so many decisions with no result," Ryzhkov wailed. People could see (presumably on television) that Western stores were overflowing with vegetables, but all there was on Soviet shelves was "straw." An urgent March 2 Politburo meeting featured sharp criticism of past ills and the current mess, but offered no cure. Ryzhkov had warned grimly in January that if agricultural output didn't start growing rapidly, so that people could see and feel a real increase, "the conversation is over." Even the ever optimistic Gorbachev seemed at a loss. If agriculture couldn't be resurrected, he warned, then "nothing can save us." If all he and his colleagues could do was complain and blame one another, then "we might as well close down perestroika." The countryside needed a complete "turnabout in people's brains." After nearly four years of reforms, the Soviet peasant remained "nothing more than a serf, in fact worse off."[21]

While the economy was failing, Baltic nationalism was rising. Until February 1989, Russian was the official "state language" in all three Baltic republics; now they declared their own languages to be "state languages." Soon their Supreme Soviets proclaimed economic "autonomy" (still undefined) and pledged to limit immigration of Russians and other non-Baltic nationalities, who were approximately half the population in Latvia and nearly reached that level in Estonia. Moscow had counted on Baltic Communist parties to suppress ethnic separatism, but those parties were now moving closer to "national front" groups in each republic. Lithuanian party stalwarts tried to move against Sajudis, the Lithuanian front, at a February plenum of the Lithuanian Central Committee, but hard-liners lost every seat they contested in the March elections for the Congress of People's Deputies.[22]

The election results in the Baltics shocked the Politburo. Six members prepared a memorandum that Chernyaev described as "alarmed and defeatist; everything is collapsing, power is slipping away to the popular fronts." At a Politburo meeting on May 11, the three Baltic Communist leaders were, according to Chernyaev, "put through hell." But Gorbachev remained calm, if not entirely confident: "We trust all three of them, there is no other way. . . . We shouldn't identify the popular fronts, which are supported by 90 percent of the population, with extremists. We have to learn how to communicate with them. [. . .] We have to trust in people's common sense." We have to "think, think, think how in practice to transform our federation. Otherwise everything will really collapse." Yet, even to prevent that, "the use of force is out of the question."[23]

Meanwhile, far to the south, ethnic unrest exploded in Tbilisi, the capital of Soviet Georgia. On the warm night of April 9, Ministry of Interior and regular army troops "wielding sharpened entrenchment shovels and gas canisters" charged a crowd of demonstrators. As later reported by U.S. Ambassador Matlock: "Persons who had fallen to the pavement were beaten to death and gas was sprayed directly into the faces of prostrate, unarmed individuals. Scores of people were hospitalized, many suffering from gas poisoning." In the end, up to twenty were killed and hundreds injured.[24]

This was precisely the kind of tragedy that Gorbachev had feared. How did it happen and what was his role? Demonstrations demanding greater Georgian autonomy had begun in the fall of 1988. By April 1989, militant groups were calling for Georgia to secede from the "Russian-Soviet empire" and appealing to the U.S. Congress and NATO to help end the "Bolshevik occupation" of Georgia. Thousands gathered in front of Government House in Tbilisi on April 4. Over the next three days, protestors seized city buses to blockade the square. Whether the demonstrations turned violent, and if so, how much, is not clear from conflicting accounts. Equally unclear are the deliberations in Tbilisi and Moscow that led to Ministry of Interior and army troops being sent in to quell the disturbances. During the afternoon of April 7, Ligachev chaired a special session of the leadership without Gorbachev and Shevardnadze, who were in London. They didn't fly back until very late that evening, when they were met at Vnukovo Airport by the Politburo. Earlier that day, Georgian party leader Dzhumber Patiashvili requested that troops be sent, but Ligachev denies authorizing their dispatch. Gorbachev insists his response upon returning was to send Shevardnadze to try to calm the situation. But Shevardnadze didn't go, because Patiashvili reportedly changed his mind and proclaimed that he had the situation under control.[25]

People in a position to know differ about Gorbachev's role. Premier Ryzhkov, who didn't attend Ligachev's afternoon meeting on April 7 but was at Vnukovo in the evening, insists General Ivan Rodionov, who led the troops into Tbilisi, would never have acted without permission of Defense Minister Yazov, who in turn wouldn't have approved without orders from higher up. But even former Gorbachev chief of staff Boldin, who regularly depicted his boss in the worst possible light, says Gorbachev "knew much," but not "everything," and that Patiashvili, who insisted the decision to suppress the demonstrations had been "agreed on," did not say "with whom." According to the Central Committee international department's first deputy head, Brutents, Ligachev authorized sending troops to Tbilisi, but Gorbachev didn't countermand that order. To further complicate the picture, Patiashvili may have rejected Shevardnadze's help because he couldn't bear the thought of his predecessor as Georgian leader coming to his rescue in Tbilisi. Or as Gorbachev put it to Chernyaev, the Georgian leadership "dropped a load in its pants and sent the troops in against its own people."[26]

The most objective assessment is probably that of a commission set up by the Congress of People's Deputies under the chairmanship of Anatoly Sobchak, with Sergei Stankevich as secretary. Both men were politically closer to Yeltsin than to Gorbachev, but rather than blaming Gorbachev, the commission found Igor Rodionov, the hard-line general in charge of the operation, and two other generals commanding the troops on the spot, to be "personally responsible" for the carnage, and Patiashvili and another Georgian party secretary to be "politically responsible."[27]

IN FEBRUARY, GORBACHEV invited workers from around the country to meet with him in the Kremlin. Renowned in Bolshevik song and story for its "vanguard" role in "building Communism," the proletariat had long been passive as the Communist party and its chieftains seized leadership in its name. But not on February 14. Gorbachev began by depicting perestroika "on a great highway with broad horizons before it," but hastened to admit it faced "complex problems." What followed when he invited questions from his audience was a flood of complaints: empty shelves, food rationing, terrible housing, miserly pensions, decisions not implemented, laws that didn't work, operators of the new cooperatives getting rich at the people's expense.[28] Gorbachev himself had been lamenting just such troubles, but to hear about them from workers who implied he was at fault was especially painful.

Several days later, during a not-so-grand tour of Ukraine, Gorbachev heard more of the same from workers in Kiev, including a grievance that was particularly hurtful for a long-winded orator: "We've had it with talking. It's time for deeds." Gorbachev had received a letter, as Stalin would have, attributing widespread shortages to sabotage, prompting him to object that their real sources were more complicated than that. A more ironic exchange could hardly be imagined. The letter writer's sympathetic attempt to blame "enemies of the people," rather than Gorbachev, only showed how primitive he was. Gorbachev's more sophisticated analysis was almost certainly too abstruse for his listeners and hadn't helped him to find a solution either.[29]

The intelligentsia, rather than the proletariat, was Gorbachev's main constituency. But its members, too, were talking back. On the eve of 1989, several well-known intellectual and cultural figures published an open letter to Gorbachev in *Moscow News*. In Stalin's time, they wrote, officials who didn't implement his orders were removed or even shot, but Gorbachev not only tolerated them; he continued to trust them. Chernyaev shared the view that Gorbachev should be tougher, but instead of acting on the criticism, Gorbachev was "just irritated" by it. When he and the rest of the Politburo met with 150 leading intellectuals on January 6, Gorbachev spoke for two and a half hours and seemed on the defensive. It was not true, as conservatives charged, that perestroika was "leading to chaos," that it had "no strategy and plan," that what the country needed was a "strong hand," as in the "good, old days." But liberals were equally misguided in their calls for "political pluralism, multiple parties, even private property." Adopting a centrist political line came naturally to someone temperamentally inclined to compromise. But something deeper was visible in Gorbachev's response to the intellectuals' reproaches. No matter how much he sought out their advice, probably just because he so valued it, he was "always," as Chernyaev testifies, "dissatisfied with his relations with the intelligentsia."[30]

Apart from the places where they worked (institutes, universities, mass media, theaters, and so on), those in the liberal intelligentsia had no organizational base for political activities, but they were building one in the spring of 1989, especially in large cities. Andrei Sakharov, Yuri Afanasyev, and others had founded the Moscow Tribune Club in late 1988. Dozens of activists around the country created the "Memorial" Society to honor victims of Bolshevik terror, many of them also hoping to play a broader political role. Memorial's first conference, held in Moscow in October 1988, attracted 338 delegates from fifty-nine cities.[31] Ligachev warned at an October 24, 1988, Politburo meeting against "the political ambitions" of founders of movements like Memorial.[32] But hardliners had the most powerful base of all—the party Central Committee. Although Gorbachev still set its agenda, chaired its meetings, and managed to elicit unanimity in its resolutions, party conservatives used it as a platform against him.

Gorbachev received no applause at the March 1989 plenum, and several other speakers failed even to mention his name. In April, in an old-style, bureaucratic power play, he informed another plenum that more than a hundred Central Committee members and candidate members who had retired from their day jobs in the party and state sector had now "volunteered" to leave the Central Committee as well. Most of the "volunteers" meekly thanked Gorbachev for his support and trust. But other members leaped into the breach, directly condemning Gorbachev policies (failure of economic reforms, toleration of nationalism, press slander of party officials, the disintegration of the army) in what Medvedev called "the first mass assault on the Gorbachev leadership." Gorbachev cursed his critics the next day and accused them of conspiring against him: "Look," he told Chernyaev, "the speeches were all coordinated, like from a script." But he didn't fight back at the plenum or afterward, managing instead to rationalize the row at the plenum as a sign that the party was returning to the healthy, open debates of Lenin's time.[33]

Such restraint was tactical. Even though, as he put in his memoirs, the party was turning from "a vanguard into a rearguard," Gorbachev wanted to jolly it along while erecting new institutions to take on its former functions. In that sense, his self-control reflected his confidence that danger was still outweighed by possibility. But beyond the tactics were real mood swings. "We're walking on the razor's edge," he had warned aides on January 17. But "we're doomed to work out solutions," he remarked a week later. Comments he made to Vadim Medvedev from a Black Sea coast vacation in early February reflect anxiety—about Sakharov's prediction to a French newspaper that Gorbachev might soon be ousted by hard-liners, and about Lithuania's increasing restlessness. During that vacation, he escaped from his anxiety by working on yet another book—to be titled "1988: The Turning Point Year." He dictated the main ideas at Pitsunda, turned over the drafting to a Chernyaev-led team of writers, and received a 400-page manuscript on March 9. But by that point 1989 was too troubling to ignore, so work on the book was never completed. Gorbachev seemed in a particularly good mood in early April when he reflected on what it took to become a leader, but his self-image was so inflated as to imply he might be struggling to buttress his self-esteem. "Anyone can become a politician," he told Chernyaev, but "there has to be a foundation—a vessel. The contents will come with experience, but the vessel comes from God. Take me, for example. Have I changed much since childhood? Not really, I'm essentially the same as I always was."[34]

Contrast that with Chernyaev's sense of "anxiety and sadness" and the feeling of "coming crisis," recorded in his diary on May 2. Gorbachev had said many times that he was "prepared to go far." But "the fear of losing the levers of power" held him back. He was "sticking to familiar methods" of dealing with the party, using "velvet gloves," because he had no clear "concept of what he is moving towards."[35]

MAY 25, THE OPENING DAY of the Congress of People's Deputies, dawned clear and warm with the lush grass of Kremlin lawns shining in the sunlight. The Palace of Congresses, built in the International Modern Style in 1961 with marble and glass walls, contrasts sharply with the fifteenth-century churches that surround the adjacent Palace Square. The great hall of the palace, which seats six thousand people, had hosted all Communist party congresses since 1961, while also serving as a second stage for the Bolshoi Ballet and Opera. Rank-and-file deputies encountered friendly crowds as they walked toward the Kremlin. High-ranking party and government officials blew by them in black cars and limousines, as did foreign diplomats, including Ambassador Matlock in his "discreetly armored Cadillac with the Stars and Stripes fluttering over the right fender." At party congresses, Politburo members always sat in serried ranks on the stage facing the audience. Now, for the first time, they were relegated to seats in the auditorium facing the stage along the wall on the left side. When the session started precisely at 10:00 a.m., Gorbachev and his deputy for the Congress, Anatoly Lukyanov, sat in the first row alongside other deputies from Moscow, while the chairman of the Central Electoral Commission, Vladimir Orlov, alone on the stage, brought the meeting to order and read his report on the election results.[36]

Orlov had just finished when a Latvian deputy, a physician from Riga with gray hair and beard, confidently strode up to the podium and asked the audience to rise in tribute to those who had recently perished in Tbilisi. Then he lodged an official "deputy's inquiry" about who gave the order "to slaughter" peaceful demonstrators with "poisonous substances." Gorbachev looked puzzled, but applauded and stood for the minute of silence. Other Politburo members took a while to register their shock. "They all thought it was part of the script," recalled Galina Starovoitova, a liberal deputy who lived and worked (as scholar of the Caucasus) in Moscow but represented a district in Armenia.[37]

It was not part of the script. In fact, in many ways, the Congress had no script at all. There was an agenda, there were rules of procedure, there was even an electronic system for tallying votes, but much of the time the scene was near chaos. "It was like Shakespeare on an epic scale but not written beforehand," recalled essayist Yuri Chernichenko. "The script was created as it went along, nobody knew what was going to happen five minutes later, who was going to kill whom and who was going to die in convulsions." Instead of waiting for their marching orders, trying not to nod off while preassigned speakers droned on, deputies listened intently to spontaneous debates and argued passionately with one another. "Decades of pent-up emotion" spilled out, remembered Vadim Medvedev. "Waves of hate" was how writer and liberal deputy Yuri Karyakin put it.

"The hall swarmed with activity, like an anthill," Boldin remembered. So did hallways during recesses, where young Soviet reporters, following the lead of Western journalists, besieged Politburo members, as well as military and KGB leaders, with embarrassing questions. "For decades," noted *Washington Post* correspondent David Remnick, "no one had dared ask them about the weather, much less the erosion of the Communist Party. Now they were being chased to the bathrooms" for "accountings of themselves." In the mammoth buffet on the top floor, hitherto inaccessible party bosses (not Politburo members, who had private dining rooms, but others just below that level) were reduced to ordinary mortals chowing down at 140 tables covered with food.[38]

All Congress sessions were televised live from gavel to gavel with most of the country watching, as people skipped work to do so and debated in their homes what they saw and heard on the screen. There had been some opposition to this in the leadership, and initially newspaper TV listings included only opening and closing ceremonies, but in the end Gorbachev insisted on transmitting in full what the country had never seen before—the political decision-making process. It took a while for untutored deputies to learn to preen for the cameras, but their initial innocent directness made the viewing even more addictive.[39]

The first major business of the Congress was electing its chairman, who would not only direct its deliberations but serve, like previous chairmen of the old, submissive Supreme Soviet, as titular head of state. Gorbachev, who already had that title, was the obvious choice. The process of reanointing him went relatively smoothly, but not as easily as he expected. Shortly after the unexpected motion to memorialize the Tbilisi victims, Gorbachev, who was temporarily in the chair, recognized Andrei Sakharov, who presented another unscripted proposal— that candidates for the job present their views on the main issues of the day before the vote was held, as was the practice throughout the world. The notion that there might be more than one candidate was near heresy. Sakharov himself supported Gorbachev, he said, but his endorsement was "conditional." Gorbachev chided Sakharov for speaking more than the five-minute maximum, Sakharov's remarks were met with loud, angry buzzing in the hall, and Gorbachev was soon elected by an overwhelming margin—2,123 (95.6 percent) in favor, 87 against.

But not before he felt compelled briefly to justify perestroika policies, to explain that his role in the Tbilisi tragedy was only to have ordered Shevardnadze into the breach, and to defend his lavish new Black Sea villa at Foros, saying it wasn't his but the whole leadership's and that other dachas he and his family had used had been transformed into sanatoriums. In the end, Gorbachev faced only nominal opposition from a Leningrad deputy, an engineer/designer with an old, aristocratic name, Aleksandr Obolensky, who nominated himself for chairman.[40]

Being chosen chair was much easier than chairing the Congress. Ales Adamovich, the Byelorussian writer, had an up-front seat from which he could watch the action. Previously, the general secretary "had only to move his eyebrow," Adamovich recalled, "and the whole audience would know what to do, jump to their feet, applaud. . . ." Now Gorbachev "had to steer" the cart as it veered left or right or careened downhill "on the verge of destruction." Adamovich remembered watching Politburo member Viktor Nikonov, whose "mouth was wide open, staring in amazement and fear" as if Gorbachev was "playing a dangerous game with snakes." The writer Daniil Granin thought Gorbachev performed his new role brilliantly, like a "trickster: you see a question and then you don't; an issue is supposed to be voted on and suddenly there is no issue." Even Boldin had to admire the way his boss persevered day after day, "maneuvering this way and that, placating, calming or encouraging." It helped that Gorbachev's staff pampered him; arriving thirty to forty minutes before the Congress convened (having already conferred with other leaders on his car phone), he was ushered through a special entrance and up to a small third-floor study where special aides were waiting: medical personnel, a masseur, and, Boldin is at pains to point out, a hairdresser ready to wash his hair, shave the back of his neck and his sideburns "ever so slightly," and then dry and comb his hair. Gorbachev had so little hair to be shampooed, dried, and combed, and Boldin was so hostile, that this part of the latter's account may not be trustworthy. But the strain of trying to keep order during Congress sessions was immense, so when Gorbachev retired to the presidium lounge during intermissions, he doubtless was, as Boldin says, "in a state of utter exhaustion."[41]

Gorbachev's greatest challenge was that the Congress split into two camps. Party apparat stalwarts outnumbered liberals (or democrats, as they often called themselves and were referred to in the press), who were themselves divided internally, not so much by ideology as by prior political affiliations with (in the case of Moscow deputies) the Academy of Sciences' voters' club, or Boris Yeltsin's staff, or other would-be leaders like Yuri Afanasyev. In addition, there were nationalist-minded deputies from the Baltics and other non-Russian republics. What was originally called the "Moscow Deputies Group" morphed into the "Interregional Deputies Group," which grew from about 60 liberal deputies to 150 toward the end of the Congress. Moreover, liberals mobilized their backers with daily mass rallies at which leading deputies reported on congressional proceedings. One of the first of these rallies, held at Luzhniki Park outside Lenin Stadium, drew tens of thousands, many of them uncertain how to behave, "whether and when to applaud," deputy Starovoitova recalled, and "what to shout in the pauses between speeches."[42]

Still thinking of themselves as champions of perestroika, liberals hoped to cooperate with Gorbachev in his struggle against conservatives. And in some ways he reciprocated. Although 85 percent of the deputies were party members, he made clear there would be no party discipline, that they would be free to vote their consciences. He called on liberals to speak, especially Sakharov, more often than their numbers seemed to justify. He was patient, up to a point, when they spoke too long, and sought compromises when they challenged his views. But under intense pressure from the other side, and committed to his own centrist line, he found himself increasingly isolated from both sides as they warred with each other.

Gorbachev's dilemma was visible when the Congress chose members of its smaller, full-time surrogate, the new Supreme Soviet. Leading liberals like Sakharov, Afanasyev, and Popov were defeated, as was Yeltsin, despite his huge victory in the March elections, prompting Afanaysev to lash out at the Congress's "aggressively obedient Stalinist-Brezhnevite majority." Polarizing rhetoric of that kind didn't serve Gorbachev's purposes, and he wasn't pleased with the outcome either. So when a little-known Siberian deputy named Aleksei Kazannik tried to yield his Supreme Soviet seat to Yeltsin, Gorbachev acceded to the maneuver.[43]

Was Gorbachev tempted by an alliance with Yeltsin? He offered him a ministerial post in mid-May and toyed with the idea of making him Russian Republic deputy premier. He agreed to Yeltsin's chairing the Supreme Soviet's committee on construction and architecture. But Yeltsin rejected the ministry and would have refused the deputy premiership. He disdained his committee chairmanship, although his aides used its downtown office to advance his cause. Yeltsin abstained in May when the party Central Committee decided to nominate Gorbachev as Congress chairman, and came close to having his own name placed in nomination. In his first speech to the Congress, he called for a yearly national vote of confidence (or nonconfidence!) in the chair. In all these ways, Yeltsin continued to be difficult, but his own shortcomings made him seem less threatening to Gorbachev. Yeltsin quarreled with other leaders of the Interregional Group: he wanted to be sole leader, but had to settle for being one of five cochairs. His biographer Timothy Colton judged Yeltsin to be a "listless lawmaker." According to U.S. embassy observers, who attended Supreme Soviet sessions and observed Yeltsin closely from the balcony, he was "an aloof legislator," who "rarely took the floor," attended "fewer than half of the sessions" in the fall of 1989 and "fewer than ten" the next spring, and "rarely devoted attention to the proceedings, evidently preferring to page through newspaper and magazines."[44] So Gorbachev's motive for easing Yeltsin's way into the Supreme Soviet was less to win him over than to avoid the scandal of leaving millions of his voters unrepresented, and to keep up pressure on the party hard-liners.[45]

Sakharov also proved a thorn in Gorbachev's side. The father of the Soviet H-bomb turned dissident wasn't really a politician. In some ways, he was the antithesis of one: he was a symbol of moral courage, who was maddeningly immune to both threats and blandishments. Older and frailer than his nearly seventy years, Sakharov was a terrible public speaker; he stammered, paused, struggled for the right word, spoke in a high-pitched voice. Tall, gaunt, and bent, with unkempt thinning hair, he sometimes trembled, but he was determined to follow the truth wherever it led. His critics in the Congress tried to silence him—hissing, whistling, clapping, shouting, roaring him down, but he ignored them and plowed on.[46]

Sakharov greatly valued Gorbachev, who in four years "had completely changed the situation in the country," and saw no alternative to him as Soviet leader. Certainly not Yeltsin, whom Sakharov regarded as "a figure of an altogether different [i.e., lesser] caliber." But Sakharov wished Gorbachev had moved faster toward private property and in dismantling the party dictatorship; he feared the concentration of power even in Gorbachev's hands. Like other Moscow intellectuals, Sakharov also felt superior to Gorbachev. According to Adamovich, who spent a lot of time talking with Sakharov in private, Sakharov felt "older and more experienced" than Gorbachev. He had "seen more and knew more," but he also understood how much "depended on this person from Stavropol, this onetime party cadre, onetime Komsomol member, onetime tractor driver." The seeming contradiction between Gorbachev's uninspiring background and his enormous achievements puzzled Sakharov, as it did so many. One day, speaking with both "bitterness and embarrassment," he told Adamovich, "I don't understand Gorbachev."[47]

Gorbachev regarded Sakharov as "an idealist not always in touch with real possibilities and consequences," a description not so inapt for Gorbachev himself. But he, too, hoped to work with, not against, his sometime antagonist. On the first day of the Congress, Aleksandr Yakovlev approached Sakharov in a hallway and begged him "to help Gorbachev," who was "transforming the country almost single-handedly," while the task took "a huge human toll on him." Gorbachev kept calling on Sakharov to speak even when he didn't like what he said, and he tried to persuade the angry majority to let Sakharov be heard. "By God, I wanted to be impartial," Gorbachev insisted later, but Sakharov "kept opening himself up to criticism, so it became harder and harder for me to pacify the raging hall."[48]

The two men's views of each other soured as the Congress proceeded, especially after a tête-à-tête that Sakharov contrived to arrange. It occurred late one night after an evening session of the Congress. Sakharov had been sending word all day that he wanted to meet, but Gorbachev claims he didn't get the message. So Sakharov waited alone in the vast, dimly lit Great Hall until Gorbachev, accompanied by Lukyanov, walked by on his way out. The men pulled three chairs together on the stage and sat down. Both Gorbachev and Sakharov were exhausted, but Gorbachev paid close attention—"without," Sakharov remem-

Gorbachev and Andrei Sakharov during the first Congress of People's Deputies, May 1989.

bered, "the half-benevolent, half-condescending smile on his face that he usually directed toward me." Sakharov said Gorbachev faced a choice between speeding up change or preserving the old system; the centrist path Gorbachev was on led nowhere, and in the meantime, his "personal authority" had fallen to "almost nothing." Sakharov was also worried about rumors, obviously spread by Gorbachev's enemies, that the Soviet leader had accepted massive bribes when he was Stavropol party boss.

Nothing good came of this meeting, recalled Sakharov. All Gorbachev remembered, or cared to recall, about it was his response to the charge of corruption: "Andrei Dmitrievich, you needn't lose sleep over this. Gorbachev has never done anything like this." Or as Sakharov remembers Gorbachev's words: "I am completely pure. I will never submit to any attempt to blackmail me, whether they come from the right or the left."[49]

Whatever his own view, Gorbachev had to take account of the hardline majority's fury at Sakharov. But he also came to believe that "radical democrats" were exploiting Sakharov's naïveté, "manipulating him," goading him to speak endlessly so that Gorbachev would have to shut him up, "showing the nation" how crudely "the powers that be treated a man of honor."[50]

On the next to last day of the first Congress, June 8, Gorbachev was conducting more or less routine business when he announced that Sakharov was "insistently asking to speak." The reaction, according to the transcript, was *"noise in the hall."* Although he had already spoken seven times, Gorbachev added, Sakharov was now requesting fifteen minutes. *"Noise in the hall."*

"Shall we give him the floor?" Gorbachev asked. [*"Noise in the hall."*] "Wait a minute," Gorbachev continued. "It seems to me we should ask him to limit his remarks to five minutes." [*"Noise in the hall."*]

Five minutes it was. But it wasn't. Sakharov worried aloud that Gorbachev had too much power, about a coming "economic catastrophe," rising ethnic tensions, and a "crisis of trust in the country's leadership." Therefore, Congress "must take power into its own hands."

"Just a moment," interjected Gorbachev, but Sakharov couldn't be stopped.

Gorbachev: "Finish up, Andrei Dmitrievich."

Sakharov: "I am finishing. I'm skipping a lot that I wanted to say."

Gorbachev: "That's it. Time's up. Excuse me, but time's up."

Sakharov: [*"Not audible."*]

Gorbachev: "That's all, Comrade Sakharov. Comrade Sakharov, do you respect the Congress? Good. That's all."

Sakharov: [*"Not audible."*]

Gorbachev: "That's it." [*"A bell rings."*]

Sakharov: [*"Not audible."*]

Gorbachev: "I ask you to conclude. I ask you to finish. That's it." Gorbachev cut off Sakharov's microphone, leaving the speaker orating into a void. [*"Applause."*][51]

Pleading with Sakharov to finish instead of forcibly exiling him to Gorky—How much had changed under Gorbachev! Draining and frustrating though the Congress might be, Gorbachev was, his Politburo critic Vorotnikov noticed, "on a roll." From his perch near the stage, Adamovich could see that the Congress "was his brainchild, he had invented it all. His brainchild was a capricious child, a malicious child, a child that wanted to bite and spit in his face," but although he was a little "offended and indignant," he had a "caring attitude, a loving attitude."[52]

Gorbachev hailed the Congress in his memoirs as "a sharp turn, a real *volte-face*." "It changed the history of the country," recalled Yakovlev. But if the institutional turnabout was all-important, so was Gorbachev's starring role in it. This was true glasnost—the kind he had dreamed of and worked so long and hard to bring about. This was the successful culmination at the highest level of all his abortive attempts, beginning in godforsaken villages around Stavropol, to solve social problems through discussion rather than fiat. Gorbachev was trying to develop a true "parliamentary culture" in a country that never had one, Shakhnazarov recalled, so he stayed on after sessions ended, meeting with deputies, hearing them out, seeking to understand them and their concerns. The fact that the country's chief executive was doubling as the speaker of its parliament, taking valuable time off from running the country and its foreign policy to referee novice legislators' endless, unruly debates, was in a sense madness. Some of his supporters warned him that by doing so he was lowering his prestige and weakening his authority. But who else could tutor the deputies and the millions watching on television in the culture of parliamentary governance? Who else could attend like a virtuoso to all the necessary political nuances? He was sure no one could, and he was probably right. And it flattered his ego to do it so well. The Kyrgyz writer/deputy Chingiz Aitmatov rhapsodized about Gorbachev in supporting his nomination to chair the Congress. Gorbachev quoted Aitmatov's encomium at length in his memoirs—"not to flatter myself," he insisted, but because "with his writer's gift, Aitmatov was able to find the right words to describe what happened"—how into the "sleeping kingdom" of the old order, "there came a man," a man "fate willed to arrive . . . just in time," a man who "could have sat calmly and triumphantly, read aloud from the rostrum texts written for him by others, and everything would have rolled along smoothly." But instead this man "dared what seemed impossible . . . dared to follow the path of social renewal on which he now stands in the sharp wind of perestroika."[53]

IT WAS "RIGHT AFTER" perestroika peaked at the first Congress that, according to Chernyaev, it "began its decline."[54]

Instead of improving as Gorbachev had hoped, basic economic indicators got worse, especially the gap between rising household incomes and the falling availability of goods. By the end of the year, only 11 percent of 989 consumer goods monitored by an economic research organization were readily obtainable. Almost entirely absent from stores were televisions, refrigerators, washing machines, most household cleaning products, furniture of all sorts, electric irons, razor blades, perfumes and cosmetics, school notebooks and pencils.[55] Taking stock of shortages and inflation on June 29, Gorbachev told his Politburo colleagues, "We have two years, maximum" to fix this. "Otherwise, we'll have to resign."[56]

Coal miners' strikes that summer reflected deteriorating economic conditions and aggravated them by reducing the output of coal. There had been rumblings before then—warning strikes in March, mining region party bosses defeated in March elections, alarms sounded by deputies at the Congress—but the Kremlin wasn't prepared on July 10 when a work stoppage at a single mine in the Kuzbass city of Mezhdurechensk sparked 158 other strikes (involving 177,862 miners) in the same region and then spread to Karaganda, Pechora, Lvov, Rostov, and the all-important Donbas. The strikes were spontaneous, but the ferment of the elections and fiery speeches at the Congress encouraged the strikers to act. Many strike committee leaders were young party members still waiting for perestroika to improve their lives. Thousands of strikers occupied city squares, sweltering in steel helmets, dust-coated clothes, and rubber boots, but gaining in confidence as Moscow emissaries arrived promising better housing, improved working conditions, and, perhaps most important, soap so that miners could wash their faces after emerging from the pits.[57]

Most of the promises weren't kept, but they temporarily satisfied the strikers. It never occurred to Prime Minister Ryzhkov to use force, he recalled, since the miners "would have risen up and all other industries along with them." Gorbachev was convinced that outside agitators from the Interregional Deputies Group in Moscow were inciting strikes and thus "stabbing perestroika in the back," but, according to Ryzhkov, Gorbachev supported him "all the way" in not using force.[58] Gorbachev himself never went to meet with the miners.

The economic crisis was the subject of numerous high-level meetings throughout the summer and fall—Politburo sessions, Central Committee conferences and plenums, even two large gatherings to which

Gorbachev invited leading economists with various views, patiently listening to them discourse at great length. But all these occasions were longer on depressing reports about current conditions than proposed solutions. "We're standing still," complained Gorbachev after lunch during a six-hour Politburo meeting on October 12. "None of our agricultural reforms are being realized." "Why can't we feed ourselves?" Ryzhkov moaned on November 3. "We import more grain every year, but the situation gets worse and worse."[59]

Toward the end of the year, nearly five years into grappling unsuccessfully with the economy, Gorbachev took the long-overdue step of hiring an economic adviser, the liberal, market-minded economist Nikolai Petrakov. "I know about your views," Gorbachev told him, "and they can provide just the kind of help I need." He and Petrakov would work in an atmosphere of "complete open and mutual trust," Gorbachev added, and then, after a meaningful pause, asked, "Do you [second-person singular again] trust me?" Petrakov replied that he did, but asked, "Do you [second-person plural] trust me, Mikhail Sergeyevich?" Gorbachev laughed.

After two days of pondering whether Gorbachev was truly open to market-based reforms, Petrakov signed on, and early in January 1990 attended his first Politburo meeting. Gorbachev, Yakovlev, Shevardnadze, and Yevgeny Primakov (the Gorbachev adviser who was by now speaker of the lower house of the Supreme Soviet), Petrakov observed, towered intellectually above all the rest. The level of the discussion was "low." So was the quality of materials prepared for the meeting. Many of the participants were "hopelessly narrow" in their views. Instead of confronting the country's crisis, they blamed it on the mass media, the "democrats," and the Interregional Deputies Group.[60]

Discourse on "the nationality question" wasn't much better. By the end of 1989, various ethnic crises had worsened (Azerbaijan was blockading railroad traffic to Armenia), while new ones erupted: rumblings of Ukrainian and even Russian separatism, and bloody pogroms against Meskhetian Turks in Uzbekistan's Fergana Valley, to which Stalin had deported them from Georgia during World War II. Meanwhile, the Baltics were rushing toward independence. In June, Lithuania's Communist youth league withdrew from the Soviet Komsomol. In July, the Lithuanian Communist party discussed creating "an independent, democratic, law-based Lithuanian state." On August 23, the fiftieth anniversary of the 1939 Nazi-Soviet agreement to divide the Baltics between them, some two million Estonians, Latvians, and Lithuanians, about 40 percent of the total Baltic population, held hands in an unbroken human chain linking the capitals of Tallinn, Riga, and Vilnius. On December 20, Lithuanian Communists seceded from the Communist Party of the Soviet Union. When former White House national security adviser Zbigniew Brzezinski asked Aleksandr Yakovlev that fall what it would mean if the Baltic republics declared their independence, Yakovlev answered, "That would be the end of perestroika." When the party Central Committee finally held a special plenum on nationality in September 1989, which Gorbachev had first called for in February 1988, the speeches were too little and too late. The Politburo's discussions that fall often disintegrated into squabbling about who or what was responsible for national unrest (past repression or an insufficiently tough response to current ethnic extremism?), mixed with woe-is-us predictions of doom, at which Premier Ryzhkov particularly excelled: "It smells of a general collapse," he warned on November 9. Gorbachev's own reaction alternated between lashing out verbally at Baltic separatists and cautioning against forcible action against them. The separatists were pushing their people into "an historical dead end." But the answer was not to act according to the Bolshevik adage used to justify Stalin's purges: "When you chop wood, chips fly." "I know how to chop wood," he told a special plenum called in December to discipline Lithuanian Communists. "In 1941, when snow covered us all, I chopped down half the trees in [my grandfather's] orchard in order to survive." But "politics isn't about chopping wood."[61]

In the face of rising economic and ethnic tensions, the Interregional Deputies Group held a kind of mini-convention in late July, followed by a second general conference in September. Several of the group's leaders established contact with striking miners. At first the miners were leery of consorting with politicians, recalls liberal leader Gavriil Popov, but eventually each side learned from the other. Deputies pressed the miners to make political as well as economic demands. The miners taught the liberals, Popov says, to focus on mobilizing "the masses."[62]

Meanwhile, conservative dissatisfaction with Gorbachev escalated.

Reaction to his speech at a June Central Committee plenum approached (even if it didn't equal) the kind of "noise in the hall" (including shouts of disagreement) that had been reserved for the likes of Sakharov at the first Congress of People's Deputies. At other plenums that fall, Central Committee staffer Brutents sat in the back of the hall, where he could hear members grumbling as Gorbachev spoke: "Chatterbox." "Narcissist." "Diva." "Playing the barrel-organ again." On December 9, Kemerovo party boss Aleksandr Melnikov dared to sneer that "the whole bourgeois world, all our past and present opponents, and even the pope himself" were hailing the "critical situation in our country" brought about by perestroika. To which Gorbachev replied, "If the Central Committee needs new leadership, a new Politburo . . . then that should be resolved right here and now. . . . If we've gone as far as accusations that the bourgeoisie and the pope hail us, then it's time to dot the i's and cross the t's."[63] But the Central Committee did not act.

THIS WAS NOT THE FIRST or only time in 1989 that Gorbachev mentioned stepping down. Chernyaev first heard such talk during the Gorbachevs' Pitsunda winter vacation. "Shouldn't I give up, step aside? Now that they've got their freedom, let those others show that they know how to use it." Chernyaev was sure Gorbachev didn't mean it then, but by his August vacation in Foros, Gorbachev seemed "serious." What his wife told Gorbachev sounded to Chernyaev like "the continuation of a conversation they'd been having": "It's time, Mikhail Sergeyevich, to devote yourself to private life, to retire and write your memoirs. You've done your job."[64] And the same conversation apparently continued, for Gorbachev at least twice assured Shakhnazarov the next year that "the main deed has been done" and that "the only issue now" was to make sure that the "future proceeds as painlessly as possible, without blood."[65]

Gorbachev didn't step down. But perhaps he should have—for his own sake, and especially for the good of his wife, who internalized the stresses and strains far more than he did. The pressure on him was mounting, and his behavior during the rest of the year reflected the toll. Memoranda he dictated at Foros reveal a man trying to convince himself that despite all his troubles there was no need to panic, that what was needed was to "calmly evaluate" the current situation without "falling into extremes," to "see the whole picture realistically, the totality of interacting factors, to define carefully where we are and what actions follow logically from that analysis."

But what Chernyaev observed in Foros was "an increasing loss of orientation and control," "giving in to emotions" toward the Baltics, in violation of Gorbachev's own golden rule, "overreacting to the press" for what he called "stirring up trouble," "flirting with the [ultra]-nationalist right" (including Yuri Bondarev, the writer who compared perestroika to a plane that took off without knowing where it would land), and "clinging to the old levers of power, like Nikita [Khrushchev] before him," as if he were "afraid of an uncontrollable market, of liberalized prices, afraid to abolish collective and state farms, although he saw that leasing [of land] could never be effective until that happened," "afraid to dismiss the Politburo, where the majority was obviously against him."[66]

Chernyaev himself was promoting a liberal agenda. The disarray he detected in Gorbachev reflected his own disappointment. If Chernyaev had spelled out that disappointment, Gorbachev would have chided him in return for being too radical, for not appreciating the herculean efforts it took to keep the conservatives at bay. But Chernyaev was right that Gorbachev's ego was bruised and needed bolstering. In late September, Gorbachev asked Chernyaev to find a filmmaker to make a "Portrait of Gorbachev," not to include, Gorbachev insisted, "clichés and banalities," and not to be released in the USSR (only in Italy) as yet, because he had to "earn the right for a portrait through achievements," but the producer should "get started on it right now."[67]

Meanwhile, Gorbachev went after Vladislav Starkov, the editor of *Argumenty i fakty*, which received 5,000–7,000 letters a day from its 20–30 million readers and had examined 15,000 of them to see how they rated deputies at the first Congress. Sakharov came in first, followed by Yeltsin, Popov, and Afanasyev. Gorbachev came in sixteenth. Previously, Gorbachev had ignored hard-line demands that liberal editors, like *Ogonyok*'s Vitaly Korotich, be fired. Now, at a meeting with mass media leaders, he berated Starkov: "In your place, as a Communist, I would go into retirement after such a publication." To make sure Starkov resigned, the Central Committee Secretariat summoned him, but he refused to go.

Gorbachev was overreacting to Starkov's poll numbers. They reflected the views of a self-selected sample. According to more reliable polling, it wasn't until May 1990 that Yeltsin overtook Gorbachev as the most popular politician in Russia and the Soviet Union. After the foreign press picked up the Starkov story (with a little help from *Argumenty i fakty* editors), Gorbachev backed off.[68]

AS THE AUTUMN PROGRESSED, several observers noticed, or later claimed to have, a dismaying turn in Gorbachev's demeanor. Politburo member Vorotnikov, increasingly hostile toward Gorbachev, detected more of a previously visible pattern: inflated self-importance, self-assurance, and peremptoriness; disrespectful to colleagues; "in love with the logic and music of his own words." Aleksandr Yakovlev, ostensibly Gorbachev's closest ally, complained to Chernyaev in October about Gorbachev's ingratitude. "He [Yakovlev] has not received a single 'Thank you' in their five years of working together." True, the two men had a "friendly relationship (and sometimes a pretense of trust)." For "the umpteenth time," Yakovlev told Chernyaev, Gorbachev had "asked my advice" as to whether he should retire. But "not a hint of recognition or reward." Brutents, the Central Committee international department's first deputy chief, complained to Chernyaev that Gorbachev increasingly injected "personal issues" into politics, for example, his open attack on editor Starkov, and his obvious animus toward liberal leader Yuri Afanasyev. Even Chernyaev himself was "losing [his] desire to serve Gorbachev."[69]

If something like this was Gorbachev's state of mind, how did he cope with the two very different men who had become his nemeses? On the first morning of the second Congress of People's Deputies, which met from December 12 through 24, Sakharov rose to make the case for altering the Constitution to allow debate on land and property ownership and repealing Article 6, which established the Communist party as the "leading and guiding force" of Soviet society and "the nucleus" of its political system. "But my impression," Gorbachev responded from the chair, "is that you don't know how to implement your own proposal, so we won't know either."

"But the proposal is very simple," Sakharov started to reply.

"Those articles that you propose to repeal—Who will define which they are?"

"We'll present a list," Sakharov said.

"No, I don't think that will do. Well, all right. Let's leave it that way."

"As for Article 6," Sakharov tried to continue, "I'll submit 6,000 telegrams which I've received. . . ."

"Come up later on," Gorbachev interrupted again. "I'll give you thousands of similar telegrams."

"But I have 6,000. I'd give them to you."

"Let's not pressure each other by manipulating public opinion. That's not the way to do it. Next speaker, please."[70]

This wasn't as brutal as cutting off Sakharov's microphone, but it was humiliating enough and again visible on national television. Sakharov so despaired that later that day at home he wrote out his own proposed new constitution for a Eurasian commonwealth in which membership was voluntary and the Communist party was not the only one. Two days later, he looked exhausted at a meeting of the Interregional Deputies Group, where he repeated his refrain that Gorbachev was "leading the country into catastrophe." That night, after telling his wife he was going to take a nap and then write a speech because "tomorrow there will be battle," he collapsed in the hallway outside his study.[71]

Gorbachev did not announce Sakharov's death to the Congress the next day—a serious error. He left that to Vorotnikov, as chairman of the session, who hailed Sakharov's "great and unique contribution" to the USSR's "defense capability," but left it to "history" to provide "an objective analysis" of "various other aspects of his public activities." Nor did Gorbachev support adjourning the Congress that day in Sakharov's honor. Before the session convened, Ilya Zaslavsky, the crippled, thirty-year-old deputy from Moscow, asked Gorbachev for a day of mourning, only to be told this was "not a tradition"; general secretaries got three days, and Politburo members, one, but academicians got none. Zaslavsky hobbled up to the podium anyway, at which point Gorbachev ordered him to "sit down." As Zaslavsky refused to do so, *Washington Post* newsman David Remnick, who was watching through binoculars, "could see the fury in Gorbachev's eyes." Gorbachev gave in and let Zaslavsky propose a day of mourning, and Vorotnikov promised it would be considered, but then dropped the matter. When it was finally decided that the Congress would take a break for a few hours on the day of Sakharov's funeral, Remnick reports, hard-line deputies "hissed."[72]

Gorbachev did pay tribute to Sakharov ("I always valued his openness, straightforwardness and sincerity.") in an interview with *Moscow News*, and offered to arrange a general secretary's funeral, complete with lying in state at the Hall of Columns near the Kremlin. But Sakharov's widow, Elena Bonner, chose a less official venue at the vast Pioneer Palace in southwest Moscow, where for five hours people flowed by his bier in a continuous stream. The next day, when Sakharov's body was brought to the Academy of Sciences, Gorbachev was waiting with other Politburo members in a cold drizzle. In a brief conversation, Bonner told him that with Sakharov gone, he had lost his most loyal opposition. Gorbachev didn't agree, but he removed his gray fur hat and approached the coffin. A member of the honor guard had lifted the lid. After staring for several minutes at Sakharov's face, Gorbachev entered the academy building and signed the memorial book "in a bold script," Remnick reported, while "the rest of the Politburo signed in more modest hands." Before he could leave, a reporter asked Gorbachev about Sakharov's 1975 Nobel Peace Prize, which had been dismissed by Brezhnev and company as an international blessing for subversion of the Soviet state. "It is clear now," Gorbachev replied, "that he deserved it."[73]

Sakharov's death opened the way for Yeltsin to lead the no-longer loyal opposition, a result Gorbachev had expected for some time.[74] But Yeltsin looked less formidable at the end of the year than when he swept to victory in March, partly owing to his misbehavior during an American trip, and another scandalous episode in Moscow.

Yeltsin mentioned to Ambassador Matlock in June that he was eager to see the United States. Matlock sought out a congressional committee willing to invite a leading Soviet deputy, but received no answer over the summer. So Yeltsin arranged his own trip, a ten-day lecture tour beginning on September 9, sponsored by the Esalen Institute in California and the director of its Soviet-American exchange program, Jim Garrison. A New Age landmark on the Pacific in Big Sur, Esalen welcomes guests seeking "to discover ancient wisdom in the motion of the body, poetry in the pulsing of the blood." There wasn't much poetry in Yeltsin's tour, it turned out, but plenty of motion and pulsing.[75]

Yeltsin's original schedule called for making "just" two to four speeches a day, sometimes in different cities, but he ended up making six or seven appearances a day while barnstorming through eleven cities in nine states. More than anything, he wanted to meet American leaders, who, he assumed, were equally eager to meet him. Secretary of State James Baker would meet him at the airport, wouldn't he? If not, then New York Governor Mario Cuomo? Matlock disabused him on both counts. Yeltsin expected to be received by President Bush, and the president did indeed want to see him, but Bush didn't want to give him "ammunition to use against Gorbachev." So he decided on a "drop-by," meaning that he would ostensibly bump into Yeltsin when dropping by National Security Adviser Brent Scowcroft's office.[76]

The White House visit exhibited some of the Yeltsin traits that drove Gorbachev wild. He refused to get out of the car unless Scowcroft aide Condoleezza Rice assured him he would see the president. She did not. Once in Scowcroft's office, a pouting Yeltsin droned through a long monologue—about how the Soviet Union should be reformed and how Washington could help—so "self-absorbed," recalled Robert Gates, "so oblivious" to the impact on his audience, that he didn't seem to notice that his host had dozed off. When Bush arrived, Yeltsin was transformed, "Chameleonlike," says Gates, suddenly "alive, enthusiastic, interesting," paying rapt attention to someone "plainly worth talking to—someone really powerful."[77]

The trip had other low points. In Miami, where Archer Daniels Midland mogul Dwayne Andreas put up Yeltsin in a seaside residence usually occupied by his daughters, Yeltsin found women's underwear in bedroom drawers. Sensing a CIA plot to blackmail him, he exploded, calming down only after an hour on the phone with Washington power broker Robert S. Strauss.[78] His appearance at Johns Hopkins University, in Baltimore, was described by *Washington Post* feature writer Paul Hendrickson this way: "That he could stand up, let alone be engaging and sound urgent, seemed a little miraculous. It wasn't just the two hours sleep he was going on. It was the amount of Tennessee whiskey he had knocked back overnight"—"a quart and half" of Jack Daniels' black label. "Like "a circus bear on a skateboard," Hendrickson continued, in a piece headlined "Yeltsin's Smashing Day," Yeltsin "came swaying and galumphing and bassooning and mugging and hugging and doom-warning through the greater Baltimore–Washington corridor."[79]

This account wasn't entirely accurate. According to Johns Hopkins President Steven Muller, Yeltsin shared the Jack Daniels with several other colleagues. Jim Garrison told the *Post* that Yeltsin was suffering from severe jet lag. (Many years later, though, Garrison recalled that after Yeltsin arrived in Baltimore on David Rockefeller's private plane he "turned around and urinated on the plane's back tire.") Yeltsin's interpreter said sleeping pills also accounted for Yeltsin's "zombie state." But Vittorio Zucconi, Washington correspondent of the left-wing Italian paper *La Repubblica*, didn't get the word. Instead, he repeated the most damaging charges from Hendrickson's account and added a few more of his own, some of them collected at second or third hand from unreliable Soviet émigrés and from at least one source, allegedly an Esalen official, who did not exist. "For Yeltsin," Zucconi reported, "America is a holiday, a stage set, a bar 5,000 kilometers long."[80]

Gorbachev and his inner circle of aides (Yakovlev, Chernyaev, Boldin, Medvedev, and Frolov) were at the villa in Novo-Ogaryovo when they discussed whether to republish the *La Repubblica* piece in the Soviet press. Almost all favored doing so, recalls Shakhnazarov; Yeltsin had dug his own hole, after all, so why should they spare him? Someone warned that piling on would only evoke more sympathy for him. Gorbachev paced the floor ruminating and then returned to the table where the others were waiting.

"It doesn't sit right with me. There's something unethical about it. Of course, we can expect anything from Boris, but we shouldn't mimic him." Gorbachev's aides tried to change his mind, but he held firm until someone said, "What if some paper decides on its own to reprint the piece? We have freedom of the press now, so no one need be ordered."

Gorbachev spread out his hands in a gesture of helplessness. Medvedev informed TASS, the Soviet press agency, that there would be no instructions as to whether or not to reprint. *Pravda* reprinted it, which Yeltsin and nearly everyone else interpreted as Gorbachev's latest attempt to discredit Yeltsin. It wasn't, insists Shakhnazarov, recalling how many times Gorbachev "rejected with disgust" proposals for "petty intrigues" against his rival, let alone really dirty tricks. And *Pravda's* ploy did indeed backfire. The newspaper actually apologized to Yeltsin (in a small correction on the bottom of page 7), citing errors in Zucconi's article. And Gorbachev told off *Pravda* editor Viktor Afanasyev. "I had a talk with him," Gorbachev told Medvedev. "I told him that when he has something to say, he should say it himself, and not invoke pieces of that kind."[81]

Soon after this, Afanasyev was sacked. But meanwhile, Soviet television showed footage of Yeltsin at Johns Hopkins (which Gorbachev also previewed, according to Medvedev) during prime time. What does the whole episode say about Shakhnazarov's generous take on Gorbachev's treatment of Yeltsin? Didn't Gorbachev know that Afanasyev would grab at a chance to "heap filth" (a familiar Soviet expression usually applied to Western "slanderers" of the USSR) on Gorbachev's rival, especially since it came from an Italian paper, rather than an American one, which might be thought to be fronting for the CIA? And that Soviet television, left to its own devices would do the same? Did Gorbachev just use this incident as an excuse to dump Afanasyev, about whom he had had reservations for quite some time? What the episode actually suggests is that as Gorbachev paced the floor at Novo-Ogaryovo, pondering how to treat his rival, he was trying to resist the temptation to eviscerate Yeltsin, but he didn't succeed.

Fortunately for his conscience, Gorbachev didn't have to restrain himself in his rival's next escapade, since Yeltsin did all the damage to himself. This time the curtain rises on the guardhouse of the Uspenskoye dacha compound on the Moscow River west of the capital, at about ten in the evening on September 28, 1989. Enter Yeltsin, soaking wet, telling the police that he had been bushwhacked by mysterious thugs, who threw a sack over his head and dumped him off a bridge into the river. "The water was terribly cold," Yeltsin recalled in his memoirs. "I got cramps in my legs and was barely able to swim to the shore, although the distance was only a few hundred yards. As I climbed up onto the bank, I collapsed and lay on the ground for some time, recovering my senses. Then I got up, shivering in the brutal cold. I realized I could never make it to my friend's house on my own, and I staggered to the nearby police station."

Yeltsin was being driven from a political rally to the dacha of a friend from Sverdlovsk whom he had known since the 1960s. He was carrying two bouquets of flowers he had taken from the rally. He called his family from the guardhouse and asked them to come and get him, and as he left, he asked the police to say "nothing to anyone about what had happened."[82]

Of course, word got out and created a storm of rumors, ranging from an attempted tryst in which Yeltsin's would-be paramour, a servant in his friend's dacha, dumped a pail of water on him, to a KGB plot to assassinate him. When the Supreme Soviet met on October 16, Gorbachev called on Minister of Internal Affairs Vadim Bakatin to "clear up the political speculation" about what had happened. With Yeltsin looking stricken as he sat among other deputies, Bakatin reported, among other things, that no one could have survived being thrown off the nearly fifty-foot high bridge into less than five feet of water, and that in a September 30 conversation with him, Yeltsin had admitted that no attempt to assassinate him had in fact occurred. After Bakatin spoke, Yeltsin grimly confirmed to his fellow deputies that "no attack on me occurred" and that "I make no accusations against the police. That's all I have to say."[83]

After this public confession, Yeltsin fell ill for two weeks and canceled several public appearances, while aides informed him that his popularity rating had dropped sharply.[84] Well might Gorbachev have felt, as the end of the year approached, that at least the Yeltsin threat had receded.

But not for long.

CHAPTER 13

1989:
TRIUMPH AND TROUBLE
ABROAD

I N THE LONG RUN, THE FALL of the Berlin Wall was inevitable. How could Germans remain forever separated when they were so attached (occasionally too attached) to their shared nationhood? But when and how the wall fell was not predictable. It did not fall because in the summer of 1987 President Reagan declared, "Mr. Gorbachev, tear down this wall!" Nor because Gorbachev decided on his own to order the East Germans to do so. Rather, the actual fall resembled the theater of the absurd.[1] Under pressure from massive opposition demonstrations in early November 1989, the East German Politburo opted for new, temporary travel rules permitting "permanent exit" from the German Democratic Republic. Drafting of the regulations was entrusted to bureaucrats, who authorized travel only for those with a passport, who also obtained a visa, a process taking at least another four weeks. The new rules were to be announced at four o'clock in the morning of November 10, by which time the offices that would process visa applications could be prepared to handle the initial traffic.

Some (but not all) East German Politburo members approved the draft during a smoking break from an all-day Central Committee meeting on November 9. Egon Krenz, who had replaced Honecker as party leader in October, gave the draft to another Politburo member, Günter Schabowski, with instructions to mention it at an international press conference at 6:00 p.m. Schabowski hadn't read the document by then, so he held off mentioning it until 6:53 p.m., when a journalist's question prompted the following exchange:

Schabowski: "This travel regulation—it is still not in effect, it's only a draft. A decision was made today, as far as I know . . . that allows every citizen of the German Democratic Republic (um) to (um) leave the GDR through any of the border crossings."

Journalists: "When does that go into effect? . . . Without a passport?"

Schabowski (scratching his head): "You see, comrades, I was informed today (puts on glasses as he speaks) that such an announcement had been (um) distributed earlier today." Schabowski reads: "Permanent exit is possible via all GDR crossings to the FRG."

Question: "When does it come into effect?"

Schabowski looks through his papers: "That comes into effect, according to my information, right away, immediately."

Question: "Does this also apply to West Berlin?"

Schabowski shrugs, frowns, and looks at his papers: "So (um)." Reads aloud: "Permanent exit can take place via all border crossings from the GDR to the FRG and West Berlin respectively."

Explosion of noise in the room. Questions from all sides.

Schabowski: "I'm expressing myself carefully because I'm not up to date on this question. I was given the information just before I came over."

Several journalists dash from the room to report the stunning news.

Question: "What is going to happen to the Berlin Wall now?"

Schabowski: "It has been brought to my attention that it is 7:00 p.m. That has to be the last question. Thank you for your understanding."

Several hours later, besieged by crowds of East Berliners, border guards opened the gates, letting crowds swarm across the border, where they were greeted ecstatically by West Germans, with many from both sides soon climbing atop the wall to celebrate by starting to chop away at it with pickaxes.

WHEN THE GATES OPENED at approximately 11:30 p.m. Berlin time (1:30 a.m. Moscow time) on November 9, 1989, Mikhail Gorbachev was asleep. Given the confusing reports coming in from Berlin, his aides did not wake him up.[2] According to Grachev, Gorbachev's "secret dream" had been to "wake up one morning and learn that the wall had fallen of its own accord," rather than at his command, and "that's essentially what happened." Told the next morning that the gates to West Berlin had been opened, Gorbachev responded, "They did the right thing."[3] Looking back in 2012, he said, "It wasn't unexpected. By then everything had become clear."[4] But no more than other leaders East and West had he foreseen that the wall would fall so soon, reshaping the political map of Europe with breathtaking speed.

A long, painful Soviet Politburo meeting on November 9 had addressed not the Berlin wall but turmoil in the Baltics, the upcoming second session of the Congress of People's Deputies, preparation of a new Communist party program, and how to cope with strikes at coal mines near the former hard-labor camps in Vorkuta, close to the Arctic Circle. It was at this session that Prime Minister Ryzhkov warned his colleagues that although the Baltics were boiling over, "what we should fear is not the Baltics, but Russia and Ukraine. I smell an overall collapse." The meeting paid no attention to East Germany.[5] After the wall fell, Gorbachev never summoned the Politburo (which decided not only matters of the greatest importance but minor matters as well) to a special session, of which there were plenty throughout his years in office. He did send a message to Mitterrand, Thatcher, and Bush that, while praising East Germany's "correct and forward-looking decision" to open the wall, struck some in the Bush administration as betraying "barely disguised panic." His November 10 message to Kohl warned of "a chaotic situation" that could have "unforeseen consequences." But Gorbachev seemed reassured the next day when Kohl told him by telephone that "we want the people of the GDR to stay home," that most of the hundreds of thousands who had entered West Berlin were "just visitors," and that West Germany did not want "a destabilization of the situation in the GDR." Gorbachev responded, "I take the words you have spoken in our conversation today very seriously. And I hope you will use your authority, your political weight and influence to keep others within limits that are adequate . . . for the requirement of our time."[6]

The main "requirement of our time," in Gorbachev's view, was that East Germany remain a viable socialist state for a lengthy interval so that eventual reunification would fit into the common European home that he had long favored. But Chancellor Kohl did not use his "authority, political weight and influence" in the way Gorbachev wanted; a mere seventeen days after their conversation, he began a process that ended with West Germany swallowing East Germany the following fall. Long before then, all the other Communist regimes in Eastern Europe had collapsed. In Poland, even before the Berlin Wall fell, the anti-Communist movement, Solidarity, triumphed in June 1989 elections, and a non-Communist prime minister, Tadeusz Mazowiecki, took power in August. In Hungary, the Communist party endorsed a multiparty political system in June. In Bulgaria, the grizzled party boss, Todor Zhivkov, fell on the same day as the Berlin Wall (although he was replaced by a Communist reformer). In Czechoslovakia, the president, by the end of the year, was playwright and longtime dissident Václav Havel. In Romania, dictator Nicolae Ceauşescu and his wife were overthrown and executed on December 25, 1989.

The collapse of Communism in Eastern Europe would be held against Gorbachev for decades by Russians proud of the Soviet empire. But Gorbachev remarkably, though characteristically, remained optimistic throughout 1989. The year had begun on a high note following his rapturous reception at the United Nations in New York. He fully expected incoming president George H. W. Bush to pick up where Ronald Reagan had left off, to meet with him early on and sign further disarmament agreements. Instead, Bush and his advisers declared a "pause" in U.S.-Soviet relations that lasted at least until the summer; their first summit meeting occurred only in December, on the island of Malta. As the "pause" stretched on, Gorbachev began to suspect that the new administration was seeking to undermine perestroika. The Malta summit didn't resolve any outstanding substantive issues, including the German question. Yet Gorbachev found a way to feel elated rather than discouraged by his meeting with Bush.

Why all this hope in the face of such seeming adversity? Partly because Gorbachev wasn't paying complete attention to foreign affairs; he was too distracted by the domestic developments described in chapter 12. "Even in the most dramatic moments," Chernyaev recalled, "even in the period of German reunification, [foreign policy] took up only five or six percent of the considerations of Gorbachev and the Politburo, of their time and their nerves." Georgy Shakhnazarov was Gorbachev's chief adviser on East European policy, but he spent most of his time writing memos and reports on domestic issues, as well as drafting new legislation and Gorbachev's speeches to the Congress of People's Deputies. The Kremlin leadership was so focused on internal Soviet problems, Shakhnazarov remembered, that "Eastern Europe was on the back burner." He and his boss still believed that "if our internal situation improved," then East European countries would be able to cope with their problems "faster and easier, and that would bring them closer to [the USSR]." On the other hand, if the domestic Soviet situation deteriorated, then Moscow would be unable to help its allies, who would "run away from us anyway, and to the West." Hard as it is to believe, "Gorbachev really did not have time, and so [the issue of Eastern Europe] was for us of secondary importance."[7]

Another factor was Gorbachev's vision of Europe's future. He had long hoped reform Communists like him would eventually come to power in Eastern Europe and adopt their own versions of perestroika. So he was delighted, rather than dismayed, to see Honecker, Husák, Zhivkov, and Ceauşescu go. He didn't despair when non-Communists took over, as long as they kept their countries in the Warsaw Pact and the Council for Mutual Economic Assistance (Comecon). Gorbachev's vision of Europe reflected something former French president Valéry Giscard d'Estaing told him in January 1989, when a delegation from the Trilateral Commission, a nongovernmental group promoting cooperation among the United States, Europe, and Japan, visited the Kremlin. Western Europe, too, Giscard said, was undergoing its own "perestroika," integrating itself to the point that in five, ten, or twenty years, it would constitute a "federative state." Gorbachev quoted Giscard to a Politburo meeting three days later, after citing Henry Kissinger's question to him: "How will you react if Eastern Europe wants to join the European Union?"[8]

Gorbachev didn't answer this question directly, either to Kissinger or to the Politburo. But he dreamed the two Europes would eventually come together, with the Soviet Union leading the way. Speaking to the Council of Europe in Strasbourg in July 1989, he almost applied for admission, citing Victor Hugo's vision of the day when France, Russia,

Britain, and Germany, "all of you, all nations of the continent, will merge tightly, without losing your identities and your remarkable originality, into some higher society and form a European fraternity," when "markets open to trade, and minds open to ideas, will become the new battlefields." Gorbachev didn't lay out a blueprint, but talked about ruling out the use of force or threat of force, creating a "vast economic space from the Atlantic to the Urals," protecting the environment and respecting human rights.[9]

By linking this vision to his oft-repeated notion of a "common European home," Gorbachev gave his speech a propagandistic air. But he was deadly serious. For the foreseeable future, the two Europes would remain separate, each with its own different political and economic system and its own security pact. Over time, however, their societies would come to resemble each other. NATO and the Warsaw Pact would become less military and more political, eventually to be replaced by a new collective security system based on the continent-wide Conference on Security and Cooperation in Europe (CSCE). This was the context in which Gorbachev imagined the two Germanys gradually converging, confederating, and finally uniting. That was what he meant when he told German interlocutors that he was not against German reunification in principle, but that history would decide when and how it occurred.

Unfortunately for Gorbachev, history decided a lot faster than he expected. But as 1989 ended, it was still possible (barely possible) for him to think time was on his side. It took all his considerable capacity for optimism to remain as hopeful as he did—optimism reinforced by his pressing political and psychological need, given his travails at home, to find not just comfort and hope abroad, but continuing confirmation that he was ending the cold war and bringing peace to the world.

ON JANUARY 17, 1989, four days before his inauguration as president, George H. W. Bush wrote a letter to Gorbachev that Kissinger delivered in Moscow. Bush reiterated "what I said to you last year, when you came to the United Nations." Bush was "still serious about moving our relationship forward," and believed that "we should elevate the dialogue, especially between you and me, above the details of arms control proposals, and discuss more general issues of more extensive political relations to which we should aspire." Bush added that he would need "some time to think through the entire range of issues" and to "formulate a solid and consistent American approach," but he reassured Gorbachev, "We are not talking about slowing down or reversing the positive process that has marked the last four years."[10] Five days later, Bush followed up with a phone call, which, Gorbachev recalled, also had "an optimistic tone." As a result, he expected that his relationship with the president would "not only proceed in a constructive fashion, but with all necessary speed."[11]

Gorbachev had made his expectations clear even before coming to New York in December 1988. Anatoly Dobrynin told secretary of state–designate James Baker that what Gorbachev "really wanted" was "a meeting with George Bush. We're happy to be dealing with you guys [rather than a new Democratic administration]. You are known quantities."[12] Gorbachev assumed he was also a known quantity to Bush; by then, as Chernyaev puts it, his boss "counted on" Bush and other Western leaders "taking his word" that he was sincere in his peaceful intentions and "responding accordingly."[13] But although Reagan had taken his word, and Thatcher and Mitterrand still did, Bush, or rather some of his key advisers, did not.

"I was probably less suspicious of Gorbachev than were others in my incoming team," Bush recalled. "I thought, as Prime Minister Thatcher had once said about him, that this was a man I could work with." Bush felt Gorbachev was "sincere" in his desire to change the Soviet Union and East-West relations. He knew Gorbachev was "carefully watching to see if we would veer off to a harder line than Reagan had taken at the end of his Administration." Yet that is exactly what Bush did.[14]

Bush might well have been a believer in Gorbachev. He had transformed the Soviet political system, discarded the ideological underpinnings of Soviet foreign policy, signed one disarmament treaty (INF) and moved toward another (START), announced a cut in conventional forces in Europe, moved to withdraw from Afghanistan, and recognized universal human rights. No wonder Thatcher declared the previous November, "We're not in a cold war now," and Secretary of State Shultz considered that by the end of 1988 the cold war was "all over but the shouting."[15]

But more than shouting continued in Washington. General Brent Scowcroft, Bush's national security adviser, remained "suspicious of Gorbachev's motives and skeptical of his prospects," as did Scowcroft's deputy Robert Gates and Secretary of Defense Dick Cheney. Had the old men in the Politburo been "all wrong," General Scowcroft asked, in thinking that Gorbachev would revitalize the system rather than overturn it? "Not likely," Scowcroft thought in 1989. In fact, Gorbachev's reforms made him potentially even "more dangerous" than his predecessors, whose overly aggressive moves spared the West the consequences of "its own wishful thinking."[16] Scowcroft believed, as he recalled several years later in a letter to two of his White House colleagues, that Gorbachev was "trying to smother us with kindness," that his December 1988 UN speech was "an attempt to lure the West into disarmament by taking measures that looked impressive but made a negligible difference in the capability of Soviet forces in Eastern Europe."[17] To Scowcroft, Reagan's born-again faith in Gorbachev, not to mention his effort to abolish the nuclear weapons that deterred a Soviet attack on Western Europe, seemed naïve. James Baker, who had been Reagan's White House chief of staff and then treasury secretary, reportedly thought Shultz had been a "flabby negotiator," who paid for concessions that Gorbachev "might have made for free," while other Bush officials anonymously denounced Shultz to reporters as "the worst secretary since Edward Stettinius" (whom FDR appointed three months before his death in 1945).[18] In contrast to Shultz, who had pressed for summit conferences and welcomed their results, Scowcroft feared Gorbachev would "exploit" an early meeting to pretend the cold war was over and thus "only abet the current Soviet propaganda campaign." Scowcroft knew that Bush "wanted to sit down with Gorbachev at an early date," and was relieved when his boss "did not press the idea," even though "he periodically came back to the issue as the months passed."[19]

Scowcroft, Gates, and Cheney were right to doubt Gorbachev's prospects for remaining in power over the long term. But they were wrong about how much he had accomplished by 1989. And furthermore, his longevity in office might well have been extended if he had received more help from the United States—help that they resisted rendering to him.

If Bush trusted Gorbachev more than some of his advisers did, why didn't he override Scowcroft? Why did he instead order an across-the-board reassessment of U.S. policy toward the USSR, which dragged on through the spring? Partly because, as Dana Carvey's *Saturday Night Live* Bush double would have put it, "Wouldn't be prudent!" Bush was cautious and more than a little insecure. "I don't want to do anything dumb," he told Scowcroft in late January.[20] He also had a complicated relationship with Reagan and Reaganism that held him back. Bush wanted to emerge from Reagan's shadow as his own man, "to put his own fingerprint on the country's foreign policy," as Baker later put it. But he also feared right-wing attacks for being more liberal than Reagan, which he could avoid by being tougher on the Russians than Reagan had been. Bush knew from the letter that Kissinger brought back from Moscow that Gorbachev was (in Bush's words) "ready to pick up immediately from where the Reagan administration had left off," but instead Bush decreed the "pause."[21]

Gorbachev was puzzled, then "offended" (according to Grachev), that "his newly discovered 'friend George' was not ready to render him the support he so badly needed," "afraid" (Chernyaev recalled) that "everything he had achieved with Reagan" might be "lost."[22] He could tolerate a short delay, but weeks and months? Ignorant of the ways of Washington (John F. Kennedy had similarly resisted Nikita Khrushchev's push for talks soon after the presidential inauguration in 1961, agreeing to meet only in June in Vienna), Gorbachev and his close aides did not understand, Chernyaev admits. The Foreign Ministry did understand, according to Shevardnadze's aide, Sergei Tarasenko, but apparently the Kremlin didn't get the word.[23] Meantime, Gorbachev was under pressure from Kremlin conservatives who, he recalls, interpreted the pause as "evidence that Washington intended no good toward our country."[24] The KGB was quick to portray the delay in the most negative light. Gorbachev had called KGB chief Kriuchkov's agency on its worst-case interpretation of Baltic nationalism—"packaged as truth," Gorbachev labeled it, adding, "Vladimir Aleksandrovich, I am looking at you!"[25] But he proved less able to resist erroneous charges (which he repeated to West German Chancellor Kohl and Italian Communist leader Achille Occhetto) that a special CIA group had the secret mission of discrediting perestroika and Gorbachev personally, and so did the BBC in Great Britain.[26]

Gorbachev was "in a hurry," Grachev writes, to show in foreign affairs the kind of positive results that were so painfully absent at home. He virtually admitted as much in a poignant confession to Kissinger that Kissinger reported to Bush: "I lead a strange country. I am trying to take my people in a direction they do not understand and many do not want to go." Gorbachev originally thought perestroika "would be completed by now. Instead economic reform had just begun." "It was easy to see what was wrong," he admitted, but "harder to find out what works." In the meantime, "I need a long period of peace."[27]

A cry for help! But help wasn't forthcoming when Gorbachev badly needed it. The Bush administration's strategic review eventually came up with what Scowcroft called a "four-part approach for coping with Gorbachev." First, "to appear confident about our purposes and agenda." Second, "to signal that relations with our allies were our first priority" by underscoring "the credibility of our nuclear deterrent through modernization." Third, to place a higher priority on relations with Eastern Europe than with the USSR, since the region had become "a potential weak link in the solidarity of the Soviet bloc." Fourth, to promote regional stability in a place like Central America, although the Kremlin had shown "no signs of abating its support for Communist military activities [there]."[28]

The list did not include helping Gorbachev transform his country and close out the cold war. Because the overriding purpose of American foreign policy, as understood by the "realists" around Bush, "should not be how can we help perestroika or Gorbachev, but how can we promote the interests of the United States." The words are those of Ambassador Jack Matlock Jr. in the third of three cables he sent from Moscow in February 1989. Actually, Matlock did want to help Gorbachev, but he couched his advice carefully so as to preserve his credibility; his first cable's main message was that what Gorbachev was doing was itself in the American national interest: "In sum, the Soviet Union has, in effect, declared the bankruptcy of its system, and just as with a corporation which has sought the protection of Chapter XI, there is no turning back."[29]

To be sure, there were other objections to "helping" Gorbachev— that Washington should focus on the USSR, not on its individual leader; that regardless of his achievements, or rather, just because of them, Gorbachev faced mounting opposition and probably eventual ouster; and that in the meantime, Washington didn't know enough about Moscow politics to be of effective assistance. But as Bush himself later said of Gorbachev, "This guy *is* perestroika"—to which one might add that for the time being the Soviet leader's position was secure; that he himself was identifying the assistance he needed (i.e., early talks leading to the kind of strategic nuclear arms control agreement, START I, that Bush eventually signed in July 1991); and that by the spring of 1989 he was already satisfying "conditions" for such talks stipulated in U.S. National Security Directive 23, which was drafted in April and May, but not issued until September: Soviet "deployment of a force posture that is smaller and less threatening"—announced by Gorbachev at the UN in December. "Establishing a firm Soviet domestic base for a more productive and cooperative relationship with the free nations of the world"—see the political reforms of 1988 and 1989. "Self-determination for the countries of East-Central Europe"—already underway in Poland.[30]

Interviewed in 2006, Bush claimed, "I have never had second thoughts about whether we should have 'responded sooner'" to Gorbachev—"none at all. I do not think that those who wanted to unseat him would have been deterred by an earlier substantive response on our part."[31] But back in April 1989, the president himself was getting antsy. During Baker's February tour of Europe, allied leaders kept telling him Bush must engage with Gorbachev. Domestic voices in Congress and the press pounded home the same message. Matlock urged an early summit on Bush at a meeting in the Oval Office on March 3. After the president brushed him off with "Interesting. Let's think about it," Matlock groused to his colleagues: "Our marching orders are clear: "Don't just do something, *stand there!*"[32] Baker realized that Gorbachev must view the Bush administration with "some concern." Not only had it "frozen the [arms control] negotiations in place while we went through the lengthy 'review,'" but on April 29, Cheney said in a CNN interview that Gorbachev would "ultimately fail." Baker didn't necessarily disagree, but he was dismayed to hear this expressed publicly, by the secretary of defense, no less, as the administration's view.[33] Reagan himself suggested in a May 6 interview that Bush was being too cautious in his approach to Gorbachev.[34] Meantime, Bush decided that "we had to regain the initiative." His "own thoughts," he recalled, "were focused on putting the United States back out in front as we tackled the challenges in Eastern Europe and the Soviet Union."[35] That sounded more like public relations than realpolitik, but the result was that Baker arrived in Moscow on May 10 to resume the high-level dialogue with Gorbachev.

Just how badly Gorbachev wanted such talks was evident in his and Shevardnadze's demeanor. Shevardnadze, who conducted the initial conversations, invited Baker and his wife, Susan, to dinner at home, in an apartment house reserved for high-ranking officials, although with the standard, small, dingy elevator that held only three passengers. Shevardnadze's wife, Nanuli, laid on a lavish Georgian feast with spicy lamb and vegetable stew, then endorsed independence for her native republic ("Georgia must be free!"). Her husband, obviously briefed on Baker's hobby of turkey hunting, gave him a twelve-gauge shotgun. Breaking with the cold war precedent of denying Soviet internal problems, lest they invite the impression of weakness, Shevardnadze recited a catalog of economic horrors from both the black market and the legal economy: repairmen paid in vodka and taxi drivers in foreign cigarettes, cheap state-subsidized bread fed to pigs, corn rotting in the fields. He also confessed that when Gorbachev came into office, "none of us had any idea of just what we were facing in the economy," and lamented that national unrest was "the most subtle and troublesome" problem facing the country. Baker's impression was that Shevadnadze's "shoulders seemed to carry the burdens of the world," his white hair made him look "older than he was," and "the patches under his eyes seemed to darken and lengthen." It would have been difficult for Shevardnadze to conceal such innate characteristics, but by going out of his way to reveal his deep anxieties, he underlined his and his country's need for a helpful, constructive partner in the United States.[36]

Gorbachev's very different mood conveyed a similar message when he greeted Baker the next day in St. Catherine's Hall. "He bounded into the room," Baker recalled, "beaming as always with energy and confidence." Baker noticed Gorbachev's "actor's gift to fill a stage with his presence" and "with his upbeat attitude." He reminded Baker of Reagan, who also "filled a room with his upbeat outlook, buoying everyone in it." Both men were "invariably positive," one reason, Baker thought, why they were "able to work together so successfully." As was the case with Shevardnadze, this demeanor came naturally to Gorbachev (although he was quite capable of grimness and anger, either real or put-on, when the situation called for it), but in this case it reflected his satisfaction that the Bush administration was finally coming around, as well as the sheer pleasure he felt when jousting again with an American leader rather than with Ligachev or Yeltsin.[37]

Baker reassured Gorbachev that he and the president had no desire to see perestroika fail. "To the contrary, we would very much like it to succeed." He admitted that "a small number" of Americans thought perestroika would fail and that the United States would "gain" as a result. But not in the administration, which believed that successful reforms would render the USSR "stronger, more stable, more open and more secure." Other aspects of the talks didn't go as well, however. Gorbachev's idea of reducing short-range nuclear forces in Europe "blindsided" Baker because it would encourage West German opposition to planned deployment of new American Lance missiles. Baker's complaints about Soviet arms shipments to Central America irritated Gorbachev, who had already ordered a halt to arms shipments to Nicaragua. Baker's response to Gorbachev's "long soliloquy" on perestroika and its problems, his recommendation that Moscow reform prices sooner than later, prompted this bittersweet rejoinder from the Soviet leader: "We were twenty years late on price reform, so two or three more years won't hurt."[38]

Gorbachev was gratified by the talks. Baker struck him as a "serious" and "constructive" man, who "firmly defended his views, but was ready to listen and even heed sensible arguments." But almost half a year had already been lost to the "pause," and talk about a summit had been further postponed until the fall. As for Baker's claim that everyone in the administration was rooting for perestroika to succeed, at least one member of Baker's delegation still had his doubts. When Gorbachev and Baker joined their colleagues after an hourlong one-on-one conversation, Gorbachev was introduced to Robert Gates. He understood, he told Gates, that the White House had a "special cell assigned the task of discrediting Gorbachev," and that "you are in charge, Mr. Gates." To Baker he added, "Perhaps if we are able to work out our problems, Mr. Gates will be out of a job."[39]

———

FOR MOST OF 1989, Gorbachev found it more gratifying to deal with West European leaders than with Americans. Their views and his had more in common. He could complain to them about Bush, hoping they'd pressure Washington to be more forthcoming. He was welcomed rapturously in European capitals, flattered by their leaders, and invited to perform in their most hallowed halls.

Gorbachev spent April 5 through 7 in London, where British Ambassador to Moscow Rodric Braithwaite observed him to be "lively, forceful and direct," despite "all his troubles." In response to Gorbachev's complaints about Bush, Thatcher described the president as "a more balanced person" than Reagan, who would pay "more attention to detail" and would "as a whole . . . continue the Reagan line." But as soon as Gorbachev departed, she informed Bush that Gorbachev had good reason to be upset with Washington's dreadfully lengthy strategic review. Thatcher praised perestroika to Gorbachev; she had been "the first to say that your success is in our interest," but she was "concerned about the immensity of your task," a burden Gorbachev confirmed when he confessed he felt as if he had "lived two full lives in the course of the last four years" with "no respite in sight."[40]

It wasn't just what Thatcher said, but how she said it—with verve and enthusiasm matching his own from the moment she and her husband met Gorbachev and his wife on a cold, rainy night at Heathrow Airport. They got on "like a house on fire," noted Ambassador Braithwaite. "Madam was magnificent," marveled Chernyaev. "For three hours I sat opposite her" as she "tried to cast a spell on him," while he, in response, "played the role of a man who was trying to make an impression."[41]

Gorbachev enjoyed performing in public as well: in front of the prime minister's residence at 10 Downing Street, he recalled, before "some three hundred journalists from the world's biggest television companies, news agencies and newspapers"; at Westminster Abbey, where he emerged from his limousine to meet "thousands who greeted our delegation with stormy applause"; at Guildhall, "one of the most prestigious national rostrums," which was vouchsafed to foreign leaders "only on extremely rare occasions"; before a gathering of the "cream of British social and political circles"; at lunch with the queen and the prince of Wales at Windsor Castle, where (according to Braithwaite) both hostess and guest were "uncharacteristically stiff and ill-at-ease," but where, after a royal guided tour of the castle's artistic treasures, the queen tentatively accepted Gorbachev's invitation to visit Russia (where her grandfather's cousin Nicky, a.k.a. Tsar Nicholas II, had been murdered by the Bolsheviks in 1918).[42]

As was his wont, Gorbachev preserved his own press notices in what he called "notoriously critical British newspapers." *Daily Express*: "The whole world has been talking about Maggie and Mikhail." *Today*: "Overwhelming majority believes Russian leader is sincere in wanting to free the world of nuclear weapons." *The Times*: "Unlike Bulganin and Khrushchev 33 years ago, President and Mrs. Gorbachev were treated by the Queen not just to a cup of tea, but a three-course meal."[43] One other item from London: Braithwaite noted that Mrs. Gorbachev stood out of range of the cameras (about five yards to her husband's right) on the steps of 10 Downing Street, "evidently determined not to attract the same kind of adverse attention back home that she got after the 1984 visit." She did, however, make an excellent impression on children at a London museum, who, according to a *Daily Mail* clipping in her husband's collection, "reacted to her with delight."[44]

As Gorbachev recalled it, West Germany's ardent embrace between June 12 and 15 exceeded Britain's: young people cheering "in solidarity with Soviet reforms"; breakfast on the banks of the Rhine with the "erudite, intelligent, well-disposed" President von Weizsäcker; streets crowded with people "overflowing with friendship and sympathy," shouting, "Gorbi! Gorbi!" and holding signs saying, "Hang in There, Gorbachev!" Plus an "unforgettable" reception on a square in Bonn, warm visits to other cities and towns around the country, and an ecstatic greeting at a steelworks in Dortmund, where a thousand workers "perched on machines, balancing on cranes and sitting on each other's shoulders," "interrupting me with approving shouts and applause after almost every sentence," seeming to understand "my words even without translation" as he dropped his prepared text and improvised, racing ahead of his interpreter.[45]

Gorbachev's talks with the massive Chancellor (Kohl stood six feet five and weighed around three hundred pounds) lacked the "Maggie" frisson, but were just as friendly. Gorbachev's idea of reducing short-range nuclear missiles (which could leave divided Germany in ruins) got a warmer reception in Bonn than in London. When Gorbachev asked whether he could count on economic assistance if urgently needed, Kohl answered yes. To Gorbachev's complaint about Bush's stalling on summitry, Kohl responded that the president was prepared to cooperate as well (adding that Bush's wife was "a steady, balanced woman" with "a calming effect on people," which "wasn't the case before"). He followed up with a June 15 phone call to Bush, urging the president to be in closer touch with Gorbachev, "who places a high premium on 'personal chemistry.'"[46]

The discussion of Europe and Germany also seemed reassuring. Gorbachev expressed his concern about Eastern Europe. No one should "poke a stick into an anthill," disrupting the process of building trust between West and East. The consequences could be "absolutely unpredictable." Kohl seemed to agree: "I am not interested in destabilizing the situation in the GDR."[47] In contrast to his formal, wooden exchanges with Communist leaders, Gorbachev and Kohl exchanged candid assessments of them; both admired Poland's Jaruzelski; neither could stand Ceauşescu. During a walk along the Rhine, Kohl compared the division of Germany to a dam on the river: just as the river would overflow and find its way to the sea, Germans would never reconcile themselves to being permanently divided. Gorbachev refrained from contradicting him. In a joint statement, the two leaders declared it their "paramount objective" to "contribute to overcoming the division of Europe." In addition, they signed eleven agreements expanding economic, cultural, and other ties.[48]

Gorbachev and Kohl met privately three times, twice at the Bonn chancellery and once at Kohl's villa on the Rhine. Kohl gave Gorbachev a medal depicting the two leaders, and a gift for Gorbachev's mother. "I've read about her in the press," said the chancellor. "I thought she might like to receive a small token of my regard."[49] At Kohl's home, the two men exchanged reminiscences about their childhoods and their families' suffering during the war. At one point, Kohl said, "I tell you once again that I like your policy and I like you as a person." As they parted, the two couples embraced each other. "For me," Kohl said later, "this evening was a pivotal experience, and I believe it was for Gorbachev, too." Said Gorbachev in Bonn, "I value the trust that is growing between us at every meeting." By the end of the visit, as one historian writes, West Germany had become Moscow's "most important partner in Europe," or as two others put it, in the face of Bush's not-benign neglect, Kohl had become Gorbachev's "main foreign partner."[50]

If French President Mitterrand wasn't Gorbachev's main European partner, he seemed his intellectual soul mate. Mitterrand, too, dreamed of overcoming the division of Europe. He, too, imagined East Europeans reforming Communism and then moving closer to an increasingly integrated Western Europe. He, too, could see the German problem eventually solved in this evolving pan-European framework, with Europe's post-bloc security guaranteed within the CSCE. Mitterrand treated Mr. and Mrs. Gorbachev like the intellectuals they felt themselves to be.[51] Gorbachev cherished his invitation to address a select portion of the French intelligentsia at the fabled Sorbonne. After paying tribute to French philosophers whose ideas shaped the French Revolution, he "philosophized" himself, defining the "fundamentally new global problems facing mankind at the end of the twentieth century," to which his "new thinking" provided answers. He must have particularly appreciated Mitterrand's confession, in a cozy, candid conversation with the Gorbachevs, that Bush had a "very big drawback as a president—he lacks original thinking altogether." He declared to Gorbachev, "I believe in you. How could I not? I well remember how you talked to me about your plans when you first took office in 1985. I see that you are keeping your promises." It was no wonder Gorbachev considered his talks with Mitterrand "a breakthrough," demonstrating that "at last Western leaders believed in perestroika."[52]

GORBACHEV'S NEXT VISIT was to China, from May 15 through 18. What happened there in Tiananmen Square and his own reaction to it shaped his approach to turmoil he faced in Eastern Europe. China's paramount leader, the octogenarian Deng Xiaoping, was also a reformer. But whereas Gorbachev concluded that economic reform was impossible without democratization and political pluralism, Deng was proceeding to introduce a market economy, while jealously guarding the party's monopoly of political power.

In both countries the reforms unleashed pressure from below for more radical change. The day that Gorbachev arrived in Beijing, thousands of students were occupying Tiananmen Square. Some held banners saluting him as "The Ambassador of Democracy." (Outside the walls of a large park where the Soviet delegation was housed in a separate residence, demonstrators chanted, "Gor-ba-chev! Come to us!")[53] The regime's planned welcome in the square had to be canceled (it was held instead at the airport), and when Deng hosted Gorbachev in the Great Hall of the People, next to the square, demonstrators broke a window trying to crash the party. Deng and his colleagues had hoped to clear the square before Gorbachev's arrival, but the demonstrators knew they would be safe as long as Gorbachev was in town, bringing hordes of foreign journalists who were covering his visit.[54]

Gorbachev hadn't come to China to lead the demonstrations, of course, but to heal the Sino-Soviet breach that had waxed and waned since the 1960s. His talks with Deng succeeded in doing just that. But the talks had an undertone reflecting the uproar in the square and the two men's differing assessments of it. Gorbachev didn't say so directly, either in Beijing or afterward, but he sympathized with demonstrators pushing for the kind of changes he had introduced at home. Deng was already moving toward his eventual decision to use massive force to clear the square. He took care to note that past Sino-Soviet ideological debates (in which he had played a leading role beginning in the sixties) were "empty words" on both sides, and had to admit that "we do not believe that our views were always correct." But he dominated the discussion, assuming the mantle of leading interpreter of Marxism-Leninism, thereby implying that his views on the proper balance (or rather, imbalance) of economic and political reform were correct.

Gorbachev talked at length with Communist party general secretary Zhao Ziyang (Deng had by now retired from that post while maintaining ultimate authority), whose vision of reform was much closer to Gorbachev's. But Zhao was replaced shortly after Gorbachev departed for Moscow. And on June 3–4, Chinese troops smashed the Tiananmen

Mikhail and Raisa Gorbachev with Deng Xiaoping in Beijing, May 16, 1989.

demonstration, killing up to several hundred in the process and wounding thousands more.[55]

Gorbachev was enough of a diplomat not to condemn the crackdown in public. But it reinforced his determination not to use force to smash demonstrations in the Soviet Union and Eastern Europe. In that sense, his Beijing visit confirmed his view that welcoming East European revolutions was the wise way to handle them, and increased his confidence that he could do so successfully. As for Deng's view, his younger son, Deng Zhifang, expressed it to an American journalist in 1990: "My father thinks Gorbachev is an idiot."[56] What he meant was that Gorbachev was risking the survival of Soviet Communism by putting the cart (political transformation) before the horse (radical economic reform).

IN EARLY OCTOBER 1988, Gorbachev's adviser on Eastern Europe, Shakhnazarov, sent him an urgent memorandum. What should Moscow do "if one or even several countries become bankrupt simultaneously?" What if "social instability" escalated in Poland, Hungary, and Czechoslovakia? "Do we have a plan in case of a crisis that might encompass the

entire socialist world or a large part of it?" It was "high time to discuss
these issues in the Politburo in the presence of experts."[57]

Gorbachev did not call an emergency meeting of the Politburo to discuss the East European situation—not then or later. It took him until
January 31, 1989, to raise these issues in the Politburo, and he did so in
a way that reflected confidence, as well as concern. The Politburo must
indeed study where its East European "friends" were "drifting." "What
is going on in Hungary, for example," where new leaders were emerging? Gorbachev was sure "the socialist basis" would be preserved in "all"
allied countries, but for a reason that underlined how weak the link
between Moscow and its friends had become. They still assumed that
Moscow would keep them on "a leash." "They simply do not know that if
they pulled harder on this leash it would break."[58]

In February, Gorbachev received formal studies of the East European
situation. One, prepared by the Institute of the Economy of the World
Socialist System, imagined a best-case scenario (that by championing
"a new model of socialism" reform Communists could maintain control),
and a worst-case vision of "the collapse of the socialist idea." Gorbachev
credited the former while ignoring the latter. Another report, from the
Central Committee's international department, counseled "a certain
vagueness" about whether Moscow would act to thwart radical change,
lest "anti-socialist forces" be tempted to "test the fundamentals of socialism." But Gorbachev kept insisting forcible intervention was out of the
question. Indeed, the "Brezhnev Doctrine"—that Moscow would inter-
vene by force, if necessary, to maintain Communist control of Eastern
Europe—was officially abrogated at the Warsaw Pact summit in Bucharest in July 1989. According to the meeting's concluding document, relations among member countries were to be characterized by "equality,
independence and the right of each country to arrive at its own political position, strategy and tactics without interference from an outside
party."[59]

Poland presented a daunting test case. It was Moscow's most important East European ally. It had a history of anti-Russian nationalism. It
was challenging the "fundamentals of socialism" more drastically than
others. Yet Gorbachev was particularly optimistic about its prospects. He
admired the Polish Communist leader, General Wojciech Jaruzelski, for

his "ability to evaluate even the most complicated situation clearly, precisely and brilliantly." He trusted Jaruzelski "almost absolutely" (according to Chernyaev) as someone who could gradually lead Poland out of a crisis as "an ally" and a "friendly state." Jaruzelski and his reform-minded colleagues trusted Gorbachev in return. When they decided in September 1988 to open talks with the opposition, they didn't consult Moscow, and Moscow didn't object. Speaking to Polish Foreign Minister Józef Czyrek, Gorbachev seemed to countenance free elections and a possible coalition government.[60] When Jaruzelski told Gorbachev he couldn't guarantee the results of such elections, Gorbachev replied, "Wojciech, we just carried out our own free elections to the Congress of People's Deputies, and I didn't know the results in advance either. And lo and behold, the sky didn't fall. So how, after that, can I object to Poles' having the same right?"[61] Polish roundtable negotiations produced an April 7, 1989, agreement to hold mostly free elections. Solidarity, the anti-Communist trade union turned political movement headed by Lech Wałesa could compete for seats in a new Senate of 100 members, but would be limited to 35 percent of the 460 seats in the more important Diet. Even Solidarity's triumph in the June elections (winning 92 of 100 Senate seats in June, and 160 of the 161 seats open to them in the Diet) didn't shake Gorbachev's faith—because, according to Grachev—"we believed that the USSR had the political means to circumscribe the processes at work." Nor did the appointment on August 24 of a non-Communist prime minister, Tadeusz Mazowiecki, who had been arrested when martial law was declared in Poland in 1981 and was one of the last prisoners to be freed in December 1982. According to Mieczysław Rakowski, who became party leader when Jaruzelski was elected president in July, Gorbachev offered "not the least objection, nor the least reservations" about the new Polish cabinet.[62] Instead, talking with Rakowski in October, he joked that now that the Polish opposition had a role in government, they would learn "it's not easy being in power."[63]

Gorbachev's joke covered a sense of apprehension. Rakowski had lamented, Gorbachev told the Politburo the next day, that despite its massive size, the Polish party was "helpless." "It's just like ours," Gorbachev continued, "an exact copy." Gorbachev also made a veiled threat that in fact was a bluff: "I told him that if affairs in Poland were to develop 'not

as they should,' we will react."[64] By autumn, according to Polish historian Paweł Machcewicz, what appeared in the summer to be the start of
lengthy negotiations, with Communists still in control, had become "the
speedy dissolution of the Communist system." But as late as December,
Gorbachev told Rakowski, "Don't forget, Mieczyslaw, your socialist ideas
have a future."

"The ideas do, but we don't have one," Rakowski answered.

Gorbachev didn't reply. He realized, Rakowski recalled, that the
socialism he was trying to promote in Poland was at "an impasse." Did
Gorbachev still believe things could be changed for the better? Rakowski
thought that he did.[65]

The pace of change in Hungary lagged behind that in Poland, but not
by much. Gorbachev showed signs of unease and uncertainty, but for the
most part supported change or, at least, refused to oppose it. In January,
reform-minded Politburo member Imre Pozgay declared in a radio interview that the Hungarian revolt crushed by Moscow in 1956 had been not
a "counterrevolution" (the official Soviet bloc description) but "a popular insurrection against an oligarchical power." He and his supporters
waited in suspense for a harsh reaction from Moscow, but it never came;
Gorbachev specifically vetoed one prepared in the Central Committee's
international department.[66] In March, when the hard-line Hungarian
party general secretary, Károly Grósz, raised the issue in Moscow, Gorbachev said that how the Hungarians evaluated 1956 was entirely up to
them. But although he endorsed democratization in Hungary, he ominously specified, again bluffing, that "the limit, however, is the safekeep-
ing of socialism and assurance of stability."[67]

On March 3, Miklós Németh, another reformer serving as Hungary's prime minister, told Gorbachev that his government had decided to
open the border with Austria since it now serves "only to catch citizens
from Romania and the GDR who are trying to escape illegally to the
West through Hungary." But to this unprecedented breach in the Iron
Curtain, which kept widening until the Berlin Wall itself fell, Gorbachev
replied only, "We have a strict regime on our borders, but we are also
becoming more open."[68] That same month the Hungarian Central Committee endorsed the principle of free elections and a multiparty system.
And when Grósz repeatedly asked Gorbachev to back his resistance to

such changes, Gorbachev "consistently and knowingly refused to do so." Grósz was tempted to use force to stop the system from unraveling, but, he recalled, "not only would we have been condemned by Western countries and subjected to sanctions, but, above all, such an action would have collided head-on with the whole thrust of Soviet foreign policy, and we would have been isolated in our own camp."[69]

It wasn't just Gorbachev who forswore the use of force in dealings with Eastern Europe. By now even Soviet hard-liners understood it was too late for that.[70] But while they despaired for the future, Gorbachev believed that the Hungarian model of democratizing socialism not only had a good chance of succeeding but could even become a model for the Soviet Union itself.[71]

If Gorbachev had illusions about Poland and Hungary, he had none about East Germany as long as it was under Erich Honecker's thumb. The two leaders' July talks in Moscow were, Grachev reports, "a dialogue of the deaf." Honecker made clear he needed no advice. Gorbachev warned that if the East German regime needed Soviet help, especially military help, to stay afloat, none would be forthcoming.[72] Honecker felt superior to the misguided Gorbachev.[73] Gorbachev privately told Chernyaev that Honecker was a "scumbag," who nonetheless regarded himself (Gorbachev later told Honecker's successor, Egon Krenz) as "No. 1 in socialism, if not in the world."[74] Raisa Gorbachev told her husband on October 1 that Soviet Cultural Fund colleagues recently returned from East Germany characterized the situation there as "five minutes to midnight."[75] No wonder that Gorbachev hesitated to attend the fortieth anniversary celebration of the GDR's founding a few days later in East Berlin, finally agreeing to go when assured he would meet with the whole GDR Politburo, not just with Honecker.[76]

Honecker put on a lavish show, but it boomeranged from the moment Gorbachev arrived at Schönefeld Airport on the morning of October 6. On the drive to Niederschönhausen Palace, where the Soviet delegation was staying, Gorbachev recalled, young people lining the route shouted, "Gorbachev! Gorbachev!"—although Honecker was sitting stone-faced "right next to me." Nor did crowds pay any attention to Honecker that afternoon when "we walked through a narrow corridor between two columns of people" to what was supposed to be gala meeting at the Palace of the Republic. That night the regime mustered a mammoth torchlight procession along the main East Berlin thoroughfare, Unter den Linden: bands playing, drums beating, light from giant projectors stabbing the sky, thousands of young people, although carefully chosen by the Communist youth league, shouting "Perestroika!" "Gorbachev, Help Us!" "Gorbi! Gorbi!" as they marched past Gorbachev, Honecker, and some twenty other Communist bloc leaders on the reviewing stand.[77]

It looked like "a boiling pot with a tightly shut lid," Gorbachev remarked to Valentin Falin, his chief adviser on Germany. Polish party leader Rakowski approached Gorbachev and whispered, "This is the end." Later, during a walk in the park near the palace, Gorbachev asked Falin, "What shall we do?" Honecker was "beside himself," Gorbachev said, he was in "a kind of trance," but Gorbachev could hardly be expected to "force the people to be silent." The next day, the two leaders met for almost three hours, during which Honecker rattled on about his regime's glorious achievements. But meeting afterward with East German Politburo members, Gorbachev told them that "a party that lags behind the times" will "harvest bitter fruit," that if it "does not react to the demands of reality, it is doomed," that "life punishes those who are too late," that "now is a good moment for you to act." Honecker listened to Gorbachev with "a slightly reddish face" and a "contorted smile," a German participant remembered. In a strained voice more high-pitched than usual, he thanked Gorbachev, but then recalled his own recent visit to Magnitogorsk, the fabled Soviet iron and steel center, where "the stores were empty and even soap and matches weren't available." Under his breath, but audible to all, Honecker muttered, "Those who brought down their own country are ready to teach us."[78]

Gorbachev's warning to the East German Politburo was the kind of intervention against an allied leader that he had eschewed until then— until it was too late (if it had ever been possible at all) to save the East German regime.[79] His listeners, many of whom had long wanted to act but didn't dare to without support from Moscow, got the message. Honecker's erstwhile protégé Egon Krenz said to Falin, "Your man said all he needed to say. Ours didn't understand anything." Falin replied, "The rest is up to you." Two weeks later, the Politburo demanded and got Honecker's resignation, and Krenz took over as party and state leader.[80]

Gorbachev left East Berlin with "mixed feelings," he recalled.[81] He had been "worried and alarmed," he later confessed to former West German Chancellor Willy Brandt. Talking to Honecker had been like "throwing peas against a wall," he told Krenz.[82] On the other hand, the sight of so many young East Germans championing change "inspired hope." Chernyaev added tellingly in his diary, "The recognition and understanding he gets 'over there' reinforces and reassures him—in contrast to the worthless treatment he gets from his own people."[83] And now the GDR had a new leader! Under whom the GDR could proceed to establish its own version of reformed socialism! On November 1 in Moscow, Gorbachev gave Krenz a warm welcome and urged him to undertake "radical reform and not just a cosmetic repair job."[84]

THE FALL OF THE BERLIN WALL eventually changed almost everything. Until then, Gorbachev was the prime initiator of change, launching reforms in his own country, delighted when they spilled into Eastern Europe, pushing Western leaders toward a new world order. Afterward, he had to react to changes initiated by others—by masses of people on the ground in the GDR, by East European politicians moving beyond Communism, by West European and American leaders ignoring or challenging Gorbachev's vision.

But these changes did not happen immediately. East Germany itself wasn't transformed overnight. Nearly nine million East Germans, a majority of the population, visited the West during the first week after the wall opened, but almost all returned home. Street demonstrations continued, some of them for German reunification rather than reformed socialism, with protesters shouting, "We are one people," instead of, "We are the people." But most East Germans still assumed the GDR should and would remain socialist, separate, and sovereign.[85] Even before the wall fell in Berlin, it had been breached when East Germans were allowed to leave through Hungary and Czechoslovakia—tens of thousands camping that summer near the Austro-Hungarian border, where the electrified barbed wire had been dismantled, until permitted to depart; thousands more swarming the West German embassy in Prague until allowed to flee across East Germany to the West in sealed trains. Now that East Germans could go and come as they pleased, that might even help stabilize the GDR under its new reformist leaders.[86]

The new East German leader, Egon Krenz, lasted only until December 3. Long viewed as Honecker's crown prince and heir apparent, deeply involved in repression as party chief of internal security, having grabbed all Honecker's posts and kept several Honecker men in the Politburo, Krenz "wasn't adequate," as Gorbachev's ally Vadim Medvedev dryly put it.[87] When Krenz's delegation left Moscow after his November 1 meeting with Gorbachev, one cynical Kremlin wag whispered, "There goes the committee to destroy the GDR."[88] But Hans Modrow, the man who replaced him, seemed to many a potential "East German Gorbachev." He had characterized his country as "ruined," warned that without new leaders it would be "lost," and on November 17 proposed a new reform program that was welcomed by dissident leaders.[89] Modrow later admitted that he and Gorbachev "still harbored illusions," that Gorbachev "thought the path was free for perestroika in the GDR."[90]

Meanwhile, the larger issue of German unification reared its head. Ever since 1949, when Stalin authorized the establishment of the German Democratic Republic to match the Federal Republic of Germany (FRG) in the West, Moscow had insisted the two Germanys were there to stay.[91] Khrushchev provoked the Berlin crisis in 1958 by trying to get the West to formally recognize that status quo. Brezhnev finally got that recognition in 1971 in return for finally taking the heat off Berlin. Gorbachev granted that Germany would eventually be reunited, but on some distant, unspecified date. Nor had the Western powers pushed for unification of a country with a long history of aggression, which would immediately become the strongest power in Europe. "Naturally we expressed our support of German reunification," former British prime minister Edward Heath reportedly said in 1989, "because we knew it would never happen."[92] But now "the German question" was back. Would West Germany push for early unification? Would it be joined by its main European allies, France and Britain, and by the United States? If so, how would Moscow react?

U.S. Secretary of State Baker worried that "Gorbachev would draw the line against change in East Germany." Having paid "an immense price" to defeat the Nazis, and with "400,000 elite troops in the GDR,"

Moscow had made clear throughout the cold war that "it would not tolerate a revived German threat."[93] Chancellor Kohl feared that Gorbachev's message to him on November 10 was "a veiled threat."[94] Said Mitterrand on November 10, "Gorbachev will never agree to go further, or else he will be replaced by a hawk." As for people fomenting demonstrations in Berlin, according to Mitterrand, they were "playing with world war without knowing what they are doing."[95]

Such fears weren't fantastical. Shortly before the wall fell, Gorbachev told his ambassador to East Germany, Vyacheslav Kochemasov, "Our people will never forgive us if we lose the GDR."[96] Later, in December, he told Mitterrand that if Germany were united, "there would be a two-line announcement that a Marshal had taken over my position."[97] But in the meantime, rather than reveal his own fears, Gorbachev chose to "display assurance," to show that "he still maintained total control of events." Gorbachev "had to make everybody believe nothing extraordinary had happened," Grachev continues. That's why he dispatched his adviser Vadim Zagladin to calm West European fears of Soviet military action in East Berlin. In fact, "confusion reigned in the Kremlin," where there was "no strategy to deal with events that were no more than the logical consequences of Gorbachev's own policy." According to Grachev, Shevardnadze and Chernyaev were "neither sensitive nor competent enough" to convey all the "complexities of the German problem," Zagladin didn't have enough "authority (or strength of character)" to do so, and Gorbachev's leading Germanist, Valentin Falin, "did not have daily access to Gorbachev."

"For at least two months" after the wall fell, Grachev reports, Gorbachev failed to see how fast German reunification was coming.[98] Western leaders contributed to his misplaced optimism by seeming more resolutely opposed to early German unification than they turned out to be. Margaret Thatcher, as usual, put it most directly to Gorbachev in Moscow on September 23, so directly that she asked that no written record be made of her remarks, although Chernyaev noted them down immediately afterward. "Britain and Western Europe are not interested in the unification of Germany. The words written in the NATO communiqué may sound different, but disregard them. We do not want the unification of Germany [which] would undermine the stability of the entire international situation and could lead to threats to our security."[99]

Once again, the medium enhanced the message. "She was beautiful, smart, extraordinary, feminine," raved Chernyaev in his diary. "It's not true that she is a woman with balls or a man in a skirt. She's a woman through and through, and what a woman!" Gorbachev may not have been quite so smitten, but it was clear to Chernyaev that "he favored her." Not only did she praise Gorbachev to his face; she did so for almost an hour on Soviet television, to which she was granted unprecedented access.[100]

Mitterrand, typically for him, was less direct. Like the British, the French had never been keen on German unification. But by November he understood that the issue demanded attention. "I am not afraid of reunification," he declared at a Bonn press conference on November 3. "I do not ask myself that kind of question as history advances. History is there. I take it as it is." But he still assumed unification would come slowly after a gradual rapprochement between the FRG and a democratizing GDR.[101] It was necessary, he told Gorbachev on the phone on November 14, "to take into account the real feelings that exist among people both in West and East Germany," but the French "would like to avoid any kind of disruption." There was "a certain equilibrium that exists in Europe, and we should not disturb it."[102]

Other European powers, such as Italy and the Netherlands, weren't eager to see Germany reunited either. But the United States had long been more open to the prospect, and in May 1989 Baker urged Bush to "get ahead of the curve" on German unity and "exceed expectations." Knowing "Bush's competitiveness from our days as doubles partners in Houston," he pressed him to "move out ahead in a way that establishes a Western anchor for this process." "I don't share the concern that some European countries have about a reunified Germany," Bush declared on October 24. He wasn't "pushing" reunification, he told an interviewer, or "setting timetables," or "making a lot of pronouncements." It "takes time. It takes a prudent evolution." But the subject was "so much more front and center because of the rapid changes taking place in East Germany."[103]

Meanwhile, however, two former White House national security advisers, one a Republican, the other a Democrat, had raised doubts in Gorbachev's mind about Washington's support for German unity. The first was Kissinger, whom Gorbachev referred to as "Kisa" (the Russian diminutive for "kitty cat") when reporting to the Politburo on their conversation in January 1989. "Kisa" had "hinted at the idea of a USSR-USA condominium" to make sure that "the Europeans do not misbehave." Kissinger warned that German nationalism could be bad for both the United States and the USSR. Zbigniew Brzezinski outdid Kissinger in an October 31 conversation with Aleksandr Yakovlev. If East Germany were to "crumble," the issue of German reunification would "immediately arise," and this would be dangerous, for a "united and powerful Germany would correspond neither to your interests nor to ours."[104] Bush and Baker rejected Kissinger's notion of condominium (in which he clearly hoped to play a leading role) as redolent of Yalta, and Brzezinski certainly didn't speak for the administration. But what they said helps explain why Gorbachev thought that not just Western Europe but "the West" as a whole "doesn't want a united Germany, but wants to prevent it with our hands."[105]

What about West Germany itself? "The FRG has no interest whatsoever in destabilizing the GDR," Kohl assured Gorbachev on October 11.[106] And he repeated that message on November 11, leading Gorbachev to tell Mitterrand three days later, "[Kohl] assured me that he would abide firmly by our previous agreements."[107] Kohl sounded more aggressive on November 16 when he insisted that East German Communists "give up their monopoly on power, allow independent parties and assure binding free elections"—steps that would open the way for East Germany to unite with the West. But East German Prime Minister Modrow proposed the next day that the two Germanys join a "treaty community," governed by a series of bilateral treaties—just the sort of gradual step that Gorbachev envisioned.[108] By the middle of November, a semblance of calm descended on the German question. On the fifteenth, Mitterrand told his Council of Ministers that unification was "no longer in the foreground," since Gorbachev could not accept it.[109] "We will not be making exhortations about unification or setting any timetables," Bush told Kohl on the seventeenth. "We will not exacerbate the problem by having the

President of the United States posturing on the Berlin wall."[110] But the calm was deceptive. Just a few days later, Kohl pressed hard for unity on his own terms, unintentionally encouraged (it turns out) by a Gorbachev adviser's attempt to prevent just that.

Valentin Falin was not your standard Soviet functionary. He was tall, aristocratic looking, with hair cut longer than was fashionable atop what a pre-twentieth-century observer might have called a noble head. Born in Leningrad in 1926 and educated at the Moscow State Institute of International Relations, he not only had a doctorate but (unlike other high Soviet officials whose dissertations were ghostwritten) he was genuinely erudite. Joining the diplomatic corps in 1950, he was by the 1960s one of the Foreign Ministry's main German hands. He even dared to push for détente with West Germany against the wishes of Foreign Minister Gromyko, surviving because Brezhnev liked Falin as well as the policy he recommended, and then serving as Soviet ambassador to West Germany from 1970 to 1978. Falin became head of the Central Committee's international department in 1988, then one of a handful of Central Committee secretaries in 1990. But instead of being by Gorbachev's side as the fate of Germany was being decided in late 1989, he was marginalized. He didn't get along with the current Soviet ambassador to Bonn, Yuli Kvitsinsky, and he didn't particularly admire Shevardnadze either. Falin wanted Moscow to count on German social democrats, particularly his old friend Willy Brandt, whereas Gorbachev followed Kvitsinsky's advice to align with Kohl and the latter's deputy and foreign minister, Hans Dietrich Genscher.[111]

Falin shared Gorbachev's hope that German unification, although unavoidable in the long run, would come gradually. But with Gorbachev apparently trying to stop the process rather than shape it, Falin conceived a too-clever trick—that an unofficial emissary be sent to Bonn (bypassing Shevardnadze and Kvitsinsky) to tell Kohl foreign policy adviser Horst Teltschik that almost "anything might become possible." Since this formulation resembled Gorbachev's "history will decide," Chernyaev "saw no harm in it," especially since (he later told Grachev) "he was looking for a way to satisfy Falin's pride, apparently wounded by his estrangement from discussions" of the German issue. What Falin didn't tell Chernyaev was that Teltschik would be presented with the idea of German confederation, which Gorbachev wasn't ready to propose, an arrangement that would guarantee the continued existence of the GDR at least for a while.[112]

Nikolai Portugalov, a chain-smoking Central Committee official who had carried out unofficial missions many times before, was chosen to deliver the message. Entering Teltschik's office on November 21, he showed him two handwritten documents.[113] One conveyed Moscow's "official position"—that the two Germanys should continue to exist "*for the foreseeable future*" (emphasis in original) and that "construction of a common European order" had "priority over the solution of the German question." The other, labeled "unofficial considerations" (to make it disavowable), said the Soviet Union was "thinking the unthinkable," and might even "in the medium term" "give the green light to a German confederation."[114]

Grachev describes Falin's operation "as bordering on political adventurism." Bordering? This was a stunning act of unauthorized prestidigitation in which Gorbachev mysteriously materialized as both the ostensible sponsor of Portugalov's unofficial message and, as Grachev points out, its actual "addressee." "Feeling incapable of persuading his boss of the merits of German confederation," Falin "was counting on the Federal Chancellor to do the job for him."[115] But the trick boomeranged. Kohl was supposed to telephone Gorbachev and obtain his approval, but instead Kohl took the seeming hint and acted unilaterally. If Gorbachev's circle was already contemplating German reunification, then, as Genscher's chief of staff recalled, "It was high time to take the initiative."[116]

Genscher wasn't informed in advance of what Kohl was planning, and neither were other Western leaders, except for Bush (at the very last minute). On November 28 in the Bundestag, Kohl presented a ten-point plan for reunification. Its most important points were that Bonn would consider developing "confederative structures between both states in Germany, with the aim of creating a federation, that is, a federal order, in Germany," and that, in the meantime, it would expand desperately needed economic aid to the GDR, but only "if a fundamental transformation in the political and economic system of the GDR is definitively accepted and irreversibly set in motion."[117]

On the surface, Kohl's plan wasn't revolutionary. It didn't set any timetables, and Kohl himself thought it would take five to ten years to achieve German unity.[118] Secretary of State Baker regarded the démarche as "relatively modest."[119] Its content "did not shock [Mitterrand] at all, although he greatly resented not being informed in advance."[120] But Kohl's ten points were, as White House adviser on Eastern Europe Robert Hutchings later put it, "an exercise in political brinksmanship" designed to set the terms and pace for German unification before British, French, and Soviet efforts to slow the process could get underway.[121] And for Gorbachev it was a bombshell. "Never before or since have I ever seen Gorbachev so agitated and bitter," said Genscher, recalling their meeting in Moscow on December 5. Chernyaev described the conversation as "unprecedented in its heat," as going beyond "any generally accepted limits for exchanges between statesmen of such high rank."[122]

Kohl's ten points were nothing less than "ultimatums," Gorbachev warned Genscher, to be "imposed on an independent and sovereign German state." Less than three weeks earlier, he and Kohl had a "constructive, positive" phone conversation in which they "reached agreement on several fundamental issues." But now Kohl "probably already thinks his music is playing—a march—and that he is already marching with it." He was "treating the citizens of the GDR, in essence, like his own subjects." ("Even Hitler did not allow himself anything like that," Shavardnadze interjected.) Kohl was preparing "a funeral for the European process." The "confederation" he proposed "implies a common defense system, a common foreign policy. Where will the FRG be, in NATO or the Warsaw Pact? Or will it become neutral? And what would NATO mean without the FRG? What will happen next, in general? Have you thought this all through? What will become of our existing agreements?"[123]

The shock of Kohl's bold move explains Gorbachev's emotional reaction. Unaware of Falin's secret initiative, he was unprepared for what seemed a completely unilateral step by Kohl. He interpreted the move, Chernyaev recalled, "as a breach of [Kohl's] promise not to push events forward or to try to extract one-sided political advantage" and "a violation of their agreement to consult each other on every new move."[124] Nor did Kohl's Western allies appreciate his unilaterally placing German reunification squarely atop Europe's agenda. Hence his "icy" reception (Kohl's description) at a December 8 European Community summit where the "interrogation" he received reminded him of a "a tribunal."[125] But once West Germany had made clear its wishes, its allies (even Thatcher) could go only so far to oppose them. Kohl's ten points "have turned everything upside down," Mitterrand complained to Gorbachev in Kiev on December 6. Mitterrand still wanted to make sure "the all-European process develops more rapidly than the German question." But neither he nor Gorbachev had a plan for doing so. All Mitterrand could suggest was that Gorbachev accompany him on a previously planned trip to East Berlin on December 20 (the sight of the two former cold war adversaries on a joint mission of this sort would have taken some getting used to), but that didn't happen. Gorbachev, the former peasant, damned Kohl as "provincial"—"acting so crudely on such a universally sensitive issue." Mitterrand salved Gorbachev's wounds by praising him for the opposite qualities: "You are loyal to your heritage, and at the same time, you continue to deepen your revolution. . . . I appreciate your courage in the struggle for the goals you have set. One has to be brave. . . . But you radiate calm, and you are even in a good mood. This gives us hope."[126]

IF THE FALL OF THE WALL was an earthquake, Kohl's ten points were a massive aftershock. But even after November 28 Gorbachev remained upbeat, his hopes lifted by the Malta summit with President Bush on December 2–3.

As late as the autumn of 1989, Bush administration skeptics still questioned Gorbachev's credentials as a reformer. He was "still a Communist," National Security Adviser Scowcroft believed, and hence "quite prepared to take advantage of us whenever the opportunity arose." Scowcroft deputy Robert Gates feared Gorbachev's reforms could be "easily reversed." Dick Cheney, according to Scowcroft, thought it was "premature to relax Cold War–style pressure. The Soviet system was in trouble and we ought to continue the hard-line policies which had brought us and it to this point. Why give up what appeared to be a winning hand?"[127]

Back in July, however, after being urged to be more forthcoming by Western leaders and reformers in Poland and Hungary, President Bush opted to meet Gorbachev "sooner rather than later. What good would it do to hold back now?"[128] Bush preferred to meet at Kennebunkport, in Maine, or Camp David, or even a rustic retreat in Alaska about half-way between Washington and Moscow, where he and Gorbachev could "put our feet up on the table," and he could "work on chemistry with the guy." But Gorbachev rejected a third trip in a row to the United States, Italy (where Gorbachev was going to be in early December) was out as a NATO member, and Cyprus was too riven by Greek-Turkish civil strife. Bush's younger brother Bucky suggested Malta, which appealed to the president because the two leaders could seclude themselves from the press aboard Soviet and U.S. ships in Marsaxlokk Bay, thus echo-ing the famous August 1941 meeting on two ships off Newfoundland at which Franklin Roosevelt and Winston Churchill produced the Atlantic Charter.[129]

Gorbachev's path to Malta led through Milan and Rome, where his welcome exceeded, if that was possible, those he had previously encountered in Western Europe. "Mass hysteria" in Milan, according to Chernyaev's diary entry. "Cars could barely move through crowds in the streets." "Everywhere people were piled on top of each other—in windows, on railings, on any protruding surface. There was a deafening roar: 'Gorby! Gorby!' The police were trampled. Security services had a heart attack." At one point, a group of well-dressed women "threw them-selves at his car windows with tears in their eyes, and when guards tried to tear them away, they broke through and tried to run back."[130] Among welcoming signs in Rome: "Gorbachev: You're Greater than Napoleon!" Pope John Paul II himself received Gorbachev and prayed not only for peace but for the success of perestroika.[131]

The summit itself was supposed to rotate among three ships in the Malta harbor: the American cruiser USS *Belknap*, where Bush bunked; the Soviet cruiser *Slava*, anchored about a mile away, where the first ses-sion was scheduled; and the big Soviet cruise ship *Maxim Gorky*, berthed at the dock, where Gorbachev was staying. But a massive storm inter-vened. With the wind howling and waves crashing, Gorbachev didn't dare try to get to the *Slava*, so the first meeting was moved to the *Gorky*, which Bush somehow managed to reach on a storm-tossed launch. (Before the gale winds came up, the president managed to cram in some fishing off the fantail of the *Belknap*.) Although one session was later canceled, the first took place on schedule on the *Gorky*, where Gorbachev greeted his guests outside the salon, looking tired but smiling, dressed in a dark-blue pinstripe suit, a cream-white shirt, and a red tie.[132]

In some ways, the Malta summit wasn't productive. At Bush's insistence, more time was devoted to Central America (reflecting the issue's electoral importance in vote-rich Florida) than to arms control, of which the American side was still leery. Gorbachev, as usual, discoursed at length about "the historic turning point" the world was going through, about "the entirely new problems facing mankind of which people in the past could not even conceive."[133] Divided Germany, the hottest spot on the planet, got relatively little attention, with nothing at all decided by the two leaders. But Malta was where Gorbachev seemed finally to achieve with Bush the kind of full understanding and trust that eluded him with Reagan, where they formed not just a friendship but the sort of partnership that might allow them to cap off the cold war and buttress reform in the Soviet Union itself.

Neither leader expected this outcome. Bush and his team feared another Gorbachev "surprise," the kind of radical disarmament proposal he sprang on Reagan at Reykjavik. Bush was "taut as he began to speak" at the first meeting, Scowcroft recalled, "clearly nervous about the import of what was happening." Gorbachev was also tense, Chernyaev remembered, "uncertain until the last minute" whether Bush would come through. Gorbachev himself recalled being "entirely focused" on Bush's "every sentence," checking to see, "as if by scratching metal with my teeth to see if it was gold," what all the months of delay would produce.[134]

Bush began with a mea culpa, confessing that when he proposed the summit back in July he was "changing my former position 180 degrees." Lest there be any doubt, "I agree completely with what you said in New York," a year before. The world would be "better if perestroika ends as a success." There were of course different points of view in the United States, but "you can be certain that you are dealing with an administration and with a Congress that wish for the crowning success of your reforms." What concretely would the administration do to help? It would seek to suspend the Jackson-Vanik Amendment, which denied "most favored nation" tariff treatment to the USSR, and to repeal the

Stevenson and Baird amendments that restricted credits that could be extended to Moscow. Neither step, Bush added tactfully, was meant to demonstrate "American superiority," to give the impression that America was "saving" the Soviet Union. Bush was talking not about aid, he emphasized, but cooperation. The United States also favored granting the USSR observer status in the General Agreement on Tariffs and Trade (GATT) to help Moscow familiarize itself with "the conditions, operation and development of the world market," plus establishing Soviet contacts with the Organization for Economic Cooperation and Development (OECD), "a good framework for cooperation on economic issues between East and West." In addition, Bush mentioned environmental protection, climate change, and student exchanges (involving as many as one thousand young people from each side). He also gave Gorbachev a list of other areas in which the United States could offer "technical cooperation," such as helping Moscow set up a banking system, a stock market, and other market institutions. "Look these over," he said. "We'll be happy to pursue any of them with you."[135]

One might dismiss this as a laundry list (some items of secondary importance, others requiring the cooperation of the U.S. Congress or of other countries to be enacted), but Gorbachev did not. He had come to Malta prepared to deliver "some sort of reproach" if the president offered more words without deeds. But "now," he said, "there is both a statement and action," or, as Chernyaev put it later, "concrete proposals" for a "new stage in U.S.-Soviet relations."[136]

On Eastern Europe, the two leaders exchanged important confessions and compliments. Bush admitted he was "shocked" by how fast things were changing, and he offered high praise for Gorbachev's "personal reaction and the reaction of the Soviet Union" to these changes. "You are catalyzing changes in Europe in a constructive way." "Look at how nervous we are," Gorbachev admitted at one point. "What form of action should we take? Collective action?" "I hope you noticed," said Bush, "that the United States has not engaged in condescending statements aimed at damaging the Soviet Union." Some in the United States accused him of being "too cautious," and it was true, "I am a cautious man, but I am not a coward; and my administration will seek to avoid doing anything that would damage your position in the world."[137]

"You cannot expect us not to approve of German reunification," Bush continued. But he admitted that "some Western allies who pay lip service to reunification" are actually "quite upset by the prospect," and he assured Gorbachev, "We are trying to act with a certain reserve." "We will not take any rash steps; we will not try to accelerate the outcome of the debate on reunification." If Kohl's public declarations sounded more radical, that was because when Germans speak of reunification, they do so "with tears in their eyes."[138]

Much of the conversation at lunch on December 2 was devoted to how perestroika was doing in the USSR. Chernyaev was "simply astonished" to see how "sincerely" Bush and Baker "wanted things to work out for us," wanted "the economy to take off and for us to cope with our troubles." "If you closed your eyes and ears and blocked out the English, you might have thought you were attending a Politburo meeting where everyone was worried about the country's fate, trying to convince each other, trying to prove their points." And this made "a big impression on Gorbachev, convincing him on an emotional level that the U.S. administration had made a choice."[139]

The Soviet sense of general comity extended to the great issue of war and peace. Gorbachev assured Bush that "the Soviet Union will not under any circumstances initiate a war," that "the USSR is prepared to cease considering the U.S. as an enemy and to announce this openly," and that far from seeking to exclude the United States from Europe (as some in the administration still feared), Moscow couldn't imagine a peaceful Europe without an American role in it. The "meeting of the minds" allowed the two sides to compromise on a description for the universal human values that loomed so large in Gorbachev's "new thinking"—not "Western" values (Bush's preference), which implied that Gorbachev was conceding defeat, but "democratic" values, which the West and the new Soviet Union could be said to share. In the new era of good feeling, the two leaders even decided to hold a joint press conference, something Soviet and American leaders had never done before.[140]

The upshot of Malta, as Gorbachev saw it, was that the cold war was finally, really over—witness the fact that several weeks later Secretary of State Baker signaled that Washington would not object if Soviet-led Warsaw Pact forces intervened in Romania to halt the bloodbath accompanying the fall of Ceauşescu. (Moscow declined to do so.) What Malta had done, Chernyaev concluded, was "secure the external conditions for the acceleration of perestroika," in other words to make the world safe for Gorbachev's reforms. The external threat was "no more. Our hands were free." The Americans had even "made a commitment to give economic support to perestroika."[141]

Not everyone in Gorbachev's entourage was so euphoric. His military adviser, former armed forces chief of staff Marshal Akhromeyev, regretted that Gorbachev hadn't opposed German reunification more aggressively. According to former ambassador to Washington Dobrynin, Gorbachev ignored a foreign ministry proposal that he insist German reunification come only after NATO and the Warsaw Pact transformed themselves from military to political alliances and disbanded by mutual agreement. Central Committee official Brutents later accused Gorbachev of falling into an American trap at Malta, by feeling he had to prove his sincerity to Washington over and over again.[142]

President Bush, according to Ambassador Matlock, considered the summit as significant as Gorbachev did. But advisers like Scowcroft and Gates did not. Scowcroft's later praise for the summit was noticeably faint: he welcomed among other things the fact that fears that had led him "to oppose a summit for months" (e.g., that Gorbachev would exploit it by playing "one-upmanship") "were not realized." As Matlock puts it, some of the president's advisers thought Bush's attempts to support Gorbachev risked "seizing defeat from the jaws of victory."[143]

Perhaps the most balanced Soviet summary of Malta came from Shevardnadze aide Sergei Tarasenko, who pointed out how Gorbachev's domestic and foreign troubles came together at the summit. By the end of 1989, Gorbachev and Shevardnadze "had a very keen feeling that we had to accomplish a huge maneuver without losing time. We felt the Soviet Union was in free fall, that our superpower status would go up in smoke unless it was reaffirmed by the Americans. With the avalanche of 1989 almost behind us, we wanted to reach some kind of plateau that would give us some time to catch our breath and look around."[144]

CHAPTER 14

COMING
APART?

1990

DURING SOVIET TIMES, the English terms "Russia" and "the Soviet Union" were often used interchangeably, but mistakenly so. Russia, officially known as the Russian Soviet Federative Socialist Republic (RSFSR), was by far the biggest of the USSR's fifteen republics, accounting for half of the union's population, two-thirds of its economy, and three-quarters of its territory. But the other fourteen were, at least formally, Russia's equals. In addition to all their external accoutrements of authority (legislatures, councils of ministers, flags, and so on), the non-Russian republics had their own Communist parties, all, however, subordinate to the Communist Party of the Soviet Union in Moscow. But just because it was so big, the Russian Republic was denied its own party, lest it be seen to dominate the CPSU, even though, in fact, it did just that.

Given Russia's dominant position in the Soviet Union (which echoed, of course, its supremacy in the pre-1917 Russian Empire), Russians were slow to develop the nationalist sense that they needed their own, separate state. But by the spring of 1990, with non-Russian nationalism flaring, particularly in the Baltics and the Caucasus, Russian nationalism was on the rise as well, and with it the case for Russia's having its own Communist party. Gorbachev himself would have preferred the status quo, because his fiercest conservative critics were pushing for a Russian party, but he had to accept a founding conclave in June. Meanwhile, his liberal critics were also playing the Russian card, working feverishly to turn the new Russian Republic Congress of People's Deputies, with members democratically elected that same spring, into a force pressing for reforms more rapid than Gorbachev wanted.

It was no surprise, therefore, that Gorbachev addressed the Russian party's founding congress on June 20, 1990. He was still the leader of the CPSU, of which the new RCP was a subordinate part. What was surprising, however, and astounded Gorbachev's aide Chernyaev, was that "for some reason Gorbachev attended the entire Congress," and that "he tolerated such abuse" and "even direct insults" from the hard-line delegates. "He sat through so much nonsense, not even reacting to the most idiotic statements." He tried to defend himself, but was inundated with "provocative, venomous, mocking, vulgar questions," which he answered "in a rambling, muddled manner," as if "he were trying to ingratiate himself with an audience that simply loathed him."[1]

Fast-forward to December 4, 1990, when Gorbachev addressed the USSR Supreme Soviet. This speech, too, according to Chernyaev, was "disastrous." "He was unrecognizable. He simply mumbled," saying nothing new. He "rambled on." His listeners "showed complete indifference, even contempt." Chernyaev, Yakovlev, and Yevgeny Primakov, listening on the radio, were all distraught: "What's happened to him, why is he doing this?" Other top aides, who attended the session, had an even more negative impression. Vadim Medvedev said, "He's overburdened, embittered, confused." Yakovlev later took Chernyaev aside and "totally distressed," whispered to him, "He's done for, now I'm sure of it."[2]

These were not the only such occasions during 1990. The Soviet Union was coming apart. Was Gorbachev himself beginning to do so? Andrei Grachev, then a loyal Central Committee aide and soon to be Gorbachev's press spokesman, recalls that Gorbachev "gradually changed during 1990 without realizing it himself, from a 'gatherer' of interesting people and the soul of society into a lonely man," whose "bombast often turned Politburo meetings into lengthy monologues," who valued seeming loyalty more than candid advice, and treated his longtime aides as mere service personnel.[3]

Not all of Gorbachev's close associates had a similar impression. His wife certainly did not. She admitted that her husband now lived "in a state of incredible tension." She never saw him back home before ten or eleven o'clock, always arriving with a pile of papers, often working until two or three in the morning. She was "extremely worried" about his health. But in her adoring eyes, he maintained his "self-possession, tolerance and self-control," sustained by his innate respect for other human beings: "He never asserts his own dignity by trampling on the dignity of other people. . . . Never in his life has he humiliated the people next to him so as to make himself taller. Never."[4]

According to Shakhnazarov, Gorbachev didn't seem to feel any fear, never "panicked," always remained "concentrated, very firm and resolute." Of course, he worried, "otherwise he wouldn't be a politician." But even when his associates quailed, Gorbachev never did. "Relax," he would say. "Of course, it's a serious matter, no panic though. Think about how we can respond to this step."[5] Gorbachev's chief military adviser, Akhromeyev, was by now disenchanted with his boss, but he continued to admire Gorbachev's "self-possession and patience" and the way he remained "organized, businesslike, and calm," even as his authority and popularity began to evaporate.[6]

To British Foreign Secretary Douglas Hurd, Gorbachev seemed "so satisfied with the way things were going that he could prose on about them for longer than you expected." In contrast to Yeltsin, who flaunted his power by having a flunky "bring in a great big decree, a parchment, which Yeltsin signed and then sent away," Gorbachev was "too busy explaining in a very easy sort of way how well things were going, how well he was doing." His eyes would "sort of dance in pleasure at his own cleverness, how he had just come from some meeting, which might have been difficult, but he explains how well he handled it. There was no sense of hurry."

Talking to Hurd was easy, the foreign secretary recalls, because "I wasn't transacting urgent business, not negotiating with him. I was just listening, really."[7] (The Kremlin's main diplomatic business in 1990—Germany and Iraq—was with Bonn and Washington.) But U.S. Ambassador Matlock didn't see any "psychological deterioration" either.[8]

Gorbachev himself confessed that he had to force himself not to lash out at critics hurling insults at him from all sides. He was tempted, he told a small group of liberals on July 27, 1990, to take legal action under a new law he had pushed through, protecting his honor and dignity as

Soviet president. Only "gradually" did he cool down in such cases, realizing (in one participant's paraphrase of Gorbachev's remark) that "when somebody throws foul language at him, this person must be boiling over and unless he lets off [steam] with the insults, he may explode."[9]

Gorbachev's feelings were contradictory. Who could have faced what he was facing with steady equanimity? He had forced through reforms, but they were being sabotaged by some and pushed too hard by others. He created a new role for himself as president of the USSR, but was unable to play it successfully. The most severe troubles he faced, like economic collapse and nationalist uprisings, couldn't be wished away, but others he could and did deny, repressing his qualms and soldiering on.

"TO BE OR NOT TO BE—1990 will be decisive for perestroika," Gorbachev warned the Politburo at its first meeting of the year, on January 2.[10] He struck Chernyaev as "cheerful and animated" on January 6.[11] But the year got off to a bad start. While incomes rose by 13 percent in 1989 and continued to balloon at that rate during the first two months of 1990, people had less and less to buy. On any given day, only 23 of 211 basic food items were available in state stores.[12] Prime Minister Ryzhkov, pessimistic as usual, put it this way in February: "We have no grain, and we have no foreign currency. The situation is hopeless."[13]

Gorbachev visited Lithuania between January 11 and 13 in a last, personal effort to halt its rush to independence. At times, he was at his best, pleading with Lithuanians to give a *real* Soviet federation, rather than the phony one they had lived under so long, a chance: "Do you even know what a federation is? [Voices: We know, we know.] How do you know if you've never lived in one?"[14]

Gorbachev thought the majority of Lithuanians would reject the extremists and listen to reason. Instead, he encountered scenes like the following, featuring an elderly factory worker holding up a sign reading, "Total Independence for Lithuania."

Gorbachev: "Who told you to write that banner?"

Worker: "Nobody. I wrote it myself."

Gorbachev: "What do you mean by 'total independence'?"

Worker: "I mean what we had in the 1920s, when Lenin recognized Lithuania's sovereignty, because no nation is entitled to dictate to another nation."

Gorbachev: "Within our large family, Lithuania has become a developed country. What kind of exploiters are we if Russia sells you cotton, oil, and raw materials—and not for hard currency either?"

Worker (interrupting Gorbachev): "Lithuania had hard currency before the war. You took it away in 1940. And do you know how many Lithuanians were sent to Siberia in the 1940s, and how many died?"

Gorbachev: "I don't want to talk to this man anymore. If people in Lithuania have attitudes and slogans like this, they can expect hard times. I don't want to talk to you anymore."

At this point, Raisa Gorbachev tried to calm down her husband, but instead further riled him.

"Be quiet," he snapped, uncharacteristically.

No wonder "fury and confusion" mottled Gorbachev's face at every meeting in Vilnius.[15] And the pressure stayed on when he returned to Moscow. In March, General Varennikov recommended treating Vilnius like Prague in 1968: using three regiments to "isolate" the separatist leaders and installing Quislings who would "invite" in the Soviet army. And the Politburo seemed to endorse the plan. Only Yakovlev and Medvedev "kept quiet," recalled Chernyaev. He himself protested to Gorbachev the next day, only to have his boss reply, "Just forget it, Tolya. Everything will be fine, everything will be all right."[16]

Everything would not be all right. Gorbachev managed to deflect the Prague scenario for the rest of 1990, although a version of it would be mounted the next year. But the strain on him was enormous. As he told visiting U.S. Senator Edward Kennedy on March 26, "You don't know what pressure I'm under. Many in our leadership want to use force right now."[17]

Whatever else Gorbachev might think of the Lithuanian separatists, their protests were at least orderly and self-disciplined. Not so in Azerbaijan, where, on the very day Gorbachev arrived in Vilnius, the Azerbaijani National Front blockaded government offices in the republic's second-largest city, Lenkoran, and mobilized huge crowds in Baku. Two days later, mobs attacked apartment houses where Armenians lived, massacring their inhabitants, throwing women and children to their death from upper-story windows. Moscow ordered troops into the area, but demonstrators blockaded the streets to keep them from entering the city. The soldiers fought their way in, killing two hundred demonstrators in the process and incurring thirty casualties of their own.

Much as he abhorred the use of force, Gorbachev justified it this time as "a last resort in extreme circumstances." But the decision to use force—which didn't end Azerbaijani separatism and in fact intensified it by providing the National Front with an additional national grievance—took a personal toll on him. Raisa Gorbachev could scarcely recognize her husband. "He had gone grey and his face was grey, too: he seemed to have suffered a nervous shock, to have gone through a mental crisis."[18]

Instead of addressing concrete problems facing the country at its January 22 meeting, the Politburo debated a new party platform, with some members endorsing radical innovations like multiparty competition, while others defended old orthodoxies like the "class basis" of Communism and the need for one-party rule.[19] For once, Gorbachev remained mostly quiet, listening to the debate instead of dominating it, as if still in shock after Vilnius and Baku. The next day, he gathered his closest aides to continue the discussion, but as Chernyaev recalled, "we spent six hours on it, [and] despite our frankness with each other and Gorbachev, we found ourselves going around in the same circles as the Politburo, looking for 'acceptable' formulas that actually obscured the issues."[20] With Baku still burning, the sterile discussion shifted to the abstract issue of what sort of property would be ideologically acceptable as the economy moved toward a market system. Yakovlev was willing to use the term itself, "private property," as long as it did not (to quote the hackneyed Soviet cliché) involve "the exploitation of man by man." Gorbachev preferred "individual labor property." It took Shakhnazarov to remind the group that, of course, "any private property presupposes the exploitation of labor." Finally, Gorbachev offered the following formulation "so that the people know we are opposed to capitalism": "The CPSU categorically opposes private-capitalist property, but believes that 'private-labor' property can contribute to the development of society."[21]

In February, attacks on Gorbachev intensified from both liberals and hardliners. It was bitter cold on February 4 when 200,000 to 300,000 demonstrators tramped along the Garden Ring Road, turned down Gorky Street, and massed in Manezh Square, right outside the Kremlin's red-brick crenellated walls. "Party bureaucrats: Remember Romania!" warned one of their banners. From a perch on a flatbed truck, historian Yuri Afanasyev shouted into a microphone, "All hail the peaceful February revolution of 1990!" Russians couldn't miss the reference to the February Revolution of 1917, which toppled the tsar and might have opened the way to democracy, if the Bolsheviks hadn't seized power in October.[22] The prospect of another massive demonstration on February 25 prompted emergency meetings at the Central Committee. This time demonstrators were barred from the city center, and troops joined with police to enforce the ban. Rumors spread that violence was likely, and Prime Minister Ryzhkov begged citizens on television to stay home. In the end, the protest was peaceful ("Seventy-two Years on the Road to Nowhere," read one banner), but as Interior Minister Bakatin warned his Central Committee colleagues, their panicky preparations didn't so much calm the situation as "kindle the psychosis."[23]

The conservative assault came at a Central Committee meeting held between February 5 and 7. Vladimir Brovikov, former prime minister of the Byelorussian Republic and now Soviet ambassador to Poland, charged Gorbachev (without mentioning his name) with reducing the country to "anarchy" and "ruin," preferring to be lionized by Western crowds rather than confronted by his own "gloomy compatriots," and turning a "celebrated world power" into a "state with a misshapen past, a joyless present, and an indefinite future"—all to the delight of the West, which, while hailing perestroika, was actually "whooping it up at the collapse of communism and world socialism." Echoing the famous words with which Gorbachev launched his reforms in 1985—"We can't go on living like this"—Brovikov warned, "We can't go on living the way we're living today."[24]

Gorbachev didn't respond to Brovikov directly at the plenum, but a week later he was still hurting. "Brovikov practically called me 'scum,'" he snarled at a session to prepare for the next session of the Congress of People's Deputies. How could "this same Brovikov" now return to Poland as Soviet ambassador? "How can he represent our foreign policy? He doesn't believe in any of it." Well, "let Shevardnadze and Yakovlev take care of it."[25] They did. Brovikov was fired. A rare instance of Gorbachev's actually dumping a critic rather than continuing to coexist with him.

Brovikov wasn't alone; the majority of the Central Committee probably shared many of his views. Nonetheless, in yet another demonstration of Gorbachev's mastery of the "old game" of nondemocratic politics, the same raucous Central Committee session endorsed his plan to further enhance his own power while reduc   ing the party's. One might have thought the creation the previous spring of a new and more democratic legislature, along with its choice of Gorbachev as its chairman, would have been sufficient. But the Congress was so divided and unwieldy that he was spending endless hours in parliamentary maneuvering rather than leading the country. And the Central Committee retained its power to oust him as general secretary, thereby overthrowing him as the country's leader. The alternative, he slowly had come to realize, was the creation of a new USSR presidency, a post he would occupy himself, while depriving the party of its constitutional mandate to rule by repealing Article 6 of the Soviet Constitution.

It was Andrei Sakharov who first proposed establishing a powerful presidency, in 1989. At that point, Gorbachev rejected it as too radical a change. Later he admitted he'd been wrong: not only was it "physically impossible" to combine chairing the legislature with all his other duties, but after decades of submission to all-powerful leaders, the people longed not for a parliamentary "speaker" but for an imposing chief executive.[26] In addition, Shakhnazarov reveals, Gorbachev hadn't wanted people to think he had "organized all these reforms only in order to attain his post," especially since that was far from the truth.[27]

When liberal critics warned, at a Supreme Soviet session on February 27, against an "imperial presidency," Gorbachev's reaction (as observed by Ambassador Matlock) resembled the meltdowns that so disturbed Chernyaev that year. His face was "drawn with fatigue," his remarks were "disjointed" and "filled with innuendo and incomplete sentences," and he grew more and more "defensive and emotional." He was "wounded by the implication that he, of all people," was seeking excessive power. "'What has all this got to do with Gorbachev?' he asked rhetorically and illogically, as if nobody had any idea that it was he who would be the new president."[28]

In a conversation with Czechoslovak President Václav Havel on February 26, Gorbachev volunteered that "only extremely arrogant people dream of becoming heads of state."[29] Did the comrade not protest too much? Matlock, who observed Gorbachev closely for several years, credited his disclaimer. "Unquestionably, he loved power. Unquestionably, he shuddered at the thought of losing it." But if power had been his only or primary goal, why hadn't he used it to cement his position, rather than risk it by transforming the country and alienating so many?[30]

If liberal critics had doubts about Gorbachev's becoming president, conservatives weren't wild about it either. But hard-liners who hadn't entirely lost faith in him saw two important opportunities: they could get him to use new presidential powers to impose law and order and crack down on national separatism, and get him to turn over his leadership of the party (which he had been using to emasculate it) to a hard-liner. Gorbachev's seeming ally Anatoly Lukyanov looked forward to the new president's taking "sharp measures, even of a negative character."[31] Liberals like Yakovlev and Chernyaev also wanted Gorbachev to step down as party leader, so as to join with more natural allies in the democratic camp. But Gorbachev still refused to do that, preferring to maintain control of the party as he continued to press for its reform.

Gorbachev initially preferred the American model for the new Soviet presidency, with the government fully subordinate to the chief executive. Then he shifted to the French, in which the president shares power with the prime minister. Finally, he compromised on a structure in which the cabinet was responsible to both president and parliament, an arrangement that invited trouble in 1991 when a conservative prime minister appealed to parliament for additional powers at the president's expense.[32]

If only Gorbachev had been popularly elected president, some say, that would have armed him with the legitimacy needed to overcome his adversaries.[33] But instead, he chose to be chosen by the USSR Congress of People's Deputies. Why? Because a long and costly campaign would have escalated political tensions just when the country needed quick, decisive presidential action.[34] The venerable deputy Dmitry Likhachev warned that direct elections would lead to "civil war." The eighty-three-year-old scholar of the literature and culture of Old Russia had lived through

1917 and the Solovki prison camps created soon after the revolution. His powerful pleading helped carry the day.[35] According to Yakovlev, Gorbachev feared he might actually lose a direct, popular election.[36] But if so, he was unnecessarily alarmed. According to the most reliable public opinion polling, in the spring of 1990 he was still the most popular Soviet politician; it was only later that year that Yeltsin's rating exceeded Gorbachev's for the first time.[37]

The Congress chose the president on March 14. Gorbachev wanted to have opposition for the sake of appearances, and in fact, Prime Minister Ryzhkov and Interior Minister Bakatin were also nominated, but they withdrew. Gorbachev received 1,329 votes, 495 were cast against him, and 313 deputies either did not vote or they cast invalid ballots, meaning Gorbachev was supported by less than 60 percent of the deputies.[38]

Gorbachev was pleased, of course, but his pleasure was tempered by the disappointing margin and the challenges still facing him. The vote was by secret ballot, with the result not announced until the next morning, but Gorbachev found out sooner than that. After the Congress adjourned, with the lights going out in the hall, he went up to his office in the Palace of Congresses, where his wife and a couple of aides were waiting to raise glasses (of coffee, he assures us in his memoirs) in honor of "my new status." But "I asked myself whether my situation had really changed at all."[39]

The next morning, after the results were announced and greeted by a standing ovation from deputies and guests, Gorbachev took the oath of office at a table bordered by a long red Soviet flag. In the future, such a flag in a special holder would flank him (as the American flag does the U.S. president) in the president's office, in conference rooms, and in other places where he was present, while the words Sovetsky Souiz (Soviet Union) would be painted on the presidential plane in the American manner.[40] Gorbachev's inaugural address was suitably resolute, but had a defensive tone when he rejected charges of usurping power and being indecisive (an odd combination). In the absence of anything positive to say about the economy, he declared that the main achievements of perestroika were "democracy and glasnost." Who could have predicted five years earlier that the Soviet leader would be able to claim with justification that democracy and glasnost (which by 1990 had become almost indistinguishable from free speech) would be products of his time in office?[41]

The other main plank in Gorbachev's platform in early 1990, the repeal of Article 6 of the 1977 Constitution, ratifying the CPSU as the nation's "ruling party," was discussed in Gorbachev's inner circle even before the Nineteenth Party Conference in June 1988. But then and for months afterward, he wasn't about to wave *this* red flag at the party bull, especially after repealing Article 6 became the battle cry of radical critics—from striking miners in Vorkuta to hundreds of thousands demonstrating in Moscow in 1989 and 1990. By March 1990, however, with power about to shift to the presidency, and "multiparty" democracy on many lips, Gorbachev got the Central Committee to ride the wave rather than resist it, recommending to the Congress of People's Deputies that

Gorbachev takes the oath as the first president of the USSR, March 15, 1990.

Article 6 be abolished, which the Congress did forthwith.[42] Yet another example of his continuing power to compel compliance from those who hated what he was doing.

In his memoirs, Gorbachev approvingly cited his aide Ivan Frolov's conclusion that the repeal symbolized nothing less than "a wholesale change" of a political system so long dominated by the Communist party.[43] One concrete expression of that change seemed to be the de facto replacement of the Politburo by a Presidential Council. From now on, according to Grachev, Politburo sessions gradually became "information meetings where no serious [state] problems" were "genuinely debated." Later that summer, the other top party body, the Central Committee Secretariat, was abolished, and Gorbachev began to turn his consultations with the rest of the party hierarchy into a "pure formality, sometimes ignoring it altogether."[44]

But while the old policy-making process was being dismantled, the new one didn't work, as the short, unhappy life of the Presidential Council showed. The eighteen-member council included an unwieldy mélange of top governmental officials who were divided among themselves (Premier Ryzhkov, Interior Minister Bakatin, KGB chief Kriuchkov, State Planning Commission chair Maslyukov, Foreign Minister Shevardnadze, Defense Minister Yazov, and Lukyanov, who was recently chosen to chair the Supreme Soviet); liberal Gorbachev aides (Yakovlev, Vadim Medvedev, Yevgeny Primakov, Gregory Revenko), but also his secretly seditious chief of staff, Boldin; assorted intellectuals representing various disciplines and clashing points of view (liberal economist and self-declared social democrat Stanislav Shatalin, physicist and Academy of Sciences vice president Yuri Osipian, Russian patriotic writer Valentin Rasputin, and Kirghiz novelist Chingiz Aitmatov); one representative from the tumultuous Baltics, Latvian farm director Albert Kauls; and one former proletarian (now head of the United Front of Workers), Venyamin Yarin, whose speeches as a people's deputy had been sharply critical of perestroika, but who toned it down when named to the council.[45]

Could it have become an admirable, Lincolnesque "team of rivals"? It looked like a Politburo manqué when it first assembled in the same Kremlin meeting room—Yakovlev to Gorbachev's right, where Ligachev used to sit, Medvedev next to him in his usual place, Ryzhkov, as always, to Gorbachev's left, other members spread out where they wished, Chernyaev and Shakhnazarov at a little table at the end of the big one, and lesser staff members seated against the wall. The members shook hands. Suitably ceremonial words were spoken. But after a couple of meetings, Gorbachev became bored with his new baby. At one point, according to Yakovlev, after several members disagreed with Gorbachev on a minor matter, he got red in the face and snapped, "Who here is the President? All of you are just consultants. Don't forget that!"[46] Shakhnazarov remembered that when the writers on the council were still waiting for offices befitting their exalted new status, someone joked, "Question: What is a member of the Presidential Council? Answer: An unemployed person receiving a presidential-level salary."

This outcome reflected Gorbachev's style, Shakhnazarov contends— "indifferent to formal institutions, even those he himself created, in fact more so to them since they reflected his penchant for willful improvisation oddly combined with respect for tradition." Not that he was shirking work; on the contrary, he was a "workaholic." But what really gave him pleasure was "to meet with scholars, writers, artists, journalists, and other creative people who were interesting to listen to and before whom he would shine." Hence, the appointment of cultural luminaries to the council, a body that turned out to be not so much "harmful as useless."[47]

Actually, that grim verdict understates the damage. The failure of the Presidential Council (and of the new Federation Council, which consisted of leaders of the various republics) to provide informed, effective policy-making further isolated Gorbachev. He had hoped that the new presidency would inherit the party's role as a "powerful political center for the country."[48] Instead, he now sat almost alone atop a still small presidential apparatus, presiding over what Shakhnazarov calls "a pseudo-businesslike bustling about combined with a monstrous amount of organization muddle."[49] Moreover, his administration was managed by Boldin, who inundated him with incriminating disinformation about democrats, including Gorbachev's close ally Yakovlev, who the KGB insisted was a CIA "agent of influence." According to Yakovlev's later account, his phone was being tapped, eavesdropping bugs had been installed in his office, he felt he was being followed, his son had been shot at in a train by an unknown assailant, and someone had set fire to his daughter's car.[50]

THE 1989 ELECTION CAMPAIGN for the new USSR Congress of People's Deputies, and the first sessions of that Congress, constituted the new, more democratic "game" that Gorbachev was still learning to play. The even more democratic elections for the Russian Republic parliament the following spring proved to be a greater challenge still. This time there were no reserved, uncontested seats for "social organizations" like the Communist party, nor party-dominated electoral commissions to filter nominees. This time democrats and liberals, mobilized in a proto-party called "Democratic Russia," were better organized. This time Yeltsin, too, was better prepared: campaigning not just for himself (for a seat in his former base, Sverdlovsk) but for like-minded candidates in other provinces. He boasted a best-selling book, *Confessions on an Assigned Theme*, which advertised his brave battle against the dark forces of power and privilege; he stood for freeing Russia from stultifying centralist rule and offered to give regions within Russia more autonomy as well. He seemed to have put his inner turmoil behind him, one observer in Sverdlovsk noted, and to have consolidated his identity as a tribune of the people— "flying into the hall filled to capacity, swiftly ascending the podium, and straightaway taking over the audience with his booming, powerful voice," the very image of a "strong, confident politician, a decisive and energetic man."[51]

The Communist party, too, tried harder this time, running fewer predictable losers, nominating younger candidates from somewhat lower ranks. But its nominees were still seen, in effect, as "incumbents" responsible for the terrible mess the country was in, and the party's campaign once again featured more last-minute improvisation than careful coordination.[52] The result was that of the deputies elected on March 4, 465 voted the Democratic Russia line most of the time (far more than democrats could muster at the USSR Congress in 1989), 417 dubbed themselves "Communists of Russia" and followed the party line, and 176 wavered back and forth between the two main blocs.[53]

Gorbachev once again failed to stall Yeltsin's ascent—this time to the post of chairman of the new Russian parliament. Ryzhkov gloomily warned the Politburo on March 22 that if Yeltsin and his allies "take Russia," they would be positioned to quickly "destroy the Soviet Union and throw out the party and state leadership," and that the "whole federal superstructure would quickly disintegrate."[54] But the functionaries Gorbachev recruited to run against Yeltsin were losers. The pallid sixty-four-year-old chairman of the old Russian Supreme Soviet, Vitaly Vorotnikov, declined to run because he, too, was disenchanted with Gorbachev and wanted to retire. With just two weeks to go before the Congress chose its chair, Gorbachev decided to back Vorotnikov's colorless replacement, former minister of the interior Aleksandr Vlasov. But then, in the light of discouraging straw polls, he shifted to Ivan Polozkov, the ultra-conservative Krasnodar province party chief, who would later lead the new Russian Communist Party against Gorbachev, but who was more acceptable to Gorbachev than Yeltsin was. Finally, Gorbachev swung back to Vlasov after Yeltsin led in the first two rounds of voting but failed to obtain the 50 percent plus one needed to win. On May 23, four days before the voting began, Gorbachev himself descended on the Congress in a last-ditch effort to stop Yeltsin. But his crude high-handed bullying alienated deputies who might otherwise have voted against Yeltsin. And then, just before the decisive ballot was held on the twenty-ninth, Gorbachev actually left town—flying off to Canada and the United States.[55]

On May 29, Yeltsin received 535 votes, leading Vlasov by 68, just 4 more than he needed. Gorbachev got the bad news somewhere over the Atlantic. Two aides suggested he congratulate Yeltsin and drafted a telegram containing the statement "You have shown yourself to be a real fighter." But Gorbachev dismissed the suggestion, saying he didn't need this kind of advice.[56] A few days later, at Camp David, the presidential retreat near Washington, Ambassador Matlock asked Gorbachev whether he thought he could work with Yeltsin. "You tell me," Gorbachev shrugged. "You've seen more of him than I have of late."

Matlock describes this response—half jibe, half flattery—as "a typical Gorbachev technique when he wanted to parry a difficult question and make a few points himself."[57] But more than that was implied: asking for advice that Matlock couldn't give after rejecting advice (to congratulate

Yeltsin) he really needed suggests Gorbachev was struggling to make sense of the Yeltsin phenomenon. "Strange things are happening," Gorbachev remarked at a Politburo meeting on April 20. "What Yeltsin is doing is incomprehensible. Both here and abroad he drinks like a fish. Every Monday his face doubles in size. He's inarticulate, he comes up with the devil knows what, he's like a worn-out record. But over and over the people keep repeating, 'He's our man,' . . . and they forgive him everything."[58]

Although Gorbachev didn't know the secret of Yeltsin's success, he still thought he could handle his rival. When Shakhnazarov urged him to get Ryzhkov to run against Yeltsin, Gorbachev dismissed that idea. The Russian parliament's choice of its leader was "nothing to be afraid of. Everything will be alright. You'll see." Aides opposed Gorbachev's trying to talk deputies out of supporting Yeltsin, but he wouldn't listen, recalls Shakhnazarov; he "counted on his charm and his arguments to be irresistible." Aides counseled against backing Polozkov, whose retrograde reputation would push many deputies toward Yeltsin, but Gorbachev accused them of trying to "help the democrats."

Gorbachev's behavior reminded Shakhnazarov of the chess grandmaster who loses to a lesser player. Such things happened, of course, but a true master made sure it didn't happen again, whereas Gorbachev "couldn't stop underestimating Yeltsin, kept convincing himself and trying to convince the public that his rival was finished." In the end, as Shakhnazarov puts it, Gorbachev's "sense of injury won out over political calculation, and his pride took precedence over common sense."[59]

With Yeltsin's victory, and the Russian parliament now out of Gorbachev's control, he tried to prevent the fledgling Russian Communist party from breaking away toward the opposite end of the political spectrum. Originally opposed to the party's formation, by early May, Gorbachev accepted its inevitability, while trying to limit the damage.

The Russian party held its founding congress from June 19 through 22, and Gorbachev attended throughout. Ironically, his main aim was to prevent the congress from choosing Ivan Polozkov as its leader, the very man whom he had put forward to challenge Yeltsin for Russian parliament chairman. But once again Gorbachev's last-minute candidate, Vladimir Ivashko, fell short and Polozkov prevailed. "It was the worst imaginable outcome," recalled Gorbachev ally Vadim Medvedev, guaranteeing a once unimaginable clash between the Soviet and the Russian parties, and producing a wave of departures from the CPSU by the very liberal-minded members Gorbachev was counting on to reform the party under his leadership.[60] Gorbachev's own performance at the Russian party congress was the first of the two public occasions in 1990 that so dismayed Chernyaev and other Gorbachev aides. Behind the scenes, Gorbachev didn't look any better. Just before Polozkov's election, Gorbachev summoned the CPSU's chief pollster (the party secretly carried out opinion surveys of its own members), who met Gorbachev in his office at 2:00 a.m. Gorbachev looked exhausted, as if he hadn't slept for several days. "His face was all gray," the pollster later told Ambassador Matlock.[61] Gorbachev subsequently came close to admitting he was depressed. By now "the Russian question had become the central question of perestroika," and it had the potential to "destroy both Russia and the Soviet Union. In a word, my heart was heavy at the prospect." Meanwhile, in the shorter run, the same conservative delegates who dominated the Russian party's founding congress would presumably constitute the majority at the CPSU's own Twenty-Eighth Party Congress, which would open in less than two weeks and decide the future of the party.[62]

DURING THE MONTHS BEFORE the Twenty-Eighth Congress, when Gorbachev was struggling unsuccessfully with huge issues like the Russian question, there were smaller signs of his deteriorating mood and its effect on his behavior. One sign was his anger. He had always been capable of blowing up for calculated effect, but now the outbursts seemed more spontaneous and indiscriminate, as if by flailing at others, he could escape the blame so many directed at him. At a March 2 Politburo meeting, he condemned radical "slanderers" and "political scum" who "represent no one," but were intent on "shattering the state"; he classified hidebound conservatives, as well, as "a bunch of bastards"; and he lashed out at his own reformist ally Vadim Bakatin for allegedly allowing "defeatists" to infiltrate his interior ministry circle.[63] Gorbachev dismissed party officials who had mobilized deputies to vote against him for president as "idiots and dolts"; he mocked Central Asian party leaders who thirsted to become "elected emirs"; and, in the midst of a long and rambling Politburo discussion, he suddenly snapped at Medvedev, another ally, "Sit down! This meeting has turned into a seminar"—which Politburo meetings had indeed become during his tenure.[64]

Gorbachev reserved special anger for the Moscow intelligentsia he had once greatly admired; now that so many of them had turned against him, he regarded them as "rotten."[65] He condemned Russians' traditional penchant for gleefully "reviling authorities," for believing that government can and should accomplish anything, for putting their faith in Tsar-the-Father or, at the other extreme, for wallowing in "nihilisim."[66] The people who he had hoped would change their lives for the better weren't ready for the "profound, revolutionary transformation we are carrying out." It was as if they wanted the government to tell them "how to hammer in a nail." They were irritated by "the slightest manifestation of initiative" by a "talented person." A successful farmer was dismissed as a "Rockefeller." "Social consciousness" was "backward."[67]

Gorbachev still defended his great project, of course. In fact, the more it stumbled and stalled, the more grandiose his descriptions of it became. A young Komsomol audience inspired him on April 10 to hail the 1980s as perhaps "the greatest turning point in world history." There was "no reason to doubt, even for a minute," that perestroika was the "correct path."[68] To aides drafting his report to the Twenty-Eighth Congress, he boasted on May 19 that perestroika met "the mature needs of civilization"; it was "not an artificial schema," but "inevitable." Soviet society had already become "new," and the whole world was "thinking differently" on the Soviet model.[69] When *Time* magazine asked how he could remain so calm in the face of so much adversity, he answered, "I'm confident because I know that what we're doing is necessary and correct. Otherwise, it would be impossible to bear this burden."[70]

Two other episodes from that spring fit this pattern. In late April, he barnstormed through Sverdlovsk, because he wanted to raise popular morale, but also because, according to Shakhnazarov, the city was Yeltsin's political base. His speech at Uralmash, the vast, heavy-machine-building plant, recognized everyday difficulties workers and their families faced, and although his audience was slow to warm to him, it applauded vigorously at the end. But that didn't merit the "sense of victory over the working class" that Chernyaev says Gorbachev brought back from Sverdlovsk, especially given the "jeers" and unflattering posters that also greeted him there. When Gorbachev violated his own rule about controlling his emotions and lambasted Yeltsin, declaring that his rival was "finished," Shakhnazarov, in charge of vetting published versions of his boss's remarks, cut out the sharpest jabs. But Gorbachev angrily reproached him, and Raisa Gorbachev chimed in: "You shouldn't have done what you did. You don't have the right."[71]

May 1 in Moscow was as sunny and bright as the political atmosphere was gloomy. Over the years, the official May Day festivities had evolved from over-the-top glorifications of Stalin and Soviet military might to a politicized Soviet version of Macy's Thanksgiving Day Parade. Under Gorbachev, the proceedings grew even more relaxed, and in 1990 informal political clubs were allowed to walk through Red Square following the organized parade of citizens, many of them factory workers mobilized at their place of work. Gorbachev and his Kremlin colleagues as usual watched the proceedings from atop the reddish-brown marble Lenin Mausoleum, standing next to one another in prearranged order. Gorbachev himself, David Remnick noted, watched with "a bored, kingly smile, as if he were pleased to live through this hour of his life without crisis." Until suddenly thousands of raucous demonstrators appeared, some with Lithuanian and Estonian flags and tsarist Russian tricolors, others carrying banners blaring, "Down with Gorbachev!" "Down with the Politburo!" "Down with the CPSU—Exploiter and Robber of the People!" "Down with the Fascist Red Empire!" "Ceausescu of the Politburo: Out of Your Armchairs and onto Prison Floors!" Still others waved red Soviet flags with the hammer and sickle ripped out. Leaders on the mausoleum reacted differently: Ligachev grim, Yakovlev expressionless, Gorbachev, Remnick observed through binoculars, showing not "the minutest flicker of anger," watching for what seemed endless minutes, chatting with those next to him as if nothing unusual were occurring, a performance "as amazing as the demonstration itself."[72]

Inwardly, Gorbachev was seething. After about twenty-five minutes, he turned on his heels and descended from the mausoleum, followed by the others, accompanied as well, Chernyaev remembered, by "jeering, laughing, whistling, and shouts of 'Shame!'" from the rowdy crowd now gathered right in front of the mausoleum. That evening Gorbachev telephoned Chernyaev, cursing the demonstrators as "scoundrels and ugly mugs." Later, on national television, he damned them as "rabble," as "extremists" of all sorts waving "flags of anarchists and monarchists and portraits of Nicholas II, Stalin and Yeltsin." Even before his May Day humiliation, the day before, in fact, he struck Chernyaev as "very tired and aging by the minute." That same day, Gorbachev complained to Chernyaev and Brutents that he had "reached the breaking point" and his head was "bursting."[73]

THE TWENTY-EIGHTH PARTY CONGRESS, which opened on July 2, dispensed with almost all the rituals of previous conclaves: no standing ovations as the party leadership filed into the hall; no salute by red-kerchiefed Young Pioneers. The only tradition that remained from Stalin's time was the provisioning of delegates with an overabundance of food and drink. When Grachev entered the hall (as an observer, not a delegate), he noticed it was "buzzing like huge hornet's nest" that someone had poked with a stick.[74] Would the Congress endorse Gorbachev's democratic reforms? Would it continue him in office in the first free election of the party leader since Stalin took power? Would the party democratize itself? Would it elect reformers to its Central Committee?

Such questions seemed irrelevant to radical democrats who had long ago rejected the party as a reactionary force. Some of Gorbachev's own aides (Chernyaev, Shakhnazarov, and Petrakov) yet again counseled him to reject the party general secretaryship, so as to free himself from the "idiotic wishes of idiotic people," and concentrate on leading the country as its president. But once again Gorbachev refused. After a sterile session with local party officials on June 11, he described them to Chernyaev as "self-interested scum, they don't want anything except a feeding-trough and power. . . ." So let them go, Chernaev urged him. "You're the president. You see what kind of Party this is." As long as Gorbachev remained its leader, he would be "its hostage, its permanent whipping boy."

"Tolya, you think I don't see it. But I do." But "I can't let this lousy, rabid dog off the leash. If I do that, all this huge structure will be turned against me."[75]

Gorbachev often told the party what it wanted to hear, and he could speak Chernyaev's language, as well. The truth was that Gorbachev despised and feared party retrogrades, but he hadn't yet given up all hope of transforming the party. What he refused to do, he told the raucous Central Committee plenum that preceded the Congress, was to tolerate "loutishness." If delegates acted like boors toward him, he would "withdraw my candidacy for party leader." "You want me to be frank?" he continued. "You should know this: I will not tolerate loutishness. [*Noise and animation in the hall.*]"[76]

But Gorbachev did tolerate loutishness. "A mob of crazed provincials and demagogues from the capital . . . thirsty for blood," is how Chernyaev described the congress.[77] "Like a drunken peasant," recalled Yakovlev, "who gets lost on his way home, falls down, gets up, crawls ahead, cursing all the way."[78]

The angry Congress demanded that Politburo reformers like Yakovlev and Shevardnadze individually account for their misdeeds. Gorbachev insisted on chairing all Congress sessions (despite having agreed earlier that Politburo members would do so in turn), even when hard-liners were "smearing his allies against the wall." His travails extended beyond the rostrum. No longer, Chernyaev noted, was Gorbachev "surrounded by hundreds of people, asking him questions, sharing their thoughts, arguing, wanting to know his opinion, making requests during breaks. Now he walked out into the corridors alone accompanied by his bodyguard." Chernyaev pitied him and felt terrible for doing so—except that by now "he is already pitied publicly, in newspapers and on television."[79] Throughout the congress, Gorbachev stayed up late plotting his next moves (until four in the morning when preparing his concluding remarks), while his wife, Raisa, told an interviewer, "I can't sleep: even in my sleep the conflicts continue."[80]

Despite all this, Gorbachev considered the Congress a victory. He was reelected party leader, although almost a quarter of the delegates voted against him. His candidate for deputy general secretary, Ukrainian party leader Vladimir Ivashko (whom Gorbachev later regretted having chosen), defeated Ligachev. At least formally, the Congress approved Gorbachev's foreign and domestic policy. He got to fill the Politburo and Central Committee with his own nominees after longtime members either stepped aside to show that their main allegiance was now to the state rather than the party (Yakovlev, Shevardnadze, Ryzhkov) or were forced out (Ligachev). Although hard-liners now felt free to speak out openly against Gorbachev, they had once again submitted to party discipline. And most of the new Central Committee members looked to Yakovlev not like stalwart reformers but like "dead souls."[81] Actually, the biggest winner at the congress was Yeltsin, whose triumph consisted of storming out of it.

Yeltsin did what Gorbachev had so far refused to do—leave the party in order to base himself entirely in the democrats' camp. Gorbachev admitted that Yeltsin gave one of the strongest proreform speeches at the Party Congress, one that coincided in many ways with his own views. But on July 12, Yeltsin announced that as chairman of the Russian Supreme Soviet he now answered to the Russian people and not to the CPSU, and with that, he marched up the Palace of Congresses' center aisle, accompanied by howls and whistles from the delegates. Later that day, when Soviet television broadcast his walkout, Yeltsin emerged from his office to watch the only wide-screen set in the building. "His face was strained," noticed a witness. "He noticed no thing or person. . . . All that was important to him was to see himself. . . ." As soon as the camera cut away, "he walked noiselessly to his desk—looking at no one, greeting no one, saying goodbye to no one."[82]

THE HIGH POINT OF 1990 for Gorbachev was the few weeks from late July to the middle of August. This was a time of near euphoria; he briefly thought he had found the glue that would keep the country together. The seeming fix was for the economy, which had so far eluded his every effort at reform; moreover, the cure was to be devised by a political coalition that until then had been beyond his reach—between Gorbachev and Yeltsin.

The State Commission on Economic Reform, headed by Prime Minister Ryzhkov's deputy, economist Leonid Abalkin (whom Ryzhkov touted as proof that his government included academicians as well as bureaucrats), had reported the previous December on three possible paths toward a market economy: an "evolutionary" approach, a "radical" option, and a "moderately radical" plan. As anyone who has ever contemplated recommendations devised in a bureaucracy will recognize, the first two proposals were designed to be rejected in favor of the third. The USSR Congress of People's Deputies, meeting in December 1989, did just that, and the next spring Ryzhkov presented a more detailed plan that Gorbachev regarded as continuing the prime minister's fight to limit the extent of economic reform. But, on the other hand, Gorbachev himself wasn't sure what to do. "Inveterate marketeers," he recalled," were pressing for a rapid transition to a market economy while providing themselves with alibis by warning against going *too* fast. Enterprise directors were predicting doom if the radicals prevailed. The new Presidential and Federation Councils resolved nothing at their meetings on April 14 and May 22. All the while the economy continued to crater. "If we can't come up with something to save consumers," he warned on May 22, "(and they're already almost destroyed), the people will explode."[83]

"Something" appeared toward the end of July in the person of a round-faced, thirty-eight-year-old, promarket economist serving as a deputy prime minister in Yeltsin's Russian government. Grigory Yavlinsky approached Gorbachev's economic adviser Nikolai Petrakov, urging that economists close to both Gorbachev and Yeltsin work together on the transition to a market. Petrakov had Yavlinsky prepare a written proposal and showed it to Gorbachev the next day. Gorbachev, who seemed preoccupied, glanced at it quickly, then focused on it more carefully, and then "suddenly came alive in an almost joyful grin."

"Where is this fellow?" he asked.

"At work," Petrakov replied.

"Where does he work? Get him here right away."

A few minutes later, Yavlinsky arrived at the Kremlin. Gorbachev was soon convinced. By forming a new market transition team, he would reach out not only to Yeltsin but to the national republics chafing under still-centralized economic rule. Of course, Ryzhkov would object, but Gorbachev was sure he could co-opt the prime minister. Yavlinsky was dispatched to recruit Yeltsin, then vacationing on a Baltic beach in Latvia. After hesitating long and hard (and getting a conciliatory Gorbachev phone call), Yeltsin signed on. At that point, Petrakov remembers, Gorbachev looked even "happier and more excited, like a chess player who, on the verge of losing, finds a way to keep playing."

The next step was to create the team and order it to come up with a plan by September 1. Uncharacteristically, Gorbachev signed Petrakov's draft directive on July 27 without making a single correction in the text. Yeltsin, too, was ready to go, until Gorbachev insisted that Ryzhkov also sign the directive, along with Yeltsin's Russian prime minister, Ivan Silayev. The trouble was that besides their drastically diverging views, Yeltsin and Ryzhkov hated each other as much as Gorbachev and Yeltsin did, if not more. It took another Yavlinsky trip to the beach to get Yeltsin on board, and Ryzhkov still hadn't yielded when Gorbachev left for his Black Sea vacation on July 30. Ryzhkov finally signed two days later.[84]

The "joint team" consisted almost entirely of market-minded economists such as Petrakov and Yavlinsky, but with Abalkin and a couple of his associates representing Ryzhkov. Chairing the group, at Petrakov's and Yavlinsky's suggestion, was Stanislav Shatalin, a veteran economist whose outspoken, iconoclastic social democratic views had long held back his career. In 1990, however, those views helped him become head of the Academy of Sciences economics division and a member of the Presidential Council. Not in good health (he lost one lung to an operation), Shatalin regarded his appointment as his "golden hour," according to Gorbachev, and his team set to work with a vengeance.[85]

Except, ominously, for Abalkin and his government associates. Yavlinsky and his colleagues lived and worked at resort cottages (complete with offices, meeting rooms, copying machines, and safes for secret documents) near Archangelskoe, outside Moscow. Shatalin was too ill to settle in with them, but he later described the scene: "There was a wonderful atmosphere. People with brains, with a heart, with a soul, people who were really concerned about what was happening, who understood their historic responsibility for what was happening to the country. They showed incredible enthusiasm. I have never seen people work like that— five hours sleep at the most."[86] Abalkin and company were concerned, too—so much so that they stayed away in protest and refused to provide Yavlinsky's group with government documents it requested, ensconcing themselves instead at another resort outside the capital, Nikolina Gora. The two groups convened together only twice, each time because Yeltsin had returned to Moscow to get an update on their joint work in progress, or rather, the lack thereof.[87]

What was at issue between the Shatalin/Yavlinsky and the Ryzhkov/Abalkin teams was how fast and in what ways to introduce elements of a market system into the Soviet economy. The Shatalin/Yavlinsky plan promised nothing less than to create a competitive market system—through large-scale privatization, freeing prices from state controls, moving to integrate the economy into the world economic system, devolving substantial power from Moscow to the republics, plus a series of other radical changes—in five hundred days. In its final form, the "500 Days" plan (as it came to be known) even laid out a detailed timetable for accomplishing the main steps along the way. Of course, the target dates were designed to spur action, not goals to be achieved on time at any price. Shatalin himself later admitted it would take "generations" to create a modern economy.[88] But in the meantime, the program was a political as well as economic declaration that socialism (never once mentioned in the plan) was dead, something that Gorbachev had hitherto not been willing to admit. Ryzhkov and Abalkin, on the other hand, wanted to proceed much more gradually, fearing that even if the "500 Days" program took longer than that to implement, it would add to the chaos that Gorbachev's political reforms had already created.

Meanwhile, at his Black Sea villa in Foros, Gorbachev inquired nearly every day about the work going on at Archangelskoe. He was "full of enthusiasm," Chernyaev recalled. "'Tolya,' he would say, 'Now the most important thing begins. This is the final breakthrough to the new phase of perestroika. . . . Now we'll be providing it with an adequate base. . . .' No matter what we were meeting about, he began every conversation on this note."[89]

"I had never seen him so engaged," Petrakov remembered. "There wasn't a single day, not even Sunday, when he didn't telephone me." Sometimes Petrakov had to report to him two or three times a day. He wanted to know about everything; he read everything Petrakov sent him and returned all the papers covered with comments.[90]

According to Shatalin, Gorbachev called him five times a day, too (almost certainly an exaggeration), asking, "How's it going? How's it going? How's it going?" Gorbachev called Abalkin at least once, but he "hardly called" Ryzhkov at all, according to the latter, "as if he weren't interested in how the work was going."[91]

Gorbachev had other things on his mind on "vacation." He wanted to write an article about socialism and the market. Accused of trying to lead the country away from socialism, he told Chernyaev, "I'd like to show that I am talking about a 'modern socialism' that is an organic part of the march of civilization." With Chernyaev's help he wrote three drafts, but never finished the piece. Gorbachev also worked on ideas for a new federal union treaty, lurching from a revival of "Lenin's concept of federalism" to "a new federation," to a "confederation," to a "union of independent states." "He's late again," Shakhnazarov complained to Chernyaev, since some republics were already lining up to leave the USSR. Then another major event demanded Gorbachev's attention: Saddam Hussein invaded Kuwait on August 2.[92]

On August 11, he invited Kremlin bosses and their wives vacationing in Crimea to a gala dinner. Kazakh party leader Nazarbayev, sounding ominously nationalistic, boasted about the natural resources of his "state," without which, he added, the other states in the union could not survive. But Gorbachev's guests dutifully pronounced toasts celebrating him and perestroika. Another evening Gorbachev invited Chernyaev and Primakov to a family dinner at his dacha. There he unloaded on Yeltsin—"a scoundrel, a man of no rules, no morals, no culture," a demagogue who promises sovereignty to constituent parts of Russia, leaving "Gorbachev to pick up the tab," a man whom no one criticized anymore in the Soviet press, but who recently went out of his way to "slam" Gorbachev in "vulgar" interviews with Swiss and Japanese newspapers. Gorbachev would have nothing to do with Yeltsin as a person, he insisted, but he would "consistently pursue a compromise [with him] because without Russia nothing could be accomplished."

As if mimicking their boss, Chernyaev and Primakov spoke equally sharply about Ryzhkov: he was leading the military-industrial complex against Gorbachev; he had publicly opposed his program to the president's; he had turned Abalkin into his "creature"; he was discrediting Yavlinsky's group. But advised to "bid farewell" to Ryzhkov, Gorbachev snapped, "You're like little kittens." Dumping Ryzhkov would create another front against Gorbachev, and "you and I would be finished."

Better to let Ryzhkov become a "natural victim of the market system's objective development," just like the party's power over the state, which would be "gone by the end of the year."[93]

AS AUGUST WORE ON, hope gave way to worry. At one point, Gorbachev confessed to Chernyaev, "I don't want to work. I don't want to do anything. I'm continuing only out of decency."[94] His optimism fading, Gorbachev cut short his vacation and returned to Moscow on August 21. Shortly before that, Ryzhkov and Abalkin met with Yavlinsky, Petrakov, and their group. Ryzhkov felt as if he were entering "the enemy camp," as if his hosts talked to him like "masters to their pupils," as if they "neither listened nor heard," as if the three-hour showdown were "senseless." Rzyhkov was "not about to bury the state with my own hands," he announced, and he would "fight you, its gravediggers, as long as I have the strength."[95]

The bad feeling carried over to Vnukovo-2 Airport, where, in keeping with tradition, Politburo and Presidential Council members awaited Gorbachev's arrival: Ryzhkov, "pale with anger" whispering something to Lukyanov; KGB chief Kriuchkov inert and impassive; Defense Minister Yazov standing stiffly at attention; the uncharming Boldin waiting to chat up Raisa Gorbacheva, as was his habit at all formal arrivals and departures. In contrast to his grim welcoming committee, a tanned Gorbachev emerged from his plane smiling, but not for long.

"You're going down in history," Ryzhkov snarled at Petrakov.

"You've already gone down in history," Petrakov shot back.

"If you keep this up," Lukyanov said to Chernyaev and Petrakov, the Supreme Soviet will oust the government, the Congress of People's Deputies will disband itself, and "you and the president will have to go."

Gorbachev played the peacemaker, but only up to a point. Ryzhkov demanded that the president meet with his group before Yavlinsky's and that he do so almost immediately, before Yavlinsky could ply him with "disinformation." Gorbachev changed the subject and, after leaving the terminal, called Petrakov from his car, summoning Yavlinsky's group to the Kremlin at ten o'clock the next morning.[96]

The meeting, which several young economists attended in short-sleeved summer shirts (having had no chance to go home and change into jackets and ties), went swimmingly for several hours. Gorbachev had read the preliminary report, Shatalin recalled, and "he asked competent, professional questions." He interrupted other speakers, but "respectfully, so as be sure he understood and was understood," and treated them as equals. When the meeting was over, "our guys felt as if they had wings." Afterward, as Gorbachev huddled with Shatalin and Petrakov, he, too, seemed in a "magnificent mood," according to Shatalin.[97]

Ryzhkov and several of his deputy prime ministers had their chance with Gorbachev the next morning. Ryzhkov insisted that Yavlinsky's plan would destroy socialism and the Soviet Union. Knowing Gorbachev's allergy to Yeltsin, Ryzhkov's men lambasted him. "You've got to get rid of him, no matter what," demanded State Planning Commission chairman Maslyukov, leaping from his chair. "Do it any way you want, Mikhail Sergeyevich, but he's got to go, at any price!"

"Stop talking nonsense," Gorbachev interrupted.[98] Shortly after that the meeting adjourned. And at some point in the next few days, Gorbachev and Yeltsin had a surprisingly amiable five-hour meeting. According to Yeltsin, they agreed never to return to the issues that had divided them, and Gorbachev "made it absolutely clear that he would support the [Yavlinsky] plan that had been prepared on our initiative."[99] Gorbachev's equally upbeat take on the meeting was conveyed right afterward to Petrakov: "You know, Nikolai, we had good man-to-man talk. It's easier for me to find a common language with Boris than with many who've only recently gotten into politics and think so much of themselves. Whereas Yeltsin and I went to the same [party] school and understand each other instinctively. Of course, at the beginning we expressed our grievances about each other. . . . But in the end we got down to business and I think it worked out."[100]

This seeming rapprochement helps explain Gorbachev's upbeat mood before the Presidential and Federation Councils met to consider rival transition plans on August 29–30. Canceling all other appointments and taking no phone calls, he went over the Shatalin-Yavlinsky materials (including tables and graphs) page by page with Petrakov, expressing some doubts (especially about the danger of inflation and public reaction to privatization of land). But he seemed inspired—not so much by the economic ideas, Petrakov concluded, but by the political possibilities opened up by an alliance with Yeltsin. "He was in an excellent mood," Petrakov recalled, "joking around, recounting episodes from his life, reciting poems and ditties from memory."[101]

In retrospect, this marked the end point of Gorbachev's August optimism. For the "500 Days" plan, the fulcrum of his seeming reconciliation with Yeltsin, not only faced fierce opposition from Ryzhkov; it soon provoked paralyzing doubts in Gorbachev himself. In fact, the plan was so radical as to suggest that his initial enthusiasm for it was more the product of desperation than of rational calculation.

When the Presidential and Federation Councils convened on August 29, their members hadn't seen final versions of either plan, just a short summary of the "500 Days" scenario, delivered late the previous evening, plus a government program, delivered during breaks in the council sessions, for implementing existing plans and budgets for 1991.[102] (Yeltsin, according to biographer Colton, "never read a page" of the two-volume final report that Yavlinsky eventually presented to him, "homing in instead on the political facets—the zippy title and the taut timetable.")[103] Petrakov suspected Boldin of stacking the joint meeting with specially invited guests—government ministers and other economic administrators, parliamentary deputies, economists and other scholars—mostly opposed to "500 Days"; Ryzhkov's adherents did indeed dominate the discussion. But representatives of the republics, especially Yeltsin, favored "500 Days," and a majority of both councils seemed to, as well. Gorbachev, according to Petrakov, also appeared "sympathetic" to the "500 Days" program, but held back from "decisively" endorsing it.[104]

For two days, Ryzhkov recalled, "we beat each other over the head."[105] Given the deep divide, plus the absence of complete texts, the councils postponed any decision. But not before a particularly hot exchange involving Ryzhkov himself. Yeltsin's Chechen deputy, Ruslan Khasbulatov, crudely demanded that the prime minister resign. "If I have to leave," Ryzhkov shouted in what Chernyaev called "the hysterical manner that had become characteristic of him over the preceding year," then "so should everyone else! We've all contributed to the collapse, the bloodshed, the economic chaos, we're all responsible. . . . Why should I be the only scapegoat?"[106] Ryzhkov warned Gorbachev, "Go ahead. Run the government yourself! Then the next blow will be against you."[107]

What followed over the next month and a half was the slow death of the "500 Days" plan and, with it, Gorbachev's hope to lead a centrist coalition in partnership, however shaky, with Yeltsin.[108] Ever the compromiser, Gorbachev commissioned his longtime economist-consultant Abel Aganbegyan to combine the two plans into something both camps could accept. But that, as Yeltsin was later to put it, was like "trying to mate a hedgehog and a snake."[109] Meantime, despite an agreement to hold off on submitting either plan to either parliament, Yeltsin presented "500 Days" to the Russian Supreme Soviet, which approved it on September 11; Ryzhkov proposed his own program to the USSR Supreme Soviet. When Aganbegyan's composite proved unsatisfactory, Gorbachev asked the Soviet parliament to choose between the plans, but it proved unwilling and unable to do so. The final death rattle was a decision to boil everything down to a short, sixty-page statement of "Basic Principles" (Gorbachev labored over this for several days), which proved sufficiently vague and indeterminate that an exhausted USSR Supreme Soviet could adopt it (356 in favor, 12 against, 26 abstain) on October 19, thus returning the whole process to square one—that is, nowhere.

During this time, Chernyaev recalled, social and economic tensions were "rising by the hour." Telegrams to the president from all over the country reported "crime running rampant," including "murders, robberies, brazen muggings and rape of children." There were "howls about the powerlessness of authorities," curses on the president "who is unable to restore order," empty stores, tobacco riots, breadlines a thousand people long, women furious, men "cursing at the very mention of Gorbachev's name," interethnic clashes growing worse, "ethnic hatred felt in the streets, on buses and in stores."[110]

"Gorbachev is at a loss," Chernyaev confided to his diary on September 4. "It looks as if he is completely confused and does not know what is going on." Chernyaev had never seen his boss in this state. "He could see power slipping from his hands." "Tolya," Gorbachev asked on September 15. "What should we do? Where's the way out?"[111]

There was no good way out—none that Gorbachev could see, and perhaps none at all. Much as he was enamored at first with the "500

Days" project, he dreaded possible economic and political consequences. One, he feared, would be to put the Soviet Union itself at risk by handing over too much power to the republics. Powerful lobbies—the party apparatus, the military-industrial complex, and the collective farm/state farm hierarchy—warned of rampant inflation, unprecedented unemployment, chaos in the marketplace.[112] Meanwhile, Ryzhkov and his government were threatening to resign. On the other hand, to openly embrace Ryzhkov's gradual approach would be to ratify the already existing economic collapse and end once and for all Gorbachev's hope of wooing back the democrats. That's why, in the end, he settled for a stalemate.

Chernyaev thought Gorbachev made a "fateful mistake" when he rejected the "500 Days" program. Yakovlev considered it Gorbachev's "worst, most dangerous mistake," because that program was "the last chance for a civilized transition to a new order," and what followed its rejection was "nothing less than a war."[113] Shakhnazarov admitted that he and other aides shared Gorbachev's fear that ordinary people would bear the heaviest burden of "shock therapy," but adopting "500 Days" would achieve a truce with the opposition, "isolate extremist hysterics," and reestablish elementary order.[114] Even if, as was likely, the plan didn't pass the Supreme Soviet, Chernyaev contends, it would have become the "the banner of reformist-democratic forces," with which Gorbachev could have led "an army," a "new Gorbachevian reform party." With the people behind him, he could have broken finally with the Communist party, scheduled elections for a new parliament, "given up on the old Soviet Union and begun serious work on [new] union treaty right then and not a year and half later."[115]

But who is to say events would have followed this course? They might just as easily have led to further chaos and suffering and the kind of attempt to oust Gorbachev that failed in August 1991 but might have succeeded in 1990.

WITH THE "500 DAYS" PROGRAM DEAD, if not yet buried, Yeltsin delivered a fiery speech to the Russian Supreme Soviet on October 16, charging that Gorbachev had reneged on his promises and warning that Russia would no longer accept its subordination to the central Soviet

government in Moscow. Gorbachev took the speech as a renewed declaration of war. The next day's Presidential Council meeting reminded
Chernyaev of what the atmosphere must have been in the Winter Palace
on October 25, 1917, as the Provisional Government that replaced Tsar
Nicholas II waited for the Bolsheviks to storm the palace. Kriuchkov
and Lukyanov called for "tough measures" (to which Shevardnadze
and Medvedev objected). "How long can we take this? No one listens to
us!" wailed Ryzhkov. "The country is out of control! We are in the midst
of a complete collapse." "Fear and hatred filled the room," Chernyaev
recalled. "Gorbachev sat there gloomily, getting angrier and angrier,"
but saying little.[116]

Gorbachev decided to counterattack Yeltsin on television. Shatalin, Petrakov, and others tried to dissuade him. Gorbachev shouted at
them, "I've already decided." If he held his fire, people "would think I'm
a coward." Yeltsin wanted Gorbachev's job. "He's turned his people loose
on me. They all deserve a good punch in the face." In the end, Gorbachev
agreed to have Lukyanov address the nation instead, after which,
according to Chernyaev, "he regained his composure and calm."[117]

This episode set the tone for the rest of the year. Gorbachev's memoirs
characterize the autumn as a turning point when he finally began to
construct an effective executive branch.[118] Not so, according to Yakovlev: "Gorbachev broke down." He "rushed about feverishly seeking
solutions," but "only ended up making mistakes." Rather than being
strengthened, Gorbachev's presidential power further eroded as republic leaders scooped it into their own hands.[119]

Yeltsin, of course, continued to torment his rival. The two men met
again in mid-November in yet another attempt at a truce, a session that
Gorbachev thought "somewhat eased the tension."[120] But the next day,
Yeltsin's report on the meeting to the Russian parliament infuriated Gorbachev, who thundered to his aides that he wouldn't take it anymore and
would himself "declare war."[121]

Meanwhile, Gorbachev's support among the intelligentsia continued to crumble. The liberal *Moscow News* published an "Address to the
People and the President," signed by a wide array of writers and scholars, which Gorbachev regarded as yet another betrayal by those whom
he had protected, promoted, trusted, and relied on.[122] At the same time,

Gorbachev leading the anniversary of the Bolshevik Revolution
demonstration on Red Square, November 7, 1990. First row, left to right:
Rafik Nishanov, Anatoly Lukyanov, Vladimir Ivashko, Nikolai Ryzhkov,
Gorbachev, Boris Yeltsin, Gavriil Popov, Ivan Silayev.

false information from Kriuchkov and Boldin was poisoning him against
Shevardnadze, Yakovlev, and Interior Minister Bakatin. Gorbachev still
trusted Yakovlev enough to show him a KGB report that was "bootlicking pure and simple, rapturous about Gorbachev and his wife," while
negative about Shevardnadze, "playing on Gorbachev's envy of [the foreign minister's] popularity." But one day, Bakatin later recalled, Gorbachev suddenly ordered that his and Yakovlev's movements be tracked,
after Boldin falsely reported that the two of them, along with Chief of the
General Staff Mikhail Moiseyev, were suspiciously "out picking mushrooms." ("I've never in all my born days picked mushrooms," Bakatin
insisted.)[123]

By mid-November, much of the press was either demanding that Gorbachev resign or predicting civil war, or both. Colonel Viktor Alksnis,
co-leader of a conservative deputies' caucus called Soiuz (Union), proclaimed that the president had "lost the army," an assessment confirmed
by Gorbachev's disastrous meeting on November 14 with more than a

thousand officers who had been elected to public posts. "Tension in the leadership couldn't have been higher," Gorbachev remembered. "Even my closest associates were hesitating and vacillating."[124]

Gorbachev faced a parliamentary uprising led by Soiuz, demanding that he give an accounting to the nation, but he seemed to take this demand in stride. "So they want me to speak," he said to his aides, "so I'll speak." The text he dictated struck Petrakov as "flaccid and amorphous," given the parliamentary frenzy. Aides urged Gorbachev to make it shorter and sharper, suggesting he read the blistering attacks to which it was a response. But he waved off their advice.[125]

The hourlong speech, delivered on November 16 and filled with abstractions and platitudes, bombed. A Politburo meeting later that same day exploded with long pent-up protests from angry members. Oleg Shenin and Oleg Baklanov demanded that Gorbachev declare a state of emergency and establish presidential rule. Moscow party leader Yuri Prokofiev warned that organized crime was taking over the market for food. Just that morning, added Leningrad party boss Boris Gidaspov, he had seen up to a thousand people waiting in line to buy provisions. The new Russian Communist party's chief, Polozkov, demanded that Gorbachev "take power in your own hands tomorrow," disperse the Presidential Council, and arrest dangerous people in the mass media. "It's your fault," Polozkov told Gorbachev, that "you began perestroika by destroying the foundation on which the party has been built." Even a Gorbachev ally, Kazakhstan President Nazarbayev, seemed to join in the assault, agreeing that the Presidential Council should be abolished, demanding to know why Gorbachev hadn't created a full-fledged presidential administration, and calling for a moratorium on all rallies and strikes.[126] So hostile was the reaction to his speech from both the Supreme Soviet and the Politburo that Gorbachev stayed up most of that night writing the sort of address he should have given the day before. Alerting his aides only at the last minute, he addressed the Supreme Soviet again the next morning. Brief and concrete, his remarks lasted only twenty minutes and outlined an eight-point program including reorganizing the government—turning its council of ministers appointed by the parliament into a cabinet answerable to the president, abolishing the Presidential Council, strengthening the role of the Federation Council, and creating a new security council. Afterward, his mood swung again; lunching with members of both the Politburo and the Presidential Council, Gorbachev seemed elated, turning the conversation to literary topics, including the poetry and last days of Vladimir Mayakovsky and Sergei Esenin, and demonstrating his detailed knowledge of both.[127]

Gorbachev wasn't the only one pleased with his speech. Conservatives welcomed what seemed to be the strengthening of the state, while democrats, according to Gorbachev's hopeful assessment, "at least those who weren't prejudiced from the start, couldn't but see that Gorbachev was fully determined to keep the reforms moving forward."[128] Some of the changes he announced had been on his agenda since he realized that becoming president wasn't enough, that he needed a stronger executive branch. But announcing them actually weakened his authority—by raising expectations that he would use his new powers to resolve the national crisis and then disappointing them when he was still unable or unwilling to do so. Two months later, he confessed to aides that he'd had "no time" to work on strengthening "presidential structures."[129]

One reason Gorbachev failed to use his new authority to keep the reforms moving forward was that his liberal allies and advisers were giving way to hard-liners who would eventually try to oust him. Shortly after November 17, when Gorbachev was in Paris, Chernyaev asked him whether anyone in Moscow was implementing his eight-point plan. Or whether "we might return to find things the same as we left them?"

"Of course, not," Gorbachev replied. "I left instructions. Drafts are being prepared on each point."

Who was doing it? "He named Lukyanov, Kryuchkov, and some others." Chernyaev continues. "I said nothing, because everything was clear."[130]

With the demise of the Presidential Council, Yakovlev faded out of Gorbachev's inner circle. On November 4, Petrakov and other members of the Shatalin-Yavlinsky team published an "open letter" in *Komsomolskaya pravda* defending their "500 Days" program. That night Gorbachev (understandably) bawled out Petrakov on the phone, after which they saw each other "very infrequently." At the end of December, Petrakov resigned, over Gorbachev's perfunctory objections.[131] For almost a year before that, Petrakov had been working without an office secretary and with an outdated identification badge listing him as an assistant to the party general secretary rather than to the president—two signs, as Chernyaev put it in his diary, that although Gorbachev had been president since the spring, he had yet to build a presidential administration.[132]

The most stunning departure was Shevardnadze's. According to his closest aides, Shevardnadze first considered resigning in 1989—he even wrote a letter doing so in the fall of that year, but never sent it. By 1990, he had many reasons: anger over official reports on the April 1989 Tbilisi massacre that implied that he had deceived his homeland; continuing hard-line attacks on his handling of foreign policy, especially arms negotiations, Eastern Europe, and German reunification; attempts by the military to cheat on agreements he had negotiated with the United States; plus his sense that the USSR couldn't join the "civilized world" unless it carried through domestic reforms that were now stalled, if not being reversed, at home.[133]

All this and more led Shevardnadze to the lectern at the fourth Congress of People's Deputies on the morning of December 20. At first, he stood there silently. After a long pause, he began speaking slowly in a muffled voice, then more passionately to his fellow "democrats: You have run away," he chided them. "A dictatorship is coming. I declare this with total responsibility. No one knows what kind of dictatorship it will be, and who will be the dictator, and what the regime will be like. I want to make the following statement: I am resigning. . . . Let this be my protest against the onset of dictatorship." At the end of his speech, he quickly left the stage.[134]

Gorbachev didn't know this was coming. Shevardnadze told no one except his aide Sergei Tarasenko. Gorbachev was shocked, "very sad and disappointed," recalled Shakhnazarov. Gorbachev's press aide Vitaly Ignatenko tried to persuade Shevardnadze to wait until Gorbachev could speak to him, but the foreign minister refused and departed. When Gorbachev appeared several minutes later he looked "tense and deep in thought." He tried unsuccessfully to reach Shevardnadze by phone. He tried again two hours later, but Shevardnadze had disappeared. Later that day, having gathered himself, Gorbachev told the Congress he was particularly distressed that Shevardnadze had not consulted him before resigning, because he had planned to nominate his foreign minister to become the nation's first vice president. Since the vice president had no specified duties, and the Congress was far from certain to approve this appointment, this was far from a cri de coeur about the loss of Shevardnadze.[135]

Gorbachev's actual choice for vice president, Gennady Yanayev, a former Komsomol leader now head of the official trade union, was another bad sign. American Ambassador Matlock had met Yanayev several times in the 1970s and 1980s and was unimpressed. After calling on the new vice president, Matlock remained so: Yanayev seemed weak and nervous, chain-smoking cigarettes, his hand trembling as he lit them. Puzzled at Gorbachev's choice, Matlock recalled Gorbachev's jealousy of Yeltsin's popularity and concluded that he wanted a number two who would never rival him for public affection.[136] Gorbachev's longtime ally Vadim Medvedev considered Yanayev a vulgarian with a weakness for feeble jokes, who particularly put off intelligentsia deputies. But when he tried to talk Gorbachev out of Yanayev (urging the much smarter, stronger, and more liberal Primakov instead), he got nowhere—probably, he thought, because the president didn't like to be shown that he was making a mistake.[137] The Congress failed to elect Yanayev on the first ballot, but after Gorbachev insisted, it did so on December 27.

On December 26, Vitaly Vorotnikov noted in his diary that neither he nor anyone else who had been in the Politburo in March 1985, when Gorbachev became general secretary, remained close to the Soviet leader.[138] More significant, since so many veterans of 1985 had long ago turned against Gorbachev, he had also isolated himself from close allies and aides who had supported him all along. "Gorbachev didn't want to talk to any of us," recalled Chernyaev, "neither Yakovlev, Primakov, Medvedev, nor his aides. He'd apparently limited himself to Lukyanov and Kryuchkov."[139]

At one point before Petrakov resigned, he cited a newspaper reporting the Soiuz faction's call for Gorbachev's resignation, and asked why Gorbachev didn't get as furious as he did when radical democrats demanded the same. "I don't need aides who give me one-sided information," Gorbachev snapped. When Primakov pointed out that the latest meeting of the Interregional Deputies Group had *not* demanded that Gorbachev resign, the latter grumbled, "Well, that's what Lukyanov told me. And he always tells me the truth."[140]

Between December 3 and 15, Gorbachev worked on his speech to the upcoming Congress of People's Deputies session, injecting several notes designed to please conservatives: praising the sacred "socialist choice" the nation had supposedly made in October 1917, referring to the Communist party as "a pillar of the people," rejecting a positive reference to private ownership of the land. "One had to see Yeltsin's sarcastic smile," Chernyaev noted later, when Gorbachev lectured the Congress on the "inadmissibility of private property."[141]

On December 24, Gorbachev took to the podium to fulminate against a draft Congress resolution that he insisted, loudly but mistakenly, ignored some of his presidential initiatives. Either he hadn't read the resolution, or he'd read an earlier version. Watching him closely from a seat in the hall, Chernyaev could see Gorbachev was disturbed that he had made this mistake.[142]

Gorbachev during an extraordinary Congress of People's Deputies session, December 20, 1990. PHOTO BY YU. LIZUNOV.

On New Year's Eve, Gorbachev recorded his annual televised greeting to the Soviet people. Afterward, he invited Chernyaev and Shakhnazarov into his Kremlin office, where he was shuffling papers, writing resolutions, making phone calls. The best any of his aides could muster for him was compassion or pity. Which, Chernyaev adds, "on top of everything else, only embittered him even more."[143]

CHAPTER 15

COMING
TOGETHER?

1990

I F ONE WERE TO GRAPH the trajectories of Gorbachev's popularity at home and abroad between 1985 and 1990 (leaving aside temporary ups and downs), the line representing his domestic approval would begin at its peak and would be plummeting by the end of 1990.[1] Meanwhile, his international reputation (especially in the West) rose steadily until, by 1990, political leaders and ordinary citizens alike regarded him as one of the greatest statesmen of the twentieth century.

Gorbachev's own demeanor reflected this contrast. In mid-January he spoke to a gathering of Soviet workers, peasants, engineers, and technologists, the next day to a global forum on the environment attended by delegates from eighty-three countries. For his domestic audience, Chernyaev noted in his diary, Gorbachev recycled "old tired wording" to which his listeners responded by "harassing him with trite and shameless questions" that implied he had no idea what was going on in the provinces. The environmental forum's rapturous welcome "sent him into ecstasy."[2] On March 25, he received a group of American schoolteachers. "Oh, what a holiday this was for his soul!" Chernyaev wrote. "He opened up, charmed them and was full of 'ideas,' just as he used to be when beginning his ascent." Soviet teachers, Chernyaev worried, would be "resentful," thinking "he has plenty of time for American teachers while we are sitting in shit."[3]

Gorbachev visited Canada and the United States between May 29 and

June 4. He was "a different person there than he is at home," Chernyaev noted, "too different" for his own good. Over there "his common sense" came through, while at home his "visceral fear" and the tactics that it spawned "are greatly damaging his policies and his entire cause."[4]

On the morning of October 17, 1990, "fear and hatred filled the room" where the Presidential Council was meeting. The day before, Yeltsin blasted Gorbachev for breaking his promise to support the "500 Days" program for creating a market economy. Now Presidential Council members urged Gorbachev to "hit back massively," as Lukyanov put it. Yeltsin wasn't "in his right mind," declared Boldin. "No agreement with him is possible," Ryzhkov warned. If "we don't show strength," he continued, "the best that would happen" is "they'll shoot us, the worst is they'll hang us from lampposts." According to Chernyaev, Gorbachev sat "gloomily" through the council session, "getting angrier and angrier," but saying almost nothing. At noon, however, at a long-planned meeting with U.S. Secretary of Defense Dick Cheney, he was "a different person. He was in charge again, the leader of a global power," commanding "hot spots" around the world, "calm about domestic affairs and seemingly sure of success." The only indication of his distress was that, according to Chernyaev, Gorbachev "didn't let the Americans get a word in edgewise, and there were seven of them." But by now Americans, like other domestic and foreign audiences, had become accustomed to his longwindedness without realizing that it helped obscure his confusion and anguish.[5]

While Gorbachev's country was coming apart in 1990, he was trying to bring the world together and to keep himself together in the process. He acquiesced in German unification and allowed reunited Germany to join NATO. He stood with President George H. W. Bush after Saddam Hussein invaded Kuwait. He broke with decades of proud, prickly Soviet independence and petitioned the West for billions in aid for perestroika in the USSR.

All these breakthroughs abroad outraged his domestic critics, whose attacks at Central Committee plenums grew increasingly fierce. Although ostensibly directed at Foreign Minister Shevardnadze, their clear target was Gorbachev. Hard-line apparatchiki had been lambasting the "shameful betrayal" of East European Communist allies. Traditionally tame high-ranking military officers had joined them. "The Soviet army is leaving without a fight the countries that our fathers liberated from fascism," declared General Albert Makashov. Others labeled Gorbachev's triumphant summit with George Bush at Malta in December 1989 a "Munich." Makashov was particularly rabid, but the general mood in the military was poisonous. British Ambassador Braithwaite, who saw a lot of them after 1989, was "amazed that they kept their tempers as long as they did."[6]

Later, when Gorbachev was out of office, several of his former aides joined the chorus. How could he allow NATO to expand into East Germany, an outcome Moscow had fought to prevent for decades? At the very least, he should have gotten much more, including a guarantee against further NATO expansion in Eastern Europe, in return. How could he abandon Iraq, Moscow's longtime Middle East client, in which it had a large financial as well as geopolitical stake? How could he lower himself to begging aid from the West, which, in the end, didn't provide anything close to what he needed? Some former aides attributed his foreign policy "failures" to the gap between his reputations at home and abroad. Anatoly Dobrynin traced Gorbachev's "unnecessary concessions" to his "efforts to sustain his weakening reputation at home by what appeared to be successes abroad."[7] According to Karen Brutents, Gorbachev had psychological as well as political motives for appeasing the West: he had long sought "praise and global glory," and "this was the period when Gorbachev's pretension to the role of Messiah reached its zenith." Having "fled" from his troubles at home, he would return from foreign trips boasting about "how well he had been received," about all the "cries of delight" his presence abroad had evoked.[8]

Gorbachev claims his policies responded to political realities (American and West European support for continued German inclusion in NATO) and military realities (Saddam's clear aggression in Kuwait). He says he was pursuing his vision of a post–cold war world in which Germany and a transformed USSR could become genuine allies, as would the Soviet Union and the United States. All this is true, but that doesn't exhaust the question of his motivation. He had indeed become psychologically dependent on being lionized abroad. Just as important, his intellectual independence was on display in his ever-warmer relation-

ships with Western leaders. Having broken decisively with Soviet orthodoxy, he had come to think like a Westerner (of the social democratic
persuasion) himself.[9]

As the year went on, Gorbachev increasingly decided foreign policy
matters on his own, consulting with a small number of associates, but
hardly ever with the Politburo or even the new Security Council, which
he founded in November but didn't convene until spring.[10] He no longer
circulated key documents, including accounts of his meetings with foreign leaders, to Politburo members. Delicate matters relating to German
reunification were "totally off limits" to the Politburo. By elevating and
isolating himself, Gorbachev made it easier to adopt policies that the
majority in the Politburo opposed, but harder to avoid problems that
experts with alternative views might have anticipated. Not only did he
further antagonize the political and military establishments; he alienated "close political allies" who sometimes learned of his decisions from
Shevardnadze's speeches or press conferences.[11]

By 1990, Gorbachev risked becoming a stranger in his own land.
Despite all the warmth, he remained a stranger in the West as well—
witness the way his Western "partners" played on his weaknesses,
both political and psychological, to advance their own interests. He
was under ferocious political pressure at home. The fact that he himself was still wedded to at least some old orthodoxies also held him back.
No wonder, then, that although he trumpeted his agreements with the
West as triumphs, his path to them was at times as tortured as his situation at home.

EAST GERMANY WASN'T DEAD YET at the beginning of 1990; it looked
as if it still might survive as a reformed socialist regime, and Gorbachev
still seemed desperate to save it.[12] He warned in December that if Germany were reunited, he would be replaced by a military dictator.[13] And
to the Central Committee he declared, "We will see to it that no harm
comes to the GDR. It is our strategic ally and a member of the Warsaw
Treaty." But by the end of January, none other than the Soviet KGB chief
and the East German leader told Gorbachev that the German Democratic
Republic was done for. Kriuchkov reported that since the regime's gov-

ernmental structures had collapsed, the GDR could no longer be considered a state.[14] Hans Modrow said much of the East German population no longer supported the separate existence of their own country.[15]

Gorbachev gathered a small group of associates (including Ryzhkov, Shevardnadze, Kriuchkov, Akhromeyev, Chernyaev, Shakhnazarov, Yakovlev, Falin) to discuss this grim situation on January 25. At the meeting, he announced two key decisions—to accept German unification (instructing Marshal Akhromeyev to start preparing to withdraw Soviet troops from East Germany) while vigorously opposing a united Germany's inclusion in NATO. But how was he to prevent that? There were still nearly 350,000 Soviet troops in East Germany, but using them or threatening to do so could mean war or renewed cold war. The alternative was hard bargaining from a position of weakness, but what could that possibly achieve?

Ironically, Gorbachev's domestic weakness strengthened his bargaining position, as did Western leaders' fear of what he might do if they didn't accommodate him. Mitterrand worried that Gorbachev might fall from power if the West Germans pressed too hard for unity and NATO.[16] West German Foreign Minister Genscher assumed Gorbachev could never agree to move NATO's borders eastward "via German unification." "No reasonable person could expect the Soviet Union to accept such an outcome."[17] President Bush's national security adviser Brent Scowcroft believed a united Germany might be so "intolerable" to the Soviets that they might "oppose it, by force if necessary. Or they would successfully impose conditions . . . which would render it unacceptable to us."[18] Gorbachev "could have played the spoiler's role," Ambassador Matlock recalled, and thereby "improved his political position at home." He "could have sulked and refused to recognize Germany's right to choose its alliances freely." If he had, Germany could have had either unity or NATO but not both—"at least, not both at that time."[19] "We kept waiting," adds former special assistant to President George H. W. Bush for European and Soviet affairs Robert D. Blackwill, "for Gorbachev to take advantage of the fact that seventy percent of Germans would have been satisfied if Germany had remained outside of NATO. Our nightmare was that Gorbachev would announce in March 1990 that he would accept Germany unity but not NATO membership. We expected this to happen any day.

It would have created enormous difficulty for us. But it didn't happen. Praise be!"[20] Gorbachev proved "more flexible than we felt he might be" was Bush's decidedly understated summary many years later.[21]

Why *didn't* Gorbachev resist German unity more forcefully? Because, he recalled, it would have been "morally" wrong to deny unity to the great German nation, "politically" a betrayal of perestroika to do so, and "strategically" disastrous to poison Soviet-German relations for the indefinite future. Nor was he willing to let Britain and France "use him" to delay German reunification, since he understood "better than they did" that to oppose what was "objectively inevitable" (i.e., German unification), "all the more so by force," would have been to "call forth the chaos that we all wanted to prevent."[22]

Why *didn't* Gorbachev bargain harder on German NATO membership? Why didn't he demand, his former adviser Brutents wanted to know, that Soviet troops remain in what had been East Germany, a concession that Margaret Thatcher might have been prepared to make? Why didn't he insist, as his former aide Georgy Kornienko wished, that NATO troops leave West Germany in return for Soviet withdrawal from the East? Why didn't he require a concession that West German Chancellor Kohl himself could conceive of—that German participation in NATO be modeled on the French, that is, committed to the defense of Europe, but not directly involved in the military organization? Why didn't he obtain a written guarantee that NATO would not expand farther into Eastern Europe?[23]

Was Gorbachev too focused on the big picture, on his vision of the Soviet Union's and Germany's coming together in a new world, to let lesser issues stand in the way? Did he accept the case made by Chernyaev in a May 4 memorandum that since one way or another Germany would end up in NATO, the only result of resisting that outcome would be to make Moscow's final agreement look like a huge defeat?[24] Did Gorbachev anticipate what Ambassador Matlock later took to be the lesson of history: that since a united Germany's army was limited by treaties it signed, and since a well-disposed Germany could be a "profitable trading partner and potential investor in the Soviet Union or Russia," Gorbachev was "utterly faithful to his country's interests when he concluded the agreements he did"?[25]

Gorbachev was torn between his hopeful vision of the future and his reluctance to cave in to the West, his hesitation intensified not only by domestic political pressure and hostile public opinion but by his own residual geopolitical instincts. As a result, he remained adamantly opposed to German NATO membership—until suddenly, to the amazement of Western leaders and the shock and dismay of some of his own advisers, he accepted it almost without preconditions.

"BASICALLY, NO ONE CASTS any doubt on it." With this answer on January 30 to an East German television reporter's question, Gorbachev seemed to signal acceptance of German unity. Although he was "struggling with perestroika" and therefore "not happy" that he had to "handle the German question now," he told Chancellor Kohl on February 10 in Moscow, they had no disagreement on the issue of German unity. "Germans themselves should decide their own future." To make sure he'd heard correctly, Kohl repeated Gorbachev's words. There was no misunderstanding. "This is the breakthrough!" Kohl's foreign policy adviser Horst Teltschik rejoiced in his diary.[26]

During a press conference that evening in Moscow, just before Kohl announced that Gorbachev had left the matter of reunification up to the Germans themselves, microphones picked up the following jubilant exchange between Kohl and Foreign Minister Genscher that neither of them meant to be public:

Genscher (giggling) to Kohl: "Let's shake hands."

Kohl (clapping Genscher's hand): "Now we can have a drink."

Genscher: "Very good! Yes! Very good! Actually, we should get drunk now."[27]

That same evening in the Kremlin's Garnet Room, after Gorbachev summarized his talks with Kohl, the chancellor glimpsed "naked horror" on the faces of Falin and another Soviet Foreign Ministry Germanist. Falin sarcastically told another Gorbachev adviser that now that the German problem had been "solved," they could retire.[28] Actually, Teltschik's elation and Falin's horror were both premature. For although Gorbachev didn't demand German "neutrality," he was still rejecting NATO membership. Moreover, on the NATO question, Gorbachev thought he had gotten what he wanted from Kohl and from U.S. Secretary of State Baker before him: a promise that NATO would not expand at all, not even into former East German territory after Germany was reunited.

Baker had been in Moscow just before Kohl. During his meetings with Gorbachev, Baker set the pattern he and President Bush would follow that year and the next—of "stroking" Gorbachev all the way to the bank. Baker was solicitous about Soviet domestic problems; he hoped progress in Soviet-American relations would "aid" Gorbachev at home. He offered free advice: an economy could be either "command or market"; there was no third way. All the excess rubles floating around the economy fueling inflation should be liquidated and a social safety net established before freeing up prices. He disavowed any intention to "lecture" his host and urged him, should Gorbachev "feel that the United States is doing something undesirable to you, to call us without hesitation and tell us about it." Baker was sincere; he and Bush genuinely admired Gorbachev and feared for his future. But that rendered all the more credible their strategy of "playing" Gorbachev (former CIA director Robert Gates's phrase) in order to outplay him.[29]

Baker's approach on Germany and NATO was to raise a specter with ominous historical overtones—of a powerful united Germany on the loose in a vulnerable Europe. "What would you prefer," he asked: "a united Germany outside of NATO, absolutely independent and without American troops; or a united Germany keeping its connections with NATO, but with the guarantee that NATO's jurisdiction or troops will not spread east of the present boundary?" Gorbachev didn't answer directly. Earlier in the conversation Baker said he'd welcome a guarantee that "*not an inch* of NATO's military jurisdiction will spread in an eastern direction" (emphasis added) or, as he also put it, that "Germany's unification will not lead to NATO's military organization spreading to the east."[30]

When Kohl saw Gorbachev the next day, he confirmed Baker's promise that NATO would not "extend its territory towards what is now the GDR." And Genscher's assurance to his counterpart, Shevardnadze, was even more expansive: "For us, it stands firm: NATO will not expand to the East."[31]

Several days before Baker and then Kohl arrived in Moscow, Genscher had told British Foreign Secretary Douglas Hurd, "the Soviet Union needs the security of knowing that Hungary, if it has a change of government, will not become part of the NATO alliance." On January 31, 1990, in a speech in Tutzing, Genscher publicly urged NATO to declare, "Whatever happens in the Warsaw Pact there will be no expansion of NATO eastward, that is to say, closer to the border of the Soviet Union."[32]

Given all this, how can it be that NATO eventually expanded not only into the former East Germany but all the way into Eastern Europe and the former Baltic republics of the USSR, alarming post-Soviet Russia and souring its post–cold war relations with the United States? The actual expansion took place after Gorbachev left office. But were Baker and Kohl offering a guarantee that could have prevented it? If so, how did it slip through Gorbachev's fingers?

Part of the answer is that almost as soon as Baker and Kohl uttered their promises, Bush began to take them back. Limiting NATO jurisdiction to only one-half of a reunited Germany was impossible, Bush concluded. Disavowing any further NATO expansion was unwise. For as Bush told Mitterrand in April, no other organization "could replace NATO as the guarantor of Western security and stability," certainly not the sort of pan-European alliance that Gorbachev hoped to build in the "common European home."

"To hell with that!" Bush told Kohl, referring to the idea of giving up too much to Gorbachev. "We prevailed. They didn't. We can't let the Soviets clutch victory from the jaws of defeat." In that case, Kohl said, they would have to find some other way to placate Gorbachev: "It will come down in the end to a question of cash." Bush replied that West Germany had "deep pockets." Or as Robert Gates put it later, the goal would be "to bribe the Soviets out" of East Germany, with West Germany paying the bribe.[33]

Unaware of all this backtracking, which neither Bush nor Kohl announced from the rooftops, Gorbachev assumed a NATO nonexpansion promise still held. Why didn't he press for a *written* guarantee? Because if it went "without saying," as he told Baker, "that a broadening of the NATO zone is not acceptable," it presumably went without writing, as well. To have pressed for a written guarantee when the Warsaw Pact still existed and there seemed no prospect of NATO expansion would have "simply been stupid," he later explained. But he himself warned Mitterrand of just such a prospect on May 25, saying, "some are pushing for countries to leave the Warsaw Pact and enter NATO." The idea of NATO expansion into, say, Poland, Chernyaev told Gorbachev in an April 5 memo, was an outdated, cold war idea in a new era. But if Gorbachev believed that, neither his Western counterparts nor his post-Soviet successors did.[34]

Baker's overall impression of Gorbachev on February 9–10 was mixed. On the one hand, he looked "buoyed by his success" in pressing for a new presidency and an end to the Communist party's monopoly on power. On the other, he seemed in denial about the "decline of the Soviet Union as a great power."[35] Shevardnadze told Baker, "The odds have to be against [Gorbachev's] survival, although we aren't about to say that in public." That helps to account for Gorbachev's demeanor on the morning of February 9 when he and Shevardnadze sat down with Baker at a long ornate table in the Kremlin's St. Catherine's Hall. "None of the usual chaff and badinage" is how an unidentified participant described it to two reporters. Gorbachev seemed "frazzled after the struggles of the week."[36]

Baker and Gorbachev agreed that further talks on Germany and NATO should involve the two Germanys plus the four former occupying powers. Moscow wanted to dub the talks "Four-plus-Two." Washington preferred "Two-plus-Four" so as to emphasize Germany's responsibility for its own future, and Gorbachev agreed. "I pocketed his assent quietly and quickly," Baker recalled.[37]

The push for German unity gathered strength in March and April. On March 18, in their first free elections, East Germans voted unexpectedly and overwhelmingly for the Christian Democratic Union and that party's preference for rapid unification, rejecting the slower path to unity promoted by the Social Democrats. Meanwhile, however, Gorbachev repeated his "no" to German NATO membership to a series of foreign leaders. "Unacceptable to us," he assured East German leader Modrow on February 28. "That would change the balance of power, would it not?" he protested to Bush on February 28. "Unacceptable, no matter what conditions are attached" was his message to an East German delegation on March 6. "An unacceptable violation of the European balance," Gorbachev told the pope on April 14. Even conventional arms reduction talks in Vienna, to which Moscow had attached great significance, could be halted, he warned Italian Foreign Minister De Michelis on April 17, "if NATO won't take our security into account."[38]

If full German NATO membership was out, what about the seemingly plausible alternatives (limited, French-style membership, or Soviet troops remain in Germany) that Western leaders feared and Soviet critics preferred? Instead, Gorbachev floated pipe dreams: united Germany in the Warsaw Pact, or in both NATO and the pact at the same time (two anchors are better than one, he contended), or the Soviet Union itself in NATO.[39] Was he so consumed by domestic politics as to be unable to focus clearly on foreign affairs? Or was he already moving to accept German NATO membership (while telling neither the world nor his own associates), partly in hope of getting German help for his domestic problems?

Gorbachev did *not* reject NATO membership when Kohl's adviser Teltschik visited Moscow in mid-May, and hinted at flexibility on the issue. He also told Teltschik and two Deutsche Bank officials that perestroika needed "oxygen" to survive for two or three more years, that is, credits worth 15 to 20 billion rubles.[40] He mentioned 20 billion dollars for loans and credits when Baker came calling again on May 18—"not such a huge amount" for the vast American economy, he added reassuringly—only to be told by Baker that Congress would balk at giving taxpayers dollars to a government that supported Cuba. Gorbachev added poignantly that in the midst of a "colossal struggle" at home, in which he was accused of conceding too much to the West, "we have the right to expect that you won't just wait until the fruit falls into your basket."

Baker's main move during this visit was to offer nine "assurances" designed to render NATO, even with united Germany in it, safe for the Soviet Union. Among his promises: NATO would become more of a political, rather than a strictly military organization; Germany would abjure nuclear, chemical, and biological weapons; for "a certain period," Soviet troops could remain on East German territory and no NATO troops would be stationed there; negotiations on limiting conventional weapons would be speeded up while talks on tactical nuclear weapons cuts would begin; the Conference on Security and Cooperation in Europe (CSCE), including all European states and the United States, which Gorbachev had hoped would eventually replace NATO, would become the "cornerstone of the new Europe"; plus, of special importance in view of Gorbachev's interest in economic credits, "the process of [German] unification will take into account the economic interests of the Soviet Union."[41]

Asked later why Gorbachev eventually accepted full German membership in NATO, Chernyaev answered curtly, "Baker's nine points."[42] But even to the diplomatically untrained eye, these "concessions" look vague, or partial, or limited. More important, then, may have been Mitterrand's visit to Moscow on May 25. Mitterrand was "brutal," as a French historian put it. Gorbachev's idea of Germany's joining the Warsaw Pact was "a political fantasy." German membership in both blocs simultaneously was "preposterous." NATO membership à la français (i.e., political rather than military) got no encouragement, either, from Mitterrand. "I do not see how to forbid unified Germany from choosing its alliances as agreed in Helsinki," Mitterrand concluded.[43] Instead of reassuring Gorbachev, Mitterrand denied him his one last hope—that the French would help him find an alternative to Germany in NATO.

Gorbachev still hadn't conceded, but he took a big step toward doing so a week later in Washington.

GORBACHEV'S AMERICAN VISIT, Chernyaev wrote later, was a large "bright spot against the bleak background of the situation in our country." In America he "opened himself up to the maximum in front of people who wanted to listen, who felt for him, and who wished both him and his cause well." Americans could see "a man with an independent mind and common sense talking sincerely and naturally." Whereas back home, he maneuvered this way and that, hiding his true feelings, issuing "appeals for compromise and unity that were already an object of ridicule."[44] Actually, the trip wasn't that rewarding, either diplomatically or in its ceremonial aspects. It was the bleak situation at home that made the visit so gratifying in comparison.

Gorbachev's plane arrived to a low-key welcome at Andrews Air

Force Base at 7:30 p.m. on Thursday, May 30. If his hopes for the summit can be measured by the size of his entourage, they were substantial. Some 140 people, including press, had accompanied him to Geneva in 1985, and nearly 200 to Washington in 1987. This time he brought 360 on eighteen aircraft, which also carried eighty tons of supplies, including all the dishes, utensils, and food for the dinner he would throw for President Bush at the Soviet embassy.[45]

The official White House welcome the next morning, by militia whose red-jacketed, Revolutionary War uniforms stood out against the fresh green grass, with a military band playing and honor guards dipping their flags as Bush and Gorbachev reviewed them, was suitably magnificent. And to Bush, Gorbachev "looked well and seemed confident" and "not at all tired" as he "greeted me with a smile and a strong handshake."[46] But while Gorbachev combined a high-minded vision of the future with a plea for aid and comfort in the present, Bush was characteristically averse to "the vision thing" and offered more comfort than aid.

"You and I turned out to be visionaries," Gorbachev said hopefully in their first one-on-one session on May 31. The world had "changed beyond recognition," he added. Perestroika was now in a "critical phase," so he was counting on the president's "understanding and cooperation." He particularly needed "reserves for maneuvering," which wouldn't amount to much "on the scale of your economy."[47]

Bush said Gorbachev's vision was "important from the philosophical point of view," but he was eager to get on to "practical aspects." He managed not to look at his watch until what he considered a "rambling" discussion had run over by twenty minutes.[48] When National Security Adviser Scowcroft reminded him that the full delegations were waiting, Bush recalled, Gorbachev "waved him off with a grin before wading back into an extensive description of the problems facing his country."[49] In response to Gorbachev's request for "understanding and cooperation," Bush cited his own "political constraints" and said he would return to the subject later.[50]

Germany and its relationship to NATO came up that afternoon with advisers to both presidents present. Bush aide Robert Blackwill noted how much less "controlled, exacting, and commanding" Gorbachev now seemed than at Malta.[51] Gorbachev tried one last time to raise alternatives to German NATO membership: new security structures in Europe, transforming both military blocs into political organizations, letting united Germany "stand on two pillars," with "some sort of associated membership not only in the West but also in the East." Predictably, Bush disagreed, but as delicately as possible: "If I am not right, then I ask you to point out where I am mistaken." If he were mistaken, if "the new generation of Germans" were to decide that they didn't want to be in NATO, then "we will pull out of Germany."

Gorbachev affirmed that the American military presence in Europe was "necessary"—a declaration that would have merited Kremlin defenestration at any point during the previous four decades. For the time being, at least, he added awkwardly but stunningly, "One probably could not do without NATO." But he still preferred double membership for Germany in both NATO and the Warsaw Pact. Gorbachev hoped he and Bush could agree because "if the Soviet people get an impression that we are disregarded in the German question, then all the positive processes in Europe . . . would be in serious danger."

Baker repeated the nine "assurances" he had presented in Moscow. But Gorbachev wanted more—the kind of Grand Coalition that had united the United States and the USSR during World War II. "Are we more stupid than Roosevelt and Stalin?" he asked. More point/counterpoint followed before the dam suddenly broke in the following exchange:

Bush: "If Germany does not want to stay in NATO, it has the right to choose a different path."

Gorbachev: "Then let us make a public statement on the results of our negotiations [where we will say that] the U.S. president agreed that sovereign Germany would decide on its own which military-political status it would choose—membership in NATO, neutrality or something else."

Bush: "It is the right of any sovereign country to choose alliances. If the government [of Germany] would not want to stay in NATO, or even tell our troops to get out, we would accept that choice."

Gorbachev: "That's how we will formulate it then: the United States and the Soviet Union agree that united Germany . . . would decide on its own which alliance she would be a member of."

BINGO! According to Bush, "the room suddenly became quiet."

Akhromeyev and Falin "looked at each other and squirmed in their seats." After Gorbachev confirmed his concession, "Akhromeyev's eyes flashed angrily as he gestured to Falin." They exchanged "loud stage whispers" as Gorbachev spoke. "It was an incredible scene," Bush continued, "the likes of which none of us had ever seen before—virtually open rebellion against a Soviet leader." Shevardnadze "tugged at Gorbachev's sleeve and whispered to him." Falin "launched into a lengthy filibuster," while Shevardnadze "kept gesticulating and whispering heatedly to Gorbachev." In response to all this, Gorbachev tried to back off and saddle Shevardnadze with pursuing the issue with Baker, only to have Shevardnadze insist that issues of this importance must be discussed by the two presidents. "Another incredible moment," according to Bush, even though Shevardnadze then gave in. Bush couldn't figure out "why Gorbachev did what he did." All he knew was that it was "an amazing performance." Scowcroft, too, "couldn't believe what I was seeing, let alone figure out what to make of it." Another Bush aide, Robert Zoellick, recalled the scene as "one of the most extraordinary" he'd ever witnessed.[52]

Why did Gorbachev concede? Many years later, James Baker and Condoleeza Rice still couldn't answer that question.[53] "Had he been insistent," Scowcroft later speculated, "perhaps" he could have kept united Germany "neutral." But that alternative, like all the others Gorbachev had proposed, now seemed at a dead end. Moreover, as his unconvincing advocacy of those alternatives indicated and he later admitted, he himself had come to share the main Western arguments—that united Germany must not be left "in a situation analogous to the one it occupied in 1918"; that united Germany in the Warsaw Pact was "impossible"; that German NATO membership would not in fact threaten Soviet security; that, "most important," Germany itself, as represented by both West and East German governments, "wanted to join NATO."[54] As Gorbachev put it in an interview: if Germany was to be "sovereign, its people should decide for themselves. As someone devoted to democracy, how could I object? To have done so would have been unworthy."[55]

Obviously, Gorbachev had not informed Akhromeyev and Falin, and perhaps not even Shevardnadze. Nor did he or Bush announce to the world what he had just done. Bush slipped into his statement at the summit's final press conference that he and Gorbachev were in "full agreement" that alliance membership was a "matter for the Germans to decide." The Soviets had a chance to object, but to the Americans' surprise, they did not do so, and the world didn't pick up on the hint.[56] From that moment on, Gorbachev later wrote, "the German question, in the form it had taken since World War II, ceased to exist," but it didn't look that way at the time. It wasn't until Gorbachev met with Kohl near Stavropol in July that Gorbachev finally and publicly proclaimed what he had seemed to accept in Washington.

MEANWHILE, THE WASHINGTON SUMMIT continued. Searching for triumphs he could hail at home, Gorbachev pushed for a trade agreement that would normalize economic relations by extending "most favored nation" benefits to the USSR. Looking "very agitated," Gorbachev told Bush after a White House state dinner on May 31 that the trade agreement would make or break the summit, that failure to sign one would be a "disaster."[57] Shevardnadze asked Baker, "almost pleading," but with "an air of resignation," "How can we explain [such a failure] to our people in Moscow when we return?" Baker was used to Shevardnadze's being emotional, but never more than this time. "I've rarely spoken like this with you," Shevardnadze implored him, "but it's just *extremely important* that this be done."[58]

The problem was that the United States had long conditioned normalized trade relations on Moscow's allowing Soviet citizens to emigrate freely. And that Bush and Baker had linked a trade agreement to the end of Soviet economic sanctions against Lithuania. But the Soviet emigration bill had been delayed until the autumn, and the Lithuanian blockade was still on. So when Gorbachev told Bush in the Oval Office the next morning that a trade agreement "would be an important political gesture," Bush replied he was "under enormous [congressional] pressure" to stand firm and didn't see "how to get out of this situation."

"We have each made our points," responded Gorbachev, "wearily," according to Bush. "I can't force you to agree with my points. You have chosen the Baltics over *me*, and let's leave it at that" (emphasis added).[59]

Bush was moved by Gorbachev's dilemma. He decided to sign a trade agreement on two conditions—that Gorbachev promise to settle the Baltic crisis peacefully, and that Bush submit the treaty to Congress only after the Soviet emigration law passed and the Lithuanian blockade was lifted. Just before a gala ceremony in the East Room at 5:30 p.m. on June 1, Gorbachev asked Bush whether they had a trade deal. "Yes," Bush replied with a smile. "This really matters to me," Gorbachev responded. Bush planned to mention his two conditions in his public statement. Gorbachev begged him not to, lest he seem in Moscow to have caved in to Washington. With his characteristic touch and tact, Bush agreed.[60]

With the biggest issues out of the way, and further discussions taking place at bucolic Camp David, Gorbachev's mood improved even more. Bush originally wanted to host the Gorbachevs overnight at his seaside compound in Kennebunkport, Maine, but in view of the crowded schedule, he settled for a day at the presidential retreat near Washington. The two presidents helicoptered there, accompanied by military aides carrying the nuclear codes that allowed each to incinerate the other's country, but at a time when Gorbachev was about to promote a Soviet market economy, most of their in-flight chitchat resembled an introductory course in real estate economics. How were houses bought and sold? Gorbachev asked. How much did this or that house cost? Who lends the money? On the flight back to the White House, Gorbachev asked more real estate questions, prompting Bush to explain the role of real estate agents. Gorbachev laughed. The big difference between the United States and the USSR, he said, was that "in our country they'd find a real estate agent and shoot him."[61]

At Camp David the two men talked while sitting at a glass-topped table outside Aspen Lodge (which overlooked a pool, golf course, and putting green), during walks in the woods, and at dinner. Meanwhile, Mrs. Gorbachev set out to explore the grounds with Mrs. Bush, wearing high heels (which she assured her hostess were her "walking shoes," but which her interpreter explained she wore in case she was photographed), prompting Mrs. Bush to suggest using a golf cart. Later, after Mrs. Bush noticed that "Raisa's poor feet looked raw," Raisa changed into black mules. She asked whether the Bush children owned their own homes, and if so, how they could afford them. Plus, Mrs. Bush recalled, "a million questions about the free enterprise system." She also asked why Barbara Bush was so popular. Because, Mrs. Bush replied, "I threaten no one—I am old, white-headed and large," and "stay out of my husband's affairs." Unlike Nancy Reagan, Barbara Bush "liked Mrs. Gorbachev a lot and felt very sympathetic." It was during their long talks at Camp David that "Raisa suddenly became a person to me and not just this woman who had done all her homework (although, as always, she had)."[62]

The two presidents' talks centered on regional issues, ranging from Cuba and Central America to the Middle East, South Africa, Afghanistan, and Korea. Gorbachev was particularly pleased when Bush agreed to cosponsor an international conference on the Middle East, and with their "nonconfrontational" conversation about Afghanistan.[63] Bush marveled at the "rancor-free atmosphere," the "feeling of give and take," the way Gorbachev "roared with laughter" at jokes, the way "he stayed energetic and fired up, and was agreeable to many of my suggestions." Gorbachev reserved his bitterness for Yeltsin. When Bush asked what role the newly elected Russian parliament chairman would play, Gorbachev replied with emotion that Yeltsin was "not a serious person" but an "opportunist," a man who "could have been with us," but had become "a destroyer."[64]

It didn't hurt that the weather was sunny and warm, that Gorbachev jettisoned his jacket and tie for a gray V-necked sweater, and that strolling by the horseshoe pit, he picked up a shoe, threw it, and got a ringer on his first-ever try. One of Bush's aides secured the orange-colored horseshoe, and put it on a plaque that Bush presented to his guest in an informal toast at dinner. Gorbachev was "very emotional and choked up," Bush recalled, when he described what the new Soviet-American relationship and his own relations with Bush meant to him. And in their telephone conversations over the next eighteen months, Bush kept coming back to Gorbachev's horseshoe feat as a way of recapturing the Camp David mood. Even a "golf-cart" incident didn't spoil the fun: the two presidents set out to tour Camp David with Gorbachev at the wheel, but when they looked over and waved at Gorbachev's old nemesis Robert Gates, Gorbachev briefly lost control, swerved to avoid a tree and nearly turned the cart over. Not even a vain effort by Gorbachev to talk about financial aid spoiled the mood. After dinner, he took Bush aside and told him he hadn't wanted to raise "the question of needing money" (Bush's paraphrase) in front of his own associates. But once again Bush stalled, citing "difficult political problems" such as Cuba and Germany, mentioning the possibility of government-guaranteed private loans, but adding that "these other matters [had] to be sorted out." What he really meant but couldn't say directly, he later explained, was that he knew Gorbachev "needed face and standing" when "everything around [him] was falling to pieces," and he was trying to give him that, but "we couldn't hand them the $20 billion of financing they wanted unless they made deep economic reforms—and even then we didn't have the money."[65]

GORBACHEV DID SOME OF HIS OWN stalling on a crucial issue that could have wrecked the summit, but that Bush chose to keep quiet—the fact that Moscow had been pursuing a mammoth program to develop biological weapons capable of causing mass destruction on the scale of nuclear weapons themselves. With a germ warfare program dating back to the 1920s, but accelerating in the 1970s and 1980s, the Soviets had built the world's first industrial-scale biological weapons factory and were trying

Gorbachev and Bush at Camp David, June 2, 1990.

to spawn bugs resistant to any and all remedies known to mankind. Exactly how much Gorbachev knew about Soviet violations of the 1972 Biological Weapons Convention, which prohibited work on such weapons, is not clear. In February 1986, he had signed off on a five-year plan for bioweapons development, and on May 15, 1990, he received a high-level report covering much, but apparently not all, of the program. But if he didn't know everything, the United States and the United Kingdom filled him in on a lot, having learned much themselves from key Soviet defectors. On May 14, 1990, Ambassadors Matlock and Braithwaite confronted Chernyaev with the evidence, and at Camp David, Bush took Gorbachev aside and leveled with him, as did Margaret Thatcher on June 8.

Gorbachev tried to stall Bush and Thatcher (by proposing an exchange of visits to Soviet and American biological research sites) as he did James Baker, John Major (Thatcher's successor as prime minister), and Bush again in 1991. And rather than making public what they knew, the Americans and British kept silent lest American hawks, already charging Moscow with violating other treaties, use the revelations to block key nuclear treaties. That allowed the Soviet program to continue until finally curbed, it would seem, after the USSR collapsed and Yeltsin took power.

Why did Gorbachev hide the truth? For fear that disclosing it would destroy the new world he was building together with the West? To pay off the military for going along with his radical nuclear disarmament proposals? Whatever the reason, his behavior shows that, idealist though he was, he was also capable of realpolitik and of appeasing Soviet hard-liners—which in turn gave ammunition to American hard-liners who remained skeptical of Gorbachev's intentions for so long.[66]

AS IN 1987, THE GORBACHEVS' American trip schedule included ceremonial occasions of all sorts, but this time not just in Washington and New York. The enthusiasm they encountered in Minnesota and California may even have exceeded what Washington and New York delivered in 1987, but this time he failed to overwhelm the capital.

One of the highlights of the Washington visit was a grand luncheon of chicken Kiev and caviar that the Soviet embassy mounted for what it described as "intellectuals and opinion leaders," the American counterpart of the Soviet intelligentsia that the Gorbachevs had long cultivated in Moscow. Although the guests included several academics and two artists (Robert Rauschenberg and Andrew Wyeth), there were more movie stars (Gregory Peck, Douglas Fairbanks Jr., and Jane Fonda) than creative writers (Ray Bradbury and Isaac Asimov). "I guess not everyone knows what intellectual means," condescendingly commented literary and cultural historian Dmitry Likhachev, who attended with a roster of Soviet luminaries. A White House official told a reporter that officials in Moscow picked the invitees and that Mrs. Gorbachev had particularly requested some Hollywood stars. It should be noted, however, that the "cultural" standing of actors in Russia is traditionally higher than in Hollywood, and their "star factor" lower, as are their salaries.

Gorbachev's opening remarks on this occasion hailed the global changes he helped to bring about—the United States and USSR moving from rivalry to genuine "partnership"; the world realizing, after being divided into "opposing camps," that it was "one civilization"—but his monologue was rambling and lasted a full half hour. To Henry Kissinger, he seemed "relaxed and at peace with himself," a simply "amazing" show of calm. But others who had attended a similar gathering in 1987 found him "less invincible" this time and "under siege." David Remnick thought Gorbachev's speech, which included warnings not to try to pressure him, "defensive," as well as "elusive and disjointed." He tried to "repeat his customary routines," Remnick noted, "flattering his guests by name and breaking into a broad grin," but the luncheon had the feel of a "not-quite-successful revival." Some Soviet attendees agreed. Gorbachev aide Primakov told Kissinger that tearing down the Berlin Wall wasn't "our" idea at all. "It was *his*," he said pointing at Gorbachev.[67]

Because of Moscow's threats and sanctions against Lithuania, Congress didn't invite him to address a joint session. So the next morning Gorbachev invited twelve legislative leaders to breakfast at the embassy. In response to Senator George Mitchell's question about prospects for raising prices in the USSR, Gorbachev delivered a lecture that consumed twenty-eight minutes, half the time allotted for Q and A. All told—introductory remarks, plus answers to four questions—he uttered about ten thousand words. Back in 1987 his political finesse had wowed a similar audience. This time Senator Bob Dole noted afterward, "He does have long answers." Added Senator Claiborne Pell, "He spoke very ably, but not very briefly."[68]

Another event that afternoon at the Soviet embassy provided more balm to the wounds Gorbachev was suffering at home. An hour and half was allotted in his schedule, but it took more time than that for him to receive five awards: the Albert Einstein Peace Prize, the Franklin Delano Roosevelt Freedom Medal, the Martin Luther King Jr. Non-Violent Peace Prize, the Man of History Award, and the Martin Luther King Jr. International Peace Award. One by one representatives of the award-presenting organizations solemnly trooped into the embassy's lavish reception hall, affixed their banners to the wall, and heaped praise on Gorbachev, as American and Soviet television cameras recorded every word. Gorbachev beamed his delight throughout.[69]

Gorbachev tried to recapture the 1987 magic in another limousine walkabout. As in 1987, a throng gathered when his car screeched to a stop, with people cheering and applauding, jumping up and down to catch a glimpse of him, screaming and shoving to get close. "I feel really at home here," he told the adoring crowd—a sentiment as ironic as it was revealing, since at home he no longer felt so at home.[70]

Mrs. Gorbachev, as usual, had her own schedule. Mrs. Bush's guided tour of the White House was as successful as Mrs. Reagan's had been disastrous: First Dog Millie "quivered with pleasure when Mrs. Gorbachev spoke to her," the first lady later reported. Mrs. Gorbachev helped open a Library of Congress exhibit of books and illuminated manuscripts that belonged to Old Believers who split from the official church in 1666. At the Capital Children's Museum, she played tic-tac-toe with a nine-year-old and read out loud in her best intermediate English the texts of exhibits in the museum's learning center. Mrs. Bush invited her to the Wellesley College commencement. On the flight there, Raisa seemed shocked to be reminded that, like Mrs. Bush, she would be giving a commencement speech; she pulled out a tiny piece of paper and started making notes. In fact, her interpreter was carrying a translation of Mrs. Gorbachev's prepared text. "Was Raisa being funny?" Mrs. Bush wondered. "How could there be such a misunderstanding?" Easy enough in the Soviet bureaucracy. But the most likely explanation was Mrs. Gorbachev's innate sense of insecurity—which helps explain why she held Mrs. Bush's hand during the commencement introductions and often leaned over later during the ceremony to grasp Barbara's hand again. Raisa's speech, which began by recalling her joy at her own graduation from Moscow University on a similar summer day, was short, sweet, and not at all preachy, except for saying that "even in the most cruel and most troubled times, women have had the special mission of peacemaking, humanism, mercy and kindness." She got a standing ovation, as did Mrs. Bush (although the announcement that she would deliver the commencement address had sparked considerable protest on the campus) after a feisty, funny speech: "I know your first choice for today was Alice Walker, known for *The Color Purple*. Instead you got me—known for . . . the color of my hair!"[71]

Minnesota's Twin Cities met the Gorbachevs with an orchestra playing Shostakovich at the airport. They were "really touched," he recalled, by the "crowds lining the roads for miles and miles, people shielding themselves from the rain with umbrellas and newspapers," tens of thousands chanting, "Gorby! Gorby!" including an "Uncle Sam" on stilts waving a Soviet flag. A block from the governor's mansion, where many

Raisa Gorbachev and Barbara Bush at the White House,
in Washington, May 30, 1990.

in the throng were waving white "Gorbachief" hankies, they emerged from the back seat of their ZIL and walked the rest of the way to the entrance, where seventy-five bell ringers were waiting. Later he invited top business executives from all over the Midwest to invest in the Soviet Union, while his wife visited two "typical" American stores (Pepito's Mexican delicatessen and Snyder's Drugs, where she asked about pay, working conditions, and product ingredients) and a "typical" American family, where five thousand or so onlookers greeted her, intoning, "Gor-ba-chev, Gor-ba-chev." At least five times Gorbachev exited his limousine and waded into rain-drenched crowds to inhale the adulation close up. "There was Gorby," a nineteen-year-old woman remembered—"the short little guy. Raisa had a great suit—magenta and blue. Raisa held onto my hand, and it freaked me out. Raisa, like, clung to my hand." "There is little that Gorbachev enjoyed more than that," his aide/interpreter Pavel Palazhchenko recalled. The frenzy reminded Chernyaev of the Gorbachevs' most ecstatic welcomes in Europe: "crowds everywhere as in Milan."[72]

They flew to San Francisco that same evening. The next morning their fifty-car motorcade roared down to Stanford University, something Gorbachev was particularly looking forward to, Palazhchenko said, since he valued so much "the process of learning as such, and the academic milieu." Thousands of students cheering "Gorby! Gorby!" lined the road onto campus. "Only" a lucky 7,100 students, faculty, and staff had won a chance to see him close up at the main quad, where the Gorbachevs were formally greeted, the Graduate School of Business promenade, where a small group talked to him, and Memorial Auditorium for his formal speech, which got almost continuous applause. "Gorbachev seemed to draw strength from the crowd," according to Palazhchenko, "their smiles, handshakes, and words of encouragement." The presence of Gorbachev's old sparring partner, former secretary of state George Shultz, who now was at Stanford, made the occasion especially sweet. "Well, George," Gorbachev said, "I see you now live in paradise. . . . You should all have to pay a tax on this weather."[73] San Franciscans weren't quite as adoring as Minnesotans: noisy Armenian demonstrators demanding the return of Nagorno-Karabakh to Armenia were in evidence. But Gorbachev addressed 150 admiring business and civic leaders, met with South Korea's president, Roh Tae Woo, and had a tender reunion with the Reagans at which Nancy and Raisa went out of their way to embrace.

At the airport that evening, with the Gorbachevs about to fly home, a choral group on the tarmac dressed as Cossacks serenaded them with a Russian version of "I Left My Heart in San Francisco." But Raisa knew what awaited them at home. Ambassador Matlock overheard her mutter, "The thing about innovations is that sooner or later they turn around and destroy the innovator."[74]

AFTER THE SUMMIT, the Soviet position on the German question, which Gorbachev had seemed to settle in Washington, hardened. At a Two-plus-Four meeting of foreign ministers in East Berlin on June 22, Shevardnadze proposed that even after unification the four former occupying powers retain their rights and that Germany in effect remain divided between NATO and the Warsaw Pact. German Foreign Minister Genscher passed a note to Baker calling the proposal "window dressing," but Baker feared Gorbachev had been overruled in the Kremlin. One of Baker's aides, Dennis Ross, challenged Shevardnadze's assistant, Tarasenko, after the meeting: "This is a total reversal. You guys just screwed us. What the hell is going on?"

What was happening was what Gorbachev had predicted in Washington—that there would be hell to pay at home for what he conceded in the White House. Tarasenko told Ross that Shevardnadze's new stance was a Politburo position that had been "overtaken by events," but could not be disowned until after the Twenty-Eighth Party Congress in early July, later adding that his boss had been forced to "go through the motions" with the "military, hard-line document." Deputy Foreign Minister Yuli Kvitsinsky, who feared that Shevardnadze was losing "one trump card after another," had prepared the tough proposals to slow the runaway train. Shevardnadze in Berlin was as "beleaguered" as Baker had ever seen him, as if overwhelmed by the domestic political struggle.[75]

Gorbachev, meantime, was desperately concentrating on domestic politics, until two events allowed him to return to the German question.

In early July, pushed hard by the United States, NATO promised changes (including cuts in conventional forces, a new defensive military strategy, and permanent liaison missions for its former enemies) that Gorbachev could cite to show it was safe for united Germany to join.[76] At almost the same time, the Twenty-Eighth Party Congress gave Gorbachev enough of a victory to strengthen his diplomatic hand. On the eve of Chancellor Kohl's July 14 arrival in Moscow, Valentin Falin made one last desperate attempt to stiffen the Soviet stance on Germany, first in a "tough memo" to Gorbachev, and then by asking for ten to fifteen minutes of his time. Gorbachev phoned him that evening. Falin warned once more against a German "Anschluss" and German NATO membership, pleading with his boss, "at the very least, to fight to the end" for political membership only on the French model. Gorbachev's response: "I'll do what I can. But I'm afraid the train has already left the station."[77]

Kohl's visit couldn't have gone more smoothly. During their one-on-one session in the Foreign Ministry's opulent neo-Gothic guesthouse on Alexei Tolstoy Street, he pledged a "new era" in Soviet-German relations.[78] Gorbachev agreed that NATO was "transforming" itself, and reported that Soviet "public opinion" was "gradually coming around." That day and the next, the two leaders finally settled the German question. United Germany would consist of the FRG and the GDR and Berlin within their current borders, thus eliminating the danger it would seek to recapture lands lost to Poland and other East European countries during the war. It would renounce nuclear, chemical, and biological weapons. Soviet troops could stay in the East for three or four more years. NATO military structures would not be extended into East Germany until Soviet troops departed. "United Germany," Gorbachev said, "can be a member of NATO."

The issue of NATO expansion farther into Eastern Europe had not come up in the latest talks between Gorbachev and Kohl. The question they were discussing was whether the territory of a NATO member, West Germany, should be enlarged. But the result of this process, as two European historians put it, was that "the Warsaw Pact would lose a member and be forced to concede territory and position," and in time "this asymmetry would prove the thin edge of a very significant geo-strategic wedge in Russia's relations with the West."[79]

"The breakthrough is accomplished!" Teltschik exulted in his diary. "What a sensation! We had not expected such clear promises from Gorbachev. . . . Who would have predicted such a result? For the Chancellor, this is an unbelievable triumph." Kohl himself, like Bush, tried to conceal his joy at getting so much of what he wanted. He, too, made concessions such as agreeing to reduce the Bundeswehr to 370,000 troops, about 130,000 fewer than West Germany had in 1989. He had previously pledged $3 billion in credits to the USSR; he would pay millions more to support Soviet troops in East Germany and house them once they returned home. But when Gorbachev's deputy prime minister Stepan Sitaryan asked Kohl's finance minister for more credits (Gorbachev being too delicate to do so himself), he was told that more would have to be considered multilaterally in a process including the International Monetary Fund.[80]

At dinner with his West German colleagues, Kohl no longer masked his elation: "Never in my life have I been so happy." But Gorbachev was delighted as well. To his critics he had betrayed the Soviet national interest. Falin privately charged that Shevardnadze had received "some sort of secret financial payoff" from the West Germans. [81] But Gorbachev now defined the Soviet national interest as joining the West in building a new, post–cold war world, and he looked forward to doing so with the support of the two most wealthy and powerful nations in the world, the United States and a united Germany.

Not only that, but he had dominated the Soviet side of the negotiations, displaying such command of the issues and of his subordinates that Teltschik thought he was formulating Soviet policy on the spot.[82] Adding to the good mood, Gorbachev took Kohl (whom he now referred to as "Helmut" and addressed in the second-person singular) on a tour of his home region. In Stavropol, he showed his guest the party office where he had once worked and strolled with him through the central square. At Arkhyz, a small VIP resort in Gorbachev's beloved Caucasus Mountains, they found Raisa picking flowers while she waited for them. There they spent the night, Chernyaev reported, "most of it at the table, and I don't mean the negotiating table." The Caucasus had the further virtue of being far from Gorbachev's many critics in Moscow when he and Kohl sealed their deal and announced it the next day at a press conference.[83]

———

GORBACHEV WAS ON his Black Sea summer holiday on August 2 when Iraq invaded Kuwait. Chernyaev got the word in a nighttime phone call from Shevardnadze, who got it in turn from James Baker, who was his guest in Siberia. In return for Baker's hosting him at the Grand Tetons in Wyoming, Shevardnadze had arranged an Irkutsk idyll: a half-day hydrofoil trip up the Angara River to Lake Baikal, the world's largest body of fresh water; fishing on the lake where Shevardnadze, who had failed to hook anything in Wyoming, delighted himself and his guest by landing a large, elusive Siberian grayling (with more than a little help from a game warden and a high-tech reel); dinner at a rustic fishing lodge; plus, of course, talks on foreign policy matters.[84]

When Baker heard that the Iraqi invasion was imminent, Shevardnadze checked with his own intelligence sources. "It would be completely irrational for Saddam Hussein to do this," he told Baker. "It's not going to happen. Don't worry about it." So when Baker confirmed that the invasion had begun, Shevardnadze, he recalled, "was thunderstruck, embarrassed for being misled by his own intelligence services and enraged by the lunacy of the deed itself."[85]

For Soviet intelligence agencies the news was too bad to be true. Iraq was Moscow's closest ally in the Persian Gulf, the two tied together with an official Peace and Friendship Treaty; it had bought billions in Soviet weapons, including advanced fighter planes, helicopters, SCUD missiles, tanks, and artillery, and still owed Moscow $13 billion; it had KGB advisers for its secret police, Soviet military advisers for its armed forces, and Soviet technicians servicing its military-industrial complex. Some nine thousand Soviet citizens and their families lived and worked in Iraq, susceptible to becoming hostages if Moscow joined with Washington against Saddam Hussein.[86]

For all these reasons, the question of how Moscow should respond to the invasion was fraught. Shevardnadze decided to return immediately to Moscow. Baker kept to his plan to fly on to Mongolia (so as not to further alarm the world), but two of his aides, Dennis Ross and Robert Zoellick, accompanied Shevardnadze. Bush hoped the Soviets would join him in condemning the invasion, and Ross and Zoellick found Shevardnadze receptive, but what would Gorbachev say? To Chernyaev's surprise, Gorbachev "stated unequivocally that this was an aggression and couldn't be justified."[87] But Shevardnadze and Chernyaev were almost alone in supporting him.

While Baker was in Mongolia, Ross and Zoellick, with Tarasenko's assistance, drafted a U.S.-Soviet joint statement condemning Iraq's invasion, which Baker (stopping in Moscow on his way back to Washington) and Shevardnadze could proclaim together. But Defense Minister Yazov and KGB chief Kriuchkov vigorously objected, as did old Middle East hands at the Foreign Ministry who were loath to abandon Iraq. The head of the ministry's Middle East desk grabbed Tarasenko, rammed him against a wall, and demanded to know what he would do if an Iraqi mob reacted to the proposed U.S.-Soviet statement by assaulting Soviet children living there.[88]

Gorbachev approved the joint statement, and during the autumn he stuck to his denunciation of the invasion. But whereas Shevardnadze, in agreement with Baker, was prepared to step up the pressure on Saddam and even threaten to use force against him, Gorbachev, according to Chernyaev, "was repelled by the mass use of modern weapons and deeply concerned to keep casualties to a minimum."[89] In this, he was strongly influenced by Yevgeny Primakov, veteran Middle East specialist, long-time Saddam Hussein acquaintance, and now close Gorbachev adviser, who kept telling him it might be possible to negotiate Saddam out of Kuwait. Things got so bad between Shevardnadze and Primakov that when Gorbachev dispatched Primakov to Washington with a "peace plan" for Iraq, Shevardnadze took it as a sign of Gorbachev's mistrust and moved to undermine the messenger, whom he also suspected of plotting to replace him as foreign minister. Shevardnadze had his own aides inform Baker's that he was against Primakov's plan. "Shit all over it" was Zoellick's interpretation of what Shevardnadze wanted Washington to do.[90]

Gorbachev was trying to have it both ways in Iraq, as he was in the USSR—to redirect history without using force. But on November 29 he finally went along with a United Nations resolution authorizing member states to use "all necessary means," including force, if Iraq refused by January 15, 1991, to cease and desist. "Aggression must not be encouraged," he wrote later, "an aggressor, no matter who, must not be allowed to emerge the victor."[91] Looking back, he declared that the Iraqi invasion constituted a "watershed" in world politics, "the first time the superpowers acted together in a regional crisis."[92]

In that sense it was a test for both Gorbachev and Bush, and particularly for each in the eyes of the other. For Bush the question was whether Gorbachev would match his highfalutin' talk of a new world with concrete action. Gorbachev would find out whether Bush was finally ready to accept the Soviet Union as a full partner, or whether, despite all his praise, he was still primarily interested in exploiting Soviet weakness.

Both seemed to pass these tests. Gorbachev did so by backing the UN resolution. Bush reversed the decades-old American policy of trying to bar the Soviet Union from the Middle East by welcoming it into the region—not just by recruiting Gorbachev as a partner against Iraq (thereby buttressing the anti-Saddam coalition Bush was organizing) but by agreeing to cosponsor an international conference on the Israeli-Palestinian conflict. When the two men met on November 19 in Paris (where they were attending a CSCE summit), Bush begged his friend "Michael" (as he now called him) for assistance in the Gulf: "I need your help." To which Gorbachev replied, "Let me say it rests on just the two of us." When the two leaders and their aides gathered for an informal dinner that evening, Bush recalled, they "joked and told stories" with Gorbachev and his usually dour defense minister Yazov "roaring with laughter." According to Bush, Gorbachev agreed with him that "it had been the best meeting we ever had, even better than Camp David."[93]

WELL MIGHT GORBACHEV have thought, given the way he accommodated the West on Germany and Iraq, that the West would reciprocate with the economic aid the USSR so desperately needed. During the summer and fall, he swallowed his pride and made that quite plain to a series of Western leaders.

"We are at the Rubicon," he told Italian Premier Andreotti on July 26. "We would like to receive from Italy about the same amount of credit that we have from the FRG. We're not asking for handouts, we will repay it all. We would also ask you to support our request to the Europeans and Americans for 15 to 20 billion."[94]

Thanks to "good will and mutual understanding," Gorbachev told Helmut Kohl on September 7, they had been able to achieve the unification of Germany. Did Kohl really mean to "blow up" all that good work by not providing all the aid Moscow needed to support Soviet troops returning from East Germany?[95] (Not the least important reason why the Soviet military were aghast at the idea of pulling their troops out of East Germany was that, absent such aid, many of them would have to be settled in tents in frozen fields.) "What happened in Eastern Europe and Germany was more difficult for us than for the U.S.," Gorbachev said to George Bush on September 9: "It took colossal efforts on our part, a huge exertion of political will." The clear implication was that Washington owed Moscow big-time financial assistance.[96] "Germany wouldn't be unified without the Soviet Union's contribution," Gorbachev told German Foreign Minister Genscher on September 12: "We don't want to bargain or extort."[97]

Meeting with British Foreign Secretary Hurd on September 14, Ambassador Braithwaite recalled, Gorbachev was "less bouncy than before, fewer jokes, fewer flashing smiles, not even bothering to tease Soviet Ambassador Zamyatin." He said he needed $2 billion in unconditional credits "right away" to stabilize the consumer market, plus $15–20 billion in credits, goods, and know-how.[98] Moscow would like to receive 15-20-30 billion dollars, Gorbachev informed Jacques Attali, then head of the European Bank of Reconstruction and Development on September 19.[99]

How did the West respond? "You helped me," Kohl told Gorbachev on September 10, "and I want to help you."[100] And the West Germans came through—by mid-1991 with about DM 60 billion.[101] But that paled in contrast with the billions more that West Germany later put into the reconstruction of East Germany, and with the DM 100–120 billion (450 billion adjusted for inflation in 1990) that longtime conservative leader Franz Joseph Strauss thought that Bonn might have to pay in 1966 for a package consisting of a neutral East Germany, a West German exit from NATO and the European Community, plus a German pledge not to raise the issue of German unification until the end of the century. In 1990 the Germans got a lot more and paid a lot less.[102]

The rest of the West put off the biggest Soviet requests until leaders of the seven most industrialized countries, the G-7, gathered in Houston on July 9. During Gorbachev's visit to Camp David, Baker aide Dennis Ross had asked Primakov, "How much do you really need?" Primakov answered, "About 20 billion dollars a year for three years." Kohl and Mitterrand urged their colleagues to ante up at least $15–20 billion, but in vain.[103] Bush contended massive aid wouldn't help Gorbachev until he had transformed the economy and drastically reduced military spending and foreign aid. ("It would have gone down the tubes," Baker later said, adding that he "personally" got the Saudis to give $4 billion to Gorbachev.)[104] Japanese Prime Minister Toshiki Kaifu, still waiting for Moscow to return the northern Japanese islands it had obtained as a result of World War II, also resisted. In the end, Bush suggested dispatching experts to help improve Soviet railroads and communications systems, grain storage, food distribution, and other services. And the seven leaders agreed to study the Soviet economy as a prerequisite for potential Western aid. In other words, as two historians put it—"a polite but thinly disguised rejection of the kind of large-scale concrete assistance Gorbachev was looking for."[105]

Could Gorbachev have gotten more out of Western leaders who owed him so much? Thatcher thought he "could have extracted much more" to cover the costs of providing for Soviet troops withdrawn from East Germany.[106] A British intelligence specialist turned cold war historian believes Gorbachev "could have squeezed far more from NATO had he played a tougher hand in the [German membership] negotiations, instead of expecting to be rewarded later for cards he gave away."[107]

If what Gorbachev was hoping for was aid on the scale of the Marshall Plan that helped rebuild Europe after the war, he was naïve. But he was also undermined by domestic political pressures. During their talks at Arkhyz, Gorbachev confessed to Kohl his fear of seeming to have "sold" German membership. "What will be said," he asked, "when [we announce] that Gorbachev has consented to Germany's entry into NATO? . . . Our consent will be interpreted as a trade for credits, as reprehensible."[108] When Bush sent Secretary of Commerce Robert Mosbacher and a group of leading business executives to Moscow in to discuss investment and trade, Gorbachev turned the group over to Yuri Maslyukov, the chairman of the State Planning Commission, who promised a list of enterprises in which they might invest, plus names for a joint liaison committee to expedite future negotiations. But Maslyukov never delivered either. Was that because he was no fan of Gorbachev's campaign for market reforms, which was then in full swing? Or was this another case of Soviet bureaucratic paralysis, which market reforms were supposed to help cure? All Ambassador Matlock knew was that whenever the embassy inquired where the lists were, the answer was always "It will be ready in a few days."[109]

THREE EPISODES toward the end of the year epitomized the gulf between Gorbachev's standing at home and his standing abroad. Soon after Gorbachev's hopes for a rapid transition to a market economy collapsed, he and his wife visited Spain: cheering crowds, new friendships with the royal family (Gorbachev greatly respected King Juan Carlos for his role in establishing democracy after the death of dictator Francisco Franco), and long discussions with socialist Premier Felipe González, "intoxicating" conversations, Chernyaev called them, "worthy of the highest theoretical forums," about "the essence and fate of capitalism and socialism," about "the new era and the fate of the world," about the importance of perestroika not just to the Soviet Union but to the whole world. "So much understanding and so many friends" was the way Raisa Gorbachev remembered the trip.[110]

In late November, the CSCE held a summit meeting in Paris, attended by leaders of all West and East European states, plus the United States, Canada, and the Soviet Union. The meeting issued a "Charter of Paris for a New Europe," for a "new era of democracy, peace, and unity." Although Gorbachev hailed the charter as portending a "transformation" in both NATO and the Warsaw Pact, those changes never matched his expectations.[111] But in Paris he was the star of the show. All the other leaders in Paris "wanted to have at least a short personal conversation" with him, Chernyaev recalled. Every time Kohl passed Gorbachev on his way to his seat, he "leaned over and whispered" to him. And when the two of them stepped aside to talk to each other, "the hall seemed to hold its breath." It was as if they were jointly projecting a message to Europe: "We're the ones who did all this for Europe. Everything depends on us."[112]

On October 15, Gorbachev won the Nobel Peace Prize. It so happened that U.S. Secretary of Defense Dick Cheney arrived in Moscow the next day and was feted at dinner that evening at the Defense Ministry by Marshal Yazov and his colleagues. When Cheney hailed Gorbachev's Nobel in a toast, his hosts fell silent. "It was as if I'd done something gross in the middle of the table," he remembered.[113]

Gorbachev recalled having "mixed feelings" about the prize. He was "flattered, of course," to follow in the footsteps of Albert Schweitzer, Willy Brandt, and Andrei Sakharov (!), but to many Russians, who had regarded Nobel awards to Boris Pasternak and Aleksandr Solzhenitsyn as "anti-Soviet provocations," this appeared like another one.[114] But he was mesmerized by the contrast between the world's admiration for his accomplishments, and the scorn they evoked at home. Chernyaev found him poring over excerpts from letters and telegrams condemning him and his prize. Gorbachev read one of them aloud: "Mister [!] General Secretary: Congratulations on receiving the imperialists' prize for ruining the USSR, selling out Eastern Europe, destroying the Red Army, handing over all our resources to the United States and the mass media to the Zionists." And another: "Mister Nobel Prize winner: Thank you for impoverishing the whole country, for earning a prize from world imperialism and Zionism, for betraying Lenin and October, for destroying Marxism-Leninism."

Chernyaev asked Gorbachev why KGB chief Kriuchkov "collected all these and put them on his desk," while regularly supplying him with polls showing that 90 percent of the population disapproved of the prize.

"Do you think I haven't thought about this," Gorbachev replied, continuing to stare at his hate mail as if riveted to it.

"Mikhail Sergeyevich," Chernyaev continued, "Do you really want to spend your time and your nerves on this junk? As President, you should 'soar above' this ignorance."

Gorbachev did not reply.[115]

Loath to be seen and photographed accepting the prize, he sent First Deputy Foreign Minister Anatoly Kovalev to Oslo to pick it up—an exception to the usual Nobel procedure—on December 10. After resisting for months, he finally agreed to deliver his Nobel Lecture, on June 5, 1991, the last day he was eligible to do so. In it, he reaffirmed his commitment to the course he was on. "I have long ago made a final and irrevocable decision. Nothing and no one, no pressure, either from the right or from the left, will make me abandon the positions of *perestroika* and new thinking. I do not intend to change my views or convictions. My choice is a final one."[116]

CHAPTER 16

TO THE
COUP

January–August 1991

IMPRESSIONS OF GORBACHEV from Anatoly Chernyaev's diary in early 1991: January 2: "His self-confidence is becoming ridiculous, even laughable." January 7: "He no longer thinks seriously about foreign policy." "He doesn't prepare for anything; he repeats the same thing ten times." January 14: Gorbachev's speech on Lithuania at the Supreme Soviet was "pitiful, inarticulate, full of pointless digressions." March 14: "M. S. is growing more petty and becoming more irritable. And he is less informed." March 20: "He used to read articles and books . . . and thus develop himself." Now "he has exhausted himself intellectually as a politician. He is tired. Time has passed him by—his own time, created by him."

Chernyaev's reactions may have been particularly emotional, but he wasn't the only one who detected that the rush of events and ferocious cross pressures were making life almost intolerable for Gorbachev. "By the winter of 1990–1991," recalled Grachev, even Gorbachev's "strategic reserve of optimism seemed to be on the verge of exhaustion." "It was as if everything was too much for him."[1]

Secretary of State James Baker, visiting Moscow in mid-March, found Gorbachev "fixated" on Yeltsin, "positively neuralgic." When Baker said he was thinking of meeting with Yeltsin, Gorbachev "went through the roof."[2]

Richard Nixon arrived a few days after Baker. At their first meeting five years earlier, Gorbachev was confidence personified. Now he struck Nixon as downcast, defensive, and drained.[3]

Gorbachev's embrace of hard-liners, visible in his estrangement from Yakovlev and Shevardnadze and in his choice of Yanayev as vice president, also included the appointment of Valentin Pavlov as prime minister. Ryzhkov had suffered a heart attack on December 25, 1990. Shakhnazarov and Chernyaev suggested several possible replacements: Leonid Abalkin, the professional economist who resisted the "500 Days" plan earlier that autumn; Arkady Volsky, a talented party functionary, Gorbachev's point man on the Nagorno-Karabakh dispute, who had become an industrialist and entrepreneur; and Anatoly Sobchak, formerly a democratic firebrand in parliament, now mayor of St. Petersburg.[4] But Gorbachev settled on Pavlov, his short, rotund, crew-cut finance minister, whom British Ambassador Braithwaite described as "cynical, miserly with the truth and . . . incompetent as an economist as well." American Ambassador Matlock found Pavlov "erratic and not totally serious" (since he scoffed at the idea that the massive "ruble overhang" that generated inflation was a real problem), but the new premier was more mischievous than that. His idea of economic policy, just when Gorbachev was desperately seeking Western loans, was to accuse "foreign banks" of planning to subvert the Soviet government by flooding the nation with billions of rubles that they were hoarding for that purpose.[5]

Early in January, Gorbachev began increasing pressure on Lithuania. The Ministry of Defense sent a detachment of paratroops, supposedly to detain Lithuanian draft dodgers. On January 10, Gorbachev issued an ultimatum demanding the Lithuanian Supreme Council "immediately . . . rescind unconstitutional acts adopted previously." Soviet forces started to occupy Vilnius buildings the next day. On Sunday morning, January 13, Soviet troops stormed the television tower, killing fifteen of the several hundred Lithuanian demonstrators who were defending it and wounding many more.

The result was a political crisis. Yeltsin flew to Vilnius, where, along with the presidents of Lithuania, Latvia, and Estonia, he condemned the attack. In Moscow, demonstrators carried banners reading, "Gorbachev Is the Saddam Hussein of the Baltics" and "Give Back the Nobel

Prize," while democratic leader Yuri Afanasyev blamed the "party dictatorship," at the head of which stood "Mikhail Sergeyevich Gorbachev."
Several days later, thirty famous intellectuals who had once been Gorbachev favorites condemned him in the liberal weekly, *Moscow News*,
for another "Bloody Sunday," a reference to the tsarist police massacre
of demonstrators in St. Petersburg in 1905. Even his closest aides came
close to quitting. Grachev, whom Gorbachev was about to appoint head
of the Central Committee's international department, decided to reject
the offer. Chernyaev, "in complete despair," wrote, but in the end didn't
send, a letter of resignation that ended this way: "Since I've been with
you, I never thought I would ever again be tortured by such burning
shame for the policies of the Soviet leadership as I was under Brezhnev
and Chernenko. Alas! That is what it has come to." After waffling for
more than a week, Gorbachev finally declared that what happened in
Vilnius was not his policy, enraging those who planned and carried out
the operation. They later claimed that Gorbachev himself had authorized it.[6]

What *was* Gorbachev's role in the Vilnius massacre? He had been
bombarded, he recalled, by demands that he declare a state of emergency and proclaim presidential rule, but he had never done so. The military used force without his permission, he insisted, in "a provocation"
designed to "discredit" him at home and abroad. Or as he put it later
to Zdeněk Mlynář, the hard-liners' aim was "to establish a blood bond
with me, to subordinate me to a kind of gangsters' mutual protection
society." But, if so, why didn't he follow his aides' advice to fly immediately to Vilnius, place wreaths on the graves, and address the Lithuanian parliament? He went so far as to ask Yakovlev to draft a speech for
him to give there. But after seemingly agreeing to go, he acted the next
morning as if he had never discussed such a trip. KGB chief Kruichkov
apparently told him he couldn't guarantee Gorbachev's safety in Vilnius. Yakovlev (according to Grachev) thought Gorbachev's wife feared
a "provocation" or even a special operation against her husband in Vilnius. Gorbachev explained to Chernyaev on January 17 that he "could
not openly dissociate myself from [the army] and condemn them" after
Lithuanian nationalists had "humiliated them and their families in the
garrisons."[7]

Hard evidence concerning Gorbachev's responsibility is lacking. And testimony from those in a position to know (or perhaps not to know, but willing to say anyway) is contradictory. Kriuchkov cited a meeting in Gorbachev's office where "it was decided to use force against the extremists in Latvia and Lithuania."[8] Gorbachev's press aide Vitaly Ignatenko concluded, after his boss pretended not to recall their conversation about flying to Vilnius, that Gorbachev had not been "misinformed" about the Vilnius operation and was (in Chernyaev's paraphrase) "carrying out his plan of intimidating the Balts."[9] Vadim Bakatin, the former, liberal-minded minister of interior, concluded that Gorbachev "could not have not known," but that he must have been assured, since his opposition to the use of force was well known, that Lithuanians could be cowed bloodlessly.[10] One would have thought that his embittered chief of staff, Boldin, would claim Gorbachev knew all about it, but Boldin wrote later that he wasn't sure to what extent Gorbachev was involved.[11]

Whatever his responsibility, the Vilnius bloodbath (along with the killing of four more demonstrators in the Latvian capital, Riga, several days later) left Gorbachev facing a double backlash from liberals and hard-liners alike, and more bitter than ever about both sides. "Now they're calling me a criminal and murderer," he complained about the authors of the *Moscow News* attack.[12] "That son of a bitch!" he exclaimed after Yeltsin flew to Vilnius. "What's to be done about him?"[13] As for those he labeled "provocateurs" but didn't name, they apparently included not only Kriuchkov and Boldin but Prime Minister Pavlov and Central Committee secretaries Baklanov and Shenin. All of the above reportedly convened in Boldin's Kremlin office on the evening of January 11 in a meeting that broke up shortly after the Vilnius shooting began. But even if Gorbachev knew that, he wasn't yet ready to break with them.[14]

Gorbachev's "right turn" continued until the end of March, but with signs he had doubts about it. On January 29, he ordered the military to join local police in patrolling cities to guard against demonstrations. When Chernyaev and Ignatenko objected, he shouted, "Mind your own business! Don't you have anything better to do? You don't understand! This is nothing special. It's normal practice. You're always fussing and panicking, just like your intellectuals." But after berating his aides, he modified the order to include supervision by republic legislatures, many of which proceeded to ban such patrols on their territories.[15]

On February 19, Yeltsin unloaded on Gorbachev for forty minutes on television, ending with a call for his resignation. But this time Gorbachev's reaction was denial: Yeltsin's song was sung, Gorbachev told aides; people expected big things from Yeltsin, but he couldn't get anything done; he was panicking; his own aides were cursing him; his own parliament refusing to be his herd of sheep.[16]

Unrest in the Russian parliament threatened to provoke another confrontation, this time in the streets of Moscow. Hard-line Communist members prepared to try to impeach Yeltsin; his supporters mobilized in his defense. Gorbachev banned demonstrations while shifting control of Moscow's police force from liberals in city hall to hard-line Interior Minister Boris Pugo. By March 27, the center of the city looked like "an armed camp." More than fifty thousand Interior Ministry troops were deployed with water cannons and tear-gas launchers; rows of empty buses and troops cut off access to Manezh Square, outside the Kremlin. The next morning, as thousands of pro-Yeltsin demonstrators gathered, the smell of civil war was in the air. What if the protest turned violent? What if KGB provocateurs triggered that violence in order to justify a crackdown? If any of the demonstrators had been killed, Yakovlev said later, "all of Moscow would have been in the streets." In the end, both sides showed restraint and the demonstration ended peacefully. Gorbachev was lucky, but not before he showed himself susceptible to the KGB disinformation that prompted him to issue the ban in the first place. Demonstrators were planning to storm the Kremlin walls using "hooks and ladders," he was told, even though Moscow Mayor Popov later joked that given the shortages of nearly everything, there wouldn't have been enough rope in the city to allow the attempt.[17]

Like the Vilnius bloodshed and the order for joint military-police patrols, Gorbachev's ban on demonstrations backfired, intensifying liberals' disillusionment with him without convincing hard-liners he was their man. Why, then, did he seem to align himself with hard-liners in the first place and pursue that path so long? Because, he took pains to explain, he was maneuvering between them and liberals to maintain his moderate centrist course. In January, after the events in Vilnius alarmed

Washington, he told Ambassador Matlock (and through him President Bush) that "we are on brink of civil war" and that to prevent that, he would have to engage in "zigs and zags" that might seem inexplicable. "I wanted to gain time by making tactical moves," he said later, "so as to allow the democratic process to acquire sufficient stability" and "bring the country to a stage where any such attempt to seize power would be doomed to failure."[18]

On the surface, this tactic seems reasonable: a coldly Machiavellian way to advance his democratic ideals. Moreover, Gorbachev would insist, it worked. But this leaves out the turbulent emotions that lay beneath his tactic, as evidenced in a peculiar pattern that Matlock noted that winter and spring. Matlock was used to political leaders who were "irascible in private," but project a "calm, thoughtful and empathetic" image in public. By contrast, Gorbachev had become "exceedingly irritable" and "less cogent" in public, while remaining "collected, even judicious" in his private conversations with the ambassador.[19]

One might say both were calculated poses—railing against liberal critics as a way to woo conservatives; calmly confident to reassure Washington. But Gorbachev's rage at Yeltsin and radical democrats, and especially against intellectuals who had turned against him convinced that he had turned against them, wasn't entirely rational. It was as if, when he was speaking to and about them in public, he couldn't contain his anger, whereas, in private conversations with Westerners, with whom he now felt so comfortable, he could better control his emotions.

AFTER THE ZIG TO THE RIGHT came the zag to the left. On April 23, at the lavish government estate in suburban Novo-Ogaryovo, Gorbachev and nine republic presidents (minus those of Latvia, Lithuania, Estonia, Moldova, Georgia, and Armenia) jointly pledged to prepare forthwith a treaty establishing a Union of Sovereign (*not Soviet*) States and to follow its signing by adopting a new constitution. In addition, the ten leaders called for and got an end to miners' strikes, which were then raging around the country.[20] Suddenly, thought Gorbachev's aide and interpreter Palazhchenko, he had "pulled another rabbit out of his hat."[21] Hard-liners, who had been getting too powerful, were now isolated.

Republic leaders, including Yeltsin, who were getting too ornery, were back on board. Moreover, by involving the many so-called autonomous republics within Russia in the initial stages of "the Novo-Ogaryovo process," Gorbachev complicated Yeltsin's ability to speak for Russia as a whole.

This trick wasn't easy to pull off and wasn't guaranteed to succeed. Gorbachev had to contain his anger and swallow his pride, and so did Yeltsin. But the two men needed each other—Gorbachev to lead what he called "the center-left," Yeltsin to position himself as de facto co-leader of the union treaty drafting process. The party Politburo wasn't even informed and resented its nonrole. A nationwide March 17 referendum on the future of the union seemed very important at the time. It asked whether citizens considered necessary "the preservation of the Union of Soviet Socialist Republics as a renewed federation of equal sovereign republics in which the rights and freedoms of any nationality will be fully guaranteed," and 76.4 percent answered, "Yes." But the six republics that refused to sign the April 23 declaration didn't take part; and in Russia a separate question as to whether the republic should have an elected president of its own—in all likelihood Yeltsin—was approved by more people than voted for the union.[22]

Gorbachev arrived at Novo-Ogaryovo (built under Khrushchev in the 1950s in the style of a nineteenth-century gentry estate) ten minutes or so before the April 23 session was to start. Yeltsin's car demonstratively pulled up at the last minute—no second fiddle he, waiting for the first violin to arrive. When the meeting convened in an elegant room under a crystal chandelier on the second floor, Gorbachev took the chair, with parliamentary speaker Lukyanov and Yeltsin immediately to his right and other republic leaders seated in alphabetical order by their domains. The result was, as Grachev puts it, another example of Gorbachev's "virtuoso tactical mastery." Before departing, the assembled leaders dined together, toasting their joint achievement with champagne, Gorbachev and Yeltsin clinking glasses, all "feeling relieved," Gorbachev thought, "feeling hope."[23]

The Novo-Ogaryovo process continued until July 23, when the leaders agreed upon the draft union treaty to be signed in Moscow on August 20. And for at least some of this period, the good feeling remained. Yeltsin damned Gorbachev with faint praise, but that was better than what he usually dished out. "For the first time," he told the *Washington Post* after the April 23 meeting, Gorbachev "has spoken like a human being." "Gorbachev and I bore the entire burden of hashing out controversial issues," he later recalled, although "I usually had to seize the initiative myself if a fundamental issue was involved. . . ." Their debates never turned into "unpleasant scenes or fights," Yeltsin continued, even though "something seemingly intolerable for a man such as Gorbachev was happening—the restriction of his power."[24]

Gorbachev, too, kept his temper, although he told Shakhnazarov on May 8, "I don't believe [Yeltsin] at all. The man lives for one thing only—to seize power, even though he has no idea what to do with it."[25]

Yeltsin became even more powerful on June 12, when he was elected president of Russia with 59 percent of the vote—just the sort of popular mandate that Gorbachev, chosen Soviet president by the Congress of People's Deputies, lacked. Having tried awkwardly and unsuccessfully to prevent Yeltsin's 1990 appointment as Russian parliamentary speaker, Gorbachev behaved better this time. But he denied Yeltsin permission to project his July 12 inauguration, complete with a twenty-four-gun salute and an oath on the bible, onto a jumbo screen in Red Square; and he arrived late and spoke clumsily at the ceremony. As the two men approached each other onstage to shake hands, Yeltsin ostentatiously stopped, forcing Gorbachev to come to him. Afterward, Gorbachev marveled to Shakhnazarov at his rival's political touch, and admitted his own lack thereof. "Such . . . a simpleminded yen for the scepter! I'm at my wit's end to understand how he combines this with political instinct. God knows, maybe this is his secret, maybe this is why he is forgiven everything. A tsar must conduct himself like a tsar. And that I do not know how to do."[26]

Apart from their personal animosity, Gorbachev and Yeltsin disagreed on the nature of the new union. Gorbachev wanted a strong federation in which the central government, while conceding considerable authority to the republics, retained substantial powers. Yeltsin preferred a much weaker union, although it wasn't until autumn that he explicitly demanded a confederation. The draft treaty approved on July 23 was a compromise, but closer to what Gorbachev wanted. Although the republics would share in defining domestic and foreign policy, the new union state would be responsible for defending the country's sovereignty and territorial integrity, implementing its foreign policy, preparing and implementing the union budget, and adopting a new constitution.[27]

Gorbachev rejoiced at the outcome and prepared for the formal signing ceremony on August 20. "Everything was ready," he recalled in September. "Many of the republic representatives were already in Moscow. The seating arrangements had been discussed as well as where the banners would be. We were even shown the pens that would be used at the signing."[28]

On July 30, Gorbachev invited Yeltsin and Kazakhstan President Nazarbayev to dinner at Novo-Ogaryovo to plan for next steps after the treaty was signed. With more than a little help from liquor, the mood was euphoric. On a summer night, the conversation, punctuated by loud toasts, could be heard through open windows, but just in case, the KGB had the room well bugged. Gorbachev later recalled Yeltsin's sensing danger, getting up and looking around, and warning them to be careful as they talked of replacing Kriuchkov and Pavlov after the treaty was signed. But it was too late. Kriuchkov, Boldin, and company already regarded the new union treaty as a "grave threat" to the USSR. Now they would act to save themselves as well.[29]

YELTSIN'S WASN'T THE FIRST warning. Several times that spring hardliners challenged Gorbachev with breathtaking brazenness. But instead of moving to oust them, he managed to convince himself that they posed no mortal threat.

The first such occasion was a Central Committee plenum that opened on April 24. Gorbachev anticipated a right-wing assault; that was one reason, in fact, why he "zagged" left on April 23. On the eve of the plenum, hundreds of local party bosses demanded an extraordinary party congress to call Gorbachev to account, and thirty-two of seventy-two province party bosses called for his resignation.[30] The plenum's draft resolution, prepared in advance by a new cadre of younger Central Committee secretaries whom Gorbachev himself had appointed, condemned his policies.[31] Moscow, St. Petersburg, and Ukrainian party leaders delivered especially biting plenum speeches that had been "orchestrated" in advance.[32] Ukrainian leader Stanislav Gurenko charged Gorbachev with "doing to the country what its enemies have not been able to do." Byelorussian party boss Anatoly Malofeyev demanded that Gorbachev declare a state of emergency or resign.[33]

At this point Gorbachev rose from his chair, muttered, "OK, that's it, I'll answer everything," and, without asking the chair's permission, stalked toward the rostrum. The hall suddenly fell silent—until, alarmed at the unusual sight of an enraged Gorbachev, someone shouted, "Let's take a break."

"Don't worry," Gorbachev snarled, "I won't take long. You'll make it to lunch." And then: "I'm leaving. I'm retiring." After that he walked out.[34]

Pandemonium followed. Several generals started shouting, "Go ahead, leave! Get out! Beat it!"[35] Gorbachev supporters frantically mobilized to defend him, but they didn't have to. The Politburo caucused without Gorbachev and decided to "remove the issue [of his removal] from discussion." And he agreed to return. Yet again, he had to decide whether to split the party, leading his supporters into a new party and leaving opponents to fend for themselves. Chernyaev thought the latter had "shat in their pants" at the thought of having to cope without the leader they hated. So they should be told to "go fuck their mothers." But although Gorbachev defended his cause passionately to the plenum, he once again shrank from a split. "I would have preferred to resign," he recalled, "but I didn't have the right to give up my attempt to reform the party, just when reforms were threatened with defeat."[36]

How long would his conscience "require" him to keep enlightening those who didn't want to be reformed? Or was this another tactical maneuver to keep the rabid dog on a leash? Whatever it was, it had another unfortunate consequence. Although the plenum shook him ("What should I do now, Tolya?" he asked Chernyaev on the phone late that night), his opponents' retreat further buttressed what Shakhnazarov called Gorbachev's "artless confidence" that when push came to shove, he could and would prevail.[37]

The next shove came on June 17. Prime Minister Pavlov asked the USSR Supreme Soviet to give to his government additional powers that had previously been President Gorbachev's or that the national parliament had shared with republic or local governments: to propose legislation on its own; a larger role in economic and social policy-making; control over the State Bank and the taxation inspectorate; and a special mandate to go after organized crime. Pavlov said the president was already working eighteen hours a day and had more duties than he could handle. When deputies asked whether Gorbachev, who wasn't present, agreed, Pavlov insisted he had no "basic disagreement" with the president.

Pavlov's challenge was stunning, but what came next even more so. After parliament declared itself in a closed session, the "power" (*siloviki*) ministers—Yazov (defense), Pugo (interior), and the KGB's Kriuchkov—warned in the darkest terms of the crisis facing the nation. Kriuchkov cited Yuri Andropov's 1977 warning to the Politburo that the CIA had been recruiting Soviet citizens, organizing their education, and then moving them into position to run the country in accordance with American wishes. As a result, he continued, the current reforms were "not what they look like to us, but rather, they've been devised across the ocean." Kriuchkov said he'd presented "complete, sharp, objective warnings to the country's leadership, along with concrete recommendations for action." But the leadership's reaction had been "inadequate."[38]

One could hardly imagine a more brazen challenge. Kriuchkov didn't name Aleksandr Yakovlev (whose year as an exchange student at Columbia University in 1958 and ten years as Soviet ambassador to Canada made him the obvious candidate to be the CIA's agent), but he didn't have to. Soviet politicians were past masters at reading between the lines.

But for a while Gorbachev didn't object. He let Vice President Yanayev tell the deputies the next day that the president was following matters closely and "didn't see any political subtext" to the closed session.[39] Gorbachev told visiting European Commission President Jacques Delors there was no difference between him and Pavlov, that "you couldn't get a piece of cigarette paper between them." But privately, recalled Shakhnazarov, his boss "recognized this as an overt attack on him" and was "extremely angry." He said, "This is what it's all come to—they're openly attacking us now, our so-called 'comrades-in-arms.'" Press aide

Ignatenko remembered Gorbachev had a "rough talk" with Pavlov and company. And on June 21, Gorbachev scolded his ministers at the Supreme Soviet, watched as the deputies gave them "a good thrashing" by voting down Pavlov's recommendations 262 to 24, and then, with his wayward ministers standing grimly beside him, told reporters with a grin, "The 'coup' is over."[40]

Why didn't Gorbachev go farther and fire Pavlov and the power ministers? Was it because (as he put it to Chernyaev) he had to use all sorts of people if his cabinet was to reflect divided opinion in the country? Or because, Chernyaev wondered, Gorbachev couldn't admit that he'd erred in appointing them? Or because (Ignatenko's guess) Gorbachev's "innate kindness" prevented him from telling them to go? It was probably all of the above, plus his accursed overconfidence again, that sense of superiority that persisted despite, or perhaps because, of all his problems. Gorbachev "couldn't believe these people would betray him," Shakhnazarov later wrote, because he thought "they couldn't do without him," that they were "incapable of doing anything without their leader."[41]

Ambassador Matlock found Gorbachev's inaction "inexplicable." Searching for an explanation, he invited liberal Moscow Mayor Popov and others to lunch on June 20. But Popov asked to come by earlier, and upon arrival, while talking of other things, he scribbled a note on a piece of paper and handed it to Matlock: "A coup is being organized. We must get word to Boris Nikolayevich."

Yeltsin was in Washington. Matlock, while conversing as naturally as he could, wrote that he'd send a message, and then added, "Who is behind this?" Popov replied, "Pavlov, Kriuchkov, Yazov, Lukyanov." Popov proceeded to pick up the paper he'd written on, tear it into small pieces, and shove it into his pocket.

Matlock urgently conveyed the warning to Bush and Scowcroft, who replied that the president would convey it to Yeltsin, but that Matlock should warn Gorbachev. Matlock immediately requested a meeting and was received by Gorbachev that same evening in his Kremlin office. Seated at a long table next to Chernyaev and opposite Matlock, Gorbachev was in a jocular mood, and in no hurry to hear Matlock's urgent message, Gorbachev greeted him as "Comrade Ambassador" and then listened as Matlock said, "Mr. President, President Bush has asked me to notify you of a report that we have received which we find greatly disturbing, although we cannot confirm it. It is based on more than rumor, but less than hard information. It is that there is an effort underway to remove you and it could happen at any time, even this week."

Matlock, Chernyaev recalled, was "pale as a sheet" when he entered the office. But his solemn warning prompted Gorbachev to "start laughing." Matlock started to apologize, saying he couldn't not deliver his president's message. Then Gorbachev turned serious: "Tell President Bush I am touched. I have felt for some time that we are partners, and now he has proved it. Thank him for his concern. He has done what a friend should do. But tell him not to worry. I have everything well in hand. You'll see tomorrow." After that, according to Matlock, Gorbachev "lapsed into the sort of soliloquy of which he was fond": the situation was complicated; Prime Minister Pavlov was inexperienced; some hotheads in parliament might have been talking about overthrowing the government. But Matlock would see the next day that he (Gorbachev) had matters under control, that in fact, the coup he'd been warned about was "100 percent unlikely."[42] The "proof" that Gorbachev promised "tomorrow" was the Supreme Soviet's misleadingly sharp slap-down of Pavlov's request for additional powers.

Two more red flags appeared before Gorbachev's departure for a Black Sea vacation in early August, but he dismissed one and took the other as a sign of hope rather than of danger. On July 23, the reactionary newspaper *Sovetskaya Rossiya* (which had published Nina Andreyeva's philippic in March 1988) printed "A Word to the People," signed by General Varennikov, Vasily Starodubtsev, the head of an agricultural lobby, and Aleksandr Tizyakov, a military-industrial lobbyist), plus a collection of Russian nationalist politicians and writers. "Our motherland is dying, breaking apart and plunging into darkness and nothingness." The "bones of the people are being ground up and the backbone of Russia is snapped in two." "How is it that we have let people come to power who do not love their country, who kowtow to foreign patrons and seek advice and blessings abroad?"

Gorbachev was angry and indignant. But when Chernyaev and Ignatenko pointed out that signers included generals subordinate to him as commander in chief (including General Boris Gromov, formerly Soviet

commander in Afghanistan and now deputy minister of the interior),
Gorbachev replied, "Well, they're also people's deputies, members of parliament." The spectacle of generals and colonels sitting in parliament,
unheard of in other democracies, was the country's problem. The fact
that Gorbachev seemed not to recognize the danger posed by the speakers was his problem.[43]

The second danger sign came at another Central Committee plenum,
held on July 25–26. The focus at the session was Gorbachev's plan for a
new party program that was in fact social democratic rather than Communist: it would endorse a market economy and a democratic polity and
thus, in his view, "constitute a final break with the past." His defense
of the program was strong and clear. So the surprise wasn't that delegates continually interrupted him with objections but that the plenum
approved the draft in the end. At the time, he felt as if he'd won a "final
battle." "I thought I had strengthened my position against the opposition," he recalled twenty years later, "that society was now on my side.
Now I understand that was arrogance on my part."[44] Only later did he
realize that his hard-core opponents had been biding their time in July:
having given up on voting him out of office, they were preparing to oust
him by force.[45]

IN THE PAST, FOREIGN AFFAIRS offered Gorbachev comfort as his troubles mounted at home. That pattern continued in 1991, but the satisfying
moments were fewer and farther between because the Western powers,
and particularly the United States, had less and less reason to accommodate him—first, because he had already conceded what they most
wanted from him, and second, because his chances of remaining in control of his country continued to diminish.

"The Gorbachev era is effectively over," began a CIA assessment in
April. Deputy National Security Adviser Robert Gates thought Gorbachev's "time was running out." Gates and Secretary of Defense Cheney
were already salivating at the thought of "the Soviet Union broken up,
thereby reducing the chance it could ever threaten our security again."
But President Bush was, as ever, more cautious. Gorbachev was "still all
we've got," he said, "and all *they've* got, too." His view, as expressed in his

diary on March 17, was "you dance with who is on the dance floor—you don't try to influence the succession, and you especially don't do something that would [give the] blatant appearance [of encouraging] destabilization." So he and National Security Adviser Scowcroft focused on "locking in" gains Gorbachev had already allowed them to make rather than anticipating a post-Gorbachev era.[46]

For a while, at least, President Bush's bad impression of Yeltsin reinforced his positive attitude toward Gorbachev. Bush still hoped the two men could work together, so when Yeltsin lashed out at Gorbachev on February 28, Bush was disappointed although not surprised: "This guy Yeltsin is really a wild man, isn't he?"[47] Baker's experience in Moscow in March (when Yeltsin nixed at the last minute a short meeting with the secretary of state and rudely demanded a longer session) didn't alter this impression.[48] But Yeltsin's visit to Washington in June as newly elected Russian president did. Bush was "greatly relieved and surprised" when Yeltsin "sang [Gorbachev's] praises." He found Yeltsin "engaging and fascinating, and his infectious laugh made him easy to like." Yeltsin even seemed to have learned that a proper president should be properly attired. "In contrast to his previous trip," Bush noted, Yeltsin had "taken a page from Gorbachev's book and arrived well-tailored and -pressed."[49]

Back in January, when Yeltsin wasn't yet danceable, the White House went relatively easy on Gorbachev during the Lithuanian crisis. Doing so wasn't cost-free, because of right-wing pressure on Bush to stand behind the Lithuanians. But although Bush quietly called off planning for a possible February summit, and sent Gorbachev a private letter threatening to cut off all economic assistance, the administration avoided criticizing him in public. Baker thought Gorbachev "knew more about what had gone on [in Vilnius] than he wanted [Bush] to believe."[50] But Bush believed Gorbachev at the time, and still did in 1998 when he wrote his memoirs.[51] Furthermore, Baker admits, "while we couldn't ignore Soviet behavior [in the Baltics], neither could we afford to lose the Soviets on the eve of the Gulf War."[52]

The Bush administration did *not* accommodate Gorbachev on the Gulf War. Throughout February, with Washington poised to transform its massive bombing campaign into a ground war against Saddam Hussein, Gorbachev tried "relentlessly" (James Baker's word) to prevent that.

He sent Yevgeny Primakov, whom Baker regarded as "an apologist" for Hussein, to Baghdad several times, and welcomed Hussein's foreign minister, Tariq Aziz, to Moscow. Almost to the very last moment, Gorbachev bombarded Bush on the phone and in writing with peace proposals. But with more than a little help from Hussein, who held out for peace terms that the Americans weren't willing to concede, Washington and its allies launched their ground offensive on February 23, informing Gorbachev early on Sunday morning, February 24.

Why did Gorbachev try so hard to prevent it? Because, Baker contends, Gorbachev wanted to buttress his domestic position by playing the peacemaker, and to show the world that "his crumbling union retained its stature in the international arena."[53] Undoubtedly so, but the Gulf crisis was an acid test of Gorbachev's whole new approach to foreign affairs—of whether the United States and the USSR could cooperate to rein in an aggressor and do so without shedding a sea of blood.[54] Granted, the Americans wanted Gorbachev's support to show that East and West were united against Iraq. But he needed them more than they needed him, and they knew it. Which helps to explain why, even though Bush was greatly irritated by Gorbachev's last-minute diplomatic maneuverings, he rebuffed them "more in sorrow than in anger"; the United States "could not let him interfere with our Gulf diplomacy or our operations at a critical moment," Bush recalled, but "we tried to say no as gently as possible without causing him difficulty." "I want you to know," he told Gorbachev on February 21, "that nobody here thinks you are doing anything other than trying to be extra helpful and working toward peace." Bush thanked Gorbachev again in a March 10 letter whose handwritten postscript further salved Gorbachev's ego: "I am signing this letter at Camp David, and I am recalling our most relaxed and pleasant discussions here. I often think about the problems you face at home." Bush hoped Gorbachev would tell Baker, scheduled to be in Moscow five days later, "if there's anything you'd like me to know on a very private basis. As you know, I consider myself lucky to be your friend."[55]

But friendship was one thing and economic assistance was another. How much did Gorbachev need? How much did he want? How much did he actually expect to get? None of these questions has a clear answer. The need, given the Soviet economic collapse, was overwhelming—unless, as most Western leaders believed, the still unreformed Soviet economic system was so far gone that nothing short of a total transformation could save it. What Gorbachev really wanted wasn't clear, because he hesitated to beg for huge sums that hard-line critics would label surrender and Western governments might reject anyway. As for his expectations, they rose and fell depending on signals from Western capitals, and on his own mood, especially when desperation, oddly overlaid with his innate optimism, led him to hope for more than he could reasonably expect. In March, Gorbachev wrote Bush requesting $1.5 billion in loans with which to buy American grain. But when Bush stalled, Gorbachev's bitter reaction revealed how much he really had in mind: "When they started the war in the Gulf," he told aides, "they had no problem finding $100 billion. Now, when it's not a matter of going to war, but assisting a new strategic partner, it becomes problematic." Or as he put it to foreign visitors: "Why wouldn't they come up with $70 to $100 billion to help perestroika in the USSR, something that is ten, a hundred times, more important [than the Gulf War] to the world's future?"[56]

The moment of truth came in July when the leaders of the seven main Western powers, the G-7, met in London. Gorbachev lobbied hard for an invitation, particularly pressing Mitterrand and Kohl to work on their American ally, and got one. But he failed to get the massive aid he wanted in London, and his bumbling attempt to get it was partly responsible for that failure.

Gorbachev was delighted with the invitation, but somewhat prickly when British Ambassador Braithwaite extended it on June 15. He was "no petty shopkeeper," he told Braithwaite, and wasn't going to London to "haggle" when what was needed was a "major, principled discussion." He knew there would be "no money on the table," but he was preparing the case for it with the help of an unexpected expert tandem: Grigory Yavlinsky, the young Soviet economist who had helped to prepare the doomed "500 Days" reform plan as Yeltsin's first deputy prime minister of Russia, and Graham Allison, Harvard political scientist from the Kennedy School of Government.[57]

Yavlinsky and Allison first met in November 1990 soon after Yavlinsky resigned his Russian government post, convinced that the Russian Republic alone would not be able to carry out thoroughgoing reform.

They assembled a joint working group of Soviet and American academics, which put together a program called "Window of Opportunity: The Grand Bargain for Democracy in the Soviet Union." The plan assumed that Soviet economic transformation required massive Western economic support, but that such support would be forthcoming only if Moscow was engaged in such a transformation. So it suggested a series of mutually reinforcing parallel moves. In a first phase ("institution building," 1991–early 1992), the Soviet side would develop the political and legal framework for a market economy (mainly by agreeing on a new union treaty and removing limitations on private economic activity), and prepare for macroeconomic stabilization by controlling social spending and government credit. In return, Moscow would receive associate membership in the World Bank and International Monetary Fund, food and medical aid, technical assistance of all sorts, and trade liberalization of the kind that had been provided to Eastern Europe. In 1992, in return for strict macroeconomic control, large-scale price liberalization and initial privatization, the West would support convertibility of the ruble and provide balance-of-payments help, including foodstuffs and medicines, cash grants and loans, credits to the new private sector, and investments in infrastructure and industry. And so on and so forth until 1997, when Soviet structural reform would be in full flower and less foreign assistance would be needed. How much money overall would the West contribute? Yavlinsky and Allison didn't say, lest mentioning a huge sum abort the whole scheme. But what was involved would be a modern-day Marshall Plan consisting of tens of billions of dollars.[58]

Would Gorbachev endorse such a scheme? Could he, in fact, do so when his prime minister, Pavlov, was championing a much less drastic, more incremental program? Yavlinsky thought he had Gorbachev's support, especially, he told Matlock, after attending a cabinet meeting in early May at which Gorbachev sharply criticized Pavlov's "anticrisis" program five times, adding that Bush, Mitterrand, and Kohl had all told him that the program wouldn't work. But Chernyaev wasn't so sure after Gorbachev defended Pavlov to him on May 17: "For now we need precisely someone like him—willing to sacrifice himself, ready to bow out at a moment's notice, someone who, now that he's started the job, will stick to it like a bulldog. It takes that kind of person to get anything done with a people like ours."[59] The truth was that Gorbachev was uncertain, drawn to both conflicting programs, and unable to decide between them—not only because of the political and economic risks of choosing one or the other but also because he didn't know enough economics to do so. Yavlinsky and Allison met with him several times to go over their plan and were stunned by the "dumb" questions Gorbachev asked, especially about private property, with which Gorbachev had so little experience in his private as well as public life.[60]

One thing that attracted Gorbachev to Yavlinsky and Allison was that they helped open the door to London. After meeting with Chernyaev on May 17, Allison and Yavlinsky returned to the United States to continue work on their program and lobby the Bush administration on its behalf. Later, they visited the six other Western capitals to do the same, traveling on a private jet put at their disposal by liberal-minded oil heiress Ann Getty. Bush had been pleased when Gorbachev told him on May 11 that he was sending Yavlinsky to Washington to discuss the "cooperation in the G-7 framework," but dismayed that Primakov (a thorn in Washington's side during the countdown to the Gulf War and now Gorbachev's point man for international economics) was coming as well. Moreover, it began to look as if Primakov's main Washington mission was to defend Pavlov's anticrisis program, along with Pavlov's principal deputy, Vladimir Shcherbakov, official head of the Soviet delegation.[61]

Ambassador Matlock emphasized bluntly to Primakov that Bush and Baker were "mainly interested in hearing Yavlinsky's ideas." Primakov replied (Matlock's paraphrase) that "Gorbachev would not approve any program his government could not stomach," so "if there were to be economic reform, it would have to be implemented with Pavlov's cooperation, not in opposition to it." When Bush met the Soviet delegation in Washington on May 31, he singled out Yavlinsky and asked for his views. But Primakov condemned those views as "too radical" and stressed it was he who spoke for Gorbachev. On July 6, shortly before Gorbachev was to depart for London, Matlock drove out to Volynskoe to tell him yet again how much Bush liked Yavlinsky's program, which the president was sure Gorbachev and his colleagues were "making good use of." But by that time Gorbachev had turned the program over to his longtime Kremlin colleague Vadim Medvedev, who fancied himself an economist but wasn't in the same league with Yavlinsky. Gorbachev had assured Yavlinsky that Medvedev would use "all the good parts" of his plan in combination with those of others. Those others included Pavlov, Primakov, and Shcherbakov, whom Matlock noticed lounging around at Volynskoye, waiting for their meeting with Gorbachev to resume. Praising the program he was taking to the G-7, Gorbachev told Matlock he looked forward to "some very important discussions, some critical decisions." The "pleasure of his anticipation," Matlock recalled, "seemed genuine." If he was in fact as "remarkably relaxed and confident" as he seemed to Matlock, Gorbachev was blissfully ignorant of what awaited him in London.[62]

"500 Days" revisited! Once again, Gorbachev flinched. Once again, he wasn't crazy to do so, since adopting the Yavlinsky program (which Yeltsin had approved, even though his Russian Republic foreign minister, Andrei Kozyrev, quietly urged Washington not to subsidize the central government in Moscow) would have triggered a showdown with Pavlov and company and then led to an upheaval as the economy was transformed. But that showdown was coming anyway.[63]

London, it followed logically, was an anticlimax. As usual, Gorbachev was welcomed warmly. Descending from his plane on July 16, he was "full of beans," Ambassador Braithwaite noticed, although Mrs. Gorbachev looked "grey and badly run down," as if exhausted from acting as her husband's "emotional shock absorber." The Gorbachevs were cheered at Covent Garden (before the first act of Rossini's *Cenerentola*) and in the street outside. Prime Minister John Major praised him effusively at a Downing Street reception for the London elite and held a small candlclight dinner at Admiralty, which the Gorbachevs entered holding hands. Gorbachev held separate talks with each Western leader, the G-7 as a whole welcomed him to a special session (since they weren't ready to accept the Soviet Union as a member of an expanded G-8), and Bush huddled with him for breakfast and lunch on July 17, the day of the G-7 session, and then into the afternoon at Winfield House, the American ambassador's residence. But when it came to the main aim of his mission—mobilizing massive, concrete Western economic support—Gorbachev failed miserably.

Gorbachev meeting with leaders of the Group of Seven in London, July 17, 1991. First row, left to right: George H. W. Bush, Gorbachev, John Major, François Mitterrand, Helmut Kohl. Second row: Jacques Delors, Giulio Andreotti, Brian Mulroney, Toshiki Kaifu, Ruud Lubbers.

He had previously sent a detailed plan for economic reform to G-7 leaders, and he summarized it at their meeting. It struck Ambassador Braithwaite, who sympathized greatly with the Soviet leader, as "very frank" about the Soviet Union's difficulties, but "flatulent in the Russian way" about solutions, "words, no action, again."[64] Gorbachev listed reforms he intended to carry out, Bush recalled, including price liberalization and ruble convertibility, but was "vague on details." As if anticipating rejection of a request for massive aid he hadn't explicitly made, he asked G-7 leaders with some heat, "Will you be well-wishers, onlookers, or active supporters? I'll answer your questions, but I want you to answer mine." Bush's response to Gorbachev was stunningly short—"I don't have much to say"—and his praise for Gorbachev's "outstanding presentation" was hollow. Nor were other leaders more helpful. Jacques Delors, president of the European Commission, peppered Gorbachev so aggressively with tough questions that Bush, ever alert to proper decorum, "tried to explain to Mikhail that he shouldn't take the preachy approach personally," that his peers "simply had legitimate questions on economic issues that they wanted answered before they could support aid."[65]

They didn't get answers, at least not those they wanted. So the only aid they supported was technical assistance—on energy, defense conversion, agriculture, and food distribution—plus "special associate" status for the USSR at the IMF and the World Bank.[66] Gorbachev was deeply frustrated after the meeting, but in fact he had been frustrated before it. He had the impression, he told Bush beforehand, that the president of the United States hadn't yet decided what sort of Soviet Union he wanted to see, that "my friend George is watching us, but doesn't really see what we're doing, that what he's saying, in effect, is 'Atta boy, Gorbachev! Keep going, we wish you success, but in the end, you've got to boil in your own pot, because it doesn't concern us.'"[67]

Bush "turned red," Chernyaev recalled, "and his eyes darkened," but he continued eating while Gorbachev plowed on. "It's very strange. A hundred billion gets thrown at a regional conflict [the Gulf War], but [not] for the transformation of the Soviet Union from an adversary and threat to a member of the world community and international economy."[68]

Bush's reply was cold and brusque: "It appears I have not laid out my policies convincingly enough if you're not clear what sort of Soviet Union we would like to see. I could understand if a question arose as to how the United States could best help the Soviet Union. But if we are again discussing how the United States would like to see the Soviet Union, I will try to answer one more time."[69]

Chernyaev couldn't comprehend Gorbachev's behavior, and still couldn't a decade later. Bush was stumped, too. "It's funny," he said on returning to Washington. Gorbachev had "always been his own best salesman, but not this time. I wonder whether he isn't kind of out of touch." Matlock concluded, "It was the wail of a desperate man whose control over his country was slipping away—and even more disturbing of one who no longer understood what he was trying to achieve." Why *did* Gorbachev antagonize the man whose support he so desperately needed? Because he so desperately needed it and knew, despite his surface optimism, that he wasn't going to get it.[70]

Margaret Thatcher would have reacted differently. She made that quite clear when, no longer prime minister, she visited Moscow as the Gorbachevs' personal guest in late May. Granted, the American and European economies were struggling, with little cash to spare for Moscow, and Japan was loath to open its purse until it got back the northern islands it had been forced to yield to the Soviets after World War Two. But the former prime minister leveled with the British and American ambassadors: "Please get a message to my friend George," she told Matlock. "We've got to help Mikhail. Of course, you Americans shouldn't have to do it all by yourselves, but George will have to lead the effort, just as he did in Kuwait." Thatcher remembered what Reagan's successor seemed to forget. "Just a few years back, Ron and I would have given the world to get what has already happened here." If the West did not come to Gorbachev's aid, "history will not forgive us."[71] Later, in September, at the United Nations General Assembly, where she had come as a private citizen, Thatcher urged anyone who would listen to compare the destruction of Nazism and the fall of Communism. The former cost the world tens of millions of lives; the Soviet people accomplished the latter themselves, and almost bloodlessly. So it would be a terrible mistake not to assist them.[72]

Matlock agreed with Lady Thatcher. "One can find many excuses for doing nothing," he wrote in his diary, but "our leaders will be bereft of wisdom or courage, or both, if they fail to respond to the challenge." Of course, he added later, there were "sound reasons" not to "throw money indiscriminately," but these were "excuses for not trying to devise a rescue effort that could succeed." What the West needed to do was to tie "very substantial aid" to "specific projects and objectives," to "work with Gorbachev (and Yeltsin) to build an international structure that would encourage steps to transform the Soviet economy."[73]

By this standard, the Gorbachev-Bush summit that took place in Moscow on July 30–August 1 was also a failure. It had all the usual pageantry: a warm airport welcome by Yanayev, who Bush had been told was "something of a hardliner," but found to be entirely "engaging and pleasant, with a good sense of humor," although "not a heavy hitter";[74] a splendid arrival ceremony in the Kremlin's St. George's Hall; formal talks in St. Catherine's Hall; a joint stroll with Gorbachev, reminiscent of Reagan's, through Cathedral Square on a beautiful summer day; a grand state dinner; a lovely Camp David–like interlude at Novo-Ogaryovo, where the leaders and their aides dressed informally and talked outside on a veranda; a majestic signing ceremony for the START treaty limiting strategic nuclear weapons.[75] But the visit, as Gorbachev aide and interpreter Palazhchenko observed it close up, was "almost anti-climactic."

The issue of Western economic aid came up in St. Catherine's Hall, where the two leaders talked for two hours, followed by lunch with their delegations. Using words that no previous leader of the proudly autarchic Soviet Union would ever have uttered, Gorbachev announced, "We want to depend much more on the U.S. in economic terms—not slavishly or out of weakness. We want to develop and build our relationship. We should be predictable for you. When countries are linked by economic cooperation at a certain level, they become more predictable. It might seem a paradox that we want to depend more on you—but that's our line."[76] He reportedly complained that the G-7 hadn't offered Moscow the *full* membership in the IMF that a "major power" deserved. And that although Bush said plenty of "nice words about how you want us to succeed, when it comes to specifics, you put up roadblocks."[77] But when Bush fobbed him off with talk of the billions in private investment Moscow could attract if it would just improve its business practices, Gorbachev subsided. Bush was greatly relieved that Gorbachev turned out to be "pragmatic and resigned to the fact that he would not get funds."[78]

The Novo-Ogaryovo intermezzo seemed to Chernyaev like "the culmination" of everything Gorbachev had been working toward in foreign affairs, a demonstration of the superpowers' new relationship that was all the more striking because the conversation was simple but serious and "devoid of any formality or pretension." Even when there was disagreement, Chernyaev remembered, the meeting "never resembled the 'tug of war' of the past." Instead, Gorbachev and Bush talked about "partnership," about "practical collaboration with a *common* goal on every specific question," with a warmth between them that had never existed with Moscow's Communist allies: "no hypocrisy and self-righteousness, no paternalism, pats on the back and obedience."[79]

Gorbachev's vow to stay the course was stirring. "No dogma will stop me." "There will be no ideological constraints." U.S. leaders would be his "strictest judge." But Bush was impatient with Gorbachev's lengthy opening monologue, during which he "barely managed to squeeze in a comment." And the mood was spoiled when Bush informed Gorbachev of news to which an American diplomat had just alerted him—that unknown assailants had murdered six Lithuanian customs agents on the Byelorussian border. "A pall fell over the meeting," Bush recalled. Gorbachev was shaken by the news—which may well have been the intent of those who ordered the killings. The conversation continued, Bush remembered, but Gorbachev's "ebullient spirit was gone."[80]

Gorbachev characterized the START treaty signing as "a moment of glory." But it was "less joyous," Palazhchenko remembered, than the INF signing in Washington in December 1987. Gorbachev had expected that to be followed in 1988 or, at the latest, in 1989 by a START treaty, which could have helped him politically at home far more than it did in the summer of 1991.[81]

It didn't help that Yeltsin intruded on the summit—first, the specter of him as conjured by the KGB, then the man himself. A week before Bush arrived, Gorbachev confided to Chernyaev information he had obviously received from the KGB—that after breakfasting with Gorbachev in London, Bush had told associates, "Gorbachev's tired and nervous, he's not in charge, not sure of himself, that's why he suspects me of being disloyal. It looks like its time to shift our attention to Yeltsin."[82] Despite this suspicion, Gorbachev invited Yeltsin and Kazakhstan President Nazarbayev to a working lunch with Bush in Moscow. But Yeltsin declined to be part of a "faceless mass audience." He insisted instead on receiving Bush in his own office in the Kremlin, but he kept the president waiting for nearly ten minutes, stretched their conversation from the allotted fifteen minutes to forty, and then sprang a press conference on his guest without warning. Not to mention that he also arrived late at the state dinner, sent his wife through the reception line with Mayor Popov, and then tried to escort Barbara Bush to her table in the Chamber of Facets as if he, not Gorbachev, were the host. "Everyone was dumbfounded" by Yeltsin's behavior, Gorbachev recalled—"except for me. I knew Boris too well." The night before, Yeltsin had asked Gorbachev to be allowed to enter the hall along with him and Bush. "Naturally," Gorbachev recalled, "I refused. Why had he even asked?"[83]

From Moscow, Bush flew on to Kiev, where his reception was more

**Gorbachev with Yeltsin and Bush during the Moscow summit,
July 31, 1991.**

fervid by far than in Moscow. By now Ukrainians had caught the independence fever as evidenced by signs they waved as Bush drove by: "Moscow has 15 colonies"; "The evil empire is alive"; "If being part of an empire is so great, why did America get out of one?" Still loyal to Gorbachev, and worried about the fratricide that was beginning to tear Yugoslavia apart, Bush warned against a bloody breakup of the USSR: "Freedom is not the same as independence. Americans will not support those who seek independence in order to replace a far-off tyranny with a local despotism. They will not aid those who promote a suicidal nationalism based on ethnic hatred."[84]

Fine words—though hardly enough to dissuade Ukrainian nationalists whose push for Ukrainian independence would eventually help to finish off the USSR and Gorbachev as its leader.

MEANWHILE, A MORE IMMEDIATE threat to Gorbachev was being hatched in Moscow. As early as the spring, KGB chief Kriuchkov commissioned planning for a possible state of emergency and establishment of a State Committee on Emergency Rule. At the same time, he quietly sounded out officials in other agencies who were disillusioned with Gorbachev. Central Committee secretary Valentin Falin (whose advice Gorbachev hadn't followed on Germany) recalled a "strange" telephone call in which Kriuchkov referred to Gorbachev's "inadequate behavior" that so "disturbs everyone." Falin agreed that the president's foreign policy left much to be desired, but suggested that Gorbachev be approached directly on such matters. Kriuchkov dropped the subject and never called back.[85]

Gorbachev left Moscow for a much-needed Black Sea vacation on August 4. The next day, at a lavish KGB facility on the outskirts of Moscow (officially an "Archival-Bibliographical Center," but boasting a pool and a sauna and protected by a high fence and security guards inside and outside the building), Kriuchkov secretly met with Defense Minister Yazov, who arrived in an unmarked car, and Gorbachev's chief of staff, Boldin. Over the next week or so, KGB and military personnel prepared scenarios for emergency rule, plus pronouncements and decrees that the State Committee would issue beginning on August 18.

Future participants in the August 1991 coup congratulating Gorbachev on his sixtieth birthday, the Kremlin, March 2, 1991. Clockwise from Gennady Yanayev, who is facing Gorbachev: Dmitry Yazov, Vladimir Kriuchkov, Boris Pugo, Anatoly Lukyanov, Aleksandr Bessmertnykh (who did not oppose the attempted coup), unidentifid, Valery Boldin, Valentin Pavlov.

The evening before that, Kriuchkov summoned other top officials to the "Archival-Bibliographical Center." Kriuchkov, Yazov, General Valentin Varennikov, commander of Soviet ground forces, and Deputy Defense Minister Vladimir Achalov arrived undercover. Boldin drove up in another unofficial car with Communist party Central Committee secretaries Shenin and Baklanov, who also served as Gorbachev's deputy on the Defense Council. Prime Minister Pavlov came late after a cabinet meeting. Once assembled, the plotters agreed on the makeup of a delegation that would fly to Gorbachev's Black Sea villa the next day to confront him.[86]

CHAPTER 17

THE
COUP

August 1991

T HE TOWN OF FOROS is located near the southern tip of the Crimean Peninsula, between Tesseli and Cape Sarych, and about twenty-five miles west of Yalta, where the last Russian tsar, Nicholas II, had a summer palace in which Joseph Stalin, Franklin Roosevelt, and Winston Churchill famously conferred in 1945. It was in Foros that Mikhail Gorbachev had a palace of his own, called Zarya (Dawn), on a rocky bluff high above the Black Sea.[1]

The bare cliffs had to be covered with earth brought in by convoys of heavy trucks and then replenished each year after winter wind and rain took their toll in erosion. The only greenery that would grow on the escarpment was a particularly hardy breed of junipers. To protect the main house from the winds, a huge space for it was gouged out of the rock by dynamite. On the first floor was a great hall, decorated in marble and gilt, with two doors opening toward the sea, one for the Gorbachevs, the other for service personnel. The second floor, which appeared to be the ground floor to those approaching from the main road and the mountains beyond it, contained the formal entrance and bedrooms for the Gorbachevs' thirty-four-year-old daughter, Irina, and her husband, Anatoly, and for their two granddaughters, Ksenia (age eleven) and Anastasia (Nastya, for short, age four), plus a room for communications equipment. On the third floor, with a magnificent view of the sea, were the Gorbachevs' bedrooms, his office, and a dining room seating as many as twelve. This floor had two large balconies, one facing the sea, where the Gorbachevs breakfasted, the other, the mountains. Opening onto the mountain-side veranda was a large hallway furnished with sofa and chairs. In addition, another small bedroom was fitted out for massages, to which Gorbachev resorted frequently for a bad back.

North of the main building was a two-story guesthouse where Vladimir Medvedev, the head of Gorbachev's security detail, was based, along with his deputies, the Gorbachevs' physicians, communications officers from the Ministry of Defense, and other personnel. Two hundred seventy or so yards beyond that was a three-story building for Gorbachev's other bodyguards, numbering about thirty; it contained a cafeteria, a small movie hall for service personnel, and a basement garage, and was a little less than a mile from the gates leading to the main east–west road.

The main house's south-facing doors opened onto two walkways: a cinder path to an outdoor movie theater, covered by a light aluminum roof, with six chairs for the Gorbachev family, the other trail leading down to the sea. The descent to the beach involved a steep climb, but that wasn't the only way down. A covered escalator provided an alternative route to a clearing with two huts, one with a toilet, the other with chairs and a telephone. Closer to the rocky beach, under a large awning, were two more rooms for changing and for hot and cold showers. Not far from the water were chaise lounges and trestle beds. Close by was a tent for bodyguards and the on-duty doctor. There was also a swimming pool, about twenty-five yards long, with seawater refilled every three days, and next to it an artificial grotto cooled to a constant, comfortable temperature by an air conditioner.

Zarya wasn't the Gorbachevs' only summer option. During his first summer in office, 1985, they had retreated to Yalta, as Stalin, Khrushchev, and Brezhnev, following in Tsar Nicholas's footsteps, had occasionally done. Another destination was the lavish dacha complex on the Black Sea coast near Pitsunda in Abkhazia, where Khrushchev regularly vacationed. Yet a third possibility was available on the Moscow River near Archangelskoe; construction began when Gorbachev took power and finished in record time. Gorbachev wasn't the only Soviet leader who enjoyed access to multiple, magnificent villas in his far-flung domain.

And if Zarya cost untold millions (which, of course, weren't disclosed), neither did his predecessors stint in spending on themselves.

But Gorbachev was supposed to be different—personally more modest, politically democratic—so much so that his closest aide, Chernyaev, was stunned by his first exposure to Zarya in 1988. He had once vacationed in nearby Tesseli and swum below the same rocky cliffs, but now that vast swath of rock had given way to a spread that made Yalta's Livadia Palace look like "a barn." Chernyaev delicately asked Gorbachev whether he liked it there. Gorbachev said he did, despite certain "unnecessary extras" built for his predecessors. But local residents told Chernyaev that Zarya had gone up in a great hurry during the last year and a half. Until he saw Zarya, Chenyaev, who remained faithfully at Gorbachev's side to the end of his reign and for more than twenty years afterward, had viewed his boss as the "selfless" hero of perestroika. Now, confronting "the perquisites" at Foros, Chernyaev wasn't sure what to think.[2] Asked about Zarya in early 2016, Gorbachev responded that the decision to build it was taken before he became general secretary, that neither he nor Raisa were involved in the design, and that neither of them particularly liked it.[3] The escalator to the beach, clearly designed for his elderly frail predecessors, Brezhnev, Andropov, and Chernenko, would seem to support Gorbachev's version.

Zarya (Dawn), the Gorbachevs' villa at Foros.

———

MIKHAIL AND RAISA GORBACHEV arrived in Crimea on August 4, 1991, accompanied by Irina, Anatoly, Ksenia, and Nastya, along with Chernyaev and two secretaries, Olga Lanina and Tamara Aleksandrova. The family desperately needed a vacation: "I'm tired as hell," Gorbachev confessed to Chernyaev on August 3.[4] "We needed a vacation," his wife had insisted. "If not now, then when would we get another chance?"[5]

But the same troubles and strains that had worn them down in Moscow made it risky to leave the capital. Raisa had encountered a small sign of rank-and-file party apparatchiki's disdain for her husband that spring when she paid her party dues at a district party office in Moscow. Upon entering the office, she could feel "tension in the air." When she looked the district party boss in the eye, she saw "hatred"—"not for me but for Mikhail Sergeyevich." They hadn't welcomed her husband's reforms, she told his interpreter, Palazhchenko, "and now they're embittered and afraid."[6]

The Gorbachevs departed for Crimea from Vnukovo-2 Airport in Moscow. As usual, a suite of high officials saw them off. The last two to arrive, even after the Gorbachevs did, were Presidential Chief of Staff Boldin and Prime Minister Pavlov. Soviet Vice President Gennady Yanayev was also in attendance. Raisa Gorbachev and her physician daughter, Irina, noticed spots of eczema on Yanayev's hands. Knowing someone who had long suffered from the same ailment, Raisa resolved to recommend a doctor to Yanayev as soon as she returned from Foros.[7]

When their plane landed at Belbek military airbase, the Gorbachevs were met by Ukrainian and Crimean leaders who, in accordance with custom, insisted on treating them to a long, tiresome luncheon. The Black Sea Fleet commander's toast, Raisa noted in her diary, assured Gorbachev that Soviet armed forces were ready to defend their commander in chief and "to carry out his orders at any hour, at any minute."[8]

Once at Foros, the Gorbachevs settled into their regular routine as established by Raisa: up at about eight o'clock, breakfast at nine, down to the beach about ten (preceded by children and grandchildren), Gorbachev wearing a light shirt and shorts, sandals, and a light khaki cap. Suffering from a bad back, he liked to read—materials sent from

Moscow, newspapers, and books—while standing in the sun in his bathing trunks. His wife preferred to read lying down by the beach. After a couple of hours, they entered the water together, he, in a plastic cap, swimming out a considerable distance and then gamboling in the waves before turning back, she calmly doing regular laps. After about forty minutes, she usually asked a nearby bodyguard, "How long have we been swimming?" Upon hearing his answer, she would declare, "Time to get out, Mikhail Sergeyevich," addressing him by his first name and patronymic, as she usually did in public.

Next came showers, then massages, first, his, then hers. They took lunch on the veranda facing the mountains, free from the sun's glare, at about three o'clock. After lunch, he worked until five on documents sent over by Chernyaev, who was housed at a nearby sanatorium but had an office in the service building next to the Gorbachevs' villa. Then the Gorbachevs took a vigorous one- or two-hour walk around the grounds or along the shore, both wearing shorts, she in a sun hat, he wearing a cap, both followed at some distance by guards with bottles of sparkling water for the Gorbachevs, plus walkie-talkies and machine guns. Dinner, which was usually served at about seven, was itself followed by another vigorous stroll or swim, and then a movie, television, or more reading. The couple's highest priority, according to Raisa, was a good night's sleep.[9]

The first two weeks at Foros were unremarkable. The weather, as usual, was extremely hot when they arrived, the trees and flowers wilting in the heat, the mountains obscured by haze. Gorbachev contemplated writing an article refuting the charge that perestroika had led to catastrophe and that he had sold out to "American imperialism." As was his habit, he was reading several books at the same time, including one on attempts to reform Russia under the last tsar, and a translation of American scholar Robert C. Tucker's biography of Stalin. Raisa was reading Roman Gul, a Russian émigré writer and editor who had fought the Bolsheviks during the Russian civil war, and Mikhail Bulgakov's wicked satire of Soviet life in the 1920s, *Heart of a Dog*, banned for decades until it was published in 1987. Gorbachev consulted republic leaders on the phone about the upcoming union treaty signing, and he and Raisa entertained Ukraininan Communist leader Leonid Kravchuk and his wife, Antonina, who were also vacationing in Crimea. Gorbachev was suffering from lumbago, which somewhat limited their daily walks, but not the sort of intellectual conversations in which he and Raisa often engaged, for example: What shapes political leaders' behavior more—personality or circumstances? Their conclusion: Situations elevate leaders, often turning traits that ordinarily look like weakness into strengths.[10]

Two weeks after their arrival, late on Sunday afternoon, August 18, Gorbachev was working in his office as usual. Among other officials, he telephoned Vice President Yanayev, who promised to meet him at the airport in Moscow the next day. Then he resumed polishing the speech he planned to give at the union treaty signing ceremony the day after that, consulting on the phone with another close aide, Georgy Shakhnazarov, who was based at another local sanatorium. Their last conversation ended at about 4:30. When Shakhnazarov tried to call back a few minutes later, Gorbachev's line was dead.[11]

A few minutes after that, at about 4:50, Gorbachev's chief bodyguard, Medvedev, knocked on his office door. He found his boss sitting in a comfortable chair at a big desk, reading a newspaper, dressed in a thick robe to keep his sore back warm.

"A group has arrived," Medvedev announced: Gorbachev's chief of staff, Boldin, Central Committee secretaries Shenin and Baklanov, and General Varennikov. With them as well was Yuri Plekhanov, head of the KGB directorate in charge of the president's security, the Soviet equivalent of the U.S. Secret Service.

Gorbachev wasn't expecting them. Nor, said Medvedev, was he. Gorbachev was immediately suspicious. "Don't leave me," he ordered Medvedev. "Stay with me and carry out my orders only."[12]

Gorbachev picked up the phone, but the line was dead, as were a second, third, fourth, and fifth that he tried, along with the dacha complex's internal line. After a long pause, Gorbachev left his office and walked into the bedroom suite where his wife was reading a newspaper. "Something bad has happened," he told her, "perhaps, terrible." He named the visitors. He hadn't invited them, but they were already there. The phone lines were cut. What did it all mean? A conspiracy? Had they come to arrest him? If so, he wouldn't give in to threats or blackmail. In which case, he added, "It may end badly for us for all of us, the whole family. We've got to be ready for anything."

"Whatever you decide," his wife answered, "I'll be with you, no matter what." Irina and Anatoly, whom they summoned, were equally resolute.[13]

Meantime, the delegation, which had been impatiently waiting in Medvedev's office, entered the dacha, climbed to the third floor, and settled itself in Gorbachev's office—"unceremoniously," Gorbachev remembered, "an unheard of lack of respect," "as if the place belonged to them."[14] Gorbachev found Baklanov and Varennikov seated next to a small table along the wall near the door, Shenin and Boldin leaning against the window sill. Plekhanov was with them, but Gorbachev ordered him out of the office. All his "guests" were his own people, appointed and trusted by him, especially Boldin, who had been a family confidant since 1982.

Gorbachev demanded to know who sent them.

"The Committee," Baklanov replied.

"What Committee?"

The State Committee on Emergency Rule, the body that had been set up in Moscow because, Baklanov said, the country was sliding into a catastrophe. The committee included KGB chief Vladimir Kriuchkov, Defense Minister Dmitry Yazov, and Vice President Yanayev, Gorbachev was told, plus Anatoly Lukyanov, parliamentary speaker, whom Gorbachev had known for nearly forty years since they first met at Moscow State University. As for Boris Yeltsin, who Gorbachev might have hoped would come to his defense despite the bad blood between them, he had been arrested, Gorbachev was told, or rather, Baklanov corrected himself, Yeltsin would be arrested that evening upon his return from Alma-Ata, capital of the Soviet republic of Kazakhstan.

The delegation demanded that Gorbachev sign a document proclaiming a state of emergency. Or if he refused, that he authorize Vice President Yanayev to do so. As if sympathetically, Baklanov lamented Gorbachev's ill health—his fatigue and his back problems. "You don't have to do anything yourself. Just stay here and rest. We'll do all the 'dirty work' ourselves. Then you can return to Moscow."

Gorbachev refused. "Then it's time for you to resign!" demanded Varennikov. Earlier, Gorbachev tried to explain to the group that his own response to the country's crisis was the new union treaty. "There will be no union treaty," he was now told. His face flushed, he unleashed a volley of curses. When Boldin tried to tell him he didn't understand the situation in the country, Gorbachev snapped, "Shut up, you asshole, who are you to lecture me on what's going on?"[15]

Failing to convince him, the delegation decided to return to Moscow and report to the committee. As they exited Gorbachev's office at about six o'clock, they passed his family, who had been huddled in the hall outside it, trying to catch bits of the conversation. Varennikov passed them without a glance. Boldin kept his distance. Baklanov and Shenin greeted Gorbachev's wife, and Baklanov held out his hand, but she looked away. When she and Irina entered the office, they were shocked to find it empty. Fearing the worst, they rushed onto the balcony where they found Gorbachev indignant, his wife recalled, "not only about the ultimatum, but about the peremptoriness and effrontery" of his visitors. To Chernyaev, who soon afterward found his boss standing by the back door of the dacha, Gorbachev described the group as "suicidal" and "murderers."[16]

Chernyaev reported on his conversation with Plekhanov's deputy, KGB General Vyacheslav Generalov. The latter's orders were to detain everyone at the dacha. Anyone who tried to leave would be immediately seized by border guards arrayed in triple, concentric arcs around the dacha. The main Yalta–Sevastopol road was closed. The helipad had been blockaded with fire trucks and street-cleaning machines, and other trucks blocked the main entrance to the compound. Several ships were stationed offshore. The plane that had arrived to take Gorbachev to Moscow the next day had been sent back to the capital. The garage had been sealed and was guarded by a new set of machine-gun-wielding security men. Contrary to Gorbachev's orders, his chief bodyguard, Medvedev, had left obediently with the delegation, but the rest of Gorbachev's original security detail remained, and would soon reaffirm its allegiance to him. Generalov also told Chernyaev that the "nuclear briefcase" (Generalov called it "the line"), whose handlers accompanied Gorbachev always and everywhere, would be removed to Moscow the next day.[17]

By now Gorbachev was calmer. His wife was not—particularly about Boldin, who she said was "like a relative to us; we trusted him with even the most intimate things." When Gorbachev, who was always polite in the presence of women, mentioned that he had called Boldin a *mudak* (scumbag), Irina, a physician, laughed and said the word "mutant" might fit Boldin better.[18]

The next morning the State Committee on Emergency Rule officially proclaimed that it was taking control of the country, and that since President Gorbachev was ill, his authority was being exercised by Vice President Yanayev. The Russian Republic's television and radio stations went off the air, and tanks and troops rolled into Moscow. Hearing the news on an old radio one of his secretaries had found, Chernyaev entered the main house at Zarya, where there was no sign of the Gorbachevs. Eventually, Nastya, their little granddaughter, took him upstairs where her grandfather was lying in bed, writing in a notebook after a rubdown for his sciatica. "This may not end well," Gorbachev said sadly. But he had "faith in Yeltsin." "He won't give in to them, he won't compromise," he added on the basis of painful, personal experience. "But that means blood."[19] Yeltsin, it turned out, had not been arrested that morning. He was allowed to drive to the White House, the huge building of the Russian government and parliament on the banks of the Moscow River, where he began to organize resistance to the State Committee.

Gorbachev asked Chernyaev to come back after dinner. Because Raisa kept repeating that the house was bugged, the three of them descended to a covered beach-side pavilion, where Gorbachev began dictating to Chernyaev a series of demands to his new "protectors": that they immediately restore communications and recall the presidential plane so he could return to Moscow. Not surprisingly, neither order, nor others he issued the next day, was obeyed.

That evening Gorbachev dictated a statement to his wife in which he denounced the emergency declaration as a crime and denied that he was ill. In the dark of night, he secretly recorded his statement four times on videotape, after which, between four and six in the morning, Irina and Anatoly separated the four sections with manicure scissors, carefully wrapped each in paper, and hid them in various places in the dacha, hoping to find a way later to smuggle them out of the complex.

The Gorbachevs didn't sleep that night, and the tension rose even higher the next day. Trying to reassure their granddaughters, they wanted to act normally. They also wanted to show anyone watching from ships offshore that Gorbachev wasn't ill, so they descended again to the shore, but "holding on to each other," Raisa Gorbacheva recounted in her diary, since "anything could happen." High-strung to begin with, she was now taut as a wire. She had previously decided they were not to eat any food delivered to the dacha on the eighteenth or afterward. Now she decreed they would limit themselves to food from their guards' own supplies and would eat only cooked items. When Chernyaev arrived at the villa, she immediately pulled him out to the balcony, pointing to the furniture, maps, and ceiling to remind him yet again that they were bugged. Trying to lighten the mood, he offered as a joke to attempt swimming the three or even six miles to Tesseli, carrying one of the wrapped videotape segments with him. But the couple took him seriously, and Gorbachev nixed the idea: "Even if they don't fish you out of the water, when you come out you'll be practically naked, and then what? They'll send you to the nearest police station and the film will be lost."[20]

Later, as Gorbachev and Chernyaev stood by a balcony railing, they could see telescopes atop watchtowers rotate in their direction, while a border guard on a nearby cliff trained his binoculars on them. They could hear another guard below the house reporting, "The object under observation is out on the balcony, the second one on the left."

According to Chernyaev, the Gorbachevs' mood oscillated with foreign news broadcasts picked up on old radios that bodyguards found in service areas and rigged up with aerials, and on Anatoly's pocket Sony. Gorbachev was certain Western leaders would condemn the junta and bankrupt the country by canceling all credits they had extended to him. The guards also managed to get a TV to work, and the Gorbachevs watched a press conference by members of the state of emergency committee. The fact that two members looked drunk and Vice President Yanayev's hands shook as he spoke gave them hope. But when Yanayev repeated that the president was ill, Gorbachev warned, "They will make reality match the lie they told publicly."[21]

The tide turned in Moscow early on the morning of August 21. By then, tens of thousands of citizens had come to protect the White House against an attempt to storm it, which they, along with Yeltsin and his team inside, feared would come at any moment. In the end, however, the emergency committee lost its nerve and the storming never happened.

In a desperate attempt to appease Gorbachev, several members, including Kriuchkov and Yazov, flew to the Crimea to beg his forgiveness. But the Gorbachevs, their communications still cut off, didn't know this—or that Yeltsin's own men, led by Russian Republic Vice President General Aleksandr Rutskoi, were also racing to Foros to try to prevent an attempt by Kriuchkov and company to kidnap or kill Gorbachev.

What the Gorbachevs did know was that three young men had died overnight in Moscow, crushed by tanks in an underpass near the White House. "Has the worst of the worst begun?" Raisa wrote in her diary. At about ten in the morning on August 21, she and her husband noticed several more ships joining those stationed offshore, including three landing craft that roared toward the shore but then turned away at the last minute. Two Gorbachev bodyguards ordered the family to stay indoors, lest they get caught in a crossfire their captors might try to provoke. At three that afternoon, the BBC reported that a Kriuchkov-led delegation was flying to Foros to confirm that Gorbachev was in fact gravely ill— which the Gorbachevs took to mean he soon would be. He ordered his guards to blockade the doors, to admit no one without his permission, and to use force if necessary; they took up positions, with guns drawn, outside, and inside on the stairs. Meanwhile, Irina and Anatoly locked themselves and their daughters inside one of the interior rooms.

At this point, with thoughts about where and how to hide her husband racing through her mind, Raisa's left arm went numb and she found herself unable to speak. "A stroke," she thought, as her family gently lowered her into bed.

At five o'clock several cars drove up to the dacha. Two of Gorbachev's guards walked toward them with Kalashnikovs raised. "Stop!" they shouted, as did several more guards who emerged from the bushes. "Don't move!" the guards yelled as two men stepped out of the first car. After consulting with someone in the dacha, the guard directed the cars to park behind the service building where Chernyaev's office was located. Stepping out on its balcony, he saw Kriuchkov, Yazov, Baklanov, Lukyanov, and Gorbachev's deputy leader of the Communist party, Vladimir Ivashko, enter the service building downstairs. "They looked beaten," Chernyaev recalled.[22]

Informed of their arrival, Gorbachev ordered they be detained, and no one admitted to the villa until his communications had been restored. "Stop or we'll shoot," snapped a guard when Plekhanov approached the main house. "And they will," muttered Plekhanov as he retreated.

Communications were finally restored at five forty-five, some seventy-three hours after they had been cut off. Gorbachev immediately called Yeltsin, who exclaimed, "Dear Mikhail Sergeyevich, so you're alive! We've been ready to fight for you for 48 hours."[23] Gorbachev also called Nursultan Nazarbayev and Leonid Kravchuk, presidents of Kazakhstan and of Ukraine, he called Moscow and ordered that the plotters be barred from the Kremlin and that all their communications be cut off, and he called President George H. W. Bush in Kennebunkport, Maine, who exclaimed, "Oh my God, that's wonderful, Mikhail! My God, I'm glad to hear you."[24] Initially during the coup attempt, however, Bush had hesitated to condemn it outright, lest it succeed and he have to do business with its leaders.[25]

A short while later loud, happy voices rang out in the second-floor hallway—the Rutskoi delegation had arrived. Gorbachev greeted them in the dining room wearing a light gray sweater and khaki pants. He was trembling with excitement. Chernyaev would remember the scene "for the rest of my life": "exclamations and shouts; Rutskoi and Ivan Silayev (Yeltsin's prime minister) embracing Gorbachev; everyone interrupting each other, including those who had railed against him in parliament and the press, who had argued with him and protested indignantly against him. Now misfortune revealed that they were part of a whole, which is just what the country needed."[26]

Gorbachev looked "amazingly well," recalled Silayev. Raisa, however, according to another member of the Russian delegation, "was in horrible condition," "wobbling" as she tried to walk down the stairs, but "making sure to kiss all of us."[27]

Gorbachev refused to see anyone in the Kriuchkov delegation except parliamentary speaker Lukyanov and deputy party chief Ivashko. Either one, he told them, could have stopped the coup, but all Lukyanov wanted was to succeed Gorbachev as president, while the party Secretariat ordered local party organs to support the putsch. Lukyanov tried to argue that he had resisted the coup. "Cut the bullshit," Gorbachev snarled. "Stop pulling the wool over my eyes."[28] Meanwhile, Kriuchkov and the others waited glumly for five hours in a service building room with a television playing in the background.

Gorbachev suggested that the Russian parliamentary delegation stay over and return with him to Moscow the next morning. They insisted on flying that night, taking Gorbachev and his family (plus Kriuchkov as a hostage) in the Russian plane, lest someone try to shoot down the presidential plane, in which the rest of the plotters would travel under strict guard. "What a bunch of good-for-nothing old cowards!" muttered Plekhanov, seating himself at some distance from his fellow conspirators in the second plane. "But I fell in with them like a chicken ready to be plucked."[29]

The Gorbachevs departed at 11:00 p.m. on August 21. The usual departure ceremony, in which female staff members presented them with flowers had to be improvised this time—the flowers pulled from a cold storage room. Little Nastya, who had been awakened from a deep sleep, asked why there were no flowers for her. At the Belbek airbase, the two planes waited about half a mile apart—the presidential Ilyushin 62 with "Sovetsky Soiuz" on its side, the smaller Tupolev 134 surrounded by MiG-29 fighter jets—while limousines raced back and forth between them to confuse anyone trying to pinpoint the one Gorbachev would take. The scene on the Russian plane was quietly joyous—Gorbachev sitting in the forward cabin with his family, conversing softly with Rutskoi and others who had come to his rescue; Raisa lay next to him, Nastya was sleeping on the seat next to Irina, and Ksenia was asleep on the floor. Kriuchkov was under guard in a separate, rear compartment.

When the plane landed at Vnukovo-2 Airport at two in the morning, Gorbachev was told to wait while his guards with machines guns surveyed the scene. Then the family slowly descended the steps. Gorbachev looked hale but not hearty in a beige windbreaker. Behind him came Raisa, weak but ambulatory, her arms around Ksenia.

At the foot of the stairs, television cameras were waiting. "No, Mikhail Sergeyevich is tired," objected Gorbachev associate Yevgeny Primakov. "We should go." But Gorbachev wouldn't move. On the plane he had said, "We're flying to a new country." Now he wanted "to breathe the air of freedom in Moscow."[30]

Gorbachev thanked Yeltsin personally, along with all the other Rus-

Gorbachevs returning from Foros after abortive coup, August 22, 1991.

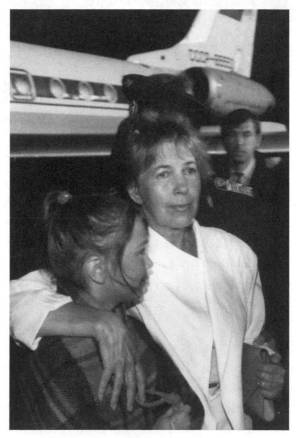

Raisa Gorbachev with her granddaughter Ksenia, returning to Moscow from Foros after the attempted coup, 2 a.m., August 22, 1991.

sians who had defended the constitutional order in the streets. He called for cooperation between Moscow and the restive Soviet republics to surmount the economic and political crisis. The main obstacle that foiled the coup was the fact that "our society and people have changed. . . . And that is the greatest victory of perestroika."[31]

Gorbachev being interviewed after his return to Moscow from Foros, August 22, 1991.

Meanwhile, thousands of jubilant Muscovites were celebrating the victory near the White House, where they had waited for hours to greet Gorbachev. At that moment, a leading democrat, Galina Starovoitova, later recalled, Gorbachev was "more popular than he had ever been or would be again."[32] But instead of celebrating their joint triumph with them, Gorbachev got into his car and went home.

WHY DIDN'T GORBACHEV rush to the White House rally to be hailed by the crowd, yelling, "PREZ-I-DENT! PREZ-IDENT!," that had been waiting for him all night? Out of concern for his wife? Because he was exhausted? That is not the only question about the coup that has lingered for years afterward. What made the coup plotters think that Gorbachev would agree to declare a state of emergency or authorize Yanayev to do so? Why did he allow himself to be held under house arrest rather than order his armed guards to detain his uninvited guests? Is it remotely conceivable that Gorbachev himself was somehow complicit in the coup? The latter charge seems incredible on its face, but it has been pushed hard for more than two decades by those who plotted against him, and it could still be heard in Moscow in 2016 from his ill-wishers.

Parliamentary speaker Lukyanov, who supported the coup without formally joining the State Committee, maintained that Gorbachev knew about it in advance "and took not a single step to stop it." According to Premier Pavlov, "Gorbachev decided to play a game that he could not lose. If he stayed there [in Foros] and the state of emergency worked, he would come back to Moscow later, having recovered from his illness and taken charge. If it didn't work, he could come and arrest everyone. . . . In either case he would show the people that his hands were squeaky clean."[33]

Even two Western accounts take such charges seriously. Historian John B. Dunlop writes, "It appears that Gorbachev permitted the coup to go forward while declining to associate himself with it openly." Amy Knight asks, Why didn't Gorbachev's thirty-two guards, who still had their weapons, resist their captors? "Did it not occur to Gorbachev to ask them for help?" Was he really as isolated at Foros as he claimed? Dunlop wonders. How could he be if he reportedly used a telephone that wasn't cut off to call Arkady Volsky in Moscow at 6:00 p.m. on August 18? Or did he isolate himself in order to wait out "an exceptionally cunning and risk-ridden game"? First, he would let the coup leaders suppress Yeltsin, the Russian "democrats," and leaders of the most rebellious republics; next he would double-cross Kriuchkov and company; and then, having disposed of adversaries on both extremes, he would resume his moderate reform course.[34]

Even some of Gorbachev's associates initially wondered whether he was somehow involved, recalled his Politburo ally Vadim Medvedev. "Where is Gorbachev?" his former and future foreign minister Shevardnadze asked at a huge Moscow rally protesting the coup. "Is he involved in this in some way?"[35]

Chernyaev condemns such charges and insinuations: "When I read or hear that communications weren't cut off, that we weren't all under arrest there, that we could freely go wherever we pleased, and that Gorbachev had nearly a battalion of heavily armed loyalists ready to free him from captivity . . . I take this as a cynical, obnoxious lie. . . ."[36]

In the swirl of conflicting accounts, two crucial things are clear. One is that the coup plotters did not need Gorbachev's agreement in advance to embark on their adventure. It was enough for them to recall his undeclared alliance with them throughout the winter and spring of 1991 to conclude he might support their plan. All his tactical maneuvering to keep hard-liners on the leash, all the contingency planning for a state of emergency that he never actually declared, all this worked too well: it convinced the plotters he was still with them, even when he was not.

It is also clear why Gorbachev made no attempt to detain his captors or to try to escape. According to his daughter, Irina, the family discussed that possibility several times. But apart from not being sure exactly which guards were with them and which not, they concluded the idea was "absurd."[37] "What was he supposed to do? Clamber through the mountains with his wife and two little grandchildren? Or leave us, Mama and the kids, as hostages, while rushing off into a trap, where he would likely encounter a 'stray bullet' and thus solve the plotter's problem for them?"[38] If his wife, whom he dearly loved, collapsed at the thought of plotters coming to poison them, imagine how she would have reacted while making a break for freedom, or waiting to hear whether her husband was shot while doing so![39]

Why did Gorbachev persist in trusting the plotters until they arrived at his Foros door? He wasn't the only one who thought they were dummies. "A bunch of losers," proclaimed CIA Soviet expert Fritz Ermarth when informed of the coup. "Muppets," Ambassador Braithwaite's wife, Jill, declared after watching a State Committee press conference. "Marx Brothers," Brent Scowcroft opined afterward. To Gorbachev aide turned critic Brutents, the failed coup resembled "an amateur operetta." Even some of the sinners thought so. "We never discussed what we'd do if Gorbachev didn't accept our proposals," lamented General Varennikov.[40]

By Machiavellian standards, the coup was indeed a terrible botch. The plotters never seized full control of the media. They never arrested Yeltsin and isolated other opposition leaders. They never commandeered communications and transport. They didn't take advantage of early support from party leaders, republic presidents, and most Soviet ambassadors abroad. The State Committee's August 19 press conference was a farce; Yanayev's hands did indeed shake and several other men appeared drunk. And they couldn't bring themselves in the end to storm the Russian White House. To be sure, tens of thousands of citizens were massed there, but few elsewhere in the city, and even fewer defended Gorbachev in the provinces. There would have been a bloodbath, but that hadn't stopped Deng Xiaoping in Tiananmen Square.

Kriuchkov later insisted he and his colleagues wanted to avoid bloodshed.[41] Rather than arresting Yeltsin, whom the KGB had surrounded in his Archangelskoe dacha on the morning of the nineteenth, they wanted to whisk him away to private talks, presumably about cooperating against Gorbachev. But crossed signals allowed him to escape to the White House and lead the resistance. Up until the last moment, the plan was to have tanks and troops clear the White House square so that the KGB's "Alpha" team could seize the White House and neutralize or kill defenders inside. Gorbachev aide Shakhnazarov thought that if the coup leaders had been "more resolute and less worried about the consequences, and had given the order to fire on the crowd, things could have turned out differently."[42] In the end, however, after several army generals and their men went over to Yeltsin's side, and several KGB commanders themselves balked, Yazov and his generals called off the operation. "I'm not an old fool," Yazov said. "I didn't fight at the front during the war to end up in an adventure with a bunch of drunkards, to shoot my own fellow citizens. I'll fly to Foros to tomorrow to confess to Gorbachev and Raisa Maksimovna."[43] In that sense, Gorbachev's revolution had changed not only the tens of thousands who now dared to confront the troops and tanks but also the generals and policemen who no longer dared to smash them.[44]

In the end, the plotters failed to seize the day. But so did Gorbachev after he returned to Moscow. Why didn't he rush to the White House rally? Because his wife was sick ("You had to see her eyes," Grachev recalled. "They were the eyes of a mortally wounded human being."), and he wanted to take her home.[45]

CHAPTER 18

FINAL DAYS
August–December 1991

RAISA GORBACHEV NEVER FULLY recovered from the trauma of the coup. Whatever it was that struck her down (probably a ministroke, her physician daughter concluded) left her exhausted and demoralized. She was hospitalized several times during the autumn and spent much of the rest of the time sitting on the veranda at home reading or staring off into the distance. She blamed herself for insisting that her husband take the vacation at Foros. Determined never again to let vandals ransack her family's private world, she collected fifty-two letters he had sent to her while traveling on party business early in his career, reread them, and on August 27 burned them one by one. Gorbachev found her in tears when he returned from work. "I've just burned all our letters," she told him. "I can't imagine someone reading them if another Foros were to happen." He, too, trying to comfort and reassure her, burned twenty-five notebooks of his own, "not a personal diary," he recalled, but planning notes containing "nuances and assessments of his associates." Over the next few years, Raisa's health seemed to improve (although hemorrhages in both eyes impaired her ability to judge distances and the depth of stairs), until it suddenly deteriorated in 1999 when it was discovered she had leukemia.[1]

If Gorbachev's absence at the early morning rally on August 22 (for which "I've been criticized for twenty years," he noted in 2011) was the result of love for his wife,[2] his remarks at a press conference later that day were an unforced error. He did not yet realize how fully party leaders had compromised themselves by supporting the coup. He hadn't gotten to sleep until five or six that morning, only to be awakened at seven to catch up on what had happened in Moscow during the coup. During the flight back to Moscow, he had said that he was "returning to a new country."[3] But his press conference pledge to reform the now discredited Communist party left the impression of a man who didn't understand how much his country had changed. Only after agonizing for two days did he resign as party general secretary and call upon the Central Committee to disband. He remained convinced, he told journalists, that the party was still filled with people "who are real democrats devoted to perestroika . . . who will neither surrender nor bend." But in the meantime angry anti-Communist crowds were gathering at party headquarters, forcing Central Committee officials like Chernyaev to flee through underground passages, and at the mammoth KGB complex on Lubyanka Square, where the forbidding statue of its founder, Felix Dzerzhinsky, would soon be toppled.[4]

Gorbachev finally began to purge his opponents. Three of them did the job for him. One of the conspirators, Minister of Internal Affairs Boris Pugo, shot his wife and then himself. Former armed forces chief of staff Marshal Sergei Akhromeyev, who had broken with military hardliners to become Gorbachev's arms control adviser, but later grew disillusioned with his boss, had cut short his vacation and rushed to Moscow to support the coup. Now he confessed what he had done in a letter to Gorbachev, then wrote a note saying, "I can no longer live when my Fatherland is dying and everything I have worked for is being destroyed," and hanged himself in his office. Nikolai Kruchina had been in charge of the Communist party's secret stashes of funds as the Central Committee's general manager. "I am not a conspirator," he wrote, "but I am a coward. Please report that to the Soviet people." Kruchina jumped to his death from his apartment window.[5]

Gorbachev fired Kriuchkov and Yazov and replaced them with Kriuchkov's deputy, Leonid Shebarshin, and Army Chief of Staff Mikhail Moiseyev. But he had to reverse himself almost immediately, since both men had backed the coup. When Moiseyev entered Gorbachev's office, Yeltsin was standing there, too. "Explain to him that he's not a minister any longer!" Yeltsin ordered Gorbachev. Gorbachev repeated Yeltsin's words; Moiseyev listened and left.[6]

Another debacle followed on August 23 when Gorbachev appeared before the Russian Supreme Soviet. Catcalls greeted his attempt to explain how the coup came about. When Gorbachev contended Pavlov's cabinet had resisted the coup, Yeltsin rose dramatically from his seat on stage, stalked over to Gorbachev at the podium, and, with the country watching on television, shoved in his face a transcript of the August 19 cabinet meeting at which nearly all ministers, all Gorbachev appointees, had endorsed the coup.

"Go on, read it now," Yeltsin barked, towering over his victim, jabbing his right forefinger in Gorbachev's face.

Gorbachev "crumpled," one of the deputies recalled, and obeyed.

**Yeltsin bullying Gorbachev at the August 23 session of
the Russian Supreme Soviet.**

For his next trick, Yeltsin announced with a broad grin that, "on a lighter note," he would now sign a decree banning the Russian Republic's Communist party. Gorbachev tried to talk over the thunderous applause, trying to get Yeltsin's attention by repeating the latter's first name and patronymic three times, trying to say he hadn't read the decree. But Yeltsin signed anyway with a characteristic flourish, exacting revenge by humiliating the man who had so humiliated him.[7]

"It's all over," Scowcroft told Bush after contemplating Yeltsin's torment of Gorbachev at the Russian Supreme Soviet. "I don't think Gorbachev understands what happened." Bush agreed: "I'm afraid he may have had it."[8]

Six days later, when Gorbachev summoned the British ambassador to his office to renew his plea for economic aid, he struck Braithwaite as "overwrought, almost incoherent: his Southern accent is stronger than ever, his sentences ever more complex and elliptical. I can barely understand him. He and [Vadim] Medvedev [who was with him] seem close to panic."[9]

In retrospect, Gorbachev aides think he was done for after the coup. Gorbachev lost even as he won, Chernyaev concluded—"lost the remains of his own power" when "he rejected the 'services' of the traitors," who "represented the last of the old levers of power." "Everything was predetermined" after the coup, according to Shakhnazarov. Republic leaders "no longer needed an alliance with the President or the union he supported," recalled Grachev, who became Gorbachev's press spokesman after the coup. Gorbachev was "the only member of his own team," Grachev continued, "who believed (or pretended to) that nothing had been lost" in the coup and "tried to inspire his crew with his optimism." Chernyaev later compared Grachev's press office to the orchestra playing on the deck of the *Titanic*. Gorbachev insisted to the end and afterward that "the union could have been preserved," but even he had to admit that his administration was almost powerless, that the "mechanism of power was so disordered that no decisions, even the most optimal ones, had a chance to be implemented." Boldin, for all his sins, had been an efficient chief of staff; his replacement, former Kiev party boss Grigory Revenko, was overwhelmed trying to transform the party's general department into a genuine presidential administration, recruit a new set of advisers, prepare and outfit new Kremlin offices for the presidential staff, transfer the presidential security service from the KGB to the Kremlin, and apportion party and government property between the federal and the Russian republic governments.[10]

Despite all this, Gorbachev's hopes rose during September. The hard-liners had surrendered; the party no longer had to be appeased; the republics remained to be dealt with, but Yeltsin, the most difficult republic leader, disappeared on vacation for much of the month, and when he reappeared seemed disposed to cooperate. He and Gorbachev agreed on such key provisions of a new union treaty as a rapid transition to a market economy, a common currency, and central control over nuclear weapons. Gorbachev praised Yeltsin's "courage" to Secretary of State Baker in the middle of the month. Yeltsin described Gorbachev to Baker as a "changed man," adding that the two of them constantly talked on the phone. Each had an interest in assuring the Americans that they were working together. Gorbachev seemed more "human" again to Chernyaev, as well—"the way he had been at the beginning of perestroika," as if some of his overweening self-confidence, "stemming from his international fame and the corruption of power, had faded away."[11]

GORBACHEV'S FATE IN THE FALL OF 1991, as well as that of the union, hinged on his renewed attempt to negotiate a union treaty. The draft federation he and republic leaders had agreed on in late July was a sufficiently drastic departure from the centralized USSR to have triggered the August coup. The draft he and republic leaders worked on that autumn pointed toward a mere confederation: no constitution except the union treaty itself, the division of powers between the center and the republics left undefined, a president with virtually no executive functions.[12] By November, Gorbachev was reduced to trying to preserve almost any kind of union at all. Moreover, this new fight required him to play yet another political "game." Up to and including 1988, he had excelled at manipulating colleagues in the Politburo. After that, he proved less adept at democratic electioneering and at balancing between hard-liners and radicals in parliament and in the streets. Now the arena had narrowed again—to a newly established State Council where he was almost alone in a struggle with republic leaders propelled by (and themselves propelling) rising nationalism in their realms.

Gorbachev threw himself into this fight with almost all his remarkable energy. He was "devilishly tired," he remembered, but, according to Chernyaev, he wasn't "demoralized" and hadn't "lost his self-control."

It was as if his final battle lifted him out of the malaise into which he had descended earlier in the year. He convinced himself that the Soviet people wanted unity, but this was "sincere self-deception," as Chernyaev saw it, from "a person always prone to overestimate the significance of his 'partial' victories along perestroika's torturous path." Gorbachev's point man for union treaty negotiations, Shakhnazarov, informed him on September 27 that the treaty could be signed "no earlier than December, God willing." But Gorbachev wanted it much sooner than that.[13]

The State Council's first real working session took place on October 11 in the Kremlin suite where the Politburo used to meet. Gorbachev wanted the meeting to symbolize the country's new commitment to unity. Without consulting other members, he invited state television to broadcast the session live, so it was embarrassing, to say the least, when Yeltsin, a master of passive aggressiveness as well as the more active kind, failed to arrive on time. Gorbachev waited for five minutes and then began to orate on the importance of the new union treaty. Yeltsin strolled in just as Gorbachev was finishing, muttered something about why he was late, and seated himself, looking (according to Grachev) "even more sullen than usual at finding himself in the glare of spotlights that had not been cleared with him ahead of time."[14]

When Gorbachev asked whether the live broadcast should be continued, the State Council demurred. After Yavlinsky laid out the case for a common economic community, everyone waited for Yeltsin's reaction. Russia would join other republics in signing an economic agreement, he said, but not ratify it until it was fully satisfied with all practical details. And "from now on," Yeltsin declared with his finger jabbing the air, "we are going to stop financing the organs of government that are not provided for in the treaty."

Despite his bluster, Yeltsin's readiness to sign an economic treaty buttressed Gorbachev's position. And he joined with Gorbachev in lamenting Ukrainian leader Kravchuk's announcement that Kiev would cease working on the full union treaty until a December 1 referendum decided whether the republic should be fully independent. None of the other republic leaders was prepared to challenge Gorbachev, who ran the meeting as if he still ran the country. But his display of dominance sowed seeds of their later revolt. "He knew the situation in the country better than [they] did," noted Bakatin, who was present, "but he shouldn't have flaunted that. He should have kept silent and let them talk more." During a break in the meeting, Bakatin overheard republic leaders muttering, "It's the same old talkfest." Gorbachev had been advised not to try to impose his views on the others, and he had agreed not to, but he couldn't seem to help himself.[15]

Gorbachev confessed to aides on October 21, "Nothing will pass without [Yeltsin's] agreement. His people are telling him that crafty Gorbachev is resurrecting the Center to deprive Yeltsin of the fruits of his August triumph." If he ever believes that, if he "feels deceived or discarded, he's capable of ripping up everything."[16]

Yeltsin began "ripping" in a speech to the Russian Congress of People's Deputies on October 28: he announced that he would cut the Soviet Foreign Ministry staff tenfold. "This was to be expected," Chernyaev wrote in his diary; "M. S. was the only one who did not expect it." Rather, "he kept thinking that by talking to [Yeltsin] and maintaining good relations, he could channel him, as M. S. likes to say."[17]

Gorbachev had what he called a "man-to-man" talk with Yeltsin on November 2. "You keep changing your policy," he told him, "you keep rejecting everything we've agreed on. If you're that impatient to take the reins in your own hands, there's no point to the State Council or an economic agreement. If that's how it is, then go ahead and govern by yourself. I'll resign. I'll tell you and the other [republic] leaders: I led you all to independence and now you no longer seem to need the union. So go ahead: Live as you wish and fire me."

Yeltsin denied he'd changed his tune and promised to keep his word. As for the 90 percent purge of the Foreign Ministry, that was just a "rough" estimate. It could be 90 percent or, say, 70 percent, he not so graciously conceded.

"Come on, Boris," Gorbachev objected. "Someone keeps egging you on, pushing you to extremes, and then you have to take the rap. Why do you keep doing that? You've got to be more careful when you speak!"[18]

Gorbachev was "clearly satisfied" with this conversation, according to Shakhnazarov. But Yeltsin wasn't, and it showed at the next State Council meeting, on November 4. Again he arrived late. Again he was outraged to find the session televised. Gorbachev, who was passionately exhorting his colleagues to save the country, went on for forty minutes. Yeltsin "just sat there," according to Gorbachev, acting as if the mess the country was in "didn't bother him." When Yeltsin did speak, he demanded the meeting return to its formal agenda. Gorbachev asked others to comment, but no one did. It was like a scene in the forest, Grachev recalled, "where the pack waits for the confrontation between the two strongest wolves to find out who will be their leader." In the end, Yeltsin agreed with Gorbachev that the new union needed a unified army, and he settled for "only" a 30 percent cut in Foreign Ministry personnel.[19]

Gorbachev called the next State Council session, on November 14 at Novo-Ogaryovo, where he had reached out to disaffected democrats in April, an obvious attempt to re-create the good mood of the spring. Yeltsin didn't arrive late this time (although he got there last), but he did arrive mad—incensed by Gorbachev's criticism of his hostile reaction to Chechen demands for independence. "Our new relationship has lasted all of three months," Yeltsin snarled at Gorbachev, "and now it's over." But then he calmed down, and the meeting confronted the central issue. Gorbachev still wanted a "union state"; Yeltsin, supported by Byelorussian President Stanislav Shushkevich, insisted on a "union of states," a confederation. "If there are no effective state structures," Gorbachev asked, "then what good are a president and a parliament? If that's what you decide, then I'm ready to resign."

"You're getting carried away," Yeltsin retorted.

"Not at all, I'm too exhausted for that."

After more tense exchanges, a compromise was found: a "confederative state" or, as Yeltsin put it when Gorbachev pushed him forward to brief journalists who were waiting outside, "a democratic, confederative state." But the compromise that saved this day at least was a classic oxymoron: the new union could be a state or a confederation, but not both. Something had to give.[20]

It did when the State Council met at noon on November 25. "We're here to sign it," said Gorbachev, referring to a treaty text reflecting the November 14 compromise. But immediately Yeltsin objected: his parliament would not approve *any* kind of union state, not even a "confederative state." Gorbachev "couldn't believe his ears," Grachev recalled.

Yeltsin's veto "would wipe out everything we've already agreed on," Gorbachev cried, "all the language we debated for hours last time," everything "we announced to the country [that] we had worked out together."

Quickly republic leaders split into two camps. Only Kazakhstan and Kyrgyzstan supported Gorbachev. The others backed Yeltsin. The atmosphere was heated. In other tense situations, Grachev recalled, Gorbachev's stolid, peasant-like composure was such that "he sometimes had to simulate strong feelings," but on this day genuine "indignation seeped from every pore." Didn't the other leaders know what they were doing? They were "creating a kind of poorhouse instead of unified state" at a time when "we're already drowning in shit!"

Gorbachev walked out, announcing, "A break!" so as not to confuse it with a final rupture. Downstairs in "the fireplace room," he and his aides composed yet another compromise: instead of signing the treaty, the leaders would collectively appeal to their parliaments to do so. Soon the republic leaders, who remained upstairs, sent down their negotiators, Yeltsin and Byelorussian President Shushkevich.

"And so," proclaimed Yeltsin, "we have come to kowtow before the Great Khan of the Union."

"You see, Tsar Boris," Gorbachev replied with a smile, "everything can be resolved through honest cooperation."

Or so it seemed. Yeltsin allowed the phrase "unified confederal state" to remain in the draft, to be discussed along with other amendments by the republic parliaments. The leaders agreed to tell their legislatures that they expected them to ratify the treaty by the end of the year. But leaving it up to multiple parliaments was a recipe for indefinite delay.[21]

Ukraine was the key. The largest republic had not been among the republics attending the last two State Council sessions: Russia, Byelorussia, Kazakhstan, Kyrgyzstan, Tajikistan, Turkmenistan, and either Azerbaijan (on November 14) or Uzbekistan (on November 25). Ukraine awaited its crucial December 1 vote, which would elect a president of the republic as well as decide on independence from what was left of the union. In one of their spats on November 25, Yeltsin warned Gorbachev there could be no union without Ukraine. Without a union, Gorbachev shot back, separatists would triumph in Ukraine and everywhere else.[22]

As December 1 approached, public opinion polls showed a growing majority for Ukrainian independence, including ethnic Russians in eastern and southern regions. Ukrainian Communists themselves latched onto independence as a way to rebuild their tattered reputation, led by Kravchuk, campaigning for president, who had morphed overnight from a Communist into a nationalist. Even President Bush, who still supported Gorbachev's attempt to preserve a democratic union, succumbed to electoral pressure from Democrats and Ukrainian émigré voters and told a Ukrainian American group on November 27 that he would recognize Ukrainian independence quickly without clearing it with Moscow. After the group leaked the news to the *Washington Post*, Gorbachev felt betrayed and told Bush he did, but gently, as befit a man who still depended on his "friend" in Washington.[23]

The results of the Ukrainian referendum were stunning: an election turnout of 84 percent; more than 90 percent voting for independence; more than 83 percent in the eastern city of Lugansk, nearly 77 percent in Donetsk, even 54 percent in Crimea, where ethnic Russians accounted for 60 percent of the population, 57 percent in Sevastopol, headquarters of the Soviet Black Sea Fleet.[24]

Despite all the signs, Gorbachev had expected Ukrainians to reject independence.[25] Even after they didn't, he hoped Ukraine, like other republics that previously declared their independence after the August coup, would continue to negotiate a new union treaty. So when Yeltsin proposed the next day a four-member union consisting of Russia, Ukraine, Byelorussia, and Kazakhstan, Gorbachev retorted, "And what would be my place in it? If that's the deal, then I'm leaving. I'm not going to bobble like a piece of shit in an ice hole."[26]

Gorbachev scrambled to set up a meeting with Yeltsin, Kravchuk, Shushkevich, and Nazarbayev on December 9, only to learn that Yeltsin, Kravchuk, and Shushkevich had decided the fate of the nation without him on December 8. They did so at Belovezhskaya Pushcha, a wooded resort area a few miles north of Brest on the Polish-Byelorussian border. Created as a habitat for the last descendants of European bison, it boasted a luxurious lodge where Soviet and Warsaw Pact leaders used to gather for hunting (presumably not of the bison) and consultations. The three

Slavic leaders, too, may have planned only to consult. Yeltsin had promised Gorbachev that he would try to persuade Kravchuk to support the latest union treaty draft, and he apparently did so, although with how much enthusiasm isn't clear. But Kravchuk refused to sign on, and with that, the three leaders set to work, apparently with the help of material conveniently prepared by Yeltsin aide Gennady Burbulis, to establish an alternative—a Commonwealth of Independent States. On paper, the CIS resembled the last November draft of the union treaty (including, for example, a "sphere of joint activities," plus "unified command" of armed forces), but by replacing the union president, parliament, state council, and government with "coordinating organs of the Commonwealth," the three mutineers in fact abolished the USSR.[27]

The deed was done in "utmost security," as Yeltsin put it, guarded by "a special security division." Tension was high because they feared Gorbachev's reaction. "After all," remarked the head of the Byelorussian KGB, "it would take just one battalion to nail all of us here."[28]

Gorbachev didn't learn what happened until Shushkevich telephoned him on the eighth. Yeltsin had previously called Soviet Defense Minister Yevgeny Shaposhnikov and gained his support by appointing him commander in chief of the new entity's armed forces. Yeltsin also called President Bush, who listened politely and promised to study the text of the agreement. It was only then that the triumvirate deigned to inform Gorbachev.

None of the three wanted to call him. "I will not be talking to Gorbachev today," Yeltsin announced abruptly. Shushkevich took on the dreaded assignment. "Do you realize what you've done?" Gorbachev erupted. "Who gave you the authority? Why didn't you warn me? How could you take such a decision without me! This is totally arbitrary! Don't you understand that the world community will condemn you? Once Bush finds out about this, what then?"

"Boris Nikolayevich has already told him," Shushkevich responded, "and [Bush] reacted calmly."

"You talked to the President of the United States of America and your own president doesn't even know what's going on!" Gorbachev exploded. "That's a disgrace."[29]

AS GORBACHEV STRUGGLED to preserve some semblance of a union, as well as his own position in it, the world watched with fascination. Throughout the fall, he received a steady stream of foreign visitors and continued his foreign travels, partly to address pressing world problems, partly to buttress what was left of his domestic authority, partly still seeking foreign aid, but also in search of a sympathetic audience to whom he could tell his troubles. He tried to convince them that he would eventually prevail. He was also trying to convince himself, but in the end he convinced no one, for the image he conveyed, despite his best efforts to appear optimistic, was of a man going down for the last time.

International Monetary Fund chief Michel Camdessus met with Gorbachev in Moscow in early October. For all his "bounce," Gorbachev struck him as "pathetic and lonely." British Ambassador Braithwaite saw Gorbachev on November 12: he "seems tired, resigned, as if he were above the struggle, an elder statesman on the verge of becoming at best a constitutional monarch."[30]

The big diplomatic gathering of the fall was the conference on the Middle East, cosponsored by the United States and the Soviet Union and held in Madrid from October 30 to November 1. In the past, such a gathering would have been a triumph for Gorbachev. It seemed to cede the USSR a leading role in the region, something Washington had sought to deny Moscow for decades. It also brought together Israeli Prime Minister Yitzhak Shamir and Palestinian leader Yasser Arafat (the Palestinians were part of a joint Jordan-Palestinian delegation), along with leaders of other Arab countries. But the conference made no progress on Middle East issues, and Gorbachev's effort to seem upbeat about his situation at home fell flat.

He assured Bush that most Soviet people favored a market economy, that even "the Baltic leaders are increasingly reminding us of the need for cooperation," that what Bush might have heard from Ukraine, was "not the real Ukraine," and that the draft treaty he had worked out with Yeltsin "calls for a unitary state, not a free commonwealth." He granted that Yeltsin's October 28 speech called for practically eviscerating the

Foreign Ministry, but Yeltsin's endorsement in the same speech of radical economic reform was "dramatic and brave."[31]

Bush's verdict was typically gentle: "Gorbachev looked well. The smile was there, but not with quite the same zip as before." Baker's was less so: "Unfocused," careening back and forth between the Middle East and his domestic problems, "he seemed like a drowning man, looking for a life preserver. It was hard not to feel sorry for him."[32] Gorbachev's plea for economic aid produced the familiar runaround ending with a nasty needle from Baker: Gorbachev mentioned $10–15 billion; Bush offered $1.5 billion in agricultural credits; Baker whispered to interpreter/aide Palazhchenko, "Take the 1.5 billion. It's hard cash. Take it before we change our mind."[33]

Instead of dollars, Gorbachev got strokes. "I have an awful year ahead of me, an election year," Bush told him. "And yet, Mikhail, my problems don't even begin to compare with the gigantic task you are accomplishing. It's a riveting drama. We're all following it with bated breath, and we wish you success."[34] This was, in effect, an example of what C. Boyden Gray, White House counsel under Bush, much later described as the code of the Bush dynasty: "You would be generous to a loser, you would not boast about your victory, you would be civil during an engagement, but you'd use every trick you had, every skill, to win."[35]

Gorbachev did enjoy what he called a "strikingly open, 'masculine'" conversation with Bush, King Juan Carlos of Spain, and Spanish Prime Minister Felipe González. In Grachev's view, Gorbachev was "his own best listener—he persuaded himself more than he did other people." But on this occasion their warmth even evoked a bit of empathy for Yeltsin. "Let's give him credit," Gorbachev said, "for his willingness to embark on radical economic reforms"—a sentiment that probably reflected Gorbachev's relief at having someone to shoulder the responsibility for such reforms' unpopular consequences. "In his soul," Yeltsin sincerely favored the union. But although he seemed "strong and confident," he is "easily influenced." "You work with him, come to an agreement, and then it turns out you have to start everything all over again. But I do not want us to be completely disappointed in him."[36]

Gorbachev particularly enjoyed González, with whom, he told Grachev, he could speak more openly than with anyone else, anywhere, including at home in the USSR. According to Grachev, Gorbachev loved "Felipe's temperament, his openness, his youth, his penchant for abstract, philosophical thinking. And especially his attachment to socialism, which provided further support for the Gorbachevian 'socialist choice.'" The most important product of the trip, Grachev concluded, wasn't its diplomatic results, but "psychotherapy" for his boss.[37]

Gorbachev stopped overnight at Mitterrand's farm, at Latche in the Pyrenees, on the way back to Moscow. The seemingly modest place reminded Chernyaev of a Russian village: "squat houses with small windows and straw roofs," "damp, dark, green and cool," with goats and chickens patrolling the grounds. Gorbachev was touched to learn that he and his wife would stay in a small room with shuttered windows, which ordinarily only Mitterrand's family members used. Mitterrand warned them that roosters, donkeys, and goats would awaken them in the morning with their crowing, braying, and bleating.

Inside a narrow barn-like building, to which Mitterrand guided them along a narrow path lit only by flashlights, was an elegant salon where the two presidents conferred. Gorbachev lamented that the August coup ruined everything, but vowed to fight on for a new democratic, federal union. Mitterrand, in his wise, world-weary way, urged his guest to take the long view: Gorbachev had "already done the main thing," he said. "You destroyed the system that hasn't worked for a long time." Did Mitterrand's generosity reflect the fact that, back in August, he had seemed ready to live with the August coup and what he had called at the time "the new Soviet leaders"?[38]

Dinner, in another small building, was for family only, plus Chernyaev and his French counterpart. Coffee and cognac followed in a space where there wasn't enough room for everyone to sit down. The pleasant, informal chatter touched on whatever came up. Gorbachev, Chernyaev remembered, "could not stop talking. Mitterrand, sitting in a large chair, would occasionally stop the disorderly conversation . . . with a kindly, indulgent smile on his tired face."[39]

On the flight home to Moscow, Gorbachev invited Chernyaev, Grachev, Palazhchenko, and a couple of other aides to lunch with him in the plane's conference room. He seemed buoyed by Western leaders' support for his struggle to save the union. "They understand it better than those guys back home," he said. He would cite their support to Yeltsin and the others as he continued to push for a union treaty. His aides agreed with this tactic, even "the skeptical Chernyaev," recalled Palazhchenko. Only Gorbachev's wife seemed pessimistic about the chances for success.[40]

GORBACHEV'S WIFE WAS RIGHT. From December 8, when he learned that Yeltsin, Kravchuk, and Shushkevich had founded the Commonwealth of Independent States, until December 25, when he resigned his office, Gorbachev's political trajectory was steadily downward. But his state of mind gyrated wildly. He desperately sought alternatives, even as he realized there was no hope. He contained his emotions—except when they burst forth. He reached out to Yeltsin, who seemed to reach out to him, but their mutual bitterness prevailed in the end. His wife suffered more than he, as she always had, but her pain transmitted itself to him. World leaders rallied round, expressing deep compassion and genuine admiration in a series of farewell phone calls, but they had long been stronger on sympathy than on actual support.

On the morning of December 9, Grachev found Gorbachev "composed, well rested and ready for action." He was waiting to receive Yeltsin and Nazarbayev. Kravchuk and Shushkevich had refused his summons to Moscow to explain what they had done at the Belovezhskaya resort. Yeltsin had called to say he feared he'd be "arrested in the Kremlin." "Are you crazy?" Gorbachev replied. "I'm not," Yeltsin shot back, "but somebody else might be."

Yeltsin came; Gorbachev interrogated him; Yeltsin objected, "What is this, a cross-examination?" Gorbachev calmed down: "OK, sit down. But tell me this—what are you going to say to people tomorrow?"

"I'm going to say that I'm going to take your place," Yeltsin retorted.

The crossfire continued. Nazarbayev was "ashamed to be present," he recalled. Afterward, Yeltsin told Kravchuk, "I never want to have that kind of conversation with anyone ever again."[41]

Gorbachev hoped society would react to this new, Byelorussian "coup" as it had to the August putsch—that parliaments would reject decisions they hadn't made, that media would defend the man who had liberated them, that intellectuals, in particular, would rally to his side. But none of this happened. What he wanted most was a "constitutional" way back to the status quo. Instead, the Ukrainian and Byelorussian Supreme Soviets ratified the CIS agreement on December 10, followed by the Russian legislature on the twelfth. As for the USSR Supreme Soviet, Gorbachev himself forbore to call it into session once he realized he lacked support among its members.[42]

Did Gorbachev ever contemplate the use of force to save the union? Of course not, he later insisted, "It never came into my head, because if it had, I wouldn't have been Gorbachev."[43] But he would have been mad not to at least explore this possibility, and, in fact, he halfheartedly did. Back in November, he had called Soviet Defense Minister Shaposhnikov to the Kremlin, put him at ease with tea and sweets and a few minutes of friendly joshing, and then mentioned a radical way to cope with the nation's crisis: "What if you military men were to take power in your hands, set up a government convenient for you, stabilize the situation, and then move off to the side?"

"Yeah, straight into prison," Shaposhnikov grunted. "Something just like that already happened in August."

"What do you [second-person singular, as usual] mean, Zhenya," Gorbachev objected. "I'm not proposing anything to you, I'm just canvassing alternatives, thinking out loud."

On December 8, just after Yeltsin called from Byelorussia to inform Shaposhnikov about the CIS, the defense minister's phone rang again. "You just talked to Yeltsin," Gorbachev said accusingly. "What's going on in Byelorussia?" Shaposhnikov hesitated, but then conveyed what Yeltsin had told him, as well as his approval of what Yeltsin and company had done.

"It's no business of yours," Gorbachev snapped. "I'm warning you."

Gorbachev called Shaposhnikov twice on December 9, before and after seeing Yeltsin and Nazarbayev. The first time, he apologized for blowing up the day before. The second time, he assured Shaposhnikov that nothing would come of the CIS, that he might well call another round of talks at Novo-Ogaryovo with those still willing to sign the union treaty. Later the same day, Gorbachev visited the Defense Ministry, where Shaposhnikov and commanders of the country's military districts greeted him coldly. The next day, Yeltsin held his own meeting with military leaders in which he promised to raise their pay and to lead the nation out of chaos. That meeting went very well.[44]

Gorbachev issued a statement on December 10 condemning the action of the three presidents as "illegal and dangerous." But that same evening he sounded helpless at a meeting with advisers.[45] On December 13, he surprised Ambassador Braithwaite by being in "bouncy form." Braithwaite and a senior British Foreign Office official had arrived "looking apologetic," noted Chernyaev, "with glum, funereal expressions." But their host cheered them up by joking, "Well, are you here to find out what country you're in and who I am these days?"

Gorbachev compared himself as a "statesman" to the "highwaymen" with "hairy faces" who were challenging him, but then led the conversation "cheerfully and self-confidently, as if nothing had happened." Chernyaev knew his boss was "grasping the slightest excuse to conclude that all was not lost." Braithwaite, too, could see that the "charm Gorbachev bubbled with was verbose and hectic," and that Yakovlev, who was there as well, "looked more and more gloomy" as his leader "built castles in the air."[46]

In two other encounters on the thirteenth, Gorbachev seemed even more resigned. Strobe Talbott and Michael Beschloss, who were writing a book on the end of the cold war, approached his office through empty Kremlin corridors that were "deathly quiet." The Gorbachev they met was angry: "Who has the right to cut this country into pieces?" But "the main purpose of my life has already been fulfilled. I feel at peace with myself." He told President Bush that same day that he would "abide by the decisions of the republics." He regarded the CIS as "the work of amateurs"; that's why he hoped the United States and the West would join him in helping "the commonwealth come alive with real institutions."[47]

By this time, Chernyaev and Grachev were pressing Gorbachev to step down, partly so he wouldn't seem desperate to hang on to personal power. But the boss "keeps dragging it out, hoping for something," Chernyaev grumbled to his diary on December 15.[48]

Secretary of State Baker came to town again on December 16. Yeltsin showed him who was now boss by receiving him in St. Catherine's Hall with Marshal Shaposhnikov seated beside him. Gorbachev later hosted

Baker in the same hall, but whereas Yeltsin had "swaggered," Gorbachev was "subdued." Since Baker had already talked to Yeltsin, Gorbachev asked pathetically, "What do you plan to discuss with me today?" Gorbachev's face was flushed, suggesting to Grachev that he either had a fever or his blood pressure was high. Baker noticed and passed Gorbachev what Grachev took to be some medication, but it was a Velamint, Baker remembered, because his throat was dry and he guessed Gorbachev's might be, too. Baker thought to himself that history would be "kind" to Gorbachev—especially if he stepped aside quickly and gracefully.[49]

Gorbachev was almost ready to go. The next day, at a Kremlin reception for participants in an international conference called "The Anatomy of Hatred," he looked like someone from whom a burden had been lifted. It was good, he said, that a new generation of politicians was "coming along" (not, obviously, including Yeltsin, who was, in any case, a month older than Gorbachev). "Maybe they will appreciate that we had the courage to begin—which means that we had some worth." At the end of a German television interview following the reception, Gorbachev quoted the poet Aleksandr Blok: "Peace comes to us only in our dream"—quickly amending Blok's line with "Actually, we no longer have peace, even in our dreams."[50]

As of December 18, he still hadn't finally decided to resign. He was waiting for a December 20 meeting in the Kazakhstan capital, Alma-Ata (to which he had not been invited, but to which he sent a long memorandum listing what the CIS would have to do to succeed), at which other republics would decide whether to join Russia, Ukraine, and Byelorussia in the CIS. Eight of them did, all the former Soviet republics, except Georgia and the Baltics. That completed the roster of former Gorbachev supporters who, he said many years later, remained silent as he sought to save the union: "deputies in republic parliaments, the army, the intelligentsia, the press—all of them."[51]

At 11 p.m. on Saturday, December 21, Gorbachev gathered Yakovlev, Chernyaev, and Shevardnadze to help him write his farewell speech. "We got carried away," Chernyaev noted in his diary, "as if we were at Volynskoe or Novo-Ogaryovo composing yet another speech for the Supreme Soviet or something like that, arguing about words, as if forgetting that this was an obituary." As always with Gorbachev, who was emotional about not showing his emotions in public, passionate passages suggested by Chernyaev were cut—"castrated," their author complained. Gorbachev grumbled while he worked: Yeltsin was reminding him every day to vacate his office in the Kremlin. The most important thing for Yeltsin was to "occupy the Kremlin," Gorbachev sneered. Everything else was "secondary." Yeltsin and his men were "mediocrities" and "complacent and irresponsible," to boot. They would crow about signing up eleven republics compared with the seven Gorbachev had mustered for the union treaty, "but still, they will fail."[52]

The republic presidents in Alma-Ata left it to Yeltsin to work out details of the transition with Gorbachev. So on December 23 the two men huddled in the Kremlin's Walnut Room—for almost ten hours, according to Grachev, who was waiting in suspense with other aides. The session got off to a bad start when Yeltsin found a Soviet-American television crew waiting to tape the scene. Gorbachev had welcomed a farewell series of press and television interviews, and was allowing an American TV crew to tape his final days in office. He had offhandedly approved Grachev's proposal to tape Yeltsin's arrival, but the latter snorted, "Out of the question. Otherwise, I'll cancel the meeting."[53]

The meeting itself went better. Yeltsin behaved "appropriately," Gorbachev told aides afterward. The two men "argued," recalled Yakovlev, who attended part of it as a sort of mediator, "but without getting irritated." Ten days earlier, Gorbachev's interpreter, Palazhchenko, had asked Beschloss and Talbott to convey a secret message to Bush or Baker, urging them to caution Yeltsin against taking revenge against Gorbachev. The message also asked the Americans to recommend that Gorbachev play some role in the CIS. Baker did urge Yeltsin to handle the transition "in a dignified way—as in the West." And Yeltsin mostly did so, at least on December 23.[54]

The two men agreed that Gorbachev would formally announce his resignation as president and commander in chief on the evening of December 25. After that, Yeltsin and Shaposhnikov would arrive to take custody of the nuclear briefcase. Gorbachev and his aides would vacate their offices by December 29, and the Soviet flag would come down from the Kremlin tower on December 31.

Gorbachev with Yeltsin in the Kremlin, December 1991. Yeltsin's bodyguard, Aleksandr Korzhakov, is at left. Yegor Yakovlev stands with back to camera.

Yeltsin refused fully to meet Gorbachev's requests for pension and staff. He agreed only that Gorbachev could keep his current salary, 4,000 rubles a month, quite high as Soviet salaries went, but plummeting toward a measly $40 at the black-market exchange rate. He would have a Moscow apartment, but smaller than the one he currently occupied, and a country dacha outside the city, with two cars at his disposal and a twenty-person household staff, including bodyguards. Two days later, Yeltsin boasted publicly about how he denied Gorbachev's "exorbitant" request (which Gorbachev denied ever making) to extend his presidential immunity from prosecution: "If he is guilty of something, he should acknowledge it now while he is still president."[55]

Gorbachev wanted to establish a think tank on the model of the RAND Corporation, and for that he would receive the large building complex of the Central Committee's Social Science Institute on Lengradskii Prospekt (complete with classrooms, cafeterias, gyms, and a hotel), which had previously hosted activists from other Communist parties. According to Yeltsin's chief bodyguard, his boss had "no idea of the actual dimensions of the complex," but he was worried, according to Gorbachev, that it would become "a nest of opposition" to the new regime. Yeltsin asked Gorbachev "not to criticize him for the next six months." Gorbachev pledged his support for "as long as Yeltsin continued on the course of democratic reform."[56]

The two men also agreed on the transfer of the supersecret archives documenting Stalin's most awful crimes. One of those was the massacre of thousands of Polish war prisoners, ordered by secret police chief Lavrenti Beria and approved by Stalin, in Katyn Forest in the spring of 1940. The official Soviet position had long been that the Nazis had slaughtered the Poles after occupying the area, but how long could the truth be concealed? Prompted by Andropov, Valentin Falin started searching for incriminating documents in 1982, but the KGB resisted and Andropov, their former chief, dropped the matter. Chernyaev urged Gorbachev to provide a full accounting, but got no reply from his boss. Aleksandr Yakovlev and Falin learned that documents establishing Soviet responsibility for the killings were in Soviet archives, and Falin even got KGB chief Kriuchkov to confirm as much to him. But Gorbachev denied that Kriuchkov had so informed him, and Kriuchkov quickly backtracked. Eventually, the truth got out, thanks to digging by the Soviet press and pressure from the Poles, but if Gorbachev didn't entirely block it, he didn't reveal it either.

Something similar happened to secret protocols attached to the Nazi-Soviet Pact of 1939. The pact itself, which delayed Hitler's invasion of the USSR for almost two years while freeing him for a blitzkrieg to the west, remained controversial enough. But its long-denied secret protocols, which divided lands lying between Germany and the Soviet Union between them, and consigned the Baltic states to Stalin's tender mercies, were particularly explosive in 1989 and 1990 when the Baltics were pushing for independence. Foreign Minister Gromyko had twice vetoed proposals to admit and release those protocols in 1968 and 1978. In 1986, Gorbachev did so again, insisting he would not take political responsibility for releasing them until he could be shown that original copies of the protocols actually existed. In 1988, when Yakovlev and Falin confronted him with proof (although not with the originals themselves), Gorbachev replied with a smile and a grin, "Do you think you're telling me something new?," and then walked away into his inner office. In 1989, the new Congress of People's Deputies formed a commission, chaired by

Aleksandr Yakovlev, to study and assess the Nazi-Soviet Pact. But Gorbachev prevented Yakovlev from providing a full accounting.[57]

Ambassador Matlock summarizes how "dirty secrets" like Katyn and the secret protocols were handled: they were "exposed, half denied, then not contested, then finally admitted officially," the last act occurring after Gorbachev left office.[58] In other words, glasnost applied only slightly more to Katyn and the secret protocols than to Moscow's secret biological warfare program. In retrospect, Chernyaev still doubted that Gorbachev had ever seen a document with Stalin's signature on it condemning Polish prisoners to extermination. Gorbachev was "too violently emotional when dealing with these kinds of things to keep these emotions to himself. I remember his rage when he saw execution lists from 1937 to 1938 with the signatures and comments" of Stalin and other leaders. "And on Gorbachev's instructions, [those lists] were made public. So why would he conceal yet more evidence of Stalin's crimes?"[59]

Perhaps because Gorbachev faced so many other urgent tasks, so many obstacles to accomplishing them, so many other flammable controversies. Why should he further inflame already anti-Soviet Poles? Why should he court more resistance from the Soviet old guard by fully revealing what they had labored so long to conceal? Much better to allow speculation and debate to go on without releasing the "smoking guns" themselves.

On December 23, Gorbachev opened his personal safe, extracted a pile of secret file folders, and tried to hand them to Yeltsin. "Stop! Please!" Yeltsin says he insisted. "Just hand in those papers to the archives, and they'll make you sign for them. I don't intend to be held responsible for them. Why should I take charge of them? You are no longer the General Secretary, while I have not been one and will not be."[60]

When the meeting finally ended, Gorbachev downed two shots of vodka, confessed he wasn't feeling well, and disappeared into a back room. Yeltsin and Yakovlev continued drinking, eating and talking until Yeltsin strode off down the empty parquet corridor like a conqueror, Yakovlev remembered, "as if he were marching along a parade ground." When Yakovlev looked in on Gorbachev, he found him lying on a couch with tears in his eyes.

"So you see, Sash," he said. "This is how it goes."

Gorbachev asked for some water. He said he wanted to be alone.[61]

The next day Gorbachev addressed aides, advisers, and other members of his presidential staff (about forty to fifty in all) in the large room where the Politburo and later the State Council used to meet. His session with Yeltsin had been tough, he told them. Yeltsin had refused to grant them severance pay, but would extend their access to the Kremlin polyclinic for a year. Gorbachev urged his people to follow his example: "Restrain your emotions as much as possible."[62]

Gorbachev arrived at the Kremlin later than usual on December 25. By prior arrangement, an American TV crew headed by Ted Koppel of ABC was waiting to accompany Gorbachev to his office. "I'm feeling absolutely calm, absolutely free," Gorbachev told Koppel. "Only my role is being changed. I am not leaving either political or public life. This [peaceful transition] is happening probably for the first time. Even in this I have turned out to be a pioneer."[63]

According to Koppel, Gorbachev "showed little emotion throughout, he was very businesslike, very self-contained and dignified." Pausing at the door to the Senate Building, where his office was located, Gorbachev quoted Winston Churchill: "The politician thinks about the next election—the statesman thinks about the next generation."[64]

On the way up to his third-floor office, Gorbachev passed checkpoints already manned by Yeltsin guards, who had ordered Gorbachev staffers not to lock their desks or offices, and had begun searching their bags as they entered and departed the premises. Vasily Gusenkov, Raisa Gorbachev's main aide, had been detained until he threatened to complain to the president. Chernyaev, seemingly protected by his age and military bearing, was able to remove some documents. No telephones were ringing in Gorbachev's reception room. Yeltsin's aides had already disconnected most lines, except for one on Gorbachev's dark cherrywood desk.

Chernyaev and Grachev entered Gorbachev's office at about three o'clock to get his signature on farewell letters to foreign leaders, but found it empty. Gorbachev was resting in his back room, but when he appeared five minutes later he looked fresh and fit despite some "slight redness of the eyes." Grachev showed him the front page of a Moscow newspaper with a headline from Pushkin: "No, I shall not die completely." Smiling, Gorbachev completed the stanza: "My soul, my lyre, will survive me and escape corruption."[65]

After Chernyaev departed with the signed letters, Gorbachev read the final version of his speech aloud, still making last-minute changes. He had been writing and rewriting it for several days, working with drafts prepared by Yakovlev and Chernyaev. Yakovlev's version tried to appease Yeltsin and confessed some of Gorbachev's own mistakes. Chernyaev's avoided what he called "capitulation and whining," and Gorbachev adopted this one. He wanted to avoid pronouncing the words "I resign," so he would begin with "I cease my activities as President of the USSR."[66]

Shortly after this, the one working phone in his office rang. His wife was calling in high dudgeon from their dacha to say new security men there had given her and her husband twenty-four hours to remove their "personal belongings." Gorbachev shoved the pages he was editing aside and "flew into a rage," Chernyaev recalled. "His face covered with red spots, he called one official after another, cursing them out." "You're talking about someone's home," he shouted angrily at the new security chief. "Do I have to report all this to the press? Stop this madness!" The man said he was just following orders, lamented the excessive zeal of his subordinates, and promised to call a halt to what amounted to an eviction. "It took the President awhile to calm down after that," Grachev remembered. It must have taken his wife a lot longer.[67]

Ted Koppel and his TV producer, Rick Kaplan, who had been interviewing Gorbachev when his wife called, were ordered to leave the room. They had asked him whether he could have retained power if he had wanted to. Gorbachev replied he wasn't the kind who sought power for its own sake, but that if he had "wanted to remain in government more than anything else, that would not be too difficult to achieve." That would have been true earlier, but in 1991 it was more a reflection of wounded pride than a realistic assessment. "It was evident that he wanted to be perceived as in control," Kaplan recalled, "not in control of the Soviet Union or Russia, but in control of himself."[68]

At five o'clock, two hours before his speech, Gorbachev called President Bush, the next to last in a series of phone conversations he had with Western leaders. The calls reflected his determination to step down in a dignified manner, as well as his remarkably warm relationship with all his interlocutors. Mitterrand telephoned on December 21, shortly after the Alma-Ata decision sealed Gorbachev's fate. According to Grachev, who witnessed the conversation, "Gorbachev needed such an understanding and sympathetic listener." And Mitterrand was so "uncharacteristically emotional" that Gorbachev had to reassure *him*: "I am calm. I am doing what I can to make what is happening here as painless as possible."

Chancellor Kohl had called the previous day. "I don't believe they will succeed," Gorbachev said referring to the CIS, "but I would like them to." Besides expressing his country's everlasting gratitude, Kohl invited his dear friend to come and live in Germany. Gorbachev thanked him but said, "I will live here."

"I want to help Yeltsin," even "defend him from attacks," Gorbachev assured Prime Minister Major, who called in the middle of Gorbachev's long session with Yeltsin on the twenty-third. Major and his wife, Norma, "sincerely love you and Raisa," the prime minister told him. "Raisa Maksimovna and I fell in love with you and Norma," Gorbachev replied. "That sort of weakness isn't characteristic of me, but I can't not tell you that."

Canadian Prime Minister Brian Mulroney hailed Gorbachev's "unique and heroic" contribution to history when he called on the twenty-fourth. Not only had Gorbachev earned the gratitude of Germans, Foreign Minister Genscher told him on Christmas day; he had "won their hearts for all eternity."

Bush was celebrating Christmas with his family at Camp David when Gorbachev reached him. "George, my dear friend, it is good to hear your voice," he said, adding that he wasn't going to "hide in the taiga," but to continue to be active in political and social life. Bush responded with equal warmth, reaffirming "the friendship [with the Gorbachevs] that Barbara and I value very, very much," welcoming Gorbachev's continued counsel, "perhaps right back up here at Camp David"—even going so far as to assure Gorbachev that "the [Camp David] horseshoe pit where you threw that ringer is still in good shape." Of all the phone calls they had exchanged, this was "the most emotional," Bush recalled, even more than after the August coup attempt ended. "He was emotional. I was emotional. I felt I was losing a good friend from the scene." Bush was, however, surprised to learn that Koppel and his ABC crew were videotaping the call in the Kremlin. Bush shook his head at the thought that his friend in Moscow was still performing for an international audience.[69]

Gorbachev delivered his farewell address in Room Number 4 rather than his real office so as to give crews from Russian television and CNN two hours to prepare before he spoke. But the fake office resembled the real one: a green carpet, a large desk with a high-backed chair in front of it and four telephones, none of them connected, beside it, the Soviet flag hanging from a ten-foot pole in front of a painting of the Kremlin, a large chandelier overhead. Made up for the camera by a stylist who brushed powder on his familiar red birthmark, Gorbachev entered the room carrying a leather briefcase containing his speech and a decree formalizing his resignation as commander in chief of the armed forces. After having been unsure whether to sign the decree before or after speaking, he now signed it with a flourish and put it aside, unseen by the world (since the cameras weren't yet live) as he yielded up his nuclear power.

Just before 7 p.m. Gorbachev took off his glasses, wiped them, put them back on, and began reading from his typed text: "Dear compatriots! Fellow citizens! In view of the current situation and the formation of the Commonwealth of Independent States, I am ceasing my activities

Gorbachev delivers his farewell speech on television,
December 25, 1991. PHOTO BY YU. LIZUNOV.

as president of the USSR." His voice sounded "unnatural and hollow," Grachev remembered. "It seemed on the verge of trembling, as did his chin." But he "gained control of his emotions" and his words "resonated with conviction and dignity."[70]

Gorbachev started by regretting the breakup of the Soviet Union, but pledging to do all he could to end the crisis and promote social accord. He had tried to transform society because it couldn't keep living as it had and partial reforms wouldn't work. He named his achievements: political and spiritual freedom, an end to totalitarianism, a break-through to democracy, the turn toward a market economy, and an end to the cold war, the arms race, and the "mad militarization" of the country. He explained why things had gone wrong: resistance from the entrenched party-state structure, old habits and ideological prejudices, "our impatience, the low level of political culture, and fear of change," plus, of course, the August coup that drove the country "to the breaking point." Gorbachev understood people's deep unhappiness with him, but reminded them that fundamental change can't come without "pain, dif-ficulties, and shocks." Granted, "much could have been done better, and some mistakes probably could have been avoided," but he was sure that "sooner or later our common efforts will bear fruit and our people will live in a prosperous democratic society."[71]

This last part was the closest Gorbachev came to the kind of repen-tance that might have won the hearts of Russians, who tend to prize penitence and atonement. Yeltsin would express shame and remorse when he gave up the Russian presidency nine years later, after prom-ising renewal but driving Russia even deeper into a ditch. Gorbachev didn't mention Yeltsin in his farewell, crediting neither his contribution to democratization nor his role in the defeat of the August coup, and fail-ing to wish him well. And at least two passages seemed to target Yelt-sin indirectly. The fateful decision to "dismember the country and the state" should have been taken only on the basis of the "popular will." The "democratic gains of the last years, won only after all the tragic suffering that preceded them, must not be abandoned under any circumstances or for any reason."

Yeltsin wasn't the type to miss or forgive slights. "Switch if off," he barked, pointing to the television, "I don't want to watch it anymore."

He refused to go to Gorbachev's office to take custody of the nuclear briefcase. "I can't go to Gorbachev," he told Shaposhnikov. "You go by yourself."

Shaposhnikov objected. This was a delicate matter, and he and Yeltsin ought to go together. Besides, he wasn't sure Gorbachev would agree to transfer the "property" to him alone.

"If there are complications, call me and we'll discuss options," Yeltsin replied.[72]

One last opportunity to stick it to Yeltsin! What would Yeltsin do if Gorbachev refused to cooperate—come begging for the nuclear button? Shaposhnikov arrived in Gorbachev's office (where ABC television was waiting to tape the turnover, this time with Yeltsin's prior approval) and announced Yeltsin wasn't coming. Instead, Yeltsin proposed that the handover take place in St. Catherine's Hall, where the president usually met with foreign leaders. "This was not only ridiculous, it was stupid," Gorbachev recalled. He rejected the idea and instead handed the briefcase and what looked like a portable telephone to Shaposhnikov and two colonels, "very ordinary-looking men in civilian clothes," according to Grachev, who disappeared down the corridors to deliver it to their new chief.[73]

After Shaposhnikov left, Chernyaev and the two Yakovlevs (Aleksandr and Yegor) entered Gorbachev's office. They found him "agitated and red-faced." The men drank some cognac and then moved to the Walnut Room, where Grachev joined them for a farewell supper in "an empty, half-lit room." Much cognac was drunk, Grachev remembered. "The atmosphere was solemn, sad. There was something of a feeling of a big thing accomplished. There was a kind of feeling of everyone sharing." The "party" ended before midnight. "There were no other formal farewells," Gorbachev recalled, "of the sort conducted in civilized countries. Not one of the presidents of the now sovereign republics, men with whom I'd had close comradely relations for many years, deigned to come to Moscow or even call me on the phone."[74]

Gorbachev looked "somber" when he arrived at the Kremlin the next morning. The Soviet flag over the Kremlin had come down at 7:32 the night before, and he was no longer the country's president. By agreement with Yeltsin, he had access to his office for three more days, but his

ZIL limousine had been removed overnight. He'd had to badger body-guards to get a replacement to take him to the Kremlin. "They're throwing me out of the dacha, and they've taken the car away," he complained angrily when he reached his office, where the Soviet flag still hung on a pole behind his desk.[75]

Two events on December 26 somewhat raised Gorbachev's spirits. That morning, two sympathetic Italian journalists offered him the opportunity to reflect calmly on his years in power. This was "the first time" Grachev heard him "try to summarize his mistakes." He should have moved faster to a market economy; he should have started negotiating a union treaty sooner; he should have tried earlier to consolidate the democrats; he should have dismantled totalitarianism faster and moved more quickly to construct a new system. Simply to list these roads not taken is to realize they were probably impossible to traverse successfully. But Gorbachev was sure he made "the right choice." "It's as if I've lived several lives over the past seven years. I myself changed along with the country, but I helped the country to change." In that sense "my fate has been unique," and "I don't regret it." What about his family? How did they feel about his resignation? Were they relieved? Gorbachev's answer was brief: "I am grateful to my family for having endured all this."[76]

That evening Grachev arranged what he hoped would be the sort of fond farewell that hadn't occurred the previous evening. He called it a "final briefing for journalists by the presidential press service," and staged it in the ballroom of the five-star President Hotel, formerly known as the October Hotel and used by high-level officials and visiting dignitaries from other Communist parties. Grachev invited three or four hundred Russian and foreign media representatives. Although many had been sharply critical of his boss, they were "the only interlocutors capable of appreciating the true role of Gorbachev and were not embarrassed to express their appreciation." The hotel's director didn't fit that description. A protégé of a former high party apparatchik, he refused to book the event, claiming the president's account was "closed." When Gorbachev's aides tried to pay cash, he found another excuse, but by now the hotel was a private, rather than state, enterprise, so he finally accepted payment.[77]

The event was a way to distract Gorbachev, another of his aides remembered, "to prevent him from having a heart attack."[78] As he climbed the wide marble stairs to the ballroom, he looked exhausted, but he was greeted by an ovation that brought him back to life. Hugs for old comrades, "men of the sixties," who had waited so long for a reformer like him to lead them. Quick interviews, warm wishes, requests for autographs. Two hours of questions and answers. What would he do now? "For the next two weeks, I'll disappear. Not physically [*laughter*], just need the time to come to." Would he lead the opposition? "To whom?" Not to Yeltsin as long as he hewed to democratic reforms. As for criticism of his own role, well, "I evaluate my own role no less critically than many of you do." How was his mother reacting to what had happened? "She's been saying to me for a long time, 'Throw it all over. Come home.' I'm going to call her today. She'll probably say, 'Thank God, time to take a rest.'"[79]

Friday, December 27. Gorbachev was scheduled to arrive at his office at 11 a.m. for an interview with Japanese journalists. But at 8:15 Yeltsin marched into Gorbachev's reception room accompanied by his deputy prime minister, Gennady Burbulis, his press and information minister, Mikhail Poltoranin, and the speaker of the Russian parliament, Ruslan Khasbulatov. Overnight, the plaque on the office door reading, "The President of the USSR, M. S. Gorbachev," had been removed.

Yeltsin ordered the receptionist to open the office: "Well, show it to me." Upon entering, he pointed toward Gorbachev's desk. "There used to be a marble pen holder here. Where is it?"

Trembling, the woman explained, "There was no pen holder. Mikhail Sergeyevich never used pens; we always put a set of markers on his desk."

"Oh, alright," Yeltsin conceded. "What's in there?" he demanded pointing to the back room where Gorbachev used to rest. There he found another desk and began rifling through its drawers until he found one that was locked.

"Why is it locked? Call the Commandant!"

Someone ran in with key and opened the drawer. It was empty.

"Alright, alright," Yeltsin conceded.

Returning to the main office, he and his entourage seated themselves at the large oval table. "Bring us some glasses," he commanded.

Almost instantly a man materialized with a bottle of whisky and glasses, which the "guests" filled and downed.

"Now, that's better," Yeltsin said. "I won't bother with the Walnut Room and the place where the State Council and the Politburo used to meet. I've been there, I've been there."

Yeltsin's men laughed. As they strolled out of the office, Yeltsin warned the receptionist, "Watch what you're doing. I'll be back later today."[80]

"The triumph of the plunderers," Gorbachev called it in his memoirs.[81]

When Shakhnazarov arrived a while later to make sure Gorbachev's reception room was ready for the Japanese interview, he discovered that Gorbachev's things had already been removed from his office; the premises were to be ready for their new occupant by ten o'clock. Gorbachev received the Japanese journalists in his chief of staff's office, one floor below.[82] Afterward, he called Chernyaev about letters that had come in from British Prime Minister John Major and from Japanese Premier Kiichi Miyazawa, and a book signed by members of the Vakhtangov Theater. Gorbachev was "excited," Chernyaev recorded in his diary. "Such signs of attention are balm for him now."

Gorbachev told Chernyaev he was getting sick, probably from the flu. But he now had to move out of his dacha, so he had to get to work sorting through his books and things. He asked Chernyaev to start working on a "chronicle of new thinking" based on records of his conversations between 1985 and 1991. After that, he got into the car his guards had commandeered and left the Kremlin.[83]

CHAPTER 19

OUT OF
POWER

1992–2016

ALL BUT ONE OF GORBACHEV'S predecessors as Soviet leader managed to die in office. Stalin had a little help from Kremlin "friends" who, while they apparently didn't poison him, delayed calling the doctors after he had a catastrophic stroke.[1] Politburo colleagues of Brezhnev, Andropov, and Chernenko insisted they stay on, although aging and ill, until they dropped dead. Khrushchev lived for seven years after being ousted in 1964, but under what amounted to house arrest. Gorbachev's postpresidency, on the other hand, has lasted more than a quarter of a century and resembled those of American presidents like Jimmy Carter and Bill Clinton, who devoted decades to good works at home and abroad.

The Carter Center in Atlanta aims to fight "disease, hunger, poverty, conflict, and oppression around the world." The Clinton Foundation strives to "improve global health and wellness, increase opportunity for women and girls, reduce childhood obesity, create economic opportunity and growth, and help communities address the effects of climate change."[2] Shortly after leaving office, Gorbachev founded the International Foundation for Socio-Economic and Political Studies, otherwise known as the Gorbachev Foundation, which has pursued a variety of charitable endeavors, particularly supporting treatment of children with leukemia. It has also been a kind of "think tank" with its own staff of specialists, and has sponsored multiple conferences and publications on issues domestic (e.g., education, inequality, federalism, civil society) and international (Russian-American relations, Russia and Europe, world poverty, ecology, climate change, economic development). Gorbachev has also chaired Green Cross International, which, in the face of "insecurity, poverty and environmental degradation," promotes "a sustainable and secure future," and the World Political Forum, which, seeking to emulate the Davos-based World Economic Forum, brings together world and other leaders to discuss global problems.[3]

Most retired world leaders comment from time to time on contemporary politics, particularly the irrepressible Clinton, who has campaigned almost nonstop for his party's candidates, especially his wife. But Gorbachev has been just as political, in fact, more so. Many of his foundation's conferences and publications, most of which he chaired or edited, have concerned Russian politics, often focusing on his own era or on policies of his successors. After a brief hiatus in early 1992, he began lambasting the Yeltsin regime, regularly volunteering his opinions in interviews and at press conferences. In 1996 he went so far as to run for president against Yeltsin (and the Communist candidate, Gennady Zyuganov) and later worked to create and to try to sustain a political party, the Russian Social Democratic Party.

In a sign of the changing times, Yeltsin never arrested or banished Gorbachev, but he hounded him mercilessly, at least until Gorbachev's pitiful performance in the 1996 presidential election proved that he posed no real threat. Gorbachev welcomed Vladimir Putin's ascendance to the presidency, in part because he viewed him as the "anti-Yeltsin," but after their initial honeymoon, the two men soured on each other.

This is not to say that Gorbachev's postpresidential years were entirely embattled. Free at last from the pressures of ruling, he was able to relax, go to the theater, watch movies, and travel the world (spending up to one-third of his time abroad), basking in fervid welcomes for having liberated his country from totalitarianism and the world from cold war and nuclear fear, but also soaking up sights and sounds as a tourist. Moreover, his view of himself and his mission somewhat mellowed. Of course, he continued vigorously to defend perestroika and his "new thinking" on world politics, but he admitted numerous tactical mistakes and even concluded that the democratization of his country, which he had hoped to accomplish in a few years, might take decades. But this reassessment reflected his fraught relations with his successors. If, as Gorbachev insisted, Yeltsin nearly destroyed the state, then Putin deserved praise for rebuilding it, even when he used authoritarian methods to do so.

The best part of retirement was being able to spend more time with his beloved wife and family.

THE INITIAL PERIOD AFTER Gorbachev's resignation was particularly depressing for him and his wife. The Gorbachevs were allowed to privatize their in-town apartment on Kosygin Street, but it was very small, and they hadn't lived there anyway. Their forced march out of the lavish presidential dacha (carried out by bodyguards using their own cars when the Gorbachevs were denied state-supplied moving vans) brought them back to a lesser one they had occupied between 1978 and 1986. (The next resident after them in 1986 had been Boris Yeltsin.)[4] Located on Rublevskoe Shosse, it boasted about ten acres of wooded grounds near the Moscow River, but the dacha itself was "decrepit and crumbling," according to Gorbachev, and his daughter remembers that the authorities "didn't lift a finger" to improve it. "Mama refused to humiliate herself by asking for help." Let it all fall apart, grumbled the woman who had prided herself on keeping all her other homes perfectly shipshape. After Gorbachev's resignation, his daughter remembers, "the telephones went silent. Even people they regarded as close to them dropped them." Among the Gorbachevs' few visitors during the first months were Aleksandr Yakovlev and Yegor Yakovlev and their wives. They were struck by how lonely the Gorbachevs seemed— their residence isolated down a long driveway protected by guards, their phones silent all evening. The privacy that they had preserved so zealously now seemed like torture. Raisa couldn't stop thinking about Foros. The family's incarceration there had been a "moral Golgotha," she would later say, and "thoughts of what we went through in those days torment[ed] me constantly."[5]

Raisa had always wanted her family to be close by; indeed, when they returned from Stavropol in 1978, Irina and her husband, Anatoly, lacking an apartment of their own, lived with her parents at their riverside villa. But later, after Ksenia was born, they moved into the city apartment to which Gorbachev was entitled but rarely used. Her mother was "terribly against this move," Irina recalled. After her father's ouster from power, Irina's mother was "emotionally defenseless. Perhaps that's why she wanted me to be near her—to serve as a safety valve or shock absorber. She didn't want to be entirely dependent on him. She pitied him, she loved him, she needed to talk everything through, to cast everything off. But with whom? Whom else could she talk to? Strangers? All she had was me."[6]

Gorbachev warded off depression with work. He had formally to register his foundation and appoint its staff: Aleksandr Yakolev and Grigory Revenko, Gorbachev's last presidential chief of staff, as initial vice presidents; other staffers included longtime associates Vadim Medvedev, Chernyaev, and Shakhnazarov. The foundation was officially a nonpartisan "think tank." But in due course, Shakhnazarov admitted, it amounted to an "intellectual, if not political, opposition to the regime."[7] In fact, its initial aims, as Gorbachev later summarized them, sounded explicitly political: to analyze and publish materials on the history of democratization under perestroika, to "defend that history from slander and falsifications," to "monitor" life in post-Soviet Russia while suggesting "alternative paths of development," and to study international and global processes as well.[8]

Gorbachev celebrated the foundation's grand opening on March 3, 1992 (the day after he greeted his sixty-first birthday quietly at home with his family), surrounded by old comrades like Shevardnadze, Yakovlev, and Primakov, by actors, artists, and writers who were the cream of the Moscow intelligentsia, plus (a sign of the temporary cease-fire between him and Yeltsin) the country's vice president, Aleksandr Rutskoi. The foundation's premises were beyond imposing. On the surface, it resembled the kind of presidential library, archive, and museum that former U.S. presidents since Franklin Roosevelt have erected and had maintained with help from the U.S. government. But, in the absence of Russian government subsidies, which Yeltsin cut off later in 1992, Gorbachev financed his foundation by lecturing for large fees around the world. He also applied his celebrity to selling pizzas and Louis Vuitton bags in print and television advertisements; along with his lecture fees and book royalties, these very occasional appearances in advertisements were the main way of keeping his foundation in existence. "I was against his doing these advertisements," his wife later said, "but I understood why he did them."[9]

The cease-fire between Gorbachev and Yeltsin followed Gorbachev's promise to refrain from criticizing the Russian president as long as he pursued democratic reforms. For a while, Gorbachev praised Yeltsin for his courage, boldness, and decisiveness during the August 1991 coup, and beseeched the West to support the struggling new Russian state. But privately he nursed his loathing for Yeltsin, growling to journalist Dmitry Muratov, "When they hang me, make sure that they don't hang Yeltsin from the same birch tree."[10]

The truce soon broke down. Yeltsin's decision to free prices totally in January triggered raging inflation. By the end of 1992, prices were nearly thirty times higher than in January, wiping out the savings of ordinary people almost overnight, bringing them out into the streets, where they lined the sidewalks, forlornly holding out family belongings they hoped to sell for a pittance. Gorbachev had shrunk from this sort of radical reform out of fear it would produce just such consequences. But for a while he held his fire. His foundation was not a "shadow cabinet," he told Muratov on February 24, and he personally was "not in opposition."[11] But at a late April press conference he not only condemned the Yeltsin administration's "flagrant errors"; he equated them with the way the Bolsheviks had driven people, "like a herd of cattle," into collective farms in the late 1920s and early 1930s.[12]

Didn't this harsh criticism violate Gorbachev's pledge to Yeltsin? Muratov asked him in late May.

"Listen," Gorbachev responded, "Yeltsin isn't Jesus Christ." "I won't conceal my disagreements [with him]. I won't keep silent."[13]

Yeltsin quickly struck back. Gorbachev had a right to express his views, Yeltsin's press secretary declared on June 3, but it ill-behooved someone who "never found the courage to undertake economic reform" to criticize his successor, who did. The declaration warned Gorbachev that Yeltsin was prepared to "take necessary and lawful steps to defend his reforms."[14] Later the same month, Minister of Press and Information

Mikhail Poltoranin called Gorbachev a "criminal" who, as Soviet Communist leader, had financed international terrorism. "We could knock him out in one blast" of incriminating evidence from the archives, Poltoranin warned, but why bother, since Gorbachev was "finished as a politician."[15]

Whether or not he was "finished" at home, he certainly wasn't abroad. In Japan in 1992, huge crowds hung on his every word, holding children aloft as if to capture Gorbachev's karma, and Prime Minister Kaifu hosted a gala dinner at which hundreds of guests serenaded the Gorbachevs with "Moscow Nights." Several universities granted him honorary degrees, at one of which his wife told some twenty thousand students how she and her husband fell in love at Moscow University. Gorbachev hinted that he might someday return to political life. "The last time French President de Gaulle returned to power he was 68 years old, but I'm only 61."[16]

Gorbachev toured the United States that spring in the Forbes corporate jet, *The Capitalist Tool*, spoke to adoring crowds, collected huge honoraria to support the Gorbachev Foundation, and held a last, nostalgic get-together with Ronald and Nancy Reagan, drinking wine, eating chocolate-chip cookies, and recollecting how the two leaders ended the cold war.[17] But at Harvard's Kennedy School, where he spoke at the Forum, he seemed to Bruce Allyn, who had been part of the Yavlinsky/Allison team in 1990, like a "man disoriented," as if in "some kind of substitute reality," as if "he could not find words to accurately describe where he was and where he was going." After his talk, "he failed to show up for a private reception with wealthy and powerful sponsors of his Harvard visit, and instead dined alone at a corner table in the Charles Hotel with his wife."[18]

In Spain, crowds shouted not only "Gorbi! Gorbi!" but "Torrerro," as if welcoming a victorious matador, while Gorbachev broke away from his security detail to press the flesh and sign autographs. At the Seville World's Fair, "Expo-92," the usually formal Gorbachev dressed informally in light brown trousers and a green, short-sleeved shirt, his wife in a colorful, gauzy blouse and dark brown pants. The Gorbachevs actually took a real vacation in the Canary Islands and visited his dear friend

Spanish Premier Felipe González and his wife, Carmen Romero, at their summer home on Mallorca.[19]

During an eight-day visit to Germany in March, crowds followed the Gorbachevs chanting his name. Politicians of all stripes—Chancellor Kohl and President von Weizsäcker, and former chancellors Willy Brandt and Helmut Schmidt—lined up to be seen with the man whom so many Germans wanted to thank for helping to reunite their country. Kohl, rarely failing to mention that he was on a first-name basis with "Misha," hailed his friend: "We Germans, and I in particular, will never forget what you did for us." The trip's official sponsor was Gorbachev's German publisher, Bertelsmann, which made a large donation to the Gorbachev Foundation. Raisa, exhausted from accompanying her husband to most of his appointments, skipped a sightseeing trip or two. When he declared he was "a free man now," she quipped, "I haven't noticed you're a free man. Not according to your calendar. He is always working. We have no time to work together. I hope all this will come."[20]

Meanwhile, back in Moscow, Yeltsin regretted he had granted the Gorbachev Foundation so much space in the former Social Science Institute. Soon the place was under siege. First, state scrutiny of whether the foundation was illegally using funds of the former Communist party. Then, confiscation of funds the foundation had inherited from the school, forcing Gorbachev to cut back on staff. Next, removal of the hotel formerly attached to the school—another potential source of income for the foundation. Finally, on the morning of October 7, 1992, an obviously nonspontaneous protest in front of the foundation by several dozen demonstrators who said they'd been brought from outside Moscow, and who threatened to "come down hard on your 'gang'" and "give a licking to those swine." Gorbachev, who was en route to the foundation when he learned of the blockade, called a press conference to challenge it—only to discover that Yeltsin had already decreed a further reduction of foundation space, from 38,000 square feet to 8,600.[21] Police surrounding the building barred Gorbachev staffers from entering it.

Gorbachev fired back. "President Yeltsin has completely isolated himself," he told *Der Spiegel*. "Or, as we say, he's gotten himself into a mess."[22] Later in 1993, Yeltsin ordered the military to bombard the White House, where the rebellious Russian Duma was holding out against him. "The Commonwealth of Independent States hasn't worked out," Gorbachev declared, "the country has been torn to pieces, its economy has collapsed," and "70 percent of the population is on the edge of poverty." The trouble with this indictment was that it described what so many Russians took to be Gorbachev's own legacy. Which rather reduced the appeal of his declaration that if the situation required him to "save the country," he was now ready "to do so."[23]

After the December 1993 parliamentary elections, in which two pro-Yeltsin parties lost badly, Gorbachev called upon Yeltsin to resign— just as Yeltsin had demanded of Gorbachev.[24] When President Yeltsin reviewed the troops at a huge military parade on May 9, 1995, the fiftieth anniversary of victory in World War Two, and held a gala reception attended by U.S. President Clinton and German Chancellor Kohl, Gorbachev wasn't invited.[25]

Meanwhile, two judicial battles raised the tension surrounding Gorbachev. In 1992, after thirty-seven deputies to the Duma asked Russia's Constitutional Court to reject Yeltsin's outlawing of the Soviet Communist party, fifty-two anti-Communists countered by claiming that the party itself was unconstitutional. In the chaotic context of the time, with one state (the USSR) being replaced by another (the Russian Federation) and constitutional norms up for grabs, the resulting trial, in which the court combined the two suits, was a political struggle with Gorbachev caught in the middle—portrayed by the Communists as having betrayed the party, and by Yeltsin's prosecutors as having ruined the country. Gorbachev adamantly refused to testify in court as a matter of principle, but he was mortally offended, as David Remnick found in an interview. "He wore his resentment like a pistol," Remnick reported. "Look," Gorbachev said, "I am not going to take part in this shitty trial."[26]

The other trial, the last formal echo of the August 1991 coup attempt, wasn't much better, but Gorbachev agreed to take part. All the plotters had been offered amnesty by the Duma in February 1994; all accepted except General Varennikov, who insisted on being judged. Varennikov, paradoxically, wanted to show not only that the plotters had tried to save the country from Gorbachev but that Gorbachev himself had encouraged the coup. Gorbachev, who testified for eight hours as a witness in Varennnikov's trial before the Military Collegium of the Russian Supreme Court, denounced this version of history. The whole experience was a horror. Pro-Varennikov demonstrators outside the courtroom cried, "Judas! Judas!" Varennikov, who conducted his own defense, shouted at Gorbachev, "You are a renegade and a traitor to your own people." "Arrogant lies! Lies and slander!" Gorbachev shouted back, with coup plotters Kriuchkov, Yazov, and Lukyanov sitting close by in the visitors' gallery. At least one prosecutor conceded that Gorbachev was partly responsible for the coup attempt, but a second prosecutor disagreed—another sign of disorder in the court. In the end, Varennikov was acquitted (to shouts of "Thank You" from his assembled followers), on the grounds that he was merely following the orders of civilian superiors, and that his intention had been to save his country, not betray it.[27]

All the tension and strain took a toll on Gorbachev. Muratov, the journalist turned close friend whom Gorbachev came to treat as a kind of "adopted son," swore in a 2013 interview that he never saw Gorbachev in a state of "emotional aggression," even in response to fierce attacks.[28] But Remnick had found him in just such a state at the Gorbachev Foundation during the Communist party trial—"furious, obsessed," like "Lear raging about plots against his underappreciated self."[29]

The year 1995, the tenth anniversary of the start of perestroika, gave Gorbachev a chance to make his case to the country, at least to that part of it that would listen. He staged a conference on the theme "The Intelligentsia and Perestroika" at his foundation, and afterward felt better than he had in a long time about the intellectuals who abandoned him in 1990 and 1991. He proposed to the Duma a law that would rein in powers of the president that Yeltsin had expanded in the new 1993 constitution. He met in Novosibirsk with scholars, students, workers, and entrepreneurs and found them receptive. Likewise, he visited St. Petersburg, where the year before he had found his host, Deputy Mayor Vladimir Putin, to be "attentive, tactful, and knowledgeable." His reception at a factory in Kursk in 1995 was less friendly; the angry crowd, many of them women with children, didn't allow him to speak until he descended from the stage, approached people in the first row, and said, "Did you come here to make noise or to converse? If the former, we can end this right now." After that, he recalled, they talked for two hours, and he got vigorous applause at the end. In the Chuvash Autonomous Republic, west of the Volga River in European Russia, the crowd shouted down anti-Gorbachev demonstrators and asked so many questions that the discussion "seemed to go on forever." And in the evening, the Chuvash president, who three short years before, as Russian minister of justice, had threatened to drag Gorbachev before the Constitutional Court in handcuffs, invited him to dinner and seemed, according to Gorbachev, to have "become a wiser man."[30]

THE RUSSIAN PRESIDENTIAL ELECTION was scheduled for June 16, 1996, with a second round, if necessary, to be held on July 3. All through 1995, Gorbachev later recalled, people kept asking whether he would run. In retrospect, the idea seems preposterous. At the time, according to Gorbachev, "the majority of my colleagues and friends were against my running," and some of them, including Yakovlev and Vadim Medvedev, said so publicly. Shakhnazarov remembered thinking that all the campaign would bring his boss was "more blows to his self-esteem and a further fall in his already not very high ranking in his own country."[31] As for his closest adviser of all, his wife, she expressed "not only doubts but fears," Gorbachev remembered.[32] Fearing that he would encounter a media blockage, she warned him, "They won't even let you utter a squeak."[33] In the end, when he did run, "the psychological burden on her wasn't easy," he admitted, especially when the campaign turned into a "game without rules." But one may be excused for thinking the toll much greater than that. She was "categorically against" his running, Gorbachev admitted, but having failed to convince him, "I submitted," she said. "After all, I am his wife."[34] She "couldn't stand" the thought of his confronting again the terrible strain of the late perestroika years, Gorbachev confessed in May 1996. But having admitted as much, he made light of her objections in a campaign speech: "I'm acting in accord with the principle: listen to women (in this case my wife and friend) and then do the opposite of what they tell you."[35]

He insisted on running because "I couldn't reconcile myself to the election coming down to a choice between Yeltsin and [Russian Communist party leader Gennady] Zyuganov." Yeltsin had "destroyed the Soviet

Union, shot up the Russian parliament, merged the state and business, and given the green light to criminality." Zyuganov still endorsed Stalinist totalitarianism, approved of the August 1991 coup, and had encouraged his colleagues to back the Belovezhskaya agreement that finished off the USSR. Faced with this choice, "I did not have the right to stand aside."[36]

Fine, but what possessed him to think he had a chance to prevail? Well, there were the big crowds that greeted him with increasing warmth as he barnstormed the country.[37] Plus, there were people who "200 percent guaranteed" that if he ran for a Duma seat in their district, he would easily win.[38] But, asked a journalist, wasn't he "fiercely hated" by pro-Communists who had lifted Zyuganov's party to victory in the 1993 Duma elections? "Labels don't interest me," Gorbachev replied. Besides, "a majority of Russians" didn't want a return to the past that Zyuganov's party represented.[39] Didn't polls show that less than 1 percent of the population supported Gorbachev's candidacy? asked another interviewer. "I have other data," Gorbachev retorted.[40]

Actually, Gorbachev didn't expect to win the election outright. What he hoped to do was help create a centrist bloc including other candidates like Yabloko party leader Grigory Yavlinsky, renowned eye surgeon Svyatoslav Fyodorov, and famed military commander General Aleksandr Lebed. He granted that Yeltsin and Zyuganov could each count on a substantial vote, but a silent majority of 65 to 70 percent could still garner "colossal support."[41] As for who would actually become president if his bloc prevailed, Gorbachev didn't think any of his allies had "a real claim to that role." But he was fully prepared to give them and their supporters, especially younger ones, high posts in his new administration—generosity that his putative allies didn't necessarily appreciate.[42]

Gorbachev didn't spare himself in his campaign. He established "an initiative group" in February 1996 to collect the necessary one million signatures. On March 21, by which time 1.5 million had been gathered, he formally announced his candidacy and began barnstorming the country. From then until the middle of June, he campaigned continuously, holding several rallies in each of twenty cities, including St. Petersburg, Nizhny Novgorod, Novosibirsk, Krasnoyarsk, Irkutsk, Ulan-Ude, Kemerovo, Barnaul, Omsk, Volgograd, Rostov-on-Don, Stavropol,

Samara, Yekaterinburg, Kazan, Ufa, and Vladimir. Pro-Yeltsin local officials put up road blocks almost everywhere—boycotting him themselves, barring local media from covering him, closing off meeting halls or changing them at the last minute, refusing him access to higher educational institutions, including the Stavropol Agro-Economic Institute, where he himself had received a degree. And in many places, his audiences weren't much friendlier. In Omsk, anti-Gorbachev demonstrators barred the door to the hall, and local police advised him to sneak in through a back entrance, but Gorbachev marched through the hecklers to the stage. Inside, some two thousand people were waiting, including an angry young man who slapped Gorbachev across the face. Faced with catcalls, Gorbachev remained silent for a long time and then suddenly shouted full force, "So this is how fascism comes to Russia!" He wasn't afraid for himself, he later said, but rather for "normal people" filling about half the hall, who had come to listen to him. So he turned and left the building. As for his wife, she accompanied him on all his campaign trips.[43]

Some places gave him a friendlier reception, for example, the Altai region, at the junction of Siberia, Kazakhstan, and Mongolia, where he

Gorbachev campaigning for the presidency of Russia, Volgograd, May 9, 1996. PHOTO BY A. STEPIN.

actually got to appear on local television. That helped him to believe that up to 70 percent of the electorate was still making up its mind and might yet vote for him, Yavlinsky, Fyodorov, or Lebed. Meanwhile, however, that would-be bloc fell apart—if indeed it ever existed—at which point, insists Gorbachev, "I had no choice but to campaign on to the finish," with at least one chance to make his case on central television, not in debate with Yeltsin and Zyuganov, which wasn't allowed, but in a recorded speech of his own.[44]

The election wasn't entirely rigged, but it certainly was corrupted by the all-out support Yeltsin got from rich oligarchs. In return for helping to save their property as well as their country from a return to Communist rule, they got even more property—"shares" (in mammoth, undervalued state enterprises) in return for massive "loans" to Yeltsin's campaign.[45] In the end, Yeltsin and Zyuganov each got about a third of the votes in the first round, trailed by Lebed with about 14 percent, Yavlinsky with 7.5, Zhirinovsky 5.8, and Fyodorov 0.9. Gorbachev got 0.5 percent, or about 386,000 votes in all. After Yeltsin prevailed in the two-man runoff with 54.4 percent, Gorbachev consoled himself with the thought that Yeltsin had cheated, in part by suborning Lebed with an offer to make him his national security adviser, and that the cleanest elections in Russian history had been those that Gorbachev himself had presided over in 1989 and 1990. Moreover, his thunderous defeat had a positive result. According to Shakhnazarov, it "reduced Yeltsin's pathological fear" of his rival, so that, although Yeltsin's anger "didn't morph into charity," a kind of "hostile neutrality" broke out between them, and for the rest of his time in office (until 1999) Yeltsin, increasingly hobbled by ill health as well, more or less left the Gorbachev Foundation alone.[46]

RAISA NEVER FULLY ADJUSTED to her post-Kremlin existence. It wasn't that she missed her husband's power and the pomp that went with it. On the contrary, the memory of all the betrayals at the top deepened her misery, and what was worse, her daughter remembers, the perfidies continued as Gorbachev's accomplishments were ignored and he was accused of corruption or even treason. To be sure, she continued to find satisfaction in charitable activities, such as supporting the Russian Chil-

Raisa
Gorbachev,
1996.

dren's Hospital and an association called Hematologists for Children of
the World. In 1998, she organized a concert to benefit the Children's Hospital, but when Russian businessmen failed to support it substantially,
she contributed her own funds. Meanwhile, she helped her husband prepare his memoirs, published in 1995, and several other books as well—
gathering material in his archive, collating his correspondence, editing
and retyping his manuscript—so much so that she considered herself his
de facto coauthor. And she collected tens of folders with materials and
notes for her own memoirs, picking up where her 1991 book, *I Hope*, left
off. She worked on twenty-three chapters for a volume with the tentative
title "Why My Hearts Aches," but gave up when contemplating the past
revived "thoughts of what we endured during those years [which] torment me constantly," she told an interviewer in 1999.[47]

Raisa had a small office near her husband's at the Gorbachev Foundation, where in 1997 she established a subdivision called Raisa Maksi-

movna's Club (with herself as president and her daughter, Irina, as vice president), to promote women's welfare in Russia; its first conference was titled "Contemporary Russia: Women's Views." Despite her ailments and depression, she prepared for club conferences with all her usual meticulousness, drafting her own remarks on small file cards that she kept in front of her even though she had memorized their contents, speaking clearly and simply without the rhetorical flourishes that her husband also sought to avoid in formal speeches.[48] But at work, too, thoughts of past and present oppressed her. Her immediate worry in 1997 was that the foundation was being forced (by its ever-shrinking space in the former Social Sciences Institute) to find a new home. Gorbachev had been reserving funds from his lecture fees for a new building, but couldn't collect enough—until he met Ted Turner in California. Raisa couldn't contain herself and described the dilemma to Turner. He asked how much money they would need for construction. Gorbachev himself didn't answer, but his wife declared, "One million dollars." After quickly consulting with his then wife, Jane Fonda, Turner agreed to provide that and more for a beautiful building on Leningradskii Prospekt that was completed after Raisa died.[49] Later, when the Gorbachev Foundation lacked funds to pay for all its expenses, it began renting out space in its new building to Russian business firms.

The Gorbachev Foundation's new building in Moscow, 2001.

According to Olga Zdravomyslova, the sociologist hired to direct the Raisa Maksimovna Club, who later became the foundation's executive director, Raisa kept returning in their conversations to past humiliations and perfidies. "You can't imagine what it was like" in the Kremlin, she told Zdravomyslova: she was "alone, surrounded by men, only men, in black suits." And she kept recalling her fear during the August 1991 coup that the plotters would kill her entire family, especially when she suddenly remembered that her grandfather had been arrested on that very same date in 1937.[50]

A doting grandmother, Raisa treasured Ksenia and Nastya, keeping close track of all their activities, noting memorable things they said, collecting the drawings they made for her and her husband's birthdays. She was extremely distressed, therefore, when Irina and her husband divorced in 1994. Their marriage had been "far from ideal" for some time, Raisa's sister, Ludmila, later revealed, but not wanting to hurt her mother, Irina kept the bad news from her. Raisa took the divorce "very hard," Ludmila continued. "She regarded it as her daughter's tragedy."[51] Meanwhile, Raisa herself turned against her oldest friend from Stavropol days. Lydia Budyka's husband was dying from cancer when an American documentary filmmaker offered to help him obtain treatment in the United States in return for Lydia's agreeing to be interviewed. When she asked Raisa whether she had any objections, Raisa did, and she never forgave Budyka for ignoring her wishes.[52]

Accompanying her husband on his 1996 presidential campaign trips was a remarkable act of love and will. But that was the family tradition—never to let Gorbachev travel alone, always to have his wife or daughter with him. In early 1999, although increasingly tired, Raisa convinced him that they should accept an invitation to a song festival in San Remo, Italy. And when he prepared a speech, which Italian friends sensed would be out of place, she delicately urged him to take his cue from them, who "know better." In Rome that same April, she confessed to the same Italian friends, "I'd much rather stay home. But Mikhail Sergeyevich doesn't like to travel alone. If I said, 'I won't go,' he'd be very upset. And that pleases me, of course."[53]

In late May 1999, Raisa traveled with her husband all the way to Australia. Invited there many times, they had always declined, but in a recent Australian public opinion poll, some 75 percent of respondents had named Gorbachev as "the man of the twentieth century." Gorbachev was "stunned," he recalled, and accepted the next invitation so as to "respond to all of Australia." The trip "left us with many wonderful memories," he remembered, not just visits to Melbourne and Perth and a speech to the Australian parliament, but a walk in a eucalyptus forest where the local koala bears seemed positively "tipsy," reminding him

Mikhail and Raisa Gorbachev, late 1990s.

and his wife of all too many of their Russian compatriots. But the flight back was "long and difficult," Gorbachev continued in an autobiography, *Alone with Myself,* written a decade after his wife's death, "and to this day I am haunted by the thought that the trip exacerbated processes that were brewing within Raisa."[54]

Her full medical checkup early in 1999 revealed no problems, but in

July, Raisa complained about sharp pain in her back. She informed Gorbachev's aide Karen Karagezian, who was helping her with her memoir project, that she was ceasing work on it. The back pain was so bad, she said, that at times her legs felt as if they had turned to cotton and she collapsed.[55] Even before then, she had a premonition. Once when she and her husband were talking about the future, she abruptly announced, "I don't want to be left without you. I wouldn't be able to live. And you? What about you? You'll remarry and live on."

"What are you talking about?" he replied. "Why are you thinking like that? Who's talking about death? You're young. Just look at yourself in the mirror. Listen to what people say about you: you're just tired."[56]

On July 22, a Russian doctor diagnosed leukemia. Gorbachev immediately contacted Karagezian, who also served as his main German specialist and was then vacationing in Munich, asking him to recruit the best German hematologists, and authorizing him to contact German Chancellor Gerhard Schröder's office for help in getting German doctors to Moscow. The next day in Moscow, two German specialists confirmed the diagnosis. Whereupon, Gorbachev called Schröder and President Clinton, who both invited Raisa to be treated in their best hospitals. Gorbachev opted for the cancer center in Münster, Germany, because it was closer to Moscow.[57]

In accordance with Russian custom, Gorbachev didn't tell his wife the whole truth: "The doctors call it 'an acute blood disease,'" he said.

"Is this the end?" she asked, looking him in the eye.

"No. We've decided to fly to Germany tomorrow for more tests, to get the full picture. They'll decide on the treatment there."[58]

The Gorbachevs flew in a private plane, arriving on July 25 in Munich, where an ambulance was waiting on the tarmac. Raisa lay on a stretcher, but was strong enough to joke about it.

For the first ten days in the hospital, Gorbachev stayed with his wife around the clock, neither of them managing to sleep at night; he helped nurses turn her over in bed every ten minutes or so. After their daughter, Irina, arrived with her daughters, the routine eased somewhat. She attended her mother all morning, Gorbachev came early in the afternoon and stayed through the evening, and Karen Karagezian and a Russian woman with a medical background who was married to a German alternated on the overnight shift, sleeping on an easy chair in an examination room, while Raisa was attended by nurses.

After an initial series of tests, chemotherapy commenced. Because the patient's immunity was severely compromised, the air in her room had to be purified and visitors had to disinfect their hands and clothes and don sterile masks. Raisa was in deep pain, too weak even to read, but she retained her sense of the absurd. Once when her husband was holding her, she dozed off and he gently removed his arms.

"Don't go, don't leave me," she begged. "Hold me a bit longer."

"I need a bit of rest," he replied. "My back can't stand it."

"Oh, Gorbachev," she retorted, "there was a time when you absolutely adored me, and now you can't even support me."[59]

But support her he did psychologically. When she complained to her doctors about pain, one of them asked whether there was anything at all that comforted her. She rejoiced at her husband's visits, she answered.

One day Irina summoned her father to the hospital, saying her mother needed him. He feared a crisis, but when they were alone, Raisa said, "I want us to see more of each other and to talk more."[60]

The conversations that followed ranged over their life together. Their first meeting at Moscow University. Their first kiss: Did he remember it, she asked. Of course, he said, but he should have done it sooner. Whose fault was that? "Yours, of course," she said laughing.

Why, he asked, had Raisa wanted to break off their relationship before it really began? Because her roommates had chided her for dating another man so soon after she broke up with Anatoly. And because Elvira, a girl from Azerbaijan, "had designs on you, and I got in her way."

"So, you gave up?" asked Gorbachev.

"You can see that I didn't. We're together."

"And what if I hadn't insisted and persevered?"

"Well, I knew that you would, and you did."

"That's called, 'female logic,'" he countered.

"Yes," she retorted. "You men think everything goes according to your plans."

The next question was his: "When did we become husband and wife?"

"Legally on September 25."

"True enough, but in actual fact?"

In the new dormitory on Lenin Hills, she replied.

"When?"

"I don't remember."

"You see. I remember. It was on October 5, 1953."

Throughout their lives, Gorbachev recalled in *Alone with Myself*, he and his wife "engaged in a dialogue that never stopped"; even when he was Soviet leader and away at the office or traveling, they called each other several times a day. Except that sometimes it did stop, he slyly and suggestively recalled, as happened one morning when they were doing their exercises in their separate bedrooms. When she called him in to witness her do a headstand, he worried she "might break your neck." As for him, she shot back, she needed to give his combine driver's muscles "some constant and serious attention."

"Give me your hand," she continued.

"Oops!"

"Hold me tight," she said. "We still have plenty of time: you won't be late and neither will I."

"We took a shower," he recalled, "and then entered the bedroom."

"She was keen to know my opinion about many things," reads the next sentence of *Alone with Myself*—followed shortly by a waggish account of what made his wife so attractive to him: Once, when Raisa and her daughter were in Crimea, they visited the Khan Girei's palace and looked in on the place where the harem used to be. "Mama," asked ten-year-old Irina. "Why did the Khan have so many wives and Papa has only you?"

"Ask Papa when we get home. Let him tell you whether I'm his only woman and why."

Irina asked, and her father answered, "You know, Khan Girei had many wives. But not one was a philosopher."

Actually, he goes on in *Alone with Myself*, Raisa was "a beautiful woman, and not only in my eyes." She was also "elegant, charming, wonderfully feminine," and "innately aristocratic. A person with a huge sense of dignity." Not "aloof," as she appeared to some who didn't know her well, but "tactful, considerate, and with an obliging nature," a "serious and interesting person to talk to," who "liked people with a sense of humor." She was "sensitive and perceptive" and "open to discussion, but very intolerant of slander, which made her suffer."[61]

As Raisa's condition worsened, the slander ceased. Thousands of sympathetic letters poured into the hospital from Russia, former Soviet republics and around the world, along with books and other gifts, including supposedly miracle cures, half filling the room where Karagezian, who was in charge of sorting through them, was stationed. So did telegrams from world leaders like Schröder (who also came to Münster to visit Gorbachev), Clinton, French Premier Lionel Jospin, Kazakhstan President Nazarbayev and his wife, George H. W. Bush, Margaret Thatcher—even from Boris Yeltsin, who hadn't addressed himself directly to his predecessor for the last eight years. Yeltsin's "words were good," Gorbachev told his friend Italian journalist Giulietto Chiesa, who visited him in Münster. "A very nice gesture."[62]

The Russian newspaper *Izvestiia* published an article headlined "Lady Dignity." It read in part, "Fragile and elegant, with a refined taste for beautiful clothes, she became a symbol of a country liberating itself from drabness. But we didn't understand her. Perhaps because we didn't want to understand her. Perhaps we demanded too much of this family when they were in power. But we didn't break them. . . . And meanwhile, we ourselves have changed; we've become human beings. It turned out we had forgotten how to share a stranger's grief. But now, for the saddest of reasons, we are showing respect for two people who love each other— Raisa and Mikhail."[63]

Gorbachev took the article into Raisa's room (despite the prohibition against foreign objects) and read it to her. She listened and wept. Then she whispered, "It turns out you have to die to be understood."[64]

One day Raisa's doctors convened a meeting of specialists from other hospitals to review the results of her treatment and discuss future plans. Late in the meeting, which took several hours, they invited Gorbachev to join them. When he returned to his wife's room, she said, "You had a very long meeting. Things are bad? You must be holding something back from me. They probably don't know what to do next."

Neither Gorbachev nor Irina hinted to Raisa (or admitted to themselves) that her situation was almost hopeless. Now they had decided on a bone marrow transplant with Raisa's sister, Ludmila, as the donor.

"Why are we wasting time, then?" Raisa asked.

Because she had to get stronger before they could operate. "If they saw no grounds for hope," he said, "they wouldn't have decided on the transplant. So you shouldn't waste your strength worrying."

She seemed to calm down and closed her eyes. But the next day she announced, "I want to go home. What will be will be. Do you hear me? I want to go home. I will lie in our bedroom on our bed. I hate all this."[65]

She did not go home. Ludmila arrived from Ufa and took up residence in a nearby hospital room waiting for Raisa to be ready, but never visiting her sister, who didn't want to be seen in her devastated state. Instead of gaining strength, Raisa weakened. On the evening of September 12, she was suddenly rushed to the intensive care unit and attached to an artificial breathing machine. After that she could no longer speak, but doctors urged Gorbachev and Irina to speak to her so she could hear their voices and feel their presence. Irina "did not close her mouth for hours," Gorbachev recalled, "but I sat there as if I were a statue."[66] On the night of September 20, two days before the transplant had been scheduled, five days, Gorbachev remembered, before the forty-sixth anniversary of the date they obtained their marriage license, he and Irina stood beside Raisa's bed while she lay in a coma.

"Don't go, Zakharka," pleaded Gorbachev, calling her by the nickname he often used at home. "Can you hear me?" He took her hand, hoping she would somehow respond with a squeeze. But "she was silent," he recalled. "She was dead."[67]

ONCE DURING HER HOSPITAL STAY, Raisa said to her husband, "When I get well, if I get well, let's find a little house not far from the sea, where the sun shines a lot, where we can enjoy our last years together." This wasn't the first time she had said so. She had often said it before. Gorbachev had asked friends to start looking for such a cottage. But it was too late.[68]

"Of course, I'm guilty," Gorbachev declared a year and half later in an interview. "I'm the one who did her in. Politics captivated me. And she took it all too much to heart. If only our life had been more modest, she would be alive today."[69]

Gorbachev
with his
daughter, Irina
Virganskaya/
Gorbachev,
during the
burial of Raisa
Gorbachev.

Gorbachev's
daughter, Irina
Virganskaya/
Gorbachev, with
her daughters,
Anastasia (left)
and Ksenia, at her
mother's funeral.

For more than a year, Gorbachev was deeply depressed. "I felt so alone," Gorbachev recalled eight years later. "I didn't want to live, quite frankly. I once said so aloud; I couldn't hold it in, although that kind of lack of restraint isn't characteristic of me. Only Irina, Ksenia, and Nastya were my salvation. I kept calling my daughter by my wife's name, Raya."[70]

Irina, whose marriage to Virgansky had collapsed in 1994 and who was raising her two daughters on her own, packed up their Moscow apartment and moved in with her father. She understood, she recalled, that "he must not live alone, simply must not." Several years before that she had given up her cardiological research career and then, after finishing a business school, started working full-time at the Gorbachev Foundation with full authority to run the foundation. For the next two

Gorbachev with his daughter and granddaughters, 2009, in photo taken by his son-in-law, Andrei Trukhachev.

years, she spent almost all her time with her father at home, at work, and on the road—until it became awkward for Ksenia and Nastya to invite friends to their grandfather's home, and he began to worry if they weren't home by nine o'clock. At that point, Irina sold her Moscow apartment and bought a small house for herself and her daughters just five minutes away by car from her father's.[71]

Gorbachev changed almost nothing at home after his wife died. All her books remained in place when he and Irina reduced the vast family library, even the two small volumes on her bedside table. So did the knickknacks she loved to collect while traveling, and the piece of paper on the wall with one of her favorite aphorisms written in her perfect script: "It's not those who get tired who perish, but those who stop." He couldn't bring himself to look at her papers, including twenty-five family folders. But he couldn't resist entering her closet. He had given some of her clothes to Ludmila, but most remained, still smelling of her perfume, each linked in his mind with a time in her life; she had even kept the gray suit with cherry-colored blouse she wore as a student. He looked at a box, hesitated to open it, but then did and recoiled in surprise. Her tights! All labeled as to the outfits with which they went. Typical of a woman who was a perfectionist in the way she coordinated her clothing, as in so much else, who didn't let her husband see her in the morning until she was suitably coiffed and arrayed, who stealthily threw out some of the worn-out old clothes he liked to wear at home, but gave him the last word on her own wardrobe. If all he said was, "OK," that item was doomed. When he gave a "thumbs up," he remembered, she beamed.[72]

Asked in 2001 whether he would ever consider remarrying, Gorbachev replied, "No. I will continue to live with her. Our dialogue continues." Had some of the grief begun to ebb? "No. This kind of calamity doesn't go away. She was lucky; she died first. We used to argue about who was more fortunate. I would say she was—to have found me. She would say I was—to have found her. We never settled this issue, but I think we'll meet again and continue our discussion."[73]

At some point, Gorbachev "forced myself not to remain in the past," to think instead of all he still had to do: run his foundation, convene the World Political Forum, preside over Green Cross International, write a monthly column syndicated by the *New York Times*, try to found a social democratic party, and cochair the new "Petersburg Dialogue" between high-ranking Russians and Germans.

This last assignment he took on at the request of "Vladimir Vladimirovich," that is, Boris Yeltsin's successor, the new Russian president, Vladimir V. Putin.

Gorbachev with Vladmir Putin and Angela Merkel at a meeting of the St. Petersburg Dialogue Forum in Wiesbaden, Germany, 2007.

IN THE BEGINNING, recalled his close friend Dmitry Muratov, Gorbachev "treated Putin carefully. Was that because he really admired Putin's policies? Or because he wanted the president of the country to respect him?" The answer appears to be both.[74]

Yeltsin appointed Putin as acting prime minister and anointed him as his successor in August 1999, a designation approved by the Russian people when they elected Putin president on March 26, 2000. Gorbachev's initial reaction when Putin became premier was to view him as a "black box," a man without high-level experience whose future behavior was unpredictable.[75] Just before the election, Gorbachev in effect endorsed him, telling the Italian newspaper *La Republica* that, faced with a choice between democracy and authoritarianism, Putin was likely to "choose correctly." Gorbachev considered himself a democrat, but since Yeltsin had left the country in chaos, he recalled, it needed "strong, firm leadership," in other words, "a certain dose of authoritarianism."[76]

Gorbachev's attitude toward Putin soon warmed even more. He was invited to attend Putin's May 7, 2000, inauguration (the first time Gorbachev had entered the Kremlin since December 1991) at which Putin praised him as well as Yeltsin for behaving "worthily" not only while in office, but since leaving it.[77] Russian representatives abroad began receiving the last Soviet president (inviting him to stay at the Russian embassy in Washington and hosting him at the Russian consulate in New York), something that never happened while Yeltsin was president.[78] But soon Putin's dose of authoritarianism turned out to be too big. When masked policemen descended on the offices of the independent-minded NTV television network and its owner, the Media-Most company, barking out orders—"Hands up!" "Down on the floor!"—Gorbachev leaped to NTV's defense. The police action crossed the line between "moderate and hard authoritarianism," he charged in an interview on the network itself. He agreed to chair NTV's Public Advisory Council, whose other members formed an all-star cast of perestroika's champions. Gorbachev didn't blame Putin publicly, however, and Putin reciprocated by inviting Gorbachev to meet with him in September. Putin told him the NTV affair merely reflected an economic spat between Media-Most and Gazprom-Media in which he had not interfered, and that he firmly favored independent and objective television. Gorbachev welcomed those words, but soon came to his own conclusion—that what Putin really wanted the media to do was: "Submit! Follow orders!"[79]

Despite this conclusion, Gorbachev continued to support the president—"not unconditionally," he insisted, "but firmly," telling not only Russian and foreign journalists but Gorbachev's own friends that Putin was "devoted to democracy," but had to use "tough measures" to rebuild the state and stabilize the economy. This endorsement partly conveyed Gorbachev's fellow feeling for a chief executive faced with overwhelming challenges. But it also reflected Putin's support for Gorbachev's latest great cause—a new social democratic political party.[80]

Even before he left office, Gorbachev had become a kind of social democrat—believing in, as he later put it, equality of opportunity, publicly supported education and medical care, a guaranteed minimum of social welfare, and a "socially oriented market economy"—all within a democratic political framework. Exactly when this transformation occurred is hard to say, but surely by 1989 or 1990 it had taken place.[81] He hadn't broadcast his new allegiance while in power, but in the year 2000 he helped form the Russian United Social Democratic Party, which three years later merged with the Social Democratic Party (first headed by Gorbachev's old comrade Aleksandr Yakovlev and then by Konstantin Titov, governor of Samara province) to form the Social Democratic Party of Russia.[82]

Gorbachev with his granddaughter Anastasia, marching in a demonstration of the Social Democratic Party of Russia, May 1, 2001.

As these rapid name changes suggest, Russia's social democrats had trouble gaining traction, partly because, like most other Russian political groupings, they were divided among themselves over tactics and personal ambitions. Gorbachev wanted the party to compete in the 2003 parliamentary elections, but Titov, who did not, prevailed. By 2005 they had both resigned as leaders, and before long the party disbanded, or rather was disbanded by higher authorities as a result of not having enough members to register and run in elections.

The larger irony is that social democrats, who might seem to have offered a moderate left alternative to Communism, turned out to be discredited by Communism's failures. The more personal irony is that Gorbachev came to regard the social democratic project as "the most important project of his life" (according to his aide Olga Zdravomyslova), that he traveled the country making speeches on its behalf, and that for a while he cherished the encouragement he got for the project from Putin. When they met on June 17, 2002, Putin remarked that Russian society needed a center-left party and that he was open to cooperation with it. "That fully corresponded with my intentions," Gorbachev recalled, although, he added, it turned out that what the Kremlin really wanted was not "powerful, independent parties," but weak ones that it would "easily ignore, subordinate, or liquidate."[83]

Gorbachev's mixed view of Putin in 2002 was on vivid display in a *Novaya gazeta* interview with Muratov. Hadn't perestroika been replaced by its opposite, Muratov asked, "rule of law by wheeling and dealing," "glasnost by talk shows," "personal freedom by the transformation of the state into the personal fief of its leaders"? Not so, Gorbachev objected. He still thought Putin aimed to "find a way out of the chaos he inherited." "I've been in the same skin. That's what allows me to say that what he's done is in the interest of the majority." But Gorbachev was "no apologist for the president," he insisted. He continued to criticize Putin on particular issues (he found Yukos oil company oligarch Mikhail Khodorkovsky'a arrest in October 2003 "stunning and incomprehensible"), but he went so far as to reassess his own record in the light of Putin's experience. Gorbachev had long pondered whether he had moved too slowly or too fast in revolutionizing Soviet state and society. Now he told Muratov in a November 2003 interview that the kind of fundamental transformation he still hoped was taking place could require "not ten days or five hundred days but decades, perhaps even the whole twenty-first century." Especially in Russia, where "either left-wing radicals seize power or even more radical right-wingers. It's madness."[84]

Gorbachev condemned as "shameless" the way Putin's political party,

United Russia, connived to win the 2003 parliamentary election and then "emasculated" the Duma. But he welcomed Putin's election to a second term in 2004.[85] And two years later, even before Putin fired his first anti-Western fusillade at the 2007 Munich Security Conference, Gorbachev launched his own attack. The West had "quietly applauded" the collapse of the USSR, he contended, "dancing with and around" Yeltsin while Russia's "army, education and health systems collapsed." So "we should not pay too much attention to what the West is saying" about Putin, who had in fact "stabilized the country." The United States wanted "to continue as the sole superpower in charge of the world"; that was why "it doesn't want Russia to rise."[86]

Several Gorbachev friends and associates tried to explain why he praised Putin. "I think he's secretly worried" about the Gorbachev legacy, said his friend Muratov. "The values of perestroika . . . are being savagely destroyed." But if so, then why was Gorbachev "allowing himself to be used by the Kremlin"? as another friend, Ludmila Telen, put it. Because, she continued, "he will keep balancing as long as he can." If Gorbachev were "to position himself against the president," added former Moscow mayor Gavriil Popov, that would limit his freedom to maneuver.[87]

Gorbachev denied he was being manipulated by Putin.[88] Even so, Dmitry Medvedev's election as president in 2008 came as a relief. It was Putin, of course, who chose Medvedev (so as to avoid violating the Constitution's ban on a consecutive third term) and then shoved him aside to grab a third term for himself in 2012. But for a while at least, Medvedev's liberal tone convinced more than a few Russians that he represented a new course, and he reached out to Gorbachev in a way Putin had not. He invited Gorbachev to the Kremlin on several occasions, he welcomed him to his suburban residence as well, and he celebrated the former president's eightieth birthday by personally awarding him one of Russia's highest honors—the Order of St. Andrew the Apostle the First-Called—although Medvedev's praise on that occasion was noticeably faint: "You led the country in very complicated and dramatic times. You took on a difficult challenge. What you accomplished can be evaluated in various ways, as you well know. But what you did was indeed fundamental and complex work."[89]

Grateful as he was for Medvedev's attention, Gorbachev continued to criticize "the degradation of the state and demoralization of society," "cosmetic" rather than real reforms, United Russia party conclaves that reminded him of Brezhnev-era and even Stalin-era party congresses, and the results of December 4, 2011, parliamentary elections, obviously falsified to favor Putin's party, which Gorbachev demanded be annulled and reheld. And when thousands of Muscovites took to the streets on December 10 to protest those results, Gorbachev rejoiced that the seeds of democracy planted under perestroika were again bearing fruit, that "a new generation," a "powerful, united movement of voters," was echoing the famous words he uttered in 1985, "We can't go on living like this!"[90]

PUTIN'S THIRD TERM still lay ahead. Meanwhile, Gorbachev was starting to feel his age. "I felt very good until I turned seventy-five," he remarked late in 2014, although beginning in 2002 he had four serious operations: for a benign enlarged prostate that year, on his carotid artery in 2006, on his spine in 2011, and oral surgery early in 2014. A bad fall on the ice resulted in hospitalization in early 2007, his hearing deteriorated, and in 2014 at a formal presentation of his latest book, *After the Kremlin*, he invited the big crowd in the Moskva Bookstore to join him again on his ninetieth birthday, when he'd likely arrive in a wheelchair. For more than fifty years, he had daily taken long, vigorous walks daily (usually about three miles, he recalled, though much longer in the mountains), but he cut back after Raisa died, even before his legs couldn't manage anymore. Often, he would descend from the second to the first floor in his home to get something, but forget what it was before he arrived. The morning was now his best time of day: arising at about six or six thirty, he would straighten the bed and then lie back down to do "the simplest exercises," stretching and arching, not sure, he added with characteristic good humor, whether his cat, who was doing the same sort of thing, was imitating him or vice versa. The medication he was taking had ballooned his weight and swollen his face. "I always look like a bulldog in photos now," he told *Der Spiegel* interviewers in declining to be photographed early in 2015. "In some ways," Gorbachev added, "I feel old, but in others I still feel young."[91]

His globe-trotting slowed down, but didn't stop until 2015. He staged

Gorbachev in a photo by his son-in-law, Andrei Trukhachev.

fund-raisers in London (attracting the likes of Madonna, J. K. Rowling, and Naomi Campbell) to support the Gorbachev Foundation's fight against leukemia; he chaired World Political Forum meetings, such as one in Turin in 2005, attended by former world leaders like Germany's Helmut Kohl, Poland's Lech Wałesa, and Brazil's Fernando Cardozo; he pressed for nuclear abolition at a Harvard Kennedy School of Government forum that same year. For some of his lectures, he reportedly received low six-figure fees. Other appearances, such as a trip to the south of France with a Russian billionaire friend to recruit Elton John to perform at a benefit, and his visit with tourists on a Baltic Sea cruise, cashed in on Gorbachev's celebrity.

Still other occasions were specifically designed to celebrate him and his achievements. After dinner at a 2005 tribute in Washington on the twentieth anniversary of perestroika, Gorbachev swiveled his chair to look up at the lectern behind and above him, lapping up panegyrics from former president Clinton and former secretaries of state Colin Powell and Madeleine Albright. On his seventy-fifth birthday, guests toasted him at a banquet hall on the edge of Moscow; Putin was not present, although he had sponsored Yeltsin's seventy-fifth birthday gala in the Kremlin a few weeks before. Most elaborate of all was a four-and-a-half-hour eightieth birthday gala in London's Royal Albert Hall in 2011, with proceeds going to the Raisa Gorbachev Foundation. Actors Sharon Stone and Kevin Spacey were genial hosts, although their attempts at American humor mostly fell flat with a largely émigré Russian audience. Shimon Peres, Lech Wałesa, former French premier Michel Rocard, and Arnold Schwarzenegger offered tributes in person; Bill Clinton, George Shultz, and Bono prerecorded theirs. Gorbachev presented "Man Who Changed the World" awards (obviously named after him) to Ted Turner, World Wide Web inventor Tim Berners-Lee, and the African inventor of cheap, solar-powered lamps, Evans Wadongo. Musical interludes featured Valery Gergiev conducting the London Symphony Orchestra, baritone Dmitry Hvorostovsky, Shirley Bassey (singing "Diamonds Are Forever"), Paul Anka (singing "My Way," whose lyrics he wrote, which became a signature number for Frank Sinatra), at least one crooning Spice Girl, plus assorted Russian performers and a German rock band, the Scorpions.[92]

Actually, Gorbachev insists, he would have preferred to celebrate his eightieth quietly "in the company of family and close friends." But his family persuaded him to go public, and his older granddaughter, Ksenia, who had studied public relations, entered European high society at the prestigious Crillon Haute Couture Ball in Paris in 1992, and

**Gorbachev with President Barack Obama and Vice President Joseph Biden
at the White House, March 20, 2009.**

married in style in Moscow in 2003, coproduced the London extravaganza. She and Gorbachev's other granddaughter, Nastya, who studied journalism, appeared at a 2007 party in Moscow with Donatella Versace in gowns chosen by the designer. Ksenia and Nastya, like their mother, Irina, inherited Raisa Gorbachev's elegant taste in clothes—but also her attachment to a close-knit family. When Gorbachev sold his house and a Moscow apartment and moved into a new house outside Moscow, the three women moved in as well, along with Irina's new husband, Andrei Trukhachev. And it was Irina, at a smaller, quieter celebration in Moscow of her father's eightieth, who offered a tribute more personal and touching than any uttered in London: "You've not only had the courage to remain in Russia, where they overthrew you and for years they've slandered not only you but your wife, trying to make you answer for everything the Communist party dictatorship ever did. You also courageously continue to work for the good of the country and all its people. As a human being, you are far wiser and stronger than those who slander and judge you. We are proud of you. You are the foundation of our lives."[93]

GORBACHEV'S RELATIONS WITH PUTIN "soured," he recalled, even before Putin won his third term in 2012. "We had kept in contact all along, but then things got complicated. I don't know why."[94] It can't have helped that Gorbachev had opposed a third term for the president, and he watched with dismay as Putin now "tightened the screws": arresting participants in massive protest demonstrations; getting the Duma to establish huge fines for lesser demonstrators, forcing nongovernmental organizations to register as "foreign agents," a term used to label "class enemies" slated for liquidation in the 1930s and now intended, according to Gorbachev, to force NGOs into a kind of "straitjacket." Putin's administration aimed to "completely subordinate society" to the Kremlin, Gorbachev said; the president's party, United Russia, with its "monopoly on power," now "embodied the worst bureaucratic features of the Soviet Communist party."[95]

Gorbachev and Putin had no direct encounters after 2011, except for shaking hands in passing on Russian Independence Day, June 12, 2012.

Gorbachev proposed a meeting, but Putin was always too busy. "After that," recalled Gorbachev, "I gave up and stopped calling him."[96] "I've criticized him a lot in public," Gorbachev explained in 2013. "He sometimes loses his temper. Once he said, 'Gorbachev's tongue should be cut short.'"[97] But Gorbachev also continued to praise Putin. He "is a statesman," he told the *Moscow Times* in November 2014, going so far as to rank him with two foreign leaders Gorbachev admired: Ronald Reagan and Margaret Thatcher.[98]

The praise reflected Gorbachev's sense that he himself was not without sin: "Putin," he admitted in June 2016, "suffers from the same disease from which I used to suffer: self-assuredness."[99] But Putin also deserved praise for rescuing Russia when, thanks to Yeltsin, it was "disintegrating."[100] And also, ironically, for damning Western leaders, with whose predecessors Gorbachev had been so close. Gorbachev's attacks on Western post–cold war behavior tracked closely with Putin's. Gorbachev, too, condemned Western attempts to "turn us into some kind of backwater" after the cold war, with "America calling the shots in everything."[101] He, too, continued to censure NATO's expansion up to Russia's borders, along with NATO bombing of Yugoslavia without United Nations authorization, and the American invasion of Iraq under President George W. Bush. Gorbachev welcomed Russia's takeover of Crimea, calling it a "happy moment" in accord with the "will of the people."[102] He refused to single out Putin's role in sparking the Ukrainian war, preferring to blame both sides, as well as Kiev's Western allies, for the carnage.

Why did Gorbachev turn so sharply against the West? It was not he who changed, he would say, but the Western powers, particularly the United States, which abandoned cooperation with Moscow. In Gorbachev's view, neither side "won" the cold war, which damaged both sides and which both sides cooperated to end. He thought his friend President Bush shared that view, especially after Bush refrained from crowing over the fall of the Berlin Wall and the collapse of Communism in Eastern Europe. But in 1992, Bush declared, "By the grace of God, America won the cold war."[103] Moreover, Gorbachev added bitterly in 2014 interviews, the Americans began to betray him even before he left office. Back in 1990, he insisted, he and other world leaders (President Bush and Pope John Paul II, for example) talked of creating a new world order that would be more just, humane, and secure than its predecessor. But the Americans continued to play the old game so as to create a "new empire headed by themselves." They "patted us on the shoulder, they kept saying, 'Well done, well done,' you're doing the right thing. But all the while, they were tearing us down, looting us, tearing us apart."[104]

AS HIS EIGHTY-FOURTH BIRTHDAY approached, Gorbachev remained himself. Fearful of a new cold war, he called for a U.S.-Russian summit. If he and Reagan could agree, why couldn't Obama and Putin? But, in a sign of his dwindling clout, Gorbachev got no response from either president. Did he now believe that "everything you pushed for in your political life has fallen into ruin under Putin?" asked *Der Spiegel*. "I take an entirely different view," Gorbachev retorted. "Glasnost isn't dead and neither is democracy." A new generation had grown up "much freer than in the Soviet Union. The clock can no longer be turned back." Was he ready at last to admit that, as a leader, he had been too irresolute and indecisive? Of course not. "How did this allegedly indecisive Gorbachev manage to push through perestroika against immense resistance?" How had he managed to allow freedom of speech and religion and travel? How could an indecisive leader have decided to end the nuclear arms race by completely eliminating medium-range missiles and reducing long-range missiles by half?

In February 2015, an interviewer asked him whether he was happy. A few years before, he had said there are no happy reformers. But he hadn't been "in the best of spirits" back then and had allowed himself "to get carried away." As for now, "Yes, I am a happy person."[105]

Was he really? Warmly receiving American visitors in his office in mid-October 2015, Gorbachev was clearly debilitated physically—rising from his desk with great difficulty, limping with the aid of a cane. But his mind was clear and his demeanor almost jolly.

Several friends and colleagues of his were divided about his state of mind. According to film director Aleksandr Gelman, Gorbachev felt hurt and offended that so many Russians still blame him for destroying the USSR. But his aide and interpreter Palazhchenko insisted that Gorbachev's "thick skin" insulated him from such a sense of grievance. He didn't see himself as a tragic figure, said Palazhchenko. He well knew the value of his great achievements at home and abroad, added Gorbachev's close friend Dmitry Muratov, and that sustained him. Although Gorbachev now granted that it may take a hundred years for democracy to take hold in Russia, he was proud that he was the one who opened the way.

In his family life, too, Gorbachev had reason to be depressed. After decades of being supported by the companionship of his wife, daughter, and granddaughters, he lived mostly alone. Irina Gorbachev, her second husband, Andrei Trukhachev, and her two daughters now spent most of their time in Germany—leaving Gorbachev to be attended in his large suburban villa by government-provided servants: cooks, guards, and drivers. But Gorbachev understood why Irina wanted to move away— because she and her daughters, unlike him, could no longer take the slings and arrows that he had so long endured. (She also moved because her husband needed medical care in Germany.) In fact, according to Muratov, Gorbachev was relieved that Irina had been able to distance herself at last from the hostile environment that so oppressed her.[106]

If all this was so, if Gorbachev indeed convinced himself that he was happy, then the pattern that characterized so much of his life continued almost to the end of it. Despite occasional doubt and despair, he managed for the most part to ward them off, to suppress them, to ignore how they have marred his mood and twisted his actions, to remain on the whole the confident, optimistic man he had always been.

The truth is that Russia under Vladimir Putin largely abandoned Gorbachev's path at home and abroad and returned to its traditional, authoritarian, anti-Western norm. But that only underlines how exceptional Gorbachev was as a Russian ruler and a world statesman.

UNDERSTANDING GORBACHEV

ORBACHEV WAS A VISIONARY who changed his country and the world—though neither as much as he wished. Few, if any, political leaders have not only a vision but also the will and ability to bring it fully to life. To fall short of that, as Gorbachev did, is not to fail.

Gorbachev succeeded in destroying what was left of totalitarianism in the Soviet Union; he brought freedom of speech, of assembly, and of conscience to people who had never known it, except perhaps for a few chaotic months in 1917. By introducing free elections and creating parliamentary institutions, he laid the groundwork for democracy. It is more the fault of the raw material he worked with than of his own real shortcomings and mistakes that Russian democracy will take much longer to build than he thought. After all, the American Revolution succeeded at the price of preserving slavery, which it took a bloody civil war to abolish.

In foreign affairs as well as domestic, Gorbachev had huge accomplishments to his credit. He reduced the danger of a nuclear holocaust. He allowed East European countries to become their own masters. He dismantled an empire (or acquiesced in its dismemberment) without the orgy of blood and violence that has accompanied the breakup of so many others, including the British Empire—in India, Kenya, Malaysia, and elsewhere.[1]

Gorbachev was a master politician when it came to consolidating power and using it to transform the Soviet system and end the cold war.

But the forces he let loose and the people he helped free both at home and abroad overwhelmed him in the end.

He became "Gorbachev" with the help of his own native gifts: innate optimism and self-confidence, a substantial intellect, a fierce determination to prove himself, and his ability to maneuver to get what he wanted, charming people in the process. But his environment shaped him as well. Part of this was generational. Many in his demographic cohort, peasant boys rising in the post–World War II era of rapid urbanization and mass education, had not only an optimistic worldview but, as historian Vladislav Zubok has described it, "a naive belief" in the "cultured discourse and ideology, in comparison to sophisticated, cynical, double-thinking urbanites."[2]

Even more important were the personal influences on Gorbachev: his parents (especially his father) and grandparents (especially his maternal grandfather), who loved and encouraged him rather than trying to dominate him; the rural schools he attended, where his special gifts stood out; Moscow State University, which opened up not only his intellectual but his social and political horizons. All these contributed to the extraordinary self-esteem and trust in others without which he wouldn't have dared to try to change the world.

Gorbachev made it to the top by seeming to be an ideal product of the Soviet system. Powerful figures like Andropov, Kulakov, Suslov, Kosygin, even Brezhnev (to the extent he was still compos mentis), aware of the cynicism and corruption all around them, were thrilled to discover an idealistic, energetic, educated young party leader who still sincerely believed in Communism. What Gorbachev concealed was that the Communism he believed in wasn't the carcass of Stalinism over which they presided. He wanted to do what his Moscow University friend Zdeněk Mlynář had sought to do in the Prague Spring—give Communism a human face.

How did Gorbachev's ideals survive the nearly three decades he spent climbing the party ladder? What emerged from this time of testing was the remarkable combination of characteristics described by editor and critic Igor Vinogradov: "the readiness, despite years of political play-acting, to behave sincerely and even gullibly"; the difficulty he had "lying outrageously and pushing aside those [who seemed] loyal to him";

"the heightened belief in the powers of persuasion, which made him so immensely talkative."[3] All these qualities were strengths, but they were also weaknesses, especially in the eyes of Russians for whom an "iron hand" is the mark of strong leadership.

Gorbachev often told Aleksandr Yakovlev and Anatoly Chernyaev that he was prepared to "go far," and in the end he abandoned Communism altogether. But because of his initial uncertainty, his sworn commitment to gradualism and his fear of alarming Politburo colleagues, he settled at first for mild economic reforms, plus a strong dose of glasnost. Only when the reforms stalled and the glasnost began to provoke conservative opposition did he determine to embark full bore on democratization. In doing so, he did indeed change signals on his initial Kremlin supporters, whom he then maneuvered, with more than a little help from Communist party discipline, into reluctantly tolerating his more radical program. He tried to steer liberals, too, until their radicalism outpaced his and they abandoned him.

In 1985, when he first became the leader of what was still a post-totalitarian state, Gorbachev enjoyed the kind of power of which Western leaders can only dream. But with that power came the responsibility for a far broader range of domestic and international problems than Western leaders face. American presidential historian Jeremi Suri has written, "Because of the breadth of responsibilities and the ever-faster movement of international development, the contemporary president is in perpetual crisis mode, constantly running to catch up with events"— with the result that "the president simply does not have the power, at home or abroad, to match expectations." Yet, to all the responsibilities that came with his job, Gorbachev added the challenge of transforming the Soviet system and reshaping world politics. No wonder he could not live up to his own expectations.[4]

Until the end, Gorbachev reiterated his belief in socialism, insisting that it wasn't worthy of the name unless it was truly democratic. But the effect of trying to democratize the Soviet experiment in socialism was to break it apart. In this sense, Gorbachev helped bury the Soviet system by trying to make it worthy of praise, by seeking to make it live up to what he saw as its original ideals.

Gorbachev disdained detailed plans or blueprints because he associated them with the iron schema the Bolsheviks had forced on the Russian people. But his Communist training accustomed him to the idea that society could be drastically transformed almost overnight. A sworn opponent of Bolshevik-style social engineering, he tried to engineer his own anti-Bolshevik revolution by peaceful, evolutionary means. He trusted the people to embrace self-governance, and their elected representatives to shape democratic institutions—until it turned out that they didn't know how and no longer trusted him.

Gorbachev was indeed a brilliant tactician. He was convinced from the start that the main danger he faced was the kind of hard-line revolt that dumped Khrushchev in 1964. So he went out of his way to keep Kremlin hard-liners on board—much too far, his liberal critics contended. The fact that he got the Communist party to vote away its monopoly on power was a tour de force accomplished without the use of force. His training and experience in the party apparatus prepared him to accomplish this feat—but Boris Yeltsin, whom Gorbachev regarded as inferior, as a loose cannon, turned out to be better at the new, populist political game. In a further irony, Yeltsin's electoral success owed much not only to his populism (at which Gorbachev sneered) but also to his reminding Russian voters of a gruff, strong-minded, authoritarian tsar—in stark contrast to the much milder, more garrulous, consensus-seeking Gorbachev.

Hard-nosed, cold-blooded politicians often assume that morality and politics can't coincide. But Gorbachev's decent moral instincts consistently animated his political leadership. Did that make him a utopian idealist? Yes and no. He gave up Moscow's East European empire without firing a shot and allowed a reunified Germany to remain in NATO—self-inflicted wounds to the Russian national interest, according to his Russian critics. But Gorbachev understood that national interest differently: he imagined building a "common European home" for free European peoples, and a new world order based, as far as possible, on the renunciation of force. In retrospect, that looks impossible to Western "realists" as well as to his Russian detractors. But the world might be better off had it followed his lead. Vladimir Putin has blamed the West for expanding NATO right up to Russia's borders—and used that to justify aggression in Georgia and Ukraine. What if, instead of rejecting Gorbachev's vision as a dream, the West had joined him in creating a new pan-European security structure? It is possible, of course, that Putin or some other Russian leader would have found other reasons to feel aggrieved, and to justify aggression in response, no matter what the West had done. But what looked and still looks utopian to "realists" may have been a last chance that was missed.[5]

As for drastically curbing the use of force in international relations, is that, too, impossible? George W. Bush's Iraq war is now viewed by many as unnecessary and endlessly bloody in its consequences. In contrast, his father's Gulf War to oust Saddam Hussein from Kuwait, which Gorbachev tried so hard to prevent, has been hailed as necessary, swift, and limited. But it certainly didn't feel that way to the thousands of Iraqi soldiers and civilians who were incinerated by overwhelming American military power. Nor was Gorbachev alone in preferring to threaten Iraq out of Kuwait. Plenty of tough-minded American leaders did, too.[6]

Gorbachev's character helps to explain both his successes and his failures. His overconfidence in himself and his cause gave him the courage to reach so high that he overreached—and then warped his judgment when what he was trying to build started to shatter. When the results clashed with his idealized self-image as a great statesman, he too often reacted by denying reality or rationalizing it away—whether it was Eastern Europe's failure to adopt its own version of Gorbachevian perestroika, united Germany's beginning the process of NATO expansion, or the crumbling of his authority at home. Given his historic accomplishments, he could have rested on his laurels, even if they haven't received the recognition they deserve in Russia. Instead, so determined was he to advance his cause and his reputation, even after his fall from power, that he insisted on undertaking a hopeless campaign for president in 1996. Even when his beloved wife could barely keep up, he continued to ignore her pleas to throw off politics and retire to a cottage, whether by the sea or not.

Gorbachev's brave undertaking may have been doomed from the start. But what was the alternative? If the Soviet Union had tried to muddle through without change it might have survived another ten or twenty years. But what then? Would an all-out Yugoslav-type civil war between Russia and Ukraine (playing the bloody roles of Serbia and Croatia, respectively) have made the later, limited conflict between Moscow and Kiev look tame? Would Communists and anti-Communists have settled scores in a bloodbath? Would the masters of the Kremlin have been murdered like the last Russian tsar and his family, or like Romania's Communist leader Nicolai Ceaușescu and his wife? Theoretically, there was another alternative: more rapid economic reforms without political democratization, with the Kremlin gradually privatizing property and buying off Communist apparatchiki by encouraging them to become oligarchs. Sounds a lot like China![7] But, as Gorbachev correctly understood, the Soviet Union wasn't China. Russians and Chinese have radically differing political histories and social traditions.

Another Soviet leader might have refused to make the concessions that Gorbachev made to Reagan and Bush. But if so, the cold war would have continued and even worsened—not the kind of "cold war" that broke out twenty-three years after Gorbachev left office, however nasty it has been, but the real thing, with massive nuclear arsenals still on hair-trigger alerts. Another Soviet leader might have pushed die-hard East European Communist leaders out of office, or prompted East European reformers to seize power. But would either strategy have avoided Communism's eventual collapse? Probably not, given the anti-Communist, anti-Russian sentiment that built up over so many years in East European countries, and the post–Prague Spring generation's thirst not just for "socialism with a human face" but for full Westernization. What if Gorbachev had used force to preserve the Soviet empire? That could have triggered another war in Europe.

The Soviet Union fell apart when Gorbachev weakened the state in an attempt to strengthen the individual. Putin strengthened the Russian state by curtailing individual freedoms. The burgeoning Russian middle class, estimated at 20 percent of the population, has Gorbachev to thank for opening the door to a better life—even if its members have been slow to recognize him as their benefactor. Too many Russians compensated for the sense of worthlessness brought on by the loss of empire with conspicuous consumption and glorification of the state. Will they or their children and grandchildren still feel the same about Gorbachev fifty years from now? Or will they come to appreciate him? Despite his flaws and his failure to achieve all his noble aims, he was a tragic hero who deserves our understanding and admiration.

CENTRAL COMMITTEE The institution within the Communist party that, in theory, directed the party between party congresses. Membership ranged from 28 in 1917 to 332 in 1986. The term also referred to the committee's extensive apparatus, which oversaw the work not only of party committees but of government agencies and enterprises and social organizations throughout the USSR.

CENTRAL COMMITTEE PLENUM The term used to designate plenary meetings of the party Central Committee.

COLLECTIVE FARM Theoretically an agricultural cooperative—i.e., a voluntary union of free peasants—but actually a regimented, state-controlled entity into which peasants were forcibly herded beginning in the late twenties.

CONGRESS OF PEOPLE'S DEPUTIES The new USSR parliament elected in 1989 to replace the old, rubber-stamp legislature, the USSR Supreme Soviet. Counterpart Congresses of People's Deputies were also created in each Soviet republic.

COUNCIL OF MINISTERS The directing agency of the Soviet government, in effect, its cabinet, consisting of the heads of its leading ministries and state committees. Counterpart Councils of Ministers also existed in each of the Soviet republics.

DACHA Summer and holiday residence outside a city.

FULL VERSUS CANDIDATE MEMBERS Both the party Central Committee and the party's ruling Politburo, like the party itself as a whole, had both full and candidate members. The former had full authority to vote at party meetings; the latter had voice but not vote.

GENERAL SECRETARY The supreme leader of the Communist Party of the Soviet Union.

KOLKHOZ Collective farm (see above).

KOMSOMOL Abbreviation of Kommunisticheskii Soiuz Molodezhi, or Young

Communist League (officially: All-Union Leninist Communist League of Youth).

KULAK Well-off peasant.

LOCAL PARTY COMMITTEE The main party body at local levels, such as district, city, province, or region, headed by the local party boss, the first secretary of party committee at that level.

PARTY CONFERENCE Special gatherings, equivalent in size and authority to party congresses, but called to decide urgent and important matters in the interim between congresses.

PARTY CONGRESS The national party congress, supposed to be held at regular five-year intervals, was theoretically the ultimate authority within the Communist party. In effect, real power initially devolved to the Central Committee in the years after 1917 and then to the Politburo and, particularly, its leader, the party's general or first secretary.

POLITBURO The political bureau of the Central Committee of the Communist party, the party's main decision-making body, theoretically only between sessions of the Central Committee, but actually in general. Consisted of fifteen members in March 1985 when it selected Gorbachev as its leader. The Politburo met once a week on Thursdays.

PRESIDENTIAL COUNCIL Advisory body to President Gorbachev created by him in March 1990.

PROCURATOR Soviet official whose duties included the equivalent of those of public prosecutors in the West, but extended more broadly to ensuring observance of law by officials and citizens.

SECRETARIAT Administrative organ of the Central Committee, headed by Central Committee secretaries charged with supervising main areas of Soviet life. Membership partly overlapped with the Politburo.

SOVIET Literally "council," the basic legislative entity at each level of the Soviet system.

STATE COUNCIL Created in September 1991 to be the highest organ of state power, consisting of President Gorbachev and the highest state officials of remaining Soviet republics.

SUPREME SOVIET Until 1989 the highest legislative organ of government in the USSR. The USSR Supreme Soviet was nominally the Soviet parliament. Counterpart Supreme Soviets existed in all Soviet republics. All were, in effect, rubber-stamp bodies. Beginning in 1989 and 1990, the Congresses of People's Deputies at the USSR level and in all republics selected smaller Supreme Soviets to do the regular job of actually legislating between sessions of the larger congresses.

ABBREVIATIONS

BBC	British Broadcasting Company
CC	Central Committee
CIS	Commonwealth of Independent States
Comecon	Council of Mutual Economic Assistance (of Communist States)
CPSU	Communist Party of the Soviet Union
CSCE	Conference on Security and Cooperation in Europe
d.	*delo* (file)
f.	*fond* (collection)
FRG	Federal Republic of Germany
GANISK	Gosudarstvennyi arkhiv noveishei istorii Stavropol'skogo kraia
GARF	Gosudarstvennyi arkhiv Rossiiskoi Federatsii
GATT	General Agreement on Tariffs and Trade
GDR	German Democratic Republic
Gensek	General'nyi secretar' (General Secretary)
GFA	Arkhiv Gorbachev-Fonda
INF	Intermediate nuclear forces
KGB	Komitet Gosudarstvennoi Bezopastnosti
Kompromat	compromising material real or, more likely, false designed to discredit a foe
l.	*list* (page)
ll.	*listy* (pages)
MTS	Machine Tractor Station
MGU	Moskovskii gosudarstvennyi universitet (Moscow State University)
NKVD	Narodnyi Komissariat Vnutrennikh Del
OECD	Organization for Economic Cooperation and Development

op.	*opis* (inventory)
PREM	Prime Minister's Office Files (UK)
PRO	Public Record Office (UK)
NSA	National Security Archive
RCP	Russian Communist Party
READD-RADD	Russian and East European Archival Documents Database
RSFSR	Russian Soviet Federative Socialist Republic
SCUD	Soviet tactical ballistic missiles
SDI	Strategic Defense Initiative
TSAOPIM	Tsentral'nyi arkhiv obshchestvenno-politicheskoui istorii Moskvy
TSRRT	"The Second Russian Revolution" transcript

NOTES

AUTHOR'S NOTE

1 See Archie Brown, *Seven Years That Changed the World: Perestroika in Perspective* (Oxford: Oxford University Press, 2007), x–xiv.

INTRODUCTION: "GORBACHEV IS HARD TO UNDERSTAND"

1 Archie Brown, *The Gorbachev Factor* (Oxford; New York: Oxford University Press, 1996), 309.

2 Dmitrii Furman, "Perestroika glazami Moskovskogo gumanitariia," in V. Kuvaldin, *Proryv k svobode* (Moscow: Al'pina Biznes Buks, 2005), 333.

3 Nikolai Ryzhkov quoted in Archie Brown, *The Myth of the Strong Leader: Political Leadership in the Modern Age* (New York: Basic Books, 2014), 173.

4 Cited in Brown, *Gorbachev Factor*, 88.

5 Cited ibid., 316.

6 See Georgii Shakhnazarov, *S vozhdiami i bez nikh* (Moscow: Vagrius, 2001), 409.

7 Andrei Grachev, *Gorbachev* (Moscow: Vagrius, 2001), 443.

8 Jerrold M. Post, "Psyching Out Gorbachev: The Man Remains a Mystery," *Washington Post*, December 17, 1989.

9 "Twenty Questions to Mikhail Gorbachev on the Eve of His Seventieth Birthday," in *A Millennium Salute to Mikhail Gorbachev on His 70th Birthday* (Moscow: R. Valent, 2001), 10.

10   Olga Belan, "Mnogikh oshibok Gorbachev mog by izbezhat'," *Sobesednik*, November 1992.

11   Olga Kuchkina, "Neuzheli ia dolzna umeret', chtoby zasluzhit' ikh liubov'," *Komsomol'skaia pravda*, October 29, 1999, in *Raisa: Vospominaniia, dnevniki, interv'iu, stat'i, pis'ma, telegrammy* (Moscow: Vagirus/ Petro-n'ius, 2000), 293.

12   "Twenty Questions to Mikhail Gorbachev," 10.

13   I owe this phrase to George Kateb.

14   "Mikhail Gorbachev: Zhenit'sia ia ne sobiraius'," *Komsomol'skaia pravda*, March 2, 2001.

15   See Aron Belkin, "Kto zhe takoi Gorbachev?," *Kul'tura*, October 19, 1991; for a later, fuller version of Belkin's view, see *Vozhdi i prizraki* (Moscow: Olimp, 2001), 176–93; Anatoly Chernyaev's admission that he "agreed with ninety percent" of Belkin's analysis is in Chernyaev's diary, October 20, 1991, entry, in *Sovmestnyi iskhod* (Moscow: Rosspen, 2008), 1002.

16   Jerrold M. Post, "Assessing Leaders at a Distance: The Personality Profile," in *The Psychological Assessment of Political Leaders* (Ann Arbor: University of Michigan Press, 2003), 83.

17   Mikhail Gorbachev, "Slishkom chasto proshchal," *Novaia gazeta*, December 25, 2003, in Karen Karagez'ian and Vladimir Poliakov, eds., *Gorbachev v zhizni* (Moscow: Ves' mir, 2016), 64–65.

18   Aleksandr Iakovlev, *Sumerki* (Moscow: Materik, 2005), 462.

CHAPTER 1: CHILDHOOD, BOYHOOD, AND YOUTH: 1931–1949

1   David Remnick, *Lenin's Tomb: The Last Days of the Soviet Empire* (New York: Random House, 1993), 52.

2   Don P. McAdams et al., "When Bad Things Turn Good and Good Things Turn Bad: Sequences of Redemption and Contamination in Life Narratives and Their Relations to Psychosocial Adaptation in Midlife Adults and Students," *Personality and Social Psychology Bulletin* 27, no. 4 (April 2001): 474–85.

3   Mikhail Gorbachev, *Zhizn' i reformy*, 2 vols. (Moscow: Novosti, 1995), 1:57.

4   Don P. McAdams, *The Person: An Introduction to Personality Psychology* (Fort Worth, TX: Harcourt Brace, 1994), 354–58. Psychologists argue that parenting (and grandparenting in Gorbachev's case) that is both "demanding" and "supportive" tends to produce well-adjusted people with high self-esteem and a developed sense of social responsibility. But also see McAdams on excessive harshness.

5   Mikhail Gorbachev, *Dekabr'-91: Moia pozitsiia* (Moscow: Novosti, 1992), 138.

6   Gorbachev, *Zhizn'*, 1:33.

7   Author's interview with Mikhail Gorbachev, April 19, 2007, Moscow.

8   Ibid.

9   Gorbachev, *Zhizn'*, 1:41.

10   These sources cited by Boris Kuchmaev, *Kommunist s bozhei otmetinoi: Dokumental'no-publitsisticheskii ocherk* (Stavropol, 1992), 17; Nikolai Zenkovich, *Mikhail Gorbachev: Zhizn' do Kremlia* (Moscow: Olma-Press, 2001), 11.

11   Author's interview with Gorbachev, April 19, 2007, Moscow.

12   Mikhail Gorbachev, *Naedine s soboi* (Moscow: Grin strit, 2012), 47.

13   Author's interview with Gorbachev, April 19, 2007, Moscow.

14   Kuchmaev, *Kommunist s bozhei otmetinoi*, 11.

15   Author's interview with Gorbachev, April 19, 2007, Moscow. Also see interview with Gorbachev, "Nado idti po puti svobody," *Eskvair* [the Russian edition of *Esquire*], no. 81, October 2012, in Karagez'ian and Poliakov, *Gorbachev v zhizni*, 583.

16   Author's interview with Gorbachev, April 19, 2007, Moscow.

17   Ibid.

18   Mikhail Gorbachev, *Sobranie sochinenii*, 25 vols. (Moscow: Ves' mir, 2008–15), 8:323.

19   Kuchmaev, *Kommunist s bozhei otmetinoi*, 21.

20   Ibid., 22.

21   Author's interview with Gorbachev, April 19, 2007, Moscow; Oleg Davydov, "Rozdenie Androgina," *Nezavisimaia gazeta*, February 22, 2001.

22   Gorbachev, *Zhizn'*, 1:38.

23   Author's interview with Gorbachev, April 19, 2007, Moscow.

24   Gorbachev, *Naedine s soboi*, 36.

25   Gorbachev, *Zhizn'*, 1:57.

26   Zenkovich, *Mikhail Gorbachev*, 23.

27   Author's interview with A. A. Gonochenko, July 5, 2005, Stavropol.

28   Zenkovich, *Mikhail Gorbachev*, 28.

29   Gorbachev, *Naedine s soboi*, 33.

30   Author's interview with Gorbachev, April 19, 2007, Moscow.

31   Ibid.

32   Zenkovich, *Mikhail Gorbachev*, 19.

33   Author's interview with Gorbachev, April 19, 2007, Moscow.

34   Author's interview with Mikhail Gorbachev, May 2, 2007, Moscow.

35   Olga Kuchkina, "Raisa Gorbacheva: 'Neuzheli,'" in *Raisa: Vospominaniia*, 297.

36   Author's interview with Gorbachev, May 2, 2007, Moscow; Gorbachev, *Naedine s soboi*, 30–31.

37   Kuchkina, "Raisa Gorbacheva," 297.

38   Gorbachev, *Zhizn'*, 1:42.

39   Kuchmaev, *Kommunist s bozhei otmetinoi*, 22.

40   Ibid.

41   See Sheila Fitzpatrick, *Stalin's Peasants: Resistance and Survival in the Russian Village after Collectivization* (New York: Oxford University Press, 1994), 296–312.

42   Gorbachev, *Zhizn'*, 1:38.

43   Ibid., 40.

44   Quoted from a January 3, 1990, conversation with aides, in Gorbachev, *Sobranie sochinenii*, 18:67.

45   Author's interview with sociologist Olga M. Zdravomyslova, executive director of the Gorbachev Foundation, October 18, 2015, Moscow.

46   Gorbachev, *Naedine s soboi*, 34.

47   Gorbachev, *Zhizn'*, 1:45; see also Mikhail Gorbachev, *Memoirs* (New York: Doubleday, 1995), 28.

48   Gorbachev, *Zhizn'*, 1:42.

49   Ibid., 43; Gorbachev, *Memoirs*, 28; Gorbachev, *Naedine s soboi*, 37; Valentina Lezvina, "Razgovor s zemliakom," *Stavropol'skaia pravda*, March 2, 2011, in Karagez'ian and Poliakov, *Gorbachev v zhizni*, 54.

50   Gorbachev, *Naedine s soboi*, 39–40.

51   Ibid., 41.

52   Gorbachev, *Zhizn'*, 1:44.

53   Author's interview with Gorbachev, April 19, 2007, Moscow.

54   Author's interview with Irina Yakovleva (widow of Yegor Yakovlev), May 7, 2007, Moscow.

55   Gorbachev, *Zhizn'*, 1:44; Gorbachev, *Naedine s soboi*, 38.

56   Gorbachev, *Memoirs*, 29.

57   Gorbachev, *Zhizn'*, 1:45.

58   Author's interview with Gorbachev, April 19, 2007, Moscow.

59   Ibid.

60   Gorbachev, *Naedine s soboi*, 44–45.

61   Gorbachev, *Zhizn'*, 1:46–47; author's interview with Gorbachev, April 19, 2007, Moscow.

62   Gorbachev, *Zhizn'*, 1:47–48; Gorbachev, *Memoirs*, 31–32.

63   Author's interview with Gorbachev, April 19, 2007, Moscow.

64   Author's interview with Gorbachev, May 2, 2007, Moscow.

65   Gorbachev, *Naedine s soboi*, 59.

66   Author's interview with Raisa Gudarenko, July 31, 2008, Stavropol.

67   Gorbachev, *Zhizn'*, 1995, 1:49; Gorbachev, *Naedine s soboi*, 49.

68   Author's interview with Gorbachev, April 19, 2007, Moscow.

69   Gorbachev, *Memoirs*, 33–34; Gorbachev, *Zhizn'*, 1:50; Gorbachev, *Naedine s soboi*, 50–52; interview with Mikhail Gorbachev in *Bild*, November 9–10, 2009, in Karagez'ian and Poliakov, *Gorbachev v zhizni*, 77.

70   Lezvina, "Razgovor s zemliakom," 53.

71   Gorbachev, *Zhizn'*, 1:51.

72   Kuchmaev, *Kommunist s bozhei otmetinoi*, 26.

73   Gorbachev, *Zhizn'*, 1:51; Lezvina, "Razgovor s zemliakom," 53.

74   Mikhail Gorbachev and Zdeněk Mlynář, *Conversations with Gorbachev: On Perestroika, the Prague Spring, and the Crossroads of Socialism*, trans. George Shriver (New York: Columbia University Press, 2002), 15.

75   Gorbachev, *Zhizn'*, 1:51.

76   Kuchmaev, *Kommunist s bozhei otmetinoi*, 27.

77   Ibid., 30.

78   Grachev, *Gorbachev*, 310; *Neokonchennaia istoriia: Tri tsveta vremeni* (Moscow: Mezhdunarodnye otnosheniia, 2005), 12; Gorbachev's talk at George Mason University, March 25, 2009.

79   Gorbachev, *Zhizn'*, 1:52.

80   Ibid.

81   Brown, *Gorbachev Factor*, 26–27; Zenkovich, *Mikhail Gorbachev*, 35.

82   Zenkovich, *Mikhail Gorbachev*, 35; Lezvina, "Razgovor s zemliakom," 53.

83   Author's interview with former Gorbachev classmate, name unknown, July 6, 2005, Krasnogvardeisk, Russia.

84   Kuchmaev, *Kommunist s bozhei otmetinoi*, 32.

85   *Neokonchennaia istoriia*, 12.

86   Remnick, *Lenin's Tomb*, 156.

87   Gorbachev, *Zhizn'*, 1:53.

88   Remnick, *Lenin's Tomb*, 156.

89   Gorbachev, *Zhizn'*, 1:53.

90   Ibid., 54.

91   Ibid.

92   Zenkovich, *Mikhail Gorbachev*, 43.

93   Gorbachev, *Zhizn'*, 1:53, 55.

94   Ibid., 55.

95   Remnick, *Lenin's Tomb*, 152.

96   Kuchmaev, *Kommunist s bozhei otmetinoi*, 30–31.

97   Gorbachev, *Zhizn'*, 1:56.

98   Zenkovich, *Mikhail Gorbachev*, 43–44.

99   Remnick, *Lenin's Tomb*, 157; also see Ruslan Kozlov's interview with Karagodina in "Ia zashchishchaiu nashu iunost'," *Sobesednik*, 1991, no. 21.

100   Zenkovich, *Mikhail Gorbachev*, 38–39; Remnick, *Lenin's Tomb*, 157.

101   Zenkovich, *Mikhail Gorbachev*, 39–40.

102   Remnick, *Lenin's Tomb*, 156, 158; Kuchmaev, *Kommunist s bozhei otmetinoi*, 34.

103   Zenkovich, *Mikhail Gorbachev*, 44.

CHAPTER 2: MOSCOW STATE UNIVERSITY: 1950-1955

1   Gorbachev, *Memoirs*, 41; Gorbachev, *Zhizn'*, 1:59.

2   See Vladislav Zubok, *Zhivago's Children: The Last Russian Intelligentsia* (Cambridge, MA: Belknap Press of Harvard University Press, 2009), 22-24.

3   Gorbachev, *Zhizn'*, 1:59; author's interviews with Gorbachev, April 19 and May 2, 2007, Moscow.

4   Author's interviews with Gorbachev, April 19 and May 2, 2007, Moscow.

5   Ibid.

6   Author's interview with Gorbachev, November 14, 2011, Moscow.

7   Author's interviews with Gorbachev, April 19 and May 2, 2007, Moscow.

8   Gorbachev, *Naedine s soboi*, 67.

9   "Molotovkskii raion VKLSM—Delo po priemu kandidatom v chleny VKP(b) Gorbacheva, M. S.," in Gosudarstvennyi arkhiv noveishei istorii Stavropol'skogo kraia (GANISK), f. 34, o. 3, khran. 647.

10 Author's interview with Gorbachev, April 19, 2007, Moscow.

11 Gorbachev, *Naedine s soboi*, 67.

12 Gorbachev, *Zhizn'*, 1:60; Gorbachev, *Naedine s soboi*, 69.

13 See Lewis Feuer, ed., *Marx and Engels: Basic Writing on Politics and Philosophy* (Garden City, NY: Anchor Books, 1959), 11, 18.

14 Author's interview with Dmitry Golovanov, July 29, 2006, Moscow.

15 Author's interview with Zoya Bekova, August 1, 2006, Moscow.

16 Author's interview with Golovanov, July 29, 2006, Moscow.

17 Author's interview with Nadezhda Mikhaleva, August 11, 2008, Moscow.

18 Rudolf Kolchanov, "Ot Stromynki do Mokhovoi," in Karagez'ian and Poliakov, *Gorbachev v zhizni*, 86.

19 Gorbachev, *Zhizn'*, 1:75-76; Gorbachev, *Memoirs*, 55.

20 Elena Zubkova, *Russia after the War: Hopes, Illusions and Disappointments, 1945-1957*, trans. Hugh Ragsdale (Armonk, NY: M. E. Sharpe, 1998), 138.

21 Gorbachev, *Zhizn'*, 1:62.

22 Zubok, *Zhivago's Children*, 30, 33-34.

23 Author's interview with Gorbachev, April 19, 2007, Moscow.

24 Marina Shakina, "'V 1991 godu ia byl slishkom samouveren,'" *Nezavisimaia gazeta*, December 12, 1995.

25 Gail Sheehy, *The Man Who Changed the World: The Lives of Mikhail S. Gorbachev* (New York: HarperCollins, 1990), 63.

26 "Protokol obshchego sobraniia partorganizatsii iuridicheskogo fakul'teta MGU, marta 1953," in Tsentral'nyi arkhiv obshchestvenno-politicheskoi istorii Moskvy (TSAOPIM), f. 487, o. 1 (3), d. 488 (191), l. 29.

27   Author's interview with Gorbachev, May 2, 2007, Moscow.

28   Author's interview with Galina Daniushevskaya, March 2007, Moscow.

29   Gorbachev recalled this at the Harvard Kennedy School Forum on December 3, 2007.

30   Gorbachev, *Zhizn'*, 1:62–63; Gorbachev, *Memoirs*, 44–45; author's interview with Gorbachev, May 2, 2007, Moscow.

31   Gorbachev, *Zhizn'*, 1:61; Gorbachev, *Naedine s soboi*, 84.

32   Sheehy, *Man Who Changed the World*, 66.

33   Author's interview with Bekova, August 1, 2006, Moscow.

34   Sheehy, *Man Who Changed the World*, 68–70.

35   Gorbachev, *Zhizn'*, 1:68.

36   Zubok, *Zhivago's Children*, 35.

37   Raisa M. Gorbacheva, *Ia nadeius'* (Moscow: Novosti, 1991), 51–52; author's interview with Gorbachev, May 2, 2007, Moscow.

38   Zdeněk Mlynář, *Nightfrost in Prague: The End of Humane Socialism*, trans. Paul Wilson (New York: Karz, 1980), 20.

39   Nina Mamardashvili's recollections in *Raisa Gorbacheva: Shtrikhi k portretu* (Moscow: Gorbachev-Fond, 2009), 24.

40   Author's interview with Golovanov, July 29, 2006, Moscow.

41   Zubok, *Zhivago's Children*, 35.

42   Gorbachev, *Zhizn'*, 1:60; Gorbachev, *Memoirs*, 42; Kolchanov, "Ot Stromynki do Mokhovoi," 86.

43   Sheehy, *Man Who Changed the World*, 66.

44   N. M. Rimashevskaia, "Pod zvuki vnutrennogo golosa," *Narodoselenie*, no. 1 (2006).

45   Sheehy, *Man Who Changed the World*, 70.

46   Kolchanov, "Ot Stromynki do Mokhovoi," 86.

47   Gorbachev, *Zhizn'*, 1:62, 64; Sheehy, *Man Who Changed the World*, 71.

48   Sheehy, *Man Who Changed the World*, 70.

49   Ibid., 75.

50   Author's interview with Gorbachev, May 2, 2007, Moscow.

51   Grachev, *Gorbachev*, 22.

52   Sheehy, *Man Who Changed the World*, 76–77.

53   Grachev, *Gorbachev*, 22.

54   Author's interview with Golovanov, July 29, 2006, Moscow.

55   Zdeněk Mlynář, "Il mio compagno di studi Mikhail Gorbachev," *L'Unità*, 1985, trans. in Kevin Devlin, "Some Views of the Gorbachev Era," RAD Background Report (Radio Free Europe Research, 1985).

56   Mlynář, *Nightfrost in Prague*, 1, 5, 8–9.

57   Ibid., 10–14, 19–20.

58   Sheehy, *Man Who Changed the World*, 72.

59   Gorbachev and Mlynář, *Conversations with Gorbachev*, 17.

60   Sheehy, *Man Who Changed the World*, 73–74.

61   Ibid., 66–67, 75–77.

62   Gorbachev and Mlynář, *Conversations with Gorbachev*, 21.

63   Mlynář, *Nightfrost in Prague*, 25–26.

64   Gorbachev, *Zhizn'*, 1:66.

65   Ibid., 66–67; Mlynář, *Nightfrost in Prague*, 27.

66   Gorbachev, *Zhizn'*, 1:68; Mikhail Gorbachev, "My prosto byli drug dlia druga. Vsiu zhizn'," *Obshchaia gazeta*, November 29, 1999.

67   Mamardashvili recollections in *Raisa Gorbacheva: Shtrikhi*, 18–39.

68   Gorbachev, *Naedine s soboi*, 93.

69   Gorbachev, "My prosto byli drug dlia druga. Vsiu zhizn'."

70   Gorbachev, *Naedine s soboi*, 94.

71   Ibid., 95; also see Gorbachev, "My prosto byli drug dlia druga. Vsiu zhizn'."

72   Gorbachev, *Zhizn'*, 1:67–70; Gorbachev, *Naedine s soboi*, 95–99.

73   Gorbachev, *Naedine s soboi*, 99; Maria Fedorina, "Slezy pervoi ledi," *Moskovskii komsomolets*, February 14, 1998.

74   *Raisa Gorbacheva: Shtrikhi*, 37–38.

75   Author's interview with Gorbachev, May 2, 2007, Moscow.

76   Raisa Gorbachev, *I Hope* (New York: HarperCollins, 1991), 11–19.

77   Irina Bobrova, "Posledniaia ledi SSSR," in *Raisa: Vospominaniia*, 284.

78   R. Gorbachev, *I Hope*, 21.

79   Ibid., 22, 46–47; also see Bobrova, "Posledniaia ledi," 285.

80   Grachev, *Gorbachev*, 26.

81   Sheehy, *Man Who Changed the World*, 78.

82   Grachev, *Gorbachev*, 26.

83   As Raisa later told her husband, the physics majors' rooms in the dorm were by far the messiest, filled with dirt and dust, and almost everyone's pants had holes. But the physicists were also the wittiest, posting signs informing the inspectors, "Dirt kills germs," and identifying the dust as "cosmic dust." Author's interview with Gorbachev, May 2, 2007, Moscow.

84   Sheehy, *Man Who Changed the World*, 78.

85   E. Kiselev, "Nashe vse: Programma o vydaiushchikhsia liudiakh Rossii za poslednie sto let. Raisa Gorbacheva," n.d., http://www.gorby.ru/rubrs.asp?art_id=25650&rubr_id=21&page=1.

86   R. Gorbachev, *I Hope*, 53.

87   Sheehy, *Man Who Changed the World*, 80.

88   Ibid.

89   Katrina vanden Heuvel and Stephen F. Cohen, "Gorbachev on 1989," *Nation*, October 28, 2009, http://www.thenation.com/article/gorbachev-1989.

90   Grachev, *Gorbachev*, 29.

91   "Slovo o Dzheffersone," *Nezavisimaia gazeta*, April 15, 1993.

92   Sheehy, *Man Who Changed the World*, 81.

93   R. Gorbachev, *I Hope*, 57–58.

94   Grachev, *Gorbachev*, 28–29.

95   Author's interview with Mikhaleva, August 11, 2008, Moscow.

96   Gorbachev, *Zhizn'*, 1:70.

97   R. Gorbachev, *I Hope*, 61–62.

98   Gorbachev, *Naedine s soboi*, 103–4.

99   Gorbachev, *Zhizn'*, 1:71; Gorbachev, *Naedine s soboi*, 104.

100 Grachev, *Gorbachev*, 30–31. Author's interview with Gorbachev, May 2, 2007, Moscow. Ten years after Gorbachev graduated from MGU's law school, the author spent 1965–1966 enrolled there as an American exchange student. I lived in the same Zone V where Gorbachev did, but when I asked him what his block number was (mine was 1715), he didn't recall.

101 R. Gorbachev, *I Hope*, 69. In retrospect, Mikhail Gorbachev dismisses his thesis as mostly an "apologia. I rewrote what others had already written, as everyone did, although I did read materials, a little even from bourgeois works, in the library, and I gathered other material at the Kiev District local soviet, where I studied the work of standing commissions and session." Interestingly enough, the research topic that I listed when I was at the MGU law school in 1965–1966 was almost exactly the same as Gorbachev's. I, too, knew that the "mass participation" in question was hardly at all what it was advertised to be in Soviet propaganda, but chose the theme as one likely to be acceptable to Soviet authorities.

102 Gorbachev, *Naedine s soboi*, 105; see also Bobrova, "Posledniaia ledi," 286.

103 Gorbachev, *Naedine s soboi*, 106–8.

104 Ibid., 114; also see Bobrova, "Posledniaia ledi," 287–88.

105 Gorbachev, *Zhizn'*, 1:75; author's interview with Gorbachev, April 19, 2007, Moscow.

106 Gorbachev, *Zhizn'*, 1:72–73.

107 R. Gorbachev, *I Hope*, 66–67.

108 Author's interview with Gorbachev, May 2, 2007, Moscow.

109 Gorbachev, *Zhizn'*, 1:74.

110 Grachev, *Gorbachev*, 32.

111 Gorbachev, *Zhizn'*, 1:74; Gorbachev, *Memoirs*, 53.

112 Author's interview with Gorbachev, May 2, 2007, Moscow.

113 Grachev, *Gorbachev*, 32.

114 Gorbachev, *Zhizn'*, 1:74–75.

115 Ibid., 75.

116 R. Gorbachev, *I Hope*, 70, 75.

117 Ibid., 70.

118   Ibid., 70–71.

119   Gorbachev, *Memoirs*, 51.

CHAPTER 3: CLIMBING THE LADDER: 1955–1968

1   R. Gorbachev, *I Hope*, 81.

2   Gorbachev, *Zhizn'*, 1:79; Kuchmaev, *Kommunist s bozhei otmetinoi*, 38.

3   Gorbachev, *Naedine s soboi*, 120.

4   Kuchmaev, *Kommunist s bozhei otmetinoi*, 39; Gorbachev, *Zhizn'*, 1:77–78. During the late 1980s, when Gorbachev ruled the Kremlin, Petukhov sent him a note saying how glad he was not to have blocked the way in 1955.

5   Kuchmaev, *Kommunist s bozhei otmetinoi*, 39.

6   Ibid., 40.

7   Author's interview with Gorbachev, May 4, 2007, Moscow.

8   Grachev, *Gorbachev*, 37–38.

9   R. Gorbachev, *I Hope*, 77.

10   Gorbachev, *Zhizn'*, 1:78; Gorbachev, "My prosto byli drug dlia druga. Vsiu zhizn'."

11   R. Gorbachev, *I Hope*, 78.

12   Ibid., 76–77.

13   Gorbachev, *Memoirs*, 56–57.

14   Gorbachev, *Zhizn'*, 1:78.

15   Ibid., 1:78–79; author's interview with Gorbachev, May 2, 2007, Moscow; also see Gorbachev, "My prosto byli drug dlia druga. Vsiu zhizn'."

16   R. Gorbachev, *I Hope*, 84; Gorbachev, *Naedine s soboi*, 119.

17   Gorbacheva, *Ia nadeius'*, 76–77; R. Gorbachev, *I Hope*, 78.

18   Grachev, *Gorbachev*, 35.

19   R. Gorbachev, *I Hope*, 79–80; Gorbacheva, *Ia nadeius'*, 78.

20   R. Gorbachev, *I Hope*, 88–91.

21   Author's interview with Liubov Dolinskaya, August 7, 2008, Stavropol.

22   Author's interview with Gorbachev, May 2, 2007, Moscow.

23   Gorbachev, "My prosto byli drug dlia druga. Vsiu zhizn'."

24   Author's interview with Lydia Budyka, August 3, 2008, Stavropol.

25   Gorbachev, *Naedine s soboi*, 136.

26   Author's interview with Irina Gorbacheva, March 18, 2010, Moscow.

27   Author's interview with Gorbachev, May 2, 2007, Moscow. Gorbachev, *Naedine s soboi*, 138.

28   See Orlando Figes, *The Whisperers: Private Life in Stalin's Russia* (New York: Metropolitan Books, 2007), 174–86.

29   R. Gorbachev, *I Hope*, 85–86.

30   Ibid., 85 (emphasis added).

31   Author's interview with Budkya, August 3, 2008, Stavropol; author's interview with Irina Gorbacheva, March 18, 2010, Moscow.

32   R. Gorbachev, *I Hope*, 77.

33   Zubok, *Zhivago's Children*, 67–70. This section draws widely on this book.

34   Brown, *Gorbachev Factor*, 339–40, see n. 51.

35   Andrei Grachev, *Gibel' Sovetskogo "titanika": Sudovoi zhurnal* (Moscow, 2015), 82.

36   Nikolai Shmelev, *Pashkov dom: Kartinki iz zhizni* (Moscow: Interdialekt, 2001), 259.

37   Aleksandr Bovin, *XX vek kak zhizn': vospominaniia* (Moscow: Zakharov, 2003), 189.

38   Cited in Grachev, *Gibel' Sovetskogo "titanika,"* 100.

39   Zubok, *Zhivago's Children*, 484.

40   GANISK, f. 63, o. 2, d. 1102.

41   GANISK, f. 52, o. 81, ed. khran 586, ll. 24–28.

42   Gorbachev, *Zhizn'*, 1:81; Gorbachev, *Memoirs*, 59.

43   Gorbachev, *Memoirs*, 60; Gorbachev, *Naedine s soboi*, 123.

44   Gorbachev, *Zhizn'*, 1:81.

45   Quoted in Brown, *Gorbachev Factor*, 39.

46   Gorbachev, *Memoirs*, 61.

47   Ibid., 62.

48   GANISK, f. 63, op. 2, ed. khran 1011, ll. 48, 53.

49   Gorbachev, *Zhizn'*, 1:84; Gorbachev, *Memoirs*, 62; Gorbachev, *Naedine s soboi*, 127.

50   Gorbachev, *Memoirs*, 63; Gorbachev, *Zhizn'*, 1:85.

51   GANISK, f. 63, op. 2, ed. khran. 1315, l. 53.

52   Gerd Ruge, *Gorbachev: A Biography* (London: Chatto & Windus, 1991), 55, cited in Brown, *Gorbachev Factor*, 41.

53   GANISK, f. 52, op. 81, ed. khran. 538, ll. 32, 35.

54   Gorbachev, *Memoirs*, 63–64; Gorbachev, *Zhizn'*, 1:86–87.

55   Gorbachev, *Memoirs*, 64–65.

56   Kuchmaev, *Kommunist s bozhei otmetinoi*, 42.

57   Grachev, *Gorbachev*, 34–35; Kuchmaev, *Kommunist s bozhei otmetinoi*, 44.

58   Kuchmaev, *Kommunist s bozhei otmetinoi*, 44.

59   Gorbacheva, *Ia nadeius'*, 103–4.

60   Gorbachev, *Zhizn'*, 1:90.

61   Author's interview with Nikolai Yeriomin, July 5, 2005, Stavropol.

62   Author's interview with Raisa Bazikova, July 4, 2005, Stavropol.

63   Author's interview with V. V. Kalyagin (and with A. A. Gonochenko), July 5, 2005, Stavropol.

64   Author's interview with A. A. Gonochenko (and with Kalyagin), July 5, 2005, Stavropol.

65   Author's interview with Kalyagin (and with Gonochenko), July 5, 2005, Stavropol.

66   Viktor Kaznacheev, *Intriga—velikoe delo* (Stavropol: Knizhnoe izda-
      telstvo, 1997), 7, 12–13; Kaznacheev, *Na perekrestkakh sud'by*, 28, 32.
67   Kaznacheev, *Na perekrestkakh sud'by*, 52–54.
68   Author's interview with Gorbachev, May 2, 2007, Moscow.
69   Vitalii Mikhailenko, *Kakim ty byl . . .* (Nalchik: Izdatelskii tsentr El'-
      Fa, 1997), 49.
70   Kuchmaev, *Kommunist s bozhei otmetinoi*, 55–56.
71   Gorbachev, *Naedine s soboi*, 150–51.
72   Grachev, *Gorbachev*, 36–37.
73   Gorbachev, *Naedine s soboi*, 150.
74   Stavropol region Komsomol conference, January 16–17, 1962,
      GANISK, f. 63, op 2, ed. khran. 1385, ll. 198–204.
75   Gorbachev, *Zhizn'*, 1:100–101, 106.
76   Hotel administrators claimed Gorbachev had no right to move in since
      he had a temporary residence permit, but he appealed to the Ukrai-
      nian Komsomol leader. See Gorbachev, *Naedine s soboi*, 142–43.
77   Ibid., 152–53.
78   Compare Gorbachev, *Zhizn'*, 1:109; Leonid Yefremov, *Renegat Gor-
      bachev—Al'ians dvurushnikov—iadovitaia chasha Iakovleva* (Stavropol:
      Izdatelstvo Gosudarstvennogo arkhiva Stavropolskogo kraia "Kres-
      tograd," 1996), 242.
79   Kuchmaev, *Kommunist s bozhei otmetinoi*, 63–67.
80   Gorbachev, *Naedine s soboi*, 164–65. Note that although Gorbachev's
      description of his telephone conversations with Kulakov and Yefre-
      mov's reaction to them do not appear in the published Russian version
      of this book, they do in an authorized English translation provided to
      the author by one of Gorbachev's aides.
81   Gorbachev, *Zhizn'*, 1:103–5.
82   Gorbachev, *Naedine s soboi*, 161; Kuchkina, "Posledniaia ledi," 292–93;
      also see Gorbacheva, *Ia nadeius'*, 113.
83   Author's interview with Olga Zdravomyslova, April 2, 2007, Moscow.
84   R. Gorbachev, *I Hope*, 94–99.
85   Gorbachev, *Naedine s soboi*, 173–74.
86   For example, Raisa found in one village that in addition to 2,350 fam-
      ilies living there, some 590 people lived alone. What also makes the
      dissertation impressive is its empirical nature, with statistical tables
      backing up its conclusions. Raisa M. Gorbacheva, "Formirovanie
      novykh chert byta kolkhoznogo krest'ianstva (po materialam sotsio-
      logicheskikh issledovanii v Stavropol'skom krae: Avtoreferat disser-
      tatsii kandidata filosofskikh nauk," Moskva—1967.
87   Author's interview with Gorbachev, May 2, 2007, Moscow.
88   Ibid.; Gorbachev, *Naedine s soboi*, 178; Zoia Eroshok, "Irina
      Virganskaia-Gorbacheva: O roditeliakh i semeinykh tsennostiakh,"

Novaia gazeta, February 25, 2011, in Karagez'ian and Poliakov, *Gorbachev v zhizni*, 113.

89   Brown, *Gorbachev Factor*, 43. See Lezvina, "Razgovor s zemliakom," in Karagez'ian and Poliakov, *Gorbachev v zhizni*, 55.

90   Author's interview with Gorbachev, May 2, 2007, Moscow.

91   Gorbachev, *Naedine s soboi*, 178, with some additional information in the English translation only.

92   Gorbachev, *Zhizn'*, 1:117–18.

93   Gorbachev and Mlynář, *Conversations with Gorbachev*, 29–30.

94   Ibid., 2, 63.

95   Ibid., 30.

96   Gosudarstvennyi arkhiv Rossiiskoi Federatsii (GARF) f. M-1, op. 19 (1), d. 425, l. 11.

97   Author's interview with Budyka, August 3, 2008, Stavropol.

98   Author's interview with Gorbachev, May 4, 2007, Moscow.

99   Gorbachev, *Zhizn'*, 1:112–13.

100 Ibid., 119. Author's interview with Gorbachev, May 4, 2007, Moscow.

101 Meeting of the Second Stavropol regional party aktiv, July 19, 1968, GANISK, f. 1, op. 27, d. 28, ll. 50–51.

102 Gorbachev, *Naedine s soboi*, 165.

103 Gorbachev, "My prosto byli drug dlia druga. Vsiu zhizn'."

CHAPTER 4: REGIONAL PARTY BOSS: 1969–1978

1   Grachev, *Gorbachev*, 40.

2   Mikhailenko, *Kakim ty byl*, 50.

3   Gorbachev, *Zhizn'*, 1:121.

4   Author's interview with Gorbachev, May 4, 2007, Moscow.

5   Gorbachev, *Zhizn'*, 1:147–48.

6   Ibid., 123; see also Evgenii Chazov, *Zdorov'e i vlast'* (Moscow: Novosti, 1992), 11.

7   Grachev, *Gibel' Sovetskogo "titanika,"* 102–3.

8   Gorbachev, *Naedine s soboi*, 182.

9   Grachev, *Gorbachev*, 41.

10   GANISK, f. 1, op. 27, d. 28.

11   Record of Session of Stavropol Regional Committee Bureau, ibid., d. 76, korobka 5.

12   Gorbachev, *Zhizn'*, 1:119.

13   Author's interview with Gorbachev, May 4, 2007, Moscow.

14   Gorbachev, *Zhizn'*, 1:119.

15   Kuchmaev, *Kommunist s bozhei otmetinoi*, 194.

16   GANISK, f. 1, op. 32, d. 36, ll. 75–78, 82.

17   Gorbachev, *Zhizn'*, 1:119–20; Gorbachev, *Memoirs*, 83. On Sadykov's life

and work, see Rustem Vakhitov, "The Life and Work of F. B. Sadykov," http://nevmenandr.net/vaxitov/sadykov.php.

18   Kozlov, "Ia zashchishchaiu nashu iunost'."

19   Shakhnazarov, *S vozhdiami i bez nikh*, 406.

20   Gorbachev, *Zhizn'*, 1:122.

21   Author's interview with Gorbachev, May 4, 2007, Moscow.

22   Gorbachev, *Zhizn'*, 1:142–45; Gorbachev, *Memoirs*, 93–95.

23   Ibid.

24   Stavropol regional party committee plenum, October 6, 1970, GANISK, f. 1, op. 34, d. 5, l. 5.

25   Stavropol regional party committee aktiv, June 8, 1977, ibid., op. 44, d. 56, ll. 6–7.

26   Transcript of eighteenth Stavropol regional party conference, 2/19–20/71, ibid., op. 35, d. 2, ll. 46, 56.

27   Quoted in Brown, *Gorbachev Factor*, 47.

28   Gorbachev, *Memoirs*, 88–89.

29   Mikhailenko, *Kakim ty byl*, 77.

30   Gorbachev, *Memoirs*, 90.

31   Gorbachev, *Zhizn'*, 1:126–27.

32   Gorbachev, *Naedine s soboi*, 192.

33   Kuchmaev, *Kommunist s bozhei otmetinoi*, 89, 106–7, 111.

34   Gorbachev, *Naedine s soboi*, 194.

35   Gorbachev, *Zhizn'*, 1:131–32.

36   Kuchmaev, *Kommunist s bozhei otmetinoi*, 101–6.

37   This section relies on Zhores Medvedev, *Gorbachev* (New York: W. W. Norton, 1986), 81–87.

38   Author's interview with Kalyagin (and with Gonochenko), July 5, 2005, Stavropol.

39   V. Pankratov, "Upravliaia zhatvoi: Rasskazyvaem ob opyte stavropol'skikh zemledel'tsev," *Pravda*, July 17, 1977.

40   "Vstrecha piataia," *Zhurnalist*, no. 12 (1991).

41   The scene is shown in the first program, "Enter Gorbachev," in the eight-part BBC documentary film series, directed by Mark Anderson, *The Second Russian Revolution*, VHS, 8 vols. (Northbrook, IL: Coronet Flim & Video, 1991).

42   Medvedev, *Gorbachev*, 82, 85.

43   Kuchmaev, *Kommunist s bozhei otmetinoi*, 138.

44   Brown, *Gorbachev Factor*, 45.

45   Gorbachev, *Sobranie sochinenii*, 1:183–205.

46   Gorbachev, *Naedine s soboi*, 217.

47   Grachev, *Gorbachev*, 42.

48   Author's interview with Ivan Zubenko, July 7, 2005, Stavropol.

49   Author's interview with Kalyagin (and with Gonochenko), July 5, 2005, Stavropol.

50 Quoted in Zenkovich, *Mikhail Gorbachev*, 166–68, 170, 177–79, 181–83.

51 Kuchmaev, *Kommunist s bozhei otmetinoi*, 121, 165.

52 Quoted in Zenkovich, *Mikhail Gorbachev*, 165, 173, 184.

53 Cited ibid., 171, 181–82, 229–30, 271, 274; A. A. Korobeinikov, *Gorbachev: Drugoe litso* (Moscow: "Respublika," 1996).

54 Author's interviews with Ivan Zubenko, July 7, 2005, August 1, 2008, Stavropol.

55 Grigory Gorlov, quoted in Zenkovich, *Mikhail Gorbachev*, 158.

56 Author's interview with Nikolai Paltsev, July 5, 2005, Stavropol.

57 Author's interview with Vitaly Mikhailenko, July 8, 2005, Zheleznovodsk; Mikhailenko, *Kakim ty byl*, 71–72.

58 Author's interview with Mikhailenko, July 8, 2005, Zheleznovodsk.

59 Ibid.

60 Ibid.; Mikhailenko, *Kakim ty byl*, 81.

61 Ibid., 79–80.

62 Ibid., 83–85.

63 Kuchmaev, *Kommunist s bozhei otmetinoi*, 198.

64 Gorbachev, *Zhizn'*, 1:148; Gorbachev, *Memoirs*, 95–96.

65 Gorbachev, *Naedine s soboi*, 210.

66 Author's interview with Gorbachev, May 4, 2007, Moscow.

67 Roi Medvedev, *Andropov* (Moscow: Molodia Gvardiia, 2006), 24.

68 Georgii Arbatov, *Moia epokha v litsakh i sobytiiakh* (Moscow: Sobranie, 2008), 40.

69 Author's interview with Oleg Bogomolov, April 11, 2007, Moscow.

70 R. Medvedev, *Andropov*, 77.

71 Arbatov, *Moia epokha v litsakh i sobytiiakh*, 44–45; Medvedev, *Andropov*, 77–79; see Fyodor Burlatsky, *Russkie gosudari—epokha reformatsii* (Moscow: Firma "SHARK," 1996).

72 Chazov, *Zdorov'e i vlast'*, 73–75, 115–17, 125–32.

73 Iu. Krasin, cited in Medvedev, *Andropov*, 142.

74 William Taubman, *Khrushchev* (New York: W. W. Norton, 2003), 296–97.

75 Arbatov, *Moia epokha v litsakh i sobytiiakh*, 52–54.

76 R. Medvedev, *Andropov*, 56–57; Arbatov, *Moia epokha v litsakh i sobytiiakh*, 54.

77 Pikhoia, *Sovestskii Soiuz*, 275.

78 Sakharov described his 1967 and August 1968 phone conversations with Andropov in his memoirs, *Vospominaniia: V dvukh tomakh*, vol. 1 (Moscow: Prava cheloveka, 1996), 382–83, 407; on Andropov's meetings with Pyotr Yakir and V. Krasin, see Roi Medvedev, *Neizvestnyi Andropov: Politicheskaia biografia Iuriia Andropova* (Moscow: Prava cheloveka, 1999), 128–30; Andropov initially had a good reputation among intellectuals because he met with many of the liberals, such as Taganka theater director Yuri Lyubimov and poets Yevgeny Yevtushenko and Andrei Voznesensky; see ibid., 89–90.

79   R. Medvedev, *Andropov*, 76.

80   R. Medvedev, *Neizvestnyi Andropov*, 187.

81   Chazov, *Zdorov'e i vlast'*, 76–79.

82   Gorbachev, *Naedine s soboi*, 211.

83   Gorbachev, *Zhizn'*, 1:148–52; Gorbachev, *Naedine s soboi*, 212.

84   Zenkovich, *Mikhail Gorbachev*, 200.

85   Ibid., 179.

86   Author's interview with Gorbachev, May 4, 2007, Moscow.

87   Gorbachev, *Zhizn'*, 1:159–60.

88   Author's interview with Gorbachev, May 4, 2007, Moscow.

89   Grachev, *Gorbachev*, 51.

90   Anatoly Chernyaev, *My Six Years with Gorbachev*, trans. and ed. Robert D. English and Elizabeth Tucker (University Park: Pennsylvania State University Press, 2000), 4.

91   Author's interview with Gorbachev, May 4, 2007, Moscow.

92   Gusenkov's recollections in *Raisa Gorbacheva: Shtrikhi*, 106.

93   Author's interview with Gorbachev, May 4, 2007, Moscow.

94   Gorbachev, *Zhizn'*, 1:167–68.

95   Ibid., 169.

96   Author's interview with Kalyagin (and with Gononchenko), July 5, 2005, Stavropol.

97   Author's interview with Budyka, August 3, 2008, Stavropol.

98   Gorbachev, *Zhizn'*, 1:169–70.

99   Gorbachev, "My prosto byli drug dlia druga. Vsiu zhizn'."; Natalia Kraminova, "Mama," *Obshchaia gazeta*, September 21, 2000; Kuchkina, "Raisa Gorbacheva: 'Neuzheli,'" 66, in *Raisa: Vospominaniia*, 294.

100 R. Gorbachev, *I Hope*, 109, 112.

101 Author's interview with Gononchenko (and with Kalyagin), July 5, 2005, Stavropol.

102 R. Gorbachev, *I Hope*, 109–10.

103 Author's interview with Irina Gorbacheva, March 18, 2010, Moscow.

104 R. Gorbachev, *I Hope*, 109–10.

105 Author's interview with Irina Gorbacheva, March 18, 2010, Moscow; Zoya Eroshok, "Irina Virganskaia-Gorbacheva: O roditeliakh I semeinykh tsennostiakh," *Novaia gazeta*, February 25, 2011, in Karagez'ian and Poliakov, *Gorbachev v zhizni*, 113.

106 Grachev, *Gorbachev*, 43.

107 Eroshok, "Irina Virganskaia-Gorbacheva," 114.

108 Kuchmaev, *Kommunist s bozhei otmetinoi*, 195; also see Kraminova, "Mama."

109 Author's interview with Irina Gorbacheva, March 18, 2010, Moscow.

110 Author's interview with Budyka, August 3, 2008, Stavropol.

111 R. Gorbachev, *I Hope*, 105.

112　Grachev, *Gorbachev*, 43–44; Kuchkina, "Raisa Gorbacheva: 'Neuzheli,'" in *Raisa: Vospominaniia*, 294.

113　R. Gorbachev, *I Hope*, 105–6.

114　Kuchmaev, *Kommunist s bozhei otmetinoi*, 195, quoting Iu. Kucherenko, deputy head of education department.

115　Ibid., 196.

116　Ibid., 197.

117　Eroshok, "Irina Virganskaia-Gorbacheva," 114; R. Gorbachev, *I Hope*, 116–20.

CHAPTER 5: RETURN TO MOSCOW: 1978–1985

1　Gorbachev, *Memoirs*, 3–5; Gorbachev, *Naedine s soboi*, 255.

2　Gorbachev, *Memoirs*, 6–9.

3　Gorbachev, *Zhizn'*, 1:22.

4　Gorbachev, *Memoirs*, 11–13.

5　Ibid.; Grachev, *Gorbachev*, 67–68; Gorbachev, *Naedine s soboi*, 329–30.

6　Gorbachev, *Memoirs*, 14–15.

7　Gorbachev, *Dekabr'-91*, 139–40, 148.

8　Vadim Medvedev, *V kommande Gorbacheva* (Moscow: Bylina, 1994), 16.

9　Grachev, *Gorbachev*, 55.

10　Gorbachev, *Zhizn'*, 1:171.

11　Grachev, *Gorbachev*, 56.

12　Gorbachev, *Zhizn'*, 1:170–75.

13　Author's interview with Budyka, August 3, 2008, Stavropol.

14　Gorbachev, *Naedine s soboi*, 258–59.

15　Gorbachev, *Zhizn'*, 1:176–77.

16　Gorbachev, *Naedine s soboi*, 259.

17　Ibid., 260.

18　Grachev, *Gorbachev*, 69.

19　Gorbachev, *Zhizn'*, 1:176; Grachev, *Gorbachev*, 70.

20　Gorbachev, *Naedine s soboi*, 261.

21　V. I. Boldin, *Krushenie p'edestala* (Moscow: Respublika, 1995), 46–47.

22　Author's interview with Budyka, August 3, 2008, Stavropol.

23　Gorbachev, *Naedine s soboi*, 261.

24　Gorbachev, *Zhizn'*, 1:190–91; Gorbachev, *Memoirs*, 124–25.

25　Grachev, *Gorbachev*, 70.

26　R. Gorbachev, *I Hope*, 124.

27　Anatolii Cherniaev, *Moia zhizn' i moe vremia* (Moscow: Mezhdunarodnye otnosheniia, 1995), 327–28.

28　BBC interview with Otto Latsis, in "The Second Russian Revolution" transcripts (TSRRT).

29　Ed A. Hewett, *Reforming the Soviet Economy: Equality versus Efficiency* (Washington, DC: Brookings Institution, 1988), 32.

30   Information in this and the next three paragraphs comes from Yegor Gaidar, *Collapse of an Empire: Lessons for Modern Russia*, trans. Antonina W. Bouis (Washington, DC: Brookings Institution, 2007), 75–105.

31   Raymond Garthoff, *Détente and Confrontation: American-Soviet Relations from Nixon to Reagan* (Washington, DC: Brookings Institution, 1994), 556–1119; Raymond Garthoff, *The Great Transition: American-Soviet Relations and the End of the Cold War* (Washington, DC: Brookings Institution, 1994), 7–194. Jack Matlock Jr., who served as President Reagan's special assistant for national security affairs from 1983 to 1986 and ambassador to the USSR from 1987 to 1991, was told that Pershing II's were designed to have a range just short of Moscow, lest the Soviets consider them a "decapitating weapon," but that Moscow thought so anyway. Personal communication from Ambassador Matlock, January 24, 2016.

32   Wolf and Fischer cited in Jonathan Haslam, *Russia's Cold War: From the October Revolution to the Fall of the Wall* (New Haven, CT: Yale University Press, 2011), 333.

33   Gordon Barrass, *The Great Cold War: A Journey through the Hall of Mirrors* (Stanford, CA: Stanford University Press, 2009), 277.

34   Ibid., 1–2, 298–305.

35   Chazov, *Zdorov'e i vlast'*, 85–87, 115–19.

36   Shakhnazarov, *S vozhdiami i bez nikh*, 228–35.

37   Grachev, *Gibel' Sovetskogo "titanika,"* 109.

38   Grachev, *Gorbachev*, 62–63. One of the lesser consequences of Brezhnev's decay involved his two ghostwritten books, *Malaia Zemlia* and *Tselina*, which shamelessly hyped his modest role in a little-known World War II battle near the Black Sea coast, and his role in developing the Virgin Lands. Both were required reading for Soviet high school students and showed up on university entrance exams. Soviet ambassadors around the world had to conduct seminars for their staffs on Brezhnev's "epochal theoretical works." On the way in which the pattern of oligarchs governing in the name of weak tsars dates back to Muscovite times before Peter the Great, see Edward L. Keenan, "Muscovite Political Folkways," *Russian Review* 45, no. 2 (April 1986): 115–81.

39   Cherniaev, *Moia zhizn' i moe vremia*, 267.

40   K. N. Brutents, *Nesbyvsheesia* (Moscow: Mezhdunarodnye otnosheniia, 2005), 24.

41   Robert D. English, *Russia and the Idea of the West: Gorbachev, Intellectuals and the End of the Cold War* (New York: Columbia University Press, 2000), 134, 289–90, n. 75.

42   Gorbachev, *Naedine s soboi*, 278.

43   Grachev, *Gibel' Sovetskogo "titanika,"* 123.

44 Eduard Shevardnadze, *Moi vybor v zashchitu demokratii i svobody* (Moscow: Novosti, 1991), 62.

45 NSA, READD-RADD collection.

46 Rudol'f Pikhoia, *Moskva—Kreml'—Vlast'*, vol. 2 (Moscow: Rus'-Olimp: AST: Astrel', 2007), 648.

47 Svetlana Savranskaya of the National Security Archive in Washington.

48 "Zasedanie Sekretariata TsK KPSS," June 2, 1981, NSA, READD-RADD collection.

49 "Zasedanie Politburo TsK KPSS," August 19, 1982, ibid.

50 Gorbachev, *Zhizn'*, 1:177.

51 Ibid., 189; Gorbachev, *Memoirs*, 122; Gorbachev, *Naedine s soboi*, 263.

52 Gorbachev, *Memoirs*, 97.

53 Ibid., 121; Gorbachev, *Naedine s soboi*, 262.

54 Gorbachev, *Memoirs*, 16.

55 Gorbachev, *Zhizn'*, 1:186–88.

56 Ibid., 183.

57 This section relies on Medvedev, *Gorbachev*, 94–118.

58 Ibid., 95.

59 Gorbachev, *Zhizn'*, 1:184.

60 Medvedev, *Gorbachev*, 113–14.

61 Shakhnazarov, *S vozhdiami i bez nikh*, 354; Anatoly Dobrynin, *In Confidence: Moscow's Ambassador to America's Six Cold War Presidents* (New York: Times Books, 1995), 617.

62 V. I. Boldin, *Ten Years That Shook the World* (New York: Basic Books, 1994), 31–37.

63 Gorbachev, *Sobranie sochinenii*, 18:153.

64 Gorbachev, *Memoirs*, 131.

65 Gorbachev, *Zhizn'*, 1:213; Gorbachev, *Memoirs*, 131–32.

66 Gorbachev, *Zhizn'*, 1:214–16.

67 Ibid., 218–22; Vitaly Marsov, "Mikhail Gorbachev: Andropov ne poshel by daleko v reformatsii obshchestva," *Nezavisimaia gazeta*, November 11, 1992.

68 Cherniaev, *Moia zhizn' i moe vremia*, 443–48.

69 Markus Wolf, *Man without a Face: The Autobiography of Communism's Greatest Spymaster* (New York: Public Affairs, 1997), 219.

70 Brutents, *Nesbyvsheesia*, 50–54.

71 Fired in December 1982, Shchelokov took his own life after criminal charges were filed against him. Medvedev, *Andropov*, 312–13; see also Grachev, *Gibel' Sovetskogo "titanika,"* 123.

72 Gorbachev, *Zhizn'*, 1:229–33.

73 Grachev, *Gibel' Sovetskogo "titanika,"* 133.

74 Gorbachev, *Zhizn'*, 1:235.

75 Ibid., 234.

76   Grachev, *Gorbachev*, 78.

77   Ibid., 81.

78   Gorbachev, *Zhizn'*, 1:236.

79   Iakovlev, *Sumerki*, 270.

80   Ibid., 316–19; Loren Graham, *Moscow Stories* (Bloomington: Indiana University Press, 2006), 223–36.

81   Jim Wright in Christopher Shulgan, *The Soviet Ambassador: The Making of the Radical behind Perestroika* (Toronto: McClelland & Stewart, 2008), 257.

82   Gorbachev was relieved to hear that the ranch received government subsidies (as Soviet farmers did, too, although much more of them) because, Whelan told him, "The agrarian sector cannot exist at the modern level without state aid." Ibid., 252–72; Eugene Whelan and Rick Arbold, *Whelan: The Man in the Green Stetson* (Toronto: Irwin Publishing, n.d.), 253–60; Gorbachev, *Zhizn'*, 1:238.

83   Iakovlev, *Sumerki*, 370; Shulgan, *Soviet Ambassador*, 266.

84   Iakovlev, *Sumerki*, 381.

85   Zaslavskaya soon fell ill with pneumonia and spent two months in the hospital; BBC interviews with Zaslavskaya and Aganbegyan, in TSRRT.

86   Yegor Ligachev, *Inside Gorbachev's Kremlin*, trans. Catherine A. Fitzpatrick, Michele A. Berdy, and Dobrochna Dyrzc-Freeman (New York: Pantheon Books, 1993), 256.

87   Ibid., 16, 26.

88   Grachev, *Gibel' Sovetskogo "titanika,"* 132.

89   Nikolai Ryzhkov, *Perestroika: Istoriyia predatel'stva* (Moscow: Novosti, 1992), 33.

90   Gorbachev, *Sobranie sochinenii*, 16:370.

91   Ryzhkov, *Perestroika*, 42.

92   Boldin, *Ten Years That Shook the World*, 56–57.

93   Boldin, *Krushenie p'edestala*, 36–37.

94   "Soveshchanie sekretarei TsK KPSS," January 1, 1983, NSA READD-RADD collection.

95   "Zasedanie Sekretariata TsK KPSS," April 20, 1993, ibid.

96   Pikhoia, *Moskva—Kreml'—Vlast'*, 2:683–85; Remnick, *Lenin's Tomb*, 518.

97   "Zasedanie Politbiuro TsK KPSS," September 2, 1983, in NSA READD-RADD collection; See Barrass, *Great Cold War*, 295–96; Dobrynin, *In Confidence*, 537.

98   Medvedev, *Andropov*, 398; Gorbachev, *Naedine s soboi*, 349.

99   Gorbachev, *Memoirs*, 152; see also Dmitrii Bykov, "Est' prostoi i nadezhnyi variant peremen sverkhu," *Sobesednik*, February 22, 2011, in Karagez'ian and Poliakov, *Gorbachev v zhizni*, 16.

100   Brown, *Gorbachev Factor*, 67–68; Anatoly Lukyanov, who became first deputy director of the Central Committee's general department

in 1983, denied that Andropov tried to designate Gorbachev as his successor. Grachev, *Gorbachev*, 93–94; BBC interviews with Arkady Volsky and Anatoly Lukyanov, in TSRRT; Gorbachev, *Memoirs*, 154; Remnick, *Lenin's Tomb*, 192.

101   Haslam, *Russia's Cold War*, 347.

102   Gorbachev, *Naedine s soboi*, 357.

103   Grachev, *Gorbachev*, 94.

104   Author's interview with Gorbachev, May 4, 2007, Moscow.

105   Gorbacheva, *Ia nadeius'*, 125.

106   Medvedev, *V kommande Gorbacheva*, 16–17.

107   "A View of Chernenko," July 4, 1984, PRO PREM 19/1934.

108   Grachev, *Gorbachev*, 86–87.

109   Ryzhkov, *Perestroika*, 60.

110   Gorbachev, *Zhizn'*, 1:251.

111   Brown, *Gorbachev Factor*, 72–73; Grachev, *Gorbachev*, 86–87; Ligachev, *Inside Gorbachev's Kremlin*, 45–46.

112   Gorbachev, *Naedine s soboi*, 363.

113   Chernyaev, *My Six Years with Gorbachev*, 13–14.

114   Vitalii Vorotnikov, *A bylo eto tak . . . iz dnevnika chlena Politbiuro TsK KPSS* (Moscow: Sovet veteranov knigoizdaniia, 1995), 40–41.

115   Iakovlev, *Sumerki*, 382; Gorbachev, *Zhizn'*, 1:254.

116   Iakovlev, *Sumerki*, 382–85.

117   Text in Gorbachev, *Sobranie sochinenii*, vol. 2, 77–114.

118   Iakovlev, *Sumerki*, 386.

119   BBC interview with Leonid Dobrokhotov, in TSRRT.

120   Medvedev, *V kommande Gorbacheva*, 22; Iakovlev, *Sumerki*, 386.

121   "Dialogue: The Musgrove Conference, May 1–3, 1998," p. 12, part of a Critical Oral History Conference, "The End of the Cold War in Europe, 1989: 'New Thinking' and New Evidence," organized by the National Security Archive at the George Washington University, Musgrove, St. Simon's Island, Georgia, May 1–3, 1998.

122   Andrei Grachev, *Gorbachev's Gamble: Soviet Foreign Policy and the End of the Cold War* (Cambridge, UK: Polity Press, 2008), 49–50.

123   Gorbachev, *Zhizn'*, 1:253–54.

124   Personal communication from Rodric Braithwaite, July 28, 2015.

125   Archie Brown, "The Change to Engagement in Britain's Cold War Policy: The Origins of the Thatcher-Gorbachev Relationship," *Journal of Cold War Studies* 10, no. 3 (Summer 2008). According to Braithwaite, those who were at the British embassy in Moscow believe it was they who first identified Gorbachev and recommended that he be invited to London. Braithwaite adds that her sarcasm about Foreign Office officials was "partly a pose," and that she had plenty of time for those she respected.

126   Ibid., 13–16.

127   Ibid., 19–22.

128   Chernyaev, *My Six Years with Gorbachev*, 15–16.

129   Grachev, *Gorbachev's Gamble*, 50–51.

130   Charles Moore, *Margaret Thatcher: At Her Zenith: In London, Washington and Moscow* (New York: Alfred A. Knopf, 2016), 237.

131   Author's interview with Lord Charles Powell, July 21, 2007, London.

132   Margaret Thatcher, *Downing Street Years* (New York: HarperCollins, 1993), 459.

133   Ibid., 461–62.

134   Ibid., 460–61; Moore, *Margaret Thatcher*, 238.

135   Bryan Cartledge, British Diplomatic Oral History Project, 2007, Churchill College Archives, Cambridge, UK, https://www.chu.cam.ac.uk/media/uploads/files/Cartledge.pdf.

136   Thatcher's recollections in *Raisa Gorbacheva: Shtrikhi*, 72.

137   Gorbachev, *Memoirs*, 161.

138   Author's interview with Lord Geoffrey Howe, July 22, 2008, London.

139   "Mikhail Sergeevich Gorbachev: A Personal Assessment of the Man during His Visit to the United Kingdom, 15–21 December 1984," by K. A Bishop, PRO, PREM 19/1394 part 7.

140   Constantine Pleshakov, *There Is No Freedom without Bread!: 1989 and the Civil War That Brought Down Communism* (New York: Farrar, Straus and Giroux, 2009), 136; Brown, "Change to Engagement in Britain's Cold War Policy," 33; Moore, *Margaret Thatcher*, 250.

141   Gorbachev, *Zhizn'*, 1:259.

142   Chazov, *Zdorov'e i vlast'*, 210.

143   Gorbachev, *Zhizn'*, 1:263–64.

144   Grachev, *Gibel' Sovetskogo "titanika,"* 135.

CHAPTER 6: WHAT IS TO BE DONE? 1985–1986

1   *What Is to Be Done?* (in Russian *Chto delat'?*) was a famous political pamphlet published by Vladimir Lenin in 1902. In the pamphlet, Lenin argues that the working class will not simply become politically mobilized overnight. Instead, Marxists must form a political party or "vanguard" to radicalize workers.

2   Witnesses' recollections vary on the exact time the meeting was called.

3   Gorbachev, *Zhizn'*, 1:266.

4   Author's interview with Georgy M. Kornienko, June 17, 2005, Moscow.

5   Cited in Ryzhkov, *Perestroika*, 80.

6   Ibid., 78.

7   Boldin, *Ten Years That Shook the World*, 57.

8   A. V. Shubin, *Ot "zastoia" k reformam: SSSR v 1917–1985 gg.* (Moscow: Rosspen, 2001), 594, quoting Ligachev.

9   Gorbachev, *Zhizn'*, 1:265; Pikhoia, *Moskva—Kreml'—Vlast'*, 2:14. Just before the meeting, Gorbachev had asked Grishin whether he would like to chair the funeral commission—realizing, Grishin said later, that he would decline to do so. See Aleksandr Prokhorov's interview with Grishin in *Nachalo*, no. 20, 1992.

10   Anatolii Gromyko, *Andrei Gromyko: V labirintakh Kremliia* (Moscow: Avtor, 1997), 83–94; Iakovlev, *Sumerki*, 458–59; Author's interview with G. M. Kornienko, July 17, 2005, Moscow.

11   Gorbachev, *Naedine s soboi*, 383.

12   Gorbachev, *Zhizn'*, 1:264–65.

13   BBC interview with Anatoly Lukyanov, in TSRRT; Boldin, *Ten Years That Shook the World*, 58; Cherniaev, *Sovmestnyi iskhod*, 608.

14   BBC interview with Ryzhkov, in TSRRT.

15   Gorbachev, *Zhizn'*, 1:265; R. Gorbachev, *I Hope*, 4–5.

16   Author's interview with Gorbachev, October 19, 2015, Moscow.

17   Gorbachev, *Naedine s soboi*, 395.

18   Gorbachev remarks to his Moscow University law school reunion on June 16, 1990, in TSRRT.

19   Gorbachev, *Zhizn'*, 1:267.

20   "Zasedanie Politburo TsK KPSS," March 11, 1985, NSA, READD-RADD collection.

21   BBC interview with Lukyanov, in TSRRT.

22   BBC interview with Vladimir Dolgikh, in TSRRT.

23   Gorbachev, *Sobranie sochinenii*, 2:158.

24   Chernyaev diary entry of March 11, 1985, in *Sovmestnyi iskhod*, 608.

25   Chernyaev notes on Central Committee plenum, March 11, 1985, GFA, f. 2, op. 2.

26   Gorbachev, *Zhizn'*, 1:270.

27   Chernayev diary entry of March 11, 1985, in *Sovmestnyi iskhod*, 608.

28   Boldin, *Ten Years That Shook the World*, 63.

29   Gorbachev, *Sobranie sochinenii*, 2:158–63.

30   David E. Hoffman, *The Dead Hand: The Untold Story of the Cold War Arms Race* (New York: Doubleday, 2009), 205.

31   Gorbachev, *Sobranie sochinenii*, 2:257.

32   Gorbachev, *Zhizn'*, 1:315–16.

33   Chernyaev diary entry of May 22, 1985, in *Sovmestnyi iskhod*, 628.

34   R. Gorbachev, *I Hope*, 135.

35   Gorbachev, *Zhizn'*, 1:270.

36   Mikhail Gorbachev, *Poniat' perestroiku . . . Pochemu eto vazhno seichas* (Moscow: Al'pina Biznes Buks, 2006), 26.

37   Author's interview with Budyka, August 3, 2008, Stavropol.

38   Gorbachev and Mlynář, *Conversations with Gorbachev*, 98.

39   See, e.g., the section "Gorbachev, Lenin and Leninism" in Brown, *Seven Years That Changed the World*, 284–94.

40   Boldin, *Ten Years That Shook the World*, 95.

41   Gorbachev, *Poniat' perestroiku*, 15–16.

42   William E. Odom, *The Collapse of the Soviet Military* (New Haven, CT: Yale University Press, 1998), 105.

43   Author's interview with Bogomolov, April 11, 2007, Moscow.

44   Gorbachev, *Poniat' perestroiku*, 17.

45   I owe this phrase to George Kateb.

46   Cited in Brown, *Myth of the Strong Leader*, 177.

47   Grachev, *Gorbachev*, 122.

48   Gorbachev and Mlynář, *Conversations with Gorbachev*, 65, 67.

49   BBC interview with Aganbegyan, June 19, 1990, in TSRRT.

50   Gorbachev, *Zhizn'*, 1:289; Grachev, *Gorbachev*, 101.

51   Gorbachev, *Zhizn'*, 1:289–90.

52   Ibid., 288.

53   Grachev, *Gorbachev*, 102.

54   Chernyaev's diary, December 8, 1985, entry, in *Sovmestnyi iskhod*, 658.

55   Gorbachev, *Zhizn'*, 1:291–92; see also Bykov, "Est' prostoi I nadezhnyi," in Karagez'ian and Poliakov, *Gorbachev v zhizni*, 16.

56   A. M. Aleksandrov-Agentov, *Ot Kollontai do Gorbacheva: Vospominaniya diplomata, sovetnika A. A. Gromyko, pomoschnika L. I. Brezhneva, Iu. V. Andropova, K. U. Chernenko i M. S. Gorbacheva* (Moscow: Mezhdunarodnye otnosheniia, 1994), 290; Brown, *Gorbachev Factor*, 98.

57   Chernyaev's diary, April 21 and June 9, 1985, entries, in *Sovmestnyi iskhod*, 622, 630.

58   Grachev in Brown, *Gorbachev Factor*, 98.

59   Ibid., 101.

60   Shakhnazarov, *S vozhdiami i bez nikh*, 276–77.

61   Ibid., 283.

62   R. Gorbachev, *I Hope*, 142.

63   Nikolai Efimovich and Saed-Shakh, "Raisa Gorbacheva: 'Ia nikogda ne vmeshivalas' v ego dela,'" in *Raisa: Vospominaniia*, 160.

64   See Brown, *Gorbachev Factor*, 35.

65   Efimovich and Saed-Shakh, "Raisa Gorbacheva," 160.

66   Author's interview with Anatoly Chernyaev, June 29, 2005, Moscow.

67   Author's interview with Vitaly Gusenkov, March 21, 2007, Moscow.

68   Vladimir Medvedev, *Chelovek za spinoi* (Moscow: Russlit, 1994), 201, 207.

69   Belan, "Mnogikh oshibok Gorbachev mog by izbezhat'."

70   Aleksandr Likhotal's recollection in *Raisa Gorbacheva: Shtrikhi*, 198.

71   Giulietto Chiesa and Fiammetta Cucurnia, "Edinstvennaia: Istoriia liubvi Gorbachevykh," *Itogi*, September 28, 1999, in *Raisa: Vospominaniia*, 253.

72   Irina Bobrova, "Posledniaia ledi," ibid., 287.

73   Shubin, *Ot "zastoya" k reformam*, 613–14.

74   Grachev, *Gorbachev*, 104–5.

75   Author's interview with Varennikov, February 28, 2006, Moscow.

76   Author's interview with Gorbachev, March 17, 2010, Moscow; personal communication from Pavel Palazhchenko, January 25, 2016.

77   Iakovlev, *Sumerki*, 460; Kriuchkov cited in Grachev, *Gibel' Sovetskogo "titanika,"* 134.

78   Afterword to Chernyaev 1985 diary entries in *Sovmestnyi iskhod*, 661–62.

79   Gorbachev, *Sobranie sochinenii*, 2:165.

80   Chernyaev's diary, March 18, 1985, entry, in *Sovmestnyi iskhod*, 612.

81   "Soveshchanie sekretarei TsK KPSS," March 15, 1985, NSA, READD-RADD collection.

82   BBC interview with Kravchenko, in TSRRT.

83   Chernyaev's diary, June 20, 1985, entry, in *Sovmestnyi iskhod*, 635.

84   Ibid., 648–49.

85   Medvedev, *Chelovek za spinoi*, 208.

86   Medvedev, *V kommande Gorbacheva*, 32.

87   Ibid., 32–34; Boldin, *Krushenie p'edestala*, 113–16; Iakovlev, *Sumerki*, 436–37.

88   Gorbachev, *Zhizn'*, 1:338–39; Gorbachev, *Naedine s soboi*, 427.

89   "Zasedanie Politburo TsK KPSS, April 4, 1985," NSA, READD-RADD collection.

90   Roi Medvedev, *Kak nachalas' perestroika* (Moscow: Prava cheloveka, 2006), 39, 43.

91   BBC interview with Dolgikh, in TSRRT.

92   Shakhnazarov, *S vozhdiami i bez nikh*, 295.

93   Grachev, *Gorbachev*, 130.

94   Author's interview with Nikolai Shmelyov, July 26, 2006, Moscow.

95   "Stranu nel'zia lomat' cherez koleno, po-kovboiski," *Obshchaia gazeta*, April 4, 1996.

96   Gorbachev, *Poniat' perestroiku*, 56, 58.

97   Grachev, *Gorbachev*, 131; Marina Zavada and Yurii Kulikov, "Mikhail Gorbachev: My s Raisoi byli priviazanny drug k drugu na smert'," *Izvestiia*, January 12, 2007, http://izvestia.ru/news/320650; also see Bobrova, "Posledniaia ledi."

98   Author's interview with Raisa Gudarenko, July 31, 2008, Stavropol.

99   "Rabochee soveshchanie u Gorbacheva," April 5, 1985, GFA, f. 10, op. 2.

100   Gorbachev, *Sobranie sochinenii*, 2:174–80.

101   Ibid., 2:181–88.

102   Chernyaev's diary, April 18, 1985, entry, in *Sovmestnyi iskhod*, 622.

103   Boldin, *Ten Years That Shook the World*, 68–69.

104   Gorbachev, *Sobranie sochinenii*, 2:305.

105   Ryzhkov, *Perestroika*, 87; BBC interview with Ryzhkov, in TSRRT.

106   Gorbachev, *Sobranie sochinenii*, 2:311.

107   Chernyaev's diary, April 23, 1985, entry, in *Sovmestnyi iskhod*, 622–23.

108   Gorbachev, *Sobranie sochinenii*, 3: 286–392, 407–12.

109   Vorotnikov, *A bylo eto tak*, 66–67.

110   Gorbachev, *Sobranie sochinenii*, 4:576, n. 204.

111   Gorbachev, *Zhizn'*, 1:343.

112   Speech in Tiumen', September 6, 1985, in Gorbachev, *Sobranie sochinenii*, 2:473, 481.

113   Gorbachev, *Sobranie sochinenii*, 3:69–70.

114   Ibid., 400.

115   Ibid., 415.

116   Ibid., 420.

117   Ibid., 433.

118   Daniel Yergin, *The Prize: The Epic Quest for Oil, Money and Power* (New York: Free Press, 1991), 731.

119   Pikhoia, *Moskva—Kreml'—Vlast'*, 2:20–26; Gaidar, *Collapse of an Empire*, 100–109.

120   N. Y. Petrakov, *Russkaia ruletka* (Moscow: Ekonomika, 1998), 96–98.

121   Gorbachev, *Sobranie sochinenii*, 3:174–77.

122   Ibid., 415.

123   Ibid., 420.

124   Chernyaev notes on Politburo meeting, March 20, 1986, GFA, f. 2, op. 2.

125   Gorbachev, *Sobranie sochinenii*, 3:488.

126   Ibid., 4:52.

127   Gorbachev, *Memoirs*, 188.

128   Gorbachev, *Zhizn'*, 1:298.

129   Urgent Report from USSR First Deputy Minister of Energy and Electrification, A. N. Makunin, in NSA READD-RADD collection.

130   For a short, incisive account, see Hoffman, *Dead Hand*, 242–53.

131   Gorbachev, *Sobranie sochinenii*, 4:92.

132   Gorbachev, *Naedine s soboi*, 442.

133   Gorbachev at Politburo, May 22, 1986, in Gorbachev, *Sobranie sochinenii*, 4:121.

134   Gorbachev, *Zhizn'*, 1:301.

135   Notes on Politburo meeting, July 3, 1986, GFA, f. 2, op. 2.

136   Grachev's paraphrase, in Grachev, *Gorbachev*, 160.

137   Gorbachev, *Zhizn'*, 1:299.

138   Grachev, *Gorbachev*, 161.

139   Notes on May 29, 1986, Politburo meeting, GFA, f. 2, op. 2.

140   Notes on June 5, 1986, Politburo meeting, GFA, f. 10, op. 2.

141   Notes on June 13, 1986, Politburo meeting, GFA, f. 2. op. 2.

142   Notes on Gorbachev's June 23, 1986, meeting with Central Committee secretaries, heads of Central Committee departments and aides, GFA, f. 10, op. 2.

143   Gorbachev, *Sobranie sochinenii*, 4:338.

144   Ibid., 416.

145   Notes on September 25, 1986, Politburo meeting, GFA, f. 2, op. 2.

146   Gorbachev, *Sobranie sochinenii*, 5:119.

147   Notes on October 30, 1986, Politburo meeting, GFA, f. 2. op. 2.

148   Gorbachev, *Zhizn'*, 1:306.

149   Cherniaev, *Sovmestnyi iskhod*, 704.

150   Gorbachev, *Zhizn'*, 1:337.

151   Notes on June 20, 1986, Politburo meeting, GFA, f. 2, op. 2.

152   Chernyaev's diary, June 29, 1985, entry, in *Sovmestnyi iskhod*, 637.

153   Gorbachev, *Sobranie sochinenii*, 5:178.

154   Aleksandr Iakovlev, *Perestroika: 1985–1991—Neizdannoe, maloizvestnoe, zabytoe* (Moscow: Demokratiia, 2008), 14.

155   Ibid., 28–38.

156   Author's interview with Aleksandr Yakovlev, May 31, 2005, Moscow.

157   Iakovlev, *Sumerki*, 471.

158   Gorbachev, *Sobranie sochinenii*, 2:160.

159   Gorbachev, *Zhizn'*, 1:318–19.

160   "V Politbiuro TsK KPSS," November 26, 1985, NSA READD-RADD collection.

161   Gorbachev, *Sobranie sochinenii*, 3:71.

162   BBC interview with Grigory Baklanov, in TSRRT.

163   *Sovetskoe kino*, nos. 1–2 (1933): 10.

164   Interview with Maya Turovskaia, in Liubov' Arkus, *Kino i kontekst*, vol. 4, *1986–88* (St. Petersburg: SEANS, 2002), 59.

165   Interview with Elem Klimov, ibid., 68.

166   Ibid.

167   Ibid., 119.

168   See Shevardnadze, *Moi vybor*, 250.

169   BBC interview with Ales Adamovich, in TSRRT.

170   See Richard Sakwa, *Gorbachev and His Reforms, 1985–1990* (New York: Prentice-Hall, 1990), 75.

171   Chernyaev, *My Six Years with Gorbachev*, 37–38, 72–74.

172   Gorbachev, *Memoirs*, 206.

173   Gorbachev, *Sobranie sochinenii*, 5:547, n. 53.

174   Ibid., 548.

175   Chernyaev, *My Six Years with Gorbachev*, 73–74.

176   Andrei Sakharov, *Memoirs*, trans. Richard Lourie (New York: Alfred A. Knopf, 1990), 599–603.

177   "Zasedanie Politburo TsK KPSS," August 29, 1985, NSA, READD-RADD collection. In the course of the Politburo discussion, Mikhail Zimyanin referred to Bonner as "a bitch-beast in a skirt, a protégée of imperialism."

178   Sakharov, *Memoirs*, 614–16.

CHAPTER 7: ONTO THE WORLD STAGE:
MARCH 1985–DECEMBER 1986

1   Boldin comment on Tape 2 of Oral History Conference organized by Ohio State University's Mershon Center for International Security Studies and the Russian Academy of Sciences, Institute for General History, "The Crash of the Bipolar World: The Perspective of Former Senior Soviet Officials Who Came to Oppose Mikhail Gorbachev and His Foreign Policy," Marco Polo Presnja Hotel, Moscow, Russia, June 21–22, 1999.

2   Grachev, *Gorbachev's Gamble*, 52, 62.

3   BBC interview with Vorontsov, in TSRRT.

4   Author's interview with Kornienko, June 17, 2005, Moscow.

5   Author's interview with Jack F. Matlock Jr., November 23, 2004, Princeton, NJ. See also Jack F. Matlock Jr., *Reagan and Gorbachev: How the Cold War Ended* (New York: Random House, 2004), 136–37.

6   Grachev, *Gorbachev's Gamble*, 30.

7   Roald Z. Sagdeev, *The Making of a Soviet Scientist* (New York: John Wiley & Sons, 1994), 264.

8   See Artemy Kalinovsky, *A Long Goodbye: The Soviet Withdrawal from Afghanistan* (Cambridge, MA: Harvard University Press, 2011), 77.

9   Svetlana Savranskaya, Thomas Blanton, and Vladislav Zubok, eds., *Masterpieces of History: The Peaceful End of the Cold War in Europe, 1989* (New York: Central European University Press, 2010), 104–5.

10 Grachev, *Gorbachev's Gamble*, 14, 34.

11 Anatolii Cherniaev, *1991 god: Dnevnik pomoshchnika prezidenta SSSR* (Moscow: Terra, 1997), 617.

12 Ibid., 623.

13 Brutents, *Nesbyvsheesia*, 127.

14 Author's interview with Chernyaev, June 29, 2005, Moscow.

15 Gorbachev, *Zhizn' i reformy*, 2:7.

16 Grachev, *Gorbachev's Gamble*, 47–48.

17 Dobrynin, *In Confidence*, 565.

18 Chernyaev's diary, April 4, April 12, and May 30, 1985, entries, in *Sovmestnyi iskhod*, 617–21; 629.

19 Gorbachev, *Zhizn'*, 2:708.

20 Aleksandrov-Agentov, *Ot Kollontai do Gorbacheva*, 287–88.

21 Chernyaev's diary, February 22 and December 8, 1985, entries and afterword to 1985, in *Sovmestnyi iskhod*, 603–4, 659, 663.

22 Grachev, *Gorbachev's Gamble*, 55.

23 Gromyko, *Andrei Gromyko*, 110.

24 Dobrynin, *In Confidence*, 571.

25 Chernyaev's diary, July 1, 1985, entry, in *Sovmestnyi iskhod*, 637.

26 Author's interview with Georgy Kornienko, June 17, 2005, Moscow.

27 Gorbachev, *Memoirs*, 180; see also Grachev, *Gorbachev's Gamble*, 76.

28 Gorbachev, *Memoirs*, 180.

29 Matlock Jr. quotes Bessmertnykh in *Reagan and Gorbachev*, 129.

30 Gorbachev, *Memoirs*, 180–81.

31 Eduard Shevardnadze, *The Future Belongs to Freedom*, trans. Catherine A. Fitzpatrick (New York: Free Press, 1991), 1–40.

32 Grachev, *Gorbachev's Gamble*, 87–88; Anatolii Kovalev, "Iskustvo vozmozhnogo" n.d., unpublished manuscript provided to the author by Peter Reddaway.

33 Gorbachev, *Zhizn'*, 2:482; Dobrynin, *In Confidence*, 619.

34 Dobrynin, *In Confidence*, 620.

35 Gorbachev quoted in Grachev, *Gorbachev's Gamble*, 88.

36 Ibid., 76–77, 88.

37 Cherniaev, *Moia zhizn' i moe vremya*, 46.

38 Chernyaev's diary, May 29, 1986, entry, in *Sovmestnyi iskhod*, 683–84.

39 R. Gorbachev, *I Hope*, 165–66. According to American Ambassador Matlock, an exception was made for Soviets, who found formal attire "bourgeois."

40 Author's interview with Chernyaev, June 29, 2005, Moscow.

41 Pavel Palazhchenko and Andrei Grachev recollections, in *Raisa Gorbacheva: Shtrikhi*, 50, 90.

42 V. Shevchenko, *Povsednevnaia zhizn' Kremlya pri prezidentakh* (Moscow: Molodaya gvardiia, 2004), 115–16.

43 R. Gorbachev, *I Hope*, 167–68.

44 Grachev recollections, in *Raisa Gorbacheva: Shtrikhi*, 95.

45 See William Taubman, *Stalin's American Policy: From Entente to Détente to Cold War* (New York: W. W. Norton, 1982).

46 See Taubman, *Khrushchev*, esp. chaps. 15 and 19.

47 Grachev, *Gorbachev's Gamble*, 46.

48 Ibid., 47.

49 Gorbachev, *Sobranie sochinenii*, 16:390.

50 Dobrynin, *In Confidence*, 477.

51 *Otvechaia na vyzov vremeni: Vneshniaia politika perestroika: Dokymental'nye svidetel'stva* (Moscow: Ves'Mir Izdatelstvo, 2010), 37–40; Gorbachev, *Sobranie sochinenii*, 3:238.

52 Chernyaev diary entry of August 9, 1985, in *Sovmestnyi iskhod*, 642.

53 Grachev, *Gorbachev's Gamble*, 71–72.

54 Ibid., 72.

55 Gorbachev, *Sobranie sochinenii*, 3:290.

56 Shevardnadze, *Future Belongs to Freedom*, 49.

57 Dobrynin, *In Confidence*, 600.

58 BBC interview with Anatoly Chernyaev, in TSRRT.

59 Gorbachev, *Sobranie sochinenii*, 4:124–34.

60 Vladislav Zubok, *A Failed Empire: The Soviet Union in the Cold War from*

Stalin to Gorbachev (Chapel Hill: University of North Carolina Press, 2007), 267.

61 Dobrynin, *In Confidence*, 500.

62 *Otvechaia na vyzov vremeni*, 516.

63 Gorbachev, *Poniat' perestroiku*, 33, 70.

64 Grachev, *Gorbachev's Gamble*, 114.

65 Chernyaev, *My Six Years with Gorbachev*, 61.

66 Savranskaya, Blanton, and Zubok, *Masterpieces of History*, 124.

67 Ibid., 107.

68 Grachev, *Gorbachev's Gamble*, 114.

69 Chernyaev in Savranskaya, Blanton, and Zubok, *Masterpieces of History*, 163.

70 Chernyaev, *My Six Years with Gorbachev*, 23.

71 Gorbachev, *Zhizn'*, 2:311–12.

72 Savranskaya, Blanton, and Zubok, *Masterpieces of History*, 137.

73 Transcript of Mikhail Gorbachev's Conference with CC CPSU Secretaries, March 15, 1985, ibid., 217–19.

74 See Svetlana Savranskaya, "The Logic of 1989: The Soviet Peaceful Withdrawal from Eastern Europe," ibid., 5.

75 Shakhnazarov, ibid., 123.

76 O. Vladimirov, "Questions of Theory: Leading Factor in the World Revolutionary Process," in *Pravda*, June 21, 1985, p. 3/4, trans. in *FBIS Daily Report—Soviet Union*, vol. 3, no. 122, June 24, 1985, pp. BB2–BB7.

77 Chernyaev's diary, July 5, 1985, entry, in *Sovmestnyi iskhod*, 638.

78 Savranskaya, Blanton, and Zubok, *Masterpieces of History*, 124.

79 Chernyaev, *My Six Years with Gorbachev*, 36.

80 See Savranskaya, "Logic of 1989," 6; Gorbachev, *Zhizn'*, 2:314.

81 Gorbachev speaking to Central Committee conference on March 10, 1986, in *Otvechaia na vyzov vremeni*, 519.

82 Chernyaev notes on June 13, 1986, Politburo session, in Savranskaya, Blanton, and Zubok, *Masterpieces of History*, 226–27.

83 June 26, 1986, memorandum from Mikhail Gorbachev to Politburo, and notes on July 3, 1986, Politburo session, ibid., 230–35.

84 Savranskaya, "Logic of 1989," 9.

85 BBC interview with Akhromeyev, in TSRRT; Kalinovsky, *Long Goodbye*, 16–73.

86 *Otvechaia na vyzov vremeni*, 599.

87 BBC interview with Arbatov, in TSRRT.

88 Chernyaev's diary, April 4, 1985, entry, in *Sovmestnyi iskhod*, 617.

89 "Zapis' besedy tov. Gorbacheva M. S. s General'nym sekretarem TsK NDPA V. Karmalym," March 14, 1985, in NSA, READD-RADD collection.

90 Chernyaev's diary, October 16 and 17, 1985, entries, in *Sovmestnyi iskhod*, 649–50.

91   Kalinovsky, *Long Goodbye*, 89.

92   Ibid., 88.

93   Ibid., 53.

94   Matlock Jr., *Reagan and Gorbachev*, 182.

95   Kalinovsky, *Long Goodbye*, 3.

96   *Otvechaia na vyzov vremeni*, 677.

97   Gorbachev, *Sobranie sochinenii*, 4:311.

98   Ibid., 5:280.

99   Pavel Palazhchenko, *My Years with Gorbachev and Shevardnadze: The Memoir of a Soviet Interpreter* (University Park: Pennsylvania State University Press, 1997), 28, 59.

100   A. Liakhovskii, *Tragedia i doblest' Afgana* (Moscow: Iskona, 1995), 523.

101   *Otvechaia na vyzov vremeni*, 601.

102   A. Benediktov interview with Gorbachev, Radio station "Ekho Moskvy," February 15, 2009, broadcast on "Ekho Moskvy."

103   Gorbachev, *Sobranie sochinenii*, 3:520.

104   Dobrynin, *In Confidence*, 480–86, 528.

105   Ibid., 491–92, 511–12, 517–18, 527.

106   Ibid., 544–58.

107   Mark Anderson and Annelise Anderson, *Reagan's Secret War: The Untold Story of His Fight to Save the World from Nuclear Disaster* (New York: Random House, 2009), 60, 63, 143, 156, 161.

108   Ibid., 94.

109   Epigraph to Frances FitzGerald, *Way Out There in the Blue: Reagan, Star Wars and the End of the Cold War* (New York: Simon & Schuster, 2001).

110   Iakovlev, *Perestroika*, 11–13.

111   George P. Shultz, *Turmoil and Triumph: My Years as Secretary of State* (New York: Charles Scribner's Sons, 1993), 528–33; Dobrynin, *In Confidence*, 567–69.

112   "Soveshchanie sekretarei TsK KPSS sostoiavsheesia u General'nogo sekretaria TsK KPSS tovarishcha Gorbacheva M. S.," March 15, 1985, in NSA, READD-RADD collection.

113   NSA, READD-RADD collection.

114   Dobrynin, *In Confidence*, 569.

115   Chernyaev, *My Six Years with Gorbachev*, 32.

116   Shultz, *Turmoil and Triumph*, 535.

117   Ibid., 563–64.

118   See Gorbachev, *Poniat' perestroiku*, 71.

119   Frédéric Bozo, *Mitterrand, the End of the Cold War, and German Unification* (New York: Berghahn Books, 2009), 14.

120   Ibid., 11–14.

121   Grachev, *Gorbachev's Gamble*, 63.

122   BBC interview with Yuli Vorontsov, in TSRRT.

123   Chernyaev, *Sovmestnyi iskhod*, 648; Chernyaev, *My Six Years with Gorbachev*, 40.

124   Grachev, *Gibel' Sovetskogo "titanika,"* 218.

125   Gorbachev, *Sobranie sochinenii*, 2:548.

126   Author's interview with Gusenkov, March 21, 2007, Moscow. Also see Gusenkov's recollections in *Raisa Gorbacheva: Shtrikhi*, 106.

127   R. Gorbachev, *I Hope*, 165.

128   Author's interview with Georgy Arbatov, May 27, 2006, Moscow.

129   Dobrynin, *In Confidence*, 585.

130   Shultz, *Turmoil and Triumph*, 586–87.

131   Ibid., 590.

132   Dobrynin, *In Confidence*, 583.

133   Shultz, *Turmoil and Triumph*, 594.

134   Dobrynin, *In Confidence*, 584.

135   Grachev, *Gorbachev's Gamble*, 64; Sagdeev, *Making of a Soviet Scientist*, 269.

136   Jack Matlock Jr., personal communication, January 25, 2016.

137   Suzanne Massie, *Land of the Firebird: The Beauty of Old Russia* (Blue Hill, ME: Heart Tree Press, 1980); Massie is also author of, with ex-husband, Robert K. Massie, *Nicholas and Alexandra* (New York: Atheneum, 1967).

138   Don Oberdorfer, *The Turn: From the Cold War to the New Era: The United States and the Soviet Union, 1983–1990* (New York: Poseidon Press, 1991), 142–43.

139   James Graham Wilson, *The Triumph of Improvisation: Gorbachev's Adaptability, Reagan's Engagement, and the End of the Cold War* (Ithaca, NY: Cornell University Press, 2014), 100. Wilson adds that since Reagan had outpaced his translator, he "had no clue what he was hearing."

140   Donald T. Regan, *For the Record: From Wall Street to Washington* (San Diego: Harcourt Brace Jovanovich, 1988), 305.

141   Dobrynin, *In Confidence*, 587.

142   Aleksandrov-Agentov, *Ot Kollontai do Gorbacheva*, 288; Regan, *For the Record*, 307.

143   U.S. government film seen at the Ronald Reagan Presidential Library.

144   Dobrynin, *In Confidence*, 588.

145   Grachev quotes Yakovlev, in Grachev, *Gorbachev's Gamble*, 64.

146   Ibid.

147   Reagan Library, Matlock MSS (Box 92137), obtained from the Margaret Thatcher Foundation.

148   Matlock Jr., *Reagan and Gorbachev*, 162.

149   Regan, *For the Record*, 310–11.

150   Ronald Reagan, *An American Life* (New York: Simon & Schuster, 1990), 14.

151   Gorbachev, *Zhizn'*, 2:21.

152   Chernyaev's diary, November 24, 1985, entry, in *Sovmestnyi iskhod*, 657.

153   Dobrynin, *In Confidence*, 620.

154   Grachev, *Gibel' Sovetskogo "titanika,"* 255.

155   Shultz, *Turmoil and Triumph*, 600–601.

156   On Gorbachev's hours, see Aleksandrov-Agentov, *Ot Kollontai do Gorbacheva*, 288.

157   Matlock Jr., *Reagan and Gorbachev*, 156.

158   Dobrynin, *In Confidence*, 591.

159   Regan, *For the Record*, 312–13.

160   Author's interview with Gorbachev, May 2, 2007, Moscow.

161   Reagan, *American Life*, 12–15.

162   Regan, *For the Record*, 315.

163   Ronald Reagan Presidential Library and Museum, "Address at Commencement Exercises at Eureka College, Eureka, Illinois, on May 9, 1982," *Public Papers of President Ronald W. Reagan*, May 9, 1982, http://www.reagan.utexas.edu/archives/speeches/1982/50982a.htm.

164   FitzGerald, *Way Out There*, 54.

165   Nancy Reagan, *My Turn: The Memoirs of Nancy Reagan* (New York: Random House, 1989), 66.

166   Ibid., 336.

167   Ibid., 44–54, on astrology; Regan, *For the Record*, 300, on the château.

168   N. Reagan, *My Turn*, 336–40.

169   Regan, *For the Record*, 314.

170   R. Gorbachev, *I Hope*, 168.

171   Matlock Jr., *Reagan and Gorbachev*, 170.

172   Grachev, *Gorbachev's Gamble*, 64.

173   Ibid., 67.

174   Gorbachev, *Sobranie sochinenii*, 3:205–17.

175   Matlock Jr., *Reagan and Gorbachev*, 177; Grachev, *Gorbachev's Gamble*, 68–69.

176   Chernyaev, *My Six Years with Gorbachev*, 59.

177   Dobrynin, *In Confidence*, 597.

178   Grachev, *Gorbachev's Gamble*, 67.

179   FitzGerald, *Way Out There*, 324; Hoffman, *Dead Hand*, 239.

180   Jack Matlock Jr., personal communication, January 24, 2016.

181   Gorbachev, *Zhizn'*, 2:22.

182   Brutents, *Nesbyvsheesia*, 140.

183   Gorbachev, *Zhizn'*, 2:23.

184   Gorbachev, *Sobranie sochinenii*, 4:105.

185   Ibid., 3:474.

186   Ibid., 4:84–85; Chernyaev, *My Six Years with Gorbachev*, 60–61.

187   Gorbachev, *Sobranie sochinenii*, 3:521.

188   Chernyaev, *My Six Years with Gorbachev*, 76.

189   Gorbachev, *Sobranie sochinenii*, 4:562–63; Chernyaev, *My Six Years with Gorbachev*, 76–77.

190   Chernyaev, *My Six Years with Gorbachev*, 77–78.

191   Gorbachev letter in "The Reykjavik File," National Security Archive Electronic Briefing Book No. 203.

192   FitzGerald, *Way Out There*, 346.

193   Regan, *For the Record*, 342.

194   Matlock Jr., *Reagan and Gorbachev*, 213.

195   Chernyaev, *My Six Years with Gorbachev*, 81; Grachev, *Gorbachev's Gamble*, 81–82.

196   Chernyaev's notes on Gorbachev's instructions to Reykjavik preparation group, October 4, 1986, in "The Reykjavik File," National Security Archive Electronic Briefing Book No. 203.

197   Dobrynin, *In Confidence*, 620.

198   Interviews with Kruichkov and Baklanov conducted in connection with the Oral History Conference "The Crash of the Bipolar World," Moscow, June 21–22, 1999.

199   Sagdeev, *Making of a Soviet Scientist*, 307–8.

200   Hoffman, *Dead Hand*, 261.

201   See both U.S. and Soviet minutes of the first Reagan-Gorbachev meeting at Reykjavik, National Security Archive Electronic Briefing Book No. 203, document nos. 9 and 10.

202   Shultz, *Turmoil and Triumph*, 760.

203   See U.S. and Soviet transcripts of second Reagan-Gorbachev session in National Security Archive Electronic Briefing Book No. 203, document nos. 11 and 12.

204   Shultz, *Turmoil and Triumph*, 762–65.

205   Reagan, *American Life*, 677.

206   U.S. Memorandum of Conversation of third meeting of Reykjavik summit, on Sunday, October 12, 1986, in National Security Archive Electronic Briefing Book No. 203, document no. 13.

207   Shultz, *Turmoil and Triumph*, 769.

208   U.S. Memorandum of Conversation on October 12, 1986, session, 3:25–6 pm in National Security Archive Electronic Briefing Book No. 203, document no. 15.

209   Thanks to N. Gordon Levin Jr. for helping to clarify these points.

210   U.S. Memorandum of Conversation on October 12, 1986, session, 3:25–6 pm in National Security Archive Electronic Briefing Book No. 203, document no. 15.

211   Chernyaev, *My Six Years with Gorbachev*, 86.

212   Gorbachev, *Zhizn'*, 2:31.

213   Shultz, *Turmoil and Triumph*, 773–74.

214   Regan, *For the Record*, 351.

215   Shultz, *Turmoil and Triumph*, 774.

216 Author's interview with Thomas Simons, November 20, 2006, Cambridge, MA.

217 Author's interview with Charles Hill, June 20, 2006, New Haven, CT.

218 Medvedev, *Chelovek za spinoi*, 210.

219 Dobrynin, *In Confidence*, 622.

220 Gorbachev, *Zhizn'*, 2:26; Grachev, *Gorbachev's Gamble*, 85.

221 Gorbachev, *Zhizn'*, 2:31–32.

222 Gorbachev, *Sobranie sochinenii*, 5:54.

223 Gorbachev, *Zhizn'*, 2:32; Gorbachev, *Naedine s soboi*, 470.

224 N. Reagan, *My Turn*, 344; Regan, *For the Record*, 344.

225 N. Reagan, *My Turn*, 344–46.

226 Matlock Jr., *Reagan and Gorbachev*, 230.

227 Gorbachev, *Sobranie sochinenii*, 5:65.

228 "Zasedanie Politburo TsK KPSS, 14 oktiabria 1986," NSA, READD-RADD collection; Chernyaev notes on Politburo session of October 30, 1986, in National Security Archive Electronic Briefing Book No. 203, document no. 23.

229 Interview with Boldin conducted in connection with the Oral History Conference "The Crash of the Bipolar World," Moscow, June 21–22, 1999.

230 Hoffman, *Dead Hand*, 273.

231 Moore, *Margaret Thatcher*, 598–605.

232 Jack Matlock Jr., personal communication, January 24, 2016.

233 Gorbachev, *Sobranie sochinenii*, 5:150.

234 Chernyaev notes on October 30, 1986, Poliburo meeting in NSA Electronic Briefing Book No. 203, document no. 23. According to Matlock, the Americans did in fact try to compare notes with Moscow on "what was agreed and not agreed," but it was the Soviets themselves who "adamantly refused" to do so. Matlock, personal communication, January 24, 2016.

235 Gorbachev, *Sobranie sochinenii*, 5:181.

236 Ibid., 190.

237 Ibid., 262.

238 Chernyaev, *My Six Years with Gorbachev*, 87.

CHAPTER 8: TWO SCORPIONS IN A BOTTLE: 1987

1 Author's interview with Mikhail Gorbachev, May 25, 2007, Moscow.

2 Cherniaev, *Sovmestnyi iskhod*, 739.

3 Vadim Medvedev's notes on meeting, November 19, 1986, GFA, f. 10, op. 2.

4 Medvedev, *V kommande Gorbacheva*, 44–45.

5 *V Politbiuro TsK KPSS: Po zapisam Anatoliia Cherniaeva, Vadima Med-*

vedeva, Georgiia Shakhnazarova, 1985–1991 (Moscow: Gorbachev-Fond, 2008), 128–30.

6   Gorbachev, *Sobranie sochinenii*, 5:391–458. Also see Gorbachev's concluding speech at plenum, in GFA, f. 10, op. 2.

7   BBC interview with Otto Latsis, in TSRRT.

8   Gorbachev, *Zhizn'*, 1:310–11.

9   BBC interview with Belyaev, in TSRRT.

10   BBC interview with Vorotnikov, in TSRRT; Vorotnikov, *A bylo eto tak*, 130.

11   Medvedev, *V kommande Gorbacheva*, 47.

12   Gorbachev, *Sobranie sochinenii*, 6:36.

13   Ryzhkov (BBC interview, in TSRRT) had a stake in this seeming success, but Abalkin (BBC interview, in TSRRT) and V. Medvedev (*V kommande Gorbacheva*, 48), cite similar progress.

14   GFA, f. 2, op. 2.

15   Gorbachev, *Zhizn'*, 1:346.

16   Ibid., 334.

17   Medvedev, *V kommande Gorbacheva*, 48–49.

18   BBC interview with Nikolai Petrakov, in TSRRT.

19   BBC interview with Latsis, in TSRRT; Gorbachev, *Poniat' perestroiku*, 108.

20   Gorbachev denied in his memoirs that the economic reforms were hasty or arbitrary, whereas Ryzhkov insisted that that's precisely what they were: Gorbachev, *Zhizn'*, 1:347; Ryzhkov, *Perestroika*, 167.

21   Gorbachev, *Zhizn'*, 1:349.

22   Vorotnikov, *A bylo eto tak*, 139; Gorbachev, *Sobranie sochinenii*, 6:371–75.

23   Gorbachev, *Zhizn'*, 1:353.

24   Chernyaev's diary, June 20, 1987, entry, in *Sovmestnyi iskhod*, 711–12.

25   Chernyaev, *My Six Years with Gorbachev*, 122.

26   Gorbachev, *Zhizn'*, 1:348.

27   Chernyaev's diary, July 5, 1987, entry, in *Sovmestnyi iskhod*, 713.

28   BBC interview with Petrakov, in TSRRT.

29   Chernyaev's diary, July 5, 1987, entry, in *Sovmestnyi iskhod*, 712–13.

30   Medvedev, *V kommande Gorbacheva*, 52.

31   *V Politbiuro*, 198–99; Gorbachev, *Sobranie sochinenii*, 7: 268.

32   *V Politbiuro*, 195.

33   Chernyaev, *My Six Years with Gorbachev*, 127.

34   Gorbachev, *Poniat' perestroiku*, 112.

35   Chernyaev's diary, July 5, 1987, entry, in *Sovmestnyi iskhod*, 715.

36   Chernyaev's diary, January 10, 1987, entry, ibid., 705.

37   Chernyaev's diary, June 14, 1987, entry, ibid., 709.

38   Gorbachev, *Zhizn'*, 1:318; Gorbachev, *Poniat' perestroiku*, 53; Grachev, *Gorbachev*, 165.

39   Notes on January 29, 1987, Politburo session, in GFA, f. 10, op. 2.

40   Notes on February 5, 1987, Politburo meeting, in ibid.

41   Gorbachev's remarks at January 27–28, 1987, Central Committee plenum, in ibid.

42   Chernyaev's diary, January 10, 1987, entry, in *Sovmestnyi iskhod*, 705.

43   Gorbachev, *Sobranie sochinenii*, 5:503.

44   Ligachev, *Inside Gorbachev's Kremlin*, 284.

45   Boldin, *Ten Years That Shook the World*, 160.

46   Ligachev, *Inside Gorbachev's Kremlin*, 97, 100.

47   Iakovlev, *Sumerki*, 400–402.

48   Ligachev, *Inside Gorbachev's Kremlin*, 101.

49   BBC interview with Leonid Dobrokhotov, in TSRRT.

50   Boldin, *Ten Years That Shook the World*, 159.

51   BBC interview with Lukyanov, in TSRRT.

52   Ligachev, *Inside Gorbachev's Kremlin*, 105–8.

53   See William Taubman and Jane Taubman, *Moscow Spring* (New York: Summit Books, 1989), 94.

54   Gorbachev, *Zhizn'*, 1:365.

55   Notes on March 24, 1987, Politburo meeting, in GFA, f. 2. op. 2.

56   *V Politbiuro*, 161.

57   Chernyaev's diary, July 5, 1987, entry, in *Sovmestnyi iskhod*, 715–16.

58   Chernyaev's diary, August 31, 1987, entry, ibid., 720.

59   See n.16 to Chernyaev's diary, August 28, 1987, entry, ibid., 720–22; Mikhail Gorbachev, *Perestroika: New Thinking for Our Country and the World* (New York: HarperCollins, 1987).

60   Chernyaev, *My Six Years with Gorbachev*, 126.

61   Notes on October 15, 1987, Politburo meeting, in *V Politbiuro*, 245–57.

62   Chernyaev's diary, October 15, 1987, entry, Russian version at NSA website, nsarchive.gwu.edu/rus/text_files/Chernyaev/1987.pdf, pp. 62–63.

63   Ibid.

64   Full text in Gorbachev, *Sobranie sochinenii*, 8:406–59; also see Grachev, *Gorbachev*, 173–74, esp. on Gorbachev's answering his grandfather and the importance of rehabilitating Bukharin.

65   Gorbachev, *Zhizn'*, 1:368.

66   Timothy J. Colton, *Yeltsin: A Life* (New York: Basic Books, 2008), 112.

67   Ibid., 110.

68   Boris Yeltsin, *Against the Grain*, trans. Michael Glenny (New York: Summit Books, 1990), 110.

69   Colton, *Yeltsin*, 108–9.

70   Ibid., 109–12.

71   BBC interview with Dolgikh, in TSRRT.

72   Colton, *Yeltsin*, 130–32.

73   Yeltsin, *Against the Grain*, 125–26.

74   Colton, *Yeltsin*, 128.

75   Yeltsin, *Against the Grain*, 178–81.

76   Chernyaev, *My Six Years with Gorbachev*, 130–31.

77   BBC interview with Gorbachev, in TSRRT; Grachev, *Gorbachev*, 231; Yeltsin, *Against the Grain*, 184–85. Note that Yeltsin does not mention Gorbachev's call from the Crimea, and that Vadim Medvedev contends that Yeltsin took Gorbachev's reference to the holiday to refer to Constitution Day, October 7, which, Medvedev adds, "no one really treated . . . as a holiday." This last speculation seems highly unlikely. See Medvedev, *V kommande Gorbacheva*, 64.

78   Brutents, *Nesbyvsheesia*, 100; Chernyaev's diary, October 21, 1987, entry, Russian version available at NSA.

79   Brutents, *Nesbyvsheesia*, 100; Vorotnikov, *A bylo eto tak*, 169.

80   Gorbachev, *Sobranie sochinenii*, 8:516–19.

81   Ibid., 519–20.

82   Brutents, *Nesbyvsheesia*, 102.

83   Yeltsin, *Against the Grain*, 195.

84   Full record of plenum speeches, in Gorbachev, *Sobranie sochinenii*, 8:516–80. Chernyaev's diary, October 21 entry (Russian version at nsarchive.gwu.edu/rus/text_files/Chernyaev/1987.pdf, pp. 74–92), culls particularly vivid passages.

85   Author's interview with Gorbachev, May 25, 2007, Moscow.

86   Gorbachev, *Naedine s soboi*, 168.

87   Two somewhat different versions of Gorbachev's and Yeltsin's concluding remarks in Gorbachev, *Sobranie sochinenii*, 8:376–84, 577–80; Chernyaev's diary, October 21 entry, Russian version at nsarchive.gwu .edu/rus/text_files/Chernyaev/1987.pdf, pp. 89–92; also see Colton, *Yeltsin*, 146.

88   Brutents enumerates these costs and others, in *Nesbyvsheesia*, 105.

89   Chernyaev's diary, October 31, 1987, entry, Russian version at nsarchive.gwu.edu/rus/text/Chernyaev/1987.pdf, p. 89; Gorbachev, *Sobranie sochinenii*, 8:405.

90   Colton, *Yeltsin*, 147. Colton quotes Yeltsin telling an interviewer in 2002 that had this been done, "history might have veered in a different direction."

91   Ibid., 148.

92   Author's interview with Gorbachev, November 14, 2011, Moscow.

93   Gorbachev, *Zhizn'*, 1:374; Colton, *Yeltsin*, 148; see also Evgenii Chazov, *Rok* (Moscow: Izdatelstvo GEOTAR-MEDITSINA, 2000), 224–25; Aleksandr Korzhakov, *Boris Yeltsin: Ot rassveta do zakata* (Moscow: Interbook, 1997), 65.

94   Gorbachev speech, in Gorbachev, *Sobranie sochinenii*, 8:485–95.

95   Colton, *Yeltsin*, 149–50.

96   Ibid., 150.

97   Brutents, *Nesbyvsheesia*, 106, 108.

98 Gorbachev, *Zhizn'*, 1:291–92.

99 Grachev, *Gorbachev*, 230.

100 Comparisons culled from observations of many. See also Colton, *Yeltsin*, 100.

101 See ibid., 15–22.

102 Yeltsin, *Against the Grain*, 182; also see Colton, *Yeltsin*, 140.

103 Grachev, *Gorbachev*, 231.

104 Author's interview with Gorbachev, November 11, 2011, Moscow.

105 Rudolf Pikhoia mentions the latter theory in *Moskva—Kreml'—Vlast'*, 2:101.

106 Boldin, *Ten Years That Shook the World*, 235–36.

107 Grachev, *Gorbachev*, 231–32.

108 Colton, *Yeltsin*, 130–31.

109 Gorbachev, *Zhizn'*, 1:375.

110 Grachev, *Gibel' Sovetskogo "titanika,"* 238.

CHAPTER 9: WHO'S AFRAID OF NINA ANDREYEVA? 1988

1 This section draws on Taubman and Taubman, *Moscow Spring*, 87–115, 127–45.

2 Ligachev, *Inside Gorbachev's Kremlin*, 285–87.

3 Ibid., 290; Grachev, *Gorbachev*, 219.

4 Gorbachev, *Naedine s soboi*, 166–67.

5 Chernyaev, *My Six Years with Gorbachev*, 150.

6 Grachev, *Gorbachev*, 220–21.

7 Gorbachev, *Sobranie sochinenii*, 9:246, 528.

8 Ibid., 9:235–36.

9 See Taubman and Taubman, *Moscow Spring*, 150–52.

10 BBC interview with Ivan Laptev, in TSRRT.

11 BBC interview with Nina Andreyeva, ibid.

12 Iakovlev, *Sumerki*, 412.

13 BBC interviews with Dolmatov, Pankov, and Andreyeva, in TSRRT.

14 BBC interview with Valery Legostayev, ibid.

15 BBC interview with Starkov, ibid.

16 BBC interview with Laptev, ibid.

17 Grachev reports province party organizations' letter writing campaign in Grachev, *Gibel' Sovetskogo "titanika,"* 149.

18 Grachev, *Gorbachev*, 221–22; Pikhoia, *Moskva—Kreml'—Vlast'*, 2:122; BBC interview with Andreyev, in TSRRT; Taubman and Taubman, *Moscow Spring*, 155; BBC interview with "Major Slava X," in TSRRT.

19 Author's email interview with Svetlana Savranskaya, June 20, 2011.

20 BBC interview with Grigory Baklanov, in TSRRT.

21 BBC interview with Daniil Granin, ibid.

22 BBC interview with Mikhail Ulyanov, ibid.

23 BBC interview with Mikhail Shatrov, ibid.

24 BBC interview with Zaslavskaya, ibid.

25 BBC interview with Dobrokhotov, ibid.

26 BBC interview with Elem Klimov, ibid.

27 BBC interview with Aleksandr Levikov, ibid.

28 Grachev, *Gibel' Sovetskogo "titanika,"* 150.

29 Taubman and Taubman, *Moscow Spring,* 159.

30 BBC interview with Georgy Shakhnazarov, in TSRRT; Gorbachev, *Zhizn',* 1:381.

31 BBC interview with Aleksandr Yakovlev, in TSRRT.

32 Ibid.; Iakovlev, *Sumerki,* 412.

33 BBC interview with Yakovlev, in TSRRT.

34 Gromyko, *Andrei Gromyko,* 145.

35 Aleksandr Yakovlev's account of March 25, 1988, Politburo meeting as told to Chernyaev, in *V Politbiuro,* 305; a fuller account is in Gorbachev, *Sobranie sochinenii,* 10:461–525.

36 Ligachev, *Inside Gorbachev's Kremlin,* 305–8.

37 Grachev, *Gorbachev,* 222–23.

38 Vorotnikov, *A bylo eto tak,* 197–98.

39 Gorbachev, *Sobranie sochinenii,* 10:461–69, 473, 482–86, 507–11.

40 Ibid., 470.

41 Ibid., 479–80.

42 Ibid., 487.

43 Ibid., 499–501; Iakovlev, *Sumerki,* 413–14.

44 Gorbachev, *Sobranie sochinenii,* 10:132–37.

45 Chernyaev, *My Six Years with Gorbachev,* 155.

46 Ibid., 153, 155.

47 Ibid., 156.

48 Taubman and Taubman, *Moscow Spring,* 188–90.

49 Ibid., 101–2.

50 Gorbachev, *Zhizn',* 1:386.

51 Brutents, *Nesbyvsheesia,* 239.

52 Iakovlev, *Perestroika,* 185.

53 Gorbachev, *Sobranie sochinenii,* 9:418.

54 Iakovlev, *Perestroika,* 157–58.

55 Gorbachev, *Sobranie sochinenii,* 9:278.

56 Ibid., 19:279.

57 See Dmitrii Furman, "Fenomen Gorbacheva," *Svobodnaia mysl',* no. 1 (1995): 72–73.

58 Gorbachev, *Zhizn',* 1:388.

59 Ibid., 387.

60 Chernyaev's diary, April 24, 1988, entry, in *Sovmestnyi iskhod,* 753.

61 Medvedev, *V kommande Gorbacheva,* 74–76.

62 Chernyaev, *My Six Years with Gorbachev,* 158.

63   Gorbachev, *Sobranie sochinenii*, 10:226.

64   Ibid., 287.

65   Ibid., 253.

66   Ibid., 228.

67   Ibid., 255.

68   Ibid., 228–29.

69   Ibid., 255.

70   Ibid., 230.

71   Ibid., 253.

72   *V Politbiuro*, 318.

73   Ibid., 343.

74   Ibid., 334–35.

75   Chernyaev's diary, April 24, 1988, entry, in *Sovmestnyi iskhod*, 751.

76   *V Politbiuro*, 338.

77   Ibid., 326–27.

78   Gorbachev, *Sobranie sochinenii*, 10:285–86; Chernyaev, *My Six Years with Gorbachev*, 159.

79   Chernyaev, *My Six Years with Gorbachev*, 159.

80   Gorbachev, *Sobranie sochinenii*, 10:310.

81   Ibid., 314.

82   Chernyaev's diary, April 26, 1988, entry, in *Sovmestnyi iskhod*, 754.

83   Chernyaev diary entry of April 24, 1988, Russian version at nsarchive .gwu.edu/rus/text_file/Chernyaev/1988.pdf, p. 24.

84   Gorbachev, *Sobranie sochinenii*, 10:318.

85   *V Politbiuro*, 365.

86   Gorbachev, *Sobranie sochinenii*, 10:530, 550–52.

87   *V Politbiuro*, 390.

88   Chernyaev's diary, June 19, 1988, entry, in *Sovmestnyi iskhod*, 755–56.

89   *V Politbiuro*, 391–99; Vorotnikov, *A bylo eto tak*, 212–14; Shakhnaz-arov, *S vozhdiami i bez nikh*, 101–3.

90   Taubman and Taubman, *Moscow Spring*, 280–82.

91   BBC interviews with Vitaly Korotich and Elem Klimov, in TSRRT; Brutents, *Nesbyvsheesia*, 245.

92   Gorbachev, *Sobranie sochinenii*, 11: 162, 186, 188, 201.

93   Ibid., 213, 539; BBC interview with Abalkin, in TSRRT.

94   *XIX Vsesoiuznaia konferentsiia kommunisticheskoi partii sovetskogo soiuza: Stenograficheskii otchet*, vol. 1 (Moscow: Izdatel'stvo politiches-koi literatury, 1988), 223–28.

95   BBC interview with Daniil Granin, in TSRRT.

96   Gorbachev, *Sobranie sochinenii*, 11:222.

97   Chenyaev diary entry of July 10, 1988, at nsarchive.gwu.edu/rus/ text_files/Chernyaev/1988.pdf, p. 32.

98   BBC interview with Otto Latsis, in TSRRT.

99   This self-pity served a political purpose when it appeared in a Yelt-

sin memoir in 1989; by then he was back on his feet and running for office. Yeltsin, *Against the Grain*, 203–5.

100   Boris Yeltsin, *The Struggle for Russia*, trans. Catherine A. Fitzgerald (New York: Crown, 1994), 15–16.

101   Yeltsin, *Against the Grain*, 216–36.

102   BBC interview with Granin, in TSRRT.

103   Gorbachev, *Sobranie sochinenii*, 11:249.

104   Colton, *Yeltsin*, 2008, 151–53, 156–57; Chernyaev diary, July 10, 1988, Russian version at nsarchive.gwu.edu/rus/text_files/Chernyaev/1988. pdf, pp. 32–33.

105   Medvedev, *V kommande Gorbacheva*, 78.

106   BBC interview with Dolgikh, in TSRRT.

107   Gorbachev, *Zhizn'*, 1:392.

108   Chernyaev, *My Six Years with Gorbachev*, 165–66.

109   Brutents, *Nesbyvsheesia*, 248.

110   Gorbachev, *Zhizn'*, 1:394, 396.

111   Hans Kohn's seminal work, *The Idea of Nationalism: A Study in Its Origins and Background*, was first published in 1944.

112   Gorbachev, *Memoirs*, 326–28; Grachev, *Gorbachev*, 258–59.

113   Chernyaev, *My Six Years with Gorbachev*, 181.

114   BBC interview with Gennady Kolbin, in TSRRT.

115   Gorbachev, *Memoirs*, 331.

116   Pikhoia, *Moskva—Kreml'—Vlast'*, 2:107–9.

117   BBC interview with Kolbin, in TSRRT.

118   See Grachev, *Gorbachev*, 262–63; Pikhoia, *Moskva—Kreml'—Vlast'*, 2:109–10.

119   BBC interview with Arkady Volsky, in TSRRT; Pikhoia, *Moskva—Kreml'—Vlast'*, 2:111.

120   Appeal in Gorbachev, *Sobranie sochinenii*, 9:394–96.

121   Grachev, *Gorbachev*, 264.

122   Gorbachev, *Sobranie sochinenii*, 9:397–98.

123   Grachev, *Gorbachev*, 264.

124   BBC interview with Zori Balayan, in TSRRT.

125   Brutents quotes a letter to Gorbachev from Andrei Sakharov, in Brutents, *Nesbyvsheesia*, 361–62; Pikhoia quotes Defense Minister Yazov, in Pikhoia, *Moskva—Kreml'—Vlast'*, 2:113; also see Grachev, *Gorbachev*, 264–65; official statistics are in Gorbachev, *Sobranie sochinenii*, 9:585, n. 273.

126   Author's interview with Nikolai Shmelyov, July 26, 2006, Moscow.

127   Pikhoia, *Moskva—Kreml'—Vlast'*, 2:113–14; Gorbachev, *Sobranie sochinenii*, 9:404–9.

128   Gorbachev, *Sobranie sochinenii*, 9:586, n. 282.

129   Ibid., 12:193.

130   Ibid., 10:70–71.

131   Ibid., 11:382.

132   Chernyaev's diary, October 9, 1988, entry, in *Sovmestnyi iskhod*, 767.

133   Gorbachev, *Zhizn'*, 1:400; Chernyaev August 7, 1988, notes on conversation with Gorbachev, in GFA, f. 2. op. 2.

134   See Chernyaev's notes on Gorbachev's dictation sessions while on vacation in *V Politbiuro*, 406–14, and in GFA, f. 2, op. 2; also see Chernyaev, *My Six Years with Gorbachev*, 173–76.

135   Chernyaev diary entry of September 14, 1988, Russian version at nsarchive.gwu.edu/rus/text_file/Chernyaev/1988.pdf, p. 42.

136   Gorbachev, *Zhizn'*, 1:413.

137   Chernyaev, *My Six Years with Gorbachev*, 170–71.

138   Gorbachev, *Sobranie sochinenii*, 11:256–58.

139   *V Politbiuro*, 417.

140   Chernyaev's diary, December 4, 1988, entry, in *Sovmestnyi iskhod*, 775.

141   Gorbachev, *Zhizn'*, 1:413–22; Gorbachev, *Memoirs*, 272–77.

142   Gorbachev, *Zhizn'*, 1:410.

143   Chernyaev's diary, December 17, 1988, entry, in *Sovmestnyi iskhod*, 775.

144   Iakovlev, *Sumerki*, 464.

145   Elena Krementsova, "Liubimaia zhena poslednego genseka," *Ekspress gazeta*, no. 39, 1997, in *Raisa: Vospominaniia*, 172.

146   Chernyaev diary entry, October 23, 1988, Russian version at nsarchive .gwu.edu/rus/text_files/Chernyaev/1988.pdf, p. 54.

147   Ibid., 34; Chernyaev, *My Six Years with Gorbachev*, 167–69.

148   Cherniaev, *Sovmestnyi iskhod*, 789.

CHAPTER 10: BEFORE THE STORM: 1987–1988

1   Documents in NSA Electronic Briefing Book, "Afghanistan and the Soviet Withdrawal 1989: Twenty Years Later." See also *Otvechaia na vyzov vremeni*, 601, 606, 609–13.

2   Ibid., 614, 616–24.

3   Chernyaev's diary, August 28, 1987, and October 28, 1988, entries, in *Sovmestnyi iskhod*, 720, 769.

4   Matlock Jr., *Reagan and Gorbachev*, 285, 288.

5   See Steve Coll, *Ghost Wars: The Secret History of the CIA, Afghanistan, and Bin Laden, from the Soviet Invasion to September 10, 2001* (New York: Penguin Press, 2004).

6   Gorbachev, *Sobranie sochinenii*, 5:291–95.

7   *V Politbiuro*, 366.

8   Notes on July 7, 1987, Politburo meeting, in Savranskaya, Blanton, and Zubok, *Masterpieces of History*, 255.

9   Notes on March 10, 1988, Politburo meeting, ibid., 266–67.

10   Notes on March 24–25, 1988, Politburo meeting, ibid., 270.

11   Preparatory notes for Gorbachev prior to Politburo meeting, October 6, 1988, ibid., 307–8.

12   Ibid., 339.

13   Jacques Lévesque, *The Enigma of 1989: The USSR and the Liberation of Eastern Europe*, trans. Keith Martin (Berkeley: University of California Press, 1997), 54.

14   Ibid., 62; Charles Gati, *The Bloc That Failed: Soviet-East European Relations in Transition* (Bloomington: Indiana University Press, 1990), 178.

15   Lévesque, *Enigma of 1989*, 61–63.

16   Gorbachev, *Sobranie sochinenii*, 6:345–47.

17   Gorbachev, *Zhizn'*, 2:353–54. See also Vadim Medvedev, *Raspad: Kak on nazreval v "mirovoi sisteme sotsializma"* (Moscow: Mezhdunarodnye otnosheniia, 1994), 141–43.

18   Lévesque, *Enigma of 1989*, 59–65.

19   Ibid., 65–68.

20   Gorbachev, *Zhizn'*, 2:319–20.

21   Savranskaya, Blanton, and Zubok, *Masterpieces of History*, 268.

22   Gorbachev, *Zhizn'*, 2:320.

23   Gorbachev, *Sobranie sochinenii*, 5:526.

24   Cited in Grachev, *Gorbachev's Gamble*, 121.

25   Gorbachev, *Sobranie sochinenii*, 11:152.

26   Grachev, *Gorbachev's Gamble*, 121–22.

27   Lévesque, *Enigma of 1989*, 55.

28   Grachev, *Gorbachev's Gamble*, 122–23.

29   Savranskaya, Blanton, and Zubok, *Masterpieces of History*, 156, 265–67.

30   Interview with Musatov, cited in Lévesque, *Enigma of 1989*, 55–56.

31   Notes on November 19, 1987, Poliburo meeting, in Savranskaya, Blanton, and Zubok, *Masterpieces of History*, 259.

32   Medvedev, *Raspad*, 48, 57.

33   Gorbachev, *Zhizn'*, 2:366.

34   Brutents, *Nesbyvsheesia*, 478.

35   Medvedev, *Raspad*, 161–72.

36   Gorbachev, *Zhizn'*, 2:405.

37   *V Politbiuro*, 190; Savranskaya, Blanton, and Zubok, *Masterpieces of History*, 253–54; Gorbachev, *Zhizn'*, 2:393–98.

38   BBC interview with Aleksandr Yakovlev, in TSRRT.

39   Lévesque, *Enigma of 1989*, 44–45, 75–76; Grachev paraphrases Shakhnazarov in Grachev, *Gorbachev's Gamble*, 126–28.

40   *Otvechaya na vyzov vremeni*, 62, 328, 300.

41   Chernayev's diary, July 5, 1987, entry, in *Sovmestnyi iskhod*, 715.

42   Gorbachev, *Sobranie sochinenii*, 7:16.

43   Ibid., 12:490–92.

44   Chernyaev, *My Six Years with Gorbachev*, 198.

45 Gorbachev, *Sobranie sochinenii*, 6:126.
46 Weizsäcker's recollection in Karagez'ian and Poliakov, *Gorbachev v zhizni*, 372; Grachev, *Gorbachev's Gamble*, 133–34; Chernyaev, *My Six Years with Gorbachev*, 114–15.
47 Gorbachev, *Sobranie sochinenii*, 7:299.
48 Ibid., 12:266–72, 532; Gorbachev, *Zhizn'*, 2:154.
49 Gorbachev, *Zhizn'*, 2:154–55.
50 Chernyaev, *My Six Years with Gorbachev*, 198–99.
51 Chernyaev diary entry, June 19, 1988, Russian version at nsarchive .gwu.edu/rus/text_file/Chernyaev/1988.pdf, p. 29.
52 Author's interview with Charles Powell, July 21, 2007, London.
53 Moore, *Margaret Thatcher*, 625.
54 Gorbachev, *Sobranie sochinenii*, 6:225.
55 Chernyaev, *My Six Years with Gorbachev*, 103.
56 Gorbachev, *Sobranie sochinenii*, 6:223–26.
57 Thatcher, *Downing Street Years*, 484; Moore, *Margaret Thatcher*, 630.
58 R. Gorbachev, *I Hope*, 185.
59 Author's interview with Lord Geoffrey Howe, July 22, 2008, London.

CHAPTER 11: SUMMITS GALORE: 1987–1988

1   Andrei Grachev, *Gorbachev's Gamble*, 94.
2   Gorbachev, *Sobranie sochinenii*, 6:556, n. 67.
3   Grachev, *Gorbachev's Gamble*, 96.
4   Hoffman, *Dead Hand*, 279.
5   Palazhchenko, *My Years with Gorbachev*, 66.
6   "Zasedanie Politbiuro TsK KPSS," October 22, 1986, in NSA READD-RADD collection.
7   Don Oberdorfer, *From the Cold War to a New Era: The United States and the Soviet Union, 1983–1991* (Baltimore, MD: Johns Hopkins University Press, 1998), 221.
8   Hoffman, *Dead Hand*, 283.
9   *Otvechaia na vyzov vremeni*, 182.
10 Gorbachev, *Sobranie sochinenii*, 6:348; Shultz, *Turmoil and Triumph*, 894.
11 Dobrynin, *In Confidence*, 623; Hoffman, *Dead Hand*, 283.
12 Anatoly Dobrynin, *Sugubo doveritel'no: Posol v Vashingtone pri shesti prezidentakh SShA (1962–1986)* (Moscow: Mezhdunarodnye otnoshe-niia, 2008), 674–75; Akhromeyev's account in S. F. Akhromeev and G. M. Kornienko, *Glazami marshala i diplomata* (Moscow: Mezhdunarod-nye otnosheniia, 1992), 132–33, is more diplomatic; also see Georgii Kornienko, "Zakonchilas' li 'kholodnaia voina'?," *Nezavisimaia gazeta*, August 16, 1994.
13 Gorbachev, *Sobranie sochinenii*, 6:347.

14   Shultz, *Turmoil and Triumph*, 891–93.

15   Oberdorfer, *From the Cold War to a New Era*, 224.

16   Author's interview with Thomas Simons, November 20, 2006, Cambridge, MA.

17   Gorbachev, *Zhizn'*, 2:51.

18   Shultz, *Turmoil and Triumph*, 893.

19   Matlock Jr., *Reagan and Gorbachev*, 259.

20   Oberdorfer, *From the Cold War to a New Era*, 244.

21   Ibid., 228–29.

22   Politburo minutes in NSA, READD-RADD collection; Oberdorfer, *From the Cold War to a New Era*, 229.

23   Chernyaev, *My Six Years with Gorbachev*, 116–19; "Zasedanie Politbiuro TsK KPSS," May 30, 1987, in NSA, READD-RADD collection.

24   Matlock Jr., *Reagan and Gorbachev*, 259–62.

25   Shultz, *Turmoil and Triumph*, 991–1001; Gorbachev, *Sobranie sochinenii*, 8:393–94.

26   Perhaps, one might add, the Soviet leader was mimicking his predecessors, whose examples he rejected in so many other areas: Stalin's talks with Western leaders inevitably included, after a fairly genial first session, a very nasty second sitting; Khrushchev specialized in threatening to blow up his interlocutors' capitals; Brezhnev, although generally calmer, blew hot and cold.

27   Shultz, *Turmoil and Triumph*, 999–1001.

28   Palazhchenko, *My Years with Gorbachev*, 73–74.

29   Author's interview with Pavel Palazhchenko, March 1, 2007, Moscow.

30   Text in "The INF Treaty and the Washington Summit: 20 Years Later," NSA Electronic Briefing Book No. 238, NSA website.

31   Reagan letter, ibid.

32   Shultz, *Turmoil and Triumph*, 1005–8.

33   In addition to sources cited in footnotes, this account draws on the daily coverage in the *New York Times*, *Washington Post*, and *Los Angeles Times*.

34   "Memorandum of Conversation, Meeting with General Secretary Mikhail Gorbachev of the USSR, December 8, 1987, 10:45 a.m. to 12:30 p.m.," in NSA Electronic Briefing Book No. 238.

35   Colin L. Powell, *My American Journey* (New York: Random House, 1995), 362.

36   "Memo of conversation between Reagan and Gorbachev, December 8, 1987, 2:30 p.m. to 3:15," in NSA Electronic Briefing Book No. 238.

37   Powell, *My American Journey*, 363; Shultz, *Turmoil and Triumph*, 1011.

38   "Memos of conversations between Reagan and Gorbachev, December 9, 1987, 10:30 to 10:45 a.m. and 10:55 to 12:35 p.m.," in NSA Electronic Briefing Book No. 238.

39   "Memos of conversations between Reagan and Gorbachev, December

9, 1987, 12 noon to 12:15 p.m. and 12:40 to 2:10 p.m.," ibid; Gorbachev, *Zhizn'*, 2:64; Reagan, *American Life*, 700.

40   Gorbachev, *Zhizn'*, 2:58; Oberdorfer, *From the Cold War to a New Era*, 259–62; Shultz, *Turmoil and Triumph*, 1009–10.

41   Gorbachev, *Zhizn'*, 2:66.

42   Shultz, *Turmoil and Triumph*, 1012–13; Gorbachev, *Zhizn'*, 2:66–67; David Remnick, "Day 2: The Gorbachev's Washington Orbit," *Washington Post*, December 10, 1987.

43   Gorbachev, *Zhizn'*, 2:64; Philip Taubman, "Prominent Americans Hear Gorbachev's World Vision," *New York Times*, December 9, 1987; David Remnick, "Gorbachev: 'Light a Fire' for U.S.-Soviet Rapport," *Washington Post*, December 9, 1987; William J. Easton, "Gorbachev Makes Bid to U.S. Intellectuals," *Los Angeles Times*, December 9, 1987; Oberdorfer, *From the Cold War to a New Era*, 264.

44   Andrew Rosenthal, "Soviet Visitor Mixes Charm with Venom," *New York Times*, December 8, 1987; Helen Dewar, "Hill Leaders Hold Freewheeling Debate with Soviet," *Washington Post*, December 10, 1987.

45   Robert A. Rosenblatt, "Gorbachev Tempts U.S. Businessmen," *Los Angeles Times*, December 11, 1987; Maureen Dowd, "As 'Gorby' Works the Crowd, Backward Reels the KGB," *New York Times*, December 11, 1987.

46   William J. Easton, "Gorbachev Hosts a Lavish Dinner, Toasts, 'Until We Meet in Moscow,'" *Los Angeles Times*, December 10, 1987.

47   Dowd, "As 'Gorby' Works the Crowd, Backward Reels the KGB"; David Remnick and Lois Romano, "Soviet Leader Stops in Name of Glasnost," *Washington Post*, December 11, 1987; George Bush and Brent Scowcroft, *A World Transformed* (New York: Alfred A. Knopf, 1998), 5.

48   Powell, *My American Journey*, 366; Gorbachev, *Sobranie sochinenii*, 9:124–26; Shultz, *Turmoil and Triumph*, 1014–15.

49   Gorbachev, *Naedine s soboi*, 474.

50   Gates later joked that "between my thugs, Kryuchkov's thugs, and the FBI, there was no room in the restaurant for anyone else," and that it was the only time he'd ever seen "an armed waiter wearing a trenchcoat." Robert M. Gates, *From the Shadows* (New York: Simon & Schuster, 1996), 423–25.

51   Powell, *My American Journey*, 360–61; N. Reagan, *My Turn*, 346–47; David S. Hilzenrath, "Raisa's Woman to Women Chat," *Washington Post*, December 11, 1987.

52   Author's interview with Rebecca Matlock, December 12, 2007, South Hadley, MA.

53   N. Reagan, *My Turn*, 347; author's interview with Rebecca Matlock, November 29, 2007, South Hadley, MA; Donnie Radcliffe and Sarah Booth Conroy, "The First Ladies' Public Truce," *Washington Post*, December 10, 1987.

54   Gorbachev, *Zhizn'*, 2:63.

55   Elaine Sciolino, "Frost in the White House for 2 First Ladies," *New York Times*, December 10, 1987.

56   *Otvechaia na vyzov vremeni*, 181–91; Gorbachev, *Zhizn'*, 2:67–68; Palazhchenko, *My Years with Gorbachev*, 79–80.

57   Palazhchenko, *My Years with Gorbachev*, 80.

58   Grachev, *Gorbachev's Gamble*, 98–100.

59   *Otvechaia na vyzov vremeni*, 192–93.

60   Gorbachev, *Zhizn'*, 2:116.

61   Matlock Jr., *Reagan and Gorbachev*, 284.

62   Shultz, *Turmoil and Triumph*, 1080–86; Matlock Jr., *Reagan and Gorbachev*, 277–79.

63   Shultz, *Turmoil and Triumph*, 1085.

64   Oberdorfer, *From the Cold War to a New Era*, 276–77; Gorbachev, *Sobranie sochinenii*, 2:373.

65   Shultz, *Turmoil and Triumph*, 1096–97; Powell, *My American Journey*, 373–74; Gorbachev, *Sobranie sochinenii*, 10:296–98.

66   Shultz, *Turmoil and Triumph*, 1097–98.

67   Gorbachev, *Sobranie sochinenii*, 10:238.

68   Ibid., 339.

69   Chernyaev's diary entry in "The Moscow Summit 20 Years Later," NSA Electronic Briefing Book No. 251.

70   Matlock Jr., *Reagan and Gorbachev*, 294.

71   He had originally planned to stop on the way from the airport to the Kremlin at the home of two "refuseniks," Tatyana and Yuri Ziman, who had long been denied permission to emigrate and about whom Nancy Reagan had heard from the wife of Russian émigré pianist Vladimir Feltsman. When Gorbachev got wind of this, he was furious. Mrs. Reagan was persuaded to see the Zimans at the American ambassador's residence, Spaso House, to which nearly a hundred dissidents had been invited to meet the Reagans. Ibid., 295–97.

72   "Memo of conversation between Reagan and Gorbachev, May 29, 1988, 3:26 to 4:37 p.m.," in NSA Electronic Briefing Book No. 251.

73   Matlock Jr., *Reagan and Gorbachev*, 298.

74   "Memo of conversation between Reagan and Gorbachev, May 31, 1988, 10:08 to 11:07 a.m.," in NSA Electronic Briefing Book No. 151.

75   Oberdorfer, *From the Cold War to a New Era*, 301–2.

76   Matlock Jr., *Reagan and Gorbachev*, 298–300; Oberdorfer, *From the Cold War to a New Era*, 301–3.

77   Memo of conversation, "The President's Meeting with Monks at Danilov Monastery, May 30, 1988," in NSA Electronic Briefing Book No. 251; Donnie Radcliffe, "The Communicator and the Communists," *Washington Post*, May 31, 1988; "Gorbachev and Reagan Toasts," *New*

York Times, June 1, 1988; Bill Keller, "The Vintage Actor Gets Great Reviews," ibid.

78   Steven V. Roberts, "President Charms Students, But His Ideas Lack Converts," *New York Times*, June 1, 1988; Bill Keller, "Presidential Stroll: Chaos and Applause," ibid., May 30, 1988; Oberdorfer, *From the Cold War to a New Era*, 297–301; Hoffman, *Dead Hand*, 312.

79   N. Reagan, *My Turn*, 352; Billington letter to Mrs. Reagan, April 19, 1988, Duberstein File, Office of Chief of State, Gorbachev meetings, Reagan Library; Donnie Radcliffe, "Nancy vs. Raisa: The Chill of It All," *Washington Post*, June 2, 1988.

80   N. Reagan, *My Turn*, 362–63.

81   Gorbachev to Politburo on June 6, 1988, in NSA Electronic Briefing Book: "The Moscow Summit"; Oberdorfer, *From the Cold War to a New Era*, 306.

82   Matlock Jr., *Reagan and Gorbachev*, 306.

83   October 31, 1988, conference with advisers, in "Reagan, Gorbachev and Bush at Governors Island," NSA Electronic Briefing Book No. 261.

84   Chernyaev's diary, November 3, 1988, entry, ibid.

85   Gorbachev, *Zhizn'*, 2:132; Gorbachev, *Memoirs*, 460.

86   N. Reagan, *My Turn*, 363–64.

87   Author's interview with Gorbachev, November 14, 2011, Moscow.

88   Gorbachev, *Zhizn'*, 2:134; Gorbachev, *Memoirs*, 461.

89   Gorbachev, *Sobranie sochinenii*, 13:18–37; Oberdorfer, *From the Cold War to a New Era*, 316–18.

90   Matlock Jr., *Reagan and Gorbachev*, 307.

91   Chernayev diary, December 17, 1988, entry, at nsarchive.gwu.edu/rus/text_file/Chernyaev/1988.pdf, p. 66.

92   Gorbachev, *Memoirs*, 462.

93   Donnie Radcliffe and Lois Romano, "Lunchtime Détente for the First Ladies," *Washington Post*, December 8, 1988; Oberdorfer, *From the Cold War to a New Era*, 319; Jonathan Fuerbringer, "Dollar Surges after Speech by Gorbachev," *New York Times*, December 8, 1988.

94   Oberdorfer, *From the Cold War to a New Era*, 320.

95   Memorandum of conversation, "The President's Private Meeting with Gorbachev," December 7, 1988, 1:05–1:30 p.m., in NSA collection, EBB, "Reagan, Gorbachev and Bush at Governors Island" in NSA Electronic Briefing Book No. 261; Oberdorfer, *From the Cold War to a New Era*, 321; Bush and Scowcroft, *World Transformed*, 6–7.

96   Gorbachev, *Zhizn'*, 2:135; Palazhchenko, *My Years with Gorbachev*, 105.

97   Gorbachev, *Zhizn'*, 2:135; Palazhchenko, *My Years with Gorbachev*, 107–8.

98   BBC interview with Vano Siradegian, in TSRRT.

CHAPTER 12: 1989: TRIUMPH AND TROUBLE AT HOME

1   Author's interview with Lev Gudkov, director of the Levada Center, June 7, 2016, Moscow.

2   Gorbachev, *Sobranie sochinenii*, 13:84 and 18:58; Chernyaev, *My Six Years with Gorbachev*, 201.

3   Gorbachev, *Zhizn'*, 1:423; Gorbachev, *Poniat' perestroiku*, 180.

4   Chernyaev, *My Six Years with Gorbachev*, 211; Boldin, *Ten Years That Shook the World*, 214; Iakovlev, *Sumerki*, 416; Medvedev, *V kommande Gorbacheva*, 88.

5   Boldin, *Ten Years That Shook the World*, 215.

6   Chernyaev's diary, January 15, 1989, entry, in *Sovmestnyi iskhod*, 779.

7   Andrei Sakharov, *Vospominaniia: V dvukh tomakh*, vol. 2 (Moscow: Prava cheloveka, 1996), 376–81; Viktor Sheinis, *Vzlet i padenie Parlamenta*, vol. 1 (Moscow: Moskovskii tsentr Karnegi fond INDEM, 2005), 214–23.

8   BBC interview with Sergei Stankevich, in TSRRT.

9   BBC interview with Anatoly Sobchak, ibid.

10 Colton, *Yeltsin*, 159.

11 Yeltsin, *Against the Grain*, 18.

12 See Colton, *Yeltsin*, 163–66; Jack F. Matlock Jr., *Autopsy on an Empire: The American Ambassador's Account of the Collapse of the Soviet Union* (New York: Random House, 1995), 207–10.

13 Gorbachev, *Sobranie sochinenii*, 13:530–31, nn. 198 and 200; Matlock Jr., *Autopsy on an Empire*, 210–12; Medvedev, *V kommande Gorbacheva*, 85–86.

14 Gorbachev, *Sobranie sochinenii*, 13:425, 431, 444; Vorotnikov, *A bylo eto tak*, 254; Savranskaya, Blanton, and Zubok, *Masterpieces of History*, 429; Gorbachev, *Memoirs*, 280.

15 Author's interview with Gorbachev, May 25, 2007, Moscow.

16 Notes on March 28, 1989, Politburo meeting, in Savranskaya, Blanton, and Zubok, *Masterpieces of History*, 425–28.

17 Chernyaev, *My Six Years with Gorbachev*, 218.

18 Shakhnazarov, *S vozhdiami i bez nikh*, 331.

19 Medvedev, *V kommande Gorbacheva*, 87.

20 Gorbachev, *Sobranie sochinenii*, 13:241–44, 514, n. 119.

21 Ibid., 507, n. 97, pp. 313–14.

22 Matlock Jr., *Autopsy on an Empire*, 232–33.

23 Chernyaev, *My Six Years with Gorbachev*, 226–27; Savranskaya, Blanton, and Zubok, *Masterpieces of History*, 451.

24 Matlock Jr., *Autopsy on an Empire*, 238.

25 Gorbachev, *Sobranie sochinenii*, 14:547, n. 92; Ligachev, *Inside Gorbachev's Kremlin*, 149–68; Gorbachev, *Zhizn'*, 1:514.

26 Ryzhkov, *Perestroika*, 214–17; Boldin, *Ten Years That Shook the World*,

221, 223; Brutents, *Nesbyvsheesia*, 369; Palazhchenko on Patiashvili, in Palazhchenko, *My Years with Gorbachev*, 125; Chernyaev's diary, April 16, 1989, entry, in *Sovmestnyi iskhod*, 789.

27   The commission's report is in "Istoricheskii arkhiv," no. 3 (1993); also see Brown, *Gorbachev Factor*, 264–67.

28   Gorbachev, *Sobranie sochinenii*, 13:227–29.

29   Ibid., 13:272–73.

30   Chernyaev, *My Six Years with Gorbachev*, 208; Gorbachev, *Sobranie sochinenii*, 13:97–101.

31   Sheinis, *Vzlet i padenie Parlamenta*, 1:121–26.

32   "Zasedanie Politbiuro TS K KPSS," October 24, 1989, in NSA READD-RADD collection.

33   Brutents, *Nesbyvsheesia*, 264, 270; Gorbachev, *Sobranie sochinenii*, 14:121; Pikhoia, *Moskva—Kreml'—Vlast'*, 2:136; Chernyaev, *My Six Years with Gorbachev*, 223–25; Gorbachev, *Sobranie sochinenii*, 14:152.

34   Gorbachev, *Zhizn'*, 1:430; Chernyaev's notes on January 17 conversation with aides, in GFA, f. 2. op. 2; "doomed to work out solutions," in Gorbachev, *Sobranie sochinenii*, 13:193; Medvedev's notes on phone conversations with Gorbachev, in GFA, f. 10, op. 2; about Gorbachev's new book, in Chernyaev's diary, January 20, February 19, March 8, March 11, 1989, entries, and "vessel from God," in Chernyaev's diary, April 3, 1989, entry, in *Sovmestnyi iskhod*, 781–87.

35   Chernyaev's diary, May 2, 1989, entry, in *Sovmestnyi iskhod*, 792.

36   Boldin, *Ten Years That Shook the World*, 219; Matlock Jr., *Autopsy on an Empire*, 201.

37   *Pervyi s'ezd narodnykh deputatov SSSR: 25 maia–9 iunia 1989, stenograficheskii otchet*, vol. 1 (Moscow: Izdanie verkhovnogo soveta SSSR, n.d.), 6; BBC interview with Galina Starovoitova, in TSRRT.

38   Gorbachev, *Zhizn'*, 1:435; BBC interview with Yuri Chernichenko, in TSRRT; Medvedev, *V kommande Gorbacheva*, 97; Yurii Kariakin, *Peremena ubezhdenii* (Moscow: Raduga, 2007), 219; Boldin, *Ten Years That Shook the World*, 219; Remnick, *Lenin's Tomb*, 221; Conor O'Clery, *Moscow, December 25, 1991: The Last Day of the Soviet Union* (New York: Public Affairs, 2011), 72.

39   BBC interviews with Mikhail Nanashev and Vladislav Starkov, in TSRRT.

40   *Pervyi s'ezd narodnykh deputatov SSSR*, 1:9–11; Gorbachev, *Sobranie sochinenii*, 1:294–301.

41   BBC interviews with Ales Adamovich and Daniil Granin, in TSRRT; Boldin, *Ten Years That Shook the World*, 224–26.

42   G. Popov, *Snova v oppozitsii* (Moscow: Gapaktika, 1994), 60–67; BBC interview with Starovoitova, in TSRRT.

43   Popov, *Snova v oppozitsii*, 66; Colton, *Yeltsin*, 2008, 168.

44   Embassy Moscow to Department of State, Telegram 20097, June 19,

1990, D900557-0718, Central Foreign Policy Files, RG 59: General Records of the Department of State in U.S. National Archives.

45 Yeltsin, *Against the Grain*, 246–47; Popov, *Snova v oppozitsii*, 66; Colton, *Yeltsin*, 158–60.

46 BBC interviews with Yuri Afanasyev, Aleksandr Yakovlev, and Sergei Stankevich, in TSRRT.

47 Sakharov, *Vospominaniia*, 2:397–98; BBC interview with Ales Adamovich, in TSRRT.

48 Gorbachev, *Zhizn'*, 1:447; Sakharov, *Vospominaniia*, 2:406; Gorbachev, *Poniat' perestroiku*, 197.

49 Sakharov, *Vospominaniia*, 2:416–18; interview with M. S. Gorbachev, in Aleksandr Babenyshev, ed., *Sakharovskii sbornik* (Moscow: Rossiiskii gosudarstvennyi gumanitarnyi universitet, 2011), 270–71.

50 Gorbachev, *Zhizn'*, 1:449; Gorbachev, *Memoirs*, 299.

51 Gorbachev, *Sobranie sochinenii*, 14:454–55, 520–24.

52 Vorotnikov, *A bylo eto tak*, 276; BBC interview with Ales Adamovich, in TSRRT.

53 Gorbachev, *Zhizn'*, 1:439; BBC interview with Aleksandr Yakovlev, in TSRRT; Shakhnazarov, *S vozhdiami i bez nikh*, 332.

54 Chernyaev, *My Six Years with Gorbachev*, 230.

55 Gaidar, *Collapse of an Empire*, 141.

56 *V Politbiuro*, 509.

57 Theodore H. Friedgut and Lewis H. Seigelbaum, "The Soviet Miners' Strike: Perestroika from Below," *Carl Beck Papers in Russian and East European Studies*, no. 804 (March 1990); BBC interviews with miners, in TSRRT.

58 BBC interview with Nikolai Ryzhkov, in TSRRT; Gorbachev, *Zhizn'*, 1:461.

59 Notes on October 12, 1989, Politburo meeting, in Gorbachev, *Sobranie sochinenii*, 16:240; notes on November 3, 1989, Politburo meeting, in *V Politbiuro*, 550.

60 Petrakov, *Russkaia ruletka*, 103–5.

61 Matlock Jr., *Autopsy on an Empire*, 235–36, 270, 282; Gorbachev, *Sobranie sochinenii*, 16:39–77 and 18:24, 40; *V Politbiuro*, 515, 525–33.

62 Popov, *Snova v oppozitsii*, 70, 74.

63 Brutents, *Nesbyvsheesia*, 266, 270; Gorbachev, *Sobranie sochinenii*, 17:332, 533, n. 181.

64 Chernyaev, *My Six Years with Gorbachev*, 245.

65 Gorbachev's remarks to Shakhnazarov, on December 5 and 7, 1990, are in Gorbachev, *Sobranie sochinenii*, 23:185, 305.

66 Gorbachev, *Sobranie sochinenii*, 15:461–68, with quoted lines on p. 465; Chernyaev, *My Six Years with Gorbachev*, 228–29.

67 Chernyaev's diary, October 9, 1989, entry, in *Sovmestnyi iskhod*, 807.

68 BBC interview with Vladislav Starkov, in TSRRT; Brutents, *Nesby-*

vsheesia, 299. In 1995, at a U.S. embassy reception in Moscow, Gorbachev clapped Starkov on the back, as if, says Brutents, apologizing for what happened in 1989. On various poll results, see Brown, *Gorbachev Factor*, 270–71, and Brown, *Seven Years That Changed the World*, 325–28.

69   Vorotnikov, *A bylo eto tak*, 294–96; Chernyaev's diary, October 29, 1989, entry, in *Sovmestnyi iskhod*, 814–15.

70   *Vtoroi s"ezd narodnykh deputatov SSSR, 12-12 dekabria 1989, stenograficheskii otchet*, vols. 1–2 (Moscow: Izdanie verkhovnogo soveta SSSR, n.d.), 1:32.

71   Remnick, *Lenin's Tomb*, 282.

72   *Vtoroi s"ezd narodnykh deputatov SSSR*, 2:145; Remnick, *Lenin's Tomb*, 283–84.

73   Gorbachev, *Sobranie sochinenii*, 17:406; Remnick, *Lenin's Tomb*, 286–87.

74   Shakhnazarov, *S vozhdiami i bez nikh*, 365.

75   Matlock Jr., *Autopsy on an Empire*, 247–48.

76   Ibid., 248–49; Bush and Scowcroft, *World Transformed*, 142.

77   Bush and Scowcroft, *World Transformed*, 143; Gates, *From the Shadows*, 479.

78   Colton, *Yeltsin*, 174–75.

79   Paul Hendrickson, "Yeltsin's Smashing Day," *Washington Post*, September 13, 1989, D1.

80   Eleanor Randolph, "Yeltsin's 'Spree' Denied," *Washington Post*, September 20, 1989; Garrison quoted in O'Clery, *Moscow, December 25, 1991*, 86; "Writer Admits Yeltsin Source Is Nonexistent," *Washington Post*, September 21, 1989.

81   Shakhnazarov, *S vozhdiami i bez nikh*, 371–72; "'Repubblika' o B.N. El'tsine," *Pravda*, September 18, 1989; "V sviazi s publikatsiei o B.N. El'tsine v gazete 'Repubblika,'" ibid., September 21, 1989; remark to Medvedev in the latter's notes on September 19–20 Central Committee plenum, in GFA, f. 10, op. 2.

82   Yeltsin, *Against the Grain*, 258–59.

83   Gorbachev, *Sobranie sochinenii*, 16:249, 518–20.

84   Yeltsin, *Against the Grain*, 260–61.

CHAPTER 13: 1989: TRIUMPH AND TROUBLE ABROAD

1   The following account is based on Hans-Hermann Hertle, "The Fall of the Wall: The Unintended Self-Dissolution of East Germany's Ruling Regime," *Cold War International History Project Bulletin*, no. 12/13 (Fall/Winter 2001): 131–40, 153–58; also see Mary Elise Sarotte, *1989: The Struggle to Create Post–Cold War Europe* (Princeton, NJ: Princeton University Press, 2009), 35–45; Mary Elise Sarotte, *The Collapse: The Accidental Opening of the Berlin Wall* (New York: Basic Books, 2014).

2   As East Germans rushed toward the wall, East German leader Krenz contacted Soviet Ambassador Kochemasov, who tried to reach Shevardnadze in Moscow but didn't get through. He did reach Kovalev at the Foreign Ministry, but when Kovalev insisted on receiving a formal telegram with the news, Kochemasov concluded that meant Moscow did not oppose opening the border. See Haslam, *Russia's Cold War*, 390.

3   Grachev, *Gibel' Sovetskogo "titanika,"* 161.

4   Personal communication from Gorbachev to the author, October 26, 2012.

5   See William Taubman and Svetlana Savranskaya, "If a Wall Fell in Berlin and Moscow Hardly Noticed, Would It Still Make a Noise," in *The Fall of the Berlin Wall: The Revolutionary Legacy of 1989*, ed. Jeffrey A. Engel (New York: Oxford University Press, 2009), 70.

6   Bush administration reaction, in Philip Zelikow and Condoleezza Rice, *Germany Unified and Europe Transformed: A Study in Statecraft* (Cambridge, MA: Harvard University Press, 1997), 107; Gorbachev messages and phone conversations, in Christian F. Ostermann, ed., "The End of the Cold War," *Cold War International History Project Bulletin*, no. 12/13 (Fall/Winter 2001): 158–60.

7   Chernyaev and Shakhnazarov in Savranskaya, Blanton, and Zubok, *Masterpieces of History*, 146, 151; Vladislav Zubok, "New Evidence on the Soviet Factor in the Peaceful Revolutions of 1989," *Cold War International History Project Bulletin*, no. 12/13 (Fall/Winter 2001): 10.

8   Gorbachev, *Sobranie sochinenii*, 13:198, 475.

9   Text of Strasbourg speech, in Savranskaya, Blanton, and Zubok, *Masterpieces of History*, 492–96; and in Gorbachev, *Sobranie sochinenii*, 15:156–59.

10 Savranskaya, Blanton, and Zubok, *Masterpieces of History*, 347–48.

11 Gorbachev, *Zhizn'*, 2:137.

12 James A. Baker III, *The Politics of Diplomacy: Revolution, War and Peace, 1989–1992* (New York: G. P. Putnam's Sons, 1995), 62–63.

13 Chernyaev, *My Six Years with Gorbachev*, 215.

14 Bush and Scowcroft, *World Transformed*, 9.

15 Zelikow and Rice, *Germany Unified*, 19.

16 Bush and Scowcroft, *World Transformed*, 13.

17 Brent Scowcroft to Condoleezza Rice and Philip Zelikow, February 27, 1995, Box 1, Zelikow-Rice Papers, Hoover Institution Archives.

18 Michael R. Beschloss and Strobe Talbott, *At the Highest Levels: The Inside Story of the End of the Cold War* (Boston: Little, Brown, 1993), 27–28.

19 Bush and Scowcroft, *World Transformed*, 46.

20 Ibid., 21.

21 Ibid., 27; Author's interview with James A. Baker III, October 8, 2006, Houston, TX.

22 Grachev, *Gorbachev's Gamble*, 177; Savranskaya, Blanton, and Zubok, *Masterpieces of History*, 192.

23 Tarasenko remarks in Savranskaya, Blanton, and Zubok, *Masterpieces of History*, 195; on Kennedy and Khrushchev, see Taubman, *Khrushchev*, 480–93.

24 Gorbachev, *Zhizn'*, 2:137.

25 Notes on Politburo meeting of April 20, 1989, in Savranskaya, Blanton, and Zubok, *Masterpieces of History*, 447.

26 Ibid., 476; Gorbachev, *Sobranie sochinenii*, 13:300.

27 Cited in Bush and Scowcroft, *World Transformed*, 27–28.

28 Ibid., 40.

29 Matlock telegram, "The Soviet Union over the Next Four Years," February 3, 1989, in Savranskaya, Blanton, and Zubok, *Masterpieces of History*, 383.

30 Matlock himself noted and credited these further objections in his February 22, 1989, telegram, "U.S.-Soviet Relations: Policy Opportunities," ibid., 400; Thomas Blanton cites NSD 23 and argues that Gorbachev had already satisfied its conditions, in "U.S. Policy and the Revolutions of 1989," ibid., 71.

31 Author's interview (via email) with George H. W. Bush, September 19, 2006.

32 Beschloss and Talbott, *At the Highest Levels*, 34.

33 Baker III, *Politics of Diplomacy*, 70.

34 Lou Cannon, "Reagan Is Concerned about Bush's Indecision," *Washington Post*, May 6, 1989.

35 Bush and Scowcroft, *World Transformed*, 44.

36 Baker III, *Politics of Diplomacy*, 72–80; Beschloss and Talbott, *At the Highest Levels*, 63–65.

37 Baker III, *Politics of Diplomacy*, 79.

38 Beschloss and Talbott, *At the Highest Levels*, 65; Gorbachev, *Zhizn'*, 2:139; Baker III, *The Politics of Diplomacy*, 81–82.

39 Gorbachev, *Zhizn'*, 2:141; Beschloss and Talbott, *At the Highest Levels*, 66.

40 Entry for April 7, 1989, in unpublished manuscript of Rodric Braithwaite, "Moscow Diary, 1988 to 1992," n.d.; Savranskaya, Blanton, and Zubok, *Masterpieces of History*, 438–41; Beschloss and Talbott, *At the Highest Levels*, 49; Gorbachev, *Sobranie sochinenii*, 14:43.

41 Braithwaite's diary, April 6, 1989, entry, in "Moscow Diary, 1988 to 1992"; Chernyaev's diary, April 16, 1989, entry, in *Sovmestnyi iskhod*, 788.

42 Gorbachev, *Zhizn'*, 2:84–85. Queen Elizabeth eventually did visit Russia, but only in 1994, when Yeltsin was president.

43 Ibid., 2:80–86.

44 Braithwaite's diary, April 6, 1989, entry, in "Moscow Diary, 1988 to 1992"; Gorbachev, *Zhizn'*, 2:85.

45 Gorbachev, *Zhizn'*, 2:157–59; Gorbachev, *Memoirs*, 521–22.

46 Zelikow and Rice, *Germany Unified*, 33; Chernyaev, *My Six Years with Gorbachev*, 223; Savranskaya, Blanton, and Zubok, *Masterpieces of History*, 488. Also see "Gespräch des Bundeskanzlers Kohl mit Generalsekretär Gorbatschow, Bonn, 12. Juni 1989," in Hanns Jürgen Küsters and Daniel Hofmann, eds., *Deutsche Einheit: Sonderedition aus den Akten des Bundeskanzleramtes, 1989/90*, Dokumente zur Deutschlandpolitik (Munich: R. Oldenbourg Verlag, 1998), 281.

47 Savranskaya, Blanton, and Zubok, *Masterpieces of History*, 465–66; Küsters and Hofmann, *Deutsche Einheit*, 283.

48 Savranskaya, Blanton, and Zubok, *Masterpieces of History*, 465–66; Hannes Adomeit, *Imperial Overstretch: Germany in Soviet Policy from Stalin to Gorbachev* (Baden-Baden: Nomos Verlagsgesellschaft, 1998), 398–99.

49 Gorbachev, *Sobranie sochinenii*, 14:600, n. 362; Küsters and Hofmann, *Deutsche Einheit*, 279.

50 Adomeit, *Imperial Overstretch*, 396, 399; Gorbachev, *Zhizn'*, 2:161; Savranskaya, Blanton, and Zubok, *Masterpieces of History*, 475.

51 Bozo, *Mitterrand*, 62–65.

52 Savranskaya, Blanton, and Zubok, *Masterpieces of History*, 490–91; Gorbachev, *Sobranie sochinenii*, 15:529, n. 86; Gorbachev, *Zhizn'*, 2:93.

53 Kirill Lavrov, "No byt' zhivym, zhivim i tol'ko . . . ," in Karagez'ian and Poliakov, *Gorbachev v zhizni*, 231.

54 Ezra Vogel, *Deng Xiaoping and the Transformation of China* (Cambridge, MA: Harvard University Press, 2011), 616–32.

55 See excerpts from transcripts of Gorbachev-Deng and Gorbachev-Zhao talks, in Gorbachev, *Sobranie sochinenii*, 14:203–5; and in Gorbachev, *Zhizn'*, 2:435–47.

56 Cited in Vogel, *Deng Xiaoping*, 423.

57 Shakhnazarov notes for Gorbachev prior to October 6, 1988, Politburo meeting, in Vladislav Zubok, "New Evidence on the 'Soviet Factor' in the Peaceful Revolutions of 1989," *Cold War International History Project Bulletin*, no. 12/13 (Fall/Winter 2001): 15.

58 Chernyaev notes on January 21, 1989, Politburo session, ibid., 16–17.

59 A third report on Eastern Europe, by the Foreign Ministry, consisted mostly of boilerplate, confirming that the ministry's role in Eastern Europe was subsidiary to that of the Soviet party's Central Committee. Texts of all three reports, as well as an article explicating them, Lévesque, "Soviet Approaches to Eastern Europe at the Beginning of 1989," are ibid., 49–72; the Bucharest declaration is cited in Hertle, "Fall of the Wall," 133.

60 Gorbachev, *Zhizn'*, 2:347; Chernyaev remark at Musgrove conference, in Savranskaya, Blanton, and Zubok, *Masterpieces of History*, 127–28; Savranskaya, "Logic of 1989," ibid., 41–43; record of Gorbachev-Czyrek talks, September 23, 1988, ibid., 292–305.

61   Grachev cites Jaruzelski's account of this conversation, in Grachev, *Gibel' Sovetskogo "titanika,"* 165–66.
62   Lévesque, *Enigma of 1989*, 122, 125.
63   Gorbachev, *Sobranie sochinenii*, 16:212, 233.
64   Savranskaya, Blanton, and Zubok, *Masterpieces of History*, 550.
65   Paweł Machcewicz, "Poland 1986–1989: From 'Cooptation' to 'Negotiated Revolution,'" *Cold War International History Project Bulletin*, no. 12/13 (Fall/Winter 2001): 94; Rakowski cited in Lévesque, *Enigma of 1989*, 123–27.
66   Lévesque, *Enigma of 1989*, 129–30.
67   Memorandum of conversation between Gorbachev and Grósz, in *Cold War International History Project Bulletin*, no. 12/13 (Fall/Winter 2001): 78.
68   Record of conversation between Gorbachev and Németh, March 3, 1989, in Savranskaya, Blanton, and Zubok, *Masterpieces of History*, 412.
69   Lévesque, *Enigma of 1989*, 131–33.
70   See Akhromeev and Kornienko, *Glazami marshala i diplomata*, 219–20.
71   Lévesque cites interviews with Aleksandr Yakovlev, Vadim Medvedev, and Central Committee official Vadim Zagladin, in *Enigma of 1989*, 137.
72   Grachev, *Gorbachev's Gamble*, 136–37.
73   Brutents, *Nesbyvsheesia*, 473.
74   Chernyaev's diary, October 11, 1989, entry, quoting Gorbachev, in Savranskaya, Blanton, and Zubok, *Masterpieces of History*, 548; Memorandum of conversation betwewen Gorbachev and Krenz, November 1, 1989, in *Cold War International History Project Bulletin*, no. 12/13 (Fall/Winter 2001): 142.
75   Gorbachev, *Zhizn'*, 2:410.
76   V. M. Falin, *Bez skidok na obstoiatel'stva* (Moscow: Respublika, 1999), 439.
77   Gorbachev, *Zhizn'*, 2:411–12.
78   Gorbachev's remark to Falin cited in Grachev, *Gorbachev's Gamble*, 138; Rakowski's to Gorbachev in Gorbachev, *Zhizn'*, 2:412; Falin, *Bez skidok na obstoiatel'stva*, 440–41; Gorbachev remarks to East German Politburo, in Savranskaya, Blanton, and Zubok, *Masterpieces of History*, 544–46; Günther Schabowski's recollection, in Adomeit, *Imperial Overstretch*, 412.
79   According to Shakhnazarov, Gorbachev's remark to East German leaders wasn't so much a warning to them as a reference to the Soviet Union's own experience. See Grachev, *Gibel' Sovetskogo "titanika,"* 174.
80   Lévesque, *Enigma of 1989*, 156.
81   Gorbachev, *Poniat' perestroiku*, 215.
82   Adomeit, *Imperial Overstretch*, 413–17.
83   Chernyaev's diary, October 8, 1989, entry, in *Sovmestnyi iskhod*, 806.
84   Shakhnazarov's recollection in Grachev, *Gorbachev's Gamble*, 138.

85   Zelikow and Rice, *Germany Unified*, 104.

86   The mass flight of East Germans through Hungary happened despite the efforts of the East German Politburo to prevent it; when East Berlin realized it could not halt the exodus, it ended the ability of East Germans to travel to Hungary at all. As for Prague, the GDR sealed its borders on October 3, 1989. On flight through Hungary and Prague, see Adomeit, *Imperial Overstretch*, 388–90; Sarotte, *1989*, 28–33; Pleshakov, *There Is No Freedom*, 181–84. "Prague Communists Called for the Wall to Open on November 8, 1989," NSA Electronic Briefing Book No. 294, document nos. 11, 16, 18, 19, 21, 26.

87   Medvedev, *Raspad*, 192.

88   Zelikow and Rice, *Germany Unified*, 91.

89   Ibid., 110–11; Adomeit, *Imperial Overstretch*, 430.

90   Cited in Adomeit, *Imperial Overstretch*, 455.

91   With the exception of Stalin's almost certainly false 1952 offer of reunification of Germany in return for its neutralization. See John Lewis Gaddis, *We Now Know: Rethinking Cold War History* (New York: Oxford University Press, 1997), 125–29.

92   Zelikow and Rice, *Germany Unified*, 96.

93   Baker III, *Politics of Diplomacy*, 2, 161.

94   Hertle, "Fall of the Wall," 139.

95   Mitterrand aide Jacques Attali's recollection, cited in Grachev, *Gorbachev's Gamble*, 142.

96   Zelikow and Rice, *Germany Unified*, 98.

97   Robert L. Hutchings, *American Diplomacy and the End of the Cold War: An Insider's Account of U.S. Policy in Europe, 1989–1992* (Washington, DC: Woodrow Wilson Center Press, 1997), 104.

98   Grachev, *Gorbachev's Gamble*, 142–43.

99   Chernyaev's notes, in Savranskaya, Blanton, and Zubok, *Masterpieces of History*, 532.

100   Chernyaev's diary, September 23, 1989, entry, in *Sovmestnyi iskhod*, 803.

101   Bozo, *Mitterrand*, 58, 98.

102   Record of telephone conversation between Gorbachev and Mitterrand, in Savranskaya, Blanton, and Zubok, *Masterpieces of History*, 593–94.

103   Zelikow and Rice, *Germany Unified*, 94.

104   Records of Kissinger conversation with Yakovlev, January 16, 1989, and Brzezinski, October 31, 1989, in Iakovlev, *Perestroika*, 305, 377; English translation of Yakovlev-Brzezinski conversation in Savranskaya, Blanton, and Zubok, *Masterpieces of History*, 566.

105   Chernyaev notes on November 3, 1989, Politburo meeting, in GFA, f. 2, op. 2.

106   Gorbachev, *Sobranie sochinenii*, 16:516, n. 200.

107   Ibid., 16:436.

108   Adomeit, *Imperial Overstretch*, 439.

109   Bozo, *Mitterrand*, 116.

110   Record of Bush-Kohl telephone conversation, in Savranskaya, Blanton, and Zubok, *Masterpieces of History*, 596.

111   Grachev, *Gorbachev's Gamble*, 143–44.

112   Ibid., 145–46.

113   Sarotte, *1989*, 70–71.

114   Texts of "official" and "unofficial" Soviet positions, in "The Soviet Origins of Helmut Kohl's 10 Points," in NSA Electronic Briefing Book No. 296, NSA website.

115   Grachev, *Gorbachev's Gamble*, 146.

116   Frank Elbe and Richard Kiessler, *A Round Table with Sharp Corners: The Diplomatic Path to German Unity* (Baden-Baden: Nomos Verlagsgesellschaft, 1996), 48.

117   See http://germanhistorydocs.ghi-dc.org/docpage.cfm?docpage_id=116.

118   Zelikow and Rice, *Germany Unified*, 123.

119   Baker III, *Politics of Diplomacy*, 166.

120   Bozo, *Mitterrand*, 124.

121   Hutchings, *American Diplomacy*, 99.

122   Genscher cited in Adomeit, *Imperial Overstretch*, 449; Anatolii Cherniaev, *Shest' let s Gorbachevym* (Moscow: Izdatel'skaya gruppa "Progress"—"Kul'tura," 1993), 308.

123   Transcript of Gorbachev-Genscher talks, in Savranskaya, Blanton, and Zubok, *Masterpieces of History*, 653–56; see also Cherniaev, *Shest' let s Gorbachevym*, 306–7.

124   Grachev, *Gorbachev's Gamble*, 149–50.

125   Kohl cited in Adomeit, *Imperial Overstretch*, 457.

126   Savranskaya, Blanton, and Zubok, *Masterpieces of History*, 657–59; see also Adomeit, *Imperial Overstretch*, 459–60; Bozo, *Mitterrand*, 134–36, esp. n. 131 on pp. 137–38.

127   Bush and Scowcroft, *World Transformed*, 154.

128   Baker III, *The Politics of Diplomacy*, 168.

129   Beschloss and Talbott, *At the Highest Levels*, 127–30.

130   Chernyaev's diary, January 2, 1990, entry, in *Sovmestnyi iskhod*, 833.

131   Gorbachev, *Sobranie sochinenii*, 17:184, n. 85.

132   Bush and Scowcroft, *World Transformed*, 161–62.

133   Soviet transcript of Malta Summit, December 2–3, 1989, in Savranskaya, Blanton, and Zubok, *Masterpieces of History*, 625.

134   Chernyaev, *My Six Years with Gorbachev*, 233; Bush and Scowcroft, *World Transformed*, 162; Gorbachev, *Zhizn'*, 2:143.

135   Savranskaya, Blanton, and Zubok, *Masterpieces of History*, 620–24; Beschloss and Talbott, *At the Highest Levels*, 155. In fact, the Jackson-Vanik Amendment would not be lifted during the George H. W. Bush

administration, nor even after the collapse of the Soviet Union, but only well into the Obama administration.

136   Soviet transcript of Malta summit, in Savranskaya, Blanton, and Zubok, *Masterpieces of History*, 626; Chernyaev's diary, December 10, 1989, entry, in *Sovmestnyi iskhod*, 823; Chernyaev, *My Six Years with Gorbachev*, 234.

137   Soviet transcript of Malta Summit, in Savranskaya, Blanton, and Zubok, *Masterpieces of History*, 627, 641.

138   Soviet transcript, ibid., 627, 634–35, 640.

139   Chernyaev, *My Six Years with Gorbachev*, 234; Chernyaev's diary, December 10, 1989, entry, in *Sovmestnyi iskhod*, 825.

140   Soviet transcript, in Savranskaya, Blanton, and Zubok, *Masterpieces of History*, 636, 645–46.

141   Chernyaev, *My Six Years with Gorbachev*, 235.

142   Akhromeev and Kornienko, *Glazami marshala i diplomata*, 253–54; Dobrynin, *In Confidence*, 630; Brutents, *Nesbyvsheesia*, 153–54.

143   Personal communications from Jack Matlock Jr., April 4 and 8, 2016; Bush and Scowcroft, *World Transformed*, 173.

144   Beschloss and Talbott, *At the Highest Levels*, 153–54.

CHAPTER 14: COMING APART? 1990

1   Chernyaev, *My Six Years with Gorbachev*, 275–76.

2   Ibid., 311–12.

3   Grachev, *Gorbachev's Gamble*, 330–31.

4   R. Gorbachev, *I Hope*, 189, 191–92.

5   BBC interview with Georgy Shakhnazarov, in TSRRT.

6   Akhromeev and Kornienko, *Glazami marshala i diplomata*, 330–31.

7   Author's interview with Douglas Hurd, July 22, 2008, London.

8   Author's interview with Jack F. Matlock Jr., October 18, 2007, South Hadley, MA.

9   Anatoly Strelyany, "Five Hours with Gorbachev," in Lev Timofeev, ed., *The Anti-Communist Manifesto: Whom to Help in Russia* (Bellevue, WA: Free Enterprise Press, 1990), 88.

10   Gorbachev, *Sobranie sochinenii*, 18:62.

11   Chernyaev's diary, January 6, 1990, entry, in *Sovmestnyi iskhod*, 836.

12   Leon Aron, *Yeltsin: A Revolutionary Life* (New York: St. Martin's Press, 2000), 354–55.

13   Cited in Petrakov, *Russkaia ruletka*, 106.

14   Gorbachev, *Sobranie sochinenii*, 18:95.

15   Remnick, *Lenin's Tomb*, 301.

16   Chernyaev, *My Six Years with Gorbachev*, 264–65.

17   Beschloss and Talbott, *At the Highest Levels*, 200.

18   BBC interviews with Vadim Bakatin, Yevgeny Primakov, and Georgy

Shakhnazarov, in TSRRT; Matlock Jr., *Autopsy on an Empire*, 300–304; Gorbachev, *Memoirs*, 518–20; R. Gorbachev, *I Hope*, 174–75.

19 Notes on meeting, in *V Politbiuro*, 572–78.

20 Chernyaev, *My Six Years with Gorbachev*, 255–56.

21 Cherynaev notes on "Meeting of the working group on the discussion in the Politburo of the CPSU platform," January 23, 1990, in GFA, f. 2, op. 2.

22 Remnick, *Lenin's Tomb*, 302.

23 Vadim Medvedev notes on meeting at the Central Committee, February 24 and 25, 1990, in GFA, f. 10, op. 2

24 *Materialy plenuma tsentral'nogo komiteta KPSS, 5–7 fevralia 1990 goda* (Izdatel'stvo politicheskoi literatury, 1990), 83–85.

25 "Meeting of the Central Committee for the questions of the emergency Congress of People's Deputies of the USSR and the preparation of materials for XXVIII Congress of the CPSU," February 13, 1990, in GFA, f. 10, op. 2.

26 Gorbachev, *Zhizn'*, 1:484; Gorbachev, *Poniat' perestroiku*, 236–37.

27 BBC interview with Shakhnazarov, in TSRRT.

28 Matlock Jr., *Autopsy on an Empire*, 321.

29 Gorbachev, *Sobranie sochinenii*, 18:330.

30 Matlock Jr., *Autopsy on an Empire*, 334.

31 *V Politbiuro*, 600.

32 Shakhnazarov, who presented Gorbachev with these options, preferred the French model. See Shakhnazarov, *S vozhdiami i bez nikh*, 351–52.

33 See, e.g., Brown, *Gorbachev Factor*, 204.

34 Medvedev, *V kommande Gorbacheva*, 110.

35 Gorbachev, *Sobranie sochinenii*, 19:524, n. 114.

36 Iakovlev, *Sumerki*, 424.

37 Author's interview with Lev Gudkov, June 7, 2016, Moscow.

38 Matlock Jr., *Autopsy on an Empire*, 336–37.

39 Gorbachev, *Zhizn'*, 1:489–90.

40 Boldin, *Ten Years That Shook the World*, 248–51; O'Clery, *Moscow, December 25, 1991*, 91.

41 Gorbachev, *Sobranie sochinenii*, 19:55.

42 Gorbachev, *Zhizn'*, 1:481–82.

43 Ibid., 482.

44 Grachev, *Gorbachev's Gamble*, 186–87.

45 Medvedev, *V kommande Gorbacheva*, 165; Sheinis, *Vzlet i padenie Parlamenta*, 1:338.

46 Iakovlev, *Sumerki*, 504.

47 Shakhnazarov, *S vozhdiami i bez nikh*, 357.

48 Author's interview with Gorbachev, May 25, 2007, Moscow.

49 Shakhnazarov, *S vozhdiami i bez nikh*, 353–61.

50   Richard Pipes, *Alexander Yakovlev: The Man Whose Ideas Delivered Russia from Communism* (DeKalb: Northern Illinois University Press, 2015), 64.

51   Cited in Aron, *Yeltsin*, 364.

52   Sheinis, *Vzlet i padenie Parlamenta*, 1:264–69.

53   Ibid., 280–83.

54   Chernyaev notes on Politburo meeting, March 22, 1990, in GFA, f. 2, op. 1.

55   Of course, that trip couldn't easily be postponed, but how to explain the inept anti-Yeltsin campaign that preceded it?

56   Palazhchenko, *My Years with Gorbachev*, 189.

57   Matlock Jr., *Autopsy on an Empire*, 367–68.

58   Shakhnazarov notes on Politburo meeting, April 20, 1990, in GFA, f. 10, op. 2.

59   Shakhnazarov, *S vozhdiami i bez nikh*, 366–68.

60   Medvedev, *V kommande Gorbacheva*, 143.

61   Matlock Jr., *Autopsy on an Empire*, 376–77.

62   Gorbachev, *Poniat' perestroiku*, 261–63.

63   Chernyaev notes on Politburo meeting, March 2, 1990, in GFA, f. 2, op. 2.

64   Chernyaev notes on Politburo meeting, March 29, 1989, ibid.

65   Chernyaev notes on Politburo meeting, April 9, 1989, ibid.

66   Gorbachev in conversation with Bulgarian leader, Andrei Lukanov, in Gorbachev, *Sobranie sochinenii*, 19:107–9.

67   Speech to party members in Moscow's Frunze district, ibid., 19:441.

68   Ibid., 195.

69   Gorbachev, *Sobranie sochinenii*, 20:31–32.

70   Ibid., 73.

71   This was the only time Gorbachev's wife berated him in this way, Shakhnazarov comments, adding that Gorbachev himself apologized for his outburst once he learned that so few lines had been censored. In Shakhnazarov, *S vozhdiami i bez nikh*, 368–71.

72   Remnick, *Lenin's Tomb*, 324–27.

73   Chernyaev, *My Six Years with Gorbachev*, 270; Chernyaev's diary, April 30 and May 5, 1990, entries, in *Sovmestnyi iskhod*, 852–55; Aron, *Yeltsin*, 372.

74   Grachev, *Gibel' Sovetskogo "titanika,"* 195.

75   Chernyaev, *My Six Years with Gorbachev*, 277–78, 280.

76   Gorbachev, *Sobranie sochinenii*, 20:488.

77   Chernyaev, *My Six Years with Gorbachev*, 279; Chernyaev's diary, July 8, 1990, entry, in *Sovmestnyi iskhod*, 861.

78   Iakovlev, *Sumerki*, 441–42.

79   Chernyaev, *My Six Years with Gorbachev*, 280; Chernyaev's diary, July 8, 1990, entry, in *Sovmestnyi iskhod*, 861.

80   R. Gorbachev, *I Hope*, 182.

81   Grachev, *Gorbachev's Gamble*, 190; Iakovlev, *Sumerki*, 451.

82   Colton, *Yeltsin*, 184.

83   Gorbachev, *Poniat' perestroiku*, 276–77; Gorbachev, *Sobranie sochinenii*, 20:62.

84   Petrakov, *Russkaia ruletka*, 133–38.

85   Gorbachev, *Zhizn'*, 1:572–73.

86   BBC interview with Shatalin, in TSRRT.

87   Leonid Abalkin, *Neispol'zovannyi shans: Poltora goda v pravitel'stve* (Moscow: Politizdat, 1991), 198–205.

88   Remnick, *Lenin's Tomb*, 359.

89   Chernyaev, *My Six Years with Gorbachev*, 286.

90   Petrakov, *Russkaia ruletka*, 139.

91   Abalkin, *Neispol'zovannyi shans*, 202; Ryzhkov, *Perestroika: Istoriya predatel'stva*, 329.

92   Chernyaev, *My Six Years with Gorbachev*, 284–85.

93   Chernyaev's diary, August 21, 1990, entry, in *Sovmestnyi iskhod*, 867–68.

94   Chernyaev's diary, August 26, 1990, entry, ibid., 869.

95   Ryzhkov, *Perestroika*, 328.

96   Petrakov, *Russkaia ruletka*, 152–53; Palazhchenko, *My Years with Gorbachev*, 289. These accounts differ in some details.

97   BBC interview with Shatalin, in TSRRT; Stanislav Shatalin, "500 dnei—I drugie dni moei zhizni," *Nezavisimaia gazeta*, April 2, 1992.

98   Petrakov, *Russkaia ruletka*, 154.

99   BBC interview with Yeltsin, in TSRRT.

100 Petrakov, *Russkaia ruletka*, 155–56.

101 Ibid., 155.

102 Abalkin, *Neispol'zovannyi shans*, 213; Petrakov, *Russkaia ruletka*, 156; Medvedev, *V kommande Gorbacheva*, 158.

103 Colton, *Yeltsin*, 219–20.

104 Petrakov, *Russkaia ruletka*, 156–57.

105 Ryzhkov, *Perestroika*, 332.

106 Chernyaev, *My Six Years with Gorbachev*, 289–90.

107 Gorbachev, *Zhizn'*, 1:574.

108 This abbreviated account drawn from ibid., 578–79; Abalkin, *Neispol'zovannyi shans*, 214–40.

109 "Flying Blind in the Kremlin," *New York Times*, September 30, 1990, http://www.nytimes.com/1990/09/30/opinion/flying-blind-in-the-kremlin.html.

110 Chernyaev, *My Six Years with Gorbachev*, 290.

111 Ibid., 291; Chernyaev's diary, September 4 and 15, 1990, entries, in *Sovmestnyi iskhod*, 871–72, 873–74.

112 See Petrakov, *Russkaia ruletka*, 158–60.

113 Remnick, *Lenin's Tomb*, 371.

114   Shakhnazarov, *S vozhdiami i bez nikh*, 399.

115   Chernyaev, *My Six Years with Gorbachev*, 293–95. One foreign observer who regretted the demise of "500 Days" was Harvard economist and later U.S. Secretary of the Treasury Lawrence Summers, who said, "Economic reform is like riding a bicycle. You've got to keep pedaling hard or you'll fall over." Personal communication from Strobe Talbott, December 28, 2015.

116   Petrakov, *Russkaia ruletka*, 164; Chernyaev, *My Six Years with Gorbachev*, 299.

117   Chernyaev, *My Six Years with Gorbachev*, 300.

118   Gorbachev, *Zhizn'*, 1:581.

119   Iakovlev, *Sumerki*, 502.

120   Gorbachev, *Zhizn'*, 1:584.

121   Chernyaev, *My Six Years with Gorbachev*, 308–9.

122   Ibid., 309.

123   Grachev, *Gorbachev*, 333.

124   Chernyaev, *My Six Years with Gorbachev*, 309; Matlock Jr., *Autopsy on an Empire*, 422; Gorbachev, *Zhizn'*, 1:583–84.

125   Petrakov, *Russkaia ruletka*, 171–72.

126   Official transcript of Politburo meeting, in Gorbachev, *Sobranie sochinenii*, 23:424–46.

127   Georgy Shakhnazarov's recollection, ibid., 492, n. 102.

128   Gorbachev, *Zhizn'*, 1:585.

129   See Gorbachev, *Sobranie sochinenii*, 24:403.

130   Chernyaev, *My Six Years with Gorbachev*, 309–10.

131   Petrakov, *Russkaia ruletka*, 167–70, 175–76.

132   Chernyaev's diary, January 2, 1991, entry, in *Sovmestnyi iskhod*, 898.

133   BBC interviews with Shevardnadze closest aides, Teimuraz Stepanov and Sergei Tarasenko, in TSRRT.

134   Scene described in Vorotnikov, *A bylo eto tak*, 417; speech in *Chetvertyi s"ezd narodnykh deputatov SSSR, 17–27 dekabria 1990*, vol. 1 (Moscow: Izdanie verkhovnogo soveta SSSR, 1990), 410.

135   BBC interviews with Shakhnazarov and Vitaly Ignatenko, in TSRRT; Gorbachev speech, in *Chetvertyi s"ezd narodnykh deputatov SSSR*, 1:453–56.

136   Matlock Jr., *Autopsy on an Empire*, 434.

137   Medvedev, *V kommande Gorbacheva*, 170–71.

138   Vorotnikov, *A bylo eto tak*, 419.

139   Chernyaev, *My Six Years with Gorbachev*, 314.

140   Ibid., 310–11.

141   Chernyaev's diary, December 19, 1990, entry, in *Sovmestnyi iskhod*, 890.

142   Chernyaev's diary, December 24, 1990, entry, ibid., 893.

143   Chernyaev, *My Six Years with Gorbachev*, 316.

CHAPTER 15: COMING TOGETHER? 1990

1   Polling by the All-Union Public Opinion Center (headed by Raisa Gorbachev's MGU friend sociologist Yuri Levada) showed Gorbachev's approval rating dropping from 52 percent in December 1989 to 21 percent by October 1990. At the end of the year, 32 percent backed Yeltsin as "Man of the Year" and only 19 percent Gorbachev. Cited in Matlock Jr., *Autopsy on an Empire*, 447.

2   Chernyaev's diary, January 21, 1990, entry, in *Sovmestnyi iskhod*, 837.

3   Chernyaev's diary, March 25, 1990, entry, ibid., 846.

4   Chernyaev's diary, June 24, 1990, entry, ibid., 859.

5   See Chernyaev and Shakhnazarov notes on Presidential Council meeting, in Gorbachev, *Sobranie sochinenii*, 22: 450–56; Cherniaev, *Shest' let s Gorbachevym*, 382.

6   Grachev, *Gorbachev's Gamble*, 184–85. Personal communication from Braithwaite, July 28, 2015.

7   Dobrynin, *In Confidence*, 628.

8   Brutents, *Nesbyvsheesia*, 434–35.

9   See Archie Brown, "Did Gorbachev as General Secretary Become a Social Democrat?," *Europe-Asia Studies* 65, no. 2 (March 2013): 198–220.

10   Chernyaev, *My Six Years with Gorbachev*, 338.

11   Grachev, *Gorbachev's Gamble*, 186–89. Grachev adds that Gorbachev kept Defense Minister Yazov informed, though "not systematically," about "his most important foreign policy moves," especially relating to disarmament; a commission representing the foreign and defense ministries, the KGB, the military-industrial complex, and the Central Committee international department continued to function, but mostly by holding "technical" discussions of purely military subjects rather than drafting written instructions for negotiations with the West.

12   Zelikow and Rice, *Germany Unified*, 153–54.

13   See Hutchings, *American Diplomacy*, 104.

14   Kriuchkov's January 25 report, in Chernyaev's diary, January 28, 1990, entry, in *Sovmestnyi iskhod*, 840.

15   Meeting with Gorbachev in Moscow on January 30, 1990, in Gorbachev, *Sobranie sochinenii*, 18:599, n. 130.

16   Bozo, *Mitterrand*, 168.

17   Zelikow and Rice, *Germany Unified*, 175.

18   Bush and Scowcroft, *World Transformed*, 213.

19   Matlock Jr., *Autopsy on an Empire*, 387.

20   Blackwill talk at Council on Foreign Relations Symposium on the 25th Anniversary of the Fall of the Berlin Wall, November 4, 2014, New York City.

21   Author's interview with Bush (via email), September 19, 2006.

22   Gorbachev, *Poniat' perestroiku*, 241–43.

23   Brutents, *Nesbyvsheesia*, 488–89, 506; G. M. Kornienko, *Kholodnaia voina: Svidetel'stvo ee uchastnika* (Moscow: Mezhdunarodnye otnosheniia, 1994), 268; Kornienko, "Zakonhilas' li 'kholodnaia voina'?"; Zelikow and Rice, *Germany Unified*, 207, 214.

24   Chernyaev memo, in Gorbachev, *Sobranie sochinenii*, 19:502.

25   Matlock Jr., *Autopsy on an Empire*, 388.

26   Excerpts from Gorbachev-Kohl talks on February 10, 1990, in Gorbachev, *Sobranie sochinenii*, 18:273; "Gespräch des Bundeskanzlers Kohl mit Generalsekretär Gorbatschow, Moskau, 10. Februar 1990," in Küsters and Hofmann, *Deutsche Einheit*, 803.

27   *Gorbatschow und die Deutsche Einheit* (ZDF Enterprises, 2005), accessed October 2015, http://www.zdf.de/ZDFmediathek/beitrag/video/2339972/Gorbatschow-und-die-Deutsche-Einheit#/beitrag/video/2339972/Gorbatschow-und-die-Deutsche-Einheit. This video clip is from a German documentary on unification. The first ninety seconds of it show a Moscow press conference that Kohl called on the night of February 10, 1990, right after speaking to Gorbachev. Kohl does not seem to have asked Gorbachev to appear with him.

28   Adomeit, *Imperial Overstretch*, 481–90; Gorbachev, *Sobranie sochinenii*, 18:273.

29   Gates used the phrase to describe Bush's handling of Gorbachev at Malta in Gates, *From the Shadows*, 484.

30   Savranskaya, Blanton, and Zubok, *Masterpieces of History*, 680–83.

31   Kohl's remark in Küsters and Hofmann, *Deutsche Einheit*, 799; Mary Elise Sarotte, "What the West Really Told Moscow about NATO Expansion," *Foreign Affairs* 93, no. 5 (October 2014): 93; Genscher's speech cited in Kristina Spohr and David Reynolds, *Transcending the Cold War: Summits, Statecraft, and the Dissolution of Bipolarity, 1970–1990* (Oxford: Oxford University Press, 2016) 211.

32   Sarotte, "What the West Really Told Moscow," 91–92.

33   Bush quoted ibid., 94–95.

34   Baker's explanation, in Jack Matlock Jr., *Superpower Illusions: How Myths and False Ideologies Led America Astray—and How to Return to Reality* (New Haven, CT: Yale University Press, 2010), 319, n. 9; Gorbachev, *Poniat' perestroiku*, 246; Gorbachev to Mitterrand, in Gorbachev, *Sobranie sochinenii*, 20:128–29; Chernyaev's memo, ibid., 18:502. Mark Kramer contends that the whole issue of NATO expansion in East Europe never came up: Mark Kramer, "The Myth of No-NATO Enlargement Pledge to Russia," *Washington Quarterly* 32, no. 2 (2009): 39–61. One should add that even if Gorbachev had obtained a written promise, it is unlikely that it would have been confirmed in Washington and all other NATO capitals and then sustained by future Western leaders.

35 Baker III, *Politics of Diplomacy*, 205.

36 Beschloss and Talbott, *At the Highest Levels*, 182.

37 Baker III, *Politics of Diplomacy*, 205.

38 Gorbachev, *Sobranie sochinenii*, 18:280, 361, 393, and 19:226, 262, 270.

39 Ibid., 19:226, n. 461 on p. 592, and 20:20.

40 Ibid., 19:464; also see "Gespräch des Ministerialdirektors Teltschik mit Präsident Gorbatschow Moskau, 14. Mai 1990," in Küsters and Hofmann, *Deutsche Einheit*, 1115.

41 Gorbachev, *Sobranie sochinenii*, 20:518, n. 7; Baker III, *Politics of Diplomacy*, 249.

42 Chernyaev quoted in Adomeit, *Imperial Overstretch*, 517.

43 Bozo, *Mitterrand*, 253; Gorbachev, *Sobranie sochinenii*, 20:533, n. 97.

44 Cherniaev, *Shest' let s Gorbachevym*, 351; Chernyaev, *My Six Years with Gorbachev*, 275.

45 Oberdorfer, *From the Cold War to a New Era*, 412.

46 Bush and Scowcroft, *World Transformed*, 279.

47 Soviet notes on meeting, in Gorbachev, *Sobranie sochinenii*, 20:195–201.

48 Oberdorfer, *From the Cold War to a New Era*, 414.

49 Bush and Scowcroft, *World Transformed*, 280.

50 Record of Bush-Gorbachev conversation, May 31, 1990, 10:45 a.m. to 12:45 p.m., in Svetlana Savranskaya and Tom Blanton, eds., *The Last Superpower Summits: Gorbachev, Reagan and Bush at the End of the Cold War* (Budapest: Central European University Press, 2016), 663.

51 Paraphrase of Blackwill, in Beschloss and Talbott, *At the Highest Levels*, 220.

52 Record of Conversation between M. S. Gorbachev and G. Bush, May 31, 1990, 16:00 to 18:00, in Savranskaya and Blanton, *Last Superpower Summits*, 664–76; Bush and Scowcroft, *World Transformed*, 282–83; Zelikow and Rice, *Germany Unified*, 278. Note that Bush's memoirs include exchanges from his conversation with Gorbachev that are not included in the Soviet transcript as translated in Blanton and Savranskaya, *Last Superpower Summits*.

53 Author's interview with James Baker III, October 8, 2006, Houston, TX. Personal communication from Condoleezza Rice, December 14, 2015.

54 Bush and Scowcroft, *World Transformed*, 301–2; Gorbachev, *Poniat' perestroiku*, 250–51.

55 Author's interview with Gorbachev, May 25, 2007, Moscow.

56 See Beschloss and Talbott, *At the Highest Levels*, 227.

57 Bush's paraphrase, in Bush and Scowcroft, *World Transformed*, 283–84.

58 Beschloss and Talbott, *At the Highest Levels*, 218.

59 Bush and Scowcroft, *World Transformed*, 284.

60 Ibid., 285–86; Beschloss and Talbott, *At the Highest Levels*, 222–24.

61 Bush and Scowcroft, *World Transformed*, 286, 288.

62   Barbara Bush, *Barbara Bush: A Memoir* (New York: Charles Scribner's Sons, 1994), 342–44.

63   Gorbachev, *Poniat' perestroiku*, 258.

64   Beschloss and Talbott, *At the Highest Levels*, 226.

65   Bush and Scowcroft, *World Transformed*, 276–77, 286–87; Gates, *From the Shadows*, 493.

66   Hoffman, *Dead Hand*, 298–303, 341, 345–47.

67   Oberdorfer, *From the Cold War to a New Era*, 415; Beschloss and Talbott, *At the Highest Levels*, 218–19; Bill Keller, "Washington Summit: Over Caviar, Gorbachev Relaxes and Charms," *New York Times*, June 1, 1990; David Remnick, "Embassy Guests See a New Gorbachev: Tired and Defensive," *Washington Post*, June 1, 1990; Gorbachev's remarks, in Gorbachev, *Sobranie sochinenii*, 20:213–18.

68   Maureen Dowd, "Masters of the Sound Bite Cede Match to Gorbachev," *New York Times*, June 2, 1990; Eleanor Randolph, "Accidental Dose of Glasnost? TV Cameras Catch Gorbachev's Blunt Talk with Hill Leaders," *Washington Post*, June 2, 1990; Gorbachev, *Sobranie sochinenii*, 20:221–31.

69   Beschloss and Talbott, *At the Highest Levels*, 222.

70   Oberdorfer, *From the Cold War to a New Era*, 418; Beschloss and Talbott, *At the Highest Levels*, 221.

71   B. Bush, *Barbara Bush*, 340, 538–42; Sarah Booth Conroy et al., "Raisa's Day: Tea Talk, Treasures and a Wagging Tail," *Washington Post*, June 1, 1990; Donnie Radcliffe, "Barbara Bush, Wowing Wellesley, with Raisa Gorbacheva on Hand," ibid., June 2, 1990.

72   Gorbachev, *Memoirs*, 543; David Maraniss and John Lancaster, "Chilly Weather, Warm Welcome in the Twin Cities," *Washington Post*, June 4, 1990; Maureen Dowd, "Gorbachev Passes Up Stunts But Dazzles the Heartland," *New York Times*, June 4, 1990; Michael Ross, "Minnesotans Are Hosts to First-Lady Diplomacy," *Los Angeles Times*, June 4, 1990; Steve Berg, "A Calm Capital Contrasts with a Frantic, Fidgeting Gorbachev-Crazed Twin Cities," *Minneapolis Star Tribune*, June 1, 1990; Palazhchenko, *My Years with Gorbachev* 194; Chernyaev's diary, June 17, 1990, entry, in *Sovmestnyi iskhod*, 858.

73   Jane Gross, "The Gorbachevs Will Get a Close Look at the America beyond Washington: San Franciscans to Give a Big Party," *New York Times*, June 3, 1990; Palazhchenko, *My Years with Gorbachev*, 196; Beschloss and Talbott, *At the Highest Levels*, 229.

74   Beschloss and Talbott, *At the Highest Levels*, 230–31.

75   Baker III, *Politics of Diplomacy*, 256–57; Beschloss and Talbott, *At the Highest Levels*, 232–33; Zelikow and Rice, *Germany Unified*, 295–96.

76   See Zelikow and Rice, *Germany Unified*, 303–24.

77   Falin, *Bez skidok na obstoiatel'stva*, 448–49.

78   "Gespräch des Bundeskanzlers Kohl mit Präsident Gorbatschow

Moskau, 15. Juli 1990," in Küsters and Hofmann, *Deutsche Einheit*, 1342.

79   Spohr and Reynolds, *Transcending the Cold War*, 221.

80   Aleksandr Galkin and Anatolii Cherniaev, eds., *Mikhail Gorbachev i germanskii vopros: Sbornik dokumentov, 1986–1991* (Moscow: Ves'Mir Izdatelstvo, 2006), 495–503; Zelikow and Rice, *Germany Unified*, 335–38.

81   Beschloss and Talbott, *At the Highest Levels*, 239–40.

82   Zelikow and Rice, *Germany Unified*, 339, 341.

83   Ibid., 338; Cherniaev, *Shest' let s Gorbachevym*, 359; text of Gorbachev-Kohl joint press conference, in Galkin and Cherniaev, *Mikhail Gorbachev i germanskii vopros*, 525–41.

84   Grachev, *Gorbachev's Gamble*, 191; Matlock Jr., *Autopsy on an Empire*, 409–10.

85   Oberdorfer, *From the Cold War to a New Era*, 432.

86   Ibid., 432–33; Barrass, *Great Cold War*, 366.

87   Beschloss and Talbott, *At the Highest Levels*, 245; Chernyaev, *My Six Years with Gorbachev*, 283.

88   Beschloss and Talbott, *At the Highest Levels*, 246–47; Oberdorfer, *From the Cold War to a New Era*, 433–34; Palazhchenko, *My Years with Gorbachev*, 210.

89   Grachev, *Gorbachev's Gamble*, 193.

90   Ibid., 193–95; Beschloss and Talbott, *At the Highest Levels*, 274.

91   Gorbachev, *Poniat' perestroiku*, 287.

92   Gorbachev, *Zhizn'*, 2:241.

93   Bush and Scowcroft, *World Transformed*, 408–9.

94   Gorbachev, *Sobranie sochinenii*, 21:340, 586, n. 366.

95   Galkin and Cherniaev, *Mikhail Gorbachev i germanskii vopros*, 556–57.

96   Ibid., 560.

97   Ibid., 570–71.

98   Braithwaite's diary entry, September 14, 1990, in Braithwaite, "Moscow Diary, 1988 to 1992," 201.

99   Cited in Brutents, *Nesbyvsheesia*, 425.

100 Galkin and Cherniaev, *Mikhail Gorbachev i germanskii vopros*, 563.

101 Including grants to support the continuing presence of Soviet troops in East Germany, their withdrawal to the USSR, and their resettlement there (almost DM 20 billion); credits and credit guarantees (almost DM 20 billion); and funds to cover East Germany's debts.

102 Chronology of Soviet–West German negotiations about aid, aid totals, and comparisons, in Adomeit, *Imperial Overstretch*, 539–53.

103 Beschloss and Talbott, *At the Highest Levels*, 237.

104 Author's interview with Baker III, October 8, 2006, Houston, TX.

105 Beschloss and Talbott, *At the Highest Levels*, 237.

106 Thatcher, *Downing Street Years*, 798.

107   Barrass, *Great Cold War*, 365.

108   Adomeit, *Imperial Overstretch*, 554–56.

109   Matlock Jr., *Autopsy on an Empire*, 412–15.

110   Cherniaev, *Shest' let s Gorbachevym*, 392; Chernyaev's diary, October 31, 1990, entry, in *Sovmestnyi iskhod*, 884; R. Gorbachev, *I Hope*, 183.

111   Gorbachev, *Sobranie sochinenii*, 23:158.

112   Chernyaev, *My Six Years with Gorbachev*, 308.

113   Beschloss and Talbott, *At the Highest Levels*, 273.

114   Gorbachev, *Zhizn'*, 2:214–15.

115   Chernyaev's diary, October 23, 1990, entry, in *Sovmestnyi iskhod*, 883–84.

116   Gorbachev, *Zhizn'*, 2:215; "Mikhail Gorbachev—Nobel Lecture," *Nobelprize.org*, accessed February 7, 2015, http://www.nobelprize.org/nobel_prizes/peace/laureates/1990/gorbachev-lecture.html.

CHAPTER 16: TO THE COUP: JANUARY–AUGUST 1991

1   Cherniaev, *Sovmestnyi iskhod*, 897–98, 902, 927–28, 930; Grachev, *Gorbachev*, 339.

2   Baker III, *Politics of Diplomacy*, 476–77.

3   Beschloss and Talbott, *At the Highest Levels*, 356.

4   Chernyaev, *My Six Years with Gorbachev*, 316–17.

5   Rodric Braithwaite, *Across the Moscow River: The World Turned Upside Down* (New Haven, CT: Yale University Press, 2002), 200; Matlock Jr., *Autopsy on an Empire*, 464.

6   Matlock Jr., *Autopsy on an Empire*, 449–54; Michael Dobbs, *Down with Big Brother: The Fall of the Soviet Empire* (New York: Alfred A. Knopf, 1997), 336–46; Aron, *Yeltsin*, 410–14; Chernyaev, *My Six Years with Gorbachev*, 317–27; Grachev, *Gibel' Sovetskogo "titanika*," 198.

7   Gorbachev, *Zhizn'*, 1:504; Gorbachev, *Poniat' perestroiku*, 292–93; Gorbachev and Mlynář, *Conversations with Gorbachev*, 132; Grachev, *Gibel' Sovetskogo "titanika*," 198.

8   Vladimir Kriuchkov, *Lichnoe delo*, vol. 2 (Moscow: Olymp, 1996), 30.

9   Chernyaev's diary, January 15, 1991, entry, in *Sovmestnyi iskhod*, 903.

10   V. Bakatin, *Doroga v proshedshem vremeni* (Moscow: Dom, 1999), 235; Grachev, *Gorbachev*, 349.

11   Boldin, *Ten Years That Shook the World*, 273.

12   Chernyaev's diary, January 17, 1991, entry, in *Sovmestnyi iskhod*, 907.

13   Beschloss and Talbott, *At the Highest Levels*, 307.

14   Dobbs, *Down with Big Brother*, 347.

15   Chernyaev, *My Six Years with Gorbachev*, 335–36; Chernyaev's diary, January 29, 1991, entry, in *Sovmestnyi iskhod*, 912.

16   Chernyaev's diary, February 19, 1991, entry, in *Sovmestnyi iskhod*, 919.

17   Remnick, *Lenin's Tomb*, 420–22; BBC interview with Aleksandr Yakovlev, in TSRRT.

18   Matlock Jr., *Autopsy on an Empire*, 471; Mikhail Gorbachev, *The August Coup: The Truth and the Lessons* (New York: HarperCollins, 1991), 13.

19   Matlock Jr., *Autopsy on an Empire*, 472.

20   See *Soiuz mozhno bylo sokhranit': Belaia kniga: Dokumenty i fakty o politike M. S. Gorbacheva po reformirovaniiu i sokhraneniiu mnogonatsional'nogo gosudarstva* (Moscow: Izdatel'stvo AST, 2007), 224–27.

21   Palazhchenko, *My Years with Gorbachev*, 281.

22   Matlock Jr., *Autopsy on an Empire*, 494.

23   Georgii Shakhnazarov, *S vozhdiami i bez nikh*, 404–6; Grachev, *Gorbachev*, 362; Gorbachev, *Zhizn'*, 1:533.

24   Yeltsin, *Struggle for Russia*, 26–27, 36.

25   *Soiuz mozhno bylo sokhranit'*, 234–35.

26   Colton, *Yeltsin*, 194.

27   Text of draft treaty, in *Soiuz mozhno bylo sokhranit'*, 268–83.

28   BBC interview with Gorbachev, in TSRRT.

29   Grachev, *Gorbachev*, 364–65; Gorbachev, *Poniat' perestroiku*, 326–27; BBC interview with Gorbachev, in TSRRT; Boldin, *Ten Years That Shook the World*, 278.

30   Gorbachev, *Zhizn'*, 1:535; Brutents, *Nesbyvsheesia*, 584.

31   Chernyaev's diary, April 27, 1991, entry, in *Sovmestnyi iskhod*, 937.

32   BBC interview with Yevgeny Primakov, in TSRRT.

33   Gorbachev, *Poniat' perestroiku*, 312–13.

34   Grachev, *Gorbachev*, 358–59.

35   As overheard by writer Daniil Granin. See Karagez'ian and Poliakov, *Gorbachev v zhizni*, 443.

36   Chernyaev's diary, April 27, 1991, entry, in *Sovmestnyi iskhod*, 937; Gorbachev, *Zhizn'*, 1:540.

37   Chernyaev's diary, April 27, 1991, entry, in *Sovmestnyi iskhod*, 938; Shakhnazarov, *S vozhdiami i bez nikh*, 425.

38   Sheinis, *Vzlet i padenie Parlamenta*, 1:480–81.

39   Ibid., 480.

40   Ambassador Braithwaite quotes Delors's paraphrase of Gorbachev, June 20, 1991, entry, in Braithwaite, "Moscow Diary, 1988 to 1992," 335; BBC interview with Shakhnazarov, in TSRRT; "good thrashing" is how Gorbachev later described it to President Bush, see Bush and Scowcroft, *World Transformed*, 506; on the June 21 session, see Remnick, *Lenin's Tomb*, 428–29; Beschloss and Talbott, *At the Highest Levels*, 400.

41   Aleksandr Yakovlev had also warned Gorbachev in April that "preparations are underway for a revolution from the right," only to be told by Gorbachev, "You, Aleksandr, overestimate their intelligence and

courage." As cited in Pipes, *Alexander Yakovlev*, 76; BBC interviews with Chernyaev, Ignatenko, and Shakhnazarov, in TSRRT.

42   Matlock Jr., *Autopsy on an Empire*, 540–44; Chernyaev, *My Six Years with Gorbachev*, 352.

43   Remnick, *Lenin's Tomb*, 438–39; BBC interview with Chernyaev, in TSRRT.

44   Vitalii Tsepliaev, "Narod nash ne bydlo!," *Argumenty i fakty*, March 2, 2011, in Karagez'ian and Poliakov, *Gorbachev v zhizni*, 627.

45   Gorbachev, *Zhizn'*, 1:240–49; Pikhoia, *Moskva—Kreml'—Vlast'*, 2:299–300.

46   CIA Directorate of Intelligence, "The Gorbachev Succession, April 29, 1991," NSA Summits Collection; Gates, *From the Shadows*, 501–2; Beschloss and Talbott, *At the Highest Levels*, 346; Bush and Scowcroft, *World Transformed*, 499–500. Margaret Thatcher's adviser on foreign policy and intelligence, Percy Cradock, agreed that Gorbachev was "doomed." Author's interview with Cradock, July 23, 2008, Richmond, UK.

47   Beschloss and Talbott, *At the Highest Levels*, 349.

48   Baker III, *Politics of Diplomacy*, 476–77.

49   Bush and Scowcroft, *World Transformed*, 504.

50   Baker III, *Politics of Diplomacy*, 380.

51   Bush and Scowcroft, *World Transformed*, 496.

52   Beschloss and Talbott, *At the Highest Levels*, 319–20; Baker III, *Politics of Diplomacy*, 380–81; Bush and Scowcroft, *World Transformed*, 496.

53   Baker III, *Politics of Diplomacy*, 402.

54   Chernyaev, *My Six Years with Gorbachev*, 331.

55   Bush and Scowcroft, *World Transformed*, 470; for a critical view of Gorbachev's handling of the Iraq crisis in 1990 and 1991, see Kornienko, "Zakonchilas' li 'kholodnaia voina'?"; "Telecon with President Gorbachev, February 21, 1991, 6:45–7:20 pm," in NSA Summits Collection; Bush letter to Gorbachev of March 10, 1991, George H. W. Bush Presidential Records, Scowcroft, Brent, Collection, Special Separate USSR Note Files, Gorbachev Files, Gorbachev-Sensitive January–June [3], George H. W. Bush Presidential Library, College Station, TX.

56   Bush and Scowcroft, *World Transformed*, 503; Grachev, *Gorbachev's Gamble*, 207; Chernyaev, *My Six Years with Gorbachev*, 348.

57   *V Politbiuro*, 701–2; June 15, 1991, entry in Braithwaite, "Moscow Diary, 1988 to 1992," 333.

58   See Graham Allison and Grigory Yavlinsky, *Window of Opportunity: The Grand Bargain for Democracy in the Soviet Union* (New York: Pantheon Books, 1991), 39–66.

59   Matlock Jr., *Autopsy on an Empire*, 534–35; Chernyaev's diary, May 17, 1991, entry, in *Sovmestnyi iskhod*, 942.

60   Author's interview with Graham Allison, May 27, 2014, Cambridge, MA.

61   Telecom with President Mikhail Gorbachev of the Soviet Union, May 11, 1991, 9:03–9:47, Camp David, in Savranskaya and Blanton, *Last Superpower Summits*, 828 ; Matlock Jr., *Autopsy on an Empire*, 547.

62   Matlock Jr., *Autopsy on an Empire*, 548–51.

63   Grachev reports Kozyrev's message, in *Gorbachev's Gamble*, 207.

64   Braithwaite diary, July 14, 1991, entry, in Braithwaite, "Moscow Diary, 1988 to 1992," 344.

65   Memorandum of Conversation, G-7 Meeting with President Gorbachev, July 17, 1991, in Savranskaya and Blanton, *Last Superpower Summits*, 855–63; Bush and Scowcroft, *World Transformed*, 507–8.

66   Bush and Scowcroft, *World Transformed*, 508.

67   *V Politbiuro*, 718–22.

68   Chernyaev's diary, July 23, 1991, entry, in *Sovmestnyi iskhod*, 966; *V Politbiuro*, 719.

69   Chernyaev's diary, July 23, 1991, entry, in *Sovmestnyi iskhod*, 967.

70   Chernyaev, *My Six Years with Gorbachev*, 357; Beschloss and Talbott, *At the Highest Levels*, 407; Matlock Jr., *Autopsy on an Empire*, 554.

71   Matlock Jr., *Autopsy on an Empire*, 537.

72   Cited in Boris Pankin, *The Last Hundred Days of the Soviet Union* (New York: I. B. Taurus, 1996), 181–82.

73   Matlock Jr., *Autopsy on an Empire*, 538–39.

74   Bush and Scowcroft, *World Transformed*, 510; Beschloss and Talbott, *At the Highest Levels*, 416.

75   Bush and Scowcroft, *World Transformed*, 510.

76   Record of conversation between Bush and Gorbachev, July 30, 1991, 12:55 to 1:22 p.m., in Savranskaya and Blanton, *Last Superpower Summits*, 880.

77   Beschloss and Talbott, *At the Highest Levels*, 411.

78   Bush and Scowcroft, *World Transformed*, 511.

79   Chernyaev, *My Six Years with Gorbachev*, 362; Chernyaev's diary, August 1, 1991, entry, in *Sovmestnyi iskhod*, 969.

80   Bush and Scowcroft, *World Transformed*, 513–14; Matlock Jr., *Autopsy on an Empire*, 564; Palazhchenko, *My Years with Gorbachev*, 304.

81   Gorbachev, *Memoirs*, 623–24; Palazhchenko, *My Years with Gorbachev*, 299.

82   Chernyaev, *My Six Years with Gorbachev*, 361, n. 45.

83   Beschloss and Talbott, *At the Highest Levels*, 412–13; Matlock Jr., *Autopsy on an Empire*, 563–64; Gorbachev, *Memoirs*, 624.

84   Serhii Plokhy, *The Last Empire: The Final Days of the Soviet Union* (New York: Basic Books, 2014), 58–64.

85   Grachev, *Gorbachev's Gamble*, 370.

86   V. Stepankov, *GKChP: 73 chasa, kotorye izmenili mir* (Moscow: Vremya, 2011), 28–33, 42–46.

CHAPTER 17: THE COUP: AUGUST 1991

1   The main sources for the following description of Zarya and the Gorbachevs' routine are a memoir by Gorbachev's chief bodyguard, Medvedev, *Chelovek za spinoi*, 251–60, and an article by another Gorbachev bodyguard, Jan Kasimov, "Krymskie kanikuli," *Moskovskie novosti*, April 23, 1992; brief descriptions also in Plokhy, *Last Empire*, 80; Remnick, *Lenin's Tomb*, 453; V. I. Varennikov, *Nepovtorimoe. V 7 tomakh.*, vol. 6 (Moscow: Sovetskii pisatel', 2001).

2   Anatoly Chernyaev diary, September 13 entry, in *Sovmestnyi iskhod*, 758; Chernyaev, *My Six Years with Gorbachev*, 167.

3   Personal communication from Mikhail Gorbachev via Pavel Palazhchenko, January 14, 2016.

4   Chernyaev's diary, August 3, 1991, entry, in *Sovmestnyi iskhod*, 969.

5   Raisa Gorbachev's diary, August 4, 1991, entry, in *Raisa: Vospominaniia*, 117.

6   Pavel Palazhchenko's recollections, in *Raisa Gorbacheva: Shtrikhi k portretu* (Moscow: Gorbachev-Fond, 2009), 53–54.

7   Raisa Gorbachev's diary, August 4, 1991, entry, in *Raisa: Vospominaniia*, 118.

8   Ibid.

9   Medvedev, *Chelovek za spinoi*, 268–69; Gorbachev's former aide and biographer Andrei Grachev notes that Raisa Gorbacheva established the family's Zarya routine. See Grachev, *Gorbachev*, 366; also see excerpt from Raisa Gorbachev's diary, August 5, 1991, entry, in *Raisa: Vospominaniia*, 119.

10   Raisa Gorbachev's diary entries, August 10 and 13, 1991, in *Raisa: Vospominaniia*, 120.

11   Gorbachev, *Zhizn'*, 2:557; Shakhnazarov, *S vozhdiami i bez nikh*, 442.

12   Medvedev, *Chelovek za spinoi*, 276. The rest of this account is based on several sources, which are specifically cited only with reference to particular quotations: Gorbachev, *Zhizn'*, 2:557–75, including excerpts from Raisa Gorbacheva's diary; Gorbachev, *August Coup*, 17–39; Chernyaev, *My Six Years with Gorbachev*, 374–78; Cherniaev, *Sovmestnyi iskhod*, 970–84; Grachev, *Gorbachev*, 366–82; Plokhy, *Last Empire*, 80–130; Remnick, *Lenin's Tomb*, 447–90; V. Stepankov and E. Lisov, *Kremlevskii zagovor* (Moscow: Ogonek, 1992); Stepankov, *GKChP*; Varennikov, *Nepovtorimoe*, 6:195–277.

13   Gorbachev, *Zhizn'*, 2:561–62.

14   Ibid., 558.

15 See ibid., 559; Gorbachev, *August Coup*, 19–23; Varennikov, *Nepovto-rimoe*, 6:206–12; Gorbachev's remark to Boldin was later recounted by Gorbachev to Chernyaev. See Chernyaev diary entry of August 21, 1991, in *Sovmestnyi iskhod*, 973.

16 Gorbachev, *Zhizn'*, 2:562.

17 Chernyaev, *My Six Years with Gorbachev*, 375.

18 Chernyaev, *Sovmestnyi iskhod*, 973.

19 Chernyaev, *My Six Years with Gorbachev*, 376.

20 Cherniaev, *Sovmestnyi iskhod*, 978.

21 Ibid., 979.

22 Ibid.

23 Gorbachev, *Zhizn'*, 2:570.

24 Telecon with Gorbachev, August 21, 1991, 12:19–12:31 p.m., in NSA READD-RADD collection, document no. 171.

25 See Beschloss and Talbott, *At the Highest Levels*, 422–37.

26 Remnick, *Lenin's Tomb*, 487; Cherniaev, *Sovmestnyi iskhod*, 983.

27 Remnick, *Lenin's Tomb*, 488.

28 Ibid.

29 Stepankov, *GKChP*, 285.

30 Plokhy, *Last Empire*, 134; Remnick, *Lenin's Tomb*, 490; see also Dobbs, *Down with Big Brother*.

31 *Pravda*, August 23, 1991.

32 Unpublished Mickey Berdy interview with Galina Starovoitova, date not indicated.

33 Lukyanov and Pavlov cited in John B. Dunlop, *The Rise of Russia and the Fall of the Soviet Empire*, with a new postcript by the author (Princeton, NJ: Princeton University Press, 1993), 204; Amy Knight, *Spies without Cloaks: The KGB's Successors* (Princeton, NJ: Princeton University Press, 1996), 19; Vladislav Manakhov, "Valentin Pavlov: 'Esli khotite sam Mikhail Gorbachev byl i chlenom GKChP," *Pravda*, April 12, 1996.

34 John B. Dunlop, "The August 1991 Coup and Its Impact on Soviet Politics," *Journal of Cold War Studies* 5, no. 1 (2003): 103; Knight, *Spies without Cloaks*, 22–24; Dunlop, *Rise of Russia*, 202–6; also see Amy Knight, "The Coup That Never Was," *Problems of Post-Communism* 58, nos. 4–5 (2011): 66–74.

35 Medvedev, *V kommande Gorbacheva*, 193; Palazhchenko, *My Years with Gorbachev*, 313.

36 Chernyaev, *My Six Years with Gorbachev*, 402.

37 Author's interview with Irina Gorbacheva, March 18, 2010, Moscow.

38 Grachev, *Gorbachev*, 374.

39 For a full and devastating rebuttal of the notion that Gorbachev was complicit in the conspiracy against himself, see Brown, *Seven Years That Changed the World*, 322–24.

40 Beschloss and Talbott, *At the Highest Levels*, 431; Braithwaite diary entry, August 19, 1991, in "Moscow Diary, 1988 to 1992"; Bush and Scowcroft, *World Transformed*, 534; Brutents, *Nesbyvsheesia*, 613; Varennikov, *Nepovtorimoe*, 6:197.

41 Kriuchkov, *Lichnoe delo*, 2:131.

42 Cited in Grachev, *Gorbachev*, 379–80.

43 Grachev, *Gibel' Sovetskogo "titanika,"* 208.

44 For a fuller account, see Stepankov, *GKChP*, 113–22, 127–39, 183–98, 207–65.

45 Grachev, *Gorbachev*, 381, 386.

CHAPTER 18: FINAL DAYS: AUGUST–DECEMBER 1991

1 *Gorbachev: Izbrannyi (sbornik)* (Moscow: Novaia gazeta, 2011), 25–26; Mikhail Gorbachev, *Posle kremlia* (Moscow: Ves' mir Izdatelstvo, 2014), 346.

2 *Gorbachev: Izbrannyi (sbornik)*, 26.

3 Excerpt from Chernyaev's diary, in *Raisa: Vospominaniia*, 156.

4 Press conference transcript in *FBIS Daily Report—Soviet Union*, August 23, 1991, pp. 20–30.

5 Stepankov, *GKChP*, 301–21.

6 Gorbachev replaced Shebarshin with former minister of the interior Vadim Bakatin, and Moiseyev with Air Force Commander Yevgeny Shaposhnikov. See Korzhakov, *Boris Yeltsin*.

7 Transcript of session, in *FBIS Daily Report—Soviet Union*, August 26, 1991, pp. 59–69; deputy's comment cited in Colton, *Yeltsin*, 203; Remnick, *Lenin's Tomb*, 1993, 494–95; Dobbs, *Down with Big Brother*, 415–16.

8 Scowcroft and Bush cited in Beschloss and Talbott, *At the Highest Levels*, 365–67.

9 Braithwaite diary, August 29, 1991, in Braithwaite, "Moscow Diary, 1988 to 1992," 365–67.

10 See Chernyaev, *My Six Years with Gorbachev*, 378; Shakhnazarov, *S vozhdiami i bez nikh*, 460–61; Andrei Grachev, *Final Days: The Inside Story of the Collapse of the Soviet Union* (Boulder, CO: Westview Press, 1995), xvi, 5–6; Grachev, *Gibel' Sovetskogo "titanika,"* 214–15; Gorbachev, *Poniat' perestroiku*, 339.

11 Baker III, *Politics of Diplomacy*, 527–28; Chernyaev's diary, July 23, 1991, entry, in *Sovmestnyi iskhod*, 987.

12 Sheinis compares the July and autumn drafts, in Sheinis, *Vzlet i padenie Parlamenta*, 1:594–96.

13 Gorbachev, *Zhizn'*, 2:587; Chernyaev, *My Six Years with Gorbachev*,

379–83; Shakhnazarov-Gorbachev conversation, in *Soiuz mozhno bylo sokhranit'*, 325.

14 Grachev, *Final Days*, 36.

15 Bakatin, *Doroga v proshedshem vremeni*, 357.

16 Fuller account of State Council meeting, in Grachev, *Final Days*, 33–40; Shakhnazarov notes on October 21, 1991, Gorbachev meeting with aides, "Soveshchanie v Orekhovoi komnate posle vystupleniia Gorbacheva na Verkhovnom Sovete," in GFA, f. 10, op. 2.

17 Chernyaev's diary, November 3, 1991, entry, in *Sovmestnyi iskhod*, 1014.

18 Gorbachev cites the conversation in Gorbachev, *Zhizn'*, 2:592; Shakhnazarov's fuller account, as told to him by Gorbachev, is in Shakhnazarov, *S vozhdiami i bez nikh*, 475–76.

19 Shakhnazarov, *S Vozhdiami i bez nikh*, 476; Gorbachev, *Zhizn'*, 2:592; Chernyaev's diary, November 5, 1991, entry, in *Sovmestnyi iskhod*, 1016–17; Chernyaev's notes on November 4, 1991, meeting of State Council, in GFA, f. 2, op. 2; Grachev, *Final Days*, 87–96.

20 Grachev's notes on November 14, 1991, State Council meeting, in GFA, f. 10, op. 2; Grachev, *Final Days*, 106–11.

21 Grachev's notes on November 25, 1991, State Council meeting in GFA, f. 10, op. 2. Also see Grachev, *Final Days*, 119–26; for text of draft treaty as of November 27, 1991, see *Soiuz mozhno bylo sokhranit'*, 395–405.

22 Shakhnazarov, *S Vozhdiami i bez nikh*, 478.

23 Beschloss and Talbott, *At the Highest Levels*, 448–49; Record of conversation between Bush and Gorbachev, November 30, 1991, 9:01 a.m. to 9:37 a.m., in Savranskaya and Blanton, *Last Superpower Summits*, 971.

24 Plokhy, *Last Empire*, 292–93.

25 Matlock Jr., *Autopsy on an Empire*, 634.

26 Plokhy, *Last Empire*, 294.

27 Excerpts from published interviews with participants in the meeting are in *Soiuz mozhno bylo sokhranit'*, 422–24, 434–50; on comparing the union treaty and the CIS, see Sheinis, *Vzlet i padenie Parlamenta*, 1:597–98; also see S. S. Shushkevich, *Moia zhizn', krushenie i voskreshenie SSSR* (Moscow: ROSSPEN, 2012), 191–215.

28 Yeltsin, *Struggle for Russia*, 112; Plokhy, *Last Empire*, 311–12.

29 *Soiuz mozhno bylo sokhranit'*, 456; Plokhy, *Last Empire*, 314–15; Grachev, *Final Days*, 145.

30 Braithwaite summarized Camdessus's impression in his diary, October 7, 1991, in Braithwaite, "Moscow Diary, 1988 to 1992," 391–92; his own impression in November 12, 1991, entry, pp. 409–11.

31 Records of conversations between Bush and Gorbachev, Madrid, Spain, October 29, 1991, 12:30 to 1:15 p.m. and 1:20 p.m. to 2:35 p.m., in Savranskaya and Blanton, *Last Superpower Summits*, 940, 945;

Cherynaev's diary, November 2, 1991, entry, in *Sovmestnyi iskhod*, 1006.

32   Bush and Scowcroft, *World Transformed*, 548; Baker III, *Politics of Diplomacy*, 559.

33   Chernyaev's diary, November 2 and 3, 1991, entries, in *Sovmestnyi iskhod*, 1016.

34   Grachev, *Final Days*, 573.

35   Ashley Parker, "Manners Fit Jeb Bush, If Not an Uncouth Race," *New York Times*, January 17, 2016.

36   Gorbachev, *Zhizn'*, 2:606; Grachev, *Final Days*, 69–70. Gorbachev's eagerness to share responsibility for economic reform with Yeltsin is even clearer in a later conversation with Hungarian President József Antall. See excerpts from "Gorbachev Conversation with President of Hungary Antall, December 6, 1991," in GFA, f. 2, op. 2.

37   Grachev, *Final Days*, 74; Grachev, *Gibel' Sovetskogo "titanika,"* 215.

38   See Grachev, *Gibel' Sovetskogo "titanika,"* 217.

39   Chernyaev's diary, November 2, 1991, entry in *Sovmestnyi iskhod*, 1009–14; Grachev, *Final Days*, 83.

40   Palazhchenko, *My Years with Gorbachev*, 343–44.

41   Grachev, *Final Days*, 147; *Soiuz mozhno bylo sokhranit'*, 465–66.

42   Grachev, *Final Days*, 150.

43   Gorbachev, *Poniat' perestroiku*, 344.

44   E. I. Shaposhnikov, *Vybor: Zapiski Glavnokomanduiushchego* (Moscow: PIK, Novyi Arbat, 1993), 128, 138; *Soiuz mozhno bylo sokhranit'*, 472; Plokhy, *Last Empire*, 325.

45   *V Politbiuro*, 758–59.

46   Braithwaite diary, December 13, 1991, in Braithwaite, "Moscow Diary, 1988 to 1992," 429–31; Chernyaev's diary, December 14, 1991, entry, in *Sovmestnyi iskhod*, 1036.

47   Beschloss and Talbott, *At the Highest Levels*, 453; record of telephone conversation between Bush and Gorbachev, December 13, 1991, 3:37 p.m. to 4:11 p.m., in Savranskaya and Blanton, *Last Superpower Summits*, 978.

48   Chernyaev's diary, December 15, 1991, entry, in *Sovmestnyi iskhod*, 1037.

49   Baker III, *Politics of Diplomacy*, 163.

50   Grachev, *Final Days*, 165–66.

51   Dmitrii Muratov, "Vokrug Gorbacheva opiat' bushuiut strasti," *Novaia gazeta*, February 21–23, 2005, in Karagez'ian and Poliakov, *Gorbachev v zhizni*, 260.

52   Chernyaev's diary, December 22, 1991, entry, in *Sovmestnyi iskhod*, 1040.

53   Grachev, *Final Days*, 180–82.

54 Ibid., 184; Iakovlev, *Sumerki*, 506; Beschloss and Talbott, *At the Highest Levels*, 455–56; Baker III, *Politics of Diplomacy*, 572.

55 Chernyaev's diary, December 27, 1991, entry, in *Sovmestnyi iskhod*, 1042–43.

56 Grachev, *Final Days*, 184; Plokhy, *Last Empire*, 368–70; Grachev, *Gorbachev*, 416; Korzhakov, *Boris Yeltsin*, 129.

57 Falin's recollections concerning both Katyn and the Nazi-Soviet Pact, and including Gorbachev's response to him and Yakovlev, are in *Bez skidok na obstoiatel'stva*, 371–78, 401–7; Yakovlev's are in *Sumerki*, 417–22; Chernyaev's are in *My Six Years with Gorbachev*, 129–30; for a brief excerpt from notes on a July 31, 1989, Politburo session that seems to have considered the pact, see *V Politbiuro*, 518–19; for Vadim Medvedev's notes on an August 3, 1989, conversation with Gorbachev, during which the latter bawled out Yegor Yakovlev for condemning both the Katyn massacres and the pact's secret protocols in *Moscow News*, see "Razgovor Medvedeva s s Gorbachevym," August 3, 1989, in GFA, f. 10, op. 2. Also see transcript of first meeting of the Congress of People's Deputies Commission on the Nazi-Soviet Pact, and Aleksandr Yakovlev's notes for his remarks at the July 31, 1989, Politburo meeting, in Iakovlev, *Perestroika*, 321–31, 344–51.

58 Matlock Jr., *Autopsy on an Empire*, 284.

59 Chernyaev, *My Six Years with Gorbachev*, 130, n. 39.

60 Yeltsin quoted in Pankin, *Last Hundred Days*, 86; Yeltsin, *Struggle for Russia*, 122; Plokhy, *Last Empire*, 369; Dobbs, *Down with Big Brother*, 447–48.

61 Iakovlev, *Sumerki*, 508–9.

62 Notes by Shakhnazarov and Medvedev on December 24, 1991, Gorbachev meeting with aides and advisers, in GFA, f. 10, op. 2. Also see Beschloss and Talbott, *At the Highest Levels*, 459.

63 O'Clery, *Moscow, December 25, 1991*, 27.

64 Ibid., 28.

65 Grachev, *Final Days*, 186.

66 *V Politbiuro*, 768–70; O'Clery, *Moscow, December 25, 1991*, 99–100.

67 Chernyaev's diary, December 27, 1991, entry, in *Sovmestnyi iskhod*, 1042; Grachev, *Final Days*, 186–87.

68 O'Clery, *Moscow, December 25, 1991*, 102.

69 Russian phone transcripts of conversations with Mitterrand, Kohl, Mulroney, and Major, in GFA, f. 10, op. 2; Record of telephone conversation between Bush and Gorbachev, December 25, 1991, 10:03 to 10:25 a.m., in Savranskaya and Blanton, *Last Superpower Summits*, 991–93; also see Grachev, *Final Days*, 178–89; Bush and Scowcroft, *World Transformed*, 559–61; Beschloss and Talbott, *At the Highest Levels*, 460–63, on Bush's being taken aback by the videotaping of Gor-

bachev's call; Bush's recollection of Gorbachev's final phone call in his interview with the author, September 19, 2006.

70   See O'Clery, *Moscow, December 25, 1991*, 225–28, 247; Grachev, *Final Days*, 189.

71   Full text in *V Politbiuro*, 768–70.

72   O'Clery, *Moscow, December 25, 1991*, 257–59; Shaposhnikov, *Vybor*, 136.

73   Grachev, *Final Days*, 190; Gorbachev, *Zhizn'*, 2:621–22.

74   Chernyaev's diary, December 27, 1991, entry, in *Sovmestnyi iskhod*, 1042; Grachev, *Final Days*, 191; O'Clery, *Moscow, December 25, 1991*, 275; Gorbachev, *Dekabr'-91*, 120.

75   O'Clery, *Moscow, December 25, 1991*, 262, 284; Grachev, *Final Days*, 192.

76   Excerpts from interview with Giulietto Chiesa and Enrico Siniger, in Gorbachev, *Dekabr'-91*, 145–48; Grachev, *Final Days*, 192–93.

77   Grachev, *Final Days*, 193–94; Chernyaev's diary, December 27, 1991, entry, in *Sovmestnyi iskhod*, 1043.

78   Author's interview with Karen Karagezian, April 6, 2007, Moscow.

79   Gorbachev, *Dekabr'-91*, 122–24.

80   Chernyaev's diary, December 27, 1991, entry, in *Sovmestnyi iskhod*, 1043–44.

81   Gorbachev, *Zhizn'*, 2:622.

82   Shakhnazarov, *S vozhdiami i bez nikh*, 486.

83   Chernyaev's diary, December 28, 1991, entry, in *Sovmestnyi iskhod*, 1044.

CHAPTER 19: OUT OF POWER: 1992–2016

1   See Taubman, *Khrushchev*, 236–40.

2   "Former President Jimmy Carter and the Carter Center Launch a Site on the Internet's World Wide Web," *Carter Center*, April 27, 1995, http://www.cartercenter.org/news/documents/doc724.html; "The Clinton Foundation," *Clinton Foundation*, accessed October 31, 2015, https://www.clintonfoundation.org/front.

3   "The International Foundation for Socio-Economic and Political Studies (The Gorbachev Foundation)," *Gorbachev Fond*, accessed October 31, 2015, http://www.gorby.ru/en/.

4   Natali'ia Zelnorova, "Ia nauchilas' prosto zhit'," in *Raisa: Vospominaniia*, 318.

5   Gorbachev, *Posle kremlia*, 31, 346; Zavada and Kulikov, "Mikhail Gorbachev"; Vladimir Malevannyi, "Molitva bez svechei," *Nezavisimaia gazeta*, September 10, 1999, 168 edition, sec. 9, http://www.gorby.ru/gorbacheva/publications/show_25914/; recollections of Aleksandr Likhotal and Vitaly Gusenkov, in *Raisa Gorbacheva: Shtrikhi*, 115, 196; Zoia Eroshok, "Irina Virganskaia-Gorbacheva: O roditeliakh

i semeinykh tsennostiakh," *Novaia gazeta*, February 25, 2011, in Karagez'ian and Poliakov, *Gorbachev v zhizni*, 115.

6   Author's interview with Irina Gorbacheva, March 18, 2010, Moscow.

7   Georgii Shakhnazarov, *S vozhdiami i bez nikh*, 523.

8   Gorbachev, *Posle kremlia*, 34.

9   Maria Fedorina, "Slezy Pervoi ledi," Moskovskii komsomolets, February 14, 1988, in *Raisa: Vospominaniia*, 176.

10   Gorbachev began cowriting a newspaper column and would later found a newspaper with Muratov, *Novaya gazeta*. Author's interview with Dmitry Muratov, May 12, 2013, New York City.

11   D. Muratov and V. Fronin, "Suda ia ne boius'," *Komsomol'skaia pravda*, February 24, 1992.

12   Sergei Svistunov, "Plius Burbulizatsia vsei strany?," *Pravda*, April 30, 1992.

13   D. Muratov and Iu. Sorokin, "Pravitel'stvo pora vykhodit' iz podpol'ia," *Komsomol'skaia pravda*, May 29, 1992.

14   "Rezkoe zaiavlenie v adres Gorbacheva," *Izvestiia*, June 3, 1992.

15   "Nad byvshim prezidentom SSSR sgushchaiutsia tuchi," *Golos*, June 22, 1992.

16   Shakhnazarov, *S vozhdiami i bez nikh*, 531–32; Vasilii Golovin, "Eks-Prezident v Iaponii," *Nezavisimaia gazeta*, April 24, 1992.

17   Remnick, *Lenin's Tomb*, 501.

18   Author's email interview with Bruce Allyn, May 4, 2015.

19   Valerii Alekseev, "I otdykhaia v Ispanii, Gorbachev dumaet o Rossii," *24*, August 28, 1992.

20   Stephen Kinzer, "Gorbachev the Tourist Finds Admirers in Germany," *New York Times*, March 10, 1992; "Gorbachev Jokingly Offers to Sell Subs," *United Press International*, March 11, 1992; "Gorby and Raisa Go After Laughs," *Toronto Star*, March 8, 1992.

21   Shakhnazarov, *S vozhdiami i bez nikh*, 517–19; Gorbachev, *Posle kremlia*, 59.

22   Cited in Aleksandr Vasil'ev, "Trudno byt' byvshim," *Komsomol'skaia pravda*, January 1, 1992.

23   Mikhail Gorbachev, "Esli nado budet spasat' stranu—ia vernius'," *Komsomol'skaia pravda*, October 3, 1993.

24   Vitalii Tret'iakov, "Mikhail Gorbachev zavtra vystupit no protsesse po delu Generala Varennikova," *Nezavisimaia gazeta*, July 6, 1994.

25   Shakhnazarov, *S vozhdiami i bez nikh*, 523.

26   Remnick, *Lenin's Tomb*, 506.

27   Carey Goldberg, "I'm No Coup Plotter, Gorbachev Thunders," *Los Angeles Times*, July 8, 1994; Adam Tanner, "Witness Gorbachev Finds Himself on Trial," *Moscow Times*, July 9, 1994; Alessandra Stanley, "Trial of Coup Plotters against Gorbachev Takes an Odd Turn," *New York Times*, July 10, 1994.

28   Author's interview with Muratov, May 12, 2013, New York City.

29   Remnick, *Lenin's Tomb*, 527–28.

30   Gorbachev, *Posle kremlia*, 95, 105–8.

31   Shakhnazarov, *S vozhdiami i bez nikh*, 523.

32   Gorbachev, *Posle kremlia*, 110–14.

33   Chiesa and Cucurnia, "Edinstvennaia," in *Raisa: Vospominaniia*, 255.

34   Nikolai Efimovich and Saed-Shakh, "Raisa Gorbacheva: Ia nikogda," ibid., 160.

35   "Mne nikto ne strashen," *Obshchaia gazeta*, May 16, 1996.

36   Gorbachev, *Posle kremlia*, 110.

37   Valerii Vyzhutovich, "Mikhail Gorbachev: K prezidentskim vyboram nuzhno sozdat' shirokuiu koalitsiiu demokraticheskikh sil," *Izvestiia*, December 28, 1995.

38   Marina Shakina, "'V 1991 godu ia byl slishkom samouveren,'" *Nezavisimaia gazeta*, December 12, 1995.

39   Vyzhutovich, "Mikhail Gorbachev."

40   "Stranu nel'zia lomat' cherez koleno, po-kovboiski."

41   "Mne nikto ne strashen."

42   Ibid.

43   Krementsova, "Liubimaia zhena," in *Raisa: Vospominaniia*, 168.

44   See Gorbachev, *Posle kremlia*, 115–22.

45   See David E. Hoffman, *The Oligarchs: Wealth and Power in the New Russia* (New York: Public Affairs, 2002), 296–364.

46   Shakhnazarov, *S vozhdiami i bez nikh*, 523.

47   Author's interview with Olga M. Zdravomyslova, April 2, 2007, Moscow; Vladimir Malevannyi, "Molitva bez svechei," in *Raisa: Vospominaniia*, 180–82. Malevannyi's interview was conducted before Gorbacheva became critically ill in July 1999.

48   Olga Zdravomyslova's recollections, in *Raisa Gorbacheva: Shtrikhi*, 132.

49   Recollections of U.S. television executive Pat Mitchell, ibid., 167–68.

50   Author's interview with Zdravomyslova, April 2, 2007, Moscow.

51   Irina Bobrova, "Posledniaia ledi," in *Raisa: Vospominaniia*, 290.

52   Author's interview with Luydia Budyka, August 3, 2008, Stavropol.

53   Chiesa and Cucurnia, "Edinstvennaia," 252–53.

54   Mikhail Gorbachev, *Naedine s soboi* (Moscow: Grin strit, 2012), 233. Translation here and below draws on working English translation by Pavel Palazhchenko.

55   Author's interview with Karen Karagezian, April 6, 2007, Moscow.

56   Gorbachev, *Naedine s soboi*, 13.

57   Author's interview with Karagezian, April 6, 2007, Moscow.

58   Gorbachev, *Naedine s soboi*, 16, 233.

59   Ibid., 234–35.

60   Author's interview with Karagezian, April 6, 2007, Moscow.

61   Gorbachev, *Naedine s soboi*, 240–46.

62 Giulietto Chiesa, "Grustnaia missiia Gorbacheva," *Nezavisimaia gazeta*, August 20, 1999. Yeltsin wrote the following: "I want to express my deep anxiety about the severe trial which your family is enduring. I well know how hard it is for anyone to suffer an illness. During such times, mutual support, warmth and care are more than ever needed. I wish you strength and fortitude, respected Mikhail Sergeyevich, and to Raisa Maksimovna, courage as she battles her illness and a speedy recovery."

63 Cited ibid.

64 Zavada and Kulikov, "Mikhail Gorbachev."

65 Gorbachev, *Naedine s soboi*, 235–37.

66 Chiesa and Cucurnia, "Edinstvennaia," 254.

67 Gorbachev, *Naedine s soboi*, 12–13; author's interview with Karagezian, April 6, 2007, Moscow.

68 Chiesa, "Grustnaia missiia Gorbacheva"; Chiesa and Cucurnia, "Edinstvennaia," 254.

69 "Mikhail Gorbachev: Zhenit'sia ia ne sobiraius'," *Komsomol'skaia pravda*, March 2, 2001.

70 One can see Gorbachev's grief in his face in a film made by Vitaly Mansky in 2000. Sitting in tall grass in a meadow, wearing a black shirt and a blue cap, he speaks to the camera in a muffled tone, his face darkened by grief. "I don't want to live. Honestly, I don't want to live." Vitaly Mansky, *Gorbachev: After the Empire*, 2001.

71 Eroshok, "Irina Virganskaia-Gorbacheva," 116.

72 Zavada and Kulikov, "Mikhail Gorbachev."

73 "Mikhail Gorbachev: Zhenit'sia ia ne sobiraius'."

74 Author's interview with Muratov, May 12, 2013, New York City.

75 As conveyed to former ambassador Matlock, who called on Gorbachev a few days after Yeltsin named Putin prime minister. Personal communication from Matlock, April 3, 2016.

76 Gorbachev, *Posle kremlia*, 141.

77 As recalled by Vitaly Tretiakov, in Karagez'ian and Poliakov, *Gorbachev v zhizni*, 542.

78 Personal communication from Jack Matlock, April 3, 2016.

79 Gorbachev, *Posle kremlia*, 142–44.

80 Ibid., 146–47.

81 See Brown, "Did Gorbachev as General Secretary Become a Social Democrat?"

82 Gorbachev, *Posle kremlia*, 148–52.

83 Author's interview with Zdravomslova, April 2, 2007, Moscow; Gorbachev, *Posle kremlia*, 158–59.

84 Ibid., 159–63, 184.

85 Ibid., 175–76.

86 "Soviet Union 'Should Have Been Preserved,'" *USA Today*, April 6, 2006.

87   Gregory L. White, "Gorby's Choice," *Wall Street Journal*, December 1, 2007.

88   Ibid.

89   "Gorbachevu vsego lish' vosemdesiat," *Izvestiia*, March 3, 2011.

90   Cited in Gorbachev, *Posle kremlia*, 248–58.

91   Ibid., 402, 404; Matthias Schepp and Britta Sandberg, "I Am Truly and Deeply Concerned," *Der Spiegel*, January 16, 2015, http://www.spiegel.de/international/world/gorbachev-warns-of-decline-in-russian-western-ties-over-ukraine-a-1012992.html; also see Lezvina, "Razgovor s zemliakom," in Karagez'ian and Poliakov, *Gorbachev v zhizni*, 53.

92   The author was present at the World Political Forum in Turin, the Harvard nuclear abolition conference, the 2005 Washington tribute, Gorbachev's seventy-fifth, and the London birthday gala in 2011.

93   Natasha Singer, "Rubles, a Girl's Best Friend," *New York Times*, December 9, 2007; Irina Gorbachev's remarks, quoted in Gorbachev, *Posle kremlia*, 240–41.

94   Lezvina, "Razgovor s zemliakom," 58.

95   "Soured" cited by Steve Rosenberg, "Mikhail Gorbachev Denounces Putin's 'Attack on Rights,'" *BBC News Europe*, March 7, 2014, http://www.bbc.com/news/world-europe-21695314; Gorbachev, *Posle kremlia*, 267, 269.

96   Aleksandr Braterskii, "Mikhail Gorbachev predstavil svoiu novuiu knigu," *Gazeta.ru*, November 21, 2014; Irina Skvortsova, "Mikhail Gorbachev: Ia ne boius' kritiki, potomu chto v politike nel'zia obizhat'sia," *Sobesednik*, December 17, 2014.

97   Rosenberg, "Mikhail Gorbachev Denounces Putin's 'Attack on Rights.'"

98   Ivan Nechepurenko, "Gorbachev on Russia and Ukraine: We Are One People," *Moscow Times*, November 21, 2014.

99   Neil MacFarquhar, "Reviled, Revered and Still Challenging Russia to Evolve," *New York Times*, June 2, 2016.

100 Nechepurenko, "Gorbachev on Russia and Ukraine."

101 Simon Shuster, "Gorbachev Blames the U.S. For Provoking 'New Cold War,'" *Time*, December 11, 2014, http://time.com/3630352/mikhail-gorbachev-vladimir-putin-cold-war/.

102 Nathan Gardels, "Why Gorbachev Feels Betrayed by the Post–Cold War West," *Huffington Post*, November 7, 2014.

103 George H. W. Bush, "STATE OF THE UNION; Transcript of President Bush's Address on the State of the Union," in *New York Times*, 1992, http://www.nytimes.com/1992/01/29/us/state-union-transcript-president-bush-s-address-state-union.html?pagewanted=all.

104 Anna Beligzhanina, "Mikhail Gorbachev: 'Ia rad, chto Krym prisoedinilsia k Rossii,'" *Komsomol'skaia pravda*, March 18, 2014, http://msk.kp.ru/print/26207/3093031; Nechepurenko, "Gorbachev on Russia

and Ukraine"; Andrei Arkhangelsii, "Mikhail Gorbachev: 'Nado izme-nit' atmosferu'," *Ogonek*, February 2, 2015.

105   Schepp and Sandberg, "I Am Truly and Deeply Concerned."

106   Author's interviews with Gorbachev, October 19, 2015, Pavel Palazh-chenko, October 22, 2015, Dmitry Muratov, October 23, 2015, all in Moscow.

CONCLUSION: UNDERSTANDING GORBACHEV

1   Thanks to Pavel Machala for helping to clarify these points.

2   Zubok, *Failed Empire*, 311; Zubok cites N. N. Kozlova, *Gorizonty povsednevnosti sovetskoi epokhi: Golosa iz khora* (Moscow: Institute of Philosophy, 1996).

3   Vinogradov, "The Paradox of Mikhail Gorbachev," in *Millennium Salute to Mikhail Gorbachev on His 70th Birthday*, 46.

4   Jeremi Suri, "To Get Big Things Done We Should Strip Demands on the President," *Dallas Morning Star*, December 4, 2015.

5   To be sure, it must be admitted that the East European countries and former Baltic republics of the USSR, which were later admitted to NATO, wished to join the alliance.

6   Among others whose grave reservations about the first Gulf War resembled Gorbachev's were Zbigniew Brzezinski, former chairman of the U.S. Joint Chiefs of Staff Admiral William J. Crowe Jr., former president Jimmy Carter, and Senator Daniel Patrick Moynihan. See Micah L. Sifry and Christopher Cerf, eds., *The Gulf War Reader: History, Documents, Opinions* (New York: Times Books, 1991), 225–27, 234–37, 251–54, 284–86; also see Robert W. Tucker and David C. Hendrickson, *The Imperial Temptation: The New World Order and America's Purpose* (New York: Council on Foreign Relations Press, 1992), 94–98.

7   See Zubok, *Failed Empire*, 308.

BIBLIOGRAPHY

_____

ARCHIVAL SOURCES

Arkhiv Gorbachev-Fonda (GFA), Moscow, Russia
British Library of Political and Economic Science, London School of Economics, London, UK, "The Second Russian Revolution" transcripts (TSRRT)
George Bush Presidential Library, College Station, TX
Gosudarstvennyi arkhiv noveishei istorii Stavropol'skogo kraia (GANISK), Stavropol, Russia
Gosudarstvennyi arkhiv Rossiiskoi Federatsii (GARF), Moscow, Russia
Hoover Institution Archives
National Security Archive (NSA), Washington, DC, Russian and East European Archival Documents Database (READD-RADD Collection)
Public Record Office, Kew, London, UK
Ronald Reagan Presidential Library, Simi Valley, CA
Tsentral'nyi arkhiv obshchestvenno-politicheskoi istorii Moskvy (TSAOPIM), Moscow, Russia
United States National Archives, Washington, DC

PERIODICALS

_24_
BBC News Europe
Carl Beck Papers in Russian and East European Studies
Cold War History
Cold War International History Project Bulletin
Diplomatic History
Europe Asia-Studies

Foreign Affairs
Gazeta.ru
Golos
Huffington Post
Izvestiia
Journal of Cold War Studies
Komsomol'skaia pravda
Kul'tura
Los Angeles Times
Minneapolis Star Tribune
Moscow Times
Moskovskie novosti
Moskovskii komsomolets
Narodoselenie
Nation
New York Times
Nezavisimaia gazeta
Obshchaia gazeta
Ogonek
Personality and Social Psychology Bulletin
Pravda
Problems of Post-Communism
Radio svoboda
Russian Review
Sobesednik
Der Spiegel
Svobodnaia mysl'
Time
Toronto Star
L'Unità
United Press International
USA Today
Wall Street Journal
Washington Post
Zhurnalist

PUBLISHED DOCUMENTS AND PUBLISHED COLLECTIONS OF DOCUMENTS

Cherniaev, Anatolii. *1991 god: Dnevnik pomoshchnika prezidenta SSSR*. Moscow: Terra, 1997.
—————. *Sovmestnyi iskhod*. Moscow: Rosspen, 2008.
Chetvertyi s"ezd narodnykh deputatov SSSR, 17–27 dekabria 1990. Vol. 1. Moscow: Izdanie verkhovnogo soveta SSSR, 1990.

Devlin, Kevin. *Some Views of the Gorbachev Era*. Radio Free Europe Research, 1985. RAD Background Report.

Galkin, Aleksandr, and Anatolii Cherniaev, eds. *Mikhail Gorbachev i germanskii vopros: Sbornik dokumentov, 1986–1991*. Moscow: Ves' mir, 2006.

Gorbachev: Izbrannyi (sbornik). Moscow: Novaia gazeta, 2011.

Gorbachev, Mikhail. *Izbrannye rechi i stat'i*. Moscow: Izdatel'stvo politicheskoi literatury, 1987.

——————. *Sobranie sochinenii*. 25 vols. Moscow: Ves' mir, 2008–15.

Iakovlev, A. A., ed. *Perestroika: 1985–1991: Neizdannoe, maloizvestnoe, zabytoe*. Moscow: Mezhdunarodyi fond, "Demokratiia," 2008.

Karagez'ian, Karen, and Vladimir Poliakov, eds. *Gorbachev v zhizni*. Moscow: Ves' mir, 2016.

Küsters, Hanns Jürgen, and Daniel Hofmann, eds. *Deutsche Einheit: Sonderedition aus den Akten des Bundeskanzleramtes, 1989/90*, Dokumente zur Deutschlandpolitik. Munich: R. Oldenbourg Verlag, 1998.

Materialy plenuma tsentral'nogo komiteta KPSS, 5–7 fevralia 1990 goda. Moscow: Politizdat, 1990.

Mnogaia leta . . . Mikhailu Gorbachevu—70. Moscow: "R. Valent": 2001.

Otvechaia na vyzov vremeni: Vneshniaia politika perestroika: dokymental'nye svidetel'stva. Moscow: Ves' mir, 2010.

Pervyi s'ezd narodnykh deputatov SSSR: 25 maia–9 iunia 1989, stenograficheskii otchet. Vol. 1. Moscow: Izdanie verkhovnogo soveta SSSR, n.d.

Raisa Gorbacheva: Shtrikhi k portretu. Moscow: Gorbachev-Fond, 2009.

Raisa: Vospominaniia, dnevniki, interv'iu, stat'i, pis'ma, telegrammy. Moscow: Vagirus/Petro-n'ius, 2000.

Savranskaya, Svetlana, and Tom Blanton, eds. *The Last Superpower Summits: Gorbachev, Reagan and Bush at the End of the Cold War*. Budapest: Central European University Press, 2016.

Savranskaya, Svetlana, Thomas Blanton, and Vladislav Zubok, eds. *Masterpieces of History: The Peaceful End of the Cold War in Europe, 1989*. New York: Central European University Press, 2010.

Sifry, Micah L., and Christopher Cerf, eds. *The Gulf War Reader: History, Documents, Opinions*. New York: Times Books, 1991.

Soiuz mozhno bylo sokhranit': Belaia kniga: Dokumenty i fakty o politike M. S. Gorbacheva po reformirovaniiu i sokhraneniiu mnogonatsional'nogo gosudarstva. Moscow: Izdatel'stvo AST, 2007.

Tsentral'nyi komitet KPSS, VKP(b), RSDPR(b): Istoriko-biograficheskii spravochnik. Moscow: Parad, 2005.

V Politbiuro TsK KPSS: Po zapisam Anatoliia Cherniaeva, Vadima Medvedeva, Georgiia Shakhnazarova, 1985–1991. Moscow: Gorbachev-Fond, 2008.

XIX Vsesoiuznaia konferentsiia kommunisticheskoi partii sovetskogo soiuza: Stenograficheskii otchet. Vol. 1. Moscow: Izdatel'stvo politicheskoi literatury, 1988.

UNPUBLISHED DOCUMENTS

CIA, Directorate of Intelligence. "The Gorbachev Succession." 29 April 1991.

MEMOIRS

Abalkin, Leonid. *Neispol'zovannyi shans: Poltora goda v pravitel'stve*. Moscow: Politizdat, 1991.

Akhromeev, S. F., and G. M. Kornienko. *Glazami marshala i diplomata*. Moscow: Mezhdunarodnye otnosheniia, 1992.

Aleksandrov-Agentov, A. M. *Ot Kollontai do Gorbacheva: Vospominaniya diplomata, sovetnika A. A. Gromyko, pomoshchnika L. I. Brezhneva, Iu. V. Andropova, K. U. Chernenko i M. S. Gorbacheva*. Moscow: Mezhdunarodnye otnosheniia, 1994.

Arbatov, Georgii. *Moia epokha v litsakh i sobytiiakh*. Moscow: Sobranie, 2008.

Bakatin, V. *Doroga v proshedshem vremeni*. Moscow: Dom, 1999.

Baker, James A., III. *The Politics of Diplomacy: Revolution, War, and Peace, 1989–1992*. New York: G. P. Putnam's Sons, 1995.

Boldin, V. I. *Krushenie p'edestala*. Moscow: Respublika, 1995.

————. *Ten Years That Shook the World*. New York: Basic Books, 1994.

Bovin, Aleksandr. *XX vek kak zhizn': Vospominaniia*. Moscow: Zakharov, 2003.

Braithwaite, Rodric. *Across the Moscow River: The World Turned Upside Down*. New Haven: Yale University Press, 2002.

Brutents, K. N. *Nesbyvsheesia*. Moscow: Mezhdunarodnye otnosheniia, 2005.

Bush, Barbara. *Barbara Bush: A Memoir*. New York: Charles Scribner's Sons, 1994.

Bush, George, and Brent Scowcroft. *A World Transformed*. New York: Alfred A. Knopf, 1998.

Cherniaev, Anatolii. *Moia zhizn' i moe vremia*. Moscow: Mezhdunarodnye otnosheniia, 1995.

————. *My Six Years with Gorbachev*. Translated and edited by Robert D. English and Elizabeth Tucker. University Park: Pennsylvania State University Press, 2000.

————. *Shest' let s Gorbachevym*. Moscow: Izdatel'skaia gruppa "Progress" – "Kul'tura," 1993.

Dobrynin, Anatoly. *In Confidence: Moscow's Ambassador to America's Six Cold War Presidents*. New York: Times Books, 1995.

————. *Sugubo doveritel'no: Posol v Vashingtone pri shesti prezidentakh SShA (1962–1986)*. Moscow: Mezhdunarodnye otnosheniia, 2008.

Falin, V. M. *Bez skidok na obstoiatel'stva*. Moscow: Respublika, 1999.

Gates, Robert M. *From the Shadows: The Ultimate Insider's Story of Five Presidents and How They Won the Cold War*. New York: Simon & Schuster, 1996.

Gorbachev, Mikhail. *The August Coup: The Truth and the Lessons*. New York: HarperCollins, 1991.

—————. *Dekabr'-1991: Moia pozitsiia*. Moscow: Novosti, 1992.

—————. *Kak eto bylo*. Moscow: Vagrius, 1999.

—————. *Memoirs*. New York: Doubleday, 1995.

—————. *Naedine s soboi*. Moscow: Grin strit, 2012.

—————. *Poniat' perestroiku . . . Pochemu eto vazhno seichas*. Moscow: Al'pina Biznes Buks, 2006.

—————. *Posle kremlia*. Moscow: Ves' mir, 2014.

—————. *Zhizn' i reformy*. 2 vols. Moscow: Novosti, 1995.

Gorbachev, Raisa. *I Hope*. New York: HarperCollins, 1991.

Gorbacheva, Raisa M. *Ia nadeius'*. Moscow: Novosti, 1991.

Grachev, Andrei. *Final Days: The Inside Story of the Collapse of the Soviet Union*. Boulder, CO: Westview Press, 1995.

—————. *Gibel' Sovetskogo "titanika": Sudovoi zhurnal*. Moscow: 2015.

Graham, Loren. *Moscow Stories*. Bloomington: Indiana University Press, 2006.

Gromyko, Anatolii. *Andrei Gromyko: V labirintakh Kremliia*. Moscow: Avtor, 1997.

Hutchings, Robert L. *American Diplomacy and the End of the Cold War: An Insider's Account of U.S. Policy in Europe, 1989–1992*. Washington, DC: Woodrow Wilson Center Press, 1997.

Iakovlev, Aleksandr. *Sumerki*. Moscow: Materik, 2005.

Kariakin, Yurii. *Peremena ubezhdenii*. Moscow: Raduga, 2007.

Kaznacheev, Viktor. *Intriga - velikoe delo*. Stavropol: Knizhnoe izdatelstvo, 1997.

—————. *Na perekrestkakh sud'by*. Pyatigorsk: Kavkaskaia zdravnitsa, 2003.

Korobeinikov, A. A. *Gorbachev: Drugoe litso*. Moscow: "Respublika," 1996.

Korzhakov, Aleksandr. *Boris Yeltsin: Ot rassveta do zakata*. Moscow: Interbook, 1997.

Kriuchkov, Vladimir. *Lichnoe delo*. Vol. 2. Moscow: Olimp, 1996.

Liakhovskii, A. *Tragedia i doblest' Afgana*. Moscow: Iskona, 1995.

Ligachev, Yegor. *Inside Gorbachev's Kremlin*. Translated by Catherine A. Fitzpatrick, Michele A. Berdy, and Dobrochna Dyrzc-Freeman. New York: Pantheon Books, 1993.

Matlock, Jack F., Jr. *Autopsy on an Empire: The American Ambassador's Account of the Collapse of the Soviet Union*. New York: Random House, 1995.

Medvedev, Vadim. *Raspad: Kak on nazreval v "mirovoi sisteme sotsializma."* Moscow: Mezhdunarodnye otnosheniia, 1994.

—————. *V kommande Gorbacheva*. Moscow: Bylina, 1994.

Medvedev, Vladimir. *Chelovek za spinoi*. Moscow: Russlit, 1994.

Mikhailenko, Vitalii. *Kakim ty byl . . .* Nalchik: Izdatelskii tsentr El'-Fa, 1997.

Palazhchenko, Pavel. *My Years with Gorbachev and Shevardnadze: The Memoir of a Soviet Interpreter*. University Park: Pennsylvania State University Press, 1997.

Pankin, Boris. *The Last Hundred Days of the Soviet Union*. New York: I. B. Taurus, 1996.

Petrakov, N. Y. *Russkaia ruletka*. Moscow: Ekonomika, 1998.

Popov, G. *Snova v oppozitsii*. Moscow: Galaktika, 1994.

Powell, Colin L. *My American Journey*. New York: Random House, 1995.

Reagan, Nancy. *My Turn: The Memoirs of Nancy Reagan*. New York: Random House, 1989.

Reagan, Ronald. *An American Life*. New York: Simon & Schuster, 1990.

Regan, Donald T. *For the Record: From Wall Street to Washington*. San Diego: Harcourt Brace Jovanovich, 1988.

Riabov, Viktor. *Zhizn' v TSK ili TsK iznutri*. Moscow: Zhizn' i mysl, 2005.

Ryzhkov, Nikolai. *Perestroika: Istoriia predatel'stva*. Moscow: Novosti, 1992.

—————. *Tragediia velikoi strany*. Moscow: Veche, 2007.

Sagdeev, Roald Z. *The Making of a Soviet Scientist*. New York: John Wiley & Sons, 1994.

Sakharov, Andrei. *Memoirs*. Translated by Richard Lourie. New York: Alfred A. Knopf, 1990.

—————. *Vospominaniia: V dvukh tomakh*. 2 vols. Moscow: Prava cheloveka, 1996.

Shakhnazarov, Georgii. *S vozhdiami i bez nikh*. Moscow: Vagrius, 2001.

Shaposhnikov, E. I. *Vybor: Zapiski Glavnokomanduiushchego*. Moscow: PIK, Novyi Arbat, 1993.

Shevardnadze, Eduard. *Moi vybor v zashchitu demokratii i svobody*. Moscow: Novosti, 1991.

Shultz, George P. *Turmoil and Triumph: My Years as Secretary of State*. New York: Charles Scribner's Sons, 1993.

Shushkevich, S. S. *Moia zhizn': Krushenie i voskreshenie SSSR*. Moscow: ROSSPEN, 2012.

Taubman, William, and Jane Taubman. *Moscow Spring*. New York: Summit Books, 1989.

Thatcher, Margaret. *Downing Street Years*. New York: HarperCollins, 1993.

Varennikov, V. I. *Nepovtorimoe. V 7 tomakh*. Vol. 6. Moscow: Sovetskii pisatel', 2001.

Vorotnikov, Vitaliy. *A bylo eto tak . . . iz dnevnika chlena Politbiuro TsK KPSS*. Moscow: Sovet veteranov knigoizdaniia, 1995.

Wolf, Markus. *Man without a Face: The Autobiography of Communism's Greatest Spymaster*. New York: Public Affairs, 1997.

Yefremov, Leonid. *Renegat Gorbachev—Al'ians dvurushnikov—Yadovitaya chasha Yakovleva*. Stavropol: Izdatelstvo Gosudarstvennogo arkhiva Stavropolskogo kraya "Krestograd," 1996.

Yeltsin, Boris. *Against the Grain*. Translated by Michael Glenny. New York: Summit Books, 1990.

—————. *The Struggle for Russia*. Translated by Catherine A. Fitzgerald. New York: Crown, 1994.

UNPUBLISHED MEMOIRS

Braithwaite, Rodric. "Moscow Diary, 1988 to 1992."
Cherniaev, Anatolii. "Dnevniki A. C. Cherniaeva: 1972–1991." *National Security Archive*, 2003. http://nsarchive.gwu.edu/rus/Chernyaev.html.
Chernyaev, Anatoly. "The Diary of Anatoly S. Chernyaev: 1987–1988." Translated by Anna Melyakova, edited by Svetlana Savranskaya. *National Security Archive*, May 23, 2008. http://nsarchive.gwu.edu/NSAEBB/NSAEBB250/index.htm.

AUTHOR'S INTERVIEWS

Allison, Graham. May 27, 2014. Cambridge, MA.
Allyn, Bruce, May 4, 2015 (via email).
Arbatov, Georgy. May 27, 2006. Moscow.
Baker, James A., III. October 8, 2006. Houston, TX.
Bazikova, Raisa. July 4, 2005. Stavropol.
Bekova, Zoya. August 1, 2006. Moscow.
Bogomolov, Oleg. April 11, 2007. Moscow.
Brutents, Karen. April 23, 2007. Moscow.
Budyka, Lidiya. August 3, 2008. Stavropol.
Burlatsky, Fyodor, June 30, 2005, Moscow.
Bush, George H. W. September 19, 2006 (via email).
Chernyaev, Anatoly. May 30, 2005. Moscow.
Collins, James. March 3, 2007. Moscow.
Cradock, Sir Percy. July 23, 2008. Richmond, UK.
Daniushevskaya, Galina. July 2006. Moscow.
Dolinskaya, Liubov. August 7, 2008. Stavropol.
Golovanov, Dmitry. July 29, 2006. Moscow.
Gonochenko, A. A. July 5, 2005. Stavropol.
Gorbachev, Irina. March 18, 2010. Moscow.
Gorbachev, Mikhail. April 19, 2007. Moscow.
———. May 2, 2007. Moscow.
———. May 4, 2007. Moscow.
———. May 25, 2007. Moscow.
———. March 17, 2010. Moscow.
———. November 14, 2011. Moscow.
———. October 19, 2015. Moscow.
———. June 7, 2016, Moscow.
Grachev, Andrei. June 28, 2005. Pushkino.
Gudarenko, Raisa. July 31, 2008. Stavropol.
Gudkov, Lev. June 7, 2016. Moscow
Gusenkov, Vitaly. March 21, 2007. Moscow.
Hill, Charles. June 20, 2006. New Haven, CT.

Howe, Lord Geoffrey. July 22, 2008. London.

Hurd, Douglas. July 22, 2008. London.

Kalyagin, V. V. July 5, 2005. Stavropol.

Karagez'ian, Karen. April 6, 2007. Moscow.

Kisilev, Evgeny. June 7, 2007. Moscow.

Kornienko, G. M. June 17, 2005. Moscow.

Lown, Bernard. May 29, 2014. Chestnut Hill, MA.

Luers, William. February 12, 2016. New York.

Matlock, Jack F., Jr. November 23, 2004. Princeton, NJ.

————. October 18, 2007. South Hadley, MA.

Matlock, Rebecca. November 29, 2007. South Hadley, MA.

————. December 7, 2007. South Hadley, MA.

Mikhailenko, Vitalii. July 8, 2005. Zheleznovodsk.

Mikhaleva, Nadezhda. August 11, 2008. Moscow.

Muratov, Dmitri. May 12, 2013. New York.

————. October 23, 2015. Moscow.

Palazhchenko, Pavel. March 1, 2007. Moscow.

————. October 22, 2015. Moscow.

Paltsev, Nikolai. July 5, 2005. Stavropol.

Powell, Lord Charles. July 21, 2007. London.

Savranskaya, Svetlana. June 20, 2011 (via email).

Shevardnadze, Eduard. May 14, 2007. Tbilisi.

Shmelyov, Nikolai. July 26, 2006. Moscow.

Shultz, George. August 21, 2007. Stanford, CA.

Simons, Thomas. November 20, 2006. Cambridge, MA.

Varennikov, V. I. February 28, 2006. Moscow.

Yakovlev, Aleksandr. May 31, 2005. Moscow.

Yakovleva, Irina. May 7, 2007. Moscow.

Yeriomin, Nikolai. July 5, 2005. Stavropol.

Zdravomyslova, Olga. April 2, 2007. Moscow.

————. October 18, 2015. Moscow.

Zubenko, Ivan. July 7, 2005. Stavropol.

————. August 1, 2008. Stavropol.

OTHER INTERVIEWS

A. Benediktov interview with Gorbachev. February 15, 2009. Radio station "Ekho Moskvy."

Cartledge, Bryan. British Diplomatic Oral History Project. 2007.

Telen', Liudmila. "Mikhail Gorbachev: 'Chert poberi, do chego my dozhili!'" *Radio svoboda* October 22, 2009. Radio station "Ekho Moskvy."

Other interviews are contained in various articles in the Soviet and Russian press listed below.

BBC INTERVIEWS IN THE SECOND RUSSIAN REVOLUTION TRANSCRIPTS (TSRRT)

Abalkin, Leonid
Adamovich, Ales
Afanasyev, Yuri
Aganbegyan, Abel
Akhromeyev, Sergei
Andreyeva, Nina
Arbatov, Georgy
Bakatin, Vadim
Baklanov, Grigory
Balayan, Zori
Chernichenko, Yuri
Chernyaev, Anatoly
Dobrokhotov, Leonid
Dolgikh, Vladimir
Dolmatov, Vladimir
Gorbachev, Mikhail
Granin, Daniil
Ignatenko, Vitaly
Klimov, Elem
Kolbin, Gennady
Korotich, Vitaly
Kravchenko, Leonid
Laptev, Ivan
Latsis, Otto
Legostayev, Valery
Levikov, Aleksandr
Lukyanov, Anatoly
"Major Slava X"
Miners
Nanashev, Mikhail
Pankov, Vladimir
Primakov, Yevgeny
Ryzhkov, Nikolai
Shakhnazarov, Georgy
Shatalin, Stanislav
Shatrov, Mikhail
Siradegian, Vano
Sobchak, Anatoly
Stankevich, Sergei
Starkov, Vladislav
Starovoitova, Galina

Stepanov, Teimuraz
Tarasenko, Sergei
Ulyanov, Mikhail
Volsky, Arkady
Vorontsov, Yuli
Yakovlev, Aleksandr
Yeltsin, Boris
Zaslavskaya, Tatyana

BOOKS

Adomeit, Hannes. *Imperial Overstretch: Germany in Soviet Policy from Stalin to Gorbachev*. Baden-Baden: Nomos Verlagsgesellschaft, 1998.

Allison, Graham, and Grigory Yavlinsky. *Window of Opportunity: The Grand Bargain for Democracy in the Soviet Union*. New York: Pantheon Books, 1991.

Anderson, Mark, and Annelise Anderson. *Reagan's Secret War: The Untold Story of His Fight to Save the World from Nuclear Disaster*. New York: Random House, 2009.

Arkus, Liubov'. *Kino i kontekst*. Vol. 4, *1986–1988*. St. Petersburg: SEANS, 2002.

Aron, Leon. *Yeltsin: A Revolutionary Life*. New York: St. Martin's Press, 2000.

Babenyshev, Aleksandr, ed. *Sakharovskii sbornik*. Moscow: Rossiiskii gosudarstvennyi gumanitarnyi universitet, 2011.

Barrass, Gordon. *The Great Cold War: A Journey through the Hall of Mirrors*. Stanford, CA: Stanford University Press, 2009.

Belkin, Aron. *Vozhdi i prizraki*. Moscow: Olymp, 2001.

Beschloss, Michael R., and Strobe Talbott. *At the Highest Levels: The Inside Story of the End of the Cold War*. Boston: Little, Brown, 1993.

Bozo, Frédéric. *Mitterrand, the End of the Cold War, and German Unification*. Translated by Susan Emanuel. New York: Berghahn Books, 2009.

Breslauer, George W. *Gorbachev and Yeltsin as Leaders*. New York: Cambridge University Press, 2002.

Brown, Archie. *The Gorbachev Factor*. Oxford; New York: Oxford University Press, 1996.

—————. *The Myth of the Strong Leader: Political Leadership in the Modern Age*. New York: Basic Books, 2014.

—————. *The Rise and Fall of Communism*. New York: HarperCollins, 2009.

—————. *Seven Years That Changed the World: Perestroika in Perspective*. Oxford: Oxford University Press, 2007.

Burlatskii, Fedor. *Russkie gosudari—epokha reformatsii*. Moscow: Firma "SHARK," 1996.

Bush, George, and Brent Scowcroft. *A World Transformed*. New York: Alfred A. Knopf, 1998.

Chazov, Evgenii. *Rok*. Moscow: Izdatelstvo GEOTAR-MEDITSINA, 2000.

————. *Zdorov'e i vlast'*. Moscow: Novosti, 1992.

Cohen, Stephen F. *Soviet Fates and Lost Alternatives: From Stalinism to the New Cold War*. New York: Columbia University Press, 2009.

Cohen, Stephen F., and Katrina vanden Heuvel. *Voices of Glasnost: Interviews with Gorbachev's Reformers*. New York: W. W. Norton, 1989.

Coll, Steve. *Ghost Wars: The Secret History of the CIA, Afghanistan, and Bin Laden, from the Soviet Invasion to September 10, 2001*. New York: Penguin Press, 2004.

Colton, Timothy J. *Yeltsin: A Life*. New York: Basic Books, 2008.

Dobbs, Michael. *Down with Big Brother: The Fall of the Soviet Empire*. New York: Alfred A. Knopf, 1997.

Dunlop, John B. *The Rise of Russia and the Fall of the Soviet Empire*. With a new postscript by the author. Princeton, NJ: Princeton University Press, 1993.

Elbe, Frank, and Richard Kiessler. *A Round Table with Sharp Corners: The Diplomatic Path to German Unity*. Baden-Baden: Nomos Verlagsgesellschaft, 1996.

English, Robert D. *Russia and the Idea of the West: Gorbachev, Intellectuals, and the End of the Cold War*. New York: Columbia University Press, 2000.

Feist, Jess, and Gregory J. Feist. *Theories of Personality*. Boston: McGraw-Hill, 1998.

Feuer, Lewis, ed. *Marx and Engels: Basic Writing on Politics and Philosophy*. Garden City, NY: Anchor Books, 1959.

Figes, Orlando. *The Whisperers: Private Life in Stalin's Russia*. New York: Metropolitan Books, 2007.

FitzGerald, Frances. *Way Out There in the Blue: Reagan, Star Wars and the End of the Cold War*. New York: Simon & Schuster, 2001.

Fitzpatrick, Sheila. *Stalin's Peasants: Resistance and Survival in the Russian Village after Collectivization*. New York: Oxford University Press, 1994.

Gaddis, John Lewis. *We Now Know: Rethinking Cold War History*. New York: Oxford University Press, 1997.

Gaidar, Yegor. *Collapse of an Empire: Lessons for Modern Russia*. Translated by Antonina W. Bouis. Washington, DC: Brookings Institution, 2007.

Garthoff, Raymond. *Détente and Confrontation: American-Soviet Relations from Nixon to Reagan*. Washington, DC: Brookings Institution, 1994.

————. *The Great Transition: American-Soviet Relations and the End of the Cold War*. Washington, DC: Brookings Institution, 1994.

Gati, Charles. *The Bloc That Failed: Soviet-East European Relations in Transition*. Bloomington: Indiana University Press, 1990.

Gorbachev, Mikhail. *Perestroika: New Thinking for Our Country and the World*. New York: HarperCollins, 1987.

Gorbachev, Mikhail, and Zdeněk Mlynář. *Conversations with Gorbachev: On Perestroika, the Prague Spring, and the Crossroads of Socialism*. Translated by George Shriver. New York: Columbia University Press, 2002.

Grachev, Andrei. *Gorbachev*. Moscow: Vagrius, 2001.

————. *Gorbachev's Gamble: Soviet Foreign Policy and the End of the Cold War.* Cambridge, UK: Polity Press, 2008.

Haslam, Jonathan. *Russia's Cold War: From the October Revolution to the Fall of the Wall.* New Haven, CT: Yale University Press, 2011.

Hewett, Ed A. *Reforming the Soviet Economy: Equality versus Efficiency.* Washington, DC: Brookings Institution, 1988.

Hoffman, David E. *The Dead Hand: The Untold Story of the Cold War Arms Race.* New York: Doubleday, 2009.

————. *The Oligarchs: Wealth and Power in the New Russia.* New York: Public Affairs, 2002.

Kaiser, Robert G. *Why Gorbachev Happened: His Triumph and Failures.* New York: Simon & Schuster, 1991.

Kalinovsky, Artemy. *A Long Goodbye: The Soviet Withdrawal from Afghanistan.* Cambridge, MA: Harvard University Press, 2011.

Knight, Amy. *Spies without Cloaks: The KGB's Successors.* Princeton, NJ: Princeton University Press, 1996.

Kuchmaev, Boris. *Kommunist s bozhei otmetinoi: Dokumental'no-publitsisticheskii ocherk.* Stavropol: n.p., 1992.

Kuvaldin, V. *Proryv k svobode.* Moscow: Al'pina Biznes Buks, 2005.

Lévesque, Jacques. *The Enigma of 1989: The USSR and the Liberation of Eastern Europe.* Translated by Keith Martin. Berkeley: University of California Press, 1997.

Matlock, Jack F., Jr. *Reagan and Gorbachev: How the Cold War Ended.* New York: Random House, 2004.

————. *Superpower Illusions: How Myths and False Ideologies Led America Astray—and How to Return to Reality.* New Haven, CT: Yale University Press, 2010.

McAdams, Don P. *The Person: An Introduction to Personality Psychology.* Fort Worth, TX: Harcourt Brace, 1994.

Medvedev, Roi. *Andropov.* Moscow: Molodaia Gvardiia, 2006.

————. *Kak nachalas' perestroika.* Moscow: Prava cheloveka, 2006.

————. *Neizvestnyi Andropov: Politicheskaia biografiia Iuriia Andropova.* Moscow: Prava cheloveka, 1999.

Medvedev, Zhores. *Gorbachev.* New York: W. W. Norton, 1986.

A Millennium Salute to Mikhail Gorbachev on His 70th Birthday. Moscow: R. Valent, 2001.

Mlynář, Zdeněk. *Nightfrost in Prague: The End of Humane Socialism.* Translated by Paul Wilson. New York: Karz, 1980.

Moore, Charles. *Margaret Thatcher: At Her Zenith: In London, Washington and Moscow.* New York: Alfred A. Knopf, 2016.

Neokonchennaia istoriia: Tri tsveta vremeni. Moscow: Mezhdunarodnye otnosheniia, 2005.

Oberdorfer, Don. *From the Cold War to a New Era: The United States and the*

Soviet Union, 1983–1991. Baltimore, MD: Johns Hopkins University Press, 1998.

————. *The Turn: From the Cold War to a New Era: The United States and the Soviet Union, 1983–1990.* New York: Poseidon Press, 1991.

O'Clery, Conor. *Moscow, December 25, 1991: The Last Day of the Soviet Union.* New York: Public Affairs, 2011.

Odom, William E. *The Collapse of the Soviet Military.* New Haven, CT: Yale University Press, 1998.

Pikhoia, Rudol'f. *Moskva—Kreml'—Vlast'.* Vol. 2. Moscow: Rus'-Olimp: AST: Astrel', 2007.

————. *Sovestskii Soiuz: Istoriia vlasti, 1945–1991.* Novosibirsk: Sibirskii khronograf, 2000.

Pipes, Richard. *Alexander Yakovlev: The Man Whose Ideas Delivered Russia from Communism.* DeKalb: Northern Illinois University Press, 2015.

Pleshakov, Constantine. *There Is No Freedom without Bread!: 1989 and the Civil War That Brought Down Communism.* New York: Farrar, Straus and Giroux, 2009.

Plokhy, Serhii. *The Last Empire: The Final Days of the Soviet Union.* New York: Basic Books, 2014.

Remnick, David. *Lenin's Tomb: The Last Days of the Soviet Empire.* New York: Random House, 1993.

Ruge, Gerd. *Gorbachev: A Biography.* London: Chatto & Windus, 1991.

Sakwa, Richard. *Gorbachev and His Reforms, 1985–1990.* New York: Prentice-Hall, 1990.

Sarotte, Mary Elise. *1989: The Struggle to Create Post–Cold War Europe.* Princeton, NJ: Princeton University Press, 2009.

————. *The Collapse: The Accidental Opening of the Berlin Wall.* New York: Basic Books, 2014.

Sheehy, Gail. *The Man Who Changed the World: The Lives of Mikhail S. Gorbachev.* New York: HarperCollins, 1990.

Sheinis, Viktor. *Vzlet i padenie Parlamenta.* Vol. 1. Moscow: Moskovskii tsentr Karnegi fond indem, 2005.

Shevardnadze, Eduard. *The Future Belongs to Freedom.* Translated by Catherine A. Fitzpatrick. New York: Free Press, 1991.

Shevchenko, V. *Povsednevnaia zhizn' Kremlia pri prezidentakh.* Moscow: Molodaya gvardiya, 2004.

Shmelev, Nikolai. *Pashkov dom: Kartinki iz zhizni.* Moscow: Interdialekt, 2001.

Shubin, A. V. *Ot "zastoia" k reformam: SSSR v 1917–1985 gg.* Moscow: Rosspen, 2001.

Spohr, Kristina, and David Reynolds. *Transcending the Cold War: Summits, Statecraft, and the Dissolution of Bipolarity, 1970–1990.* Oxford: Oxford University Press, 2016.

Shulgan, Christopher. *The Soviet Ambassador: The Making of the Radical behind Perestroika.* Toronto: McClelland & Stewart, 2008.

Stepankov, V. *GKChP: 73 chasa, kotorye izmenili mir.* Moscow: Vremya, 2011.

Stepankov, V., and E. Lisov. *Kremlevskii zagovor.* Moscow: Ogonek, 1992.

Taubman, Philip. *The Partnership: Five Cold Warriors and Their Quest to Ban the Bomb.* New York: Harper, 2012.

Taubman, William. *Khrushchev: The Man and His Era.* New York: W. W. Norton, 2003.

———. *Stalin's American Policy: From Entente to Détente to Cold War.* New York: W. W. Norton, 1982.

Timofeev, Lev, ed. *The Anti-Communist Manifesto: Whom to Help in Russia.* Bellevue, WA: Free Enterprise Press, 1990.

Tucker, Robert W., and David C. Hendrickson. *The Imperial Temptation: The New World Order and America's Purpose.* New York: Council on Foreign Relations Press, 1992.

Vogel, Ezra. *Deng Xiaoping and the Transformation of China.* Cambridge, MA: Harvard University Press, 2011.

Volkogonov, Dmitrii. *Sem' vozhdei.* Moscow: Novosti, 1995.

Whelan, Eugene, and Rick Arbold. *Whelan: The Man in the Green Stetson.* Toronto: Irwin Publishing.

Wilson, James Graham. *The Triumph of Improvisation: Gorbachev's Adaptability, Reagan's Engagement, and the End of the Cold War.* Ithaca, NY: Cornell University Press, 2014.

Yergin, Daniel. *The Prize: The Epic Quest for Oil, Money and Power.* New York: Free Press, 1991.

Zelikow, Philip, and Condoleezza Rice. *Germany Unified and Europe Transformed: A Study in Statecraft.* Cambridge, MA: Harvard University Press, 1997.

Zenkovich, Nikolai. *Mikhail Gorbachev: Zhizn' do Kremlia.* Moscow: Olma-Press, 2001.

Zubkova, Elena. *Russia after the War: Hopes, Illusions and Disappointments, 1945–1957.* Translated by Hugh Ragsdale. Armonk, NY: M. E. Sharpe, 1998.

Zubok, Vladislav. *A Failed Empire: The Soviet Union in the Cold War from Stalin to Gorbachev.* Chapel Hill: University of North Carolina Press, 2007.

———. *Zhivago's Children: The Last Russian Intelligentsia.* Cambridge, MA: Belknap Press of Harvard University Press, 2009.

ARTICLES

Alekseev, Valerii. "I otdykhaia v Ispanii, Gorbachev dumaet o Rossii." *24,* August 28, 1992.

Arkhangelsii, Andrei. "Mikhail Gorbachev: 'Nado izmenit' atmosferu'." *Ogonek,* February 2, 2015.

Belan, Olga. "Mnogikh oshibok Gorbachev mog by izbezhat'." *Sobesednik*, November 1992.

Beligzhanina, Anna. "Mikhail Gorbachev: 'Ia rad, chto Krym prisoedinilsia k Rossii.'" *Komsomol'skaia pravda*, March 18, 2014. http://msk.kp.ru/print/26207/3093031.

Belkin, Aron. "Kto zhe takoe Gorbachev?" *Kul'tura*, October 19, 1991.

Berg, Steve. "A Calm Capital Contrasts with a Frantic, Fidgeting Gorbachev-Crazed Twin Cities." *Minneapolis Star Tribune*, June 1, 1990.

Braterskii, Aleksandr. "Mikhail Gorbachev predstavil svoiu novuiu knigu." *Gazeta.ru*, November 21, 2014.

Brown, Archie. "The Change to Engagement in Britain's Cold War Policy." *Journal of Cold War Studies* 10, no. 3 (Summer 2008).

————. "Did Gorbachev as General Secretary Become a Social Democrat?" *Europe-Asia Studies* 65, no. 2 (March 2013): 198–220.

Cannon, Lou. "Reagan Is Concerned about Bush's Indecision." *Washington Post*, May 6, 1989.

Chiesa, Giulietto. "Grustnaia missiia Gorbacheva." *Nezavisimaia gazeta*, August 20, 1999.

Conroy, Sarah Booth, Donnie Radcliffe, Roxanne Roberts, and Judith Weinraub. "Raisa's Day: Tea Talk, Treasures and a Wagging Tail." *Washington Post*, June 1, 1990.

Davydov, Oleg. "Rozdenie Androgina." *Nezavisimaia gazeta*, February 22, 2001.

Dewar, Helen. "Hill Leaders Hold Freewheeling Debate with Soviet." *Washington Post*, December 10, 1987.

Dowd, Maureen. "As 'Gorby' Works the Crowd, Backward Reels the KGB." *New York Times*, December 11, 1987.

————. "Gorbachev Passes Up Stunts But Dazzles the Heartland." *New York Times*, June 4, 1990, sec. 1.

————. "Masters of the Sound Bite Cede Match to Gorbachev." *New York Times*, June 2, 1990.

Dunlop, John B. "The August 1991 Coup and Its Impact on Soviet Politics." *Journal of Cold War Studies* 5, no. 1 (2003): 94–127.

Easton, William J. "Gorbachev Hosts a Lavish Dinner, Toasts, 'Until We Meet in Moscow.'" *Los Angeles Times*, December 10, 1987.

————. "Gorbachev Makes Bid to U.S. Intellectuals." *Los Angeles Times*, December 9, 1987.

Fedorina, Maria. "Slezy pervoi ledi." *Moskovskii komsomolets*, February 14, 1998.

"Flying Blind in the Kremlin." *New York Times*, September 30, 1990. http://www.nytimes.com/1990/09/30/opinion/flying-blind-in-the-kremlin.html.

Friedgut, Theodore H., and Lewis H. Seigelbaum. "The Soviet Miners' Strike:

Perestroika from Below." *Carl Beck Papers in Russian and East European Studies*, no. 804 (March 1990).

Fuerbringer, Jonathan. "Dollar Surges after Speech by Gorbachev." *New York Times*, December 8, 1988.

Furman, Dmitrii. "Fenomen Gorbacheva." *Svobodnaia mysl'*, no. 1 (1995): 60–74.

Gardels, Nathan. "Why Gorbachev Feels Betrayed by the Post–Cold War West." *Huffington Post*, November 7, 2014.

Goldberg, Carey. "I'm No Coup Plotter, Gorbachev Thunders." *Los Angeles Times*, July 8, 1994.

Golovin, Vasilii. "Eks-Prezident v Iaponii." *Nezavisimaia gazeta*, April 24, 1992.

"Gorbachev and Reagan Toasts." *New York Times*, June 1, 1988.

"Gorbachev Jokingly Offers to Sell Subs." *United Press International*, March 11, 1992.

Gorbachev, Mikhail. "Esli nado budet spasat' stranu—ia vernius'." *Komsomol'skaia pravda*, October 3, 1993.

————. "My prosto byli drug dlia druga. Vsiu zhizn'." *Obshchaia gazeta*, November 29, 1999.

"Gorbachevu vsego lish' vosemdesiat." *Izvestiia*, March 3, 2011.

"Gorby and Raisa Go after Laughs." *Toronto Star*, March 8, 1992.

Gross, Jane. "The Gorbachevs Will Get a Close Look at the America beyond Washington: San Franciscans to Give a Big Party." *New York Times*, June 3, 1990.

Hendrickson, Paul. "Yeltsin's Smashing Day." *Washington Post*, September 13, 1989.

Hertle, Hans-Hermann. "The Fall of the Wall: The Unintended Self-Dissolution of East Germany's Ruling Regime." *Cold War International History Project Bulletin*, no. 12/13 (Fall/Winter 2001).

Hilzenrath, David S. "Raisa's Woman to Women Chat." *Washington Post*, December 11, 1987.

Iakovlev, Egor. "Stoish' po koleno v navoze, a v mechtakh daleko-daleko." *Obshchaia gazeta*, March 7, 2001.

Kasimov, Jan. "Krymskie kanikuli." *Moskovskie novosti*, April 23, 1992.

Keenan, Edward L. "Muscovite Political Folkways." *Russian Review* 45, no. 2 (April 1986): 115–81.

Keller, Bill. "Presidential Stroll: Chaos and Applause." *New York Times*, May 30, 1988.

————. "The Vintage Actor Gets Great Reviews." *New York Times*, June 1, 1988.

————. "Washington Summit: Over Caviar, Gorbachev Relaxes and Charms." *New York Times*, June 1, 1990.

Kinzer, Stephen. "Gorbachev the Tourist Finds Admirers in Germany." *New York Times*, March 10, 1992.

Kiselev, E. "Nashe vse: Programma o vydaiushchikhsia liudiakh Rossii za poslednie sto let. Raisa Gorbacheva," n.d. http://www.gorby.ru/rubrs. asp?art_id=25650&rubr_id=21&page=1.

Knight, Amy. "The Coup That Never Was." *Problems of Post-Communism* 58, nos. 4–5 (2011): 66–74.

Kornienko, Georgii. "Zakonchilas' li 'kholodnaia voina'?" *Nezavisimaia gazeta*, August 16, 1994.

Kozlov, Ruslan. "Ia zashchishchaiu nashu iunost'." *Sobesednik*, 1991, no. 12 edition.

Kramer, Mark. "The Myth of No-NATO Enlargement Pledge to Russia." *Washington Quarterly* 32, no. 2 (2009): 39–61.

Kraminova, Natalia. "Mama." *Obshchaia gazeta*, September 21, 2000.

Lévesque, Jacques. "Soviet Approaches to Eastern Europe at the Beginning of 1989." *Cold War International History Project Bulletin*, no. 12/13 (Fall/ Winter 2001).

MacFarquhar, Neil. "Reviled, Revered and Still Challenging Russia to Evolve." *New York Times*, June 2, 2016.

Machcewicz, Paweł. "Poland 1986–1989: From 'Cooptation' to Negotiated Revolution." *Cold War International History Project Bulletin*, no. 12/13 (Fall/ Winter 2001).

Malevannyi, Vladimir. "Molitva bez svechei." *Nezavisimaia gazeta*, September 10, 1999, 168 edition, sec. 9. http://www.gorby.ru/gorbacheva/ publications/show_25914/.

Manakhov, Vladislav. "Valentin Pavlov: 'Esli khotite, sam Mikhail Gorbachev byl i chlenom GKChP." *Pravda*, April 12, 1996.

Maraniss, David, and John Lancaster. "Chilly Weather, Warm Welcome in the Twin Cities." *Washington Post*, June 4, 1990.

Marsov, Vitaly. "Mikhail Gorbachev: Andropov ne poshel by daleko v reformatsii obshchestva." *Nezavisimaia gazeta*, November 11, 1992.

McAdams, Don P., Jeffrey Reynolds, Martha Lewis, Allison H. Patten, and Phillip J. Bowman. "When Bad Things Turn Good and Good Things Turn Bad: Sequences of Redemption and Contamination in Life Narratives and Their Relations to Psychosocial Adaptation in Midlife Adults and Students." *Personality and Social Psychology Bulletin* 27, no. 4 (April 2001): 474–85.

"Mikhail Gorbachev: Zhenit'sia ia ne sobiraius'." *Komsomol'skaia pravda*. March 2, 2001. http://www.kp.ru/daily/22504/7900/.

Mlynář, Zdeněk. "Il mio compagno di studi Mikhail Gorbachev." *L'Unità*, 1985.

"Mne nikto ne strashen." *Obshchaia gazeta*, May 16, 1996.

Muratov, D., and V. Fronin. "Suda ia ne boius'." *Komsomol'skaia pravda*, February 24, 1992.

Muratov, D., and Iu. Sorokin. "Pravitel'stvu pora vykhodit' iz podpol'ia." *Komsomol'skaia pravda*, May 29, 1992.

"Nad byvshim prezidentom SSSR sgushchaiutsia tuchi." *Golos*, June 22, 1992.

Nechepurenko, Ivan. "Gorbachev on Russia and Ukraine: We Are One People." *Moscow Times*, November 21, 2014.

Pankratov, V. "Upravliaia zhatvoi: Rasskazyvaem ob opyte stavropol'skikh zemledel'tsev." *Pravda*, July 17, 1977.

Parker, Ashley. "Manners Fit Jeb Bush, If Not an Uncouth Race." *New York Times*, January 17, 2016.

Radcliffe, Donnie. "Barbara Bush, Wowing Wellesley, with Raisa Gorbacheva on Hand." *Washington Post*, June 2, 1990.

————. "The Communicator and the Communists." *Washington Post*, May 31, 1988.

————. "Nancy vs. Raisa: The Chill of It All." *Washington Post*, June 2, 1988.

Radcliffe, Donnie, and Sarah Booth Conroy. "The First Ladies' Public Truce." *Washington Post*, December 10, 1987.

Radcliffe, Donnie, and Lois Romano. "Lunchtime Détente for the First Ladies." *Washington Post*, December 8, 1988.

Randolph, Eleanor. "Accidental Dose of Glasnost? TV Cameras Catch Gorbachev's Blunt Talk with Hill Leaders." *Washington Post*, June 2, 1990.

————. "Yeltsin's 'Spree' Denied." *Washington Post*, September 20, 1989.

Remnick, David. "Day 2: The Gorbachev's Washington Orbit." *Washington Post*, December 10, 1987.

————. "Embassy Guests See a New Gorbachev: Tired and Defensive." *Washington Post*, June 1, 1990.

————. "Gorbachev: 'Light a Fire' for U.S.-Soviet Rapport." *Washington Post*, December 9, 1987.

Remnick, David, and Lois Romano. "Soviet Leader Stops in Name of Glasnost." *Washington Post*, December 11, 1987.

"Rezkoe zaiavlenie v adres Gorbacheva." *Izvestiia*, June 3, 1992.

Rimashevskaia, N. M. "Pod zvuki vnutrennogo golosa." *Narodoselenie*, no. 1 (2006).

Roberts, Steven V. "President Charms Students, But His Ideas Lack Converts." *New York Times*, June 1, 1988.

Rosenberg, Steve. "Mikhail Gorbachev Denounces Putin's 'Attack on Rights.'" *BBC News Europe*, March 7, 2014. http://www.bbc.com/news/world-europe-21695314.

Rosenblatt, Robert A. "Gorbachev Tempts U.S. Businessmen." *Los Angeles Times*, December 11, 1987.

Rosenthal, Andrew. "Soviet Visitor Mixes Charm with Venom." *New York Times*, December 8, 1987.

Ross, Michael. "Minnesotans Are Hosts to First-Lady Diplomacy." *Los Angeles Times*, June 4, 1990.

Sarotte, Mary Elise. "What the West Really Told Moscow about NATO Expansion." *Foreign Affairs* 93, no. 5 (October 2014): 90–97.

Schepp, Matthias, and Britta Sandberg. "I Am Truly and Deeply Concerned." *Der Spiegel*, January 16, 2015. http://www.spiegel.de/

international/world/gorbachev-warns-of-decline-in-russian-western-ties-over-ukraine-a-1012992.html.

Sciolino, Elaine. "Frost in the White House for 2 First Ladies." *New York Times,* December 10, 1987.

Shakina, Marina. "'V 1991 godu ia byl slishkom samouveren.'" *Nezavisimaia gazeta,* December 12, 1995.

Shatalin, Stanislav. "500 dnei—I drugie dni moei zhizni." *Nezavisimaia gazeta,* April 2, 1992.

Shuster, Simon. "Gorbachev Blames the U.S. for Provoking 'New Cold War.'" *Time,* December 11, 2014. http://time.com/3630352/mikhail-gorbachev-vladimir-putin-cold-war/.

Singer, Natasha. "Rubles, a Girl's Best Friend." *New York Times,* December 9, 2007.

Skvortsova, Irina. "Mikhail Gorbachev: Ia ne boius' kritiki, potomu chto v politike nel'zia obizhat'sia." *Sobesednik,* December 17, 2014.

"Slovo o Dzheffersone." *Nezavisimaia gazeta,* April 15, 1993.

"Soviet Union 'Should Have Been Preserved.'" *USA Today,* April 6, 2006.

Stanley, Alessandra. "Trial of Coup Plotters against Gorbachev Takes an Odd Turn." *New York Times,* July 10, 1994.

"Stranu nel'zia lomat' cherez koleno, po-kovboiski." *Obshchaia gazeta,* April 4, 1996.

Suri, Jeremi. "To Get Big Things Done We Should Strip Demands on the President." *Dallas Morning Star,* December 4, 2015.

Svistunov, Sergey. "Plius Burbulizatsia vsei strany?" *Pravda,* April 30, 1992.

Tanner, Adam. "Witness Gorbachev Finds Himself on Trial." *Moscow Times,* July 9, 1994.

Taubman, Philip. "Prominent Americans Hear Gorbachev's World Vision." *New York Times,* December 9, 1987.

Taubman, William, and Svetlana Savranskaya. "If a Wall Fell in Berlin and Moscow Hardly Noticed, Would It Still Make a Noise?" In *The Fall of the Berlin Wall: The Revolutionary Legacy of 1989.* Edited by Jeffrey A. Engel. New York: Oxford University Press, 2009.

Telen', Liudmila. "Mikhail Gorbachev: 'Chert poberi, do chego my dozhili!'" *Radio svoboda,* October 22, 2009. http://www.svoboda.org/content/article/1858368.html.

Tret'iakov, Vitalii. "Mikhail Gorbachev zavtra vystupit na protsese po delu Generala Varennikova." *Nezavisimaia gazeta.* July 6, 1994.

vanden Heuvel, Katrina, and Stephen F. Cohen. "Gorbachev on 1989." *Nation,* October 28, 2009. http://www.thenation.com/article/gorbachev-1989.

Vasil'ev, Aleksandr. "Trudno byt' byvshim." *Komsomol'skaia pravda,* January 1, 1992.

Vorosobin, Vladimir. "Mikhail Gorbachev: Ukrainskii krisis nuzhno bylo reshat' eshche v Belovezhskoi pushche." *Komsomol'skaia pravda,* November 11, 2014.

"Vstrecha piataia." *Zhurnalist*, no. 12 (1991).

Vyzhutovich, Valerii. "Mikhail Gorbachev: K prezidentskim vyboram nuzhno sozdat' shirokuiu koalitsiiu demokraticheskikh sil." *Izvestiia*, December 28, 1995.

"We Applaud the New Thaw in the Arts." *Washington Post*, May 31, 1988.

White, Gregory L. "Gorby's Choice." *Wall Street Journal*, December 1, 2007.

"Writer Admits Yeltsin Source Is Nonexistent." *Washington Post*, September 21, 1989.

Zavada, Marina, and Yurii Kulikov. "Mikhail Gorbachev: My s Raisoi byli priviazanny drug k drugu na smert'." *Izvestiia*, January 12, 2007. http://izvestia.ru/news/320650.

Zubok, Vladislav. "New Evidence on the Soviet Factor in the Peaceful Revolutions of 1989." *Cold War International History Project Bulletin*, nos. 12/13 (Fall/Winter 2001).

ACKNOWLEDGMENTS

This book is not an "authorized" biography in the generally understood sense of that term. I did not ask Mikhail Gorbachev for permission to write it; rather, I informed him, through his longtime close aide Anatoly Chernyaev, that I was planning to write his biography and asked for his support. I am grateful to him for providing that support: submitting to several long interviews with me and my wife, Amherst College professor of Russian Jane Taubman, over the course of a decade; facilitating my use of the invaluable archive at the Gorbachev Foundation in Moscow, as well as the important assistance I received from members of the foundation's staff; welcoming the interviews Jane and I carried out in Moscow with his daughter, Irina Gorbachev (then vice president of the foundation), and other former members of his administration; inviting me to take part in several seminars at the foundation and in conferences overseas; and introducing me to people in the Stavropol region, who helped to arrange interviews with former Gorbachev associates in that area. On all these occasions, he struck me as remarkably natural and informal for a world leader of his stature, qualities that also characterized much, but not all, of his political activities.

Gorbachev's longtime aide Anatoly Chernyaev provided intellectual and practical guidance of all sorts. So, when I first started out, did Gorbachev's former press spokesman and later biographer, Andrei Grachev. Olga Zdravomyslova, the Gorbachev Foundation's executive director, was unfailingly supportive, as were Pavel Palazhchenko, Gorbachev's longtime aide and interpreter, Aleksei Litvin, the foundation's librarian, and his colleague Elena Golosovskaya. Alla Zolotukhina, then deputy head of the Stavropol government administration, arranged a long series of interviews in Stavropol and Piatigorsk, and Liubov Chavykina, deputy head of the administration in the

Krasnogvardeisky district, showed us around the village of Privolnoe, where Gorbachev was born and raised.

Svetlana Savranskaya first prompted/persuaded/browbeat me to embark on a Gorbachev biography. Herself an émigré Russian historian now working at the National Security Archive in Washington, Svetlana promised to help me track down archival and other materials, and over the course of twelve years she has done that and much more. With the blessing of the archive's director, Tom Blanton, she introduced me to Anatoly Chernyaev and others, accompanied me and Jane to interviews and archives in Moscow and Stavropol, shared with me documents that she has gathered for more than twenty years in Moscow and prepared for later inclusion in National Security Archive publications, read the first draft of my manuscript, and cheered me on throughout.

I am particularly grateful to Archie Brown, long the dean of Gorbachev studies, who generously welcomed me into that small fraternity, provided frequent, helpful advice, and meticulously read and commented on my manuscript. Stephen F. Cohen also encouraged me to write this book and kept directing me to valuable Russian sources. Among others who helped me with research were Russian scholar Yuri Aksiutin, who turned over to me his extensive collection of Gorbachev-related clippings; Dan Somogyi, who combed the British archives for me; Mark Kramer, David E. Hoffman, and James Graham Wilson, who offered helpful bibliographical advice; Roman Seebeck and Werner Brandes, who worked with me on German documents; several Amherst College students (Susanna An, Ethan Gates, Cory Merrill, Oriel Strong, and Yana Yushkin), and research assistant extraordinaire, Lauren Woodard, who labored heroically over footnotes, bibliography, glossary, and formatting the text.

During early stages of this project, I was fortunate to have a Guggenheim Fellowship and a National Humanities Fellowship. Later on, I benefited from continuous research support from Amherst College under Presidents Anthony Marx and Biddy Martin, and Deans of the Faculty Gregory S. Call and Catherine Epstein.

I'm grateful to all the people in Russia and elsewhere who agreed to be interviewed about Gorbachev. And I'm happy to say I prevailed upon an inordinate number of colleagues and friends to read and comment (often at substantial length) on a complete draft of my manuscript: Bruce Allyn, Gordon Barrass, Rodric Braithwaite, Archie Brown, Amy Demorest, Sergey Glebov, George Kateb, N. Gordon Levin Jr., Pavel Machala, Jack Matlock Jr., Pavel Palazhchenko, Constantine Pleshakov, Strobe Talbott, Philip Taubman,

Kim Townsend, and Vladislav Zubok. Mary Elise Sarotte was kind enough to read the chapters on Gorbachev's dealings with Germany and make valuable suggestions.

For secretarial and administrative assistance, I salute Theresa and Steve Laizer and Donna Simpter. Victoria Farrington and Judy Kolenda transcribed interviews conducted in English, and Bella Barmak and Alfiya Bikineyeva transcribed Russian interviews.

James Mairs, my editor at W. W. Norton, was my editorial conscience, goad, and cheerleader beginning in 1981. He kept the faith in me for the almost twenty years I labored on Nikita Khrushchev's biography, and did so again this time as I produced Gorbachev's biography in "just" eleven years. Alas, Jim died on the very day I delivered the final Gorbachev manuscript to W. W. Norton. Norton's editor in chief, John Glusman, took over from Jim during the last stages of this book; I am indebted to him and his assistants, Alexa Pugh and Lydia Brents, for the care and efficiency with which they shepherded it across the finish line, and to Otto Sonntag for meticulous copyediting. And to Norton's former president Drake McFeely, whose Amherst lineage must explain at least some of the warm attention and support he rendered to a professor/writer at his college.

Kathy Robbins has gone above and beyond the call of literary agency for this book, not only handling the business side of the project but warmly supporting me at every stage with wise counsel. Kathy and her associates, Mike Gillespie, Rachelle Bergstein, and Liza Darnton, all painstakingly read drafts of my manuscript and suggested many valuable improvements.

My wife, Jane, brought her expert knowledge to bear in interviews and archives, provided unstinting moral and material support during our many visits to Russia, and read and helped edit manuscript drafts early and late. I dedicate this book to her.

INDEX

Page numbers in *italics* refer to illustrations.